Over the last 60 years, British historian Professor Christopher Duffy has fundamentally reshaped our understanding of warfare in the late Old Regime. For much of the twentieth century, historians asserted that the military forces of Old Regime Europe were stagnant, formalised, and decorative. In this view, Old Regime armies were a lacy pastel facade destroyed by the new military prowess of Napoleon. A specialist on the Austrian, Prussian, Russian, and Jacobite armies of the mid-eighteenth century, Professor Duffy demanded that we understand the armies of the Old Regime as they were: serious and dangerous military institutions.

The Changing Face of Old Regime Warfare is a festschrift honouring Professor Duffy's legacy of writing on this pivotal period of military history. The book collects 16 essays by scholars from seven countries on three continents, which together tell the story of the dynamic nature of warfare in the Old Regime. Topics such as cavalry tactics, divisional organisation, the rise of light forces, and the effects of war-making on society accompany primary sources translated into English for the first time.

Throughout his career, Professor Duffy has written on a wide variety of subjects in over 20 books, exploring topics ranging from the Seven Years War to the First World War, from the history of fortress warfare to the experience of Marshal Suvorov. It is fitting then, that although centred on eighteenth-century warfare, this book also includes chapters which address the Napoleonic conflicts, and First World War.

The first section, Backgrounds and Retrospectives, explores the state of historical writing on eighteenth-century warfare, as well as Professor Duffy's contribution to it. The second section, Commanders and their Armies, explores the field of traditional military history. It provides coverage of tactical analyses, campaign narratives, and organisational and doctrinal changes for the armies fighting in the Old Regime. The third section, Voices from the Past, provides translations and analyses of military sources which have been previously unavailable to the public. The fourth and final section, New Perspectives, demonstrates the varied picture which methods such as archaeology, cultural history, and colonial history tell us about the imperial history of European states at war. This section contains the final essay of the great American historian Dennis Showalter, published posthumously here with the permission of the Showalter family.

The *Changing Face of Old Regime Warfare* continues Professor Duffy's legacy of studying the armies and states of Europe in the eighteenth century, and allows a host of his colleagues to honour his fine work.

Dr Alexander S. Burns is a lecturer in Modern European History at West Virginia University. In 2021, he defended his dissertation, "'The Entire Army Says Hello": Common Soldiers' Experiences, Localism, and Army Reform in Britain and Prussia, 1739-1789' which was directed by Dr Katherine Aaslestad. His research focuses on the intersection of violence, race, and the state in the Atlantic world during the eighteenth century, as well as the history of state-building and reform in German Central Europe. He has published articles on the Hessian, British, and Prussian militaries, and his next monograph explores the international culture of military professionalism that allowed the United States to triumph during the American War of Independence.

The Changing Face of Old Regime Warfare

Essays in Honour of Christopher Duffy

Edited by Alexander S. Burns

Helion & Company

For Alexander B. Rodger,
Katherine B. Aaslestad,
and all mentors and advisors taken before their time.

Helion & Company Limited
Unit 8 Amherst Business Centre
Budbrooke Road
Warwick
CV34 5WE
England
Tel. 01926 499619
Email: info@helion.co.uk
Website: www.helion.co.uk
Twitter: @helionbooks
Visit our blog at http://blog.helion.co.uk/

Published by Helion & Company 2022
Designed and typeset by Mach 3 Solutions Ltd (www.mach3solutions.co.uk)
Cover designed by Paul Hewitt, Battlefield Design (www.battlefield-design.co.uk)

Introduction © Alexander S. Burns 2022; chapters © individual contributors 2022
Maps George Anderson © Helion and Company 2022
Cover: 'European cavalry battle scene (1785)', Gouache by Oetinger, © Anne S.K. Brown Collection

ISBN 978-1-915070-38-8

British Library Cataloguing-in-Publication Data.
A catalogue record for this book is available from the British Library.

For details of other military history titles published by Helion & Company Limited, contact the above address, or visit our website: http://www.helion.co.uk

We always welcome receiving book proposals from prospective authors.

Contents

List of Maps and Plates

Contributors' Biographies

Dr Jonathan Abel has been Assistant Professor of Military History at the US Army Command and General Staff College since 2017. He received his PhD from the Military History Center at the University of North Texas in 2014. He studies the French army of the eighteenth century, and he is the author of several works on the topic, including *Guibert: Father of Napoleon's Grande Armée* and *Guibert's General Essay on Tactics*.

Kurt Baird is a PhD Candidate at the University of York, where he studies with Dr Jasper Heinzen. His thesis is entitled, 'Fighting for the Habsburgs: Community, Patriotism, and the *Kaiserlich-königliche Armee* during the Wars against France, 1792-1818'. His research interests include the Military Enlightenment, martial citizenship, the experience of war, military cultures, social militarization, conscription, and the effects of military processes and the practices on gender, regional identity, and dynastic loyalty in the Austrian Hereditary Lands.

Dr Jeremy Black is a former Professor of History at Exeter University, He is a prolific lecturer and writer, the author of over 100 books. Many concern aspects of eighteenth century British, European and American political, diplomatic and military history but he has also published on the history of the press, cartography, warfare, culture and on the nature and uses of history itself.

Dr Alexander S. Burns is a lecturer in Modern European History at West Virginia University. His publications include articles and book chapters on the American, British, Hessian, and Prussian armies between 1739 and 1789. His dissertation, '"The Entire Army Says Hello": Common Soldiers' Experiences, Localism, and Army Reform in Britain and Prussia, 1739-1789', was directed by Dr Katherine Aaslestad.

Dr Frédéric Chauviré is an associate researcher at the Tempora laboratory at Rennes University. He is a specialist in the study of warfare and cavalry and has written widely on the role of cavalry from the renaissance to modern warfare. His publications on this topic include works in French and English, including *The New Knights: The Development of Cavalry in Western Europe, 1562-1700*, published by Helion.

Dr Marian Füssel is Professor for Early Modern History with special focus on the History of Science at the University of Göttingen. His main fields of research are military history and the history of knowledge in the early modern world. In the field of military history and organized violence, he deals with eighteenth century colonial wars especially with the Seven Years War (1756-1763) as a global conflict. His recent book, *Der Pries des Ruhms,* is an ambitious global history of the Seven Years War.

Dr Jürgen Luh is the director of Research Center Sanssouci at the Stiftung Preussiches Schlösser und Gärten Berlin-Brandenburg. His wide ranging and acclaimed works have included much writing on the period of Frederick II of Prussia, including: *Der Große. Friedrich II. Von Preußen.* His most recent work examines the life of the Great Elector of Brandenburg.

James R. McIntyre is an Assistant Professor of History at Moraine Valley Community College, Palos Hills, Illinois. He serves as the editor of *The Journal of the Seven Years War Association.* He has written on numerous topics regarding the American War of Independence, including the first full length biography of Hessian Jäger commander Johann von Ewald.

Katrin Möbius is a historian and Germanist. Her main field is cultural history. She specializes in linguistic, lifeworld and psycho-historic aspects of power structures from the late Middle Ages to the twentieth century. She is a PhD candidate at the European University Viadrina. Amongst her publications are contributions and articles on military history of the eighteenth and nineteenth centuries in English, Spanish and German journals, and anthologies.

Dr Sascha Möbius is a historian and Anglicist specializing in the history of organized violence, political repression, and power structures from the late Middle Ages to the 20th century. He earned his PhD from Göttingen University. Amongst his publications are numerous books and articles on military history of the eighteenth and nineteenth centuries in English, Spanish and German.

Dr Grzegorz Podruczny is a Professor at the University of Adam Mickiewicz. His historical work has ranged from military architecture to battlefield archaeology, and he is acknowledged as the global authority on the fortresses of Frederick the Great. For the past 10 years, he has been the director of archaeology at the Kunersdorf (Kunowice) battlefield in Poland.

Dr Alexander Querengässer is a lecturer in at Martin Luther University Halle-Wittenburg. He has written extensively on military history in Europe between 1300 and 1900. An expert on the wars of Frederick the Great, he has written and edited volumes on the Battles of Kesselsdorf and Rossbach. Recently, he has released: *Before the Military Revolution: European Warfare and the Rise of the Early Modern State 1300–1490.*

Dr Frederick C. Schneid is the Herman and Louise Smith Professor of History and Chair of the Department of History at High Point University in North Carolina. He specializes in French and Italian military history. He has written extensively on the French Revolutionary and Napoleonic Wars, and the Wars of Italian Unification. Among his publications are

European Armies of the French Revolution, *The Wars of Italian Unification*, *Napoleon's Conquest of Europe*, and chapters in, *The Cambridge History of the Napoleonic Wars*.

Dr Dennis Showalter taught at Colorado College for over 40 years. He was a retired Professor of History, past President of the Society for Military History and Joint Editor of War in History specializing in comparative military history. He has written or edited two dozen books and 150 articles. Recent monographs include *The Wars of German Unification, Patton and Rommel: Men of War in the Twentieth Century* and *Hitler's Panzers*. Dennis has been given a Festschrift: Michael Neiberg (ed.), *Arms and the Man: Military History Essays in Honor of Dennis Showalter* (Leiden, Boston: Brill, 2011). He was the recipient of the 2018 Pritzker Military Museum & Library Award for Lifetime Achievement in Military Writing. Dr Showalter passed away in 2019, his chapter in this volume is published with the kind permission of his estate.

Dr Adam Storring is a post-Doctoral scholar at the Göttingen Institute for Advanced Study. His dissertation, 'Frederick the Great and the Meanings of War, 1730-1755' won the prestigious André Corvisier Prize in 2019. He has published widely on the Prussian Army, Frederick the Great, and the 1758 Zorndorf campaign.

Dr Peter H. Wilson is Chichele Professor of the History of War at the University of Oxford, a Fellow of All Souls College and Principal Investigator of a five-year research project on the 'European Fiscal- Military System 1530-1870' funded by the European Research Council. His books have been translated into Chinese, German, Italian, Polish, Macedonian, Japanese, and Spanish and include *The Holy Roman Empire: A Thousand Years of Europe's History* (Penguin/Harvard UP, 2016), and *Europe's Tragedy: A History of the Thirty Years War* (Penguin/Harvard UP, 2009) which won the Society for Military History's Distinguished Book Award. His latest book, *Lützen*, was published in 2018 by Oxford University Press in its Great Battles series.

Dr Petr Wohlmuth graduated from historical sociology and historical anthropology at Faculty of Humanities, Charles University, Prague. He received his doctorate in historical anthropology at the same faculty for a thesis, dealing with the experience of British and Russian participants in the siege of Sebastopol during the Crimean War. His research focus is the experience of combatants and other participants in wars and armed conflicts. Currently, he is a member of a team, researching the experience and memory of compulsory military service in (post)communist Czechoslovakia (1968–2004), where he combines concepts of symbolical historical anthropology and post-positivist oral history.

Acknowledgements

When working on an edited volume with many authors, it is easy for the historian to remember an ever-present fact: history writing is a collective enterprise. No historian is an island. As such, it is appropriate to first thank my fellow contributors to this volume, as we are united by our respect for Christopher Duffy's writing and legacy. Their writings were not always delivered on time, but they were always deeply engaging, and a pleasure to read and comment on. Together, we have produced a fitting volume to honour a landmark scholar in our field.

Most sincere thanks go to an individual who did not participate in the volume, but without whom it would have been impossible: Dr Ilya Berkovich. Ilya's patient advice allowed this festschrift to take its present shape. His wisdom, delivered by email and by phone (I particularly remember one conversation as I drove through rainy downtown Pittsburgh, to attend the 2018 meeting of the German Studies Association) brought many new authors to volume. Although time constraints did not allow Ilya to write a chapter for this volume, his sincere desire to honour Christopher should be remembered.

Without the constant support, encouragement, and advice of our series editor, Dr Andrew Bamford, this volume would never have appeared in print. Working with Andrew over the last five years on a variety of projects has been rewarding. His professionalism in making academic military history available to the general public sets him apart from many of his peers. Like Christopher, Andrew approaches his subject in a way that all historians should: with a dedication born of passion for his work.

My doctoral advisor, Katherine B. Aaslestad, also graciously allowed the volume to take shape when she permitted me to work on it in parallel with my dissertation project. Though she firmly warned me regarding the dangers of splitting my time, she knew that my admiration for Christopher would necessitate my involvement in his festschrift. Her insistence that I regularly attend the Consortium on the Revolutionary Era brought several authors to the Festschrift. Although she did not live to see it finished, she was a crucial part of its completion.

My wife, Noelle, graciously agreed to read sections of the book to improve clarity and conciseness. Her constant support and constructive editorial criticism, as well as her long-suffering attendance at lectures, museums, and forgotten battlefields has helped make me into the scholar I am today. My greatest debt is to her.

Alexander S. Burns

Introduction

Historians are individuals, but their lives can weave the tapestry of a generational story. When Christopher Duffy defended his doctoral manuscript at Balliol College, Oxford, in 1961, there was a vast gap in the English-language historiography of Central European history in the eighteenth century. Social history was beginning to flourish; the new military history was in its infancy. As work on his festschrift concludes 60 years later, the historiographical landscape has shifted beneath our feet. Christopher's years as an author have seen the rise of transnational history, cultural history, gender history, subaltern studies, to say nothing of material or spatial 'turns'. What is remarkable, then, is that during all that time Christopher's work has remained guided by the same principles: making history accessible to a public audience, keen analysis of historical institutions and structures, physically visiting the places being discussed, and a belief in the importance of narrative in history writing. Christopher's method of thinking about the past is rooted in the physical reality of the past: he had conversations early in life with elders who could remember the war in the Crimea. His writing makes the past come to life, whether examining the structures of states and armies, the archaeological remains of conflicts, the geological formations and weather patterns which shaped the military landscape, or the monarchical biographies of Frederick II or Maria Theresa.

This is evidenced in wide variety of scholars who leapt at the chance to take part in this volume. The authors include graduate students, young academics with the ink still wet on their diplomas, professionals in mid-career, and seasoned senior scholars in their fields. Even more surprising than the range of seniority among the authors who have come together for this festschrift is their geographical diversity. These scholars live, work, and hold academic positions in the United Kingdom, France, Germany, Poland, Czechia, Argentina, and the United States. For scholars in various stages of their careers, in seven countries on three continents, Christopher Duffy's work still holds a special place of attention. His scholarship has become the natural starting place for Anglophone scholars studying the military history of German Central Europe in the eighteenth century, as well as all scholars interested in the military history of the Jacobite 1745 Rebellion.

What is truly incredible about Christopher's professional life, however, is not the way that he has connected with fellow-scholars, but with the public. Christopher's written work, always penned in a manner that could connect to a general audience, was only one of the important ways that he reached the public. Christopher taught generations of British officers during this time at the Royal Military Academy Sandhurst from 1961 to 1996. In this period, teaching young officers alongside John Keegan, David Chandler, and Richard Holmes, Christopher thoroughly enjoyed work that he would have happily done for free. He retired as the Senior Lecturer in War Studies and spent the next several years as a research professor at De Montfort University.

In addition to writing and teaching, Christopher worked extensively in the service of a number of professional and public organizations related to his interests. He has served as a founding member and the Secretary-General of the British Commission for Military History (which he immediately pushed me to join upon our meeting) and served as the vice-president of the Military History Society of Ireland. As befits a scholar with an abiding interest in Jacobite military history, he served as the Chairman of the 1745 Association. Far from providing administration for these societies, Christopher has been at the forefront of the fight in Britain to preserve battlefields. Over the past 20 years, he has worked tirelessly with the National Trust for Scotland in order to preserve the Culloden Battlefield for posterity.

During the 1970s, Christopher worked as a military advisor with his Sandhurst colleague David Chandler for the 1972 BBC production of *War and Peace*. There, he worked tirelessly with a Serbian militia contingent of the Yugoslavian Territorial Army, to train extras for the large battle sequences. In the course of filming the Borodino sequence, the extras mutinied over working conditions, and Christopher retreated to a squad of gunners in the Raevsky redoubt, with whom he had developed a good working relationship. There the British academic and Serbian gunners waited out the end of the mutiny. Although the production was attended with difficulties, it is another sterling example of Christopher's dedication to presenting history to the widest possible audience.

In addition to service in professional organizations and media consultation, Christopher has kindly donated his time in the service of the interested public, taking on speaking engagements in the United Kingdom and the United States for private associations dedicated to the study of military history. His long connection with the Seven Years War Association fostered the study of the European Seven Years War in the United States, and Christopher developed long friendships with many members, such as the late Jim Mitchell and Dean West. Many of these interested individuals in the United States and the United Kingdom joined Christopher, as he led tours of eighteenth-century European battlefields. He has never been afraid to devote time to the public, smashing the perception that rigorous researchers are disconnected from ordinary life.

When one matches his public activities with his scholarly writing, a clear picture emerges of his scholarship. It is not an exaggeration to claim that Christopher has been in the vanguard of thought, representation, outreach, and action on the subject of eighteenth-century warfare for most of his professional life. This volume, then, is a small tribute to the life and work of a towering giant in the historical profession.

Organisation

When soliciting chapters for this volume, I was guided by one principle: the content of the chapters should connect to one of the many periods of history that Christopher has explored in his writings. Although the essays could have ranged widely, they are fortunately centred on the experience of eighteenth-century Europe. A pair of chapters considered the Revolutionary and Napoleonic eras, and one scholar focused his efforts on twentieth-century conflict, where Christopher has explored both the First and Second World Wars. Sadly, two scholars slated to explore the world of the Jacobite Rebellions withdrew from the volume as a result of other commitments, and Christopher's contribution to the world of Jacobite studies is briefly explored in the second chapter.

The Changing Face of Old Regime Warfare brings together essays from scholars who wish to honour Christopher, but the honouree is far from the only thing that unites them. Centred in the world of the Holy Roman Empire of the 1750s, most of the chapters in the volume demonstrate a focus on revision in scholarly studies on Old Regime armies between 1740 and 1789. For the authors united here, Old Regime armies were sites of reform, adaptation, and flexibility. From the French training camps of the 1770s, to the increasing importance of light forces in eighteenth-century conflict, to Frederick II 'the Great' of Prussia's grandiloquent ideas on changes in warfare after the Seven Years War: change was in the air in the late Old Regime. As a result, it is highly fitting that a festschrift with this theme should appear in a series entitled *From Reason to Revolution*.

This volume is subdivided into four sections. The first section, Background and Retrospectives, contains two essays reflecting on eighteenth-century warfare and Christopher's historiographical legacy. No living scholar has written more voluminously on eighteenth-century conflict, so it is fitting that Jeremy Black's essay, 'Eighteenth-Century War in a Global Perspective', introduces the reader to this complex world. Black's treatment of global military history provides a helpful contrast to many of the chapters which exclusively explore European military history. My own chapter, 'Writing for Pleasure: Christopher Duffy's Historiographical Legacy', places the honouree of this festschrift where he belongs: front and center. Duffy's thematic contributions to military history, as well as the broader scope of his writings, are explored in detail.

The second section, Commanders and their Armies, explores Christopher's primary field of research: traditional military history. These essays include new research from junior scholars, as well as senior historians who have known Christopher for decades. Jürgen Luh begins this section with a brief treatment of Frederick the Great's final comprehensive military treatise: the *Eléments de castramétrie et de tactique*. Peter H. Wilson gives a new window into an understudied and undervalued military state during the Seven Years War in the fourth chapter, 'The Württemberg Army in the Seven Years War'. The fifth and sixth chapters both explore the exploits of French cavalrymen, but in very different contexts. Frédéric Chauvire's 'The Crisis of the French Cavalry during the Seven Years War', examines the prestigious arm of Louis XV's military force in the 1750s. Frederick Schneid brings his considerable research to bear on the horsemen of the Battle of the Three Emperors in 'French Cavalry at Austerlitz: The Historical Narrative and Data'. This French theme is completed by the seventh chapter, Jonathan Abel's exploration of the use of divisional forces in Old Regime France. As Abel explores French experimentation with divisions, James R. McIntyre continues this journey through traditional military history in the eighth chapter, 'Pandours, Partisans, and Freikorps: The Development of Warfare and Light Troops across the Eighteenth Century'. Honouring Christopher's work on military architecture and siege warfare, Petr Wohlmuth's ninth chapter explores the world of an obscure English Engineer, Charles Bisset.

The third section, Voices from the Past, provides a unique window into the world of the eighteenth century with two essays on writing by contemporaries. Adam L. Storring begins this section with a translation of Pastor Täge's classic account of the 1758 campaign on the Oder. Katrin and Sascha Möbius provide a natural complement to this translated source with an analysis of newly rediscovered Prussian soldiers' correspondence from the early Seven Years War.

The fourth and final section, New Perspectives, demonstrates the way that methods including archaeology and cultural history have broadened the military historical field during Christopher's time in the profession. In the twelfth chapter, 'Clearing the Fog of War', Grzegorz Podruczny presents the fruits of over a decade of archaeological research on the Kunersdorf battlefield. His unique perspective brings the violence of eighteenth-century conflict to life in new and surprising ways. Kurt Baird continues the work of the so-called 'new school' on eighteenth-century common soldiers into the 1780s and 1790s in the volume's thirteenth chapter, exploring 'The Primacy of State Violence in Austro-Bohemian Lands'. The fourteenth and fifteenth chapters, from Alexander Querengässer and Marian Füssel, engage in a lively debate over the decisiveness and representation of eighteenth-century battle. The section concludes with the final essay of well-known American historian Dennis Showalter, published posthumously with the permission of his family. Showalter explores the role of empire and colonial troops in the early twentieth century.

Taken together, these essays honour Christopher's unique contribution to military history over the past 60 years. They collect the work of scholars analysing military structures, cultural history, archaeology, and narrative military history. By combining global background, specific historiographical contributions, traditional military history, new sources, and novel approaches, this volume ensures that the world of eighteenth-century Military Europe, first explored by Duffy, will be made available to a new generation of Anglophone students.

Alexander S. Burns
West Virginia University
1 September 2021

Professor Christopher Duffy. (Photo by Jeremy Sutton-Hibbert)

Christopher Duffy's Works

Facilitator and Editor

Alexander B. Rodger, *The War of the Second Coalition 1798 to 1801: A Strategic Commentary* (1961)

Contributor

East Central European Society and War in the Prerevolutionary Eighteenth-Century (1982)
The Oxford Book of Military Anecdotes (1985)

Principal Author

The Wild Goose and the Eagle: A Life of Marshal von Browne (1964)
Borodino and the War of 1812 (1972)
The Army of Frederick the Great (1974)
Fire and Stone: The Science of Fortress Warfare (1975)
The Army of Maria Theresa: The Armed Forces of Imperial Austria (1977)
Austerlitz 1805 (1977)
Siege Warfare: The Fortress in the Early Modern World, 1494-1660 (1979)
Russia's Military Way to the West: Origins and Nature of Russian Military Power (1981)
Siege Warfare: The Fortress in the Age of Vauban and Frederick the Great, 1660-1789 (1985)
Frederick the Great: A Military Life (1985)
The Military Experience in the Age of Reason (1987)
Red Storm on the Reich: The Soviet March on Germany (1991)
The Army of Frederick the Great, 2nd Revised Edition (1996)
Eagles over the Alps: Suvorov in Italy and Switzerland, 1799 (1999)
The Austrian Army in the Seven Years War: Instrument of War (2000)
Prussia's Glory: Rossbach and Leuthen, 1757 (2003)
Through German Eyes: The British and the Somme, 1916 (2006)
The '45: Bonnie Prince Charlie and the Untold Story of the Jacobite Rising (2007)
The Austrian Army in the Seven Years War: By Force of Arms (2008)
The Best of Enemies: Germans against Jacobites, 1746 (2013)
Fight for a Throne: The Jacobite '45 Reconsidered (2015)

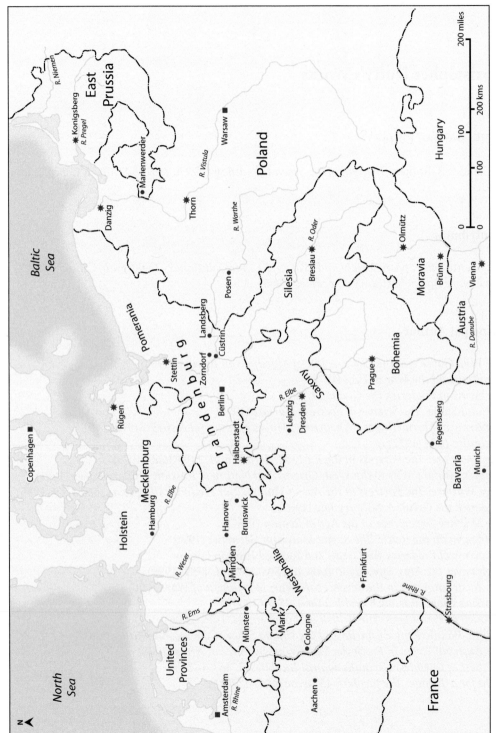

Central Europe in the mid-eighteenth century.

Section One

Background and Retrospectives

1

Eighteenth-Century War in a Global Perspective

Jeremy Black

Introduction

The customary chronology in the discussion of war and its causes was that of a decline in ideological factors between the 'Wars of Religion' and the outbreak of the French Revolutionary Wars in 1792, although bellicosity remained a key factor. However, this is very much an agenda that is set by Western concerns and developments. In that, it focuses not only on the Western interest in Western history, but also on a teleological focus on a state system supposedly created by the 'Westphalian Settlement', the Peace of Westphalia of 1648 that brought to an end the Thirty Years War. That settlement is commonly presented as a triumph of reason and restraint, in the shape of an agreement to operate an international system based on the mutual respect of sovereign powers and, in particular, an agreement to accept confessional plurality, at least in the form of different types of Christianity, as sole state religions. To contemporaries, the latter was probably more significant than subsequent secular commentators have suggested with their focus on a system of mutual respect, which is generally presented largely, or exclusively, in lay terms.

Whether respect and restraint are emphasized in secular or in spiritual terms, the reality, nevertheless, was that the Peace of Westphalia did not usher in a new age in European warfare. Indeed, attempts to advance secular and confessional interests continued in a manner that was far from limited. The Westphalian settlement also meant nothing across most of the world.

Bellicosity, Culture and Rulership

International rivalry was one of force and power, with warfare, in Europe and more generally, linked to state-forms, governmental development, and the culture of majesty, notably royal ambition. Around the world, but to a varying extent, tensions between tribal and state forms of government were significant, although, alongside contrasts between the two, there were also overlaps.[1] Across the world, *gloire*, loosely translated as the pursuit of glory, was important in causing and sustaining conflict, in setting military objectives, and in celebrating success. This reflected the extent to which the notion of 'the state' as a rational contrast to the monarch had more meaning in political theory than in practice. Military success brought exemplary purpose and fame and acted as a lubricant of obedience in crown-élite relations. Military heroism played a major role in the representation of states,[2] and this role affected literature, history, and the arts.[3] Indeed, in his 1792 treatise, *Yuzhi shiquan ji [In Commemoration of the Ten Complete Military Victories]*, the Qianlong emperor of China (reigned 1736-1796) reached 10 by including failures. The points made in this paragraph could all have been made for previous centuries which indicates the degree to which there was no real break, either in the mid-seventeenth century or at the close of the fifteenth.

War offered the possibility of strengthening the dynastic position, both domestically and internationally, and also of enhancing territorial control. This element was important to major rulers pursuing large-scale goals, but also to lesser princes, such as Max Emmanuel, Elector of Bavaria during the War of the Spanish Succession (1701-14), seeking to sell his participation in the conflict for gains in territory and status.[4] This was the buffer state or player as agent, a situation that continues to the present. In the event, Max Emmanuel's support for Louis XIV of France (reigned 1643-1715) led to defeat and the conquest by Austria of his territories which he only regained as part of the peace settlement.

A key element of Louis' bellicosity was that he had little realistic sense of how the wars he began would develop diplomatically, militarily, or politically, but then that has been true across history, as seen with the Iraqi invasions of Iran and Kuwait in 1980 and 1990 respectively and the American-led invasion of Iraq in 2003. Thus, in 1672, rather than fighting a limited war with the Dutch, who, after being invaded, were willing to offer terms, an over-confident Louis, hopeful that the war would widen to include Spain so that he could resume the conquest of the Spanish Netherlands (Belgium), issued excessive demands, including for major territorial gains and the acceptance of Catholic worship. The last reflected the extent to which religion was an important goal for all the powers, with Louis also determined to gain prestige by being seen as a champion of Catholicism, supplanting the Habsburgs in this role. In 1673-1774, the conflict changed shape and broadened, as Austria, the Dutch, Spain, and Lorraine agreed in 1673 to force Louis back to his 1659 frontiers. Louis was happy to see Spain enter the war, but not Austria, nor, in 1674, to lose the alliance with England.

Similarly, Louis miscalculated in 1688 when he assumed that his use of his army to enforce his interests in the Rhineland, notably in Cologne and the Palatinate, would lead to a limited, short, and successful conflict in which German rulers would desert Leopold I of Austria, who would be driven to terms by French triumphs. Instead, the struggle broadened

---

1   Richard Tapper (ed.), *The Conflict of Tribe and State in Iran and Afghanistan* (London: Routledge, 1983).
2   Gerald Jordan and Nicholas Rogers, 'Admirals as Heroes: Patriotism and Liberty in Hanoverian England', *Journal of British Studies*, 28 (1989), pp.201-222.
3   R.E. Glass, 'The Image of the Sea Officer in English Literature, 1660-1710', *Albion*, 26 (1994), pp.583-599; Alan McNairn, *Behold the Hero: General Wolfe and the Arts in the Eighteenth Century* (Liverpool: Liverpool University Press, 1997).
4   Philip V of Spain to Max Emmanuel, 10 September 1702, 12 October 1704, BN. NAF. 486 fols 78, 89.

out and Louis found himself facing a powerful coalition. So also with the miscalculations of the rulers of Denmark, Russia, and Saxony-Poland those who, in 1700, launched what became the Great Northern War in an attempt to partition the Swedish overseas empire.

Military command could be separated from rule, as was demonstrated by the great success and considerable importance of Prince Eugene, John, 1st Duke of Marlborough, and Marshal Saxe, leading generals for Austria, Britain, and France respectively. In addition, George Washington and the Marquis de Lafayette, both heroes of the American Revolution, were to offer a model of modern military celebrity in which political dedication to a cause they did not control was a key aspect of their appeal.[5] In the Turkish empire, military leadership on campaign was increasingly by Grand Viziers (leading ministers), and not by sultans, a pattern that had begun after Suleiman the Magnificent died in 1566: Ahmed III accompanied the army in 1715 and 1717, but remained far behind the front line, and in 1730 did not even set out on campaign, helping precipitate the rebellion that led to his overthrow.

Nevertheless, military command was generally a key aspect of rulership, a situation encouraged by the view that waging a lawful war required a declaration of war, and that only true sovereigns could declare war.[6] John Campbell's comment on Frederick William I of Prussia (reigned 1713-1740) – 'he made his troops his delight, and led all his days rather a military than a court life' – could have been repeated for other rulers. The wearing of uniform was important for monarchs in some Western states.[7] So also were military reviews. Thus, in 1777, Ferdinand I of Naples spent much time exercising his troops, including taking part in a mock campaign planned by the king that entailed constructing a camp and staging mock battles and a siege.[8]

Moreover, as for most of history, and indeed still for some states today, many of the commanders of the period were also rulers. Most, such as Peter the Great (I) of Russia (reigned 1689-1725), Frederick the Great (II) of Prussia (reigned 1740-1786), and the Kangxi emperor of China (reigned 1661-1722), inherited the right to rule, and then used war greatly to enhance their assets. Peter, in particular, transformed both army and state in order to increase Russian military effectiveness and win territory and prestige. He inherited his first war with the Turks, but deliberately started a second in 1711. As one of the allied rulers plotting to deprive Sweden of its overseas empire, Peter also played a role in beginning the Great Northern War (1700-1721) and persisted in this struggle longer than his allies. He was very much a ruler who fought, taking part in major battles, notably the crucial victory over the Swedes at Poltava in 1709 and the defeat by the Turks at the River Pruth in 1711. The Great Northern War over, Peter led an invasion of Persia in 1722, an invasion that produced territorial gains only to lead, after his death, to a withdrawal that reflected an over-extension of power in the face of a resurgent Persia.

---

5   Paul Spalding, *Lafayette. Prisoner of State* (Columbia, South Carolina: University of South Carolina Press, 2010).

6   Frederic Baumgartner, *Declaring War in Early Modern Europe* (Basingstoke: Palgrave, 2011), p.114.

7   Philip Mansel, 'Monarchy, Uniform and the Rise of the Frac, 1760-1813', *Past and Present*, 96 (1982), pp.103-132.

8   Marquis de Clermont d'Ambolise, French envoy, to Vergennes, French foreign minister, 19 April, 14 June, 1777, Archives nationales, KK 1393.

In contrast to inheriting power, Nadir Shah of Persia, having become crucial, as a commander, to military success against the invading Turks, took over a failing empire in the 1730s, declaring himself Shah in 1736, and gave Persia a military dynamism, until his assassination in 1747. Even more than Peter, he campaigned widely, leading armies against the Turks, but also, in 1739, into northern India. This was war of a type familiar to the Mongols under Chinggis Khan (c.1162-1227) and many others. Given this continuity, it is interesting to consider why any particular psychological or practical transformations in the causes of war should be anticipated in the far smaller period of time since then.

War and military activity played important roles in a culture of power to which honour and prestige were significant, let alone such related issues as insecure and provoked masculinities.[9] Concern for personal honour was particularly apparent in the case of officers, and greatly affected command practices and issues.[10] The effects, however, varied. No Western ruler matched 'Alaungpaya of Burma (reigned 1752-1760), who judged men largely by the number of heads they could produce after a battle. Moreover, unsuccessful Burmese officers were executed; a practice also seen with the enforced suicides of commanders in China. With the prominent exception of Admiral Byng, shot in 1757, after a court martial for failing to relieve the French-besieged British garrison on the Mediterranean island of Minorca the previous year, the execution of commanders was uncommon in the West until Revolutionary France, from 1792, treated failure as a demonstration of treason. The American revolutionaries had not followed this course, which was a prime instance of the less radical path followed there than in the case of France.

Again, on a longstanding pattern, the cultural dimension extended to the aesthetics of warfare, with rulers placing particular value on a good-looking army. This preference played a role in recruitment, encouraging the acceptance of tall men over short ones, notably by Frederick William I of Prussia. For the same reason, many Western rulers designed their soldiers' uniforms, with an emphasis on having the army look good, as well as seeking to assist local textile industries. Military activity also fulfilled narratives and models of imperial and royal, destiny and role. The repute of rulers and the fame of ancestors were echoed.[11] This can be very much seen in the iconography employed by Louis XIV in his new palace at Versailles, a palace that others in Europe sought to emulate, as in Berlin (Prussia) and Het Loo (the Netherlands). The ruler as warrior was the key theme, and one intended to enable Louis to outshine his predecessors and contemporaries, and to set a model for his successors.

The willingness of rulers, commanders, and combatants not only to kill large numbers, but also to accept heavy casualties, was an important feature of military culture, although the latter acceptance varied. Preserving the army was the first priority, but there was a greater willingness to take casualties than with much, although by no means all, modern warfare,

9   V.G. Kiernan, *The Duel in European History: Honour and the Reign of Aristocracy* (Oxford: Oxford University Press, 1989).

10   Rory Muir and Charles Esdaile, 'Strategic Planning in a Time of Small Government: the Wars against Revolutionary and Napoleonic France, 1793-1815', in Chris Woolgar (ed.), *Wellington Studies* (Southampton: University of Southampton, 1996), Vol.I, p.80.

11   Joanna Waley-Cohen, *The Culture of War in China: Empire and the Military under the Qing Dynasty* (London: Tauris, 2006).

and certainly as far as regular forces are concerned. Based on the cost of training modern troops and their relative rarity, a functional explanation of this current unwillingness can be advanced, one that contrasts it with the situation in the eighteenth century. However, social, cultural, and ideological factors are, and were, more significant, not least of which is the contrast between modern individualism and hedonism, both of which discourage an acceptance of casualties (even though the population is far larger), and, on the other hand, earlier concepts of duty and fatalism in a much harsher working environment. The extent to which this sense of duty and fatalism can be related to levels of habitual violence in society is unclear.[12]

The acceptance of casualties was crucial to the bellicosity of the age. On the pattern of earlier moralists, principally religious writers, Enlightenment individuals in Christian Europe and North America might criticise all, or much, of this belligerence, presenting it as a pointless and indeed dishonourable bloodlust. However, these views had scant impact on the goals and means of waging conflict. Instead, the continued normative character of resorting to warfare was more notable, and across the world. Rulers, ministers, and commanders, very much an overlapping group, tended to see their wars more as transitioning into each other, rather than as distinct conflicts punctuated by periods of distinct peace. In part, this was an objective response to particular bilateral relations, for example between China and the Zunghars, the Mughals and the Marathas, Russia and the Turks, or Britain and France. There was also the contrast between the concept of a just and lasting peace and the belief that this was likely to be illusory due to the failings of human society. War thus was normative.

Wars were believed to be not only necessary, but also, in at least some respects, desirable. In each respect, they could be presented as just. This conviction proved a key context for the eighteenth century, and also for those that preceded and followed it, again undermining the idea of significant changes through time in the longer eighteenth century. The belief in necessity also helped explain the attitude in combat zones to those who would later be called civilians. This issue included the response to conventions that restricted violence, at least within cultural zones, such as Christendom and the world of Islam.[13] In practice, these conventions were frequently ignored.

The nature of rule was a central element in the military history of the period. Military systems with political continuity and stability, and administrative strength, particularly China, France, Britain, and Russia, proved more able to sustain a projection of their power than monarchies on horseback, such as those of the Zunghars, Nadir Shah, Ahmad Shah Durrani in Afghanistan, and Napoleon, or, with the exception of their not using horses, 'Alaungpaya, and Tamsin in Siam (Thailand). Ultimately, therefore, military history is an aspect of the other histories of the period, as well as contributing greatly to them.

---

12   Julius Ruff, *Violence in Early Modern Europe, 1500-1800* (Cambridge: Cambridge University Press, 2001).

13   H. Carl, 'Restricted Violence? Military Occupation during the Eighteenth Century', in E. Charters, E. Rosenhaft and H. Smith (eds), *Civilians and War in Europe, 1618-1815* (Liverpool: Liverpool University Press, 2012), pp.116-126.

Environmental history was one such. The dependence of operations on the weather and climate was a key element, as 'the present scarcity of corn and all other provisions'[14] could delay or prevent moves or be believed likely to do so. Harsh winters and springs delayed the appearance of grass, affecting the moves of cavalry. Indeed, insofar as war could be a series of campaigns, each bounded by the weather, then the decision to start anew could be influenced by the latter. Nevertheless, alongside potent limitations, their potency in part due to their unpredictability, governmental development was significant to military capability, notably in helping produce, deploy, and sustain the necessary resources for war,[15] but, moreover, as an aspect of a system of rule that provided the political stability valuable for military activity.

Aside from serious issues in the coverage of warfare in this (and other) centuries, there are concerns about standard explanations. As a reminder, for example, of the need for care in drawing clear causal conclusions in the sphere of international conflict, and therefore suggesting a willingness to fight based on an assumption of success, governmental systems of continuity, stability and strength were not invariably successful in war. The Chinese discovered this in Burma and Vietnam, the Russians in Persia, the Afghans in Persia and the Punjab, and the British, eventually, but more centrally to their military effort than in the Chinese and Russian examples, in North America. In each case, both conflicts and failures can be regarded as those of imperial over-stretch, albeit in very different contexts, the last example, the American Revolution (1775-1783), having an element of civil war not seen in the other examples cited in the previous sentence. However, although the thesis of such an over-stretch, in aspiration and attainment, appears seductively clear, its application is not readily inherent to particular circumstances. Instead, far from being readily obvious, over-stretch emerged through the warfare of the period, warfare that helped define imperial limits and, more generally, mould, as well as register, the politics of the period.

A common requirement of the ruler-leaders in this era was the demonstration of both political and military skill in order to win *gloire*, with the military dimension closely associated with the political. As with other periods of conflict, wars were best fought sequentially, not simultaneously. It was necessary to divide opponents, to create tensions in their relationships, indeed alliances, and to fight them in sequence. This was a practice at which Frederick the Great was generally adept as, in more propitious circumstances given his far greater power, was the Qianlong emperor: war with Burma followed that with the Zunghars, and war with Nepal that with Vietnam.

Correspondingly, Louis XIV proved unable to move from a successful opening of wars to an ability to overcome the opposing coalitions to which his conflicts gave rise. With Louis, as with other cases, for example the Second World War, it is important to see two sets of 'causes' of war: those of the initial conflict and those that explain subsequent entries into the war. With Louis, there was a growing concern about his intentions, and understandably so given his disinclination to accept limits. This concern can seem a quasi-automatic response to the threat of a new hegemony, or, conversely, a reluctance to resist until success

---

14   Thomas Robinson, British envoy in Vienna, to William, Earl of Harrington, British Secretary of State, reporting views of Austrian minister Bartenstein, 22 February 1741, The National Archives, SP80/144.
15   Richard Bonney (ed.), *The Rise of the Fiscal State in Europe, c. 1200-1815* (Oxford: Oxford University Press, 1999).

seems assured. Moving from the model of hegemonic drive and resulting resistance, it is also appropriate to note the glory involved in resisting Louis. This was very much seen with the image of William III of Orange and Victor Amadeus II of Savoy-Piedmont. It was also important, for both Louis and his opponents, to hold together constituencies of interest, be they international alliances or the groups within countries backing a war effort. Doing so made the resort to war far more attractive.

The political dimension to conflict is also captured in the stress in the literature on state building, but there is a danger that that dimension of causes and consequences is approached in an overly schematic and 'modern' fashion, and without giving due weight to other political aspects of warfare and the related military aspects of politics. The notion that war makes states and states make war is seductively clear, but also begs a lot of questions about both the processes involved and the extent to which war also fulfils other purposes, as well as frequently undermining states as a result of the burdens incurred, whether resource and political, structural, or contingent.

In addition, it is important to emphasise the degree to which rulers, in making war, called upon non-bureaucratic processes to raise and support forces. These processes had significant consequences for the way in which war was pursued. Moreover, the extent to which states make war was (and is) not automatic, nor consistent, nor similar in frequency. Rather than simply viewing this question in terms of a model, whether of war, the international system, or of state-building, a model that takes precedence over particular circumstances and individual decisions, it is also pertinent to focus on these circumstances and decisions.

These circumstances and discussions are of particular significance when considering choices made between possible challenges, for these choices indicate that geopolitical and other factors also play through specific issues, with European warfare being affected accordingly. For example, by turning east against Afghanistan and India in the late 1730s, each a different military environment, Nadir Shah reduced the pressure on his former opponent, the Turks. By doing so, he enabled the latter to concentrate on war with Russia and, more successfully, Austria, and to great effect in 1739 when the Austrians, as a result, lost Belgrade. In contrast, Russia and Austria had each benefited from the end in 1735 of the War of the Polish Succession, which had reduced the pressures stemming from real or likely war on their western fronts.

Governments could also be divided over policy, as the Chinese one was over going to war with the Zunghars in the 1750s, the British over war with Spain in 1729, 1738-1739, and 1761, and with Russia in 1717-1720 and 1791, the French over war with Britain in 1770, 1778, and 1790, and the Americans over policy towards Britain and France in the late 1790s. Such division interacts with more general and more specific cultural pressures for bellicosity.

The role of ideology also has to be assessed. If religious differences played a part in rivalry between Shi'ite Persia and Sunni Turkey, they did not prevent peace between the two for most of the second half of the century; although, in the Punjab in north-west India, religious hostility between Sikhs and Afghans led, in the 1760s, to sustained and eventually successful opposition to the latter. Subsequent Afghan invasions of north-west India saw much violence directed against Sikh practices. Tension over the radical plans of the French revolutionaries may have led to war with Austria and Prussia in 1792, but Britain, the Dutch and Spain did not enter the war with France until 1793, while Prussia and Spain left it in 1795 and Spain swiftly after allied with France. In the early 1790s, Russia was more concerned about controlling Poland than opposing French radicalism, and crushed Polish opposition accordingly in 1794.

Far from there being any fixed relationship between war and politics, it is the flexible nature of the links that helps explain the importance of each to the other. Military activity certainly altered the contours and parameters of the politics that helped cause it, and sometimes of the states involved in conflict. In some cases, military activity had a comparable impact on social structures. The centrality of war as a basis of change, however, does not mean that there was a consistent pattern of cause or effect.

Wars Across Cultures

As before, there were important questions of definition when assessing wars across cultures. Although their ruling ideology was generally different, many major states were clearly hybrids, including Mughal India, Safavid Persia, Ottoman Turkey, and Manchu China. Indeed, British India was to come into this pattern. The culture, political system, ideology, and military arrangements and methods, reflected the traditions of conquerors and conquered. In part, this was a matter of assimilation and in part of the maintenance of separate practices. When the Mughals campaigned against the Uzbeks across the Hindu Kush in the 1640s or the Manchu conquered Mongolia in the 1690s, it is difficult to see such campaigns in terms of the clash of totally different cultures. Nevertheless, there had been a process of assimilation on the part of conquering Manchus, Mughals, Safavids and Ottomans, and, partly as a result, the element of cultural clash was apparent. This can be seen in the Afghan overthrow of Safavid Persia in the 1720s.

The Manchu fought to expand. Their expansionism was mostly imperial, for glory and possessions rather than for resources and trade. In contrast, the earlier Ming dynasty had fought mostly to preserve itself and its dependents, such as Korea. Manchu warfare was certainly not limited, no more than that of the Europeans against Native opponents in North America or the Russians against opponents in Siberia.

Yet, there could also be co-operation. Like the Ming, the Manchu sought the support of particular Mongol tribes, and, thus, to lessen the Mongol threat. It was also the case with European relations with Native Americans in North America. The fur trade led to the creation of political-economic networks and to the involvement of Europeans in Native wars, and vice versa, a process facilitated by, and in part due to, the increasing provision of European arms and ammunition. However, this involvement was not a case of more of the same. In North America, as elsewhere, European intrusion intensified war amongst non-state peoples.

The notion of hostility across cultures had to be qualified by a realisation of the degree to which intra-cultural wars were as important, or could take precedence. In the first half of the eighteenth century, the Russians devoted more effort to fighting Christian European neighbours, especially a life-and-death struggle with Charles XII of Sweden, than to fighting other polities, although they did devote much effort to war with the Turks in 1711 and 1736-1739. In North America, the British, French and Spaniards focused their efforts on conflict with each other, rather than with the Native Americans, and this is even more apparent if expenditure on fortifications and naval support is also considered.

In India, as a key element in European warfare, the British were more concerned about France in the late 1740s than about native states. In the Carnatic, this situation changed only after the defeat of the French in 1760-1761: the Battle of Wandewash and the fall of Pondicherry were crucial preludes to more assertive British policies towards native rulers, notably Mysore and the Marathas. The destruction in India of an Anglo-French balance and of a French threat to British interests were followed not by peaceful hegemony in regions where the British were strong but, instead, by bouts of expansionist activity.

In India, and more generally, there was no necessary pattern of continual warfare. Instead, alongside cultural and other factors that encouraged expansionism, it is more helpful to consider peace, wars, and the cause of the move from one to the other. In part, this was the case, as with all wars, of the complex relationship of fear and opportunity. Native Americans could attack European settlers because they feared their advance and despaired at the inability or unwillingness of colonial authorities to control it. This happened in the Carolinas in 1715, in what was to be Vermont in the 1720s, and in Pontiac's War in 1763-1764, a war presented by European-Americans as a rebellion or rising.

Fear also played a role in Asia. The Chinese feared the creation of a hostile Mongol confederation from the 1690s and notably the consequences in Tibet as well as Mongolia. Fear was seen elsewhere. Burmese conquest in 1767 made later Siamese (Thai) rulers fearful, encouraging them to take an aggressive stance and also to dominate the lands through which the Burmese had advanced, and might do so again.

Religion and Enlightenment

Religious tensions remained in the causes of conflict significant. In western Sichuan in China, the First Jinchuan War of 1747-1749, broke out as the Emperor sought to bring the essentially autonomous Gyalrong or Golden Stream tribes under administrative control. Religious animosity played a role, as the Golden Stream followed the indigenous, animist, Tibetan Bon religion and Tibetan Buddhism's Red Hat sect, resisting the Yellow Hat sect which the Emperor supported. In part, the conflict therefore involved a struggle between different types of prestige, magic, and providential support. This element was more generally true in East Asia, as leaders were sacral figures.[16] Similarly, in Persia, Nadir Shah's wish to resolve the schism within Islam and to integrate Shi'ism into Sunni'ism helped encourage opposition to him in Persia as well as the animosity of Turkey, whose ruler claimed religious authority as Caliph.

In Spain, the tradition of conquest for Christ remained strong and difficulties experienced in converting natives leading to a harsh attitude that also justified imperial expansion. When Nojpeten, the capital of the Maya people known as Itzas, was stormed in 1697, Martín de Ursúa, the interim Governor of Yucatán, ordered his men to plant the flag with the royal arms of Spain and religious standards among the Itza temples 'in which the majesty of God had been offended by idolatries'.[17] Ursúa thanked God for his victory and then joined soldiers and Franciscans in destroying a large number of 'idols.' If gold or silver, such idols

16   Joanna Waley-Cohen, 'Religion, War, and Empire-building in Eighteenth-century China', *International History Review*, 20 (1998), pp.336-352.
17   Quoted in Jeremy Black, *Europe and the World, 1650-1830* (London: Routledge, 2002) p.42.

were melted down. This was religious war against opponents presented as guilty of human sacrifice, cannibalism and killing priests. Five years earlier, when the town of Santa Fé was regained by the Spaniards after the Pueblo rebellion of 1680, there had also been a reimposition of Catholic control. Franciscan priests absolved natives of the apostasy and baptised those born after 1680, with the governor serving as godfather for the children. Religious identity remained crucial. Following the capture of Oran in 1732, Benjamin Keene, the British envoy, reported: 'there is scarce a Spaniard who does not think himself halfway to his salvation by the merits of this conquest' from the Muslims.[18] Large-scale Spanish attempts to capture Algiers, mounted in 1775 and 1784, failed badly. Generally forgotten, they serve, however, as a reminder of the significance of religious struggle. Although it was to be France that conquered Algeria from 1830, there is a link from the *Reconquista* to the struggle in the sixteenth to eighteenth centuries to dominate the western Mediterranean, and then on to expansionism in Morocco from the mid-nineteenth century. The values of the army can in particular be located in this context.

In these and other circumstances, opportunity, as well as fear and anxiety, played a role, but it could be a case of opportunity rather than fear or anxiety. A perception of weakness providing the chance for great gain encouraged the Afghans to attack Persia in 1722 and Nadir Shah to invade Mughal India in 1739. Both attacks were successful.

Further uncertainty arises if trying to reduce the range of contemporary attitudes to one of the 'Enlightenment view on war' or 'the Eighteenth-Century view of war'. For most contemporaries, there is no evidence of attitudes. A number of suggestions, however, can be made. First, war was normative and therefore it was likely not to have aroused attention as an unusual phenomenon requiring special attention. The role of religion was also such that attitudes towards particular conflicts as Christian or unchristian, and the views of religious bodies, were also probably significant. Given long familiarity with war, these were far more supportive of the process than is the case now.

To focus on prominent Enlightenment figures as if they defined the whole is therefore problematic. At the same time, it is useful as their views indicated a situation of flux well before the beginning of the French Revolutionary War. In particular, there were attempts to move the discussion of war from the contexts of Christian thought and royal *gloire*. These attempts spanned a range of writers from Voltaire to Adam Smith, and their preferences, and their views on rationality, were as contextual within the period as those attitudes they criticised. Nevertheless, the appeal to reason was one that looked forward to nineteenth-century views on war, albeit without the organic and biological metaphors and assumptions that were to become so important in its second half, and with scant sign that the causes of war changed. The idea of war in Europe as the guarantor of a balance of power was most clearly associated with William Robertson who, in his *History of the Reign of Charles V* (1769), wrote:

> That great secret in modern policy, the preservation of a proper distribution of power among all the members of the system into which the states are formed.... From this era we can trace the progress of that intercourse between nations which had linked the powers of Europe so closely together; and can discern the operations

---

18   Quoted in Jeremy Black, *Eighteenth Century Europe, 1700-1789* (London: Macmillan, 1990) p.201.

of that provident policy, which, during peace, guards against remote and contingent dangers; which, in war, hath prevented rapid and destructive conquests.[19]

Assessing Significance

In 1815, two of the three leading military powers were European and all three – Britain, China and Russia – were the same as the leading powers a century earlier. All the intervening fighting had had many consequences, but in the long-term it had confirmed the verdict on the conflicts in 1690-1715 that had left Britain, China, and Russia the leading powers, indeed considerably strengthening them. That, however, is neither the impression created in military history as a whole, nor that that can be readily gauged from a consideration of European military history in this period. These two observations are linked. There is a general tendency to note the significance of war in European history, but somehow to marginalise the discussion of warfighting. Instead, the relevant sub-discipline that has attracted attention is that of war and society. While interesting, it, however, offers little for the discussion of such topics as the relative effectiveness of military systems and the reasons why, in particular conflicts, certain powers succeed and others do not.

This neglect encourages a focus on an easy account in military history that serves apparently to settle the topic. The account is that of military revolutions. This popular approach draws on Hegelian-Marxist assumptions about process as well as teleological views of, and about, change. Each characteristic can be found in the case of the two prime instances for European military history: first the supposed military revolution, or rather 'Military Revolution', linked to the transition to modernity at the close of the Middle Ages; and, secondly, the supposed military revolution linked to the concept of the people under arms, a concept applied in particular to the American, French, Haitian, Latin American, and other, revolutions from 1775. This approach, however, is deeply flawed in its underlying assumptions and is wrong in specifics.

The thesis of military revolutions is also interesting for what it suggests about views about what constituted (and therefore constitutes) Europe, and how it operated, and, therefore, should operate. In particular, the established accounts focus on Western, not Eastern, Europe, and offer a core-to-periphery model of the diffusion of innovation, leadership and lessons. The key struggles apparently are those within the core. Thus, from the onset in 1494 of another group of conflicts in Italy, the 'Italian Wars,' to the end of the seventeenth century, the standard emphasis in on a struggle between Spain and France. This baton-changing approach to military history moves on to centre on Prussia from 1740, only for France to return to the fore from 1792 with the victories of revolutionary forces.

This portrayal is taken further with Napoleon's successes, only for him to fail in 1812-1815 due to his egregious mistakes, military and political, and others 'catching up' with his innovations. Moreover, as further evidence that France really 'won,' Napoleon's failure is explained in part in terms of the greater resources of his opponents; an approach that

---

19   W. Robertson, *The History of The Reign of the Emperor Charles V* (London: W. Strahan, T. Cadell, 1782), Vol.I, pp.134-135.

prefigures one of the standard (and deeply flawed) interpretations of German failure in the Second World War, and, to a degree, the First World War.

The baton-changing approach has many problems, but, again, it proves attractive because, in its clarity, it offers a high rating for that most seductive of ratios: ease of interpretation in relation to the amount of work. That is a ratio that many seek when they move to contextual points. However, in practice, as consideration of any period will reveal, there was no paradigm state of warfare, no single model of improvement. Instead, alongside borrowing, there were autonomous developments within a general context of fitness for purpose. Militaries have to respond to tasks and goals that are specific, and to do so within particular social, economic, and political parameters. In the last case, for example, the political acceptability of a large army was very different in Britain and Austria in the eighteenth century.

Turning to the eighteenth century, the key standard interpretation addresses a transition from *ancien régime* to Revolutionary warfare. This interpretation employs concepts of modernity and modernisation that are problematic, not least because employed in an essentialist and teleological fashion. The teleology for the eighteenth century sits within a broader one which assumes an inevitable development toward nationalism, peoples' warfare, the industrialisation of war, and total war. Each of these is presented as more effective than hitherto, with, in turn, even greater effectiveness derived from their interaction. From that perspective, an earlier age appears anachronistic, its warfare limited, its militaries bound to fail, or at least be superseded, and its command practices and culture outmoded, unprofessional, effete, and ready for replacement.

Always problematic, that approach looks increasingly flawed in light of the changes in conflict since the Cold War ended. There were and are also misreadings of the eighteenth century. Questions of significance are frequent. There is the repeated problem of focusing on a particular military, for example the Prussian army under Frederick the Great, and treating this military as if it defines progress and therefore importance, while its victories, in turn, underline relative capability and thus demonstrates this progress. Aside from the serious conceptual and methodological problems posed by such circular arguments, there are also those posed by a disinclination to draw sufficient attention to the failures of those supposed paradigm powers. For example, Prussia was repeatedly unable to inflict significant defeats on Austria in 1761 or 1778, and the Prussian military system collapsed in 1806.

Moreover, this approach short-changes other powers. Focusing on Prussia in mid-century leads to a downplaying of repeated French successes in the Low Countries in 1744-1748. Focusing on France in 1792-1809 leads to a downplaying of Russia's repeated successes in that period, successes that make more sense of Russia's subsequent ability to defeat France. So also with Britain's history of naval triumph and trans-oceanic power projection. British victory over France under both heads in 1793-1815 was not new but looked back on a continuity that reflected powerful institutional, doctrinal and contextual strengths, as well as the grit of experience, morale and sense of purpose.

In assessing changes, there is the repeated question of which changes to consider. Technological and tactical circumstances in European warfare were far more similar in 1715-1815 than they were to be over the subsequent century. Moreover, although the changes in 1615-1715 did not match those in 1815-1915, they were also greater than those seen in the French Revolutionary and Napoleonic Wars. Indeed, it is worth focusing on the significance of the move in 1690-1700 away from the musket-pike combination that had become dominant in Christian Europe in the sixteenth century. Turning to the latter, the particular combined armed tactics resulting from the supposed military revolution of the sixteenth and seventeenth centuries were not 'new' in the sense that both cavalry and infantry, and, for each, missile and stabbing or thrusting weapons, had long been combined. In addition, as far as the sixteenth and seventeenth centuries were concerned, successful combination proved easier to discuss in training manuals, which emphasised drill, and to attempt in combat, than they were to execute successfully under the strain of battle. Furthermore, the contrasting fighting characteristics of the individual arms – muskets, pike, cavalry, and cannon – in the sixteenth and seventeenth centuries, operated very differently in particular circumstances, which posed added problems for coordination. So also did the limited extent to which many generals and officers understood these characteristics and problems, which affected the ability to triumph in battle.

Issues of firepower and tactical coordination help explain the significance of the move in the 1690s away from the musket-pike combination to the fusion presented by firearms mounting bayonets, in which each foot-soldier carried a similar weapon. The simultaneous shift from matchlock to flintlock muskets improved their reliability as ignition systems, notably in damp weather and in the wind, and also increased the ability to rely on fire-arms to offer strong protection against cavalry and infantry attack. On the global scale, these changes possibly increased the effectiveness of Western armies more than their earlier adoption of gunpowder weaponry, an adoption shared across much of Eurasia.

Within Christian Europe, however, relative capability was not enhanced by a change shared by all armies; although this capability it was against non-regular forces. Instead, unit cohesion, experience, morale, and leadership were key elements at the tactical level. Circumstances and tactics that were particular to the individual battle, rather than formulaic to the manual, were the most significant. Command skills were involved in the choice of position, and an understanding and assessment of detailed topography were important. The topography and vegetation affected a host of factors, including the advantage of slope for all arms, and sight lines for cannon, as well as the softness of the ground, which made cavalry advances especially difficult. These factors of terrain are often difficult to appreciate today, not least because of changes in surface drainage and farming practice, which makes battlefields such as Salamanca (1812) that have seen scant change of great interest. So also, but differently, with the detailed consequences of currents, winds, shoals, and sandbanks for conflict at sea.

Linked to this, it can be very difficult to assess battles, not least because surviving sources can be scanty and can contain serious discrepancies. Indeed, with respect to Waterloo (1815), the Duke of Wellington was to point out the difficulty of recreating what had happened. This is an important qualification of much of the writing about military history with its habit of readily narrating and explaining what were often complex and obscure battles, and of running together events that could take several, if not many, hours. Indeed, most battle accounts, and for both land and naval battles, are questionable, if not highly questionable, a point underlined by Rory Muir in his treatment of Salamanca, and, somewhat differently, by Owen Connelly in his of Marengo.[20]

---

20   Rory Muir, *Salamanca 1812* (New Haven: Yale University Press, 2001); Owen Connelly, *Blundering to Glory: Napoleon's Military Campaigns* (Lanham: Rowman & Littlefield, 2008), pp.64-68.

Within Europe, the key politico-military change in the century prior to the French Revolution was the rise of Russia. Indeed, its impact for the Eurasian system was captured by Edward Gibbon when he addressed the question of whether successful 'barbarian' invasions could recur. Gibbon was most interested in this developmental characteristic, which challenged notions of cyclical change. Indeed, on the world scale, there had been a major change, one focused on the 1550s with Ivan IV's (Ivan the Terrible's) conquest of the khanates of Kazan and Astrakhan, taken on by successful expansion across Siberia to reach the Pacific in the 1630s, and, with greater difficulty, seen in Russia conquering the northern shores of the Black Sea, notably annexing Crimea in 1783.

This was yet another sphere in which the French Revolutionary and Napoleonic period saw continuity with what had gone before. Russia beat the Turks in the wars of 1768-74, 1787-1792, and 1806-1812, annexing Bessarabia (modern Moldova) as a result of the last. So also within Europe. If Alexander I reviewed a large Russian army at Chalons-sur-Marne in 1815 on the third anniversary of the battle of Borodino, Peter I (the Great) was in Copenhagen in 1716 with an army planning to invade Sweden, an invasion not in the event mounted. In 1716, 1735, 1748, 1798 and 1813, Russian troops moved into what is now Germany, and in 1760 briefly occupied Berlin. The Russians' successful emphasis on speed, notably from the 1760s, indicated that, far from being simply formulaic, as might be suggested by volley training and linear formations, there was a potential dynamism and flexibility in Western warfare. A Russian fleet moved into the Mediterranean in 1769, another following in 1798. In 1799, a Russian expeditionary force invaded Holland in combination with the British.

In contrast to Russia's success in dominating Eastern Europe, a process that by 1815 had yielded Estonia, Latvia, Lithuania, Ukraine, Finland and much of Poland, France was unable to dominate Western Europe. Looked at differently, Russia faced major challenges to its dominance, with both regional opposition and Western European intervention. Years of crisis for Russia included 1700, 1708-1711, 1720-1721, 1733-1735, 1739-1741, 1788-1791 and 1806-1812. In particular, combinations of crises, notably if in the Baltic, Poland and/or the Balkans, were of great difficulty, as was the prospect of Western European intervention, as in 1720-1721, 1739 and 1790-1791. This situation serves as a reminder of the salience of strategy (or grand strategy), and, notably, the related issues of prioritisation, and both for a power and for its opponents. These issues related to questions of skill in the management of coincident crises.

If Russia managed this successfully, there were also serious episodes, particularly Charles XII of Sweden's invasion of Ukraine in 1708-1709 and Napoleon's advance on Moscow in 1812, which can be profitably compared with the campaigning of Charles XII. After initial success, both ultimately failed totally, and, indeed, were less problematic for Russian stability than Polish intervention in the 'Time of Troubles' in the early 1610s. The Poles controlled the Kremlin for much longer than Napoleon in 1812, but, for some reason, this does not influence perceptions of military history, whether of Eastern Europe or of Napoleon.

Compared to Russia's ability to dominate Eastern Europe, an ability that lasted until the German capture of Warsaw in 1915, and that resumed in 1944-1989, France was unable to do the same in Western Europe other than in brief periods, notably 1806-1812. That underlines the questionable character of focusing on France. Ultimately the 'Western Question' that was posed from French advances, both into the lands of the Burgundian inheritance and into Italy, in the late fifteenth century, was ended in 1815, and with France failing. Moreover, the crisis was episodic between France's defeats in the War of the Spanish Succession in the 1700s and the victories of Revolutionary France from 1792. Whereas Austria, joined with Spain, had stopped France in the early sixteenth and early seventeenth centuries, and Austria, allied with the Dutch and Spain, in the 1670s, and with Britain, and the Dutch in the 1690s, 1700s and 1740s, it was Russia that was crucial, both in 1807 and in 1812-1814.

The relative failure (compared to Russia) of France to dominate its region, let alone Europe as a whole, raises questions of explanation and about how best to assess military and political effectiveness. Answers can be offered, but how best to judge them is unclear. One argument rests on the more 'multipolar' character of international relations in Western Europe, compared to East Europe.

It is also appropriate to consider the ability of France's opponents to deploy effective forces as with Marlborough and Eugene in the War of the Spanish Succession, and with French defeats in Germany at Prussian (Rossbach, 1757) and British (Minden, 1759) hands during the Seven Years' War. In 1745-1748, Saxe's victories in the Low Countries were not matched by the French in Italy or in the Rhineland. This ability remained the case into the late 1790s. Indeed, it was only in 1800-1809 that the pattern was really broken by France. So also with Prussia, which, under Frederick the Great, far from necessarily succeeding, found itself in serious difficulties from Russia and, eventually, Austria.

In trying to gauge the transition or relationship from the warfare of the *ancien régime* period to that of the Revolutionary period it is particularly valuable to focus on the last period of the *ancien régime*. To do so offers the great advantage that it is possible to avoid too static a picture of *ancien régime* warfare. That is especially valuable as it means that we thereby understand that revolution is not necessary in order to avoid substantive change, which is a rhetorical rather than an analytical position. The 'last period' of course is open to interpretation, in that the impression created may be very different depending on the years chosen. The decade ending with the outbreak of the French Revolutionary War in 1792 creates an impression centred on Russian effectiveness, while the two decades ending then gives space to French success in the War of American Independence, which for France was 1778 to 1783. The variety of European warfare certainly emerges from a consideration of particular decades, and therefore the problematic nature of assuming a common trajectory.

The development of a reform-minded intellectual climate did not begin with the French Revolution. Change was seen as a possibility to be encouraged, shaped, exploited, and harnessed, as well as a problem to overcome. There would have no Clausewitz without the Saxes, Lloyds, Guiberts, and the Schaumburg-Lippes of the eighteenth century. Discussion of strategy as a defined concept preceded the Revolution. Reform, however, scarcely began with the Enlightenment or necessarily centred on France and the German lands. Instead, the reform drive focused by Peter the Great was the most significant instance.

2

Writing for Pleasure: Christopher Duffy's Historiographical Legacy

Alexander S. Burns

Though I have spoken with Christopher Duffy many times, his philosophy in writing has never been more clearly expressed than a conversation that we had on a June afternoon in 2020, when I asked Christopher about writing in his career. He corrected me immediately: he did not view his large body of works as part of a career at all, rather, they were written for pleasure. In selecting his research, Christopher chose a series of subjects that interested him. This eccentric response, so at odds with the manner of topic selection in modern academia, gives a window into the mind of the man who has written over 20 books covering the range of modern warfare from 1500 to the Second World War. Even more importantly, Christopher Duffy's life and works, from the 1960s to the present time, have changed the face of eighteenth-century military history, demanding that we understand the armies of that period as serious military institutions.

This chapter traces the significant historiographical interventions of Duffy's work. In its style, it follows the pattern found throughout much of Christopher's writing: thematic analysis and narrative paired in different sections of the same work. Writing this chapter was a daunting task: Duffy's publications over the last 60-odd years cover a gambit of topics, from the development of roundels in early sixteenth-century siege warfare, to the influences of bourgeois and communist ideology on mechanized warfare in 1945.[1] The core of his focus, however, is the military history of Europe between 1740 and 1789: Of his 21 books as of 2021, 15 cover this period. As a result, much of the thematic focus of this chapter will be Duffy's writing on this era. Even in this short span of history, Duffy's range is impressive: topics span from the development of Russian military power to the use of Hessian *Subsidientruppen* against the Jacobites.

At the outset, it may be helpful to dwell on one important feature of Duffy's body of work which is present throughout his publications. In his writing and research Christopher Duffy

---

1   Christopher Duffy, *Siege Warfare: The Fortress in the Early Modern World* (London: Routledge, 1979), p.4; Christopher Duffy, *Red Storm on the Reich: The Soviet March on Germany* (New York: Da Capo, 1991), p.51.

has lived up to a feature that all historians should share: he divorces ego from his work and is more than willing to revise his assumptions when proved wrong. This is apparent, and indeed, self-evident in conversations with Christopher: he repeatedly instructs listeners to not care what others think of their scholarship. More tellingly, however, Duffy has substantially revised his own works on multiple occasions, changing his interpretations when new material comes to light, and perhaps more importantly, directly addressing the fact that his previous conclusions were incorrect in new forewords.[2] This sentiment is perhaps summed up best in his introduction to the 2019 edition of his first book, *The Wild Goose and the Eagle: A Life of Marshal von Browne*: 'I live in a state of permanent dissatisfaction with my own work'.[3] Christopher's humility and desire to for accuracy set a standard to which all young historians may aspire.

The Changing Face of War: Battle vs. Operations

As Jeremy Black has already suggested above, the primary interpretation of eighteenth-century military history is that the armies of the Old Regime were swept aside by the more modern, effective, and revolutionary forces of France between 1792-1807. From the perspective of what Black refers to as 'essentialist and teleological' concept of modernity the armies of the eighteenth century appear 'anachronistic…bound to fail or at least be superseded, and its command practices and culture outmoded, unprofessional, effete, and ready for replacement'. Throughout his career, Christopher Duffy, too has wrestled with the problems presented by an anticipatory teleological framework that views Old Regime warfare as waiting to fall before the forces of the Revolution and Napoleon.

This teleological problem is nothing new, however. Indeed, as early as 1976, Michael Roberts chided against the belief that Revolutionary armies were great innovators:

> If we consider the French armies which shattered the old system, and established, however briefly, a new Carolingian Empire from the Vistula to the Atlantic, we find no novel weapons to explain their achievement. Napoleon's armaments were almost identical with those of Frederick the Great. There were some important tactical innovations, *but none that had not been widely discussed and to some extent practiced by military theorists and commanders for decades before the revolutionary wars.*[4]

In examining the writings of Christopher Duffy, then, we cannot claim to find novel assertions regarding the innovations and structures of Old Regime armies anticipating

2   See, for example, Christopher Duffy, *The Army of Frederick the Great* (Chicago: Emperor's Press, 1996), p.4; Christopher Duffy, *Fight for a Throne: The Jacobite '45 Reconsidered* (Solihull: Helion & Co., 2015), p.xi.

3   Christopher Duffy, *The Wild Goose and the Eagle: A Life of Marshal von Browne* (Warwick: Helion & Co., 2019) p.ix.

4   Michael Howard, *War in European History* (Oxford: Oxford University Press, 1976) p.76, emphasis added.

Napoleonic warfare. He describes the importance of light infantry, the theoretical presence of division systems, the debates over linear and columnar formations in combat and growing importance of mobile artillery, but these continuities were all identified by Michael Howard: they are not ground-breaking.[5] What is ground-breaking, however, is Christopher's presentation of a wholly different argument. Instead of asserting that the structures of Napoleonic warfare were already in place in the Old Regime, Duffy carefully charts the way that battle itself changed during the Seven Years War. For Duffy, there are significant differences between modern and early modern armies, but the nature of how those armies fought fundamentally changed during the Seven Years War itself.

As befits a thesis put forward by the *doyen* of eighteenth-century warfare, Duffy's argument is both nuanced and shockingly easy to demonstrate. Pick up one of Christopher's books. Examine the maps of the Battles of Rossbach and Leuthen and compare them with maps the Battles of Freiberg and Burkersdorf. In the first two maps, you will find the long geometric lines and formations frequently associated with eighteenth-century warfare. In both engagements, the commanders formed their entire armies into a rigid linear pattern and engaged the enemy. In the second pairing, you will find the names of area commanders, with units grouped under their immediate command, executing independent attacks in their area of the battlefield. How does Duffy explain this change? Especially, if, during the Seven Years War, historians cannot identify great organizational innovations such as permanent divisions?

As Christopher has convincingly shown, Austrian officer Franz Moritz von Lacy pioneered a novel style of attack using the ad-hoc temporary brigades and divisions of his time. This style of attack, first used at Hochkirch in 1758, would be utilized repeatedly by the Austrians and their Prussian opponents throughout the Seven Years War. What is even more impressive is Duffy's discovery is that it was made in the middle of his career, with his first books on the Austrian and Prussian armies already written. In his 1974 survey of the Prussian army, Duffy notes:

> Just when the oblique attack was reaching its furthest development, we encounter the faint signs that the Prussians were already searching for a more flexible scheme of battle tactics. Assaults by semi-independent columns were carried out at Burkersdorf and Freiberg at the close of the Seven Years War[.] It was ironic that Frederick commanded an army which, from his own strenuous efforts, was totally incapable of ever putting such an operation into effect–an army were the infantry had been beaten into bovine submission and where the generals had lost the capacity for independent command.[6]

Here, Duffy's theoretical blinders regarding the brutal nature of subordination in the Prussian army prevent him from reaching the ground-breaking thesis of his later works. By 1985, having spent another decade of study on the Prussian army in preparation to write his military biography of Frederick II, we see a completely different picture. In this work,

---

5   Howard, *War in European History*, p.76.
6   Christopher Duffy, *The Army of Frederick the Great* (New York: Hippocrene, 1974), p.156.

we here that at Burkersdorf, 'the Prussian artillery opened up to devastating effect', while the infantry, far from a bovine performance, 'had been given precise timings and objectives [and] worked forward under the cover of the re-entrants…we have moved very far indeed from the parade-like battles of the first campaigns of the Seven Years War'.[7] Here, as we shall see below, Christopher's new appreciation for the motivation and independence of Prussian soldiers (and Old Regime soldiers generally) would enable him to present a new and convincing interpretation of the changing nature of Old Regime warfare.

In his most recent treatment of the Austrian army in the Seven Years War, Duffy continues this thread of argumentation, noting, 'It can hardly be emphasized enough that the form of attack was entirely novel, namely by means of independent converging columns, a form of grand tactics which influenced the Austrian way of making war until the 1790s.'[8] He continued:

> Hitherto the generals had been accustomed to going into battle in long continuous lines, and been assured of support on at least one flank. Now they were being called upon to act as leaders of independent bodies, and in 1758 it was probably asking too much of them to plunge into what seemed a tactical void. The necessary confidence and cohesion would have been provided if the army had been reorganized into standing formations, such as the divisions as now being explored by the French [see the chapter of Jonathan Abel, below] and advocated in the course of the war in various forms by Lacy and *GFWM*. Wartensleben.[9]

Duffy continues this pattern throughout *By Force of Arms,* noting this novel style of fighting at the Austrian attacks of Maxen, Liegnitz, and Reichenbach, and demonstrating that the Prussians quickly copied it at Torgau, Döbeln, Teplitz, Adelsbach, Burkersdorf, and Freiberg.[10] At Burkersdorf Duffy notes:

> The fighting was on much too great a scale to be considered a mere action, but the fragmented nature of the combat, in which the separate Prussian formations had been assigned precise objectives, gives it the character less of battle than an "operation," on the pattern first established by the Austrians at Hochkirch in 1758. The Prussians at Burkersdorf showed their mastery of the new techniques, and Frederick launched or held back the individual assaults in such a way that they amounted to a harmonious whole.[11]

Although they were not complemented naturally by the permanent divisions of Napoleonic warfare, this novel style of warfare did indeed present a profound change from the linear battles of the War of Austrian Succession and early Seven Years War. The obvious nature

---

7   Christopher Duffy, *Frederick the Great: A Military Life* (London: Routledge, 1985), p.316.
8   Christopher Duffy, *The Austrian Army in the Seven Years War: By Force of Arms* (Chicago: Emperor's Press, 2008), p.133.
9   Duffy, *By Force of Arms*, p.145.
10   Duffy, *By Force of Arms*, pp.199, 209, 249-250, 366-368, 285, 336, 337, 341-345, 351-362, 383.
11   Duffy, *By Force of Arms*, p.362.

of this change has been obscured by a focus on 'battle history' which emphasizes the great, set-piece encounters of Rossbach and Leuthen. In the middle and later years of the Seven Years War, commanders did on both sides of this conflict embraced a style of deployment and combat that would lay the groundwork of operational warfare for decades to come Finishing out this work, Duffy notes:

> It is clear that…the Austrians abandoned the conventional lines of battle for something altogether more fluid and ambitious, whereby their formations operated independently but within an overall design, and attack in line or column as best suited the objective. Prince Henry of Prussia was quick to grasp the advantages of the concept, and by the end of the war both sides were operating in styles fundamentally different from their first encounters.[12]

By identifying this pattern for the first time in an Anglophone history of the Seven Years War, Christopher Duffy has radically changed our understanding of late Old Regime armies. Far from clinging to a rigid linear mould that had outlived its usefulness, only to be shattered by the armies of the French Revolution, the Austrian and Prussian militaries had embraced a modern style of combat based on assaults focused on operational goals, in the middle of a supposedly static and linear period of warfare. Duffy, by challenging his own previously held misconceptions, has identified a new and fascinating sea-change in the history of battle.

The Changing Face of War: Motivation in the Old Regime

Historians often write on the daily lives of soldiers living in the nineteenth and twentieth centuries, thanks to the easy access to large numbers of typed sources. A new generation of scholars, however, has approached the daily lives of soldiers in the Old Regime with new vigour. Ilya Berkovich and Katrin and Sascha Möbius have pioneered a novel approach to the sources and founded a new school of inquiry on eighteenth-century soldiers.[13] In new works published since 2015, these scholars have shattered myths and defined this new historiographical trend, and it is worthwhile to briefly trace that historiography before discussing the experience of Christopher's work.

Before the later decades of the twentieth century, historians failed to challenge the idea that eighteenth-century common soldiers, in the turn of phrase used by the Duke of Wellington, represented 'the scum of the earth'.[14] When read back into the eighteenth century this quote

---

12   Duffy, *By Force of Arms*, p.396.
13   Ilya Berkovich, *Motivation in War: The Experience of Common Soldiers in Old Regime Europe* (Cambridge, Cambridge University Press, 2017); Katrin and Sascha Möbius, *The Psychology of Honour: Prussian Army Soldiers and the Seven Years War* (London: Bloomsbury Academic, 2019). Ilya Berkovich was extremely supportive of this volume and made a number of helpful suggestions which allowed it to take shape. The editor and all the contributors are grateful.
14   The full quote comes from Stanhope's conversations with the Duke of Wellington: 'I may say it in this room — are the very scum of the earth. People talk of their enlisting from their fine military feeling — all stuff — no such thing. Some of our men enlist from having got bastard children — some for minor

became the paradigm for understanding common soldiers. Historians asserted that soldiers were not honourable or patriotic: in this view, they were likely criminals or coerced peasants.[15] In this formerly popular view, the formulation of Frederick II, that soldiers should fear their officers more than the enemy, was the paramount authority. The traditional view was best summarized by a Professor of Strategy and Policy at the Naval War College of the United States, Andrew Wilson. He claimed, 'In general, an *ancien regime* army was a slow and unwieldy mass of disgruntled and terrorized soldiers led by untrained and unimaginative officers'.[16] This traditional view was challenged by the so-called new school of specialized historians who have driven the research on Old Regime soldiers in a different direction, arguing that these soldiers were in fact motivated by honour, religion, localism, and state patriotism.[17] In broad terms, then, the writings of the new school attempt to examine the place of common soldiers in the Old Regime with a critical and analytic sense of empathy in contrast to the dismissal of previous historiography. Soldiers appear in these studies, as individuals with stories, lives, and motivations, not simply as automata harshly controlled by their aristocratic officers.[18] Berkovich and Möbius recognized Christopher Duffy as the precursor of this new school, in addition to the writings of Timothy Blanning and Dennis Showalter. Duffy's own position on this critical issue changed during his course of his writing.

Duffy first approached the condition of common soldiers in Old Regime armies in his 1974 book *The Army of Frederick the Great*. The comments regarding 'bovine submission', quoted above, do much to illuminate his early view on common soldiers in the Prussian army. Christopher summed up his views on motivation: 'Self-respect and *esprit de corps* were useful in themselves, but in Frederick's view they were no substitute for the knowledge that the officer's sword and NCO's spontoon were pointing at your back.'[19] Though admitting that 'repression and exploitation are not the whole story', Duffy's interpretation seems to be a fairly standard view for this time, there is little to suggest that he would become a precursor to the new school.[20] In all of his writings, few subjects would be revised as completely as the motivations of common soldiers.

---

offences — many more for drink': Philip Henry Stanhope, *Notes of Conversations with the Duke of Wellington, 1831-1851* (London: J. Murray, 1889), p.18.

15   For a representative example of this view, see William Willcox and Walter Arnstein, *The Age of Aristocracy: 1688-1830* (New York: Houghton Mifflin, 2001), p.110.

16   Andrew R. Wilson, 'Masters of War: History's Great Strategic Thinkers' (Lecture, The Great Courses, Naval War College, Newport, Rhode Island, 21 February 2012).

17   Katrin and Sascha Möbius, *Prussian Army Soldiers*, pp.3-5. The author's dissertation makes a small contribution to this new school in the area of localism.

18   For some examples of this trend referencing Prussia, see: Jürgen Kloosterhuis, *Bauern, Bürger und Soldaten. Quellen zur Sozialisation des Militärsystems im preußischen Westfalen 1713-1803.* (Münster: De Gruyter, 1992); Jörg Muth, *Flucht aus dem Militärischen Alltag: Ursachen und Individuelle Ausprägung der Desertion in der Armee Friedrichs des Grossen: mit besonderer Berücksichtigung der Infanterie-Regimenter der Potsdamer Garnison* (Freiburg Im Breisgau: Rombach Verl., 2003).; Martin Winter, *Untertanengeist durch Militärpflict: Das Preussische Kantonsystem in brandenburgischen Städten im 18. Jahrhundert* (Bielefeld: Verlag für Regionalgeschichte, 2005); Beate Engelen, *Soldatenfrauen in Preußen: Eine Strukturanalyse der Garnisonsgesellschaft im späten 17. und im 18. Jahrhundert* (Münster: Lit Verlag, 2005).

19   Duffy, *The Army of Frederick the Great* (1974), p.62.

20   Duffy, *The Army of Frederick the Great* (1974), p.67.

By comparison, his assessment of common soldiers in the companion volume, *The Army of Maria Theresa*, is slightly more positive, but still traditional. Duffy quotes (aristocratic) sources which indicate that most voluntary enlistments occurred from the drunkenness, laziness, of 'worthless people'.[21] Fortunately, Duffy provides a rejoinder to this claim several pages later, quoting Henry Lloyd, an English who asserts that the Austrian force, 'is composed chiefly out of the class of labourers... they are obedient and patient, and bear without murmur the greatest hardships... by education and temper, proper to form a good soldier, and superior to any other, who are not raised by some species of enthusiasm.'[22] For Duffy, though, the reliable peasant is an Austrian phenomenon; he ends this section with the assertion: 'Here was a more lasting resource than the brittle mechanism of the Prussian military machine.'[23] Duffy's views on Prussia would change within the decade, but it would come from an unlikely source.

During his completion of *Russia's Military Way to the West* (though with a different publisher, these three works do form a trilogy), Duffy became impressed with Russian common soldiers, and began to look at the sources of their resilience. In his first truly empathetic analysis of eighteenth-century common soldiers, Duffy asserts that the Russian soldier, 'while seeming to endure so much with bovine apathy, he maintained a self-sufficiency of body and mind that were beyond the ability of his masters to crush.'[24] Here, Duffy makes a significant breakthrough: soldiers were not cows.

All humour aside, Christopher's historical empathy in describing the importance of the *artel* system in replacing the communal nature of village life in Russia stands as a significant turning point in his analysis of eighteenth-century soldiers. Christopher describes an eighteenth-century Russian soldier who was resourceful, communal, and deeply religious. Through this uncertain first step, that still relies heavily on aristocratic descriptions, we see the Russian soldier mourned in his native village, communally singing on the march, received into the comradeship of his *artel*, cared for by his *artelchiki*, engaged at amateur civilian trades while not at war, and clutching icons and talismans of his patron saint in combat. This last image, which Duffy presented with literary sources, has been confirmed by the recent archaeology on the Kunersdorf battlefield.[25] This first step into the new school would carry through into Duffy's revisionary work on other armies.

In his *Frederick the Great: A Military Life*, published four years after *Russia's Military Way*, Duffy continues his revision of the lives and motivations of Old Regime soldiers. He asserts:

> The Frederick of the Seven Years War was a consummate master of the skills of leadership... On the march he spoke to his men in their Low German dialects, and he tolerate familiarities for which he would have cashiered an ensign[.]...The other ranks were moved by religious allegiance, the "small unit cohesion" of the military sociologists, and the local and national loyalties that were evident in the

---

21   Christopher Duffy, *The Army of Maria Theresa* (New York: Hippocrene, 1977), pp.48-49.
22   Duffy, *The Army of Maria Theresa*, p.62.
23   Duffy, *The Army of Maria Theresa*, p.62.
24   Christopher Duffy, *Russia's Military War to the West: Origins and Nature of Russian Military Power, 1700-1800* (London: Routledge & Kegan Paul, 1981), p.130.
25   See the chapter of Grzegorz Podruczny, below.

Pomeranians of the regiment of Manteuffel, "upright and cheerful, strong and reliable, and loyal to their prince – in other words honest men of after the old German style."[26]

The contrast between these assertions and those which Duffy made in the first edition of *The Army of Frederick the Great* are striking. In that time, Duffy had been partially receptive to a more positive view of common soldiers in Maria Theresa's army (because of his Irish-Catholic partisanship in her cause) and made his first steps towards the creation of the new school in his study of the Russian army. He would continue his thoughtful revision of his previous work in the second edition of *The Army of Frederick the Great*.

In that 1996 work, Duffy more fully explored the tension between harsh discipline and other possible soldierly motivations. He significantly expanded the subsection 'Frederick and his Soldiers' which was the only section of his original work that considered positive leadership on Frederick's part. In a new subsection, 'Slave or Hero: The Motivation of the Frederician Private Soldier' Duffy carefully considers this question, looking at attempted desertions, the brutal nature of informal punishment officers inflicted with canes, and corporal punishments practiced in the army. Unlike the previous edition, however, he does not leave the story there. Instead, he asserts that, 'leadership of a more positive kind became evidence on campaign', and that Prussian officers frequently displayed patience and encouraged their men.[27] Duffy then turns to the most revealing source of all: the actions of Prussian prisoners of war in Austria. Here, he shows that while the *auslander* were treated leniently by the Austrians, the native Prussians and Brandenburgers were viewed as a severe problem, because of the patriotism they displayed.

Duffy would return to the theme of motivation at many points in his works, prominently quoting Timothy Blanning's exposition on this topic in *Eagles over the Alps* and returning to it in the same way, in a subsection, 'Motivation and Honour: Criminals or Heroes?' in his revisionary *The Austrian Army in the Seven Years War: Instrument of War*. Here, after discussing the traditional view and patronizing sentiments of officers, Duffy presents sources which reflect upon the importance of honour, leading him to the balanced conclusion:

> We are still left with the problem of awakening the finer instincts of the infantryman. The Austrian soldier could not be impelled by religious fanaticism, as among the Turks, or by the nationalistic hero-worship which moved the Prussians. There remained the foundation of trust and goodwill. Firm but fair, the effective officer was alive to the collective mentality of his soldiers, which did not differ in kind from that of schoolchildren or old folk. ... All that was left to the officer, therefore, was to draw out feelings of honour through his patient attention over a long period of time. He must treat his soldiers like human beings, not be afraid to encourage them by the kind word and the little joke, and maintain a discipline that was recognized as reasonable.[28]

---

26   Duffy, *Frederick the Great: A Military Life*, pp.336, 338.
27   Christopher Duffy, *The Army of Frederick the Great* (Chicago: Emperor's Press, 1996), p.88.
28   Christopher Duffy, *The Austrian Army in the Seven Years War: Instrument of War* (Chicago: Emperor's Press, 2000), pp.221, 222.

Tellingly, Duffy ends this section with the same quote from Henry Lloyd employed in his 1977 work on the Austrians. This time, instead of contrasting with this positive comment with observations on the 'brittle mechanism of the Prussian military machine', Duffy asserts that that Lloyd's observation signifies the Austrians, 'were, at the least, worthy opponents of the finest army in the world.'[29] In this passage, we can see the full evolution of Duffy's views on common soldiers in the Old Regime. The Austrians, and even the Prussians, had changed from essentially criminal elements needing discipline, to a more positive and empathetic view which places harsh discipline in tension with positive motivating factors. Once again, Duffy's willingness to approach his own previous work with a revisionary eye proves a great strength and continues makes his work the dominant interpretation of the period in his native language.

Having examined two thematic ways in which Christopher has changed our understanding of eighteenth-century warfare, the chapter will now turn to a narrative description of his many works. In attempting to grapple with his books, this narrative is divided into three subsections. The first explores Duffy's work in the early portion of his career, from his time at Oxford to his work on the *Historic Armies and Navies* series which would bring his structural analysis of the Prussian and Austrian armies to print. The next section, 'Ambitious Revisions' looks at Christopher's publications from 1979 to 1999, as he produced ground-breaking work on fortress warfare, and significantly revised his previous book on Frederick's Prussia. The third and concluding section, 'Defining Scholarship' explores his work from 2000 to 2020, when he produced the definitive two-volume study of the Austrian army, published the standard scholarly work on the late-1757 campaign, and turned his attention to rigorous studies of the Jacobite Rebellion of 1745.

The Early Works: 1960 to 1978

Duffy defended his dissertation under the direction of Dr Hans Georg Schenk in 1961. Schenk was a scholar of the romanticism in nineteenth-century German Central Europe, and Christopher was placed under his supervision by Sir Hugh Trevor Roper. During his time at Balliol, Christopher had also collaborated closely with Tutor, Dean, and Senior Fellow Alexander B. Rodger, ('the genial "Rodge"').[30] A historian with a keen interest in the Revolutionary and Napoleonic Wars, Rodger provided a great deal of inspiration for Christopher. Upon Rodger's unexpected death in August 1961, Duffy collaborated with his departed mentor's family to complete Rodger's final book: *The War of the Second Coalition 1798 to 1801: A Strategic Commentary*. The publisher summarized this unique situation in a note at the beginning of the work: 'The readiness of an old pupil, Dr. Christopher Duffy, to undertake this labour has made possible the production of the book in the form that the author would have wished. It is on him that the main burden has fallen.'[31] The work

---

29   Duffy, *Instrument of War*, p.223.
30   Christopher Duffy, *The Wild Goose and the Eagle: A Life of Marshal von Browne* (Warwick: Helion & Co., 2019) p.viii.
31   A.B. Rodger, *The War of the Second Coalition 1798 to 1801: A Strategic Commentary* (Oxford, Oxford University Press, 1964), p.iii.

was well-received, and several reviewers noted Duffy's assistance in bringing the volume to print.[32] After graduating as a Doctor of Philosophy in History from Balliol College in 1961, Christopher joined Brigadier Peter Young's Department of Military History at Royal Military Academy Sandhurst, where he would spend the next 30 years.

With his work on Rodger's final manuscript completed, Duffy turned to writing his own volumes. The first, unsurprisingly, was a revised version of his dissertation, 'Field-Marshal Maximilian von Browne, 1705-1757', published as *The Wild Goose and the Eagle* in 1964. In *The Wild Goose and the Eagle*, Duffy displayed a warm empathy for von Browne, an Irishman in the service of Maria Theresa. In justifying his volume on Browne, Duffy noted the great focus on Irishmen in French and Spanish service during the eighteenth century, and lamented that no comparable scholarly work had been performed on the '"Austrian" Irish'.[33] Furthermore, he pointed to the lack of modern scholarship on the Italian campaigns of the War of Austrian Succession and argued that this work filled an important gap in the coverage of previous historians. Finally, Duffy carefully displayed an early example of what would be a guiding feature in his future explorations of military history: 'Whenever possible, I have tried to retrace Browne's campaigning on the ground. It is a wonderful aid to judgment to lose one's way at Piacenza, or become stuck in the mud at Prague and find oneself in the company of the remains of a warrior of 1757.'[34] In his description of the Battle of Mollwitz in 1741, Duffy references the theories of Leo Tolstoy on command and control in combat.[35] His interest in Tolstoy helped to catapult him into his next work, written in the early 1970s.

In 1972, Duffy published his second book: *Borodino and the War of 1812*. In retracing the campaigns of *War and Peace*, Duffy was inspired by a visiting to the Borodino battlefield in 1970 during conference travel in the Soviet Union, as well as his 1971 work as a historical advisor on the BBC production of Tolstoy's novel, starring Sir Anthony Hopkins.[36] For a work written in the early 1970s, *Borodino* provides a solid account of the armies, campaigns, and combats of Napoleon's invasion of Russia. Duffy was writing in a time before rigorous English language accounts of the Napoleonic wars in Eastern and Central Europe had become widely available.[37] By far the most interesting part of the work, however, is Duffy's concluding chapter on Borodino in history and fiction. Here, Duffy provides a three-fold examination of the battle: the historiography, particularly Soviet work on the conflict, the presence of Borodino in Tolstoy's novel and its adaptations, and a guide to visiting the battlefield itself. Continuing the line of argumentation he took up in the introduction to *Wild Goose*, Duffy asserts, 'There is, of course, an inherent limitation to the insight which histories, novels, and films can give into a battle or campaign, and some of the missing

---

32   See, for example, Charles B. MacDonald, 'Reviewed Work: *The War of the Second Coalition, 1798 to 1801: A Strategic Commentary*', *The American Historical Review*, 71:2 (1966) p.540.

33   Christopher Duffy, *The Wild Goose and the Eagle: A Life of Marshal von Browne* (London: Chatto & Windus, 1964) p.xii.

34   Duffy, *The Wild Goose and the Eagle* (1964), p.xii.

35   Duffy, *The Wild Goose and the Eagle* (2019), p.50.

36   Christopher Duffy, *Borodino and the War of 1812* (London: Seeley, Service & Co., 1972), p.12.

37   Duffy's work on Borodino has been superseded today by a new generation of Napoleonic historians writing in English; see the works of Alexander Mikaberidze and Dominic Lieven.

elements are best supplied by a visit to the actual site.'[38] *Borodino* is also interesting for the frequent allusion that Duffy makes to other periods, and it is clear that his mind was being pulled in different directions. He compares the preservation of the field at Borodino to the American National Military Park at Gettysburg, Davout to James Longstreet, and Napoleon with Lee.[39] If his mind had turned to the history of the American Civil War (and what books that might have produced!), it was equally drawn back to his first love, the mid-eighteenth century, with frequent references to Frederick, the combats of the Seven Years War, and the way that Tsar Paul had desired to imitate, 'the mind-crushing, goose-stepping discipline of the Potsdam drill-square.'[40] It was to this imagined world of oppressive dragooned despotism that Duffy would next turn.

Duffy now moved into the classic phase of the early portion of his career, publishing *The Army of Frederick the Great* in 1974 and *The Army of Maria Theresa* in 1977 with David and Charles.[41] These early analytical studies of the two armies would make Duffy's reputation in Europe and North America, and many readers (including myself) came to Duffy's body of work as a historian by finding these books. Indeed, Duffy became the general editor of the *Historic Armies and Navies* series of which these books were a part, targeted towards a general audience, and more specifically, towards historical wargamers. The description of the goals of the series, found on the dust jacket, reads:

> We have taken into account several important developments in the reading public: the military historian is at last coming to appreciate that he must place his subject within its political and social framework, while the general historian and devotee of "war studies" are less content than before to pile generalization upon generalization when they are talking about military affairs; most important of all, we have had to recognize that the history of warfare has remained one of the fields where the serious professional researcher has kept contact with the "general public[.]"[42]

As an obvious partisan in the cause of Maria Theresa, Duffy's initial 1974 assessment of the Frederician army and kingdom was less than charitable. In describing the book, Duffy asserts that, 'students of military history will find here some object lessons in what may be accomplished by an army that is held on its course by fear and constraint rather than "inner" leadership.'[43] Indeed, the original *The Army of Frederick the Great* might be regarded one of the few times where Duffy allowed an overarching theme (brutality and a lack of positive leadership) to drive his analysis of a historical subject. In describing motivation in Frederick's army, Duffy insists that fear of officers was central, and uses descriptions of draconian punishments to reinforce this point.[44] Many of Duffy's negative comments regarding Frederick and the Prussian army generally are revised in the subsequent 1996

---

38   Duffy, *Borodino and the War of 1812*, p.172.
39   Duffy, *Borodino and the War of 1812*, pp.85, 142, 172.
40   Duffy, *Borodino and the War of 1812*, p.36.
41   Duffy, *The Army of Frederick the Great* (1974); Duffy, *The Army of Maria Theresa* (1977).
42   Duffy, *The Army of Frederick the Great* (1974), dust cover.
43   Duffy, *The Army of Frederick the Great* (1974), p.9.
44   Duffy, *The Army of Frederick the Great* (1974), p.9.

edition of the book, discussed below. In terms of organizational structure, however, this book would set the mould that Duffy would follow for many other projects throughout his career: a dual narrative-analysis approach, describing the structures of military life in addition to campaign and battle history.

While completing *The Army of Frederick the Great* and writing *The Army of Maria Theresa*, Duffy turned his attention to fortress warfare for the first time, examining European fortresses and their construction and investment in *Fire and Stone: The Science of Fortress Warfare, 1660-1860*. Here, Duffy examines the structure of fortresses in much the same way as the structure an army, with chapters on fortress placement, construction, maintenance, and defence. Finally, there is a narrative section dealing with prominent sieges, before three short appendices which describe the typology of fortress systems, how to design a wargame simulating fortress warfare in this period, and lastly, how to appropriately tour a fortress of this type. In this section, Duffy also briefly displays an early interest in historic preservation, would become a major theme of his later public work.[45]

The Army of Frederick the Great is almost the twin of Duffy's next volume, *The Army of Maria Theresa*, published in 1977. Both volumes spend approximate 150 pages discussing the structural organization of the societies, states, and armies under examination before moving to a more narrative driven chapter of 50 to 70 pages. In *The Army of Maria Theresa*, we see a great historian with a topic near and dear to his heart. The book is dedicated to James Duffy, an Austrian soldier killed at the Battle of Meissen in 1759, and as a whole, attempts to demonstrate the relative effectiveness of the Austrian military system. In his warm endorsement of the Austrian military reforms, Duffy notes that,

> In the use of its light infantry, and above all in the employment of its mighty artillery, the Theresian army foreshadowed some important aspects of Napoleonic warfare. We ought to set the record straight, now that eighteenth-century military history is attracting an increasingly wide and well-informed public.[46]

Duffy's arguments regarding the foundations of Napoleonic warfare in this volume are a small part of its overall message, and indeed, he concludes that 'the Austrian armies, trained up in the received techniques of eighteenth-century warfare, fared badly against the springy and aggressive forces of the French Revolution'.[47] His main goal, rather, was to demonstrate that the Austrian army on the whole, was more modern and effective than the Prussian force under Frederick, and, not a force that existed, 'just to give the Italians somebody they could beat.'[48] In this goal, Duffy amply succeeds with a book that, though now superseded, was exceptional for its time.

In 1977, Duffy returned to both Austrian and Napoleonic themes with the publication of *Austerlitz 1805*. The book is similar in tone and quality to Duffy's treatment of Borodino and is also addressed by Frederick Schneid later in this volume. Once again, Duffy emphasizes the importance of visiting the ground when writing a military history, noting that he

---

45   Duffy, *Fire and Stone: The Science of Fortress Warfare* (London: David & Charles, 1975), p.198.
46   Duffy, *The Army of Maria Theresa*, p.6.
47   Duffy, *The Army of Maria Theresa*, p.214.
48   Duffy, *The Army of Maria Theresa*, p.6.

visited the site with David Chandler, Richard Holmes, and Paddy Griffith in preparing the volume.[49] Once again, the concluding chapter, which melds historiographic assessment with a description of the contemporary battlefield, is the strongest.

Austerlitz 1805 also marks the end of the first phase of Duffy's career. After working for two decades, he had produced six books, with the exception of his dissertation, aimed a public audience. Though archival sources are frequently cited, these books are heavily reliant on printed sources. This grouping of works also displays characteristics which would continue to guide Duffy throughout the rest of his writing: an emphasis on seeing the ground in person, and an empathy for historical figures who were less well-known in the grand narratives of their period.[50]

Ambitious Revisions: 1979 to 1999

The late 1970s and 1980s were a fertile time in Christopher's writing. Duffy embarked on the production of a two-volume study of fortress warfare from 1494 to 1789. The results were *Siege Warfare: The Fortress in the Early Modern World, 1494-1660,* and *Siege Warfare: The Fortress in the Age of Vauban and Frederick the Great, 1660-1789.* The first volume brought Duffy to the broad attention of the academic community; it was reviewed in a dozen journals, and although some reviews were mixed, more were positive.[51] Christopher's treatment of European sieges in this period is extensive, but the book truly shines in its effort to engage in global history, with a chapter on European colonial empires and the use of fortresses and siege techniques by native peoples around the globe. In this chapter, Duffy advances an important thesis regarding European expansion:

> The thinly-spread presence of the Europeans could hardly have been supported without the help of their factory-forts, where they could refit and replenish their ships and stores and trade their goods. As the indispensable prop of the early colonial empires, the factory-fort is worth at least as close an examination as the vessels, the maps, and the navigational techniques which enabled Europeans to reach those distant shores in the first place.[52]

This claim, first made here in 1979 by Duffy, would later be echoed by noted military revolution scholar Geoffrey Parker.[53]

---

49   Christopher Duffy, *Austerlitz* (London: Seeley, Service & Co., 1977), p.xi.
50   See, for example, Duffy, *The Wild Goose and the Eagle* (1964), p.xii. and Duffy, *Austerlitz*, p.x.
51   An example of a positive review is: Gunther E. Rothenburg, 'Reviewed Work: Siege Warfare: The Fortress in the Early Modern World, 1494-1660', *American Historical Review,* 85:2 (1980) pp.383-384.
52   Christopher Duffy, *Siege Warfare: The Fortress and the Early Modern World* (London: Routledge & Kegan Paul, 1979) p.220.
53   See Geoffrey Parker, *The Military Revolution: Military Innovation and the Rise of the West* (Cambridge: Cambridge University Press, 1988) and Geoffrey Parker, *Empire War and Faith in Early Modern Europe* (London: Allen Lane, 2002) p.194-218. Duffy's first volume of *Siege Warfare* is conspicuously absent from Parker's notes; he does occasionally cite the second volume for quoted sources. However, it is clear that Parker was familiar with the work, he criticized it twice in review, once on original

With this two-volume set completed, Christopher turned books that would become the classic works of his career: *Russia's Military Way to the West: The Origins and Nature of Russian Military Power*, *Frederick the Great: A Military Life*, and *The Military Experience in the Age of Reason*. All three of these works went to the press between 1981 and 1987; in the case of *Frederick the Great: A Military Life*, the book happily appeared in 1985 just before the two hundredth anniversary of the death of the Prussian king in 1986.

Russia's Military Way, though appearing with a different publisher and containing differences in organization, is truly a continuation of the work that Duffy began in the *Historic Armies and Navies* series. The chronological sweep is longer, but the analysis along class lines (officers and men), and narrative of the various reigns is apparent. The book possesses a strong and lengthy chapter on the Russian experience of the Seven Years War, and in giving excellent coverage to Suvorov's role in the War of the Second Coalition, Duffy returned to the subject of his mentor A.B. Rodger.

The book received mixed reviews, with scholars criticizing its reliance on printed sources, but praising its accessibility and clear focus on westernization.[54] Indeed, as Duffy argues, that in the military sphere, the term modernization better describes Russian experience than westernization.[55] Duffy argues:

> How complete was the modernization of the Russian Army? With the impetus given to it by Peter, the process extended to the acquisition of Western-style ranks, tactics, weapons and (with some modifications) regimental organization and uniforms... However, certain areas remained largely untouched. It would be difficult to maintain, for example, that the Russian officers took as readily to the Western aristocratic military ethos, or a Prussian sense of responsibility, as they did to European languages and manners. More happily, the private soldier retained his primitive virtues in full measure, deriving not just from physical constitution, but a sense of community which he carried from his village life.[56]

Here, Duffy walks a nuanced middle line between the westernizing and traditional forces in Russian military life. Duffy's emphasis on the importance of village and military community in giving motivation to ordinary soldiers is also vital. He would continue this theme in his next volume, analysing the military activity of Prussian King Frederick II.

In his biography, *Frederick the Great: A Military Life*, Christopher revised his previously negative assumptions regarding Frederick and the Prussian military. Indeed, here, in the middle of the 1980s, we can see Christopher beginning the process, performed a number of times throughout his career, of revising and perfecting his previous work to a new rigorous standard. Having written extensively on the efficacy of the Austrian military, Duffy was

---

release in the *English Historical Review*, once upon re-release in *Journal of Military History*. Despite this, Duffy's assertion regarding the artillery fortress and European expansion was of sufficient quality for Parker to employ.

54   George Snow, 'Reviewed Work: *Russia's Military Way to the West: Origins and Nature of Russian Military Power 1700-1800*', *Russian History*, 10:1 (1983) pp.97-98.

55   Duffy, *Russia's Military War to the West*, p.233.

56   Duffy, *Russia's Military War to the West*, p.234.

now prepared to return to his previous assumptions regarding Frederick II and delve into what made the great king such a force to be reckoned with. The results of this new examination were a military biography of Frederick II that has still not been surpassed in English and would eventually be translated into German as *Friedrich der Große: Ein Soldatenleben*. Avoiding the trap of hagiography, Duffy carefully asserts the responsibility that Frederick bears for the violence in mid-eighteenth century German Central Europe. Despite this, his view of Frederick and the king's leadership abilities has vastly improved from their status in the 1974 *Army of Frederick the Great*.

Duffy had now completed, within the last decade, major studies of the Austrian and Russian armies, comprehensive treatments of the military architecture, and a rigorous biography of the mid-eighteenth century's most prominent military figure. With the collected material from these projects, he was now poised to write a sweeping synthesis which would become one of his defining works: *The Military Experience in the Age of Reason*. In this ambitious book, he would summarize the personal experience of European warfare from 1700 to 1789. Although briefly treating experiences in North America and India, the book remains focused on what Duffy describes as 'Military Europe'. This mélange of martial pan-European elite culture united the military experience of European states in this time. This concept, although Duffy did not carefully define the term, is one of his, and indeed this book's, important legacies. Stephen Conway has done much to further define this concept in an excellent 2010 article. However, Conway is wrong to suggest that Duffy, 'might have meant the phrase to signify no more than his intention to survey the armies of the main European powers.' [57] Rather than a mere catch-all title for his first chapter, Duffy refers to the concept of military Europe frequently throughout his text. Duffy uses language that demonstrates that military Europe could 'observe…progress', '[try] to imitate', and could be, 'taught', 'conditioned', and '[led] into the nineteenth century.'[58] This language makes clear that Duffy is referring to the literary military elite of eighteenth-century Europe, and the collective marital culture that they created during this time. Duffy's exploration of the personal nature of military Europe, and its experience of the violence of war in the eighteenth century, are the outstanding contributions of *Military Experience in the Age of Reason*.

Having completed *The Military Experience in the Age of Reason*, Christopher made his first foray into a new era of scholarship: the Second World War. In *Red Storm on the Reich: The Soviet March on Germany*, Duffy returned to his familiar eighteenth-century locales, such as Zorndorf, Kolberg, and Breslau. The result was predictable: an even treatment of writings by the Soviet and German high commands, with a particular eye to the long history of violence in area of operations. There are frequent references to the history of German-Russian conflict. At first, this seems slightly out of place, but as Duffy explains that both the Germans and Soviets viewed the Seven Years War as an emotive precedent to the conflict, the relevance becomes clear.[59]

---

57   Stephen Conway, 'The British Army, "Military Europe," and the American War of Independence', *The William and Mary Quarterly* (2010) 67:1, pp.70.

58   Christopher Duffy, *The Military Experience in the Age of Reason* (London: Routledge & Kegan Paul, 1987) pp.15, 21, 25, 191, 209, 279.

59   Christopher Duffy, *Red Storm on the Reich: The Soviet March on Germany, 1945* (New York: Atheneum, 1991) pp.43, 291-292.

The historical community received the book well, with David Glantz giving the book a favourable review in *The Journal of Military History*. While noting that the book purposefully lacked the operational detail of Earl Ziemke and John Erikson's works, Glantz welcomed Duffy's study as correcting an overemphasis on successful German operations on the eastern front between 1941 and 1943. Glantz asserts that 'Duffy focuses on the fate of German civilization in east-central Europe by chronicling the grisly fall of German cities in the region…the general reader should be more than satisfied with Duffy's imaginative treatment of this complex period.'[60] As this commentary is coming from an author who would write a definitive history of the eastern front (in cooperation with Jonathan House), Glantz' gives high praise.

Leaving the charred cities of 1945 behind him, Christopher next turned back to one of his earlier projects, the military forces of Frederick the Great. In a new 1996 work, *The Army of Frederick the Great, 2nd Edition*, published by Todd Fisher's The Emperor's Press, Duffy fundamentally revised his assessment of the Frederician military system. From the reworked chapters on Prussian origins, to a fresh analysis of Frederick's role as *roi-connétable*, Duffy provides a more sympathetic treatment based on archival sources. His reassessment of the effectiveness of Prussian light troops is one of the most telling passages of the entire book and displays his willingness to correct previous inaccuracies by quoting archival sources extensively.[61]

He comments in the introduction:

> The present book is a radical refashioning of a work which I published in 1974 under the title of *The Army of Frederick the Great*. Since then, it has been virtually re-writing itself. I have had more opportunity to see and consider how armies work. I benefitted from a reading of the many excellent studies which appeared in association with the bicentenary of Frederick's death in 1986, as the bibliography to the new edition will make clear. I refined some of my own ideas during the composition of a military biography of Old Fritz (1985). Most importantly, however, several years of work in the Austrian, Hungarian, Slovak, and French archives towards a forthcoming history of *The Austrian Army in the Seven Years War* have made me realize how ill-informed and uncharitable were some of my comments on Frederick's army. It is now clear that officers of the enemy alliance were warm in their professional admiration for Frederick's military system, and they have forced me to reappraise subjects as diverse as the Prussian style of leadership, the standard of medical care for the soldiers, and Frederick's use of light troops.
>
> The decisive encouragement to return to the theme was provided by encounters with people in many walks of life in Europe and the United States who find, like me, something of inherent appeal in the world of Fritz and Theresa. I am glad to

60   David M. Glantz, 'Reviewed Work: *Red Storm on the Reich: The Soviet March on Germany, 1945*', *The Journal of Military History*, 56:2 (1992) pp.331-332.

61   Christopher Duffy, *The Army of Frederick the Great, 2nd Edition* (Chicago: The Emperor's Press, 1996) pp.131-138.

associate myself with them as an amateur in the proper sense of the word, as a lover of history.[62]

Christopher's comments in these introductory paragraphs speak a great deal to his scholarly and professional activities at the time. This early example of his 'permanent dissatisfaction,' bore significant fruit, and remains the standard treatment on the Prussian army in English to the present day, recently republished by Helion & Company.

Duffy's comments on 'people in many walks of life in Europe and the United States', refer, in part, to his long-time association with the Seven Years War Association, a wargaming group based in the American Midwest. As early as 1992, Christopher travelled to Chicago, Milwaukee, and South Bend, to speak to this association. He also facilitated and led several tours of the battlefields of the Seven Years War, attended by this Midwestern group. Between 1995 and 2016, Christopher would travel to the meeting of this association 19 times.

With his revision on the Prussians completed, and the archival work for his study of the Austrian military underway, Christopher turned to the topic of his mentor Rodger: the War of the Second Coalition. In *Eagles over the Alps*, Duffy examines the Suvorov campaign in Italy and Switzerland during 1799. Acknowledging that the War of the Second Coalition had been widely covered by historians such as Tim Blanning, John Lynn, and Paul Schroeder, Duffy asserted that, 'What is still lacking is an old-fashioned narrative-based operational and tactical history, and the reason as that Napoleon Bonaparte was absent from the scene.'[63] Writing on the bicentenary of the events themselves, Christopher provides the most detailed coverage of Suvorov's campaign in English to date. His bibliography shows a reliance on Austrian manuscript sources, and the book is replete with black and white photographs of the battlefields being described. This feature demonstrates Duffy's continued belief in the importance of physically visiting battlefields under study.

Defining Scholarship: 2000 to 2020

In the first year of the new millennium, Christopher published his first volume of *The Austrian Army in the Seven Years War: Instrument of War*. Breaking from my purely chronological narrative, I will examine this book out of sequence with its second volume, *The Austrian Army in the Seven Years War: By Force of Arms*. These analytical works was the result of years of research in the Vienna archives, and substantial trips to other relevant archives across Europe. The introductions and acknowledgements of these volumes display years of fruitful networking with numerous German, Austrian, French, Hungarian, Italian, and Canadian academics, and public historians. In addition, Christopher once again references the contribution of the Seven Years War Association, whose, 'companionship... provided essential moral support for the present enterprise.'[64] Taken together, these two

---

62   Christopher Duffy, *The Army of Frederick the Great, 2nd Edition*, p.4.
63   Christopher Duffy, *Eagles Over the Alps: Suvorov in Italy and Switzerland, 1799* (Chicago: The Emperor's Press, 1999) p.5.
64   Duffy, *The Austrian Army in the Seven Years War: Instrument of War*, p.9.

volumes provide just under 1,000 pages of research on the Austrian military during the middle of the eighteenth century.

When these two books are examined side-by-side, Christopher's longstanding style of writing is readily apparent. *Instrument of War* contains over 400 pages analysing the structure of the Theresian army: from the origins of the Austrian state to the experience of common soldiers, to the work of the logistical, medical, and religious branches of the Austrian army. *By Force of Arms* follows the narrative of the Seven Years War in east-central Europe in a chronological manner, but also includes a 20-page chapter on the landscape and geography of the region. The second volume is replete with black and white photographs of Christopher's many battlefield walks through the region.

Like the second edition of *The Army of Frederick the Great,* Duffy's opinions originally presented in *The Army of Maria Theresa* had tempered with age. Indeed, in his introduction Christopher writes, 'I was at first puzzled by the harsh tone of many of [*Instrument of War's*] judgements on the Theresian Army.'[65] Rather than demonstrating that the military reforms of the 1740s were entirely positive, Duffy asserted:

> [T]he process of military reform was disruptive as well as creative. Thus men of all ranks found it difficult to accommodate themselves to the complicated new drills, while *Kaisertreue* was less evident among the newly regularised Croats than mass mutiny and the losing of the tactical advantage which they and the hussars had once enjoyed over the Prussians. The cuirassiers progressed marginally, if at all, and the undoubted advances among the infantry were surpassed by those among the already formidable Prussian foot soldiers.[66]

By Force of Arms, by contrast, leaves analytical commentary to the margins, and provides a detailed account of the Seven Years War. In 400 pages of narrative, Christopher gives the most comprehensive English-language analysis of the Seven Years War in east-central Europe. In its depth and complexity, this treatment is exceeded only by the work of the German General Staff before 1914 which cover the war to 1760, and the writings of Eberhard Kessel which continue the work of the General Staff from 1760 to the end of the war.[67] As noted above, Christopher clearly identifies the new more fluid pattern of warfare which broke from the previous style of unitary linear warfare in this work.[68]

In 2003, Duffy packaged a portion of the work initially slated for *By Force of Arms* into a slim but academically rigorous volume on the battles of Rossbach and Leuthen. The resulting book, *Prussia's Glory: Rossbach and Leuthen 1757,* is a mixed analysis and narrative history of the key period between July and December of 1757, when Frederick scored his two most famous victories. Duffy's writing here matches the archival rigor in *The Austrian Army in*

---

65   Duffy, *The Austrian Army in the Seven Years War: Instrument of War,* p.8.
66   Duffy, *Instrument of War,* p.422.
67   Grossen Generalstabe, *Die Kriege Friedrichs des Grossen III: Der Siebenjährigen Kriege, 1756-63* (Berlin: E.S. Mittler und Sohn, 1901-13), Vols.I-XII; Eberhard Kessel, Herausgegeben von Thomas Linder, *Das Ende des Siebenjährigen Krieges 1760-1763: Torgau und Bunzelwitz, Schweidnitz und Freiberg* (Paderborn: Ferdindand Schöningh, 2007).
68   Duffy, *By Force of Arms,* p.396.

the Seven Years War, with holdings from 11 archives in eight countries substantially framing the volume. In his introduction, Duffy emphasized the vital role of archival documents in this analysis:

> What, after all, made Frederick and his Prussians so redoubtable? The perspective of his enemies also needs to be taken into account. They were not passive targets, and we have to ask how far they contributed to their own defeats. Without such a context the talk of 'military genius' conveys nothing, just as 'inconceivable blunders' will remain inconceivable. For these reasons the present book abandons the constraints of the conventional narratives, and bases itself chiefly on original manuscripts, most of which are explored here for the first time.[69]

This is one of the few introductions where Christopher emphasizes the role of archival sources explicitly, and one of the few works where the role of the battlefield tour is not explicitly given pride of place. Despite this, Duffy's black and white photographs of the battlefields still appear frequently in text. The emphasis on archival sources, however, assisted with the book's positive reception in academic circles. Reviewing the work in *The Journal of Military History*, Thomas Barker noted, 'Duffy's persistent, thorough plumbing of non- or rarely exploited primary sources enables him not only to clarify difficult operational issues but to add incisive personal vignettes.' Barker concluded, 'it is improbable that *Prussia's Glory* will ever be surpassed as a treatment of the classic encounters of 1757. The adjective "definitive" is entirely justified.'[70] Indeed, to date, *Prussia's Glory* is Christopher's last word on the fighting in mid-eighteenth century German Central Europe. Time will tell if he returns to this subject once again.

As he finished work on *Prussia's Glory*, Christopher was also preparing a substantial volume on a new subject, much closer to home: the 1745 Jacobite conflict in Britain. This work resulted in *The '45: Bonnie Prince Charlie and the Untold Story of the Jacobite Rising*. Originally published in 2003, this book waded into the contemporary debates regarding the nature of Highland Jacobitism and Catholicism during the rising, the role of sovereignty in the conflict, the role of non-Scottish Jacobites in the '45, and the role of prominent individuals in conducting and suppressing the rebellion. Duffy is also careful to note that while the scale of the battles was 'puny' compared with contemporary encounters in the Netherlands during the War of Austrian Succession, the stakes in Britain were much higher and could have resulted in the overturning of the ruling regime.[71]

By focusing on issues of sovereignty, Duffy is able to explain why Charles Edward Stewart failed to lead a guerrilla movement after Culloden: 'The final option of prolonging the resistance in the Highlands did not commend itself to Prince Charles, even if that course had been logistically feasible, for he viewed himself only as a crown prince in command of an

---

69   Christopher Duffy, *Prussia's Glory: Rossbach and Leuthen 1757* (Chicago: The Emperor's Press, 2003), p.4.

70   Thomas M. Barker, 'Reviewed Work: *Prussia's Glory: Rossbach and Leuthen 1757*', *The Journal of Military History*, 68:3 (2004) pp.954-955.

71   Christopher Duffy, *the '45: Bonnie Prince Charlie and the Untold Story of the Jacobite Rising* (London: Phoenix, 2007) p.546.

army, and not as a the leader of a guerrilla band.'[72] Despite attempting to remain a neutral observer, Duffy is also wise enough to note: 'Nobody is so divorced from the origins and instincts as to be able to avoid "taking sides", once exposed to this subject matter.'[73] Once again, Duffy references in the importance in observing the scenes of conflicts first-hand, with tongue-in-cheek humour: 'There will always appear to be a parallel between the events of the '45, and the wild landscapes in which some of them were played out. It is as if Prince Charles turned back when the good scenery gave out.'[74] Black and white photographs of battlescapes abound.

Perhaps surprisingly considering that this was the first writing of a relative outsider in a highly contentious field, the book was positively reviewed. Writing in the *English Historical Review*, Ralph McLean noted:

> The result is a book which is able to balance the root causes and motivations of Jacobitism with a detailed and precise account of the battles which took place in the failed attempt to realize their aims. This is a piece of work which tears away the tartan veil that so often obscures an impartial viewing of this problematical topic, replacing romance with reality, and points the way to more sophisticated scholarship on a particular complex chapter of British history.[75]

In his next project, Duffy returned to the twentieth century once again. Becoming interested in German perceptions of Britain while briefly commenting on Hessian involvement in *The '45*, Christopher now turned to a full book on the subject: *Through German Eyes: The British and the Somme 1916*. Rather than a battle history of the Somme, this book focuses explicitly on the German perception and idea of the British during this period of the First World War. Using information gleaned from German interviews with prisoners taken after 15 September, Duffy demonstrates that,

> The Germans… learned a great deal from prisoners about conditions on the British home front, the tensions in Ireland, and in the Empire, together with the experience and mentality of all the British and Imperial regimental ranks, the weapons and tactics of the infantry, and every aspect of the Royal Flying Corps.[76]

In this way, Duffy seizes upon the importance of prisoner interviews in ways which match their utilization across twentieth century scholarship.[77] This interest in the German perception of Britain would continue to ferment in Christopher's mind.

---

72 Duffy, *The '45*, p.547.
73 Duffy, *The '45*, p.548.
74 Duffy, *The '45*, p.548.
75 Ralph McLean, 'Reviewed Work: *The '45: Bonnie Prince Charlie and the Untold Story of the Jacobite Rising*', *The English Historical Review*, 124: 507 (2009) p.441.
76 Christopher Duffy, *Through German Eyes: The British and The Somme*, 1916 (London: Phoenix, 2007), p.322
77 For example, see Sonke Neitzel and Harald Welzer, *Soldaten: On Fighting Killing and Dying* (London: Signal, 2012).

In 2013, Duffy returned to the Jacobite theme via a new and interesting framework. Focusing on the role of the Hessian troops and Prince Frederick of Hesse in the 1745 uprising, Christopher published *The Best of Enemies: Germans against Jacobites 1746*. Although he had utilized a small amount of material on the Hessians in his previous Jacobite volume, Duffy was assisted by Dr Günter Hollenberg, who provided intelligence on the wealth of material on the Jacobite uprising in the Hessian State Archives at Marburg. The result was a book covering an eighteenth-century German prince on the cusp of converting to Catholicism who campaigned in the Jacobite '45. It is difficult to think of a topic more to Christopher's liking. Tracing the story of Prince Frederick in a Jacobite context, Duffy demonstrates that the Hessians were a surprisingly kind adversary to the Jacobite rebels. He notes,

> The Hessians as a whole were angered by the reports of what was being done in King George's name. They opened their camp to refugees, and they were remembered in Perthshire as "a gentle race." … Frederick and his Hessians arrived on the scene of conflict as total strangers. They were not cowards (as their conduct in the great battles in Flanders was to show), but they recoiled from their assigned role as helpmates of the Hanoverians in this ugly civil war, and their revulsion must stand as one of the most telling indictments of the policies of the London government and its agents.[78]

Duffy's new foray into Hessian history had not changed his preferred methods, however. The final pages of *Best of Enemies* include instructions for a driving tour of the Hessian journey through Scotland, complete with black and white photographs of relevant terrain.

Christopher would return to the Jacobite theme once more, for his final published book (at the time of writing in 2021), *Fight for a Throne: The Jacobite '45 Reconsidered*. This book is a fitting conclusion to the works discussed in this essay, as it brings together so much of what makes Duffy's writing distinctive and commendable. Christopher writes in his preface:

> When I first tackled this subject, I believed that I had done a serviceable piece of work. I out to have remembered that history is timeless, but that once set down by the historians it turns out to be a highly perishable commodity… What astonished me, however, was just how much of the original documentation had passed me by, and this mass of material has become accessible through the help of the people who are listed in my acknowledgements. In terms of volume alone, the unexplored manuscript material exceed three times over the documentation that supported my first edition, while the quality and variety has made it possible for me to fashion what is essentially a fresh study.[79]

Writing honestly, Duffy notes that he was 'impressed more than anything else by the far-reaching challenges – political as well as military – that the Jacobite cause presented to

---

78   Christopher Duffy, *The Best of Enemies: Germans against Jacobites, 1746* (Chicago: The Emperor's Press, 2013) p.133.

79   Duffy, *Fight for a Throne*, p.xi.

the Hanoverian State.'[80] The resulting work reaches over 600 pages, and like previous revisions, is a mix of modified old writing and completely novel material. His preface ends with a reference to the ongoing need for battlefield preservation in Scotland, which became a sizable portion of his work and career at this time. Although this work remains an overtly military history, Christopher's fascination with the afterlife of Jacobitism as memorial movement is given heavy treatment in the final chapters of the work. The first three of five appendices give the fullest treatment of the contemporary natural environment to appear in one of his works, there are black and white photographs of terrain throughout the volume. Appendix III, 'Through the Land of Chiefs and Lairds', gives the reader a tour of contemporary Scotland.

Although the book is unlikely to be the last word on the Jacobite '45, Duffy anticipates and acknowledges this fact. For him, 'The Jacobite rising of 1745 may be likened to a deep well of endlessly renewing water, but when we peer inside, what swims into view will be our own reflections.'[81] Duffy's second treatment of the Jacobite movement is indeed a reflection of his style of writing: a style which emphasizes heavy use of manuscript sources, a keen attention to the natural environment and weather, and a philosophy of research which combines archival diligence with actually visiting the sites under study.

Conclusion

The picture which emerges from the body of Duffy's work is one which truly matches his expressed sentiment: they were written for pleasure, not focused on what was academically in vogue. Christopher's main qualification for success was whether *he* was pleased with a particular work, and felt that he had told the story well. The resulting body of literature is humbling. Divorced from ego, Duffy accepted the flaws in certain interpretations and gathered additional material to present a more nuanced and accurate picture. Christopher sought out networks and relationships with like-minded individuals across many countries, which pushed him to refine his research and writing. This has led to some of the finest coverage of eighteenth-century military history that has been produced.

Duffy's awareness of the importance of physically traversing the ground being studied has facilitated collaboration with many scholars, some of whom have written chapters for this volume. The importance of travel to this collaborative effort should not be understated. In addition to facilitating collaboration Christopher's travels have provided helpful photographs for his readers. This process of travelling in the same physical environment as his subject has oriented Duffy to the geographical and topographical world which he studies. This has allowed Christopher to avoid many of the novice mistakes of historians who write disparagingly of the history of battle. In writing for pleasure, Christopher has given us a glimpse into the world of the eighteenth century.

---

80   Duffy, *Fight for a Throne*, p.xi.
81   Duffy, *Fight for a Throne*, p.520.

Section Two

Commanders and their Armies

3

Military Action and Military Reflection: Some Thoughts on Frederick's *Eléments de castramétrie et de tactique* of 1770

Jürgen Luh

In 1770, King Frederick the Great of Prussia wrote a memorandum entitled *Éléments de castramétrie et de tactique*. It was composed for the benefit of the Prussian generals and published in French (1770) and in German, under the title *Grundsätze der Lager-Kunst und Tactic* (1771).[1] The paper was the very last of the king's comprehensive writings on military tactics. It succeeded his *Principes généraux de la guerre*, written in 1746, and his *Testament militaire* from 1768.[2]

The memorandum expressed the king's insights into the changing art of warfare, based on his experiences gained during the Seven Years War. The foreword of the paper is particularly important. It reveals Frederick's hindsight, and shows that he had learned from his enemies, above all from the Austrian Field Marshal Leopold von Daun, a man the king had made fun of during the Seven Years War. Thus, I will focus on this foreword in this chapter.

---

1 Johann David Erdmann Preuß (ed.), *Œuvres de Frédéric le Grand*, 30 Vols., supplemented by a Table chronologique genérale des ouvrages de Frédéric le Grand et Catalogue raisonné des écrits, qui lui sont attribués (Berlin: Rudolphe Decker, 1846-1857), Vol. 29,2: Frederick's original work *'un grand in-quarto, portant au frontispice une vignette gravée par Schleuen; il se compose d'un Avant-propos de six pages, d'une Table des matières de même étendue, que nous donnons telle que le Roi l'a faite, a et de quatre-vingt-six pages de texte, avec trente-sept plans qui tous présentent des notes explicatives, en partie très-détaillées. On lit à la fin de l'article XXXVIII et dernier: Sans-Souci, ce 12 novembre 1770, et plus bas la signature: Federic.'* The German version is entitled: *Grundsätze der Lager-Kunst und Tactic (sans lieu d'impression), 1771, quatre-vingt-quatorze pages grand in-quarto, avec la vignette de Schleuen et trente-sept plans. L'ouvrage est daté: Sans-Souci, den 12. November 1770, et signé Friderich.*
2 See Robert R. Palmer, 'Frederick the Great, Guibert, Bülow: From Dynastic to National War', in Peter Paret (ed.) *Makers of Modern Strategy from Machiavelli to the Nuclear Age* (Princeton: Princeton University Press, 1986), pp.91-119, quoting p.96. After that Frederick still wrote various instructions, but no more tactical analyses and directions.

In May 1759, for example, six months after Daun and the Austrians had defeated Frederick and his army at Hochkirch, the king published a 'Letter from the Pope to Field Marshal Daun', in which the Pope allegedly honoured Daun with a holy hat and sword. The letter was followed by fictional 'Congratulations from the Prince de Soubise to Field Marshal Daun on the sword received from the Pope', in which Frederick wrote: 'What would become of us if one day we had to wage war against you and simultaneously resist both your skills and your sacred sword?'[3] While Frederick mocked the Austrian field marshal in public, in reality he was far more impressed by 'Daun's never-failing ability to choose strong defensive positions' than he cared to admit.[4] The foreword of the *Éléments de castramétrie et de tactique* was particularly telling in this respect.

The memorandum also reveals that Frederick's style of warfare, which sought combat at any cost, was outdated and had in fact been so from the very outset of the Seven Years War. Frederick did not admit this explicitly, but, by taking a closer look, one can find that he acknowledged it between the lines.

'Before the last war', Frederick wrote at the beginning of the foreword (following the translation of Jay Luvaas),

> I had given my general officers an Instruction which at the time seemed to me suffi- cient, but the enemy, who was conscious of the disadvantage that he had laboured under in fighting us during the first campaigns, has since perfected his castram- etation, his tactics, and his artillery. Consequently, war has become more refined, more difficult, and more hazardous, for we no longer have only men to fight, but rather the prudence that tactic teaches, the strong posts, and artillery, all together. The fact alone should compel us to study these aspects of war if we are to save our former reputation and acquire new fame.[5]

Four points mentioned by the Prussian king in this passage seem to be particularly signifi- cant: The first one is that Frederick refers to 'an instruction I had given to my general officers'.[6] This clearly referred to the king's educational manual, *Les principes généraux de la guerre, appliqués a la tactique et a la discipline des troupes prussiennes* or *Die General- Principia vom Kriege, appliciret auf die Tactique und auf die Disziplin, derer Preussischen Trouppen*.[7] It was written from 1746 to 1748 – Frederick finished his work before 2 April 1748[8] – and published under its German title in 1753 for the education of his general officers, as it says in German: '*Hatte … ich meinen Generals einen Unterricht in der Kriegs-Kunst*

---

3   See Gustav Berthold Volz (ed.), *Die Werke Friedrichs des Großen in deutscher Übersetzung* (Berlin: Reimar Hobbing, 1913), Vol.5, pp.221-222.

4   See Dennis E. Showalter, *The Wars of Frederick the Great* (London, New York: Longman, 1996), p.177.

5   Jay Luvaas (ed.), *Frederick the Great on the Art of War* (New York: Da Capo Press, 1999), p.276.

6   Luvaas (ed.), *Frederick the Great*, p.276.

7   Preuß (ed.), *Œuvres de Frédéric le Grand*, Vol.28,3 and Vol.7.

8   See Adalbert von Taysen, *Friedrich der Große. Militärische Schriften, erläutert und mit Anmerkungen versehen* (Berlin: Wilhelmi, 1882), p.III. On this day Frederick finished the second revision, which significantly expanded his original text.

gegeben.[9] These 'Military Instructions to his Generals' had been an ambitious opus. They reflected Frederick's experiences from the First and Second Silesian Wars and his resulting thoughts and considerations.[10] In a letter to his brother August Wilhelm from 19 June 1748, Frederick stated: 'My very dear brother, finally I send you a work which I promised a long time ago; it is the fruit of our campaigns and of my reflections.'[11]

The work was meant to inscribe Frederick into the list of the famous theorists of war like the Roman Vegetius, the Frenchmen Feuquières, Puységur and Quincy, the Spaniard Santa Cruz y Marcenado, the Italian Montecuccoli and the German Maurice de Saxe, to name only a few writers.[12] We know this from Frederick's letter to his brother: 'I have dealt with all major aspects of war, there is no aspect which I have omitted and, in terms of the smaller details, I have these laid down in my instructions, which are in the hands of all our officers.'[13] More than this, Frederick believed that the 'Military Instructions' enshrined eternal military truths that would win him and his ideas everlasting fame: 'I can boldly claim that in no other book are things so precisely described.'[14]

However – and this seems to be the second important point arising from the passage quoted above – the Seven Years War had unfortunately proved *Les principes généraux* to be insufficient. Frederick was forced to recognise that he had neither considered everything that was possible in contemporary warfare, nor foreseen new military developments, especially in tactics and weaponry.[15] Most of all, he had overlooked the developments in field fortifications.

Frederick – and this is the third point – could not openly concede that he had not anticipated these developments. For that reason, he asserted at the very beginning of his preface that 'the enemy, who was conscious of the disadvantage that he had laboured under in fighting us during the first campaigns, has since perfected his castrametation, his tactics, and his artillery'.[16] This statement implied that his 'Military Instructions' had been wise and very advantageous for the Prussians at the beginning of the war. However, the statement was also supposed to divert attention from the fact that he had neglected the entrenchments, the tactics associated with them, and the artillery. Neither the subject of strategically located entrenchments and their selection, nor the fortification of these places with artillery had played a prominent role in Frederick's considerations. It was all irrelevant to his idea of warfare, which advocated for direct combat with the aim of

---

9   See Volz, *Die Werke Friedrichs des Großen in deutscher Übersetzung*, Vol.6 (Berlin: Reimar Hobbing, 1913), p.127. The German translation lacks three chapters: '*Des projets de campagne*', '*Des talents qu'il faut à un general*' and '*De l'attaque et de la défense des places*'.

10   Palmer, 'Frederick the Great', p.96.

11   Taysen, *Friedrich der Große*, p.IV.

12   Frederick definitely knew the works of the abovementioned military writers, and his libraries contained various editions of these. See Bogdan Krieger, Lektüre und Bibliotheken Friedrichs des Großen', *Hohenzollern-Jahrbuch*, 15 (1911), pp.168-216, p.209 and p.213; Bogdan Krieger, ‚Lektüre und Bibliotheken Friedrichs des Großen', *Hohenzollern-Jahrbuch*, 17 (1913), pp.105-155, p.144 and p.147.

13   Taysen, *Friedrich der Große*, p.IV.

14   Taysen, *Friedrich der Große*, p.IV.

15   See Palmer, 'Frederick the Great', p.95.

16   Luvaas (ed.), *Frederick the Great*, p.276.

provoking a knockout blow, because, in the words of the Chevalier de Quincy, 'battles are the making of a conqueror, and more than any other deed they endow him with the reputation of being a great captain'.[17]

But Field Marshal Daun disabused the king of his views. Only after the bloody and costly battle at Torgau in 1760, where his well-drilled army was destroyed, Frederick accepted that his military credo had no future. Because of his faulty tactics, Frederick lost most of the remaining veteran officers and men, and the Prussian army was able to win only thanks to the manoeuvres of Lieutenant General Zieten and his corps.[18] This is the fourth point that emanates from the first passage of the memorandum: the king conceded that a campaign or the outcome of a war were no longer decided in battle but rather by occupying and holding a carefully chosen, strong and impregnable position, which could be easily supplied with provisions. If one studied these aspects of war successfully, one would not only 'save our former reputation' but 'acquire new fame'.[19] Thus, Frederick accentuated something that he had not valued so far: the precise knowledge and assessment of terrain.

> The study of terrain and how its advantages and defects can be utilized constitutes one of the principal subjects to which a general officer should apply himself; for all his manoeuvres in war depend upon the posts that he should occupy with advantage, those that he should attack with minimum losses, the terrain where he should fight, … and on this science which imparts a knowledge of using troops appropriately in each situation and according to the rules that experience has taught us.[20]

After the First and Second Silesian Wars, the king had apparently attached little importance to the study of 'terrain and how its advantages and defects can be utilized.'[21] Surprisingly, Frederick's *Principes Généraux* did not expand on the general's specific need of precise knowledge of terrain and only contained general remarks about the use of terrain. Frederick stated that a commanding officer should have maps and should be able to remember the names of the villages, rivers, heights – that is, the grounds at large. The king also wrote about the importance of visual judgement. Yet one cannot find a single practical example derived from his own experience. His attitude only changed after the bitter experiences of the Seven Years War: first and foremost after the defeats at Kolin (1757), Hochkirch (1758), and Kunersdorf (1759), and after his narrow victory at Torgau in 1760.

This can be seen, for instance, in the following sentences:

> Those who are persuaded that valour alone suffices for the general officer deceive themselves greatly. It is an essential quality, beyond doubt, but it must be supplemented with much other knowledge. A general who maintains order and discipline

---

17   Quincy's quotation in Christopher Duffy, *The Military Experience in the Age of Reason* (Chatham: Wordsworth Editions, 1998), p.189.
18   See Showalter, *Wars of Frederick the Great*, pp.281-283; Jürgen Luh. *Der Große. Friedrich II. von Preußen* (München: Siedler, 2011), p.69.
19   Luvaas (ed.), *Frederick the Great*, p.276.
20   Luvaas (ed.), *Frederick the Great*, p.276.
21   Luvaas (ed.), *Frederick the Great*, p.276.

in his command is certainly praiseworthy, but that is not enough in war either. He must exercise judgement in everything.[22]

Here, Frederick re-evaluated the meaning of valour and the knowledge of terrain. In his *Principes Généraux,* a general officer was reminded that 'battles decide the fate of a nation',[23] and that 'in war it is absolutely necessary to come to decisive actions either to get out of the distress of war or to place the enemy in that position, or even to settle a quarrel which otherwise perhaps would never be finished.'[24] To follow this maxim, valour was absolutely necessary and essential for a general. However, more than 20 years later, valour had lost its prime importance as a virtue for generals in Frederick's eyes. In the passage cited, he conceded his errors in observation and judgement at Zorndorf, Hochkirch, Kunersdorf, and Torgau, admitting that he had not listened to the insight and the advice of his generals in any of these battles.[25]

However, maintaining order and discipline was not enough. Henceforth, according to Frederick's conclusion, successful warfare meant that: 'We must study castrametation, tactics, and the science of the artillery, and the way to use artillery to the greatest advantage.'[26] From now on, both generals and the king himself, should study the 'terrain and how its advantages and defects can be utilized' before anything else.[27] The study of the science of artillery came a close second. In the course of the Seven Years War, the immense impact of cannons and howitzers gradually turned the artillery into the dominating force on the battlefield. For example, in 1756, the three Prussian corps in Saxony, Silesia, and East Prussia disposed of 240 field pieces (three-pounders), sixty 12-pounder pieces, twenty-six 24 pounder battery pieces, and twenty 10-pounder howitzers, altogether 336 guns.[28] By 1762, even without the heavy battery pieces stationed in fortresses like Schweidnitz/Świdnica, Glogau/Głogów or Neisse/Nysa, the number of all Prussian field guns had doubled to a total of 662.[29]

This, in turn, had far-reaching implications for tactics.[30] An exchange of letters between Frederick and Duke Ferdinand of Brunswick, commander of the allied army during the Seven Years War, for instance, reveals that, from 1758 onwards, both commanders not only intended to employ as many guns as possible, but also that the artillery moved to the centre of their battle plans. In a moment of euphoria, Frederick even believed that he could decide the outcome of

---

22 Luvaas (ed.), *Frederick the Great*, pp.276-277.
23 Luvaas (ed.), *Frederick the Great*, p.139.
24 Luvaas (ed.), *Frederick the Great*, pp.139.
25 See Luh, *Der Große*, p.69 and pp.225-227.
26 Luvaas (ed.), *Frederick the Great*, p.277.
27 Luvaas (ed.), *Frederick the Great*, p.276.
28 See Curt Jany, *Geschichte der Königlich Preußischen Armee bis zum Jahre 1807* Second edition (Osnabrück: Biblio Verlag, 1967), Vol.II, pp.351-352 and Großer Generalstab, Kriegsgeschichtliche Abteilung II (ed.), *Die Kriege Friedrichs des Großen. Der Erste Schlesische Krieg, 1740-1742* (Berlin, Ernst Siegfried Mittler und Sohn, 1890), Vol.1 pp.118-120. The best account of the Prussian field artillery during the Seven Years War is still the one from Hans A. Bleckwenn, `Die preußischen Feldgeschütz-Typen 1756-62 in Beziehung zur allgemeinen Gefechtstaktik', *Zeitschrift für Heereskunde* 21 (1957), pp.69-74; pp.85-89; pp.116-118, and *Zeitschrift für Heereskunde* 22 (1958), pp.2-4.
29 Jürgen Luh, *Ancien Régime Warfare and the Military Revolution. A Study* (Groningen: INOS, 2000), p.171.
30 See Jürgen Luh, *Kriegskunst in Europa 1650-1800* (Köln, Weimar, Wien: Böhlau, 2004), pp.171-173; Luh, *Ancien Régime Warfare*, p.175.

a battle with artillery alone. 'If your Grace keeps your troops together as well as possible', he wrote to the duke one month before the battle of Minden, 'and concentrate all your efforts on one point where you assemble your entire artillery and can employ it with success, you will inevitably find that, despite any possible advantage, you will defeat' the French.[31]

This was undoubtedly an optimistic opinion. In retrospect, however, Frederick was proved right. At Minden, the united guns of the Allies played a crucial role in their victory over the French army. Later, it was said that the 67 heavy guns had won 'the most brilliant success over the French.'[32] The battery fire decimated the French infantry battalions, making it impossible for the French to advance against the allied wings. On the other hand, the bitter defeat at Hochkirch taught Frederick what kind of devastation Daun's superior artillery was able to cause among the Prussian troops.

The king learned his lesson: One by one, he had the regiments' 3-pounder guns replaced by 6-pounders and used heavy guns, 12- or 24-pounders, whenever possible to gain the upper hand over the enemy's artillery. According to his own words of 1759, 'to attack the enemy without superior fire is like fighting against firearms with sticks. One will have to involve as much artillery as possible, as unpractical and difficult as this may seem. ... It will make up for the shortcomings of our infantry.'[33]

Bringing our discussion full circle, Frederick acknowledged that the improved efficiency of the artillery made fortified camps in strategically crucial places increasingly important. Not even Frederick, who, in the eyes of his contemporaries, was always seeking battle, and dared to attack well-chosen positions that were defended by artillery, 'because all disadvantages are on the side of the attacker'.[34] As a result, the 'Frederician war became increasingly a war of position, the war of complex manoeuvre and subtle accumulation of small gains; leisurely and slow in its main outlines, and quite different from the short sharp warfare recommended in 1746.'[35]

First and foremost, this was what the king wanted his commanding general officers to know. On this account, he stressed his new approach repeatedly:

> It is therefore necessary to impress firmly on the mind that henceforth we shall have only a war of artillery to wage, and fortified positions to assault. This necessitates an extensive study of terrain and of the art of competently using it to every possible advantage both in the attack and in the defence.[36]

---

31   Frederick the Great to Ferdinand of Brunswick, Reich-Heinersdorf, 1 July 1759, in Ernst von dem Knesebeck, *Ferdinand Herzog zu Braunschweig und Lüneburg während des siebenjährigen Krieges. Aus englischen und preußischen Archiven gesammelt und herausgegeben* (Hannover: Hellwing'sche Hofbuchhandlung, 1857), Vol.1 p.367.

32   As quoted in Ferdinand Otto Wilhelm Henning von Westphalen (ed.), *Christian Heinrich Philipp von Westphalen: Geschichte der Feldzüge des Herzogs Ferdinand von Braunschweig-Lüneburg. Nachgelassenes Manuskript* (Berlin: Verlag der Königl. Geheimen Ober-Hofdruckerei, 1871), Vol.3, p.470.

33   Frederick the Great quoted by Johann Heilmann, *Die Kriegskunst der Preußen unter König Friedrich dem Großen* (Leipzig, Meißen: F. W. Goedsche'sche Buchhandlung (O. W. Goedsche), 1852), Vol.1, p.226.

34   Frederick the Great, 'Testament militaire', in Volz (ed.), *Die Werke Friedrichs des Großen*, Vol 6, pp.222-261, p.248.

35   Palmer, 'Frederick the Great', p.103.

36   Luvaas (ed.). *Frederick the Great*, p.277.

In 1778, during the War of the Bavarian Succession, Frederick acted in his campaign in Bohemia according to his 1770 memorandum – but with very limited success. At first, he made a long-meditated reconnaissance in force. Then he manoeuvred very carefully, but the Austrians held such strong positions beyond the Elbe that the king despite all precautions did not dare to attack.[37] This might have been due to the fact that he had missed out on yet another crucial development of late eighteenth-century warfare: the deployment of light troops, which became more and more pivotal and eventually a decisive force during the French Revolutionary Wars and the same in the following wars. Frederick had been sceptical about light troops and distrusted their success under Ferdinand of Brunswick in the western theatre of war.[38] After the end of the Seven Years War, the king either had the soldiers of his light troops enrolled in the regular regiments or dismissed them from the army, even though his brother Prince Henry had proved that one could fight very successfully with light troops. He did this primarily out of his distrust of his free battalions, not out of a lack of finances. Moreover, Frederick himself had derived all his thoughts only from the campaigns against the Russian and Austrian armies, but this was not quite enough. Light troops were again used successfully in Napoleonic times in France, Britain and Austria, but not in Prussia. So, unfortunately for Frederick's pretension and fame, his *Éléments de castramétrie et de tactique* were not made for eternity either.

Further Reading

Tim Blanning, *Frederick the Great. King of Prussia* (London: Allan Lane, 2015).

Christopher Duffy, *Frederick the Great. A Military Life* (London, New York: Routledge, Chapman & Hall, 1988).

Jürgen Luh, *Kriegskunst in Europa 1650-1800* (Köln, Wien, Weimar: Böhlau, 2004).

Jürgen Luh, *Der Große. Friedrich II. von Preußen* (München: Siedler, 2011).

Jay Luvaas (ed.), *Frederick the Great on the Art of War* (New York: Da Capo Press, 1999).

Dennis E. Showalter, *The Wars of Frederick the Great* (London, New York: Longman, 1996).

Gustav Berthold Volz (ed.), *Die Werke Friedrichs des Großen in deutscher Übersetzung* (Berlin: Reimar Hobbing, 1913), Vol. 5

---

37   Christopher Duffy, *Frederick the Great. A military Life* (London, New York: Routledge, Chapman & Hall, 1988, pp.269-271.

38   See Jürgen Luh: 'Strategie und Taktik im Ancien Régime', *Militärgeschichtliche Zeitschrift* 64 (2005), pp.101-131, p.122.

4

The Württemberg Army in the Seven Years War

Peter H. Wilson

Christopher Duffy has ranged widely across the history of European warfare, but the conflicts of the mid-eighteenth century have always been at the core of his work. His particular skill is to breathe life into the long-dead warriors, presenting them as full-rounded individuals and enabling us to glimpse the world through their eyes. This is combined with a sympathetic understanding of the armies in which they served, as well as detailed knowledge of the terrain over which they fought; often acquired through exhaustively walking the routes and battlefields. These skills are immediately apparent from his first books, a lively biography of Maximilian Ulysses von Browne (1705-57), the Austrian field marshal of Irish descent, and a history of the army of Prussia's king, Frederick II 'the Great'.[1] What follows owes much to a first edition of the latter book which I read shortly after its publication and which sparked my interest in eighteenth-century warfare. That in turn made me acquainted with the patchwork of the Holy Roman Empire over which many of the wars were fought, and ultimately brought me to the duchy of Württemberg and its army.

Württemberg played a relatively minor part in the Seven Years War which appears an ignominious episode in the duchy's history. Carl Eugen, the Catholic duke ruling this Lutheran principality, is widely presented as a merely 'playing at soldiers.' Casanova, who narrowly escaped Württemberg recruiters whilst visiting the duchy, believed 'the great subsidies which the king of France was foolish enough to pay the prince had merely allowed him to indulge in luxury and his debauches. This Württemberg corps was magnificent but throughout the war it was only distinguished by its mistakes.'[2] From the perspective of most nineteenth and twentieth-century historians, by allying with the French, Carl Eugen picked

---

1   Christopher Duffy, *The Wild Goose and the Eagle: A Life of Marshal von Browne, 1705-1757* (London: Chatto & Windus, 1964), and *The Army of Frederick the Great* (1st ed., Newton Abbot: David and Charles, 1974).

2   Quoted in Adrien Fauchier-Magnan, *The Small German Courts in the Eighteenth Century* (London: Methuen, 1958), p.209. This view was consolidated by the detailed study issued by the local history society: *Karl Eugen und seiner Zeit* (Esslingen: Württembergischer Geschichts- und Altertumsverein, 1907-9). For a modest attempt a rehabilitation, see Jürgen Walter, *Carl Eugen von Württemberg. Ein Herzog und seine Untertanen* (Mühlacker: Stieglitz, 1987).

the 'wrong' side, since Germany's future supposedly lay with Protestant Prussia, rather than Catholic Austria. More broadly, Württemberg has come to typify the popular view of the Holy Roman Empire as fragmented into petty principalities with minimal military potential. That view has now been substantially revised, indicating that the Empire functioned fairly effectively and was still capable of considerable military effort even in the later eighteenth century.[3] Nonetheless, the fact that Württemberg's involvement in the Seven Years War was scarcely glorious warrants further investigation to see what this reveals about the performance of smaller armies in mid eighteenth-century warfare.

Württemberg, the Empire and Europe

At first sight, neither Württemberg nor even the Empire appear to have mattered much in the Seven Years War and the Reichsarmee is best – if unjustly – remembered for its share in the French defeat at Roßbach.[4] In fact, both the Empire as a whole and Württemberg more specifically made substantial contributions to the Austrian-led coalition against Prussia. More importantly, imperial participation was vital to Austria's plans to dismember Prussia and eliminate it permanently as a threat. Frederick II's decisions to invade Saxony in August 1756, and much of Mecklenburg soon after, played into Austria's hands, since these were clear breaches of the Empire's public peace. By securing the support of both France and Sweden by early 1757, Austria not only obtained the necessary military support, but also the agreement of the two international guarantors of the imperial constitution. The Austrian Habsburgs, as the elected head of the Empire, thus had legal grounds to deprive Frederick of territory and rights. However, this would only be valid with the agreement of the 'imperial Estates', or component principalities and free cities of the Empire.

Across 1756-1757, Austrian and French diplomats pressured the German princes to back their interpretation of the war while their Prussian and British counterparts worked hard to ensure the imperial Estates remained neutral or, better still, supplied troops to their side.[5] Though firmly in the Empire's third rank of princes, Württemberg was the largest territory in the Swabian Kreis, the framework for coordinating the most territorially fragmented of the Empire's 10 regions. Since the later seventeenth century, Swabia had consistently supplied the largest contingent to the Reichsarmee and Württemberg was well-placed to promote or retard Swabian mobilisation.

However, the duchy's rulers had long dreamed of possessing more than regional importance. Like other German princes, they were caught in Europe's inexorable shift towards an order based on sovereign states. By contrast, politics in the Empire remained determined

3   P.H. Wilson, *The Holy Roman Empire: A Thousand Years of Europe's History* (London: Allen Lane, 2016), and his *German Armies: War and German Politics 1648-1806* (London: UCL Press, 1998).

4   Full reappraisal of the battle in Alexander Querengässer (ed.), *Die Schlacht bei Roßbach* (Berlin: Zeughaus, 2017). See also Christopher Duffy, *Prussia's Glory: Rossbach and Leuthen* (Chicago: The Emperor's Press, 2003).

5   Sven Externbrink, *Friedrich der Große, Maria Theresia und das Alte Reich: Deutschlandbild und Diplomatie Frankreichs im Siebenjährigen Krieg* (Berlin: Akademie Verlag, 2006); Eckhard Buddruss, *Die französiche Deutschlandpolitik 1756-1789* (Mainz: Zabern, 1995).

by a status hierarchy which was also being undermined by the divergence between formal rank and real power.[6] The decisive shift occurred around 1700 when three members of the Empire's elite second tier of princes, known as electors, all secured international influence through connections to foreign crowns: the personal unions of Saxony-Poland (1697-1763) and Hanover-England (1714-1837), as well as recognition of Brandenburg's sovereign duchy of Prussia, which lay beyond the Empire to the east, as a kingdom in its own right. The failure of both the Palatine and Bavarian electors to secure a crown, as well as the latter's disastrous temporary possession of the imperial title (1742-1745), signalled their growing political marginalisation. Those in the third tier, like the Württemberg dukes, were increasingly regarded by foreigners as merely the Empire's aristocracy, rather than the semi-sovereigns they had been before the mid-seventeenth century. While royal titles seemed largely beyond their reach, several hoped they could be promoted to the rank of elector and the best way to achieve this appeared to support Habsburg interests in the Empire. After all, the Hanoverians only secured electoral rank in 1692 and had done so by supplying troops to Austria against the Ottomans.

By the mid-eighteenth century, it was clear that Württemberg and Hessen-Kassel were the main contenders for the next electoral title, should one be created, as both were the largest, and most powerful secular principalities currently without one.[7] Rulers of both principalities recognised that only by making themselves useful to the emperor or his allies did they stand any hope of securing their goals. This was the real motive behind the so-called German 'soldier trade' whereby princes rented out auxiliaries or supplied recruits to foreign powers.[8] While it was always useful to make a profit, this rarely happened and most agreed to loss-making arrangements in the hope these would advance their political goals. Hessen-Kassel was the only principality to make a significant financial surplus on its supply of soldiers, but the famous 'reversal of alliances' at the start of the Seven Years War saw it dragged into the conflict allied to Britain against the emperor upon whose goodwill its political ambitions largely depended.

Württemberg had engaged in a long series of loss-making treaties since the 1670s without securing any substantial political rewards. Unlike Hessen-Kassel where the landgrave governed in a close alliance with the local nobility, Württemberg's dukes were generally at odds with their most influential inhabitants. These were a close-knit elite known as the Worthies (*Ehrbarkeit*), a network of well-educated, prosperous burghers who dominated the duchy's small market towns and Lutheran state church.[9] Since the local nobility had opted out of the duchy in the early sixteenth century, the Worthies, as the town mayors and church abbots, controlled the Estates, or representative body through which all taxes had to be negotiated. The Worthies either held most of the civil offices or were related by

---

6   Barbara Stollberg-Rilinger, *The Emperor's Old Clothes: Constitutional History and the Symbolic Language of the Holy Roman Empire* (Oxford: Berghahn, 2015).

7   Ludolf Pelizaeus, *Der Aufstieg Württembergs und Hessen-Kassel zur Kurwürde 1692-1806* (Frankfurt: Peter Lang, 2000).

8   P.H. Wilson, 'The German "soldier trade" of the seventeenth and eighteenth centuries: A reassessment', *The International History Review*, 18 (1996), pp.757-792

9   Gabrielle Haug-Moritz, *Die württembergische Ehrbarkeit. Annährungen an eine bürgerlich Machtelite der frühen Neuzeit* (Ostfildern: Jan Thorbecke, 2009).

marriage to nobles and other outsiders appointed as administrators by the duke. The army, officered primarily by nobles, was widely regarded as an alien institution which threatened the duchy's cherished 'good old laws.[10]

Matters became more complicated when the duchy passed to a junior, Catholic line in 1733 with the accession of Carl Eugen's father, Carl Alexander, who immediately tripled the army in a bid to secure Habsburg approval of electoral status and territorial acquisitions.[11] His unexpected death in 1737 was followed by a military coup staged by Lutheran officers who sympathised with the Worthies and their allies in the ducal Privy Council. Together, they overthrew the late duke's will and imposed a new regency government for Carl Eugen who was then only nine years old. The army was drastically reduced by transferring many of the regiments permanently into Austrian and Prussian service. What had appeared a logical way to reduce the duchy's military budget became potentially politically disastrous with the outbreak of the War of Austrian Succession, particularly after a Württemberg envoy proceeded to commit the duchy to providing further recruits to the Prussian army. Carl Eugen, and his two younger brothers, Ludwig Eugen (1731-1795) and Friedrich Eugen (1732-1797), were bundled off to Berlin, ostensibly for a Protestant education, but de facto as hostages for the duchy's continued compliance with Prussian interests. Eventually, Frederick II was forced to cooperate in securing Carl Eugen's premature declaration of age in 1744, to avoid the appearance he was holding the princes against their will.

The Franco-Württemberg Alliance

Carl Eugen's experience left him with an ambivalent relationship towards Prussia. On the one hand, like many of his contemporaries, he was dazzled by the glory of Frederick's victories, and soon remodelled his duchy's – now much reduced – army along Prussian lines, switching the base uniform colour from yellow to blue after 1746, and rewriting the regulations and drill manual along Prussian lines. He and Friedrich Eugen were also betrothed to two of Frederick's nieces, but Carl Eugen's marriage to Fredericke of Bayreuth in 1748 soon turned sour and he had a string of mistresses. Recognising that Habsburg support was essential if he were to become an elector, he swiftly distanced Württemberg from Prussia using the latter's good relations with France as a bridge to that power's support.

Though France could not grant an electoral title, the long-standing Franco-Austrian antagonism offered opportunities for the middling German princes to play the two powers against each other in the hope of securing concessions. More immediately, France had sequestrated nine Alsatian lordships attached to the County of Mömpelgard when the latter fell by inheritance to Württemberg in 1723, and a deal offered a way to recover these.[12]

---

10   Fuller coverage in P.H. Wilson, *War, State and Society in Württemberg, 1677-1793* (Cambridge: Cambridge University Press, 1995).

11   Paul Sauer, *Ein kaiserlicher General auf dem württembergischen Herzogsthron. Herzog Carl Alexander von Württemberg 1684-1737* (Filderstadt: Markstein, 2006); Joachim Brüser, *Herzog Karl Alexander von Württemberg und die Landschaft (1733 bis 1737)* (Stuttgart: Kohlhammer, 2010).

12   Wolfgang Scherb, *Die politische Beziehungen der Grafschaft Mömpelgard zu Württemberg von 1723 bis zur Französischen Revolution* (Tübingen: Eigenverlag, 1981).

Finally, unlike Austria which was perennially short of money, France was willing to pay well. For its part, France was eager to secure the middling German princes before these were bought up by Britain which, in the early 1750s, was still promoting Habsburg interests in the Empire.

France paid substantial financial compensation for damage inflicted on neutral Württemberg during the War of Austrian Succession, and then concluded a subsidy agreement with Carl Eugen on 4 February 1752.[13] Most accounts of this arrangement rest on a nineteenth-century misreading of the sources and present the duke as having agreed to hold 6,000 men in readiness, only to be caught out with only half that number when war actually broke out. In fact, Württemberg was obliged to maintain two infantry regiments, each of 1,500 men, in return for an annual subsidy of 130,000 florins (fl.). France released the sequestrated lordships and granted the duke a special exemption allowing him to withhold his troops in the event of a war against the Empire or the Habsburgs in their capacity as emperor. France also secretly agreed to back Carl Eugen's ambitions to become an elector. As part of the new alignment, Ludwig Eugen had already joined the French army in 1749, assuming the colonelcy of a cavalry regiment recruited from Alsatians and other 'Germans'. He subsequently participated in the French conquest of Menorca in 1756 and then served as a volunteer with the Austrians whilst remaining nominal colonel of the French cavalry regiment.

Since the subsidy was paid direct to his private purse, Carl Eugen was able to hide it from the Estates who were given a false set of accounts concealing the true size of the duchy's military expenses. The number of infantry was increased gradually from about 2,200 in 1751 to about 3,600 by late 1756. In addition, there were three cavalry units of squadron strength each, a small artillery corps, plus garrison companies in the duchy's antiquated castles of Hohentwiel, Asperg and Neuffen, making in all around 4,000 men.[14]

Württemberg's Decision for War

The reversal of alliances transformed this situation, as France sided with Austria against the new Anglo-Prussian alliance, thereby triggering the Seven Years War in Europe by August 1756. The situation was far worse than the 1740s. Then, as now, Austro-Prussian conflict threatened civil war in the Empire. The imperial Estates again wished to remain neutral, and Württemberg joined the other Protestants in January 1757 by voting for mediation through the Reichstag (imperial diet), rather than backing Austria's call to declare war on Prussia. Carl Eugen used his authority as commander of the Swabian Kreis forces to block the mobilisation of the region's contingent in December 1756. Nonetheless, the Reichstag

---

13   Hauptstaatsarchiv Stuttgart (HStAS), A202 Bü.218 and 2019. The French copy is accessible at <https://basedoc.diplomatie.gouv.fr/> under the number 17520001. The treaty was backdated to 1 December 1751. The negotiations are covered in more detail in Wilson, *War, State and Society*, pp.203-207.

14   Calculated primarily from data in HStAS A32 Bd.2; Bd.52; Bd.247; L6.22.8.1. The Garde zu Fuss, raised in 1744, was around 600 strong, while the Kreis infantry totalled 901. There were another four single-battalion line regiments, each 526 men in one grenadier and five musketeer companies.

censored Frederick for breaching the Empire's public peace and sanctioned the mobilisation of a Reichsarmee to 'execute' this verdict.

With France allied to Austria, Carl Eugen could no longer pursue the customary strategy of playing these two powers against each other to extract concessions. On the contrary, unlike the 1740s when the weak emperor, Carl Albrecht of Bavaria, had little chance of compelling the imperial Estates to support him, Austria now enjoyed French backing. The duke faced a dilemma. He could bow to Austro-French pressure and discharge his responsibilities to the Empire by supporting the imperial military action against Prussia. This would entail the expense of providing his contingent to the Swabian forces, as well as the 3,000 auxiliaries owed to France through the 1752 treaty.[15] This would commit Württemberg to the war but offer no chance of advancing ducal ambitions. Alternatively, he could offer additional support in the hope that he would be rewarded in the event of victory over Prussia.

Carl Eugen played for high stakes and took the riskier course, believing he could regain his autonomy and find a way through France to closer ties to Austria. His decision was not as foolish at it first might appear. Court expenditure grew, despite the army's urgent need for funds, but the duke was convinced he needed to appear worthy of the influence and lofty titles to which he aspired. After all, Frederick II had spent heavily on remodelling Berlin after 1745 whilst trying to persuade France to accept parity between their royal titles. Frederick would go on to build the huge Neues Palais in Potsdam in 1764 to prove that Prussia had not been bankrupted by the war.[16] Meanwhile, Carl Eugen's expansion of his army well beyond his obligations and treaty commitments was a bid to raise his status from auxiliary to ally, and thereby lay claim to a reward. Here he resembled Elector Georg Ludwig of Hanover who sought an independent command within the Allied coalition during the War of Spanish Succession (1701-1714) to enhance his chances of securing the Protestant succession to the British crowns. Again, Carl Eugen's plan was not wholly unrealistic, considering that Sweden was a full partner in the anti-Prussian alliance, yet never fielded more than 14,000 troops in Pomerania.

The duke's choice was already signalled in October 1756 when he renewed the subsidy treaty with France.[17] That month he also left his wife, indicating a growing emotional distance from Prussia. The next step came on 30 March 1757 when he bowed to French pressure and agreed a supplementary military convention, doubling his commitment to 6,000 infantry in five regiments. This was revised on 16 April when he added another 200 men at his own expense to enable the corps to be restructured as three grenadier battalions, each 400 men, and five regiments of 1,000 each.[18] On 5 May he signed the necessary orders to mobilise the Swabian Kreis troops.[19] That month, Carl Eugen travelled to Vienna to reaf-

15   The paper strength of the Swabian corps was two cavalry regiments, each 592 men, and four infantry regiments, each 1690. Württemberg owed 267 men to Dragoon Regiment Württemberg and 1,461 to the similarly titled infantry regiment.

16   Thomas Biskup, *Friedrichs Größe: Inszenierungen des Preußenkönigs in Fest und Zeremoniell 1740-1815* (Frankfurt: Campus, 2012).

17   Otto Carl Ebbecke, *Frankreichs Politik gegenüber dem deutschen Reich in den Jahren 1748-1756* (Printed PhD, Freiburg i.Br., 1931), pp.119-121.

18   HStAS, A202 Bü.2219. The French copies of the 1757 treaties are accessible at <https://basedoc.diplomatie.gouv.fr/> as number 17570001.

19   HStAS, C14 Bü.87/I.

firm his commitment to the Habsburgs and to negotiate on possible rewards. It was now agreed that the Württemberg corps, along with that of Bavaria also in French pay, would be attached to the Austrian army as part of France's support for the Habsburgs. Later, in October, Vienna gave the duke nominal command of both auxiliary contingents, raising his hopes that he would soon be named commander of the entire Reichsarmee.

Mobilisation and First Setback

Though the infantry were mobilised on 4 January, little was done to augment their peacetime establishment until 31 March, the day after the duke agreed to double his commitment. This left little time to recruit and train the additional 4,000 men needed to bring both the auxiliaries and the Kreis infantry to the required strength.[20] The French accepted that only half of the auxiliaries would be 'old ducal troops' which would provide the cadre for the new companies that would be added to the existing units. The Garde zu Fuss and four line regiments were each expanded to two battalions of one grenadier and five musketeer companies apiece, each company of 100 men. Two additional grenadier companies were added to the Garde zu Fuss Regt (also known as Werneck after its commander) to create the Grenadier Battalion Nr.1. The grenadiers of the Spitznas and Prinz Louis Regiments combined as Grenadier Battalion Nr.2, while those of Truchsess (formerly the Fusiliers) and Roeder formed Nr.3. The Kreis Regiment already had the required number of companies and simply needed to bring these to field strength. The Kreis Dragoons likewise had the requisite companies but need to double the manpower.

Württemberg sent recruiting parties to Ansbach, Speyer and neighbouring Austrian territory, but it was obvious that the bulk of the missing manpower would have to be raised locally.[21] Like most other German principalities, Württemberg relied on voluntary enlistment supplemented by limited conscription. It was accepted that the ducal household troops (*Haustruppen*) should only be volunteers, but that conscripts could be used to fill out the Kreis units since these were required to fulfil the duchy's obligations to the Empire. Military service was unattractive. The total value of an infantry private's pay, food, uniform and accommodation amounted to 60 fl annually, placing a soldier on par with a domestic servant. Knowing it was difficult to attract recruits, officers regularly detained men beyond their enlistment contracts, or demanded fees in return for a discharge. Nonetheless, the Estates only claimed that 110 men had been held against their will between the mid-1740s and the end of 1754, suggesting that the situation was not as bad as later historians believed.[22]

Recruiting difficulties had already forced the army to take a few conscripts each year to maintain peacetime strength. Conscription was organised in each of the duchy's 60 or so districts by officers and the local civil authorities using registers of all the unmarried men aged 18 to 30 who were required to draw lots to fill the quota. This process was known as 'selection' (*Auswahl*) and had been used to mobilise the militia which was no longer summoned. Prosperous householders connived with officials to ensure that troublemakers

---

20   HStAS, L5 Tom.165 fol.51b-4; L6.22.8.1.
21   Renz to Carl Eugen, 26 March 1757, A74 Bü.140.
22   List of men detained beyond their service agreements in HStAS, L5 Tom.162 fol.508-26b.

or the destitute were selected. Substitution was allowed, enabling the rich to dodge the draft if they could find and pay a replacement. The problems stemmed less from the system, and more that the doubling of the duchy's commitments necessitated sudden, heavy demands. A levy for 1,000 men was decreed on 3 May, followed by two more on 6 July and 26 October totalling another 1,700, whereas peacetime conscription seems to have averaged no more than 100 men per year.[23] The older literature stresses arbitrary measures, such as surrounding churches to seize the entire congregation.[24] In fact, the army endeavoured to ensure fair selection according to the rules, but the existing flaws in the system, combined with loud protests from the Estates, undermined the legitimacy of conscription and stirred popular hostility. Additional delays stemmed from France's failure to pay on time, forcing the Württembergers to buy everything on expensive credit.[25]

In fact, the required numbers were assembled in time for the auxiliaries to begin training in the main garrisons of Stuttgart, Ludwigsburg and Asperg in May. The army was not wholly unprepared. The bulk of the troops had camped together for field exercises in 1746 and 1747 during the armed neutrality maintained in the War of Austrian Succession.[26] The ammunition allowance for annual practice firing had been increased from 96 rounds per man to over 200 by 1752, comparing very favourably with other armies: the Austrians allowed only 10 rounds per man in peacetime in 1809.[27] The entire army had trained at an exercise camp at Osweil outside Ludwigsburg between 1 June and 20 July 1756, while the Swabian Kreis corps had camped together for three months that summer.[28]

In mid-June 1757, 4,000 infantry were concentrated in Stuttgart to complete their training, while the Kreis infantry, now 1,295 strong, were with the rest of the regional forces, totalling 5,836 effectives, at Cannstatt just to the south-east. The remaining 2,000 infantry were in Ludwigsburg, and there were another 410 troops guarding the palaces and castles.[29] Many of the junior officers were inexperienced and resorted to rough methods to maintain authority over their men.[30] Nonetheless, all seemed set and the imperial city of Ulm was notified on 20 June that the corps would shortly cross its territory to Günzberg to embark on barges for its journey down the Danube to Linz and thence on foot to the front in Silesia.[31]

The following morning, Commissioner Potier reviewed the 4,000 infantry in Stuttgart and formally mustered them into French service. Discharged from further duty that day, many men began drinking in the taverns. Drunk, one party entered the Rothebühl Gate

---

23   HStAS, A202 Bü.2007.
24   Karl Pfaff, *Geschichte des Militärwesens in Württemberg von der ältesten bis auf unserere Zeit* (Stuttgart: Schweizerbart, 1842), pp.65-66.
25   Baron Grechtler's report 4 June 1757, Haus-, Hof- und Staatsrachiv Vienna (HHStA), Kriegsakten (KA) 366 (neu). Johann Georg von Grechtler (1705-80) was entrusted by the Habsburg government with making all the arrangements to move the Württembergers to Silesia and the operation cemented his position as one of Austria's foremost entrepreneurs.
26   HStAS, A202 Bü.2280; C14 Bü.638, 639.
27   Allowance calculated from the expenditure on gunpowder in A32 Bd.1-2, and other detail in A202 Bü.2256, 2262, 2278.
28   HStAS, L6.22.8.1 15 July 1756.
29   Strengths from the report 23 June 1757 in C14 Bü.87/I.
30   Albert Pfister, 'Militärwesen', in *Herzog Karl Eugen*, Vol.I, pp.119-143 at p.126.
31   Carl Reichard, *Geschichte der Kriege und Bürgerbewaffnung Ulms von der ältesten bis auf die jetzigen Zeiten* (Ulm: J.D. Wagner, 1832), p.156.

Barracks where the Werneck Regiment was billeted. Around 200 became disorderly, refused orders and began firing their muskets. The protest spread rapidly as men smashed windows and furniture, while others stormed the guard house in front of the ducal palace in the city centre. Large groups then marched behind their regimental bands through the streets.[32] Eventually, the two grenadier companies of the Kreis infantry arrived to quell the disturbance. By the following morning, 2,000 men had deserted and only 1,000 remained under orders, of whom 600 were considered so unreliable they were granted leave.

Later historians interpreted this in religious and anachronistically nationalist terms as a reluctance on the part of the Lutheran Württembergers to fight Prussia as the Protestant German champion and cited these alleged sentiments to explain the army's subsequent poor performance. Certainly, Prussian propaganda presented the war as a religious conflict, and some local clergy preached inflammatory sermons. However, the much-feared religious tension failed to materialise in the Reichsarmee which contained a mixture of Protestant and Catholic units. Rather than religion, the primary cause was the mistaken belief amongst the men that they had been sold permanently into French service. Many publicans had given the soldiers free drinks, saying that they would never return home. A subsequent mutiny in one of the Swabian regiments was prompted by the rumour it was about to be incorporated into the Austrian army. Far from being focused on the duke, the soldiers attacked other symbols of authority, including threatening to burn the Estates' assembly hall. The mutineers also compelled some men to join them, while many soldiers hid in civilian homes to avoid becoming involved.

The authorities were initially reluctant to punish the mutineers. Carl Eugen was furious with Werneck, the senior general, who immediately issued a general pardon provided the men returned to their units.[33] Forced to abandon his negotiations in Vienna, the duke hurried home and removed Werneck, replacing him with General Spitznas on 10 July.[34] Nonetheless, Carl Eugen issued a second pardon on 14 July. The lenient policy worked, as only 356 men failed to return by 9 August when the auxiliary corps totalled 6,211.[35] Potier praised the duke's efforts in reassembling the force at short notice:

> All the troops are fine. The 1,200 grenadiers are magnificent...The clothing and equipment are new and in good condition, especially the small clothes, three times

---

32   Fuller coverage of this and the following in P.H. Wilson, 'Violence and the rejection of authority in 18th-century Germany: the case of the Swabian mutinies in 1757', *German History*, 12 (1994), pp.1-26. See also Grechtler's reports 21 and 22 June 1757, HHStA KA 366 (neu).

33   A30c Bü.1 22 June 1757. Franz von Werneck (1705-1780), a Catholic from Westphalia serving Württemberg since 1720 and rising rapidly during Carl Eugen's reign. Werneck's partial fall from grace was accelerated by a group of officers who had insisted that his refusal to shoot the rioters at the start of the mutiny had made matters worse: Immanuel M.P. Hoch, 'Württembergische Denkwürdigkeiten aus den Herzoge Carl Alexander und Carl Eugen, nach Aufzeichnungen von General Wolff und dessen Sohn', *Sophronizon*, 6 (1824), pp.16-62 at 37.

34   Hans Adolf Spitznas (1699-1758) from Thuringia who served Hessen-Kassel for over five years, before joining the Württemberg army as a lieutenant in 1728. He was actively involved in the negotiations with Prussia in 1741 and was related by marriage to Ludwig Carl von Pöllnitz, the duke's favourite adjutant.

35   HStAS, A202 Bü.2289; E31 Bü.1324. Strength from HStAS, G230 Bü.48.

as much as what a French soldier usually receives and attention is being given that they keep them as clean as possible. The officer corps is composed of the best young men who show the greatest ardour for their master's service and will surely prove this when the occasion arises.[36]

This total was only achieved by drafting over 530 men from the Kreis infantry, as well as the second levy of conscripts on 6 July. Württemberg retained its contingent when the Swabians marched to join the Reichsarmee under the Prince of Sachsen-Hildburghausen in late July.[37] Despite their presence as escort, a second, smaller mutiny occurred at Süssen as the auxiliary corps left Württemberg on 14 August under Carl Eugen's personal command. They then embarked on barges at Günzberg, making desertion much harder, but mutinied a third time when they arrived at Linz on 6 September. In all, 272 men had absconded by the time the corps reached Bohemia on 9 October.[38] This time, harsher penalties were employed: 27 men were shot and around 40 made to run the gauntlet.[39]

The incident prompted the authorities to issue revised articles of war early in 1758 which extended the punishments normally reserved for men illegally entering foreign service to apply to deserters as well. Henceforth, the government would confiscate a soldier's property, including impounding any inheritance he might be owed later. In addition, rewards were offered to civilians who turned in deserters. These measures proved effective. Though the corps arrived in Bohemian demoralised and in poor condition, there is no evidence for claims of a further mutiny in 1758.[40]

The mutiny was a huge embarrassment for Carl Eugen and a major setback to his political ambitions. The corps' departure had been seriously delayed, while the duchy had retained its Kreis contingent. Initially, the Austrians showed some understanding, accepting Carl Eugen's argument that he needed the Kreis troops to keep order. Though the duchy eventually sent around half the infantry it owed, the dragoons were retained and thus missed the debacle at Roßbach on 5 November when the understrength Württemberg Dragoon Regiment, containing only troops from the minor Swabian territories, was routed in the initial stages of the battle.[41] Short of money, Carl Eugen prioritised his auxiliaries over fulfilment of his obligations to the Empire, since the former directly supported his political ambitions. The duchy's Kreis dragoons remained at home throughout the war as a kind of gendarmerie. That it was clear that there was no intention of sending the unit to the front is obvious from the fact that the numerous Württembergers who deserted from the Prussian army after 1757 were used to keep it up to strength. This left only the two weak squadrons composed of other Swabians serving with the Kreis corps. They were eventually combined

---

36   Potier's first report, aug.1757 G230 Bü.48. The corps also had 900 horses for the company wagons: A32 Bd.11 fol.79b.
37   The other Swabian units suffered two mutinies on their way to the front: Wilson, 'Violence', p.6.
38   HStAS,A202 Bü.2289 15 September and 9 October1757.
39   See Wilson, 'Violence', p.23.
40   Alleged by Wilhelm Kohlhaas, 'Die Meuterei der Württemberger anno 1757', *Beiträge zur Landeskunde*, 5 (1971), pp.11-16. There were no further outbreaks until the Werneck Regiment mutinied in 1765.
41   HStAS, C14 Bü.87/II.

with Saxony's small Kreis contingent to provide a full regiment.[42] The official strength of the infantry regiment was unilaterally reduced in 1759 to 1,060, including 120 men from four smaller Swabian territories.[43] Carl Eugen employed various legal arguments to claim partial exemption from his imperial obligations, but his failure to send his full contingent continually angered the Austrians whom he was trying to please.

The Battle of Leuthen

The auxiliaries finally joined the Austrian army at Striegau in Silesia on 16 October when they totalled 5,737, having lost a further 227.[44] Contrary to Potier's earlier glowing comments, the Württembergers were short of clothing and, despite the winter weather, still wore their white summer gaiters.[45] Though the Württemberg artillery enjoyed a good reputation, the troops had marched without battalion guns, since these were not included in the agreements made with France. The Württembergers were attached to General Nádasdy's forces which successfully besieged the Prussian fortress of Schweidnitz from 26 October. One Württemberg grenadier company was among the nine spearheading the final assault on 11 November.[46]

The main Austrian army under Prince Charles of Lorraine joined Nádasdy to give over 80,000 men. Together, they encircled Breslau, trapping the 30,000 Prussians under the Duke of Brunswick-Bevern who had been left by Frederick to hold Silesia while he confronted the Reichsarmee and French at Roßbach. Bevern had entrenched outside Breslau. The Württembergers, along with the Bavarians and some Austrian troops assaulted the villages of Kreutern and Kleinberg which both caught fire in the fighting on 22 November. Württemberg losses were minor at three killed, 46 wounded and 38 missing.[47] Bevern retreated into the city but was captured whilst on reconnaissance two days later. The garrison surrendered, but most of the Prussians escaped across the Oder.

Thinking the campaign over, Carl Eugen already handed over to Spitznas on 18 November and went home taking the best three grenadier companies with him. These reached Stuttgart on 26 December where they were combined with two musketeer companies composed of the tallest conscripts from the third levy of 27 October, as well as tall Prussian deserters. The new unit took the title Garde zu Fuss, with the former parent unit now styled the Werneck Regiment. The new guards were expanded to two battalions in August 1758 and retained this establishment with fresh drafts when part of it was used to form a new Leibgrenadier Regiment in October 1759. Spitznas complained that the departure of the grenadiers

---

42   HStAS, C14 Bü.87/II 17 June 1759.
43   HStAS, C14 Bü.87a strength returns. The duchy at least generally maintained its infantry to this reduced establishment for the rest of the war.
44   HStAS, G230 Bü.48. Losses since 10 August totalled 474, of whom about 300 deserted or were executed, with the rest failing sick.
45   Albert von Pfister, *Denkwürdigkeiten aus der württembergischen Kriegsgeschichte* (Stuttgart: Carl Grüninger, 1868), p.183.
46   Adolf von Schempp, *Geschichte des 3. Württembergischen Infanterie-Regiments Nr.121* (Stuttgart: Kohlhammer, 1891), pp.111-113.
47   Ibid, pp.114-18.

demoralised the others who had to remain at the front.[48] However, Carl Eugen remained obsessed with his guards and repeated the measure at the end of the 1758 campaign when he again ordered the tallest men to be sent home while the others were still shivering in their billets.[49] Campaign attrition and the grenadiers' departure reduced the auxiliary corps to 1,083 grenadiers and 3,994 musketeers by 1 December 1757.[50]

The campaign was far from over, since Frederick's rapid approach from Saxony forced the Austrians to shift to a new position centred on the village of Leuthen on 4 December. Along with the Bavarians, the Württembergers were assigned to cover the extreme left of the Austrian army. The redeployment was poorly prepared and conducted in wet, foggy weather. The units arrived in confusion, deploying in an irregular line behind a stream around 11:00 p.m. They had been obliged to leave their knapsacks and baggage wagons behind and were forced to sleep in the open without straw or firewood.

As the new day dawned, Prince Charles was deceived by a Prussian feint into believing Frederick would attack his right flank.[51] Lieutenant Nicolai, adjutant to General Romann commanding one of the two Württemberg brigades, spotted this mistake early on.[52] Having attended the Prussian manoeuvres in the area in 1754, Nicolai knew that the Prussians could swing southwards and pass along the Austrian front screened by a hill in order to surprise the left. He warned Romann who informed Nádasdy who in turn requested heavy artillery and reinforcements from Prince Charles. The Austrian commander remained stubbornly convinced the attack would fall on his right, before misinterpreting the Prussians' departure from view as a retreat.

The Prussian advance guard rounded the hill about 1:30 p.m., routing the Austrian light troops on the extreme left who then fled through the Württembergers, partially disordering them. Nicolai subsequently criticised the position assigned to the corps, claiming that later maps of the battle showed marshy ground between the villages of Sagschütz and Schwriegwitz which was not in fact there, further exposing the troops' flank. The Austrian battalion guns attached to the Württembergers were short of ammunition and had to fire slowly.[53] They were soon outgunned by the Prussian heavy batteries that quickly deployed to support the rapidly advancing infantry. The three leading Prussian battalions halted at the stream where they were met by artillery fire and salvos from the three Württemberg battalions on the eastern side. The Prussians then crossed, fired a volley and advanced

48   Spitznas' reports 20 November 1757 and 9 January1758, HStAS, G230 Bü.47.

49   Roeder's report 13 December1758, HStAS, G230 Bü.49.

50   Strength return enclosed with Spitznas' report 7 December, HStAS, G230 Bü47. Of these, 500 were sick (report 4 December).

51   Christopher Duffy, *The Military Life of Frederick the Great* (London: Routledge, 1986), pp.147-154; Greater General Staff, *Der Siebenjährige Krieg 1756-1763* (Berlin: E.S. Mittler und Sohn, 1901-13), Vol.VI , pp.18-42.

52   Nicolai kept extensive campaign diaries, now in the Landesbibliothek Stuttgart, cod.milit.qt.29. See fols.75-89 for Leuthen. These form the main source for the accounts of the Württemberg campaigns published by Pfister, Schempp, and Stadlinger. For his career, see Daniel Hohrath and Rudolf Henning, *Die Bildung des Offiziers in der Aufklärung. Ferdinand Friedrich von Nicolai (1713-1814)* (Stuttgart: Württembergisches Landesbibliothek, 1990). Philipp Joachim von Romann (1702-1758) was a Calvinist from Pomerania who entered Württemberg service as a page in 1716.

53   Pfister, *Denkwürdigkeiten*, p.185.

with levelled bayonets, reaching the gun line before the Württembergers could fire another volley. Already disconcerted by the fear that Prussian cavalry were outflanking them to the left (south), the Württembergers wavered and then broke. The Prussians surged forward, shattering the Austrians and Bavarians in the second line. Prussian hussars then pursued the fugitives, while Frederick's main body turned northwards, rolling up the Austrian line and completing the victory.

Spitznas subsequently praised the officers and grenadiers, blaming the rout on the common soldiers whose 'conduct was to some extent that of the earlier Stuttgart story' (that is to say, the mutiny).[54] Spitznas ordered Becht, the senior commissariat officer, to save the pay wagon.[55] Becht ignored the order to go to Breslau, recognising that would likely fall to the Prussians, and instead joined Colonel Gablentz with the rest of the baggage.[56] Gablentz often had to draw his pistol as they forced their way through the fugitives, before they finally re-joined the corps three days later, much to the soldiers' delight.[57] However, the Austrian army lost 3,000 wagons, including the Württembergers' baggage with all the spare clothes and field equipment, as well as their knapsacks which had been left behind. Fear of the pursuing Prussians gave the fugitives no rest for three nights. They then marched for four days through rain and snow so deep they could hardly move. There was no bread for five days and no hot food during the entire retreat. The corps was always in the rear following the Bavarians who ate up everything. There were no stragglers until the fifth day, but desperation drove the men to ignore orders not to forage and they survived by digging up root vegetables and extorting civilians.[58]

The confusion was so great that there was still no clear idea in January of the losses, which were estimated at 1,200 to 1,400 men.[59] Nonetheless, a rollcall was held on 19 December which, when collated, revealed a total loss since the beginning of the month of 2,231 men, of whom 134 had been killed, 160 wounded and at least 124 captured.[60] The bulk of those missing had been captured by the Prussians who forced them to join their army. The Württemberg government considered these men deserters until 1773 when it finally conceded they had been pressed against their will and restored their property confiscated in the meantime.[61] By 27 March, 17 prisoners had escaped to re-join the corps, along with five missing and five deserters who had been recaptured. The escapees included Emanuel Schneider (1732-1806) from Bern who had joined

54   Spitznas' reports 6-8 December1757, HStAS, G230 Bü.47.
55   Philipp Ludwig Becht (1716-1786) was closely connected to the Worthies but served the duke loyally as an important military administrator.
56   Christoph Friedrich von Gablentz (1710-1794), a Saxon nobleman and brother of a Prussian general, had served Württemberg since about 1735.
57   Becht's report 20 December1757 in HStAS, G230 Bü.48, and his subsequent defence against alleged insubordination HStAS, A8 Bü.58 8 Sept.1762.
58   Reports from various officers 25 February1758, HStAS, G230 Bü.58.
59   Spitznas' report 1 January 1758, HStAS, G230 Bü.47.
60   Spitznas' report 4 January 1758, HStAS, G230 Bü.47, and Potier's report in HStAS, Bü.48. The corps numbered 2,846, including 508 grenadiers. Of this total, 450 were sick, while another 280 men were in Württemberg as a recruiting party.
61   HStAS, A202 Bü.2238, 22 March 1773.

Württemberg service as a doctor in 1755 and was captured by Prussian hussars who stole his wallet.[62]

The Austrian command redirected the Württembergers away from Prague on 24 December, sending them instead northwest to Saaz to join a force guarding the Bohemian frontier with Prussian-occupied Saxony. Another 400 men had fallen sick by the time the corps reached Saaz on 6 January, with 100 men seriously frostbitten. They had no tent poles or cooking utensils and few axes for the first nine days after their arrival.[63] Spitznas criticised the Austrian dispositions as too dispersed and vulnerable. He immediately quarantined the sick in the Saaz barracks, giving them beds, straw and full pay. They were fed 'good meat broth', rice, pearl barley, damson plums, noodles, some pork and beef from underfed animals.[64] The number of sick had risen to 600 by 17 January, forcing each regiment to establish additional hospitals in civilian homes. The senior medical officer already died on 15 January, while 12 company doctors had been captured and another seriously wounded at Leuthen and much of the medical supplies had been lost in the rout. The symptoms were described as a 'dry and fiery heat, deliria, almost insatiable thirst, weak hearing and sight, and great lethargy. Many had strong diarrhoea and swollen feet.'[65] Some had spots and a white and red rash. Doctors blamed the great exertions of the campaign, especially being forced to camp in the open during the retreat. The Saaz area was marshy and even the locals often fell sick each year. There was also no firewood, forcing the men to burn straw and often to eat cold food. One officer blamed the unfamiliar Bohemian diet of 'peas and other unthinkable ingredients'.[66]

The doctors diagnosed 'Hungarian fever' (probably typhus) and dysentery, but beyond the imperfect warm food, had little to offer beyond bloodletting and purges. The sick were dying at a rate of up to 10 a day by the end of January, and were buried in batches every three days. Grenadiers received coffins, but the musketeers were simply covered with a plank. Officers were interred close to the church with full military honours. By 24 February, only 1,040 men remained fit, while 1,436 were sick and a further 584 had already returned home, including more grenadiers recalled by the duke.[67] Those treating the sick themselves fell ill after just two days and there were no longer enough men to mount guard. Ensign Johann Caspar Schiller (1723-1796), father of the famous playwright, had some medical training and was drafted to assist as doctor and chaplain.[68]

---

62 Marc Höchner, 'Selbstzuegnisse von Schweizer Soldaten im Siebjährigen Krieg', in Rudolf Jaun et al (eds), *Schweizer Solddienst* (Birmensdorf: Schweizerische Vereinigung für Militärgeschichte und Militärwissenschaft, 2010), pp.61-103 at pp.64, 69.

63 Rieger's report 24 February1758, G230 Bü.48.

64 Rieger's report 24 February1758, G230 Bü.48. Major Bilfinger was more critical of the diet, citing no salt, bad beer and wine, heavy barley bread and lack of vegetables beyond peas and a few carrots and horseradish. HStAS, A8 Bü.58, 25 Feb.1758.

65 Rieger's report 24 February1758, G230 Bü.48.

66 Lieutenant Dertinger's report 28 Feb.1758, HStAS, A8 Bü.58. Medical information from the doctors' reports in that file.

67 Rieger's report 24 February1758, G230 Bü.48.

68 Richard Weltrich, *Friedrich Schiller* (Stuttgart: Cotter, 1899), p.5.

In response to Spitznas' pleas, Carl Eugen sent Major Rieger, the de facto head of the military administration, to assist.[69] Rieger, always keen to advance his career, conducted a thorough investigation, but put a generally positive spin on the situation which was probably improving around the time he arrived. A series of minor, practical measures were implemented to improve pay, uniforms and field equipment subsequently. Spitznas himself succumbed, dying on 22 March, the day after he received permission to hand over to General Romann and return home. He was buried with full honours, but the lack of artillery attached to the corps prevented the customary gun salute.[70] The corps finally left Saaz on 2 April, totalling 2,024 men of whom now only 400 were sick. A further 104 sick were left behind in the care of seven officers and doctors. Of the transportable sick, 94 died on the way home, while another nine men deserted.[71]

Internal Politics and Military Expansion

Leuthen and the subsequent decimation of the auxiliary corps inflicted lasting damage on Carl Eugen's ambitions and Württemberg's military reputation. Austria refused to let Carl Eugen publish his own version of events which would have inevitably revealed their own culpability in the defeat, and instead blamed the Württembergers and Bavarians for the disaster. Despite French backing, his bid to replace Sachsen-Hildburghausen as the new commander of the Reichsarmee failed early in 1758. However, the Austrians had no desire to see Württemberg retire into neutrality which might encourage other minor territories to follow suit. They continued to dangle the prospect of a new electoral title, whilst refusing to put this promise in writing.[72]

To ensure Württemberg's cooperation, Austria persuaded Carl Eugen to promote Count Friedrich Samuel von Montmartin (1712-1778) as head of a new State and Cabinet Ministry, thereby marginalising the Worthy-dominated Privy Council on 11 February 1758.[73] Montmartin had been a close confidant of the duke since 1744 and now intervened to save Werneck who retained nominal command of his infantry regiment and was promoted lieutenant general. Both men corresponded secretly with the Austrian government which even nominated Werneck as leader of a possible military coup considered in 1761 when the

---

69   Spitznas wrote 'there are no words to express my despair' 21 Feb.1758, HStAS, G230 Bü.47. Philipp Friedrich Rieger (1722-1782) came from the Worthy elite, but pursued a military career, serving Prussia in the Second Silesian War, before briefly acting as Ludwig Eugen's adjutant during the Menorca campaign earlier in 1757. As captain, he supervised the despatch of the auxiliary corps summer 1757, and then oversaw the raising of the new Garde zu Fuss. Eugen Schneider, 'Zur Charakteristik des Oberst Riegers', Literärische Beilage zum Staatsanzeige für Württemberg, (1888), pp.293-6.

70   Romann's report 23 March 1758, HStAS, G230 Bü.47.

71   Romann's reports nos.5-12 in G230 Bü.47.

72   Artur Brabant, Das Heilige Römische Reich teutscher Nation im Kampf mit Friedrich dem Großen (Berlin, 1904-31), Vol.I, pp.41-42.

73   Gabrielle Haug-Moritz, 'Friedrich Samuel Graf Montmartin als Württembergischer Staatsmann (1758-1766/73)', Zeitschrift für Württembergische Landesgeschichte, 53 (1994), pp.295-296; Hoch, 'Denkwürdigkeiten', pp.16-62.

duke fell ill. Meanwhile, to safeguard its interests, France sent Baron Franz Ludwig von Wimpffen (1732-1800) who had served with his five brothers in the French army, before arriving in Stuttgart as envoy in 1759 and joining the ducal army as colonel the following year.[74] Wimpffen's sister Josephine was briefly the duke's mistress after 1760.

All three men had divided loyalties. As outsiders, they knew their usefulness to their foreign sponsors would end with the war and that they would become scapegoats if the duke failed to achieve his ambitions. While Werneck enjoyed good connections with sections of the officer corps, the others had few local allies. Montmartin soon became locked in a personal feud with the irascible Rieger who, whilst energetically supporting Carl Eugen's plans, was careful to maintain close ties through his relations to the Estates. Montmartin allegedly forged letters purporting to show Rieger had been corresponding with the Prussians in 1762, prompting the duke to imprison him for four years.[75]

Ducal policy reached the point of no return in June 1758 as the decision to expand the army pushed war costs well beyond payments from France and existing taxes. Following the Estates' refusal to raise taxes, the ducal government resorted to a series of measures, the most spectacular of which occurred on 31 January 1759 when the Stuttgart garrison surrounded the assembly hall and seized the Estates' treasury. The Estates' legal advisor, the prominent lawyer Johann Jacob Moser, was accused of slandering Montmartin and thrown into jail in July 1759, prompting protests from other German courts.[76] However, the emperor issued a series of injunctions preventing the Estates from lodging a case in the imperial supreme court and temporarily sanctioning the increased taxes as necessary emergency measures.[77]

Determined to upgrade his status from auxiliary to ally, Carl Eugen meanwhile raised the units required if his forces were to operate independently. Whereas he had argued in 1757 he did not need expensive artillery, because this could be supplied by the Austrians, he now ordered Württemberg's field artillery corps expanded from 15 to 253 men.[78] Three heavy cavalry regiments were raised from scratch between May and October 1758, while the hussar company was expanded to three squadrons. The intention was that all four units should comprise four squadrons each, but only the Cuirassier and Dragoon regiments managed this in 1758, while the Horse Grenadiers reached only 150 and the Hussars 303 men respectively. The three provisional grenadier battalions from the 1757 campaign now became permanent units, reducing the infantry regiments each to two battalions of five musketeer companies. The auxiliary corps was swiftly rebuilt, totalling 2,194 veterans and 3,723 recruits by 22 June.[79] Details of this and subsequent increases were posted to Austrian

---

74 HStAS, A30a Bd.7 fol.384.

75 Hoch, 'Denkwürdigkeiten', pp.31-51. Another factor was Rieger's close ties to Ludwig Eugen whom Carl Eugen suspected of conspiring to replace him as duke.

76 HStAS, A8 Bü.389, 390; P.H. Wilson, 'Johann Jakob Moser und die Württembergische Politik', in Andreas Gestrich and Rainer Lächle (eds), *Johann Jakob Moser* (Karlsruhe: G. Braun, 2002), pp.1-25.

77 See Wilson, *War, State and Society*, pp.212-222.

78 Carl Eugen to Renz 12 April 1757, HStAS, A74 Bü.140. The 1758 military plan is in A8 Bü.51. See also Leo Ignaz von Stadlinger, *Geschichte des Württembergischen Kriegswesens* (Stuttgart: Hofbuchdruckerie, 1856), pp.427-428.

79 Potier's report 22 June 1758, G230 Bü.48. In addition, there were 121 senior regimental officers.

ministers, while foreign envoys were invited to review the troops and carefully-managed press releases depicted operations in a positive light.

The 1758 Campaign

As in 1757, the delay in assembling his forces frustrated Carl Eugen's hopes for an independent command operating between the French and Austrian armies. With still a year to run on his contract with France, Austria decided to release the Württembergers to join the French army facing the British and their German auxiliaries in Hessen. The main Anglo-German army under Ferdinand of Brunswick had crossed the Rhine on 1 June to attack the main French army under Clermont, leaving a small force under Prince Isenburg-Birnstein to hold Hessen-Kassel. The French command seized its opportunity and ordered its second army under the Prince de Soubise to resume its advance northwards from Frankfurt into Hessen. Soubise's advance guard under Broglie clashed with Isenburg at Sandershausen on 23 July and then occupied Kassel itself, spreading panic amongst the Allies that Soubise would push northwards into Hanover.[80]

Having mustered at Kornwestheim, north of Stuttgart, Carl Eugen and General Roeder led the Württemberg auxiliaries on 10 July to join what appeared to be a successful French campaign. The corps was accompanied by 50 cuirassiers, 40 hussars, 300 dragoons and four companies of the Garde zu Fuss, all of whom returned to the duchy when the corps reached Aschaffenburg.[81] Crossing the Main at Aschaffenburg, the corps pushed on to Marburg where it arrived on 3 August, totalling 5,994 effectives. In contrast with the previous year, desertion remained low, though 398 men were recorded as sick.[82] Nonetheless, morale was poor, and the men were kept together by harsh discipline. It can hardly have helped matters that the soldiers could see their duke travelling in style with a suite of 150 courtiers and 260 horses. The French had already eaten out the area and failed to provide sufficient supplies, forcing the Württembergers to scavenge.[83]

---

80 Von Geyso, 'Das Korps des Prinzen Johann Kasimir zu Ysenburg-Birstein unter besonderer Berücksichtigung des Gefechts bei Sandershausen am 23. Juli 1758', *Zeitschrift für hessische Geschichte und Landeskunde*, 45 (1911), pp.218-275, and more generally for the campaign: Johannes Pohler, *Kriegerische Ereignisse in der Umgebung von Cassel* (Kassel: L. Döll, 1895-7).

81 A8 Bü.251. August Gottlob Reinhard Baron Roeder (1706-1769) from Saxony, joined the Württemberg army in 1728, commanded an infantry regiment in the 1757 campaign when he was nominal second under Spitznas, but returned home after Leuthen.

82 HStAS, G230 Bü.48, contrary to reports of heavy desertion in Schempp, *Geschichte*, p.127. Rieger organised two drafts of replacement recruits in August and September totalling at least 251 men, while another 250 were sent in December. The corps lost 110 deserters between 17 August and 1 September, but thereafter the rate appears to have declined: A202 Bü.2248, 2279; G230 Bü.49. Claims that Potier and Rieger falsified muster returns, and the corps numbered only 4,000 are not corroborated by archival evidence and belong to the smear campaign to tarnish Rieger's reputation: Hoch, 'Denkwürdigkeiten', p.38. At about 6,000 effectives, the corps was at its official strength, but much smaller than the size listed in most secondary accounts of this campaign.

83 Robert Geiges, 'Mit Herzog Karl Eugen im Siebenjährigen Krieg nach dem Tagebuchaufzeichnungen des Leibmedicus Dr. Albrecht Reichart Reuß', *Besondere Beilage zum Staatsanzeiger für Württemberg*, (1928), pp.185-196, at pp.189-190.

They arrived in the French camp outside Kassel on 8 August to a polite welcome. The French had been there since 25 July and would stay inactive until early September when, after much prodding form Versailles, Soubise finally crossed into Hanoverian territory. He soon scuttled back to Kassel when Isenburg threatened his line of communications by sending General Oberg southwards to Sandershausen. Thinking the campaign over, Carl Eugen returned to Württemberg, again missing the action as in 1757. Having pinned Ferdinand, the main French army, now under the more energetic Contades, sent General Chevert with 15,000 to reinforce Soubise's 25,000.[84] With Oberg at best mustering 18,000, Soubise had no excuse and finally moved to attack.[85]

Outnumbered and discouraged by the cold, Oberg retired to a strong position on the Lutterberg heights, hoping to delay the French and then slip away in the night. Soubise sent Broglie forward early on 10 October to pin Oberg while Chevert made his way through wooded terrain to take the enemy in their left flank. The Werneck and Truchsess regiments were left with some French units to hold Kassel, but the rest of the Württembergers formed the first (righthand) column of Soubise's main force. They joined Broglie around 10:00 a.m., deploying in two lines with his troops drawn up along the marshy valley floor facing the heights. While they waited for Chevert to appear, the Württembergers were hit by some stray artillery rounds aimed at the French gendarmerie cavalry posted to their front. Chevert finally arrived around 3:00 p.m. and his Saxon infantry were particularly distinguished in a fierce fight by the woods before Oberg retreated in some disorder. Soubise ordered a general advance, either too late, or was prevented by the difficult terrain from catching the enemy to complete their destruction. The allies lost 1,200, twice that of the French, and for once Roeder was able to report a victory to Carl Eugen, even though his men had scarcely been engaged and he gave appropriate praise to the Saxons.[86]

The French soon broke off their pursuit and by 16 October the Württembergers were in winter quarters in villages around Kassel. A combined Franco-Württemberg detachment at Witzenhausen was driven in by the enemy on 14 November, but otherwise the main losses were due to the cold and desertion.[87] Soubise sent the corps south to billets around Aschaffenburg on 19 November, packing five men into each house, while the promised meat and rice failed to arrive. Only when the subsidy treaty formally expired on 15 December did he release the troops who had arrived home by the end of the month.

---

84   The Württemberg corps thus represented a quarter of Soubise's army. Chevert's force included the 9,000 Saxon and 2,400 Palatine infantry in French pay. An ensign in Ludwig Eugen's French cavalry regiment in Soubise's army left a good eyewitness account: Anton Joseph Frhr. Zorn von Bulach, *Der Fähnrich Zorn von Bulach vom Regimente Württemberg zu Pferd im siebenjährigen Kriege 1757-1758 nach seinem Tagebuche* (Strasbourg: Schlesier et Schweikhardt, 1908), in particular pp.48-51.

85   For the following, see *Bataille de Lutterbourg…le 10 Octobre 1758* (copy in HStAS, G230 Bü.49 which also contains Roeder's reports).

86   HStAS, G230 Bü.49 14 October1758. Soubise gave 10 of the 22 captured cannon to the Saxons as a reward.

87   Effectives had fallen to 4,262 including 405 sick by 14 November: HStAS, G230 Bü.49.

Another Disaster: Fulda 1759

Carl Eugen's hopes of profiting from Austro-French tensions were dashed when these powers renewed their alliance in December 1758. Austria ignored the duke's offer to campaign without payment if his political demands were met. France meanwhile refused to renew the arrangements from 1757 as it scaled back its expenses, forcing him to accept a less advantageous agreement on 9 February 1759.[88] All maintenance payments stopped, and instead Württemberg was to hold 2,000 men in readiness in return for an annual subsidy of 150,000fl across the next three years. The situation shifted dramatically with the French defeat at Minden on 1 August, as the retreat of their main army opened a gap between it and the Reichsarmee in Saxony. Meanwhile, the Saxon corps had suffered heavy desertion and the French command believed the Württembergers would be suitable replacements.[89] France signed a new convention on 3 November promising over 2 million fl for the services of 8,670 men for one year.[90]

Carl Eugen at last had the independent command he had been preparing for. The new units raised the year before were nearing full strength, while a sixth line infantry regiment (Prinz Friedrich Wilhelm) was formed in January 1759. The army approached its paper strength of 13,307 men and 2,548 horses and had been drilling at Osweil where it practiced musketry and massed artillery fire.[91] As in the previous year, Carl Eugen left his prized guardsmen at home when he set out on 28 October, a few days ahead of clinching the deal with France. Not all shared his enthusiasm, since all colonels and regiment commanders were temporarily arrested after petitioning him about the campaign two weeks before.[92] He crossed the Main at Gemünden where his corps formally mustered into French pay on 12 November.[93] Determined to make a good impression, he sent 470 men more than was required, but since 308 were sick and others were detached, effective strength was 8,740. There were also 116 transport personnel with 79 wagons and 316 horses, plus another 30 drivers and 40 horses for the artillery. The three grenadier battalions together totalled 1,213 men. Each infantry regiment was nominally 1,023. The Horse Grenadiers and Cuirassier Regiment von Phull were each 504 men, but because the Hussar Regiment only mustered three squadron s totalling 380, one squadron (122 men) from Dragoon Regiment Degenfeld was attached. The artillery totalled 134 men with 15 cannon, mainly 3-pounders with a few

---

88   HStAS, A202 Bü.2219, with the French copy accessible at <https://basedoc.diplomatie.gouv.fr/> as number 17590001.

89   Richard Waddington, *La guerre du sept ans* (Paris: Firmin-Didot et Cie, 1899-1914), Vol.III, p.102.

90   HStAS, A202 Bü.2219, with the French copy accessible at <https://basedoc.diplomatie.gouv.fr/> as number 17590002.

91   *Etat general des troupes de S.A.S. Monseigneur le Duc de Virtemberg et Theck sur pié en 1759* (n.p., 1759); Schmahl and Spemann, *Geschichte des 2. Württembergischen Feldartillerie-Regiments* (Stuttgart: Selbstverlag, 1910), p.12.

92   Seckendorf diary cited in Walter Meyer, 'Zwei Militärabschiede württembergischer Corporale (1775 und 1806) und ihr geschichtliche Hintergrund', *Ludwigsburger Geschichtsblätter*, 23 (1971), pp.56-67 at p.61.

93   The itinerary can be traced through the reports of Senior Commissar Theobald in HStAS, G230 Bü.50a.

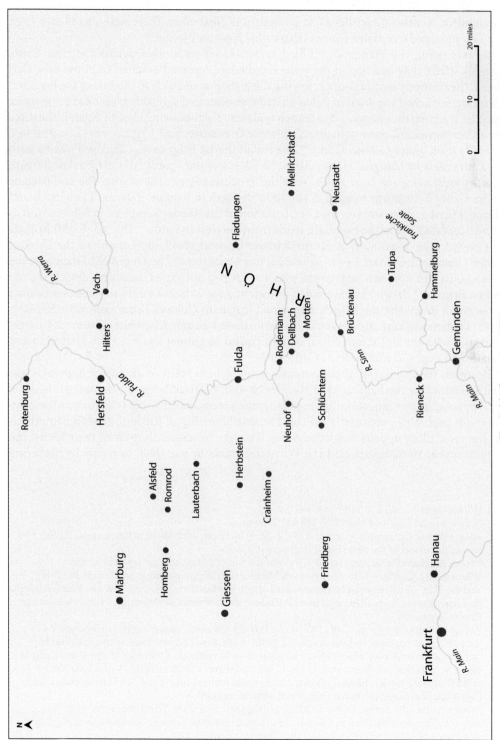

The Fulda Campaign, 1759.

6-pounders. Another 40 artillerymen arrived on 17 November. There were also 14 men from the new mounted Corps des Guides (also called Jäger zu Pferde).[94]

By this point, the French and Allied armies faced each other across the river Lahn, roughly where they had begun the year. Broglie had replaced Soubise and now gave Carl Eugen the relatively easy task of occupying the bishopric of Fulda to the east of the French.[95] Carl Eugen reached the town of Fulda on 21 November and spread his force out to interdict supplies reaching the enemy and to launch raids into neighbouring Hessen-Kassel. The three grenadier battalions, three squadrons of Horse Grenadiers and 13 guns were concentrated in Fulda itself under Colonel Gorcy.[96] The rest of the 1st Brigade was deployed nearby with the Cuirassiers in Mengen, Hartersheim, Illershausen and Pfordt, all villages downstream (northwards) along the river Fulda, with the Truchsess Regiment nearby. The 2nd Brigade under General Augé was billeted at battalion strength in hamlets between Lauterbach and Hersfeld further downstream, with one battalion of the Roeder Regiment in Schlitz, west of Pfordt, covering one of the two main roads from the west to Fulda.[97] The 3rd (Light) Brigade was posted nine hours away at Hersfeld under General Wolff and comprised the Hussars under Lieutenant Colonel Bouwinghausen, one squadron of the Degenfeld Dragoons, the Prinz Louis and Romann Regiments, plus a squadron of Horse Grenadiers detached from the 1st Brigade.[98] Broglie had seconded a weak brigade of light cavalry to maintain contact between his army and the Württembergers. Lieutenant Colonel Nordmann with 500 men was at Lauterbach, a crossroads about 20 km northwest from Fulda, while Lieutenant Colonel Wurmser with the 500-strong Royal Nassau Hussar Regiment was posted to Herbstein and Criainsfeld west and southwest of Carl Eugen.[99]

However, the chances of these outposts being able to warn of an enemy approach was much reduced by the behaviour of the French and Württembergers who antagonised the local population by requisitioning supplies without recompense in contrast to the Allies who generally paid. This particularly affected the small lordship of Riedesel around Lauterbach on the most likely approach for the Allies. Though not explicitly part of their treaty, the French appear to have expected the Württembergers to pay their own way by gathering

94   HStAS, G230 Bü.50 12 November 1759.
95   Broglie to Carl Eugen 14 Nov.1759, HStAS, G230 Bü.50.
96   Johann Baptist Gorcy de la Martiniere (1726-1791) had been a confident of Carl Eugen's mother and was made colonel of the new Hussar Regiment in 1759.
97   Johann Abraham David Augé (1698-1784) was the son of a Huguenot refugee and joined Württemberg service in 1728. He rose rapidly under Carl Eugen making general's rank in 1758: Seubert, 'Ein Württembergische General des vorigen Jahrhunderts', *Württembergische Vieteljahreshefte für Landesgeschichte*, 1 (1878), pp.150-152. His brigade comprised the Werneck, Prinz Friedrich and Roeder Regiments
98   Philipp Anton Ludwig von Wolff (1707-63), a Palatine Calvinist, joined the Württemberg army in the 1730s as an engineer and was suspected by the Austrians of pro-Prussian sympathies, but in fact appears to have been a loyal officer who was close to Werneck. Alexander Maximilian Friedrich Baron Bouwinghausen-Walmerode (1728-1796) came from a Swabian family with a long history of Württemberg service, himself initially becoming an infantry officer in 1746. Having known Carl Eugen since boyhood, he was soon favoured with promotion.
99   Nordmann had the Turpin Hussars and some dragoons. Two of the Württembergers' 15 guns appear to have been attached to his command: Strack von Weissenbach, *Geschichte der Königlichen Württembergischen Artillerie* (Stuttgart: Kohlhammer, 1882), p.108.

cash from enemy inhabitants. Wolff sent detachments downstream into Hessian territory, seizing four village mayors as hostages for a demand for 100,000 talers and 100,000 rations. Other cavalry patrols demanded 61,000 talers from the Rotenburg area and seized live-stock.[100] An attack on Rotenburg further down the Fulda was bungled when the supporting infantry failed to arrive.[101]

The Württemberg occupation of the Fulda area upset Ferdinand of Brunswick's plans and he was forced to recall various detachments he had sent to harass the main French army. As the town of Münster in Westphalia fell to his forces on 23 November, he was able to send troops south to Marburg where they collected under his nephew, the Erbprinz (Hereditary Prince) Carl Wilhelm of Brunswick (the future Prussian general defeated at Jena). Picking up additional units along the way, the Erbprinz hurried through Romrod on 29 November towards Lauterbach.

Broglie already sent word of his approach on 27 November along with the more welcome news of the recent victory over the Prussians at Maxen.[102] Carl Eugen already knew about Maxen and planned to mark this on 30 November. Some officers already started celebrating during the night of 29 November as reports arrived that the French post at Lauterbach had been driven in. The duke finally realised how exposed his forces were and ordered most of the baggage and around 80 sick evacuated to Hammelburg. There were another 147 sick already in Württemberg recuperating. The low sick rate despite the late season indicates that the commissariat functioned much better than in the previous two campaigns.[103]

Nordmann was told to regroup between Lauterbach and Fulda, while Wurmser was sent further south to Schlüchtern to cover a possible retreat via Brückenau to Gemünden. The Cuirassiers assembled from their four billets and took position west of the town between Lütters and Ober Bimbach, and orders were sent to recall the other two brigades.

In the cold dawn of 30 November, Gorcy led the Cuirassiers, two guns and several grena-dier companies forward to reconnoitre, while the rest of the grenadiers lined the town walls and secured the stone Town Bridge at the northwest end and that by Neuenburg immedi-ately to the south. Only now did Carl Eugen discover that Nordmann had ignored his orders and retreated in a wide detour to re-join Broglie at Giessen without reporting the Erbrpinz's continued advance.

The Erbprinz had far fewer troops than claimed in subsequent accounts, but given the Württembergers' dispersal, he had local superiority throughout the coming action which he used to good effect.[104] He had left Landenhausen at 1:00 a.m. heading east, splitting into

---

100 Geiges, 'Mit Herzog Karl Eugen', pp.193-194.
101 Stadlinger, *Kriegswesen*, pp.431-432.
102 HStAS, G230 Bü.50.
103 Theobald's report no.19, HStAS, G230 Bü.50a.
104 Most secondary accounts give the total as 8-9,000, whereas the paper strength of the units involved was only around 7,300, suggesting he had 6-7,000 at most consisting of the Hessian Grenadier, Mansbach and Bischhausen Regiments (each 1 battalion), the Brunswick Leib and Imhoff Regiments (both 2 battalions), 100 Hessian Jäger, the Hessian Prinz Friedrich Dragoons (4 squadrons), Hanoverian Bock Dragoons (4 squadrons), Hanoverian Luckner Hussars (1 squadron) and Prussian Ruesch Hussars (1 squadron). The Hessian Prinz Wilhelm Cavalry (2 squadrons) guarded the baggage, taking no part in the action. Some sources also list the Hanoverian Bremer Cavalry (2 squadrons), but these are not recorded in Hanoverian accounts.

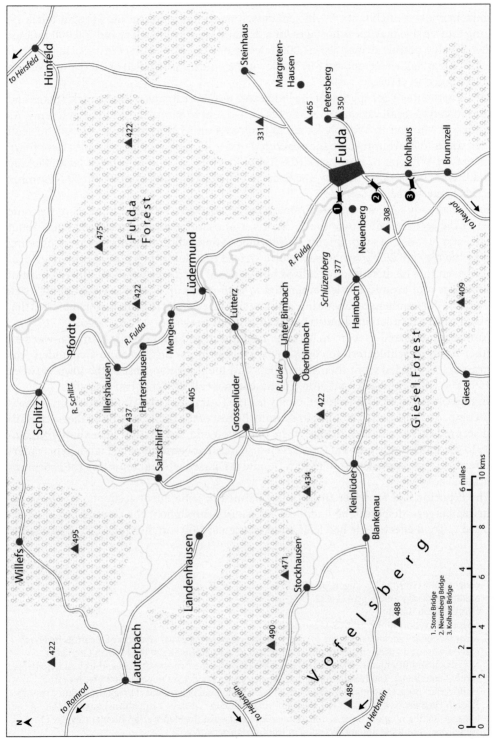

The Battlefield of 30 November 1759.

two columns to use both the southern route via Stockhausen and the Lauterbach road to the north through the woods. Both roads converged as the ground cleared just to the west of the Schulzenberg (aka Sulzberg) hill dominating the space between the trees and the Fulda River flowing south to north. The hussars and the dragoons under Major General Bock arrived first around 9:00 a.m. on the northern road and began exchanging pistol fire with the Württemberg Cuirassiers north of the hill.[105] The Württembergers retired in disorder as Bock occupied the hill. The allied infantry forming the southern column under Prince Carl von Bevern now emerged from the woods and were directed via Haimbach on the south side of the hill and towards the Neuenberg Bridge, thereby threatening to outflank Gorcy's command which was still west of the river. The allied heavy guns reached the summit of the Schulzenberg from where they opened fire on Gorcy and the bridges.[106]

It was now around midday. Carl Eugen recalled Gorcy over the river. The Cuirassiers were posted to the south towards Kohlhaus (aka Kohles), while six grenadier companies and two guns were left to defend the Town Bridge, with two more at Neuenberg and another three at the Johannis Bridge at Kohlhaus. Elements of Augé's 2nd Brigade had meanwhile arrived piecemeal during the morning and were directed through Fulda to take positions along the river between it and Kohlhaus. Only one battalion of the Prinz Friedrich Regiment was with Augé because the other was still at Neuhof, 12.5 kilometres south of Fulda, while three companies of the Werneck Regiment were also detached. The Truchsess Regiment was sent further south to hold the bridge at Lascherode (aka Löschenrod).

Bevern deployed on the higher ground opposite the Neuenberg Bridge and opened fire with his battalion guns on its defenders, while the heavier pieces bombarded the Town Bridge from the Schulzenberg. Bock advanced directly to the Town Bridge, supported by the Hessian Grenadier Regiment and two battalion guns. These forced the Württemberg grenadiers to abandon the bridge, retreat into the town and close the gates. After a few rounds from their battalion guns, the Hessian grenadiers stove in the gates with their axes and broke in. Meanwhile, Bevern's battalion guns soon quelled the resistance at the Neuenberg Bridge, allowing his infantry to cross, outflanking Fulda to the south and cutting it off from Augé's troops.

Carl Eugen decided to abandon Fulda, using his cavalry to cover the retreat of the grenadiers at Kohlhaus, and fell back southwards through Bronnzell to draw up at Laschenrode, where the terrain narrowed, facing north with his left on the river and right on a wood. Colonel Pöllnitz was directed to evacuate Fulda as best he could, leaving it to the east where he joined seven companies of the Werneck Regiment. Despatching four dragoon squadrons to pursue Carl Eugen, the Erbprinz, with Bock and the remaining six squadrons, went

---

105 Luis von Sichart, *Geschichte der Königlich-Hannoverschen Armee* (Hanover: Hahn'sche Hofbuchhandlung, 1866-1898), Vol.III, pp.572-576; Charles Pierre Victor Pajol, *Les guerres sous Louis XV* (Paris: Firmin-Didot, 1881-1891), Vol.IV, pp.474-475; Waddington, *La guerre*, Vol.III pp.102-109. The Württemberg official account can be found in G230 Bü.50 which also contains Carl Eugen's version in a letter to Broglie 1 December 1759. See also the duke's report in HHStA, KA 366 (neu) 3 December 1759.

106 Württemberg accounts claim the allies had 12-pounders which outgunned their artillery: Schmahl and Spemann, *Geschichte*, p.13.

after Pöllnitz who barely had time to form up outside the town.[107] Most allied accounts claim Pöllnitz surrendered quickly, but it is clear he offered stiff resistance lasting about 90 minutes, repulsing their attacks. However, this delayed his escape and he decided to make a stand on the Petersberg hill, east of Fulda. Supported by Bevern's infantry, the Erbprinz ringed the hill before leading a final charge, forcing Pöllnitz, who was wounded, to surrender. Allied losses were put at 60 but were probably rather higher.[108]

Now covered by his infantry, Carl Eugen meanwhile resumed his retreat through Rodemann, Dellbach and Motten. The cavalry of Wolff's brigade had reached Nisig, an hour from Fulda, when they learned of the defeat. Wolff took a detour through the hills to the east to join Carl Eugen at Kloster Tulpa on 3 December. The Württembergers blamed Nordmann's failure to inform them, but in reality, Broglie had sent accurate information about the Erbprinz's force and the duke should have recalled his detachments much sooner. Gorcy's force was too weak to defend the ground west of the river, but at least bought some time for Augé to arrive. Allied artillery superiority appears to have been decisive in making a defence of the river line untenable. The Württembergers' defeat contributed to Broglie's decision to retreat from Giessen to Friedeberg and Frankfurt on 5 December, but this was also prompted by growing supply problems. Meanwhile, Ferdinand considered the Erbprinz's position now too exposed and recalled him northwards.

Initial assessments put the total loss at 1,200 to 1,500 men, while rumours circulated in the region that the duke had been captured.[109] At an initial rollcall on 3 December, the grenadiers mustered only 558 men with 638 believed lost in the battle.[110] In all, 1,259 men including 39 officers were listed as lost. The Allies had captured up to seven companies of grenadiers and around seven of the Werneck Regiment, along with two battalion guns and 14 flags.[111] However, at least 100 prisoners had escaped to re-join the corps by 8 December, some having ransomed themselves by handing over valuables, while more came in over the following days. Rollcalls by 22 December recorded the total loss since 12 November as only 1,007, including 386 grenadiers and 571 from the Werneck Regiment.[112] Wolff's brigade did not lose a man. The allies recorded that 600 of the prisoners were wounded, while many of those returning had sabre cuts and other injuries.

The battle had begun at the point when the French were about to issue 63,000 bread rations to sustain the corps for the next four days. These were abandoned, while the capture

---

107 Three squadrons of Bock and one of Prinz Friedrich went south, while one squadron of Bock, three of Prinz Friedrich and the two hussar squadrons went northeast.

108 The Bock Dragoons alone lost 21 men and 37 horses killed and wounded: Sichart, *Geschichte*, Vol.III, p.575.

109 Theobald's report 30 Nov.1759, HStAS, G230 Bü.50a; Karl Muster (ed.), 'Memoria Digna. Aufzeichnungen des Metropolitans J.G. Vilmar zu Felsberg 1752-1769', *Zeitschrift des Vereins für hessische Geschichte und Landeskunde*, 64 (1953), pp.44-78 at p.60.

110 HStAS, G230 Bü.50a, 3 December1759.

111 The composition of the prisoners varies considerably in secondary accounts, but this is the most probable. Secondary works cite only two flags taken from the Werneck Regiment, whereas Württemberg sources admit to all 12 company flags from the grenadiers. The latter appear to have been captured, along with the grenadiers' field equipment, when allied hussars took most of the Württemberg baggage at Bieberstein on 1 December. It was primarily the Grenadier Battalion Nr.3 that was captured.

112 Geiges, 'Mit Herzog Karl Eugen', p.196; musters in HStAS, G230 Bü.50.

of several regimental quartermasters, together with their papers and pay chests, disrupting orderly administration. The troops were forced to live off the land, stripping the village of Motten of all resources as they retreated during the night.[113] Jacob Friedrich Röhm, chaplain of the Romann Regiment, only had a potato sandwich to sustain him in the three days after the battle.[114]

Unlike the aftermath of Leuthen, there was no collapse or medical emergency. Despite the defeat, the corps continued to receive contribution payments from Hessian villages, while a fresh delivery of small clothes soon arrived. The situation grew more critical as forage began to run out by the end of December, but the French refused to let the corps enter winter quarters because the enemy remained in the field. Now reinforced by their fourth squadron, the Württemberg hussars raided into Fulda and Hessian territory, seizing more hostages to secure additional contributions and taking prisoners in minor skirmishes with the Allied counterparts. Finally discharged by the French, the Württembergers retired from the Hammelburg area southwards into billets in the bishopric of Würzburg, screened by the hussars posted along the frontier.[115] The corps remained in relatively good shape, numbering around 8,400 effectives while the number of sick declined from 425 in January to 255 by May 1760.[116]

Relations with the French continued to deteriorate. The duke complained to Broglie that he lacked heavy artillery and also managed to fall out with the commander of the Saxons in French service.[117] The French supplied bread at only half the Württemberg regulation rate, forcing the corps to buy its own three days in every week.[118] The French retorted that the Württembergers' bad behaviour would turn the whole region against the coalition, and refused to let them operate independently, while Carl Eugen said he would no longer serve under Broglie. Finally, France released the Württembergers from its service on 15 May.

The Last Throw: 1760

Austria resolved to pay the Württembergers instead, rather than see the duke retreat into neutrality. Carl Eugen was ready to march but delayed hoping Vienna would improve its offer to include an electoral title, additional territory and full pay for a year. A threat to break off negotiations was sufficient to force him to accept quite poor terms on 23 July.[119] Austria would make a one-off payment of 50,000fl, waive Württemberg's contribution to

---

113 Theobald's reports 30 November and 1 December 1759, G230 Bü.50a. Carl Eugen reimbursed the villagers.

114 Von Kolb, 'Feldprediger in Altwürttemberg', *Blätter für Württembergische Kirchengeschichte*, 10 (1906), pp.22-51, 117-142, at p.125.

115 Theobald's reports in G230 Bü.50a, and Bouwinhausen's autobiography in Ernst Frhr v. Ziegesar (ed.), *Zwei württembergische Soldatenbilder aus alter Zeit* (Stuttgart: WGAV, 1904), p.82.

116 Potier's reports in HStAS, G230 Bü.50a.

117 Arnold Schäfer, *Geschichte des Siebenjährigen Krieges* (Berlin: Wilhelm Herz Verlag, 1867-74), Vol.II/II p.66; Otto Große, *Prinz Xaver von Sachsen und das Korps bei den Französischen Armee 1758-1763* (Printed PhD, Leipzig, 1907), p.61.

118 Order for General Wolff 28 January 1760, HStAS, G230 Bü.50a.

119 HStAS, A202 Bü.2236. The emperor ratified the treaty on 2 August 1760.

the Reichsarmee's operations fund for that year (saving another 56,000fl), and promised to supply free food in return for 11,000 men for that year's campaign. Since the duke had to cover all his other costs for the corps, Austria agreed that could continue his unconstitutional taxes and, in what proved a fateful decision, keep a third of all war contributions levied during the campaign.[120]

As previously, the duke was determined to make a good impression, and fielded more troops than required.[121] Two additional grenadier battalions were added to the corps from the previous year and grouped into a brigade under Carl Eugen's personal command. The additional units were a battalion each from the Garde zu Fuss and the Leibgrenadier Regiment. An additional company from the Garde zu Fuss accompanied the corps as the Flügelgrenadiere, copying Prussian practice, to guard the headquarters, making 21 companies in total numbering 2,122 grenadiers. The six line infantry regiments were grouped into three other brigades under generals Augé, Wolff and Phull.[122] General Gorcy commanded a heavy cavalry brigade, composing the Cuirassiers and Horse Grenadiers, while Colonel Bouwinghausen led the light cavalry brigade comprising the Hussars, two squadrons of Dragoon Regiment Roeder (256 men), one squadron and two companies of Feldjäger (345 men). The hussars and the two heavy cavalry regiments were each 504 men. At last, the corps included a substantial artillery component under Colonel Leger with 20 guns, and had a full set of field equipment. In total there were 20 regimental guns, 10 howitzers, six 6-pounders and four 12-pounders, with 522 artillerymen and 183 train personnel. There were another 163 baggage attendants and a total of 936 horses. As in 1759, part of the artillery joined the corps during the campaign. Two companies (totalling 201 men) of the new Staff (or Garrison) Battalion, formed in 1759 from surplus recruits, acted as baggage guards. There were 540 grenadier and artillery tents and 1,200 tents for musketeers, but none for the cavalry who were expected to lodge in villages near each camp [123]

The final, new addition to the force proved far less valuable. Perhaps concerned at the unreliability of the French light units attached to his force in 1759, Carl Eugen was keen to add his own such units. He rejected an offer from the distinguished Colonel Gschray for a full 800 men, not least because he discovered that officer was now a gouty septuagenarian who was nearly deaf. Instead, he accepted a proposal from Joachim Reinhold von Glasenapp (1717-1800), an uncouth former Prussian officer who had been serving with the French

---

120   Three Austrian commissioners were already attached to the corps on 21 July to handle provisioning and the war contributions: HStAS, G230 Bü.52.

121   Full strength was 408 above the required 11,000. Musters indicate the corps was kept to this level into mid-November: HStAS, G230 Bü.50a.

122   2nd Brigade: IRs Wolff (ex Roeder) and Werneck; 3rd Brigade: IRs Prinz Louis and Romann; 4th Brigade: IRs vacant Truchsess and Prinz Fredrich Wilhelm. The line infantry totalled 6,126 men. Ludwig Wilhelm August Baron von Phull (died 1797) belonged to a Brandenburg family serving Württemberg since 1695 but had several relations who were senior Prussian officers. Phull was also colonel of the Cuirassier Regt raised in 1758.

123   HStAS, G230 Bü.53 list of equipment 20 July 1760. The same packet contains plans of each campsite. Johann Christoph David von Leger (1701-91) came from the Worthy elite but was educated at ducal expense to become an artillery expert and military and civil architect. He was ennobled by Emperor Carl VII after he distinguished himself in the storm of Prague 1741 whilst serving as a volunteer with the Bavarians.

hussars, he agreed to raise three companies of hussars, totalling 150 men, to augment the duchy's existing hussar regiment. Glasenapp struck a poor bargain and was obliged to pay the unit himself from its muster site near the Dutch frontier until it joined Carl Eugen at Schmalkalden on 18 August. This oversight obliged him to mortgage his home to two even more shady characters whom he appointed company commanders and who claimed they knew where Frederick II had buried his treasure. Lured by the prospect of plunder, the unit soon had 270 men, of whom only 150 were mounted. The unit left a trail of smashed billets and unpaid bills and was barely under the control of its officers.[124] While Glasenapp's hussars conformed to the now growing perception of the Württembergers' poor quality, the army's general condition continued to improve and desertion and sick rates were minimal throughout the 1760 campaign.[125]

Meanwhile, Carl Eugen set out from Ludwigsburg on 27 July northwards to the river Main, then east through Würzburg territory into Thuringia.[126] His mission was to act independently as a link between a combined Franco-Saxon corps under Prince Xaver operating in Hanoverian territory around Göttingen, and the Reichsarmee under the Duke of Zweibrücken who was to clear Saxony of small Prussian garrisons and prevent Frederick wintering there.[127] If possible, the Württembergers were to sever communications between the Prussians and their Anglo-German allies to the west, as well as with their main reserve magazine at Magdeburg on the Elbe. More immediately, the Württembergers were to levy war contributions in all enemy areas along their way, and they swiftly set about this in the Hessian enclave of Schmalkalden.

Supply became more of an issue as they advanced through Gotha territory, because the French had already foraged in the area, while the Prussians held the village mayors hostage in Magdeburg to dissuade the population from cooperating.[128] Bouwinghausen's light brigade pushed ahead, rounding up all available cattle and horses. Carl Eugen appealed to the numerous Saxon deserters from the Prussian army who were said to be hiding in the woods, calling on them to join him in liberating their homeland, but in practice he left this task to Zweibrücken and instead marched northwards along the electorate's western frontier towards Nordhausen at the end of August, levying more contributions in the Hanoverian and Prussian territory along the way. The Austrian light corps under Luzinsky attached to the Reichsarmee had already levied contributions from the Prussian town of Halle. Undaunted, on 12 September Carl Eugen demanded that the town pay 250,000 talers within four days, though he eventually reduced this to 75,000. The troops were allowed to plunder freely, causing such terror that many inhabitants jumped into the river to escape.

---

124 P.H. Wilson, 'Glasenapp's Freikorps', *Seven Years War Association Journal*, 10, no.4 (1999), pp.10-19 drawing on HStAS, A8 Bü.250, 251; A202 Bü.2278. For Glasenapp's career, see Marcel Dings and Frank Poeth, *Het militaire leven van Joachim Reinhold von Glasenapp* (Tegelen, 2021), in particular pp.89-129

125 Calculated from strength returns in HStAS, A202 Bü.2221.

126 For the campaign, see HStAS, G230 Bü.51-53, especially the handwritten Journal des corps d'armee de Württemberg in Bü.53, which is partly printed in Stadlinger, *Kriegswesens*, pp.436-445.

127 The Reichsarmee, reinforced by some Austrian light troops, totalled about 30,000 facing around 11,000 Prussian field troops plus garrisons.

128 HStAS, G230 Bü.52 reports 17 and 19.

The booty and requisitioned livestock were then sold at the cattle market of Siebleben in Gotha territory at knock-down prices.[129]

The duke complained that his officers 'knew nothing and were gallant cavaliers but negligent' in their duties and had several of them cashiered for unauthorised extortion. This prompted the threat of mass resignation on 14 September, only averted when Carl Eugen apologised.[130] Delayed by waiting for the rest of the artillery to arrive, and to sell the remaining booty, the Württembergers finally moved eastwards on 20 September towards the Elbe to cooperate with Zweibrücken who had driven the Prussians under Hülsen back to Torgau. While Zweibrücken drove in the Prussian outposts still west of the river on 24 September, Luzinsky began bridging the river at Dommitzsch just downstream. Bouwinghausen led the Württemberg light troops across as Hülsen escaped northwest along the other side of the Elbe, abandoning Torgau which soon surrendered. Carl Eugen then crossed at Pretsch further downstream, following Hülsen. The Prussians counter-attacked on 31 September, forcing the Württembergers to recross the river, covered by their artillery and hussars. The duke's force comprised the grenadier brigade, one line battalion, the Hussar Regiment and two squadrons of Horse Grenadiers.

Hülsen retired further downstream to entrench facing east between Braunsdorf and Reinsdorf perpendicular to the river just north of Wittenberg on 1 October. The Reichsarmee had meanwhile crossed to the other side of the Elbe and attacked at 9:00 a.m. on 2 October, while the Württembergers launched a diversion south of the river. The Württemberg artillery was too far away to hit the Prussian baggage as it streamed westwards on the other bank, heading for Coswig. Carl Eugen ordered Bouwinghausen to cross just downstream of the town to attack Hülsen's right and thereby assist Zweibrücken by forcing the Prussians to weaken their front. The manoeuvre was very risky, because the southern bank was much higher and dangerously steep. Bouwinghausen questioned the order, but the duke insisted, so he led his hussars across the river towards the Prussian cavalry at Teuchel, immediately north of Wittenberg.[131] The Prussians faced about and counterattacked. Bouwinghausen was forced back over the river, covered by the Württemberg artillery and Austrian Colonel Zedwitz and 1,000 Grenzer (light infantry), temporarily attached to the Württembergers, who sent men over in boats to provide covering fire. Bouwinghausen lost around 50 men but took 21 prisoners and a grateful duke gave the hussars a 10,000fl reward for their bravery.[132]

Having repulsed Zweibrücken, Hülsen disengaged and retreated further westwards through Anhalt territory via Coswig, abandoning Wittenberg which surrendered on 12 October. Given that Leipzig had also now been evacuated, all of Saxony had been liberated. Meanwhile, the Russians raided Berlin, delaying a Prussian response. Zweibrücken retired southeast to join the main Austrian army under Daun which arrived at Torgau on 21 October, leaving the Württembergers to follow the Prussians through Anhalt. Coordination amongst coalition forces was poor, and Carl Eugen simply continued west to Halle hoping

---

129 Höcher, 'Selbstzeugnisse', pp.71-12.

130 Meyer, 'Zwei Militärabschiede', p.61.

131 These were Colonel Kleist with his Green Hussars, plus Dragoon Regiments Holstein and Schorlemer.

132 Hermann von Niethammer, 'Alexander Frhr. V. Bouwinhausen-Wallmerode, Generalleutnant 1728-1796', *Schwäbische Lebensbilder*, 3 (1942), pp.17-32 at pp.25-26.

to join a French force raiding the Prussian territories of Halberstadt and Querfurt.[133] Bouwinghausen and the light brigade occupied Köthen to levy contributions.

Frederick was finally able to send reinforcements, ironically commanded by Carl Eugen's brother, Friedrich Eugen, who picked up Hülsen, crossed the Elbe at Magdeburg and advanced rapidly southwards into Anhalt. With his typical timing, Carl Eugen had gone to consult Daun in Torgau, leaving the corps commanded by Wolff. The Prussians surprised Bouwinghausen's light brigade at Rothenburg on the Saale on 25 October. Surrounded by cavalry in the open, the Württemberg foot jäger surrendered after firing a volley, while Glasenapp's free hussars were cut up with only 60 men escaping. Bouwinghausen and the Hussar Regiment escaped with minimal loss to join Wolff north of Halle, and the whole force withdrew that night to Merseburg.[134]

The duke re-joined his men as they continued retreating southwest through Leipzig even before Daun was defeated by Frederick at Torgau on 3 November. Having halted for two weeks at Weimar, Carl Eugen resumed his retreat on 21 November to Erfurt, handing over to Augé the next day and hastening home ahead of his men who reached Württemberg in early January. Furious at what he regarded as a cowardly abandonment, Emperor Francis I wrote personally to Carl Eugen that he had no further use for the Württembergers.[135] The exasperated Austrians rejected the duke's offer of up to 15,000 men for the next campaign if he was given command of the Reichsarmee, and in June 1761 Austria withdrew its envoy from Stuttgart, not sending another until November 1762.[136]

The Last Years

Other than Glasenapp's unit, which was already dismissed on 7 February, all units were retained at around two-thirds strength, giving a total of over 10,000 effectives for the rest of the war.[137] Planned economies were cancelled in March 1762 when Carl Eugen believed that Spain's entry into the war opened new opportunities. Colonel Wimpffen, who had now displaced Montmartin and Rieger as ducal favourite, was sent to Madrid to offer a Württemberg corps for service against the Portuguese. Long negotiations were finally broken off in June 1763, with the Austrian ambassador noting that 'Religion is the excuse, but the real reason is the poor discipline and bad behaviour of the Württemberg troops in our service in Silesia and in French service in Hessen'.[138]

Only Württemberg's much reduced Kreis contingent remained in the field, sharing the fortunes of the Reichsarmee in its campaigns in Saxony. The Württemberg infantry escaped

---

133 Eberhard Kessel, *Das Ende des Siebenjährigen Krieges 1760-1763* (Paderborn: Schöningh, 2007), Vol.I, pp.12-15.
134 Carl Eugen claimed the Prussians numbered 15,000, HStAS, G230 Bü.53 26 Oct.1760.
135 HStAS, A202 Bü.2236 20 and 30 Nov.1760.
136 Montmartin to Straube 21 December1760, HStAS, A74 Bü.144; A8 Bü.5.
137 Monthly strength returns in HStAS, A8 Bü.54. Effectives only fell below 10,000 in April 1763 and remained over 9,000 until May 1764.
138 Count Rosenberg to Kaunitz 23 August 1762, Hans Jüretschke (ed.), *Berichte der diplomatischen Verreter des Wiener Hofes aus Spanien in der Regierungszeit Karl III. (1759-1788)* (Madrid: Görres Gesellschaft, 1970-87), Vol.III, pp186-187.

the disaster at Freiburg on 29 October 1762 where the Swabians and other Imperial troops had fought bravely before being overwhelmed in a series of Prussian attacks.[139] Carl Eugen withdrew his contingent altogether as the Reichsarmee retreated into Bohemia in November. Württemberg declared its neutrality on 4 December as part of the wider disengagement by the Imperial Estates who were disillusioned with the war.[140]

Unsurprisingly, Carl Eugen came out of the war empty handed. Württemberg was included in the Peace of Hubertusburg on 15 February 1763 only indirectly along with the rest of the Empire which, at least, secured its formal aim of restoring the pre-war status quo. Peace changed Austria's priorities which now centred on rebuilding influence amongst the smaller German principalities and polishing the Habsburgs' credentials as the Empire's benevolent overlords. In Württemberg's case, the Habsburgs skilfully inserted themselves as brokers in the duchy's growing internal problems.[141] After being led a dance by his unscrupulous agent in London during 1764, Carl Eugen finally realised that no power was prepared to hire his army.[142] Mounting pay arrears owed to officers made it difficult to disband entire units which instead were retained as cadres. Rather than compromise with the Worthies, the duke unilaterally introduced a new 'Military Tax' in March 1764. Though intended as a genuine attempt at a fairer system, the measure provoked popular unrest which the duke unwisely tried to suppress by deploying troops.[143] Capitalising on a wave of public sympathy, as well as diplomatic intervention on their behalf by Prussia, Britain and Denmark, the Estates opened proceedings in the imperial supreme court against the duke. Carl Eugen nonetheless managed to extract fresh, legal tax grants from the Estates in return for recognising the court's first verdict against him in September 1764, enabling him to pay off his officers and cut effective strength from 7,244 to 4,652 between June and September 1765.[144] A further five years of talks finally produced a settlement in 1770, fixing the duchy's taxes at the level they had been in 1739, despite a rise in population of 12 percent across the intervening years. The settlement constrained ducal ambition into the 1790s, keeping the duchy's military establishment to around 2,800 effectives.

Conclusions

Württemberg's involvement in the Seven Years War undoubtedly ended in political and military failure. Much of the blame lies with the overambitious and vainglorious Carl Eugen whose military management was often wasteful and counter-productive, as illustrated by his constant draining of the army of its best men to create ever larger guard units which rarely, if ever, took to the field. His lacklustre personal leadership and inexperience contributed

---

139 Detailed report of Colonel Baron von Auffenberg 8 Nov.1762, HStAS, C14 Bü.87a.

140 HStAS, C14 Bü.418.

141 Gabrielle Haug-Moritz, *Württembergischer Ständekonflikt und deutscher Dualismus* (Stuttgart: Kohlhammer, 1992).

142 Correspondence with the self-styled Chevalier William Stapleton, HStAS, A8 Bü.8; The National Archives (London), SP 100/17.

143 Helen P. Liebel-Weckowicz, 'The revolt of the Wuerttemberg estates', *Man and Nature*, 2 (1984), pp.109-120; Wilson, *War, State and Society*, pp.229-231.

144 HStAS, A8 Bü.54.

to the repeated setbacks, and he wasted the opportunities provided by the independent commands in 1759 and 1760 to advance his political ambitions. There were also deeper, structural constraints as Württemberg had little choice but to back France and Austria. Arguably, Carl Eugen could have limited his involvement to the 1752 treaty and Kreis troops, but that would have incurred expense for no gain other than fulfilling existing obligations. Joining Prussia would have been suicidal and served no purpose politically. Thus, decision to overcommit is understandable. Once involved, Württemberg suffered from being the weaker partner always dependent on its sponsors for funds to enable it to take the field. This was compounded by the duke's domestic political problems, as there was no support for the war from the local elite or bulk of the population. He soon passed the point of safe return and was forced to rely on illegal financial measures that merely increased his dependency on Austria.

The Württembergers also suffered from diverging expectations. Their sponsors found them costly and difficult to deal with and were often quick to pass on the blame for situations they had caused, or at least contributed to, as in the case of the Austrians after Leuthen. For their part, the Württembergers, with much justification, felt they were treated poorly and were neither paid nor fed properly. Meeting the treaty obligations cost the duchy much more than was actually provided and even if the duke had curbed his extravagant personal expenses and costly palace construction, involvement in the war would still have been a huge burden far exceeding both normal taxes and foreign payments. The Württembergers were compelled to rely heavily on contributions levied in enemy territory 1758-1760, while the logistical failures following major defeats forced the soldiers to live off the land, further worsening their reputation. The army's operations and the men's experience illustrate a more general point about the harsh reality of the Seven Years War which was far from the cliché of a 'limited war'. Finally, the army's generally poor reputation obscures the real, if modest, improvements in performance and cohesion across the war. Again, this exemplifies a broader pattern in that most German forces were cadres that had to be expanded in wartime and it took time to induct recruits and gain experience, especially given the relatively poor quality of many officers.

Further Reading

Duffy, Christopher, *Prussia's Glory: Rossbach and Leuthen* (Chicago: The Emperor's Press, 2003)

Duffy, Christopher, *The Army of Frederick the Great* (2nd ed., Chicago: The Emperor's Press, 1996)

Szabo, Franz A.S.J., *The Seven Years War in Europe 1756-1763* (London: Routledge, 2007)

Wilson, Peter H., *War, State and Society in Württemberg, 1677-1793* (Cambridge: Cambridge University Press, 1995)

Wilson, P. H., 'Violence and the rejection of authority in 18th-century Germany: the case of the Swabian mutinies in 1757', *German History*, 12 (1994), pp.1-26

5

The Crisis of the French Cavalry in the Seven Years War

Frédéric Chauviré

The Seven Years War was first perceived from the French point of view as a succession of campaigns and operations difficult to follow, punctuated by the waltz of the generals and marked by an accumulation of dishonourable defeats. The French army experienced this conflict as a humiliation whose magnitude led to a deep reflection. In the army, the cavalry was particularly shaken. The equestrian arm enjoyed until then a great reputation, built mainly during the wars of Louis XIV. This king set great store by it, often repeating that it was by his troops on horseback that his army could win in the field, especially as the infantry clashes often remained indecisive.[1]

The previous War of the Austrian Succession does not seem to have called into question the prestige of the equestrian arm. The main campaigns of that war took place on the Flanders theatre, where the cavalry did not have much opportunity to shine. The famous charges of the *Maison du Roi* at Fontenoy (1745), which certainly played a role in the victory, were able to maintain a certain illusion around its value. But another element undoubtedly contributed to preserve a relative and misleading feeling of superiority: the French, unlike the Austrians, did not have to face the Prussians, who were their allies in this conflict. They could not take full measure of the reforms implemented by Frederick II and measure the gap gradually created between the cavalry of the two kingdoms. Unlike the infantry, largely inherited from his father, the Prussian cavalry was the personal work of the king. Relying on officers of great worth, he built a formidable weapon that played a vital role in his victories.

The reversal of alliances, the 'diplomatic revolution', which marks the Seven Years War therefore had the consequence of opposing the French cavalry to its Prussian counterpart. The confrontation with the Prussian model was thus one of the main stakes of this conflict for French troopers. They were not the only ones, however. The French cavalry had to face the assertion of the fire factor on the battlefield. The increase in the number of cannon and

---

1 Bertrand Fonck, *Le maréchal de Luxembourg et le commandement des armées sous Louis XIV* (Seyssel: Champ Vallon, 2014), p.512.

the increased effectiveness of infantry firepower – particularly British and Prussian – were unavoidable phenomena that might have contributed to questioning its role in the battle. The reaction to the Prussian reforms and the new challenge of fire are thus the two main axes of this period.

To understand the framework that governs the action of the French cavalry in the war, and therefore conditions how it would face these challenges, this chapter will first consider its organization and tactics. It will then take into account the measure of its failure and the crisis it underwent through the analysis of several major defeats. Finally, it will be of interest to show that the cavalry was not ineffectual, and that these defeats produced a real awareness, prompting a deep reform in the short or medium term.

Organization of the French Cavalry

The organization and tactics of the French cavalry had changed little in relation to the previous conflict, or even since the reign of Louis XIV. The various branches of the arm, the administrative and tactical structures in particular remained unchanged. This did not, however, prevent some inflections in the field of tactics and instruction. It is therefore useful to recall the main lines of institutional frameworks and practices, distinguishing continuities and novelties.

Composition and Size

The French cavalry was still largely composed of 'light' cavalry regiments, as opposed to the *Maison du Roi* and the *Gendarmerie*. These latter troops were until the middle of the seventeenth century actually equipped with a heavier defensive armament, but that difference no longer existed in the eighteenth century. Only the different size of the horses remained, a little taller than in the 'light'. The 'light' cavalry consisted of 57 regiments at the beginning of the war. To these we must add the seven hussar regiments and 17 dragoon regiments. All these regiments were comprised of four squadrons of 160 men each, so they represent 54,000 men. It is also necessary to add on the *Carabiniers*, the *Gendarmerie* and the units of the *Maison du Roi*. The whole reached a total of nearly 60,000 men.[2]

Who were the men who made up the bulk of the cavalry? If most writers are to be believed, the ideal recruit for the cavalry was a peasant, a sturdy man who knew horses, but is this accurate? The Chevalier de Chabo, an officer who tried to give an image as faithful as possible of the composition of the French cavalry in the mid-eighteenth century, was nuanced. If it was actually preferable to recruit peasants, it was more important still that they came from the provinces which were, according to him, the best able to provide the best riders: provinces where peasants were accustomed to the horse, mainly those where it was used for agriculture. But in reality, recruits were far from being drawn predominantly from horse-familiar provinces, or even from rural provinces:

---

2   Louis Susane, *La cavalerie française* (Paris: J. Hetzel, 1874), Vol.1, pp.14-15.

More than two-thirds are, or inhabitants of the cities, people of family not accustomed to the horse, or born in the other provinces of the kingdom, from which some bring the fear of the horse rather than having an attachment to it. So, it is not an exaggerated expression to say that a third of the horsemen at most are troopers by taste, and the other two-thirds are by honour or fear of punishment.[3]

This reflection is echoed by d'Auvergne: 'Our riders have that clumsiness on horseback that the men of the nations who raise a lot of horses do not have.'[4] It seems that we are far from the recruits dreamed by theorists and officers.

A Fundamental Structure: the Company-Farm

Riders were integrated into squadrons, themselves usually composed of four companies. The squadron was an essentially tactical structure, the basic unit from an administrative point of view was the company. This one had a very special status, called 'company-farm' (*compagnie ferme*).

Historiography has sometimes been very severe with regard to this form of administration of the company, which represents for some the symbol of the malfunctions of the army under the *Ancien régime*. Edouard Desbrières condemns it without recourse, 'the proprietary captain, he says, administers his company like an estate and only seeks to benefit from it.'[5] What gave the system its 'entrepreneurial' dimension was undoubtedly its contractual aspect.[6] The captain received a commission from the king to command a company which he was obliged to keep in the best possible state, in order to best serve the interests of the sovereign. The salary and the lump sum paid to him serve both to remunerate him and to assure the maintenance of his company. So, he had to look after himself, to clothe, mount and, of course, recruit his men.

The king and his minister knew how to count on the attraction which the aristocracy of the kingdom had for the place of captain – chiefly of cavalry captain – in the royal troops, in order to offload on captains a part of the cost of the maintenance of the army.[7] It was thus not uncommon for captains to be forced to advance money in order to make up for the very great irregularity of the pay, to avoid seeing the soldiers desert. The monarchy was able to take advantage of the financial capabilities of the officers, forcing them to use their personal credit to provide a significant portion of the cash required to raise and maintain their company.[8] The task was probably not financially insurmountable in times of peace, but during wartime the financial equilibrium became much more fragile. There are many cases of captains forced to go into debt or to appeal to family generosity. This is completely

---

3   Service Historique de la Défense (SHD), GR 1M1730, 'Mémoire du chevalier de Chabo sur la cavalerie', 1749. The Chevalier de Chabo thus noted that the regions where one more readily enlisted in the cavalry are Franche-Comté, Alsace, Lorraine, Thiérache, after them Picardie, and to a lesser extent Normandie and Poitou.

4   SHD, GR 1 M1732, f°89, 'Observations sur l'équitation', par d'Auvergne.

5   Edouard Desbrières, Maurice Sautai, *La cavalerie de 1740 à 1789* (Paris: Berger-Levrault, 1906), p.8.

6   Hervé Drévillon, *L'impôt du sang, le métier des armes sous Louis* XIV (Paris: Taillandier, 2005) p.101.

7   David Parrott, *Richelieu's Army, War, Government and Society in France, 1624-1642* (Cambridge: Cambridge University Press, 2001), pp.316-317.

8   Parrott, *Richelieu's Army*, pp.329, 331.

opposed to the idea of owner captains enriching themselves with the 'exploitation' of their company.

This policy, which unburdened the treasury, had, however, a certain number of constraints and consequences more or less unfortunate. The first concerned the choice of captains. The monarchy had to be very attentive to the financial capacity of the postulants.[9] Another consequence was obviously to encourage the captains to use illegal practices to prevent their company from being understaffed ('false soldiers' or 'flying guns') and to hold back some of the money from pay. Finally, an indirect consequence with very serious implications concerns the quality of the training of the troops. Since the captains knew that the harnesses were at their own expense, and that each rider or lost horse would incur expenses that the king's allowances would not cover, they had every interest in limiting the manoeuvres, in order to spare their 'capital'.

Equipment and Armament

The most important item for personal protection was the breastplate or cuirass. Until 1733 only the regiment of cuirassiers and officers were required to wear the cuirass. Much lighter than the medieval protection of knights, its use was no less cause for some awkwardness, if we judge by the multiple calls to order of the royal ordinances.[10] This reluctance did not influence the authorities, obviously convinced of the effectiveness of this type of protection, since the ordinance of 28 May 1733 not only reminded the obligation for the officers to wear the cuirass, but commanded the brigadiers (NCOs), gendarmes, and troopers to wear a plastron (the front part of the cuirass).[11] This obligation is reiterated by the ordinance of 27 December 1743, which also mentions the necessity of wearing it in time of war as in time of peace, 'the habit of wearing cuirasses being the surest way of rendering them less troublesome.' It is not sure that this new ordinance was enough to make the concerned parties obey. As early as 1750, the King was forced to remind them that he intended the officers wear their cuirass, and the cavalrymen wear their plastron, in all the exercises, in reviews and in marches, as was stipulated by the articles of the Ordinances of 1733 and 1743.[12] Helmets and burgonets were certainly forgotten, but the head was an essential part that it was also important to protect. The order of 28 May 1733 specified that the hat would have enough depth to be able to insert under it a cap of iron, also called 'cervelière'. It was intended to protect the skull from sabre blows, but it obviously could not do anything against carbine or pistol shots.

Boots were not strictly speaking a defensive element; they were nonetheless an important point of the rider's equipment. The ordinance of 28 May 1733, put an end to the quarrel between the supporters of the stiff boots and the defenders of the soft boots by imposing on

---

9   Drévillon, *L'impôt du sang,* p140. See also Emile G. Léonard, *L'armée et ses problèmes au XVIIIe siècle* (Paris: Plon, 1958), especially p.166-168.

10   Ordinances of 16 March 1675; 1 February 1703; 28 May 1733; 27 December 1743.

11   Pierre de Briquet, *Code militaire ou compilation des ordonnances des rois de France concernant les gens de guerre* (Paris: Prault père, 1761). p.9. A first order, dating from 1703, had already established this obligation, but the war ended, the use of cuirasses and plastrons was almost completely abandoned. François Bonnefoy, *Les armes de guerre portatives en France du début du règne de Louis XIV à la veille de la Révolution* (Paris: Librairie de l'Inde éditeur, 1991), Vol.1, p.21.

12   Bonnefoy, *Les armes de guerre portatives en France,* p.20. Ordinance of 1 June 1750.

the brigadiers and troopers the wearing of soft boots.[13] This point was approved by Puységur, who regretted that it had been too long before abandoning the stiff boots. The soft boots had, according to him, many advantages, allowing for example the horsemen to be surer in the saddle, to rise more easily in their stirrups in order to swing their sword.[14]

The sword was the main offensive weapon of the cavalry. It was actually a straight sword, double edged, also called '*forte épée*'. The first regulatory model in the French cavalry dated from 1679. The blade is 95 centimetres (37.4 inches), the guard has a knuckle guard screwed to the pommel and two heart-shaped shell-guards. Some changes occurred over time. In 1733 the length of the blade decreased to 89 centimetres (35 inches), and in 1750 added a lateral branch guard to increase the protection of the hand. The *forte épée* therefore appeared as the standard weapon of the cavalry. The dragoons had the same weapon until 1767. The sabre of the hussars was regulated for the first time in 1752. The hussars were armed with a traditional weapon of the Hungarian type with curved blade, with the guard simpler than that of the cavalry.

The cavalry also carried firearms. Brigadiers and troopers were armed with a carbine and two pistols. The dragoons also had, with the carbine, a bayonet, but they had only one pistol and carried, instead of the other, a spade, bill, axe, or other instrument for entrenchment.

Instruction

If the equipment or the institutional and administrative foundations had not been profoundly modified for several decades, the War of Austrian Succession led to a certain inflection in the field of training and manoeuvring. The inadequacy of the training and the lack of uniformity in the manoeuvring became clear to many officers. Several of them, first and foremost Drummond de Melfort, disciple of Maurice de Saxe, but also La Porterie and Moustier, alerted the ministry to this subject. The minister 'awakened', according to Chabo's account, and decided to support and encourage them, triggering a positive dynamic: 'And as soon as he seemed to give some attention to this essential task, the zeal of some, the ambition of others, the self-esteem of the chiefs, and the natural inclination of the nation to perfect all things, excited everybody to a work that has become fashionable.'[15] The remarks of the Chevalier de Chabo testifies to a sense of rupture that is found repeatedly in the writings of Drummond de Melfort, which explains in particular that 'those who have not be able to see what the cavalry was before the war of 1740 are not able to judge the progress it could make.'[16] This dynamic found its consecration in the ordinance of 22 June 1755, the first official text attempting to normalize the exercise and manoeuvres of the cavalry. For the first time authorities were concerned about 'the school of the rider'; that is, individual instruction. It was, however, very succinct and too general a way for imposing a true standardization of principles and practices and to solve problems of uniformity. Harmonization

---

13   Bonnefoy, *Les armes de guerre portatives en France*, p.10. Ordinance of 28 May 1733.
14   Jacques-François de Chastenet, marquis de Puységur, *Art de la guerre par principes et par règles, ouvrage de M. le maréchal de Puységur, mis au jour par M. le Mis de Puységur, son fils* (Paris: Jombert, 1748), Vol.1, p.255. For him, the real reason for keeping the strong boot for so long is financial, the soft boot cost the captain more.
15   SHD, GR 1M 1730, 'Mémoire sur la cavalerie' par le chevalier de Chabo, 1755-1756 (?).
16   Louis Drummond de Melfort, *Traité sur la cavalerie* (Desprez: Paris, 1776), p.447.

of manoeuvres progressed appreciably, but conservatism and insufficient collective instruction limited these advances. Finally, while the tension between squire riding and military riding was becoming increasingly perceptible,[17] Melfort's remarks about the excesses of the *haute école* were not taken into account, any more than the work of Moustier.[18]

In general, it must be admitted that the efforts made, though real, were still insufficient. In most cases there was little question of instructing the riders at a pace greater than the great trot, while at the same time the Prussian cavalry was able to take the gallop, by squadron, several hundred meters from the enemy. The structural problems remained: the riders were for the most part peasants little at ease with the horses, the kingdom dependent for its remounts on foreign stock, which besides were not always of high quality. The farm-company, already mentioned, also constituted a considerable brake that limited the zeal of many officers. These difficulties were not settled in 1756, and the habit of sharply increasing the numbers at each entry into the war can only increase the effects. We understand better the half-joke of the Marquis de Castries: 'It can not be concealed that, until 1762, the king had many men and horses, but no cavalry'.[19] The difficulties were, of course, even greater during the conflict. Recruits received only brief instruction and winter quarters were rarely used to deepen drills and manoeuvres.

Tactics and Doctrine of Use

Armament and level of instruction largely determined the morphology of the charge. It relied indeed on three elements that were deeply interrelated: the choice of the main weapon, the speed and the place given to the shock. It is these which, with their own mechanisms and their interactions, determined the morphology of a cavalry charge, and presided over its course.

The ordinance of 1755 unfortunately did not allow the easy apprehension of these concepts. Regarding the weapon used for the charge, it did not decide for example on the debate between the supporters of fire and those of bladed weapons. From this point of view, it marks a certain retreat from the draft ordinance of 1753 and especially from 1733, which affirmed the principle of the superiority of the sword. In 1755 in an exercise resembling a simulacrum of a charge, it simply made do with mentioning that after sounding the charge, 'the riders will carry their sabre up as if they wanted to hit, holding the blade a little across, the point backwards, one foot higher than the hand.'[20] Can this relative shyness be explained by the desire to spare the corps leaders, by not imposing on them the manner of making

---

17   See Frédéric Chauviré and Jean-Pierre Digard, 'La naissance de l'équitation militaire', in Frédéric Chauviré and Bertrand Fonck (eds), *L'âge d'or de la cavalerie* (Paris: Gallimard, 2015), pp.146-149.

18   Edouard Desbrieres and Maurice Sautai underline how little consideration had been given to the cavalier doctrines of Drummond de Melfort, 'which the routine and inertia of the highest military personalities had stopped in his remarkable attempts.' *La cavalerie de 1740 à 1789* (Paris: Berger-Levrault, 1906), p.22. The Marquis de Moustier wrote about 1750 an *Instruction pour le Régiment de cavalerie de Moustier*, for the new recruits of his regiment. Nicole de Blomac, *Voyer d'Argenson et le cheval des Lumières* (Paris: Belin, 2004), p.191.

19   SHD, GR 1M 1732, f°91, 'Observations sur l'état dans lequel j'ai trouvé l'instruction de quelques régiments de cavalerie dans les cantonnements d'Alsace et de Metz' par le marquis de Castries, 1771.

20   Pierre Bonin, *Construire l'armée française. Textes fondateurs des institutions militaires. Tome II: Depuis le début du règne de Henri II jusqu'à la fin de l'Ancien Régime* (Turnhout: Brepols, 2006), p.251.

their troops fight? Or was it indicative of a certain hesitation about the exact place that must be reserved for firepower? One can, however, suppose that the exclusive use of the bladed weapon, without the execution of one or two preliminary salvos, was the dominant practice of the French cavalry during the Seven Years War. Indeed, the theoretical defenders of cavalry firepower seemed to lose ground starting in the beginning of the eighteenth century. The sources, both the theoretical works and the manuscript memorandums for the minister, increasingly frequently took side of the bladed weapon. In his *Essai sur la cavalerie tant ancienne que moderne*, d'Authville thus summed up most of the grievances made for the use of fire:

> This squadron that fired is broken, and being no longer able to approach the enemy without danger, it does not walk with confidence, it is much less occupied with the desire to win than ways to look for retreat. If, however, it reaches the enemy, what can this latter fear from an attack made at a moment when the men and horses of the attackers are still astonished by the noise, or their squadron is disunited, where the smoke that blinds them prevents them from parrying the blows [...]. In addition, of the 40 shots of mousquetons unleashed by a first rank, often there is not one which takes effect and we must not be surprised by this. Apart from the fact that the mousqueton is too heavy to be fired with one hand, it is usually only fired from a distance ... and the target on which it is fired is also on its side in a movement that does not allow for its easy adjustment. Moreover, when the cavalry fires, the time which it employs for this purpose also necessarily interrupts its action, and consequently diminishes its momentum.[21]

The ordinance of 1755, on the other hand, was entirely in line with the plans and instructions drawn up in previous years as regards the pace adopted in the charge. Galloping was outlawed, there was no question of going faster than the trot. Thus, *L'Instruction à l'usage de la cavalerie* of 1753 recommended to march toward the enemy 'in the best order and as slowly as possible, the charge must be done at a trot.'[22] There are only a few officers, like Melfort, to defend the idea that it is necessary to increase the pace of the charge and to start galloping 80 or 100 paces from the enemy. One of the main explanations of this conservatism is the weakness of the French cavalry in terms of individual and collective riding. French riders were not sufficiently trained to gallop without losing their cohesion. *Maréchal de Saxe*, reports Melfort, used to say, 'that it was impossible to maintain order in our cavalry once it was launched against the enemy.'[23]

These reflections allow us to better understand how to conceive the role of the shock, the last structuring principle of the charge. Recall that the shock was based on a complex balance, expressed in terms of the relationship between speed on the one hand and cohesion or mass, on the other hand. But at this time the doctrine in force still gave primacy to

---

21   Charles-Louis d'Authville des Amourettes, *Essai sur la cavalerie tant ancienne que moderne* (Paris: Jombert, 1756), p.307.

22   SHD, GR 1MR, 1734 f°55 ; 'Instruction militaire à l'usage de la cavalerie, rédigée sur l'ordre expresse du roi et conformément à son ordonnance de 1753 par les inspecteurs généraux de la cavalerie'.

23   Drummond de Melfort, *Traité*, p.434.

cohesion. Shock was a matter of order and union, of 'mass' and 'heaviness'. The riders were thus ranged in 'boot to boot' in two or three ranks (the officers forming a kind of additional rank in front of the riders), the ranks separated by a step between the rump of the front horse and the head of the one who followed him.[24] In this context there was absolutely no question of speed. It is the order, the cohesion, the thickness of a squadron, which must make the difference, explained de Vault: 'Finally, can we deny that the thickness of a body gives it strength... Two ranks will be firmer than one, three firmer than two, less subject to disorder, more difficult to break, and they will break the enemy more easily.'[25] The pre-eminence accorded to cohesion over the speed and inability of riders to support the gallop explains, as summarized by Desbrières and Sautai, that squadrons sought success 'far less by the impetuosity of their attacks than by order and cohesion pushed to the extreme.'[26]

On a larger scale, the French followed the tactical paradigms put in place since the Thirty Years War. Squadrons were usually grouped on the wings, in order to make the most of their mobility and speed. Their natural enemy was therefore the enemy cavalry, which faced them according to the pattern of the 'battle of wings'. They were most often arranged in two lines, with or without a reserve. The first line, more numerous than the second, whose squadrons kept between them sufficient distances so that the squadrons of the first could slip in among them if they were repulsed by the enemy.[27]

French Cavalry in Adversity

It was therefore without any major change in its organization and doctrine that the French cavalry began the Seven Years War. Two major challenges were not quite fully comprehended on the part French military planners: the Prussian cavalry and the fire of the Anglo-Hanoverian infantry associated with the growing power of the artillery. To analyse how it faced these challenges, and its partial failure to meet them, the chapter will focus on three significant battles, Rossbach (5 November 1757), Minden (1 August 1759) and Krefeld (23 June 1758).

The Shock of Rossbach

If there is a battle synonymous with total and humiliating defeat, it is the battle of Rossbach. If the loser, the Prince de Soubise, did not finish his military career there – for it must be remembered that he then won the battles of Sondershausen and Lutzelberg (1758) – he was the object of general ridicule in France. But we must go beyond representations to consider the tactical lessons of the battle. Had the French cavalry really fought? Was it simply jostled or rather outclassed by its Prussian opponent? The testimonies of officers who took part in the battle are an invaluable aid, they allow us to measure to what extent the success of the Prussian cavalry struck contemporaries.

---

24   Bonin, *Construire l'armée française*, p.243.
25   SHD, GR 1MR, 1731 f°8, 'Mémoire sur la cavalerie', par le général de Vault, 1750.
26   Desbrières and Sautai, *La cavalerie*, p.13.
27   Frédéric Chauviré, *Histoire de la cavalerie* (Paris: Perrin, 2013), pp.179-182.

A brief examination of the battle itself may be helpful. At the beginning of November 1757, Frederick II was in a particularly delicate situation. Defeated at Kolin (18 June 1757) by the Austrians, having lost the support of Hanover, he now had to face a Franco-Imperial army (commanded by Hildburghausen and Soubise) nearly three times more numerous than his own. Settled on the Janus Ridge, Frederick watched the movements of his opponents. The allied army took the initiative and approached in three columns to outflank the Prussian left.[28] Around noon, Prussian observers could distinguish the heads of the columns. At about 2:00 p.m. the intentions of the enemy were no longer in doubt.[29]

Frederick's reaction was as sudden as the march of the allies was slow. He immediately struck his camp, which the allies interpreted as a retreat. In reality, Frederick took advantage of the ground to put his infantry and the cavalry of the left wing behind the hill, out of sight of the enemy. The latter, too confident, continued their advance. It is therefore on units still in order of march that the cavalry of Seydlitz was thrown, supported by the artillery. It swooped *en muraille*, or closed up as a wall with no squadron intervals, 'at an incredible speed', on the French and Austrian squadrons of the right wing.[30] Some resisted, but the second Prussian line swept them in turn. The fugitives interfered with the squadrons of the left wing, who could not right the situation. The allied cavalry was offside. Meanwhile the Prussian infantry completed its deployment. Once it was over, the king made it immediately advance in echelon. Deprived of cavalry, the allied infantrymen were attacked simultaneously by the Prussian battalions and squadrons of Seydlitz, who reformed for a new charge. Escape then seemed the only way to avoid encirclement.[31] The battle lasted just two hours, and only six battalions from the Prussian left wing took part in the action.[32] Their cavalry, almost entirely grouped on the left wing, played a fundamental role in the victory.

The main point therefore lay in the surprise effect. The allied army was caught red-handed in the act of marching and could not deploy in to battle order. The responsibility of the French cavalry is of course involved in this affair. The French squadrons opened the march alongside the Austrians. Did they rise to this occasion?

The question is worth asking since the Battle of Rossbach is sometimes presented as the symbol of the decline and helplessness of the mounted troops of the King of France: the squadrons would have declined to stand against the Prussians.[33] However, testimonies like those of the Duc de Broglie or the Marquis de Castries undermine this idea. The two officers reported that the charges were 'vigorous' and that the squadrons of both sides were 'mixed for a considerable time.' Some squadrons even managed to win but then were repulsed by the second enemy line. According to them, the defeat was not due to the retreat of the French cavalry, but rather to the vivacity of the movements of the Prussian cavalry, to its superiority

---

28   As Delbrück remarks, the plan of the allied generals constitutes, in a way, a prefiguration of the movement that Frederick himself would later perform at Leuthen. Hans Delbrück, *History of the Art of War* (Lincoln and London: University of Nebraska Press, 1990), Vol.4, p.279.

29   Henry Lloyd, *Histoire des guerres d'Allemagne* (Paris: Economica, 2001), p.135.

30   Castries to Paulmy, Northausen, 9 November 1757, quoted in Desbrières and Sautai, La cavalerie, p.30.

31   Robert. B. Asprey, *Frédéric le Grand* (Paris: Hachette, 1989 for the French translation) p.434.

32   Prussian account of the battle, quoted by Lloyd, *Histoire des guerres d'Allemagne*, p.139.

33   Dominique Venner, *Les armes de combat individuelles* (Paris: J. Grancher, 1976), p.118.

'for the order and the way of manoeuvring.'[34] Desbrières also believes it necessary to recall that 'contrary to a common opinion and already prevalent in 1757, the two cavalry formations had really come into contact with each other, there was a shock and a melee, while some would believe that such a case is exceptional and usually one of them turns around before the meeting.'[35]

The losses suffered by French squadrons tend to confirm this view of the facts. The cavalry as a whole lost about 20 percent of its theoretical strength as killed, wounded and prisoners, but the figures rise to a third for the regiments of Raugrave and Saluces, and more than 40 percent for Descars and Fitz-James.[36]

If the fighting spirit of the French cavalry is not in question, we must look elsewhere for the reasons for this disaster. Would they not lie with, as Castries suggests, the tactical and manoeuvring superiority of the Prussians?

The offensive qualities of the King of Prussia's cavalry, a very effective combination of movement and shock, were, in fact, in large part responsible for the success of Rossbach. This is a truth which the French noticed at their expense. It seems that they had hitherto not taken the real measure of the Frederick's reforms nor of the superiority which they conferred on his cavalry. To read Caulaincourt and Castries, the awakening seems brutal. At this time, it was no longer a question of sticking to the usual lamentations on the numerical superiority of the enemy. The manoeuvring superiority of the Prussian cavalry had particularly marked these officers. 'We were hardly formed when all the Prussian cavalry arrived on us *en muraille*, with incredible speed', noted the astonished Castries, who also evoked 'the liveliness of the Prussian cavalry movements'.[37]

In the same way, the Prussians' desire to systematically achieve shock particularly marked the two officers. They understood that they should not expect these opponents to turn around at 20 paces, as was often the case before. 'It seems', writes Caulaincourt, 'that the custom of the enemy squadrons we are now dealing with is not to turn their backs when we approach at fifteen or twenty paces, as I have often heard that had happened in most of the cavalry fights, and it certainly will not be ours. Therefore, I do not believe that what happened in the previous wars should serve as a rule for the present moment.'[38]

The main strategic consequence of the battle was to save Frederick II's situation in the west, giving him the opportunity to turn against the Austrians in Leuthen. The French, meanwhile, despite the painful humiliation of Rossbach, continued to campaign in Germany, alternating between non-decisive victories and scathing defeats, as at Minden.

---

34   Letters from Castries and Caulaincourt to M. de Paulmy, quoted by Desbrières and Sautai, *La cavalerie*, pp.30-35.
35   Desbrières and Sautai, *La cavalerie*, p.35.
36   Rates calculated from loss figures identified by Desbrières and Sautai, *La cavalerie*, p.35.
37   Quoted by Desbrières and Sautai, *La cavalerie*, p.30.
38   Letters to M. de Paulmy, Desbrières and Sautai, *La cavalerie*, pp.35-36.

Firepower and 'The fatal day of Minden'[39]

After having taken Frankfort at the beginning of the year 1759, the French had repulsed the Anglo-German army of Ferdinand of Brunswick within Westphalia. *Maréchal* de Contades' manoeuvre to cut Brunswick's lines of communication led the latter to attack the French army at Minden on 1 August. Contades had a little more than 54,000 men against 42,000,[40] arranged in a convex circular arc between the Weser river and the village of Hahlen. Most of the French cavalry was at the centre of the deployment, in three lines (the Carabiniers and the *Gendarmerie* forming the third), facing the Anglo-Hanoverian battalions. When they moved towards the French centre, Contades engaged his cavalry to break their attack. The three lines each charged in turn. Despite the mass of troopers engaged, the assault was a bloody failure. The centre became open to the enemy, and the fierce counter-attacks (in which the cavalry still played a role) did not restore the situation. The Anglo-Hanoverian pressure becoming too strong, Contades then ordered the withdrawal by relying on his right. The strategic consequences of the Battle of Minden were quite limited, not least because the Anglo-Hanoverian cavalry did not pursue the vanquished, thus allowing them to preserve most of their army. The cavalry nonetheless paid a heavy price, elite units such as the regiment of *Carabiniers* and the *Gendarmerie* losing a little more than half of their strength.[41]

The Battle of Minden, less known perhaps than Rossbach, was also very instructive. It might even be argued that in the field of combat against infantry it was a comparable awakening moment to what Rossbach had been for cavalry combat. The experiences of Dettingen (1743) and Fontenoy (1745) do not seem to have caused any real awareness of the potential firepower of the infantry. Cavalry officers tended to be convinced of the intrinsic superiority of their weapon, relying in particular on the moral effect of the charge to impress and destabilize infantrymen. Fired inappropriately and without accuracy by frightened soldiers, musketry did not seem to them to be a really dangerous obstacle. The Battle of Minden offers the opportunity to confront this charge doctrine with the concrete realities of the battlefield.

As at Rossbach, the testimony of officers, the Chevalier de Ray and Mottin de la Balme in particular, provide valuable information on the action of the cavalry during the battle. First of all, there was the persistent gap between theoretical thinking and the reality on the ground. To begin, contrary to custom, Contades did not follow the tactical doctrine of the time, which required that the cavalry would be mostly deployed to the wings. He had placed his cavalry in the centre, in three lines, which explains why it had to charge Ferdinand's infantry. Then, this infantry did not follow the outcome of the literary simulations. It was not formed into square battalions, but deployed in line, probably without intervals between the battalions. Moreover, upsetting the certainties of certain authors, the soldiers did not seem at all 'intimidated by the appearance of horses'.[42] They did not let themselves in any case throw away their fire. Instead, the infantry, which fired at a very short distance (10 or

---

39   Augustin Mottin de la Balme, *Eléments de tactique pour la cavalerie* (Paris: Jombert et Ruault, 1776), p.107.

40   Jean-Claude Castex, *Dictionnaire des batailles terrestre franco-anglaises de la guerre de Sept Ans* (Québec: Presses de l'Université de Laval, 2006), p.380.

41   Castex, *Dictionnaire des batailles*, pp.386-387.

42   Authville des Amourettes, *Essai sur la cavalerie*, p.313.

15 paces), seems to have been effective enough to repel the first two lines of the cavalry, and to drop two-thirds of the riders of the third.[43]

One can then observe a relative diversity in the doctrines of charge. According to Ray, the second line is repulsed by the fire of the infantry without having 'fully charged' (that is to say at a gallop and until the contact with the enemy). We do not know if the cavalry employed their fire, but it is clear however that the pace of charge did not have to exceed the grand trot. Launched at a gallop, the squadrons could not have been content with a 'false charge'. It would have been impossible for them to stop the charge, turn around and come 'in order' to pass through the intervals of the third line. On the other hand, the squadrons of the *Gendarmerie*, a well-trained elite corps, charged at a gallop and with bladed weapons.

The clash between the Anglo-Hanoverian infantry and the French cavalry therefore turned into a rout for the second line. For the officers who were convinced of the superiority of the cavalry in the plain, this was an astonishing affair. Many years later, the participants were still wondering about the reasons for this defeat. For Mottin, who gave a detailed account of the action he took with the *Gendarmerie*, the failure was mainly due to the adoption of the charge *en muraille*:

> The fire of this infantry began in the centre of this phalanx, as we were no more than fifteen paces away. As the fire was progressive, starting from the centre to spread to the wings, the horses made formidable efforts to throw themselves from the right and the left and escape. The weight of this powerful compression becoming enormous, the men, controlled by their horses, rushed upon each other and piled up in such a large quantity that there remained at most only eight or ten per squadron, which were carried away in the blink of an eye very far from there ... If the squadrons had charged at half intervals, compression would have been infinitely less and there would have been much more speed.[44]

Ray's broader account does not mention this problem. According to him, the third line, made up of the *Gendarmerie* and *Carabinier*s, managed to break through the front line of the enemy infantry. 'It rushes', says the Chevalier, 'into the ranks of the enemy infantry, overthrows all that is against it and destroys the gunners behind the line.'[45] So, according to Ray, the fault is elsewhere, on the side of the general organization of the cavalry, which prevented the exploitation of success. 'But why did not this line of cavalry which had preceded us reform in the second line, behind us, to prevent, after the vigorous charge of our reserve corps, the enemy infantry to rise, to go back in line and win this battle by its destructive fire?'[46] The victorious squadrons, already well shaken, were then in a situation probably very similar to that of Dettingen. Ray's vision is therefore quite remote from Mottin's diagnosis. It is in any case reinforced by the point of view of the Comte de Lordat, major inspector of

---

43   Letters from the Comte de Lordat to *Maréchal* de Belle Isle, 11 August 1759, SHD, Ya 313.
44   Mottin de la Balme *Eléments de tactique*, pp.105-107.
45   Chevalier de Ray, *Reflexions et souvenirs* (Paris et Limoges: Lavauzelle, 1895), pp.127-128. Quotation from Frédéric Magnin, *Mottin de la Balme, cavalier des Deux Mondes et de la Liberté* (Paris: L'Harmattan, 2005), p.87.
46   Magnin, *Mottin de la Balme*, p.88.

the *Gendarmerie*, who wrote to the Secretary of State Belle-Isle that 'the eight squadrons [of the *Gendarmerie*] entered the enemy infantry, in spite of the deadly fire which threw two-thirds of them on the ground, and if, in this moment, we had had some help, we could have, with what we had left, fought very usefully.'[47]

Minden confirmed the lessons of Dettingen and Fontenoy. Infantry fire, if not insur-mountable, could be deadly when used effectively at close range. This is what Anglo-Hanoverian infantrymen knew how to do particularly well. It thus appears that, even if the battalions were not formed in squares, it was very costly for cavalry to charge an intact and determined infantry unit. If it wanted to prevail, it was essential that the coordination between the different lines of attack be flawless. Squadrons of the rear lines must be able to support those on the first line and exploit the mess they have created in the enemy infantry. On the other hand, it was no longer possible to simply advance at a trot or use the pistols before the impact. Speed must take precedence. As for preparedness or diversion attacks, they did not seem to be relevant in the case of battalions deployed in line.

The Carabiniers at Krefeld

The effectiveness of the infantry, at least when it was disciplined and trained, was therefore a reality that the cavalry could no longer neglect. But what about artillery? The Seven Years War marked a relative turning point in this field too. The power of artillery increased almost with each campaign. This development was particularly noticeable in the Eastern theatres. The Prussian and Austrian armies were accompanied by trains of 300 or 400 pieces, and Russian artillery became even more important.[48] Would not such an increase paralyze the cavalry? The charge of the *Carabiniers* at Krefeld (1758) is sometimes evoked to symbolize the impotence of the French cavalry in the face of artillery fire.

The Prince de Clermont, who commanded the French army, intended to block the advance of Ferdinand of Brunswick. He thus settled into a rather strong defensive position, the right resting on a marsh and the left on a canal. The cavalry was in the third line, behind the first two lines of infantry, and in reserve. Ferdinand tried a daring manoeuvre. He fixed the French right and centre by diversionary attacks while he began to turn their left, because he found the way to pass the channel. Clermont was completely surprised by this turning movement. The left was soon in a desperate situation. He then decided to charge with his cavalry to stop the enemy advance. The *Carabiniers* were especially relentless. They managed to cross a first line, but were then stopped by the enemy fire, in particular that of the artil-lery. The enemy's right wing was indeed furnished with a large artillery: eight heavy guns and three mortars in addition to regimental pieces.[49] The bulk of these pieces were in front of the *Carabiniers*, who thus suffered a violent grapeshot salvo added to the heavy musketry of three Hanoverian battalions. No doubt already put in disarray by their first success, they had to turn back and return through the enemy line. The other squadrons were not more successful. At least these charges helped to slow down Ferdinand's progress, allowing

---

47   SHD, Ya 313, Letter from Comte de Lordat to *Maréchal* de Belle-Isle, 11 August 1759.

48   Christopher Duffy, *The Military Experience in the Age of Reason* (Ware: Wordsworth Editions, 1998), p.231.

49   Richard Waddington, *La guerre de Sept Ans: histoire diplomatique et militaire* (Paris: Firmin-Didot, 1899-1914), Vol.2, p.102.

Clermont to prepare for withdrawal. The losses of the cavalry are estimated at 1,300 men.[50] This represents just over 10 percent of all mounted troops. However, the most engaged units experienced higher percentages. Thus, the carabineers had about 400 horsemen and officers out of action, which represents about a quarter of the theoretical strength.[51]

Thus, the three battles studied seem to strongly illustrate a form of impotence of the French cavalry. It seemed unable to meet the challenge of its Prussian counterpart, or to take the real measure of the firepower of the infantry and the artillery.

Facing the Crisis: Between Nuance and Awareness

The Seven Years War was a bitter experience for French arms. No doubt some generals had enough talent to innovate, like Broglie, who developed the system of divisions outlined by Maurice de Saxe.[52] However, the alternation of humiliating defeats and successes without result had the effect of plunging the country and the army 'in the most complete confusion'.[53] The cavalry was particularly decried. It was the cavalry, above all, that was blamed by a public opinion which no longer had confidence in its military institutions. The chapter will now discuss how the high command and the officers reacted to this humiliation. While some measures could only be implemented once peace returned, criticisms, analyses and proposals multiplied throughout the conflict and sometimes prompted some immediate adjustments. Before that, however, we will revise somewhat the impression of absolute decline that emerges from the three defeats mentioned above.

In general, the idea of a decadence of the French cavalry during the Seven Years War must be somewhat revised. The evocation of previous battles underscores the humiliation, yet, as we have seen, for some of them the responsibility of the cavalry can be nuanced. The choices and even the errors of command could mitigate these failures. For example, at Minden, where Contades deployed most of his squadrons against the infantry of the enemy centre, this departed from the traditional doctrine of use, which required that the cavalry be first employed against the enemy horse. Even more, perhaps, he ordered it against an intact, experienced infantry who were quite ready to receive it. This was again an overconfident departure from the ordinary doctrine. Indeed, at Fontenoy (1745), the charges only met some success because they were combined with the attack of the infantry and the fire of a small battery. Finally, one can point to the failure in the organization and the poor coordination of the charges, underlined by de Ray and the Comte de Lordat. At Krefeld, the fire of infantry and artillery cost the *Carabiniers* dearly. But it must be remembered, however, that this charge took place under particularly unfavourable conditions. The ground, first of all, was not the most adapted to the cavalry, and the disorganization caused by the French left having been surprised by the turning movement of Ferdinand of Brunswick must also eb taken into account. It may be added that the charge would have had a different outcome if the *Carabiniers* had been supported and the second line of cavalry had been engaged at the

50   Charles-Pierre Victor Pajol, *Les guerres sous Louis XV* (Paris: Firmin-Didot, 1885), Vol.4, p.248.
51   Waddington, *La guerre de Sept Ans*, p.111.
52   Jean-Pierre Bois, *Les guerres en Europe,1494-1792* (Paris: Belin, 1993), pp.254-255.
53   Emile G. Léonard, *L'armée et ses problèmes au XVIIIe siècle* (Paris: Plon,1958), p.220.

right moment.[54] In general, if the artillery posed an increasingly formidable threat, it did not yet hinder the cavalry to the point of preventing it from acting according to its traditional doctrine. Squadrons might suffer from cannon fire at the time of deployment, but it must be kept in mind that their primary objective was most often enemy cavalry. It was only then that they were turned against the infantry or artillery and then exposed to murderous salvos fired at close range.

On the other hand, the French cavalry also sometimes played a decisive role. This is the case for example in Lutzelberg (or Lutterberg) in 1758. In this little-known battle, the army of Soubise, about 40,000 strong, faced an Anglo-Hanoverian army of equal size (commanded by General von Oberg). Soubise gave a mission to Chevert's command (the right wing of the French battle array) to envelop the enemy's left, the rest of the army only having to commit once the manoeuvre was complete.[55] But Oberg had time to strengthen his left wing, so Chevert was faced with vigorous resistance and saw his troops pushed back. According to Mopinot de la Chapotte, Chevert's corps was then in great danger of being destroyed.[56]

Chevert decided to engage his 18 squadrons against the enemy infantry to restore the situation. The infantry salvo did not discourage them, they took the trot and then galloped and overthrew the opposing battalions. Once going through them, the French horsemen continued their advance in the plain. They successively repulsed the cavalry and the enemy dragoons, remaining 'continuously in the plain, manoeuvring at full gallop, tumbling all that gathered, and massacring all that was scattered.'[57] The Anglo-Hanoverian infantry tried to reform after the passage of the French squadrons, but Chevert intervened with his own battalions, thus preventing his horsemen from being trapped. The victory was then decided.

The role of the cavalry was essential in this battle. Chevert's squadrons engaged without restraint, executing 16 charges in succession. 'This is the most beautiful action the cavalry has ever done', says Mopinot de La Chapotte. His enthusiasm is not unfounded if we judge by the losses of the day: up to 30 or 50 percent of the force for some squadrons.[58] Lutterberg shows us that the cavalry could still take advantage of the infantry, provided it was properly supported and it charged appropriately. It should be noted that the regiments engaged were able to charge and manoeuvre at a gallop, which means that some units still had a good level of instruction. Nevertheless, the other battles analysed above were a shock to the French cavalry, particularly Rossbach. It was no longer possible to hide the structural weaknesses of the cavalry.

Beyond the feeling of humiliation, the officers were very readily aware of the previously underestimated or ignored deficiencies and backwardness of the French cavalry. The veil was torn away. A sense of rupture emerges quite clearly from their testimony, as if they wanted to point out that an era was ending, and that the cavalry charge could no longer be

---

54   Article 'cavalerie' by the Chevalier de Kéralio, *Encyclopédie méthodique, ou par ordre des matières, Art militaire* (Paris-Liège: Panckoucke- Plomteux, 1784), Vol.I, p.515.

55   Castex, *Dictionnaire*, p.328-331.

56   Lettre à Madame de***, du champ de bataille de Lutzelberg, 10 octobre 1758, quoted by Jean Lemoine, *Sous Louis le Bien Aimé, correspondance amoureuse et militaire d'un officier (Antoine-Rigobert Mopinot de La Chapotte) pendant la guerre de Sept-Ans (1757-1765)* (Paris: C. Lévy, 1905), pp.237-242.

57   Lemoine, *Sous Louis le Bien Aimé*, p.242.

58   Castex, *Dictionnaire*, p.332.

considered in the same way. Castries was fully aware that the defeat of Rossbach opened a new era, and that it forced the French cavalry into a radical questioning of its doctrine:

> In the time when the manoeuvre of the enemy demanded no accuracy in the manoeuvre of ours, everything passed because everything was in proportion, we beat, everything was finished, we did not go back to the causes, the effects were sufficient we did not ask for more. But nowadays it is different, the king's cavalry has as much advantage by the courage as than it has deficiencies of manoeuvre. Until we can perfect it, we should not increase this disadvantage by making a dangerous order of battle.[59]

In response to the defeats, criticisms and suggestions for adaptation multiplied even before the end of the conflict. They affected many fields, but we will analyse two here: the place of the officers in the squadron and the armament. It is indeed the disposal of the officers outside of the first rank that Castries refers to when he evokes 'a dangerous order of battle.' Most of the time, the captains, lieutenants and cornets were in front of their men and extended over the whole front of the squadron. The croup of their horses was placed between the shoulders of the two horses of the two horsemen who were behind them. The main reason is the representation one had of the officer and his role: that of model and example for the troopers. 'A rank of free and forward officers will bring courage to the most cowardly hearts.'[60] But at Rossbach, the confrontation with a skilfully manoeuvring Prussian cavalry, charging at a gallop and systematically seeking shock, proved deadly for them. In the Penthièvre Brigade, only one of the six squadron commanders came back from the fight. Caulaincourt and Castries both insisted on the need to no longer position the officers in front of the first rank, but to integrate them into it. This was of course to limit the losses, but also to better control the men to improve the manoeuvrability of the squadrons, one of the main weaknesses against the Prussians. Rossbach, explained the former, 'gave me an opportunity to make my opinion that it would be indispensable that the officers should be in the ranks and that the captains of the companies which close the squadron should be on both wings, also in the same ranks, in order to be able to make the right and the left march when the commander orders it.'[61] The Marquis de Paulmy, new Secretary of State for the war, seemed to agree with them in his reply to Castries' memoir:

> We admit that nothing is so bad as to put the officers outside of the ranks. The impossible has been done in the past to determine the minister to adopt a different system, and all the reasons outlined here and many others were presented vainly more than eight years ago because one listened to the cries of pain of a few captains who, incorrectly leading their troops, had their legs tight in the squadron.[62]

---

59   SHD, GR 1M 1725, f°16, 'Observations par M.de Castries', 1757 (essay written shortly after Rossbach).

60   SHD, GR 1M1734, f°98, 'Formation de l'escadron à la guerre comme à l'exercice proposé à M. le comte d'Argenson par le Sieur de Boussanelle, capitaine au régiment de cavalerie de Beauvillier', 1754.

61   Quoted by Desbrière and Sautai, *La cavalerie*, p.34.

62   SHD, GR 1M 1727, f°16, 'Observations par M. de Castries', 1757. Antoine de Paulmy d'Argenson was briefly secretary of state for war in 1757-1758, after the resignation of his uncle.

Rossbach's lessons undoubtedly outweighed the 'cries of pain' of some captains, and determined the ministry to change the use. The impact of this battle, and of the Seven Years War in general, was all the stronger as the Prussian cavalry had also evolved in this direction. Warnery testifies that, shortly before the war, the king himself recognized the necessity of placing the officers in the ranks.[63] This measure is very significant in the way Frederick II considered the role of the officers of his cavalry. To place the officers in front of the squadron led them inevitably to plunge them into the fray, which the king could not abide. Indeed, such an option reduced the officers to the level of simple trooper. But, according to Frederick, their function could not be reduced to that of a combatant. Their role was not to engage in the fight, but to ensure that the squadron was conducted it with rigor, to prevent escapes or deviations in the march.[64]

Armament is another example of a subject that officers immediately seized upon. During the war, officers and riders discovered the German arms with multiple branches and palmettes, with the most beautiful aesthetic effect. But they were especially aware of the inadequacies of their sabres in combat. The first of the observations made by the Marquis de Castries the day after Rossbach precisely concerns the sabre. He first underlined the insufficient length of the weapon, limited to 33 inches.[65] His testimony is from this very significant point of view: 'The Prussians reportedly told prisoners in praising the charges of the French cavalry that we were not armed, and indeed most of the wounds they received were very light, and our blades broke in large part. They are so short that in the shock we were cut down without being able to reach them.'[66] Castries therefore suggested lengthening them considerably (eight inches) and increasing their width in proportion. Besides the length, he regretted that the blades did not really have a point. The protection offered by the guard did not seem to be suitable either: 'the handle of our sabres does not cover the hand enough.'[67]

However, contrary to the question of the place of the officers, the marquis found himself opposed here by an outright refusal. The Minister rejected his three propositions:

> With regard to the length proposed to be carried at four feet one inch, it is believed to be extreme, those of the cavalry of the Empress Queen are not so long as ours and we are convinced that those of the King of Prussia do not approach the length of four feet one inch. It seems to me that all the sabres of the cavalry had points, and that the handle which covers the riders' hands is sufficient.[68]

The problem of the length of the swords, however, preoccupied the officers, who were not satisfied with the Minister's inertia. The following year, in 1758, a memoir of Du Ville, lieutenant-colonel at the Dampierre Regiment, raised the question again. The author was

63   Charles-Emmanuel de Wanery, *Remarques sur la cavalerie* (Paris: Anselin, 1828), p.28.
64   Brent Nosworthy, *The Anatomy of Victory, Battle Tactics 1689-1763* (New York: Hippocrene Books, 1990), p177.
65   Officers' swords were only 31 inches. Briquet, *Code militaire*, Vol.II, p.20.
66   SHD, 1MR 1725, f°16', Observations par M. de Castries', 1757.
67   SHD, 1MR 1725, f°16', Observations par M. de Castries', 1757.
68   SHD, 1MR 1725, f°16, 'Observations par M. de Castries', 1757. The minister responds directly on the brief.

extremely critical of it. 'Our sabres as they are have none of the measures, qualities, or dimensions necessary for this purpose, they are therefore useless and even harmful.'[69] His demonstration was simple: the length of a sword, including handle, was 39 inches, adding the maximum possible length of the arm one got about 79 inches. But since the distance separating two riders face to face was a little over 80 inches, the French rider was therefore in an obvious situation of inferiority. Du Ville proposed a sharp blade on both sides, 42 inches long, without including the handle that would have six inches. Another memoir of 1761 renewed this analysis and concluded in the same way: 'The sabres of our cavalry are much inferior in quality to those of our enemies, however we could use them as they are if the blades were longer. I would like to lengthen the sabres of the riders.'[70]

The French sabre criticism was also aimed at making the weapon more effective by favouring thrusts. The model that Castries called for would precisely be better to thrust, because 'pointing is the most advantageous way to fight … and by which one touches from further away.'[71] Du Ville, the following year, went further than Castries by offering a much more in-depth analysis. With a sword both strong and light, the rider could take advantage of the thrusts. This allowed him to be firmer on horseback, to recover easily if he missed his blow. He had only to bend his arm and then lengthen it; he did not waste time, was always on guard and in a state to easily change the destination of his point. On the contrary, 'to cut down with a sabre the rider is obliged to get up, throw himself on the front of his horse and to disturb his position on the saddle and the stirrups, to lower the left hand and less easily hold his horse, which causes great inconvenience.'[72] In addition, to be effective, the cutting edge of the blade must be perfectly perpendicular to the object it wants to hit. The cut must therefore be applied carefully, because 'in the event that the wrist bends right or left the sabre no longer opposes its cutting edge to the air column he wants to split, which air column, encountering a larger area, resists more and brings the sword back on its flat side.'[73]

However, it would be necessary to wait for the end of the war to see the sabre evolve in the direction wanted by the officers, under the reforms of Etienne-François, Duc de Choiseul (1719-1785). Secretary of State for the war since 1761, Choiseul was the main architect of the recovery of the years 1763–1770. The ordinance of 25 April 1767 provides for example a longer weapon, better protecting the hand through a third branch.[74]

In the field of instruction, the war clearly underlined the limits of the progress made between 1748 and 1756. It was no longer possible to be content with a profusion of initiatives without real coherence or uniformity. It was understood that it was not only necessary to raise the level of education but also to harmonize the principles, both in individual and in collective instruction. As for the former, this war electrified the consciences even more than the preceding conflict. The zeal for instruction redoubled after the Treaty of Versailles.

---

69   SHD, GR 1M 1732, f°23, 'Observation sur la cavalerie', du Ville, Lt-Colonel au Régiment de
       Dampierre, 1758.
70   SHD, GR 1M 1734, f°84, 'Mémoire sur la cavalerie', 1761, without an author name.
71   SHD, GR 1M 1725, f°16, 'Observations par M. de Castries', 1757.
72   SHD, GR 1M 1732, f°23, 'Observation sur la cavalerie', du Ville, Lt-Colonel au régiment de Dampierre,
       1758.
73   SHD, GR 1M 1732, f°23, 'Observation sur la cavalerie', du Ville, Lt-Colonel au régiment de Dampierre,
       1758.
74   Venner, *Les armes blanches*, p.119.

Five riding schools were created in 1764 to train managers.[75] Under the impetus of Choiseul, many regiments were equipped with riding schools to better instruct and exercise men and horses; almost all were equipped with them in 1770.[76]

The manoeuvring skill of the Prussian squadrons at Rossbach, as we have seen, struck the French officers singularly. It was therefore essential to deepen collective training as well. The ordinance of 1 June 1766 was the result of this realization. It marked an undeniable progress, the deployment in battle for example was now made by oblique lines, as among the Prussians. The frequency of the exercises was still limited, but the end of the farm-company, suppressed by Choiseul, could make it possible to increase their efficiency. Finally, we should note that the war made it possible to advance on the question of the school of the charge. There was indeed no real training for the charge in the French cavalry. The Duc de Choiseul introduced in the ordinance of 1766 a 'simulacrum of charge' which marks a significant progress compared to the previous ordinance.[77]

It can be seen that the officers, inspectors general, and the ministry redoubled their efforts to develop and standardize the instruction and the manoeuvres. However, we must not lose sight of the fact that these improvements were essentially aimed at one thing: to execute the charge in the best possible conditions. 'The charge', wrote the Marquis de Castries, 'is of all manoeuvres the principal, all those others to which the riders are trained are only accessories whose main object is to know how to execute that one.'[78] But the doctrine of charge had to evolve too. As in the field of instruction and manoeuvring, the Prussian model seemed to be the one which guided this transformation. Yet explicit references are quite rare, in normative texts as in theoretical writings. In a general way, the Prussian influence, though real, did not give rise to controversies as sharp as in the infantry. Perhaps the trauma was stronger in the cavalry? Perhaps this relative discretion can be explained in part precisely because a certain number of 'Prussian' reforms had already been long advocated by French officers. Still, the doctrine of the charge evolved in a sense objectively close to the Prussian criteria.

Once again, the ordinance of 1766 is quite representative of the change of mind which took place in the aftermath of the war. It explicitly mentions the charge, which is done with the sabre high and at a gallop:

> A squadron will successfully charge the enemy when it attacks the flank of the squadron that will be opposed to it, or that it will make up for it by the greatest speed … At the first command, the riders will collect their horses. At the second they will put the sword in their hands. At the third they will put their horses at a walk. At the fourth they will trot them. When, afterwards, the troop is no more than

---

75   Douai, Metz, Besançon, la Flèche and Cambrai. This decision followed, it is true, the creation of the school of the *chevau-legers de la Garde* in 1744 and that of the riding school of the Royal Military School in 1751.

76   Burnez, *Notes pour le cours de tactique appliqué à la cavalerie* (Saumur: bibliothèque de l'Ecole d'Application de l'Arme Blindée Cavalerie, 1888-1889), p.135.

77   *Ordonnance du roi pour régler l'exercice de la cavalerie du 1er juin 1766* (Beauvais: Desjardins, 1767), pp.164-166.

78   SHD, GR 1M 1732, f°56, 'Instruction pour M. le Chevalier d'Abense, maître de camp commandant le régiment du maître de camp général de la cavalerie', par le Marquis de Castries. 1770

a hundred paces from the enemy, the captain will say: high sabre, gallop. At this last command, the trumpets will sound the charge, and the cavalrymen carrying their sword high, will gallop their horses, observing to remain always tight and well aligned to arrive in order on the enemy; when they are within reach, they will rise up on their stirrups to charge them with their sabre. [79]

The exclusive use of the blade weapon should not be surprising. If Frederick II indeed advocated this point, it was also admitted by almost all French officers before the war. The use of fire was still not explicitly prohibited, but the ordinance now clearly recalls that the sword is 'the weapon of the cavalry.' Pistols and mousquetons have no place in the charge.

However, the real innovation lies rather in the adoption of the gallop. Though Langeais, de Saxe, and Melfort had long advocated it, it took Rossbach to convince the high command to evolve on this subject. This text finally drew the conclusions of the progress of the Prussian cavalry since 1741 and explicitly recommended the gallop 100 paces from the enemy. We are certainly not yet at the 500 meters at full speed of Frederick, but the morphology of the charge was well and truly revised. The harbinger of this turning point, the work of Melfort, which the 1755 ordinance had ignored, was this time, according to its author, the basis of the new regulation.[80] Thereafter all the theoretical works considered the gallop as the normal gait of the charge.

Finally, the ordinance marks a real change from the point of view of the charge against infantry. This was the first time that there was official concern about regulating this subject. Second, and above all, the principles on which this official doctrine is based were very different from those most often advocated before the war; Minden and Krefeld left their mark. To begin, the adopted tactical formation was now very clearly the column, even if the composition of said column remains unclear: 'When a cavalry corps is tasked with attacking … it will be placed on as many columns as its strength will permit.' Moreover, the preparatory attacks were improved. Finally, in the same way as for the charges against cavalry, the high command seemed to have admitted that speed must prevail over the use of the fire, so squadrons charged infantry at a gallop and with sword in hand.[81]

The confrontation with the Prussian model and with the firepower of the Anglo-Hanoverian infantry, added to the increasing weight of the artillery, thus plunged the French cavalry into a serious crisis. The structural deficiencies it suffered from, and which had previously been partially masked, associated with the circumstances and command errors, led to a succession of traumatic defeats. The arm did not collapse, as shown by the courage of the riders at Minden and Krefeld, or the example of its decisive part in the victory of Lutterberg. But the officers immediately became aware of the magnitude of the changes to be made, especially since some had advocated them for a long time. There followed, from the first defeats, an active phase of questioning, criticism, and proposals. All of them obviously could not be put into place before the end of the conflict, but the reform momentum was such that, just three years after the signing of the peace, an innovative ordinance upset the spirit and tactics of the battle cavalry. The crisis of the Seven Years War led to a profound

---

79   *Ordonnance du roi pour régler l'exercice de la cavalerie du 1er juin 1766*, pp.159-161.
80   Drummond de Melfort, *Traité*, p.2.
81   *Ordonnance du roi pour régler l'exercice de la cavalerie. Du 1er juin 1766*, p.162.

reform of the French cavalry, creating a space for debate and experimentation that continued in the following decades and created the heritage of the Revolutionary and Imperial cavalry.

Further Reading

Bois, Jean-Pierre, *Rossbach* (Paris: Economica, 2021).

Chauviré, Frédéric, *Histoire de la cavalerie* (Paris: Perrin, 2013).

Chauviré, Frédéric, *The New Knights. The Development of Cavalry in Western Europe, 1562-1700* (Warwick: Helion & Company, 2021).

Desbrières Edouard and Maurice Sautai, *La cavalerie de 1740 à 1789* (Paris: Berger-Levrault, 1906).

Duffy, Christopher, *Prussia's Glory. Rossbach and Leuthen, 1757* (London: Emperor Press, 2003).

Guinier, Arnaud, '"La malheureuse affaire du 5", Rossbach ou la France à l'épreuve de la tactique prussienne', in A. Boltanski and Y. Lagadec (eds), *La bataille, du fait d'armes au combat idéologique, XIe-XIXe siècle* (Rennes: Presses Universitaires de Rennes, 2015).

Kennett, Lee, *The French Army in the Seven Years War* (Durham: Duke University Press, 1967).

6

French Cavalry at Austerlitz: The Historical Narrative and Data

Frederick C. Schneid

I met Christopher Duffy in 1982, during my second year of High School when I wrote my first research paper on the Battle of Austerlitz. I had always loved reading military history, but had yet to delve into topics other than the Second World War or the American Civil War. Professor Duffy's book, *Austerlitz 1805*, was relatively new, published in 1977, and available in my local library. The book fascinated me and inspired a passion for the study of the Napoleonic Era that largely charted the course for my future as a military historian. Subsequently, I read his *Borodino and the War of 1812*, published five years prior to *Austerlitz*. Years later, I was equally thrilled to see Professor Duffy publish *Eagles Over the Alps: Suvorov in Italy and Switzerland 1799*. I am therefore quite pleased to have the opportunity to write a chapter in honour of Christopher Duffy's contribution to the field of military history.

Throughout his Napoleonic histories, Professor Duffy introduced the Russian dimension to students of the Napoleonic Wars. Indeed, Professor Duffy wrote in the introduction of both *Austerlitz* and *Borodino*, that his work on the television mini-series, *War and Peace*, had inspired him to explore the Russian perspective.[1] The significance of his contribution to the histories of these Napoleonic battles seems less clear in the twenty-first century, but one must fully appreciate the ability of a historian to engage with Russian sources, and visit both Austerlitz and Borodino, which were behind the 'Iron Curtain' in the midst of the Cold War. His perspectives were therefore fresh and important within the context of the historiography and the geopolitics of the twentieth century.

In this chapter I hope to honour Professor Duffy's examination of the Russian perception of the battles as juxtaposed to the French narrative. Earlier, Professor Duffy's work inspired other historians, such as Gunther E. Rothenberg, to explore the Austrian Army

---

1   See Introduction in Christopher Duffy, *Austerlitz 1805* (London: Seeley Service, 1977), p.ix, and Christopher Duffy, *Borodino and the War of 1812* (London: Seeley Service, 1972), p.12.

and their struggle against Napoleon.[2] All English-speaking historians who published books on Austerlitz and Borodino afterward, looked to Professor Duffy's histories as a starting point.[3]

As Professor Duffy introduced English-speaking readers to campaign histories that examined both Russian and French accounts, providing a new lens to view these climactic battles, it is fitting to provide an essay that also applies a new lens to historical inquiry. In the past 30 years the tectonic shift toward STEM (Science, Technology, Engineering and Mathematics) has become mantra in many academic circles, but the Humanities does not lend itself easily to the application of data. Quantitative analysis, however, can be quite useful in military history and has been applied when studying social and economic aspects of army composition and operations. Archival documents and records have yielded information, which when quantified provide patterns when placed within historical context, and may reveal new interpretations or greater depth to existing ones. In this chapter, data concerning casualties from the large cavalry actions at Austerlitz provides clear support for contemporary and subsequent narratives on the nature of cavalry combat. The findings conclude that cavalry engagements, while short and sharp, resulted in relatively light casualties in clashes of cavalry versus cavalry, or often against infantry. The heaviest casualties were incurred by artillery fire, when a regiment tried to overrun the guns, or were subject to artillery fire for even a few minutes.

The French staff system that emerged during the French Revolution and thereafter produced volumes of reports on the state of regiments, corps, and armies. Regulations demanded that generals provide an accurate accounting of their units in '*Situations*' every two weeks and this was reinforced with iron discipline. As early as the Italian campaign in 1796-1797, Napoleon had a general imprisoned for several days, for failing to submit his *Situation*. Thus, the historian of the French Revolutionary and Napoleonic Wars has ample and relatively accurate data to determine the strength, losses, attrition rates and general conditions of French forces during this era. These numbers tell a story that can be understood both in terms of analysing the data and the historical narrative.

The Battle of Austerlitz provides a valuable study in this regard, with particular attention to the fighting along the Brunn-Olmutz road. The fighting on the northern flank of the field involved the largest massed cavalry actions until the Battle of Eylau in February 1807. These clashes occurred in two distinct phases, the morning actions where the advance of *Maréchal* Jean Lannes' V Corps and *Maréchal* Joachim Murat's Reserve Cavalry were thrown onto the defensive by Russian cavalry from Prince Johann Lichtenstein and Prince Petr Bagration's columns. This first phase of the fighting began around 9:00 a.m. and concluded by 12:30 p.m. With the Russian stalling attacks repelled, Lannes and Murat began their offensive. The second phase began around 1:00 p.m. and ended three hours later. It was marked by the advance of the French V Corps and the Reserve Cavalry, having cleared enemy cavalry from their front, they pressed Bagration's forces, which withdrew to the east, all the time covering the allied right flank.

---

2   Gunther E. Rothenberg, *The Archduke Charles and the Austrian Army* (Bloomington: Indiana University Press, 1982).

3   Particularly, Robert Goetz, *1805: Austerlitz, Napoleon and the Destruction of the Third Coalition* (London: Pen & Sword, 2005).

At Austerlitz, Napoleon deployed the French Cavalry Reserve Corps under Murat to support Lannes's V Corps. Lannes' corps cavalry brigade, under *Général de Brigade* Anne-François Charles Treilhard, was combined with *Général de Brigade* Eduard-Jean Baptiste Milhaud's light brigade into an *ad hoc* division. Along with *Général de Division* François-Etienne Kellermann's light cavalry division, from *Maréchal* Jean Bernadotte's I Corps, the French massed some 7,400 mounted troops on this part of the field.[4] Opposite Lannes and Murat stood Prince Bagration's command of 13,700 men, which had the difficult task of keeping any French attacks in check, despite the numerical disparity. The Russian orders were, according to Duffy, 'as soon as Prince Bagration observes the advance of our left wing, he must attack on his own account and throw back the extreme left wing of the enemy....'.[5] Not terribly far from Bagration's position, Prince Lichtenstein's cavalry column, some 5,375 troopers, were positioned in the gap around Blaskowitz, between Bagration's position and the majority of the allied army on the Pratzen Heights. Lichtenstein was deployed to counter the masses of French cavalry surrounding Lannes's corps.[6] Yet, he had not received any orders for the morning, and 'realizing that he should have been much further to the right, he simply barged his way through the rest of the army'.[7] Bagration's cavalry, combined with Lichtenstein's late arrivals, would give the allies an overall numerical advantage in cavalry with approximately 10,000 horsemen.[8] The stage was now set.

The Problem of French Cavalry

The French cavalry fared the worst of all arms during the Revolution. An aristocratic branch by nature, emigration of nobles and resignation of officers gutted the ranks, so that the numbers of trained troopers was considerably reduced by the time the wars began. Although several of Napoleon's marshals originally hailed from the cavalry, such as Louis-Nicholas Davout, Michel Ney, and – of course – Joachim Murat, the difficulty of rebuilding an effective arm was the providing adequate mounts. Horses were in short supply. Demand for horses came from the artillery and logistical branches that needed teams to pull the caissons, wagons, and the guns. These horses, however, were not in the same category as those required for the cavalry. Cavalry horses needed to be bred and trained for combat. They had to be sensitized over an extended period to the sounds of battle, and the manoeuvres required on and off the field. The availability of such mounts was critically reduced during the Revolution when stud farms were abolished by decree in January 1790.

Stud farms were established in approximately 40 provinces of France, and owned directly by the monarchy, or French noble families. Their direct relationship with the *Ancien Regime*

---

4   The number of cavalry troopers varies slightly among historians, Duffy estimates 7,400 troopers and Robert Goetz estimates 7,500. Duffy's numbers do not include *Général de Brigade* Boyé's 3rd Dragoon Division, which began on the northern part of the field, but was deployed to support Bernadotte's corps and its attack on the Pratzen. Boyé's division was not part of the general cavalry action on the northern flank.
5   Duffy, *Austerlitz*, p.97; Duffy draws this quote from the Austrian archival documents.
6   Duffy, *Austerlitz*, p.96.
7   Duffy, *Austerlitz*, p.102.
8   Duffy, *Austerlitz*, p.194.

made them an easy target for Revolutionaries, without considering the practical military consequences. The immediate issue was the cost of state subsidies to these farms, and as France remained under severe economic duress, the abolition of state support and the law of 29 January 1790, virtually ended breeding farms for war horses.[9]

At the time of their suppression, the French stud farms produced almost 3,500 stallions. This number would have been insufficient to accommodate the exponential growth of Revolutionary armies, even if they had not been suppressed. As a comparison, consider that Russia possessed 250 stud farms by 1800, which provided ample horses for their regular cavalry – as would be seen at Austerlitz.[10] It became clear by the time of the Directory, that not only was some accommodation needed to increase the number of stallions available for military use, but that the lack of purposeful breeding programs had a profound effect on the quality of horses being bred.[11] The army acquired their mounts largely through requisitions and the services of horse traders and army suppliers. This was entirely inadequate, and the quality of horses were inferior. Although the 1790 decree was reversed in March 1795, and three national depots for military horses established, there remained a significant shortage through the campaign of 1805.[12] The dilemma of breeding high quality stallions was witnessed first-hand by Napoleon.

Napoleon had certainly been aware of the cavalry shortage during his first campaign in Italy. Yet, the terrain in the northern Italy does not lend itself to large masses of cavalry due to the numerous canals and vineyards that breakup the Padana plain formed between the Po River and the Alps. Once First Consul however, Bonaparte had to attend to the deficiencies of the national army. For the immediate needs, the Directory's depots had failed to provide, and Bonaparte returned to requisition for the 1800 campaign. Still, the quality of the horses provided were quite poor and Napoleon remarked that these depots had failed miserably, and their funds would be cut.[13] In part, requisitioning horses produced only those beasts that farmers could pawn off to fulfil the quota, and there was no quality control on those purchased by army suppliers. All of this served as the background to Napoleon's determined reorganization of the cavalry in 1803.

On 24 September 1803, Napoleon issued a decree that would reorganize the cavalry for the entirety of his reign. He established 80 regiments of cavalry, divided between light and heavy. The heavy regiments were further defined as two carabinier, 12 cuirassier and 30 dragoon regiments. The light cavalry divided among 26 chasseur à cheval and 10 hussar regiments. Each regiment was fixed at four combat squadrons with one depot squadron for training

---

9   René Musset, 'L'administratrion de haras et l'élevage du cheval en France au XVIIIe siècle (1715-1790)', *Revue d'histoire moderne et contemporaine*, 13, 1(1909), passim, and pp.55-57 for stud farm locations in 1789-1790. Eugène Gayot, *La France Chevaline* (Paris: Comptoir de Imprimeurs-Unis, 1848), Vol.I, pp.85-90, explores with greater detail the period from the suppression of stud farms into the Napoleonic era.

10   Dominic Lieven, *Russia Against Napoleon* (New York: Viking, 2009), pp.27-28.

11   Louis de Maledan, *Réflexions sur la Réorganistaion des Haras l'Amélioration des Chevaux et le Rétablissment de Manéges: d'Un Plan Organique* (Versailles: Imprimerie de Ph.-D. Pierres, 1803, and Paris: Chez Bossange, Masson et Besson, 1805), passim.

12   André Corvisier and Jean Delmas (eds), *Histoire militaire de la France: II, 1715 a 1871* (Paris: Presses Universitaires des France, 1997), pp.232-233. Seven depots were established by the new decree, but only three depots were operational.

13   Jean Morvan, *Le Soldat Impériale* (1800-1814) (Paris: Plon-Nourrit, 1904), Vol.I, p.234.

recruits.[14] Napoleon then attached one light cavalry division, or in some cases a brigade, to each corps, while the heavy cavalry was concentrated in a reserve corps under Murat.

In 1803, former cavalier Louis de Maleden published a lengthy plea for the reestablishment of stud farms, and the breeding of French horses. He provided a detailed explanation that was repeated in 1805, with the republication of his work. It is unclear if Maleden's book influenced Napoleon, and the campaign of 1805 would make clear that horse shortages had to be remedied for the imperial army.[15] Foremost among the reform, Napoleon raised a special tax for the purpose of purchasing mounts for the cavalry. Each regiment was accorded a budget, and responsible for purchasing their own horses, with the clear provision, 'do not buy any horse, and let them take one which will be in their strength in five or six years, and in the position of making several campaigns'.[16] This proviso enabled the French army to field better mounts in 1805, but the regiments were still short of horses for their full complement.[17] In the days prior to the march of the *Grande Armée* from the Channel coast to the Rhine, Napoleon wrote the Elector of Bavaria, his ally, and asked him to provide 2,000 horses, which would be paid for when the French arrived.[18] These shortages would continue to plague the army until 1806, when Prussia was defeated, and the French army captured thousands of Prussian mounts.

When Napoleon formed the *Grande Armée* at the end of August 1805, he drew the majority from the Channel Coast at the Boulogne camp and others. The dragoon divisions and light cavalry were part of the intended *Armée de Angleterre*, whereas the heavy cavalry was not intended to be transported across the Channel. The cuirassier regiments were spread across northern France in their respective barrack towns. Napoleon created two heavy cavalry divisions composed of the cuirassiers and carabiniers, which would subsequently concentrate on upper Rhine. Napoleon expected the cuirassiers to have four squadrons in the field and 500 per regiment, whereas the dragoons were projected to have three mounted squadrons per regiment.[19] Unlike the infantry at the Boulogne camp however, the cavalry regiments did not participate in mass manoeuvres at the divisional level. Certainly, the cuirassier regiments had not conducted large scale manoeuvres. Looking at the Wars of the Revolution, large cavalry actions were not commonplace, and therefore regimental tactics were of utmost concern. At Marengo in 1800, Kellermann ably conducted a delaying action with several regiments in the early hour of the battle and then a decisive charge during the counterattack in the afternoon.[20] These charges however, comprised no more than a brigade in strength.

---

14   Louis Picard, *La Cavalerie dans les guerres de la Révolution et de l'Empire* (Saumur: Librairie Militaire, 1895), pp.243-244.

15   Maledan, *Réorganistaion des Haras, passim*.

16   Morvan, *le Soldat Impériale*, p.235.

17   Charles d'Ollone, *Historique du 10e regiment de Dragons* (Paris: Berger-Levrault, 1893), p.277. The regimental history remarks that the harnessing and horses were of poor quality in 1805, and in short supply.

18   Napoleon Bonaparte, *Correspondance générale* (Paris: Fayard, 2008), Vol.V, n.10661, Napoleon to Maximilian Joseph IV, August 25, 1805, p.620.

19   Bonaparte, *Correspondance Générale*, Vol.V, n.10650, Napoleon to Berthier, 24 August 1805; the specific organization of these divisions, and these regiments were established in several letters between Napoleon and Berthier, from 24 to 26 August 1805, reprinted in full, P.C. Alombert and J. Colin, *La Campagne de 1805 en Allemagne* (Paris: Librairie Militaire, 1902), Vol.I, pp.247-258.

20   Charles Thoumas, *Les Grand Cavaliers du Premier Empire* (Paris: Berger-Levrault, 1890), pp.61-67.

In 1805, all of the cavalry divisions of the *Grande Armée* suffered from a shortage of horses. All regiments fielded only three squadrons at Austerlitz. In general, the report sent to Napoleon on the state of the Reserve Corps at the end of November 1805, indicated that while the divisions were strong if operating as a single body, but individually the regiments were significantly reduced from their intended strength. *Général de Division* Etienne-Marie Nansouty's 1st Heavy Division showed an exact number of horses equal to the troopers in the field squadrons.[21] If one spends time examining the archival *Situations* of Napoleon's armies over many campaigns, rarely – if ever – do numbers precisely correspond, either there are more horses than men, which was preferred, or the reverse. The *Situation* for 22 November then would indicate two possibilities, that Nansouty did everything possible to insure he maximized the number of mounted men, and there were no more horses to be had, or Nansouty's *Situation* is inaccurate. *Général de Division* Jean-Joseph Ange d'Hauptoul's *Situation* for the 2nd Division of Heavy Cavalry, only indicates an equal distribution for a single regiment, all others having more horses than men. All of this is intended to simply illustrate that the French heavy cavalry in the 10 days before Austerlitz, was still having difficulty maintaining sufficient mounts. Regimental strengths were, at best, 50 percent of their paper-strength by the time of Austerlitz.[22]

The low regimental strength of the cavalry by the time of the battle meant that they could not engage the Russians on equal terms. Russian light cavalry, the hussars, uhlans and chevauleger boasted 10 squadrons per regiment, usually operating in two five-squadron battalions. In comparison, Russian dragoon and cuirassier regiments fielded five squadrons. The Russian cavalry possessed well-bred mounts and were highly trained. A single Russian hussar regiment at full strength had the same number of men and horses as did an entire French cavalry division. This meant that any engagements had to be conducted with massed French cavalry attacks, and not individual regiments operating independently. The French cavalry generals understood this, and the actions throughout the day reflected it. All French cavalry charges were conducted en masse. In part, the severely reduced numbers of troopers permitted greater ability of the French to coordinate an entire division, as it had the effective strength of a single brigade.

The archival documentation on the strength of French cavalry regiments on the day of battle is imprecise. The *Situations* for the Reserve Cavalry Corps include the losses suffered by each regiment at Austerlitz, but the number of troopers present for each is not included in that record. The closest document is the *Situation* for 22 November, 10 days prior to the battle. Professor Duffy and other historians have used these figures and then deducted for detachments and attrition to estimate the number of cavalry engaged. On 22 November the *Grande Armée* was already in Moravia around Brunn. The Russians and remnants of the Austrian army were camped around Olmutz.[23] According to Duffy, Russian reports

21 Service Historique de la Défense (SHD) C2 472 'Corps d'armée sous le ordre à S.A.S. le Prince Murat, Situation sommaire du Corps d'armée au 1 Frimaire An 14 [22 November 1805]'.

22 SHD C2 472 'Corps d'armée sous le ordre à S.A.S. le Prince Murat'.

23 Duffy, *Austerlitz*, p.72.

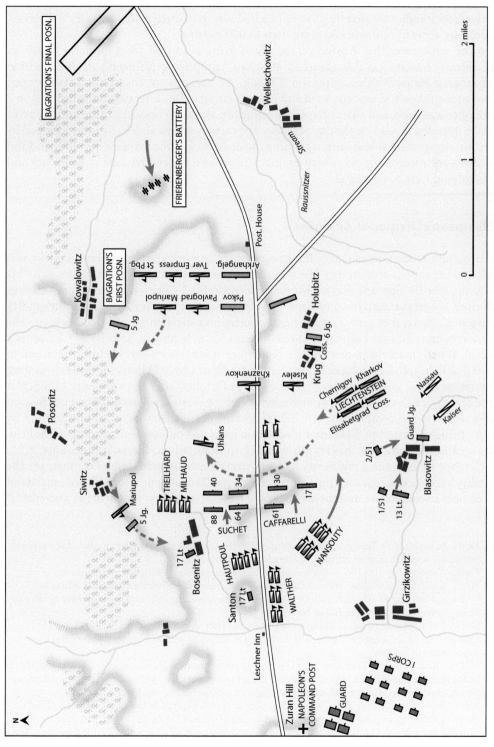

The northern flank at Austerlitz, 2 December 1805.

on the French indicated that they, 'were in a bad way, particularly their cavalry'.[24] Even so, Napoleon's army in Moravia had more than 10,000 cavalry.

In the week preceding Austerlitz, the allied army advanced from Olmutz. Napoleon had thrown Murat's cavalry ahead to Wischau, comprising Milhaud's *ad hoc* division and Frédéric Henri Walther's dragoon division. An engagement ensued on 27 November, between Bagration's advanced guard and Murat's cavalry. This foretaste of the fighting on 2 December was short and sharp. Napoleon withdrew the army toward Brunn, and the position he intended to hold on the day of battle. The cavalry action at Wischau was followed by a second engagement at Rausnitz, signalling the dance before the main event.[25] Milhaud and Walther's regiments suffered casualties, but Murat's two heavy divisions of Nansouty and d'Hauptpoul were not engaged.[26]

Kellermann's Division at Austerlitz

Kellermann's reputation as one of the finest cavalry commanders in the French army was sealed by his actions at Marengo. His performance at Austerlitz would further increase his standing. His division was part of *Maréchal* Bernadotte's I Corps, originally garrisoned in Hanover. Whereas the archival records on Murat's Reserve Cavalry corps are rather spotty between 22 November and 2 December, Kellermann's division is well documented. The division comprised four regiments, three of hussars, 2e, 4e and 5e, and the 5e Chasseurs à Cheval. When the division marched in September, it left 359 troopers behind, detached to depots, or in hospital. Among the four regimental depots, only 33 horses remained – a stark illustration of the horse shortage.[27] At the end of October, after the surrender of Mack at Ulm, and the battles that led to the encirclement of the Austrian army, Kellerman's division had a relatively full complement of 1,700 troopers, and sufficient horses, almost 1,900.[28] By the morning of Austerlitz, Kellermann's division had 1,258 officers and troopers on the field. This significant reduction in strength was due substantially to the lack of mounts. Since 26 October Kellermann's regiments had not participated in any serious combat, yet the inability to replace horses over the lengthy march meant that approximately one-quarter of the troopers were on foot, and therefore unable to serve with their regiments at Austerlitz.[29]

---

24   Duffy, *Austerlitz*, p.74. Goetz, *1805: Austerlitz*, p.100 fn., says that the Russian reconnaissance reports were quite accurate in their estimate of French cavalry strength.

25   Goetz, *Austerlitz*, pp.100-106 on the specific tactical engagements at Wischau and Rausnitz.

26   Goetz, *Austerlitz*, pp.99-104. Anon., *Histoire du 1er Régiment de Cuirassiers* (Angers: Lachèse et Dolbeau, 1889), pp.87-88, explains that the 11e Cuirassiers was the only regiment of heavy cavalry to be engaged at Rausnitz at the end of November, p.40.

27   SHD C2 474, 'État de Situation des troupes Employéer [sic]. dans l'Electorat de Hanovre, au 11 Frimaire An 14 [2 December 1805]'. The division was deployed with I Corps in Hanover, but the depots were in Holland.

28   SHD C2 474, 'Force des Troupes du 1er Corps de la Grand Armée', The document indicates that three of the four regiments had an exact number of horses to troopers. The 4e Hussards had 20 extra horses. The entire division however, had more than twice the number of horses, 239, for 96 officers.

29   SHD C2 474 'Situation des Troupes qui composant le Premier Corps de la Grande Armée à l'époque du 13 Frimaire an 14 (Deux jour après la Bataille d'Austerlitz) [4 December 1805]'. The document provides the strengths of the regiments, detached and those wounded or killed during the battle. The

The poor quality of the French horses began to show by the time the army had reached the Rhine at the end of September. *Maréchal* Ney, commanding VI Corps and a cavalryman until the Consulate, complained to Napoleon that his horses were very tired from the march, and they lacked a uniform breed causing an uneven performance. Injuries to horses were commonplace, and the inability to replace them in the field meant losing one horse and one horseman. The 1er Cuirassiers lost 65 horses to injuries before the regiment even reached the Rhine at the end of September.[30]

Table 1: Kellerman's Division at Austerlitz

	Present		
	Officers	Troopers	Total
5e Chasseurs à Cheval	20	297	317
2e Hussards	25	303	328
4e Hussards	21	259	280
5e Hussards	22	311	333
Total	**88**	**1,170**	**1,258**

	Killed		Wounded		
	Officers	Troopers	Officers	Troopers	Total
5e Chasseurs à Cheval	1	30	6	52	89
2e Hussards	0	8	3	30	41
4e Hussards	2	14	4	43	63
5e Hussards	2	6	2	13	23
Total	**5**	**58**	**15**	**138**	**216**

	Detached and No Horses	
	Officers	Troopers
5e Chasseurs à Cheval	8	306
2e Hussards	9	273
4e Hussards	14	369
5e Hussards	16	316
Total	**47**	**1,264**

Sources: SHD C2 474 'Situation des Troupes qui composant le Premier Corps de la Grande Armée à l'époque du 13 Frimaire an 14 (Deux jour après la Bataille d'Austerlitz) [4 December 1805]' and SHD C2 474 'État de Situation des troupes Employéer [sic]. dans l'Electorat de Hanovre, au 11 Frimaire An 14 [2 December 1805]'. Figures for detached and no horses do not include men at the depots. The number of men at the depots listed in 'troupes Employéer [sic]. dans l'Electorat', were deducted from the total number of detached troops listed in the master document cited first in this footnote.

---

number provided in the text is the troops present on 4 December, adding in the casualties listed for 2 December to provide the strength of the regiments on the day of the battle. Under 'Observations' it notes that the detached include those at depots and those without mounts. We know the number of troopers at depots from the previous documents cited and can therefore deduce that the remainder were dismounted.

30   Picard, *La Cavalerie dans les guerres*, Vol.I, p.260; Anon., *Histoire du 1er Cuirassiers*, p.84.

As the fog of Austerlitz gave way to the sun, Kellermann's cavalry was deployed to the front of *Général de Division* Marie-François Auguste Caffarelli's division of Lannes's V Corps. This forward position was a rather unorthodox, as Milhaud's light division was posted to the left of *Général de Division* Louis-Gabriel Suchet's regiments protecting the flank – a traditional deployment. As Bagration had screened the Brunn-Olmutz road with two regiments of Cossacks, Kellermann's cavalry was to clear the way for the infantry. The two brigades of Kellermann's division were deployed in columns by squadron. Over the course of the day the division would participate in four major actions, and conduct multiple charges against cavalry, infantry, and artillery. The casualties incurred, as reflected in Table 1, indicate a heavy engagement by the division, but do not clarify to what extent they suffered from cavalry combat or infantry and artillery fire. Here the data provides a picture of the end results of the day's events but does not provide the story of the events that led to the conclusion. Thus, a marriage of data and historical narrative are necessary to fully interpret the information.

As Kellerman began his advance sometime after 9:00 a.m., he noticed to his right the rapid movement of Russian uhlans closing in. It seems the earlier fog and the terrain obscured the movement of Liechtenstein's column, which was preceded by 10 squadrons of Grand Duke Constantine Uhlans. The first five squadrons charged Kellerman's division, catching them in flank. Rapidly ordering his troopers to change front, the uhlans set upon the French cavalry who, according to Duffy, 'scattered'.[31] Yet, the uhlans did not halt their charge, but, reinforced by the remaining five squadrons, passed through Kellermann's troopers and continued toward Caffarelli's infantry. The 2e Hussards and 5e Chasseurs à Cheval received the brunt of the Russian attack before withdrawing with the other brigade behind Caffarelli's division.[32] The uhlans recklessly continued their assault on the French infantry, only to receive musketry in response. The quality of Kellermann's troopers was clear when, after finding shelter behind the infantry, he quickly reordered his squadrons and launched a counterattack.

Kellermann maneuverer his regiments around the French infantry to the left and then descended upon the remaining uhlan squadrons in front of Caffarelli's division. As the uhlans withdrew east toward Bagration's position, Kellermann pursued, trying to clear the road for the French advance. Kellermann's pursuit was stopped by cavalry and artillery from Bagration's column along the road, while Uvarov's brigade of Liechtenstein's command met the French cavalry on the flank.[33] Kellermann's regiments conducted three separate charges during this fighting. After the initial counterattack, the 4e Hussards and the 5e Chasseurs à Cheval became embroiled in the swirling mêlée and could not break off. A second charge by the other regiments of their division extricated them. They reformed and participated in a third charge, in which the 5e Chasseurs à Cheval overran a Russian horse battery.[34] Table 1 clearly reflects the heavy casualties suffered by the 4e Hussards and 5e Chasseurs à

31   Duffy, *Austerlitz*, p.124.

32   Goetz, *Austerlitz*, pp.180-181; Picard, *La Cavalerie dans les guerres*, p.311.

33   Duffy, *Austerlitz*, pp.124-125, Picard, *La Cavalerie dans les guerres*, pp.312-313; Goetz, *Austerlitz*, pp.181-182; J. Colin, 'La Campagne de 1805 en Allemagne, VIe Partie Austerlitz', *Revue d'Histoire, Redigée à l'État-Major de l'Armée*, n.78 (June 1907), p.540.

34   Picard, *La Cavalerie dans les Guerres*, p.312.

Cheval, which were likely incurred during this phase of the cavalry action, by both sabres and artillery fire.

Dragoons and Cuirassiers enter the Fray

As the mass of Russian cavalry set upon Kellermann's division, Murat observed the danger and sent Walther's dragoons, supported by Nansouty's 1st Heavy Division, into the battle. Murat and his staff joined the combat, riding with the heavies.[35] Walther's dragoons drove straight down the road to support Kellermann's cavalry fighting Russian dragoons and hussars from Bagration's command. Nansouty's division attacked Fedor Uvarov's dragoons and hussars, which were engaged with Kellermann's other brigade toward the French front-right. During this combat Kellermann re-formed his brigades into two lines, led by the 5e Chasseurs à Cheval and 2e Hussards, with 4e and 5e Hussards in the second line. The French light cavalry conducted several charges and provided the strength necessary to break the deadlock in which Walther's dragoons were now entangled. The Russians cleared out from the road and withdrew in rapid order. The fighting had been quite fierce, with Walther suffering a wound.[36] The casualties reported after the battle were incurred largely during this action between 10:00 and 11:00 a.m.

Table 2: Walther's 2nd Dragoon Division

	Present		
	Officers	Troopers	Total
3e Dragons	24	153	177
6e Dragons	14	136	150
10e Dragons	24	183	207
11e Dragons	20	176	196
13e Dragons	23	246	269
22e Dragons	13	121	134
Total	**118**	**1,015**	**1,133**

	Killed		Wounded			
	Officers	Troopers	Officers	Troopers	Prisoners	Total
3e Dragons		5		11		16
6e Dragons		2		12		14
10e Dragons		1		16	22	39
11e Dragons			1	17		18
13e Dragons		2				2
22e Dragons	1	6	1	25		33
Total	**1**	**16**	**2**	**81**	**22**	**122**

---

35   Duffy, *Austerlitz*, 126; Colin, 'La Campagne de 1805', p.543.
36   Picard, *La Cavalerie dans les Guerres*, p.313; Walther's report on actions at Austerlitz reprinted in d'Ollone, *Historique du 10e Dragons*, pp.284-285.

Sources: C2 481 "Etat de Situation du 5 Corps de la Grande Armée aux ordres de Monsieur Le Maréchal Lannes à l'époque du 13 Frimaire an 14, avec le detail des pertes éprouvées a la Bataille d'Austerlitz, 4 December 1805'. The 13e Dragons is listed on the document, but was detached from Walther's division during the battle and did not participate in these actions.

Supporting Kellerman and Walther's divisions, Nansouty's three brigades of heavy cavalry advanced at a trot upon Uvarov's squadrons, which had swept around Kellermann's brigades, and threatened the flank and rear of Caffarelli's division. The infantry formed square and fired at the horsemen swirling around them. Nansouty's brigades attacked, sending the Russian hussars reeling. After reforming, Nansouty renewed his attack and pressed forward against Uvarov's dragoons. The Russian cavalry was supported by horse batteries that fired at the oncoming Carabinier brigade. The Russians, however, could not withstand the French horsemen and withdrew rapidly. Nansouty's heavies pursued, until they reached the Holubitz stream, beyond which Uvarov's fleeing regiments sought refuge. A Russian horse battery covered the position and offered fire as the French approached. The 3e Cuirassiers seem to have become bogged down on the banks of the stream and unable to withdraw as quickly as the other regiments. They suffered under Russian artillery fire.[37] Uvarov's two dragoon regiments were still in good shape, and upon Nansouty's withdrawal the Russian cavalry advanced across the stream and attacked again toward Caffarelli's infantry. Nansouty turned his regiments around, re-formed and charged once more, this time pressing home his attack and chasing Uvarov's remaining regiments southeast and out of the action for the remainder of the day.[38] Casualties for Nansouty's division were somewhat less than Walther's dragoons, yet the 3e Cuirassiers suffered substantially more casualties that the other regiments. Clearly, the inability to extricate the regiment under Russian artillery fire at the Holubitz stream explains these numbers.

Table 3: Nansouty's 1st Heavy Cavalry Division

	Officers		Troopers		
	Killed	Wounded	Killed	Wounded	Total
1er Carabiniers		3	2	21	26
2e Carabiniers		1		16	17
2e Cuirassiers		2	1	14	17
9e Cuirassiers		1		8	9
3e Cuirassiers	4	2	40	25	71
12e Cuirassiers		1	3		4
Total	**4**	**10**	**46**	**84**	**144**

Source: SHD C2 472 'Corps d'armée sous les ordres de S.A.S. Le Prince Murat, Situation sommaire du Corps d'armée au premier Frimaire an quatorze [22 November 1805]'.

---

37   Duffy, *Austerlitz*, p.126; Picard, *La Cavalerie dans les Guerres*, p.314; Goetz, *Austerlitz*, p.190; Colin, 'La Campagne de 1805', pp.543–544.
38   Goetz, *Austerlitz*, p.191, Picard, *La Cavalerie dans les Guerres*, p.315.

Milhaud's Division on the Left Flank

The intense cavalry actions swirling around Caffarelli's division on Lannes's right flank occupied much of Murat's attention. To the left flank however, stood Louis-Gabriel Suchet's infantry, supported by Milhaud's *ad hoc* division, which included his own and Treilhard's brigades. Bagration stalled Suchet's advance by dispatching the 10 squadrons of the Mariupol Hussars, Cossacks, and a battalion of jaeger to manoeuvre around Siwitz and then fall upon Suchet's left and rear at Bosenitz. The initial attack succeeded in throwing back French troops screening the flank, but Milhaud launched his division against the Russian hussars, and fighting ensued, giving time for Suchet to redeploy an infantry brigade.[39] The enormous size of Russian light cavalry regiments required the employment of massed French cavalry to counter, so that Milhaud's entire division was only equal in number to the Mariupol Hussars. Casualties for Milhaud's division below reflect this combat from 11:00 a.m. to noon, as well as the afternoon's actions.

Table 4: Milhaud's Division – Brigades of Milhaud and Treilhard

	Officers		Troopers			
	Wounded	Prisoner	Killed	Wounded	Prisoner	Total
9e Hussards (Treilhard)	4	2		18	17	41
10e Hussards (Treilhard)	2		1	6		9
22e Chasseurs à Cheval				4		4
16e Chasseurs à Cheval			4	51	32	87
Total	**6**	**2**	**5**	**79**	**49**	**141**

Source: C2 472 "Etat des pertes éprouvée par les Divisions composant le Corps d'Armée de S.A.S. le Prince Murat, à la Bataille du 11 frimaire an 14, à Austerlitz." Confirmed 21 Frimaire XIV or 12 December 1805. No officers were killed in this division during the battle so the column was removed.

Lannes and Murat Attack

By noon Liechtenstein's cavalry was dispersed on the French right, but Bagration's troops now switched to the defensive after their failed morning attacks. Lannes and Murat moved forward across the field and toward the Russian positions astride the Brunn-Olmutz road. Bagration did not remain passive but continued to throw his cavalry and jaeger into the battle to slow the French progress. The Pavlograd Hussars, Tver and St Petersburg Dragoons, some 18 squadrons, were sent into the attack. Sometime between noon and 12:30 p.m. Murat reordered his corps, sending Kellermann's division, Walther's dragoons, and now d'Hauptoul's 2nd Heavy Division to support Suchet's advance north of the highway. Milhaud and Treilhard advanced on their left. Altogether, this mass of French cavalry provided ample strength to overwhelm the Russian cavalry to their front. Nansouty's 1st

---

39   Duffy, *Austerlitz*, pp.127-128; Goetz, *Austerlitz*, p.192; Colin, 'La Campagne en Allemagne', p.543.

Heavy Division remained in place on the far right, keeping watch over Uvarov's squadrons on the far side of the Holubitz stream.[40]

The attack rolled over the field, as French cavalry threw the Russian hussars and dragoons back. The reinforcement of a regiment of Russian cuirassiers could not stop the French momentum. Russian infantry regiments facing Suchet's battalions stood firm, but were assailed, as three regiments of d'Hauptoul's cuirassiers crashed into their front and flank.[41] The Russian cavalry however, remained in good order, reformed and attacked, forcing d'Hauptoul's cavalry to withdraw behind Kellerman's and Walther's squadrons.[42] According to Duffy, the ebb and flow of cavalry charges and infantry attacks dotted the hours between 1:30 and 3:00 p.m.[43] The cavalry actions in this phase of the battle are rather confused to the extent of the specific timing within this period. During these 90 minutes Bagration's troops were forced back from the Siwitz-Krug line, bisected by the Brunn-Olmutz road, to a line running from Kowalowitz-Holubitz. All the sources agree that this fighting involved multiple charges by French and Russian cavalry, clashes with Russian jaeger and musketeers, and the frequent staccato of artillery fire.

With Milhaud's division on the French left, Nansouty covering the right, Kellermann and Walther pressing in the centre, d'Hauptoul carried the final cavalry charge in this part of the field. Russian infantry at the Post House along the road held firm, but their flank became vulnerable as Kellermann, and Walther pressed forward. D'Hauptoul threw his cuirassiers against the Russian flank and rear. While some of the infantry battalions broke, others formed square and stopped the cavalry with effective volleys. Suchet's infantry ultimately broke their position. The Russians managed to withdraw their remnants, covered by the Pavlograd Hussars.[44]

Table 5: d'Hautpoul's 2nd Heavy Cavalry Division

	Present			
	Officers	Troopers	Total	Horses
1er Cuirassiers	20	278	298	273
5e Cuirassiers	23	247	270	275
10e Cuirassiers	17	207	224	232
11e Cuirassiers	21	230	251	251
Total			**1,043**	**1,031**

---

40 Goetz, Austerltz, pp.236-237; Picard, *La Cavalerie dans les Guerres*, pp.316-317; Colin, 'La Campagne de 1805 en Allemagne, VIIe Partie Austerlitz', *Revue d'Histoire, Redigée à l'État-Major de l'Armée*, n. 80 (August 1907), pp.398-399.
41 Colin, 'La Campagne de 1805 en Allemagne', p.398.
42 Goetz, *Austerlitz*, p.238.
43 Duffy, *Austerlitz*, pp.129-130.
44 Duffy, *Austertitz*, p.130; Goetz, *Austerlitz*, p.241; Picard, *La Cavalerie dans les Guerres*, p.316; Colin, 'La Campagne de 1805 en Allemagne', pp.398-399; see Anon. *Histoire du 1e Cuirassiers*, pp.87-88, on Austerlitz, which also explains that the 11e Cuirassiers were the only regiment to be engaged at Rausnitz at the end of November, p.40.

	Officers		Troopers		
	Killed	Wounded	Killed	Wounded	Total
1er Cuirassiers	1	2	10	25	38
5e Cuirassiers	3	3	18	11	35
10e Cuirassiers		1	3	13	17
11e Cuirassiers		4	14	29	47
Total	**4**	**10**	**45**	**78**	**137**

Sources: C2 472 'Corps d'armée sous les ordres de S.A.S. Le Prince Murat, Situation sommaire du Corps d'armée au premier Frimaire an quatorze [22 November 1805]' and SHD C2 472 'Cav-rie Pertes à La Bataille du 11 Fre an 14' dated 24 Frimaire XIV or 15 December 1805. As with Nansouty's 1st Heavy Division, neither took part in the combats on 28 November at Wischau and Rausnitz and therefore the state of the regiments from 22 November are relatively close to what they fielded on 2 December.

Murat and Lannes continued their advance as the Russians withdrew shaken, but in good order. As the French cavalry flowed east over the field, Bagration brought up an Austrian heavy battery of 12-pounders and deployed them on the heights southeast of Kowalowitz. The sudden artillery fire halted French progress and gave Bagration time to gather what troops he could to establish a firm rear-guard. Lannes and Murat drew up their divisions as well, reordering them to prepare an assault on Bagration's last line. Desultory artillery fire was exchanged to occupy the time in between, but sometime after 4:00 p.m. the attack was prepared. French skirmishers began their advance ahead of the main body when the French marshals decided that having received no news of the events on the rest of the battlefield, they would withhold their forces. The attack was called off, effectively ending the fighting in this part of the field.[45]

Historical Narrative and Parsing Data

The combat around the Brunn-Olmutz highway witnessed all the elements of Napoleonic warfare at the tactical level. The coordination of infantry, cavalry and artillery were clearly superior on the French side. That is not a matter of opinion, but recognized by Professor Duffy, quoting *Général de Brigade* Auxonne Marie Thiard, who was on Napoleon's staff during the battle, and who observed the initial engagements between Kellermann's cavalry and the Russians:

> …you can appreciate just how much military training and experience can affect the course of an action. The troops of Caffarelli's division… opened up their intervals as coolly as if they had been on parade ground. Immediately, Kellermann's cavalry passed through they closed up again and opened fire.[46]

---

45   Duffy, *Austertitz*, pp.130-131; Goetz, *Austerlitz*, 270-271; Picard, *La Cavalerie dans les Guerres*, p.316; Colin, 'La Campagne de 1805 en Allemagne', pp.398-399.
46   Duffy, *Austerlitz*, p.124.

Russian General Alexi Yermolov, who fought at Austerlitz as an artillery officer, recalled the problem that plagued the Russians throughout the day, 'Our cavalry, like the rest of our army, acted largely without coordination, mostly on its own account, without any attempt at mutual support.'[47] Certainly, this seems the case in some of the actions, particularly the initial attack by the Constantine Uhlans upon Kellermann's and Caffarelli's divisions. Yet, throughout the day Cossacks and hussars operated quite well on the French left between Siwitz and Kowalowitz, frustrating Milhaud's movements. Similarly, the Russian cavalry's timely support of the Russian infantry attacked by d'Hauptoul's cuirassiers indicates at least local initiative and coordination.

French corps and divisional system permitted both local initiative on the part of the division commanders and those of the corps commanders. D'Hauptoul's two attacks on the flank of the Russian infantry during the afternoon reflects this initiative. Further, Murat's rapid deployment of Nansouty's and Walther's divisions to support Kellermann and Caffarelli in the morning, demonstrated the efficiency and speed of the French command structure. Bagration however, had the advantage in numbers of cavalry, and that permitted him to delay for half the day any serious movements by Lannes's V Corps along the Brunn-Olmutz road.

On tactics and the nature of cavalry versus cavalry combat, the narrative is quite clear. The data on unit strength and casualties on the day of battle provide hard evidence to the historical narrative. Cavalry regiments were generally ordered into several lines to provide depth to the assault. Hitting the enemy formation in waves was perceived as the best tactic. Beginning at a slow pace and then a trot, the charge would not be ordered until the final closing yards so as not to tire the horses.[48] Of course, situations varied, but the attack of Nansouty's division in the morning was conducted in this manner:

> Nansouty's division was disposed in two lines…. The Carabiniers pierced Liechtenstein's first line, and were repulsed on the second line, which came up in support. The 2e and 3e Cuirassiers came to the aid of the Carabiniers and hit the second line. The enemy squadrons were placed in complete disorder and their rout was complete.[49]

Cavalry combat served to disrupt enemy formations. Thousands of cavalry troopers smashing into each other and engaging in extended swordplay is the stuff of movies. More accurately, British artillery officer, Captain Alexander Cavalié Mercer described the scene when French cuirassiers and British light dragoons of the King's German Legion clashed at Waterloo:

> …we saw the charge perfectly. There was no check, no hesitation, on either side; both parties seemed to dash on in a most reckless manner, and we fully expected to have seen a horrid crash – no such thing! Each, if by mutual consent, opened their

47   Goetz, *Austerlitz*, pp.192.
48   John Elting, *Swords Around A Throne: Napoleon's Grande Armée* (New York: Free Press, 1988), pp.540-542.
49   Picard, *La Cavalerie dans les Guerres*, p.314.

files on coming near, and passed rapidly through each other, cutting and pointing, much in the same manner one might pass the fingers of the right hand through those of the left. We saw but few fall."[50]

Even the dashing French cavalry officer, Marcellin de Marbot, described in brief the charge he led against Saxon cavalry at Jena in 1806: 'I hastened to place myself at the head of our chasseurs, who were dashing on the Saxon squadrons. These latter resisted bravely, but after a short mêlée were compelled to retire with loss.'[51]

Nansouty's charge then seems quite typical of cavalry actions. According to *Général de Division* Augustin Belliard, aide-de-camp to Murat during the battle:

The prince [Murat] advanced Nansouty's cavalry division which, surged to the right of the infantry, marched on the enemy. The enemy, on his side, marched on them and there then occurred a superb and brilliant cavalry charge. During four or five minutes of sword fighting, pell-mell... the 2e Cuirassiers broke into the enemy and pushed them against their second line; we formed our cuirassier regiments, advanced; three successive charges... the enemy was overthrown.[52]

Similarly, the attack by the Constantine Uhlans on Kellermann's regiments swept through the division, scattering it and continuing on toward Caffarelli's infantry:

The charge against the right column of Kellermann's cavalry, at the front and flank, pushed into them. Part of the French cavalrymen withdrew in the interval of the [infantry] battalions; the rest escaped in disorder to the left and rallied behind the infantry.... The uhlans arrived within ten paces of our bayonets.[53]

In all of these accounts the charge serves to scatter or compel the enemy to withdraw, but is not a decisive event in terms of routing the enemy cavalry. It took many hours to clear Lichtenstein's cavalry from Lannes's right flank, and even then Nansouty's division remained posted to observe the remnants of the Russian regiments on the opposite side of the Holubitz stream.

What then can be said of the casualties incurred by multiple charges and mêlée in the cavalry versus cavalry engagements? Examining Tables 1 through 5 it seems that, with some exceptions, few regiments suffered significant casualties. Kellermann's division, which conducted at least seven charges throughout the day, and was in action for much of the battle suffered 17 percent casualties overall. Walther's dragoons and d'Hauptoul's

---

50   Mercer quoted in Rory Muir, *Tactics and the Experience of Battle in the Age of Napoleon* (New Haven: Yale University Press, 1998), p.124. The identification of the British cavalry as KGL light dragoons is in the original, Alexander Mercer, *Journal of the Waterloo Campaign* (Edinburgh: William Blackwood and Sons, 1870), Vol.I, p.306.

51   Marcellin de Marbot, *The Memoirs of Baron de Marbot* (London: Greenhill Books, 1988), Vol.I, p.231.

52   'Rapport du corps d'armée du Prince Murat pour la bataille du 11 frimaire an XIV (2 décembre 1805)' in Victor-Bernard Derrécagaix (ed.), *Le Lieutenant-Général Comte Belliard: Chef d'État-Major de Murat* (Paris: Chapelot, 1909), p.334.

53   Cited from Caffarelli's report in Colin, 'La Campagne en 1805', pp.538-539.

cuirassiers also, conducted multiple attacks throughout the day, covering the advance of Suchet's division. Their divisions both suffered 13 percent killed, wounded and prisoner. These casualty figures seem quite modest considering the action in which the cavalry was involved, its intensity and duration. This data therefore supports the anecdotal evidence that while violent, cavalry versus cavalry actions were not decisive, but served to clear the way for the infantry or guard the flanks for the main body.

This conclusion from the aggregate data provides only part of the picture. A more detailed study of the individual regimental casualties offers a better understanding of events. Within Kellermann's division the 5e Chasseurs à Cheval incurred 28 percent, and the 4e Hussards 23 percent casualties. The 3e Cuirassiers suffered 31 percent casualties in Nansouty's division. Among Milhaud's cavalry, the 16e Chasseurs à Cheval lost 43 percent of their troopers, to wounds and capture. The average casualties for all other regiments were significantly lower. The data then requires further examination of the historical record to understand this disparity. In three of the four regiments, the casualties were sustained by artillery fire. The 3e Cuirassiers became bogged down on the banks of the Holubitz stream under fire from the Russian horse battery covering Uvarov's retreat and was subsequently attacked by the Russian cavalry before it was able to withdraw.[54] The 5e Chasseurs à Cheval overran a section of Russian horse artillery during the fighting on the right of Lannes's corps.[55] The losses taken by the 16e Chasseurs à Cheval are evidently linked to the regiment having captured 13 Russian artillery pieces during the battle.[56] The 4e Hussars are an outlier as they did not attack Russian artillery. Yet, the regiment was attacked and surrounded by 800 Russian hussars and dragoons, shortly after the Constantine Uhlans were chased away. Kellermann managed to extricate the regiment with another massed charge, supported by Walther's dragoons, which forced Uvarov's squadrons back.[57]

Artillery fire appears to be the key factor in inflicting significant casualties upon the French cavalry. Infantry fire did not seem to have the same impact upon French or Russian squadrons. Kellerman's light cavalry, Walther's dragoons and d'Hauptoul's cuirassiers conducted several charges in the afternoon against Russian musketeers, some who fled, and others who formed square and offered fire. The volleys appear desultory, as casualties among those French divisions were minimal. The data from the Tables 1, 2 and 5 reflect this. In all cases, the various combats throughout the day did not render any of the regiments *hors de combat*.

The data from the contemporary archival documents provide ample quantitative proof to support the historical narrative. It does not challenge the well accepted anecdotal evidence, which appears in abundance through personal first-hand accounts, memoirs, and diaries. The military histories of this era have long described the nature of cavalry combat during the Napoleonic era, although emphasizing the impact of the tactical events, giving perhaps a more decisive role to these vivid encounters. A reader of the Napoleonic Wars is often drawn to the more dramatic events such as the massed cavalry attack at Eylau, the capture of the Great Redoubt by Saxon cavalry, the charge of the French heavy cavalry at Waterloo. This

---

54   Goetz, *Austerlitz*, p.190; Duffy, *Austerlitz*, p.126, telescopes the events.
55   Picard, *La Cavalerie dans les Guerres*, p.312.
56   *Historique succinct du 16e régiment de chasseurs* (Paris: H. Charles-Lavauzelle, 1889), p.40.
57   Picard, *La Cavalerie dans les Guerres*, p.312.

perhaps creates a different perspective of what cavalry combat was like, as opposed to the numerous charges and counter-charges and brief mêlées. Similarly, contemporary accounts emphasize the formations employed for charges were designed to hit the enemy in wave after wave, as opposed to one large crash.

Fighting in massed formation at Austerlitz clearly enabled the depleted French cavalry to meet their adversary on the battlefield, though Russian regiments possessed greater numbers and better horses. Well trained French horsemen kept their ranks, charged, rallied, and re-formed multiple times throughout the day. Their professionalism is noted in the historical record, and the data supports it as low casualty figures in most regiments meant that the troopers did not fall in swordplay and did not rout; and neither did their enemy. Further study of cavalry combat data during the Napoleonic Wars would add greater statistical support to the historical narrative. In the case of the large cavalry actions at Austerlitz, the use of data provides further depth to the analysis.

Further Reading

Alombert, P.C. and J. Colin, *La Campagne de 1805 en Allemagne* (Paris: Librairie Militaire, 1902).

Duffy, Christopher, *Austerlitz: 1805* (London, Seeley Service, 1977).

Elting, John, *Swords Around A Throne: Napoleon's Grande Armée* (New York: Free Press, 1988).

Goetz, Robert, *1805: Austerlitz, Napoleon and the Destruction of the Third Coalition* (London: Pen & Sword, 2005).

Rothenberg, Gunther, *The Art of Warfare in the Age of Napoleon* (Bloomington: Indiana University Press, 1976).

An Aspect of the Military Experience in the Age of Reason: The Evolution of the Combined-Arms Division in Old-Regime France[1]

Jonathan Abel

Christopher Duffy's *The Military Experience in the Age of Reason* remains one of the foundational texts on the period of the Military Revolution, illuminating how armies adapted its mores in search of victory. In it, he demonstrates how the eighteenth century was a time of great ferment in the French army, which reflected the social and political changes wrought by the Enlightenment and many other contemporary movements. These changes brought about consternation and a push for reform in the armies of the period. Duffy specifically notes a 'military renaissance' in mid-century France as it sought to respond to the challenges presented by all of the changes of the period.[2] Absolutist tendencies encouraged the development of army-wide doctrine and methods to better control the institution and its battlefield performance. Enlightenment ideals sparked a search for a perfect, geometric system of French tactics. Public opinion and proto-nationalist sentiment rankled at the loss of French hegemony and the rise of Prussia as the new military paradigm. The financial crisis provided urgency for reforms, particularly in the realm of cost-cutting. Finally, the defeat of France at the hands of Prussia in the Seven Years War focused these efforts into a concerted effort to bring change, often by adopting Prussian methods.

These various elements all combined to produce a reform spirit in the French army of the late Old Regime. However, reformers rarely agreed with each other on even basic principles of change. This gave rise to rival schools and vicious conflicts within the Ministry of War and the French army in general, further complicating the already complex process of institutional change they wished to affect.

---

1   Portions of this chapter were delivered as 'In Search of the Combined-Arms Division in Old-Regime France' at the Consortium on the Revolutionary Era, Atlanta GA, 2019. The author wishes to thank Rosemary Abel, Alexander S. Burns, and Bill Nance for their assistance.
2   Christopher Duffy, *The Military Experience in the Age of Reason* (New York: Atheneum, 1988), pp.5-21.

The development of the combined-arms division illustrates the process of reform and Duffy's 'military renaissance' in late Old-Regime France. The modern, operational-level warfare practiced by Napoleon and his successors required the development of echelons above regiment, like the division, because of the articulation of movement and manoeuvre they provide an army. This process was neither easy nor quick, requiring decades of proposed changes and testing, resulting in a slow and uneven evolution. As a result, the French army of the period appears to be a pre-modern organization, deploying on a single line of operation as a unitary army and lacking the echelons and doctrine for large-scale articulated warfare. To an extent, this is true: until the very end of the period, the largest organizational unit was the regiment and the largest tactical units were the infantry battalion and cavalry squadron. Simply put, the combined-arms division did not appear on an Old-Regime battlefield because it could not; the conditions simply did not exist for its creation. However, most of the ingredients necessary for creating combined-arms divisions did originate during the Old Regime period. Historiography often portrays this as a largely monocausal process, as succinctly summarized by the *Wikipedia* article 'Division (military)': 'In the west, the first general to think of organizing an army into smaller combined-arms units was Maurice de Saxe...Victor-François, [duc de] Broglie, put the ideas into practice.'[3] Others credit the ideas of Pierre-Joseph Bourcet or Jacques-Antoine-Hippolyte, comte de Guibert, particularly as inspired by Saxe.[4] These arguments, while simplistic, contain elements of truth, but only when combined: in reality, the development of the combined-arms division was a process that required many changes, especially at the tactical and organizational levels, to which many people contributed across the decades of the eighteenth century. Its development reveals the influences of the major movements of the period, the difficulties of institutional change, and the limitations of individuals to effect sweeping reform during the Age of Reason.

The notion of permanent echelons above regiment appeared in the early part of the eighteenth century, as reformers and commanders sought better methods of manoeuvring armies that remained stubbornly unitary and thus unwieldy. These men produced a wide variety of ideas and systems in an uneven process of fits and starts and false paths. The climate of the Old Regime was thus one of rapid and far-reaching change that encouraged officers to be both innovative and educated, in theory as well as the practice of large-scale manoeuvres and combat operations. This chapter will outline how the eighteenth-century French army,

---

3   'Division (military)', *Wikipedia*, last modified 6 August 2019, <https://en.wikipedia.org/wiki/Division_(military)>.

4   This argument originates from the analysis of contemporary writers and finds echoes in nearly every subsequent work on the period, most notably Jean Colin, *L'infanterie au XVIIIe siècle: la tactique* (Paris: Berger-Levrault, 1907), pp.31-58. Typical of the genre is Steven T. Ross, 'The Development of the Combat Division in Eighteenth-Century French Armies', *French Historical Studies* 4, no. 1 (1965): pp.84-94, which is more than a half-century old and devotes two pages to the period before 1789; nevertheless, Ross's conclusion is largely correct, and this chapter adopts it, with very different argumentation. See also Brent Nosworthy, *The Anatomy of Victory: Battle Tactics 1689-1763* (New York: Hippocrene Books, 1990), pp.145-154; Robert Quimby, *The Background of Napoleonic Warfare: The Theory of Military Tactics in Eighteenth-Century France* (New York: Columbia University Press, 1957), pp.49-50; and Steven T. Ross, *From Flintlock to Rifle: Infantry Tactics, 1740-1866* (New York: Frank Cass, 1996), pp.32-34.

although it could not produce combined-arms divisions, witnessed an incredible period of experimentation and testing of military theory, sowing the seeds for the division system that would emerge in the period after via institutional memory and best-practice examples.

The genesis of the division system began in the early eighteenth century, especially as authors grappled with analysing the greatly enlarged field armies and operations of the wars of Louis XIV.[5] In the early eighteenth century, commanders viewed armies as being organized into march order, consisting of a vanguard, main body, and rearguard on a single line of operation; and battle order, consisting of infantry's deploying on two lines with cavalry on the wings. Infantry and cavalry each formed their own establishment within the army akin to a modern service branch and remained largely separate, even on a battlefield. Artillery existed as an 'accessory' to these arms, generally divided between a central park and/or battery and parceled out to infantry or cavalry units. Contemporaries did not consider artillery to be an arm proper, as it could not fight on its own, only in conjunction with cavalry or infantry. During the century, a third arm emerged: the light arm. Light forces were generally a hybrid of infantry and cavalry, riding smaller horses to scout and harass enemy forces and dismounting to skirmish. Contemporary armies employed a bewildering array of these formations, usually referred to by a variety of names like hussars or *carabiniers*. Light forces were distinguished from line forces, and little crossover existed between the two and their duties. Light forces fought enemy light troops before and after battles, and on campaign, while line forces, infantry and cavalry, fought battles against enemy line forces. Dragoons occupied an uneasy interstitial space between cavalry and light, not yet acting according to the modern definition as dismounted infantry but rather as a force lighter than cavalry but heavier than light cavalry. Therefore, to refer to a 'combined-arms' formation in the eighteenth century would make little sense to a contemporary.[6]

Echelons higher than the regiment did exist, but normally as ad hoc formations, usually implemented only for the length of a single campaign and for operations other than the main effort. They were referred to by a variety of terms, including detachment, corps, brigade, and division.[7] These formations were large and unwieldy to manoeuvre, especially the transi-

5   See Colin Jones, 'The Military Revolution and the Professionalization of the French Army under the Ancien Régime', and John Lynn, 'The *trace italienne* and the Growth of Armies: The French Case' and 'Recalculating French Army Growth During the Grand Siècle, 1610-1715', in Clifford J. Rogers (ed.), *The Military Revolution Debate: Readings on the Military Transformation of Early Modern Europe* (Boulder: Westview Press, 1995), pp.149-168, 169-200, and 117-148. See also André Corvisier, *Armies and Societies in Europe, 1494-1789* (Bloomington: Indiana University Press, 1979).

6   See Jacques-Antoine-Hippolyte, comte de Guibert, *Essai général de tactique* in *Œuvres militaires* (Paris: Magimel, 1803), especially Vol.1, pp.445-447; Paul-Gédéon Joly de Maizeroy, *Cours de tactique théorique, pratique, et historique: qui applique les exemples aux préceptes, développe les maximes des plus habiles généraux, et rapporte les faits les plus intéressants et les plus utiles; avec les descriptions de plusieurs batailles anciennes* (Paris: Jombert, 1766), Vol.2, pp.70-71; and Jean-Victor Traverse, *Etude militaire pour servir d'introduction à l'instruction méthodique de l'art de la guerre* (Basle: Thourneisen, 1755), Vol.1, pp.40-41.

7   For example, Guibert, *Essai général de tactique*, 1, p.172; Guillaume le Blond, *Eléments de tactique, ouvrage dans lequel on traite de l'arrangement et de la formation des troupes; des évolutions de l'infanterie et de la cavalerie; des principaux ordres de bataille; de la marche des armées et de la castramétation, ou de la manière de tracer ou marquer les camps par règles et par principes* (Paris: Jombert, 1758), pp.239-240; and *Traité de l'attaque des places* (Paris: Jombert, 1762), pp.18-23;

tion from march to battle order, and grew more so as armies ballooned in size. Prior to the 1770s, armies maintained separate regulations for march formations and battle deployments, referred to as 'orders' in contemporary parlance. This was a direct result of the lack of uniform standards across the army, which would have allowed the union of march and battle orders. As might be imagined, the separation of the two actions added further layers of complication to both the use of armies and reform, as many later reformers would note.

A significant portion of staff work consisted of attempts to reduce the friction of the transition from one order to the other, but despite the best efforts of staff officers, deployment tended to take several hours. The chief reason for this lay in the evolution of the French doctrinal system. Colonels, who owned their regiments, maintained control over their organization, tactics, formations, and drill. They often spent little time with their units, delegating training and maintenance to junior officers. Only when the campaign began did various regiments assemble into larger armies, often with significant friction. Deployment might place two regiments with different march steps adjacent to each other. One officer's commands might differ significantly from another's, as might their methods of drill, even within the same regiment. The lack of uniformity meant that armies had to use the simplest methods of march, deployment, and manoeuvre, resulting in unwieldy formations that often took hours to form and move. To exacerbate this chaos, any suggestion of instituting army-wide methods brought immediate backlash from the nobility, which viewed such methods as tyrannical abrogations of tradition and noble privilege.[8]

Mid-century military writers dedicated much of their work to addressing these issues. Many realized that echelons above regiment could provide a solution and thus laboured to define and elaborate them, but this realization occurred only slowly and unevenly. The great late-seventeenth-century theoretician and general Antoine de Pas de Feuquières, arguably the founder of modern French military theory, does not discuss higher echelons, and he envisioned armies as being entirely traditional and unitary.[9] A military entry for 'division' first appears in the *Académie française*'s dictionary in 1718, but as 'a certain number of vessels of a navy ordinarily commanded by a general officer.'[10] However, the following year, Henri-François, comte de Bombelles, describes a situation when 'it sometimes happens that one or several brigades are detached from the command of a general officer for the purpose of making a military expedition…', although he does not explicitly name this detachment

---

Traverse, *Etude militaire pour servir d'introduction à l'instruction méthodique de l'art de la guerre*, Vol.1, pp.146-183; and Charles-Mathieu, marquis de Valfons, *Souvenirs* (Paris: Dentu, 1860), pp.209, 274, and 309-312.

8   See Reed Browning, *The War of the Austrian Succession* (New York: St. Martin's Griffin, 1995), pp.3-12; Colin, *L'infanterie au XVIIIe siècle*, pp.25-37; Nosworthy, *The Anatomy of Victory*, pp.67-72; Ross, *From Flintlock to Rifle*, pp.30-31; and Hew Strachan, *European Armies and the Conduct of War* (Boston: George Allen & Unwin, 1983), pp.10-19.

9   See Antoine de Pas de Feuquières, *Lettres inédites* (Paris: Leleux, 1845-1846), and *Mémoires contenant ses maximes sur la guerre et l'application des exemples aux maximes* (London, Dunoyer, 1736), especially Vol.1, p.142, Vol.2, pp.169, 182-183, and 360, and Vol.3, pp.9-10.

10 'Division', *Dictionnaire de l'Académie Française,* 2nd ed. (Paris: Académie Française, 1718), Vol.1, p.492. Interestingly, François Halma, *Le grand dictionnaire français et flamand* (Utrecht: 1719-1729), a near contemporary, contains entries for both 'Brigade' and 'Division'.

as a division.[11] Bombelles' definition reflects both the theory and practice of the first half of the eighteenth century – commanders in the Spanish, Polish, and Austrian Succession Wars often detached units for expeditions or to operate against an enemy flank, particularly in rough terrain, and continued past practice of referring to these by a variety of names.[12]

By mid-century, study of the military art and science reached a fever pitch in France as theorists and practitioners alike grappled with new tactics, proposed new echelons, and the position of both in the movement of armies. The Austrian Succession War created a mania for light troops, especially in imitation of various Russian Cossack units and the Austrian *Grenzer*. In addition, the rise of Prussia provided a major factor in reform, with many in France arguing that it had the new paradigm army. They contended that the Prussian military constitution rested on a foundation of discipline, training, educated and resolute officers, and elements of Prusso-German culture that lent themselves to military efficacy. Military writers in France thus looked to Prussia for new ideas, some exclusively so, while others rejected Prussian methods in favour of perfecting their own constitution based on best practice and precedent, as well as French cultural norms, while still others sought to weave the two systems together into a coherent whole.[13]

The dominant reform school of the mid-century period arose around Jean-Charles, Chevalier Folard, arguably the first important military theorist of the eighteenth century in France. He began publishing reform proposals in the 1720s and continued until his death in 1752. He attracted numerous followers, including Jacques-François de Chastenet, marquis de Puységur, and François-Jean de Graindorge d'Orgeville, baron de Mesnil-Durand. They argued for emphasizing French élan in shock attacks over Prussian-style disciplined fire. Folard went as far as to advocate for the return of the pike and deep columnar formations called *plésions*, which Puységur and Mesnil-Durand modified for their own systems. To overcome the difficulties presented by the lack of uniformity in training and drill, Folard and his followers proposed increasingly complicated geometrical structures, requiring their units to manoeuvre precisely on pre-determined lines to create perfect forms of march, manoeuvre, and deployment.[14] The result was a slow, processional deployment and combat

---

11   Henri-François, comte de Bombelles, *Mémoires sur le service journalier de l'infanterie* (Paris: Muguet, 1719), Vol.2, p.116. See also P.P.A Bardet de Villeneuve, *Cours de la science militaire, à l'usage de l'infanterie, de la cavalerie, de l'artillerie, du génie, et de la Marine* (La Haye: Jean van Duren, 1740), Vol.2, pp.18-19.

12   The best operational accounts of the listed wars are M.S. Anderson, *The War of the Austrian Succession, 1740-1748* (New York: Longman, 1995); Browning, *The War of the Austrian Succession*; John Lynn, *The Wars of Louis XIV 1667-1714* (New York: Longman, 1999), pp.266-376; and John L. Sutton, *The King's Honor and the King's Cardinal: The War of the Polish Succession* (Lexington, KY: University of Kentucky Press, 1980). Feuquières, *Mémoires*, Vol.2., provides a contemporary practitioner's account of the Spanish Succession. Louis-Hippolyte Bacquet, *L'infanterie au XVIIIe siècle. L'organisation* (Paris: Berger-Levrault, 1907), pp.51-52, posits that brigades appeared in the Thirty Years War and divisions in the wars of Louis XIV, without supporting evidence.

13   Colin, *L'infanterie au XVIIIe siècle*, and Quimby, *The Background of Napoleonic Warfare*, trace these developments in great detail. See also Duffy, *The Military Experience in the Age of Reason*, pp.268-279; and Gunther Rothenberg, *The Military Border in Croatia, 1740-1881: A Study of an Imperial Institution* (Chicago: University of Chicago Press, 1988).

14   Jean-Charles, Chevalier Folard, *Abrégé des commentaires de M. de Folard sur l'histoire de Polybe*, 3 Vols. (Paris: Gandouin, et al., 1754), and *Nouvelles découvertes sur la guerre* (Paris: Josse and

method that won many supporters but also angered others. The members of this school have become known as the 'makers of systems', and best illustrate the Enlightenment mania for definition and control in the French army of the period.[15]

In the late 1710s, Folard won over a young Saxon who would become the most important French commander of the eighteenth century. Maurice de Saxe was the illegitimate son of Augustus II, Elector of Saxony and King of the Polish-Lithuanian Commonwealth. He served in the Saxon army before making his way to France after 1715, where he would remain in the service of Louis XV for the remainder of his life. He spent much of his early career in staff positions, particularly in the planning of sieges. He also became Folard's protégé, who had established a reputation as Feuquières' successor in French military theory. Saxe rose to command in the Austrian Succession, leading the famous capture of Prague in 1742 before assuming command of the Army of Flanders and conquering much of the Low Countries before the war's end. The grateful Louis XV awarded Saxe the rank of *Maréchal-Général de France* and the storied estate of Chambord, to which he retired before dying prematurely in 1750.[16]

Saxe developed a reputation, during his life and especially after his death, as the paragon of French generalship and military prowess in the eighteenth century. This reputation rested on three pillars. The first was the most obvious path to fame: victory. Saxe defeated the British and their allies at Fontenoy, Roucoux, and Lauffeld, avenging the defeats of the Spanish Succession and Dettingen and bringing the war to a successful end. The second was the lack of competition from his fellow generals. For most of the period after 1690, France experienced a deficit of skilled generals, which became apparent especially as the eighteenth century waned. Few demonstrated the capability required to successfully manoeuvre an army on campaign, much less achieve victory. Many were political appointments originating from the often-inscrutable court and subject to the favours of the king's advisers, notably Jean-Antoinette Poisson, Marquise de Pompadour. Saxe, like his illustrious predecessor, *Maréchal-Général* Claude-Louis-Hector, duc de Villars, proved different. He won, and appeared skilled into the bargain, which made him a paragon in the eyes of most French officers, especially after the defeats of the Seven Years War. Third, Saxe published, unlike most of his contemporaries in the marshalate. He authored a work entitled *Mes Rêveries*, which was published in the mid-1750s and helped perpetuate his reputation after his death. Together, these three elements granted Saxe the highest esteem in contemporary French officers' and theorists' esteem, a reputation which has largely persisted into the present.

Labottière, 1724); François-Jean Graindorge d'Orgeville, baron Mesnil-Durand, *Fragments de tactique: ou six mémoires* (Paris: 1774); Jacques-François de Chastenet, marquis de Puységur, *Art de la guerre par principes et par règles* (Paris: Jombert, 1749). See also Colin, *L'infanterie au XVIIIe siècle*, pp.1-80; and Quimby, *The Background of Napoleonic Warfare*, pp.1-25.

15   "Makers of systems" as an epithet for Folard and his fellow writers likely originates in Guibert, *Essai général de tactique*, 1, p.331, and has been notably adopted as a category in both Quimby, *The Background of Napoleonic Warfare*, pp.26-79; and Christy Pichichero, *The Military Enlightenment: War and Culture in the French Empire from Louis XIV to Napoleon* (Ithaca: Cornell University Press, 2018), pp.25-64.

16   Jean-Pierre Bois, *Maurice de Saxe* (Paris: Fayard, 1992); and Jon Manchip White, *Marshal of France: The Life and Times of Maurice, comte de Saxe, 1699-1750* (London: Hamilton, 1967).

Saxe divides his work into two volumes, the first treating general army topics like discipline and tactics, and the second addressing more specialized ideas like sieges, mountain warfare, and passage of rivers. One of its major themes, like many contemporary works, is a lionization of Classical armies, particularly the Roman legions. He lauds the Roman commitment to discipline, especially in covering vast distances quickly, noting that 'the principle of exercise is in the legs and not in the arms; all the secrets of manoeuvres and combats are in the legs'.[17]

In this vein, the most important and celebrated chapter of Saxe's work is 'On the Legion'. In it, he calls for the formation of armies into four 'legions' of four regiments, with each regiment composed of four infantry 'centuries' with attached 'half-centuries' of cavalry and light infantry. The legion's infantry would be armed with fusils and bucklers, which Saxe argues could be used to block incoming musket fire. In addition, two of the four proposed infantry ranks would be armed with pikes to provide security against cavalry. For artillery support, Saxe calls for the creation of *amusettes*, small infantry pieces firing half-pound shot and manned by one or two gunners.[18]

At the operational level, Saxe opines that he 'would never have an army composed of more than ten legions, eight cavalry regiments, and sixteen dragoon [regiments], making 34,000 infantry and 12,000 horse; 46,000 total.'[19] In this, he claims to follow the example of Turenne, who conducted his famous Alsatian campaigns with a small army.[20] Saxe contends that armies should march quickly with scouts deployed, and skilled commanders should take advantage of all possible terrain features to gain positional advantage on the enemy. Unlike most of his contemporaries, he spends little time on the prototypical battle of two armies in an open field arrayed against each other, preferring to dedicate his work to contingencies, chiefly those involving defensive works like entrenchments or fortresses.[21]

These concepts may appear to be revolutionary, and many readers contemporary and modern have taken them as such. However, Saxe's ideas, especially on organization, tactics, and operations, are clearly drawn from the work of Vegetius. His *Epitome of Military Science* proved immensely popular during the period, feeding the neo-Classicism that formed one of the many pillars of the Enlightenment. Its status as the only surviving comprehensive Roman military manual made it required reading for all officers interested in theory and granted it an elevated position as the standard resource for military topics, both social and tactical. On the former, Vegetius castigated his late Roman society for becoming undisciplined and enervated by luxury, a favourite phrase, which led to the downfall of the once-vaunted Roman legions. Only by recapturing the spirit of the past, both its discipline and its 'Old Legion', could Rome return to its former glory.[22]

---

17   Saxe, *Mes rêveries*, Vol.1, p.23

18   Saxe, *Mes rêveries*, Vol.1, pp.33-53.

19   Saxe, *Mes rêveries*, Vol.1, p.98

20   See Carl J. Ekberg, *The Failure of Louis XIV's Dutch War* (Chapel Hill: University of North Carolina Press, 1979); and John Lynn, *The Wars of Louis XIV 1667-1714* (New York: Longman, 1999), pp.118-145.

21   Saxe, *Mes rêveries*, Vol.1, pp.81-90, Vol.2, pp.123-159 and 171-179.

22   Flavius Vegetius Renatus (trans. N.P. Milner), *Epitome of Military Science* (Liverpool: Liverpool University Press, 2001). Duffy, *The Military Experience in the Age of Reason*, p.53, opines that 'The

Mes rêveries provides an excellent example of the eighteenth-century fetish for Vegetius. Its 'On the Legion' clearly owes a debt to Vegetius's Book Two, which is often referred to as 'The Old Legion'. Saxe's arguments, including greater discipline via exercise and smaller armies, show the mark of Vegetius. Most notably, Saxe denigrates the use and efficacy of fire, a curious argument in the age of gunpowder weapons. However, it becomes explicable when the Roman example is taken into account. The Romans made little use of fire, particularly outside of sieges and skirmishes. Thus, any writer wishing to implement Roman-style discipline and tactics must also account for the shift in weaponry. Most called for a reduction in fire weapons in favour of those that delivered shock like the pike. Folard, Saxe's mentor, adopted just such an argument in his work, calling for the harnessing of French élan into shock columns that eschewed fire or used it reluctantly. Saxe has clearly been influenced by the Vegetius-Folard connection, similarly, preferring the return of pikes and shock action.[23]

As a result, Saxe's *Mes rêveries* is far less useful and foundational than is often argued. It clearly bears the mark of Vegetius, both in its form and in its argumentation. It also provides little beyond general maxims, of the kind that proliferated in the French army long before Saxe's work achieved publication in the mid-1750s. Much like Karl von Clausewitz's *On War*, *Mes rêveries* was also not finished by its author and only edited and published after his death, leading to vexing questions of authorship and intent. If *Mes Rêveries* was not the work of Saxe, it likely would not have even been published, much less have achieved the acclaim it enjoyed in the Old Regime and continues to enjoy.

Nevertheless, as is typical for heroes, Saxe's reputation has become conflated with his theory, both by contemporaries and by subsequent writers. His *Rêveries* became the pinnacle of the canon of military theory, particularly given that he did not leave campaign memoirs. His premature death also removed him from the later theoretical discussions and provided a rhetorical foil to those who castigated the French system and called for reform, much as previous writers like Caesar and Vegetius had prior to Saxe's career.

To add further complication, Saxe's campaigns illustrated how significantly his practice differed from his theory. During the campaigns from 1745 to 1748, he did not form legions, nor did he make any significant attempt to reform the organization or discipline of the forces under his command. Instead, he relied on traditional methods, his own abilities, and skilled subordinates to achieve victory. In each campaign season, he progressed according to traditional practice – he selected an important fortress and directed his main effort against it, usually culminating in a siege. During this, he detached a unit under a subordinate, usually Ulrich-Friedrich-Woldemar, Graf Löwendahl, to conduct rapid operations against other targets in the region. This would either draw off enemy support from the main target or secure the lesser prizes for the French, and occasionally both. The bulk of Saxe's

---

thought of Vegetius was absorbed so completely by the Age of Reason that he became effectively an eighteenth-century author.'

23   Folard, *Abrégé des commentaires de M. de Folard sur l'histoire de Polybe* and *Nouvelles découvertes sur la guerre*; Saxe, *Mes rêveries*, Vol.1, pp.33-53, 'On the Legion'; Vegetius, *Epitome of Military Science*, pp.29-61.

force remained in siege camp against the main target, drawing on his experience and skill at the details of siegecraft.[24]

Saxe's signal victory at Fontenoy in 1745 illustrates his tactical abilities and creativity. Rather than seeking an open field on which to engage Cumberland's Anglo-Dutch army, Saxe instead found a congested position near the town. He anchored his left on a forest and his right on a town, which he flattened. He constructed several redoubts along his position, including one in the forest and several on his right, which he filled with artillery. This was a novel use of both field fortification and artillery during the period, and even more so considering that he expected a large battle. Additionally, Saxe deployed the majority of his infantry on his flanks, leaving his large contingent of cavalry to hold the centre. When the enemy arrived and attacked, his position funnelled the Anglo-Dutch efforts into his centre, inflicting attrition on them with fire from concealed sites. While the famous British infantry 'square' nearly achieved breakthrough of Saxe's line, robust cavalry charges and enfilading fire eventually drove it off and secured the victory.[25]

Despite these significant deficiencies, Saxe's work provides important germs for future theorists and practitioners. While he desires the return of some shock weapons and action, Saxe breaks from Folard in noting that dense columns simply would not function on the contemporary battlefield; they are 'beautiful and seem dangerous for the enemy, but in execution, I found [them] in error.'[26] Instead, Saxe advocates for his legions and the rehabilitation of discipline. Unlike many of his contemporaries, Saxe did not simply view discipline as the punishment of the unruly peasants that comprised the army.[27] His view proved to be more institutional, calling for systematic changes in discipline. Most notably, Saxe declares throughout the work that the solution to much of the French army's ills is the lack of cadence in its marches and manoeuvres. To remedy the problem of regimental-level doctrine, Saxe calls for an army-wide cadence, regularizing the march and manoeuvre step of all French troops. This would provide a uniform army that, along with his organizational reforms, would be much more flexible and responsive to a skilled commander.[28]

---

24   Browning, *The War of the Austrian Succession*, pp.199-212, 282-285, 313-320, and 327-340; and White, *Marshal of France*, pp.150-245. See also Jean Colin, *Les campagnes du Maréchal de Saxe* (Paris: Chapelot, 1901-1906).

25   Browning, *The War of the Austrian Succession*, pp.206-212; and White, *Marshal of France*, pp.158-177. Writings abound on Fontenoy, particularly from English writers; see James Falkner, *The Battle of Fontenoy 1745: Saxe against Cumberland in the War of the Austrian Succession* (Barnsley: Pen and Sword, 2019), for just one recent example. Christopher Duffy, *Fight for a Throne: The Jacobite '45 Reconsidered* (Solihull: Helion, 2015), p.321, claims, in the context of the titular war, that 'multi-regimental brigades and… multi-brigade divisions had long been the basic building blocks of European armies' by 1745, unfortunately without corroborating citations.

26   Saxe, *Mes rêveries*, Vol.1, p.85.

27   For example, see Saxe's contemporary Claude-Louis, comte de Saint-Germain, to Paris du Verney, 'I lead a band of thieves, assassins to be beaten, who would flee at the first shot and who are always prepared to revolt…the King has the worst infantry under the sun, and the worst disciplined…'; see also 'Memoir on Army Failure', and 'Relation of the Battle of Rossbach', *Correspondance particulière du comte de Saint-Germain, Ministre et Secrétaire d'Etat de la Guerre, Lieutenant-Général des Armées de France, Feld-Maréchal au service de Danemark, Chevalier de l'Ordre de l'Eléphant, avec M. Paris du Verney, Conseiller d'Etat* (London: Buisson, 1789), pp.257-258 and 192-232.

28   Saxe, *Mes rêveries*, Vol.1, pp.23-25 and especially pp.81-90.

In addition, Saxe does not confine himself to ideal conditions, like many of his fellow theorists. Instead of flat terrain with symmetrical armies meeting in an archetypal battle, Saxe imagines a variety of combats that may take place in less-than-ideal conditions. These include entrenched forces, terrain features that both benefit and hinder an army's actions, and sieges. As a result of this more realistic thought and his smaller 'legionary' armies, Saxe's theory created a more dynamic army that would be more responsive to enemy action and terrain exigency. His legions also represented an early form of combined-arms formations, being supplied with line infantry, cavalry, light forces, and a measure of artillery, albeit in fanciful form.[29] Together, these ideas would inspire future reformers, although in a much more limited manner than simply following his work as gospel.

Frustratingly, Saxe's work remains ambiguous on the organization of units above the regimental level beyond his fabulous 'legions'. Several times in the work, he refers to brigades and divisions, implying that the use of such units would be understandable to a contemporary. However, he also uses the terms in multiple ways, including 'division' in the more general sense, as a subdivision of a larger unit, no matter its size.[30] At times, Saxe seems to describe operations in a prescient sense, with dispersed units operating on autonomous operational lines, but at others, he speaks of an army purely as the unitary body of contemporary practice. Indeed, his 'legions' were imagined to be armies unto themselves, or at least the core of an army not much larger than they were.[31] This ambiguity is likely rooted in the lack of standardization of terminology that persisted throughout the century and the scattered nature of *Mes rêveries*, which Saxe did not curate for publication.

Therefore, Maurice de Saxe is not the father of the combined-arms division. *Mes rêveries* occupies an awkward position in both French military theory and the development of the combined-arms division. Saxe's practice illustrated that he did not seek to implement the vast majority of the theory expressed in his writing. He made no effort to create the 'legions' espoused in the work, nor did he implement combined-arms units of any discernible sort. In fact, other than his novel use of siege elements in his battles, Saxe's campaigns were characterized by traditional methods and competence at the command level. Only the lack of the latter in most French campaigns since Turenne's death, and victory in the war, caused Saxe's to stand out. Saxe's true value lies not in his creation of the division, but rather in cultivating understanding of war. His manuscript likely circulated before its official publication, influencing a generation of young officers eager to emulate his success. Like his successor Clausewitz, Saxe encouraged his readers to better understand the social, psychological, operational, and structural aspects of warfare. If they found inspiration for echelons above regiment in his writing, it was not because he proposed them, but rather because he simply inspired further thought.

During the period in which *Mes rêveries* was published, the French army underwent its first great period of reform. In the mid-1750s, the Ministry of War under Marc-Pierre de Voyer de Paulmy, comte d'Argenson, issued sweeping changes. Foremost among these was the implementation of the cadenced step, which regularized all march and deployment practices, as desired by Saxe. In addition, the Ministry of War established the *Ecole militaire*

---

29   Saxe, *Mes rêveries*, Vol.1, pp.33-53.
30   Saxe, *Mes rêveries*, Vol.1, pp.29, 33-35, and Vol.2, p.211.
31   Saxe, *Mes rêveries*: Volume 1 generally conforms to the latter and Volume 2 to the former usage.

to educate officers and issued regulations for the grenadier units and the artillery. These reforms paid off the efforts of the early-century reformers, laying the foundation for further developments at the tactical and operational levels.[32]

As a result of both the theories of Folard and Saxe and the reforms of the 1750s, definitions of higher echelons began to crystallize in the mid-century period. The 1740 edition of the *Académie française's* dictionary defines a division as 'part of a whole army, that which is camped in order of battle.'[33] Prominent theorist Guillaume le Blond did the most to blaze this particular trail. In his seminal *Essai sur la castramétation*, first published in 1748, he refers to a division as 'nothing more than the union or liaison of several *corps* of troops destined to act together; the union of several battalions or squadrons therefore can be considered as a division of the army', a definition he later used verbatim in the *Encyclopédie* entry for 'Division'.[34] However, Le Blond immediately confuses the issue by naming a 'division of the army' a brigade, a term most commonly used to refer to a detachment under the command of an officer given the temporary rank of 'Brigadier'. This usage appears to be the standard during the Seven Years War, with brigades as a distinct and preferred echelon above regiment.[35]

During that conflict, the work of *Maréchal* de Broglie represented the next step in the formation of the division. Scion of a decorated noble family, Broglie was born in 1718 and first fought as a captain of cavalry at Parma and Guastalla in the Polish Succession before purchasing the Régiment de Luxembourg. He rose to prominence as an officer attached to Saxe in his famous seizure of Prague in 1742, which combined with his illustrious parentage to place him on the fast track to command. He held a series of increasingly important

---

32   Quimby, *The Background of Napoleonic Warfare*, pp.80-105.

33   *Dictionnaire de l'Académie Française,* 3rd ed. (Paris: Académie Française, 1740), Vol.1, p.516.

34   Guillaume le Blond, *Essai sur la castramétation, ou sur la mesure et le trace des camps* (Paris: Jombert, 1748) pp.52-54; Le Blond, 'Division', *Encyclopédie ou dictionnaire raisonné des sciences, des arts, et des métiers, par un Société de Gens de lettres* (Paris: 1751-1772), Vol.4, p.1082, Robert Morrissey (ed.), The ARTFL Encyclopédie, <https://encyclopedie.uchicago.edu>. Hereafter, *Encyclopédie.* Le Blond's previous work, *Elements de fortification* (Paris: Jombert, 1739), contains no references to echelons above regiment.

35   See 'Brigade' and 'Brigadier', *Encyclopédie*, Vol.2, p.419. *Dictionnaire de l'Académie Française*, 1st ed. (Paris: Académie Française, 1694), Vol.1, p.186, contains an entry for 'Brigade,' which includes a definition for 'Brigadier.' See also Henri-François, comte de Bombelles, *Traité des évolutions militaires: les plus simples et le plus faciles à exécuter par l'infanterie, ainsi que des divers feux dont elle peut faire usage* (Paris: Hérissant, 1754), pp.xxxii-xxxiii; Louis XV, 'Instruction du Roi au Saint-Germain du 19 Juillet 1757'; Joseph Paris du Verney to Saint-Germain, July 1757; and Saint-Germain, 'Rélation de la bataille de Lutzelberg [Lutterberg], late October 1758' in Saint-Germain, *Correspondance particulière*, Vol.1, pp.125-137, 139-140, and Vol.2, pp.65-68. Jean-Jacques-Germain Pelet-Clozeau posits that the division only came into being 'around 1770'; see 'De la division', *Spectateur militaire* (Paris: Anselin et Pochard, 1827), Vol.2, pp.260-282. To add to the linguistic confusion, during the same period, another use of 'division' arose, particularly in the works of Folard and his followers. In building their systems, they divided the battalion into sub-units that they referred to as 'divisions', a use Le Blond appears to adopt for most of his definition in the *Encyclopédie*. See Claude Bottée, *Etudes militaires concernant l'exercice de l'infanterie* (Paris: Savoye, 1750); Folard, *Abrégé des commentaires de M. de Folard sur l'histoire de Polybe* and *Nouvelles découvertes sur la guerre*; Mesnil-Durand, *Fragments de tactique*; and Puységur, *Art de la guerre par principes et par règles*. See also Colin, *L'infanterie au XVIIIe siècle*, pp.1-80; and Quimby, *The Background of Napoleonic Warfare*, pp.1-25.

positions through the remainder of the war and into the Seven Years War, where he distinguished himself with personal bravery at several battles, including Rossbach. In 1759, he received his first significant command under Louis-Georges-Erasme, marquis de Contades, which saw the French army humiliated at Minden. In October of the same year, Louis XV named Broglie *Maréchal* and sole commander of the army in Germany, which he retained until his defeat at Vellinghausen in 1762 with the war nearing its end.[36]

In his first campaign season in 1760, Broglie implemented the first true division system in the French army. His orders to his general officers read:

> The two lines of infantry will be divided into four divisions during the campaign. Each division will be composed of a quarter of the brigades of the first and second line, and they will be named at the commencement of the campaign, which will not change. Each wing of the cavalry will form one division. Each division will be commanded by a Lieutenant General, who shall be appointed for the entire campaign.[37]

Broglie's instructions for the campaign are illustrative of the ongoing transition in the French army. Brigades in the modern sense have clearly come into common use in both the infantry and the cavalry, with a semi-permanent status. Broglie simply layers an echelon on top of those brigades, dividing his army into six divisions, retaining the distinction of arms. However, each has attached artillery and light forces, making them combined-arms formations, if not all-arms. They appear to have remained in Broglie's army until his dismissal in 1762.[38] Unlike Saxe, Broglie went beyond theorizing and implemented a division system, albeit only under his direct command.

Despite appearances, they were not yet the modern division as such. The chief reason for this was Broglie's intention for them. The ponderous and laborious formations of a unitary army clogged roads and all but eliminated quick movement on campaign; Broglie determined to rectify this by dividing his force into divisions so that it could occupy several roads rather than a single line of approach. His correspondence from these campaigns clearly indicates the efficacy of such formations on the march, but it also shows that Broglie retained his belief in a unitary army arrayed on traditional lines *en bataille*. His battles saw the divisions marching independently but uniting as one army, with infantry on two lines and cavalry on the wings prior to engaging the enemy, just as his forebears had for centuries prior.[39] His application of the division system was thus not the creation of the modern system per se, but a first step towards continuing the reforms that would allow it to be possible in the future.

After the war, the course of reform quickened, both as a result of defeat and because the looming sense of impending disaster many felt in France allowed elements of noble

---

36   'Victor-François, duc de Broglie', in *Biographie universelle ancienne et moderne,* ed. Louis-Gabriel Michaud, 45 Vols. (Paris: C. Desplaces, 1842-1865), Vol.5, pp.594-596.

37   Victor-François, duc de Broglie, *Correspondance inédite avec le Prince Xavier de Saxe, comte de Lusace, pour servir à l'histoire de la Guerre de Sept Ans* (Paris: Albin Michel, 1903), Vol.1, pp.9-24.

38   Broglie, *Correspondance* inédite, passim; Colin, *L'infanterie au XVIIIe siècle*; Quimby, *The Background of Napoleonic Warfare*, pp.90-105.

39   Broglie, *Correspondance inédite*, Vol.2, pp.195-205 and Vol.4, pp.650-662.

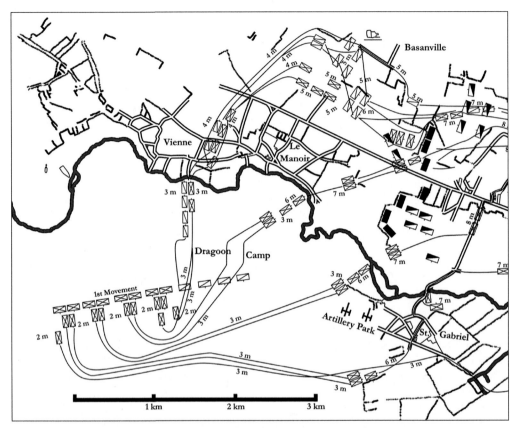

Schematic adapted from 'Fourth Grand Maneuver executed by the troops of the Camp of Vaussieux, 21 September 1778', SHAT 1 M 1819. The friendly army manoeuvres in four infantry divisions and several cavalry divisions along separate axes of approach on the enemy position before uniting in a traditional line of battle in the centre of the field.

privilege like deployment by precedence to be minimized or eliminated altogether. Broglie continued his advocacy after the war, collaborating with various Secretaries of State for War over the next three decades. In particular, he was often given command of the training camps held in spring in imitation of the Prussian tradition. During this period, the French army underwent perhaps its greatest period of change prior to the Revolution, and Broglie remained its guiding hand.

The next crucial step in the development of the division system after 1763 came as a result of two of Broglie's protégés: Charles-Benoît Guibert and his son, the soon-to-be famous Jacques-Antoine-Hippolyte, comte de Guibert. Both served in the Seven Years War and became chief reformers after it. In particular, the Guiberts made an adaptation to contemporary practice with monumental consequences. Guibert *père* suggested, and Guibert *fils* elaborated, a system that dispensed with the traditional severing of march order from battle order, combining them instead into a single system. The union of the two orders allowed commanders to march, deploy, and fight without the processionalism that marred much of

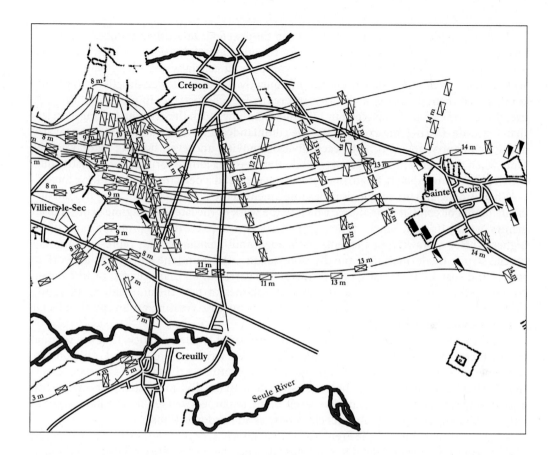

mid-century military theory in France, manoeuvring around obstacles and engaging the enemy army at an advantage.[40]

In 1776, the French army officially adopted a form of Broglie's division system, with the younger Guibert as its driving force. The kingdom was divided into 14 geographic divisions, each with a division permanently garrisoned there. It would draw from the populace and various garrisons in its jurisdiction to field a division, with several such falling under the command of a senior general or marshal. Unfortunately for the nascent system, it was quickly suppressed as a result of court intrigue and factionalism within the army.[41]

---

40   Service Historique – Armée de Terre, 1 M 1790-1794, the 'Guibert Papers', contains most of the two men's papers, including numerous discussions of contemporary issues. Colin, *L'infanterie au XVIIIe siècle*, pp.86-114, contains the most detailed analysis of this period, much of which is adapted in Quimby, *The Background of Napoleonic Warfare*, pp.80-105. See also Guibert, *Essai général de tactique*, Vol.1, pp.172-173 and Vol.2, pp.14-15 and 37-63.

41   SHAT, 1 M 1791, 13, 'Observations relatives à la nouvelle constitution'. See also Albert Latreille, *L'œuvre militaire de la Révolution: l'armée et la nation à fin de l'ancien régime: les derniers ministres de la guerre de la monarchie* (Paris: Chapelot, 1914), pp.100-106.

However, the ideas of 1776 were not lost. Over the next few years, other changes were implemented to continue laying the foundation for the adoption of divisions. Chiefly, the French army realized the need for yearly training camps with echelons above regiment in large-scale combat operations. These occurred infrequently, but they allowed Broglie, who usually commanded them, to test new theories and refine French doctrine. In particular, Broglie's exercises at the Camp of Vaussieux in 1778 illustrate how much the army had changed in less than a decade. During one exercise, Broglie commanded a force organized into one cavalry and four infantry divisions, with each division moving and even fighting autonomously. Only when the enemy has been contacted do the divisions join to form a unitary battle line, which almost immediately fragments into a larger left and a detached right flanking force.[42]

When Broglie and his contemporaries implemented the division system, they did not just create march or combat formations. Much of the work of the late Old-Regime army, like all armies, was by its staff. Much of the reform work went into creating a prototypical staff for higher echelons, drawing in elements of the *logis* and *intendance*. This represents another crucial step in the formation of the division system – the mundane and quotidian work to supply and sustain a large-scale unit, whether in garrison, on manoeuvres, or in combat. Almost every contemporary record contains volumes of pay, sustainment, and lodging information, indicating the massive effort the army put into creating prototypical staffs for echelons above regiment.

While these changes are not dramatic when compared to later practice, they are seminal for the French army of the time. As evidenced by their writings, Broglie, and other officers of the period like Henry Lloyd, clearly began to conceptualize the tactical and even operational articulation that modern theorists associate with the division system, especially with regard to march and deployment. However, many remained wedded to a unitary army in battle, and many accepted higher echelons only as ad hoc formations.[43]

In spite of disagreements, the French army had largely accepted the need for brigades and divisions of some sort by 1780. Over the next decade, these ideas were refined in a number of training camps. Broglie again commanded several, and much of his writing and the writings of others indicate that they fully appreciated the value of the division system in march, deployment, and combat. Archival documents from the 1780s reveal an army adapting to the use of higher echelons with little complaint, forming them for the season and operating with them in exercises. By 1787, Guibert could even argue that 'I do not need to dwell on the advantages of the divisional system; today, there is not one enlightened soldier, or even a good inspector, who, despite the portion of his influence that the system can take away from

---

42   Records of the Vaussieux camp are held in SHAT, 1 M 1819. See especially 19, Louis-François, baron Wimpffen-Bournebourg, 'Rélation du camp de Bayeux 1778', which contains the only complete narrative account of the camp and its exercises. 21-36 are maps of the various exercises. Guibert, *Défense du système de guerre moderne*, in *Œuvres militaires*, Vols. 3 and 4, contain his detailed account and analysis of the camp and its implications.

43   See Ludwig-Andreas Khevenhüller, graf Aichelberg-Frankenburg (trans. Carl-Gideon, baron Sinclaire), *Maximes de guerre relatives à la guerre de campagne, et à celle des sieges* (Paris: Lacombe, 1771), pp.21-22; Henry Lloyd, *The History of the Late War in Germany between the King of Prussia and the Empress of Germany and Her Allies* (London: S. Hooper, 1781); and Carl-Gideon, baron Sinclaire, *Institutions militaires ou traité élémentaire de tactique: précédé d'un discours sur la théorie de l'art militaire* (Paris: Lacombe, 1773), Vol.1, pp.9, 164-167, 185 and Vol.3, pp.13, 124-157.

him, could not recognize its usefulness and does not desire its establishment.[44] Clearly, by the end of the period, the French army had accustomed itself to the use of higher echelons, at least for march and deployment.[45]

During this same period, Pierre-Joseph Bourcet's theories on operational warfare became an influence on the development of operational-level warfare. While his works received publication during the Revolutionary and Napoleonic periods, only after 1880 did historians posit his influence on the development of the division. Jean Colin led this charge, arguing that Bourcet's writings were a primary influence on Napoleon and thus on Napoleonic operational-level warfare. Most subsequent historians have adopted this argument, ranging from Spenser Wilkinson to Robert Quimby and Claus Telp.[46] However, Bourcet's chief work was not published in his lifetime, and he confined his studies to mountainous terrain, presenting a challenge to the historian in determining its impact on the development of the division.

A lifelong staff officer, Bourcet served in the French Alps for a relatively undistinguished career. The sole, but important, exception to this is his position as chief of artillery and *génie* under Soubise for the 1758 campaign in Germany. In his frontier posting, he dedicated himself to exploring the various aspects of mountain warfare, authoring studies about it, all of which were published after his death.[47] The most famous of these is *Principes de la guerre des montagnes*, which is often presented as a work seminal to the development of operational-level warfare. In it, Bourcet argues that the restricted terrain of mountainous regions requires that armies divide into sections so as to pass simultaneously through the few available debouches, reuniting on the plains beyond. Given the difficulties of weather, terrain, and enemy action, Bourcet counsels that a staff must develop a 'plan of many branches' in order to account for blocked routes.[48]

---

44 Guibert, 'Commandements dans les provinces, organisation de l'armée, système de divisions, formation et service de ces divisions, campements annuels, suppression des étapes, marches et mouvements des troupes, refonte et application du corps des commissaires des guerres au système des divisions', SHAT, 1 M 1790, 30.

45 SHAT, 1 M 1807 and 1812 contain records of a variety of camps held after 1760, most in the 1780s at Metz and Saint-Omer. Document 75 in the former, 'Tactique' by Guy-André-Pierre Montmorency, duc de Laval, argues that 'it is absolutely necessary, after seeing a long peace, to conduct camps with the troops and exercise them for war.' See also Duffy, *The Military Experience in the Age of Reason*, pp.19-21.

46 See Jean Colin, *L'éducation militaire de Napoléon* (Paris: Chapelot, 1901), pp.32-158, which laid the foundation for subsequent interpretations of Broglie. Followers of Colin's argument include Quimby, *The Background of Napoleonic Warfare*, pp.175-184; Claus Telp, *The Evolution of Operational Art, 1740-1813* (New York: Frank Cass, 2005), pp.1-33; and Spenser Wilkinson, *The Defense of Piedmont, 1742-1748: A Prelude to the Study of Napoleon* (Oxford: Oxford University Press, 1927); *The French Army before Napoleon* (Oxford: Oxford University Press, 1915); and *The Rise of General Bonaparte* (Oxford: Oxford University Press, 1930).

47 Pierre-Joseph Bourcet, *Mémoires historiques sur la guerre des Français ont soutenue en Allemagne depuis 1757 jusqu'en 1762* (Paris: Chez Maradan, 1792), and *Mémoires militaires sur les frontières de la France du Piémont et de la Savoie depuis l'embouchure du Var jusqu'au lac de Genève* (Berlin: George Decker, 1801). See also Michaud, *Biographie universelle*, Vol.5, pp.291-292, and Johannès Pallière, 'Un grand méconnue du XVIIIe siècle: Pierre Bourcet (1700-1780)', *Revue historique des armées* (Vincennes: Service historique de la défense, 1979), pp.51-66.

48 Pierre-Joseph Bourcet, *Principes de la guerre des montagnes* (Paris: Ministre de la Guerre, 1888), especially pp.88-89.

Bourcet's work, on first glance, clearly offers a prototype for the development of the combat division and operational-level warfare. It takes little imagination to convert his theories from mountain passes to the road networks of western and central Europe, where France fought many of its wars. His divisions, which separate to pass the mountains, are simply divided onto the available roads, and reunite before meeting the enemy. This provides the operational and organizational flexibility for a skilled commander to fight what would later be recognized as operational-level warfare, particularly in the writings of Antoine-Henri, baron Jomini.[49]

However, little evidence exists as to whether or not Bourcet's work did actually prove to be a source of reform during the Old Regime. The main difficulty arises from the fact that *Principes de la guerre des montagnes* was not published until 1888, over a century after its author's death. Other works by Bourcet appeared much closer to the period, including his three-volume study of the Seven Years War.[50] Given the period's mania for military theory books, including his other works and far more esoteric works than his, it remains an open question why a study ostensibly so important to the development of military theory and practice did not warrant publication until the eve of the twentieth century. The scholarly consensus has been that Bourcet's work circulated privately or perhaps professionally, as a pamphlet available to officers within the French army. However, the earliest date for this is usually posited to be around 1775, long after others had begun the development of the division and operational-level warfare.[51]

As with Saxe's work, Bourcet's influence must therefore be relegated to the conceptual rather than the practical. His detailed and thorough studies proved invaluable to those who engaged in warfare in mountainous terrain, including Napoleon Bonaparte in 1796. However, to simply project those ideas directly into fighting in other terrain would be to give Bourcet too much credit. Instead, his influence likely joined that of Saxe and other theorists of the period in sparking thinking about warfare in its broader and more operational sense rather than providing a blueprint, as has been suggested, notably in works focused on Bonaparte.[52]

Whether influenced by Bourcet or not, the culmination of the division system in the Old Regime came just before the Revolution, when the French army implemented a permanent system of divisions. In 1787, with Guibert again leading the way, the Ministry of War divided the kingdom into 16 regions, each with a permanent division established in it and with a *lieutenant-général* commanding and three *maréchaux-de-camp* providing staff work. According to Guibert's memorandum on them, these divisions were not simply territorial divisions, as those of 1776 had been. He refused to delegate specific sub-units to each, or mandate a uniform size and strength, because the specific nature of a future war would

---

49   See Antoine-Henri, baron Jomini (trans. Charles Messenger), *The Art of War* (St. Paul: Greenhill Books, 1992), pp.72-216, especially pp.85-132.

50   Bourcet, *Mémoires historiques sur la guerre des Français*.

51   Quimby, *The Background of Napoleonic Warfare*, pp.175-184, provides an excellent summary. See also Colin, *L'éducation militaire de Napoléon*, pp.65-85.

52   Colin counts Bourcet as one of Napoleon's formative influences, along with Guibert and Jean and Jean-Pierre du Teil; see *L'éducation militaire de Napoléon*, pp.65-85. Telp, *The Evolution of Operational Art*, pp.24-25, provides an excellent example of a modern adaptation of Colin's theory.

dictate that need. This clearly indicated that Guibert intended these divisions to function in war, perhaps even as operational-level units.[53] However, Guibert would not have the opportunity to test his system, given its proximity to the outbreak of the Revolution.

Despite the advances of the period, the French army of the Old Regime did not produce a true division system. Several elements constrained its development, especially before 1763. Chief among them was the nature of the French army as an amateur, wartime force. The officer corps reflected this nature, as did the administration of the organization. In addition, French cultural and political mores further constrained development early in the century.

Throughout the Old Regime, France generally did not maintain a field army in peacetime.[54] The expense of keeping tens of thousands of men on duty was simply beyond reason, much less the resources of the French state. As a result, like many states across Europe that lacked standing armies, the army essentially reinvented itself in the early years of each war, all but eliminating the possibility of peacetime reform. In addition, the officer corps was also a significant hindrance to reform, although not for the reason often suggested. Despite theoretically being open to talented commoners, the officer corps remained almost exclusively noble until the end of the period, and the few commoners who did achieve a position rarely rose above the ranks of the junior officers. This does not indicate a form of Aristocratic Reaction, as the older historiography argues, that saw luddite officers railing against new men and new ideas. Rather, almost every officer was deeply committed to his command and to victory on the battlefield, and most sought to inform themselves of the latest military theory and modern methodologies to at least a limited degree. However, few had a deep and technical education in military theory and practice, and even fewer still had the time and energy to devote themselves to military practice in the midst of competing social and political demands. Officers often only made cursory visits to their units and delegated much of their training and daily operations to junior and non-commissioned officers.[55]

---

53   SHAT, 1 M 1790, 30, 'Commandements dans les provinces, organisation de l'armée, système de divisions, formation et service de ces divisions, campements annuels, suppression des étapes, marches et mouvements des troupes, refonte et application du corps des commissaires des guerres au système des divisions.' See also Latreille, *L'œuvre militaire de la Révolution*, pp.343-393.

54   Even Broglie's exercises, which involved in excess of 40,000 men at times, were largely drawn from the garrison units in the province of their staging. See SHAT, 1 M 1807, 1812, and 1819.

55   The 'Aristocratic Reaction' has been decisively debunked by many authors, chief among them David D. Bien, Rafe Blaufarb, Guy Chaussinand-Nogaret, and Julia Osman. However, elements of its core argument, that the French nobility acted decisively to ensure their own noble privilege against any reform and thus precipitated the Revolution, still recurs, especially in analyses of the army and the Ségur Decree of 1781 that required four degrees of nobility for officer rank. William Doyle's 'Was there an Aristocratic Reaction in Pre-Revolutionary France?', *Past & Present* 57 (1972), pp.97-122, provides an excellent summary of the debate, including footnote 1, which outlines the standard works that argue for an Aristocratic Reaction. See also David D. Bien, 'The Army in the French Enlightenment: Reform, Reaction, and Revolution', *Past & Present* 85 (1979): pp.68-98; David D. Bien, *Caste, Class, and Profession in Old Regime France: The French Army and the Ségur Reform of 1781* (St. Andrews: Centre for French History and Culture, 2010); David D. Bien and J. Rovet, 'La réaction aristocratique avant 1789: l'exemple de l'armée', *Annales histoire, science sociales* 29, no. 2 (1974): pp.23-48 and no. 3 (1974): pp.505-534; Rafe Blaufarb, *The French Army, 1750-1820: Careers, Talent, Merit* (New York: Manchester University Press, 2002); Guy Chaussinand-Nogaret (trans. William Doyle), *The French Nobility in the Eighteenth Century: From Feudalism to Enlightenment*(New York: Cambridge University press, 1989); Julia Osman, 'Patriotism as Power: The Old Regime Foundation

In addition, as officers officially owned the units that they commanded, they were expected to provide funding for necessities like clothing, food, and equipment, even on campaign. Moreover, until the 1750s, no army-wide regulations existed for details of formations or manoeuvre. Each officer was expected to train his regiment as he saw fit, in keeping with contemporary theory and practice, and any infelicities of implementation would be ironed out in spring camp prior to the campaign season.[56]

The French army was, in short, an amateur organization, particularly at the general officer level. Even if an officer wanted to dedicate himself to testing new methods and innovating his own, he simply lacked the resources of time, money, and manpower to modernize it. After 1763, the pressing need for reform became apparent to nearly everyone in France. Traditional questions of noble privilege and social mores gave way to the stark reality of defeat and submission to the new Prussian paradigm. The French army thus began the process of professionalization and reform, including the creation of a prototypical division system.

However, this produced arguably the most important impediment to change in any system: the degree to which change will undermine the fundamental values and mores of the society that produces the system. The French eagerly adopted technical Prussian innovations like the moving pivot and the deployment column wholesale. Yet they could only go so far in their enthusiasm for fear of overturning the foundation of the French social system. To create a professional military would require not only vast sums of money but also a wholesale change in the composition of the officer corps. Considering that the French state had literally been built out of the military relationship between the king and the nobility, not to mention how such a change would impact the hierarchical structures of society and the Church, such changes simply could not occur in the Old Regime system.

While they might disagree on the direction of reforms, few questioned the need for it, not just in the army, but in all of French society. Reformers in France thus did what they could within the limits placed upon them by society, finance, and propriety. As Jean Colin memorably put it, 'it is not probable that a nation, with the spirit and the *génie* that it has, can push an art and a science, in five or six years, to a greater degree of perfection than another nation that has been working on it for a century.'[57]

Despite its important innovations, the French army was at the mercy of events much larger than the institution. The kingdom's finances teetered near collapse, leaving little expenditure for the military. Also, and perhaps most importantly, France fought no wars of consequence in Europe between 1763 and 1792, and wars often provide the variety of stimuli necessary to effect major change, and quickly. The American Independence War, while significant from a strategic point of view to France, largely did not provoke the interest of most reformers; its American battles were mere skirmishes in size, and most French theorists believed that combat outside of Europe did not relate to the great Continental battles.

---

for Napoleon's Army', *International Congress of Military History Conference Proceedings* 2009 (2010); and Pichichero, *The Military Enlightenment*.

56   Colin, *L'infanterie au XVIIIe siècle*, pp.27-72; Nosworthy, *Anatomy of Victory*, pp.3-238; Quimby, *The Background of Napoleonic Warfare*, pp.7-79; and Ross, *From Flintlock to Rifle*, pp.17-50.

57   Colin, *L'infanterie au XVIIIe siècle*, p.135.

The few references to the war that do occur during and after it are generally of a Marine or philosophical bent.[58] When Revolution arrived in 1789, it swept away most of the people involved in leading the reforms and promoted its own ideas as entirely novel.

One of the major difficulties in tracing the origins of the division in Old-Regime France lies in the complex nature of the overlapping movements of the period, both constructive and destructive. The Enlightenment, absolutism, burgeoning ideas of public and nation, the financial crisis, and foreign affairs were just a few of the major events that helped define the period. Their confluence produced the French Revolution, which adds another layer of difficulty. Even after generations of revisionism, the Old Regime, particularly after 1750, is still seen as an inevitable slide towards revolution, and the Revolutionary period itself as the great time of innovation, including in military affairs.[59] This belies the actual nature of the period, which was one of intense innovation and adaption as individuals and government bodies sought to regenerate France's institutions and society, returning it to its hegemonic position. The Enlightenment provided the recipe for this: rational examination of institutions and processes followed by definition and categorization of their various elements, leading to greater control over them. Old-Regime reformers laid the foundation for later changes wrought by the Revolutionary and Napoleonic governments and is often obscured by them. The French army provides perhaps the best example of these two phenomena in that many of the reforms ascribed to the Revolution, especially in the areas of tactics, organization, and discipline, actually find their origins in the Old Regime.

The changes wrought by Old-Regime reformers laid the foundation of the modern division system in the French army, in spite of Revolutionary rhetoric to the contrary. When Revolutionary commanders began to create their own division systems in the War of the First Coalition, they had generations of writings from which to draw.[60] These began with halting efforts in the early eighteenth century to grapple with larger armies and decentralized doctrine. Folard proposed to overcome this difficulty with rigid, mathematical processionalism and geometric perfection. Others demurred, following instead the recommendation of Saxe to implement army-wide doctrine, beginning with the cadenced step in the 1750s. This allowed burgeoning ideas of echelons above the regiment to appear, first in print as divisions, brigades, corps, or detachments, and then in reality in Broglie's campaigns in the Seven Years War. Subsequent work by Guibert, Bourcet, and Broglie himself refined this process in the wake of the defeat of 1763, producing France's first division system in 1787, albeit in a nascent form. However, they had no theatre in which to demonstrate it, and the Revolutionaries picked up its pieces once the government was shattered after 1789. They also benefitted from having a war in which to test their doctrine and winnow away all but its best elements. The professional core of the Revolutionary armies was comprised

---

58   For example, see SHAT, 1 M 1792, 4, 11, and 12, Guibert, 'Mémoire sur les affaires présentes', 'Expédition d'Angleterre de 1779', and 'Notes de Lecture du comte de Guibert'. See also Julia Osman, 'Ancient Warriors on Modern Soil: French Military Reform and American Military Images in 18th Century France', *French History* 22 (2008): pp.175-196.

59   Perhaps the most coherent articulation of the inevitability thesis remains George Lefebvre, *The Coming of the French Revolution* (Princeton: Princeton University Press, 2015). See also William Doyle, *Origins of the French Revolution* (Oxford: Oxford University Press, 2013).

60   See Jordan Hayworth, *Revolutionary France's War of Conquest in the Rhineland: Conquering the Natural Frontier, 1792-1797* (Cambridge: Cambridge University Press, 2018).

of veterans of the Old Regime, men who had been raised by a generation of officers who experimented with divisions and their use. When the Revolutionaries created their system, it was not *ex nihilo*, but rather by drawing on the institutional memory of the army to which they belonged.

Further Reading

Abel, Jonathan, 'The Prophet Guibert', Michael Leggiere (ed.), *Napoleon and the Operational Art of War: Essays in Honor of Donald D. Horward* (Leiden: Brill, 2021), pp.7-38.

Anderson, M.S., *War and Society in Europe of the Old Regime, 1618-1789* (New York: St. Martin's Press, 1988).

Bacquet, Louis-Hippolyte, *L'infanterie au XVIIIe siècle. L'organisation* (Paris: Berger-Levrault, 1907).

Bien, David, 'The Army of the French Enlightenment: Reform, Reaction, and Revolution'. *Past & Present* 85 (1979), pp.68-98.

Black, Jeremy, *European Warfare, 1660-1815* (New Haven, CT: Yale University Press, 1994).

Colin, Jean, *L'infanterie au XVIIIe siècle. La tactique* (Paris: Berger-Levrault, 1907).

Duffy, Christopher, *The Military Experience in the Age of Reason* (New York: Atheneum, 1988).

Gat, Azar, *A History of Military Thought from the Enlightenment to the Cold War* (New York: Oxford University Press, 2001).

Kennett, Lee, *The French Armies in the Seven Years War: A Study in Military Organization and Administration* (Durham: Duke University Press, 1967).

Latreille, Albert, *L'œuvre militaire de la révolution: l'armée et la nation à la fin de l'ancien régime; les derniers ministres de la guerre de la monarchie* (Paris: Chapelot, 1914).

Lynn, John, *Giant of the Grand Siècle: The French Army, 1610-1715* (New York: Cambridge University Press, 2006).

Nosworthy, Brent, *The Anatomy of Victory: Battle Tactics 1689-1763* (New York: Hippocrene Books, 1990).

Olsen, John Andreas, and van Creveld, Martin (eds) *The Evolution of Operational Art: From Napoleon to the Present* (New York: Oxford University Press, 2011).

Pichichero, Christy, *The Military Enlightenment: War and Culture in the French Empire from Louis XIV to Napoleon* (Ithaca: Cornell University Press, 2017).

Quimby, Robert, *The Background of Napoleonic Warfare: The Theory of Military Tactics in Eighteenth-Century France* (New York: Columbia University Press, 1957).

Ross, Steven, "The Development of the Combat Division in Eighteenth-Century French Armies." *French Historical Studies* no. 1 (1965), pp.84-94.

Scott, Samuel, *From Yorktown to Valmy: The Transformation of the French Army in the Age of Revolution* (Boulder: University Press of Colorado, 1998).

Starkey, Armstrong, *War in the Age of Enlightenment, 1700-1789* (Westport, CT: Praeger, 2003).

Szabo, Franz, *The Seven Years War in Europe, 1756-1763* (New York: Routledge, 2013).

8

Pandours, Partisans and Freikorps: The Development of Irregular Warfare and Light Troops across the Eighteenth Century

James R. McIntyre

One factor separating the work of Christopher Duffy from many historians working in the field of eighteenth-century warfare is his close reading of the military literature of the period. Duffy often contrasts the material contained in these treatises with the actual battlefield experience of the armies under study. It seems only fitting, then, to follow this model in examining the development of various forms of light infantry across the eighteenth century, with special emphasis on the crucial period of the Seven Years War.[1] It seems only appropriate, as well, since throughout his prolific body of work, Professor Duffy often discussed the development and use of light troops in great detail. The following chapter will demonstrate that for anyone who seeks an understanding of the development and use of light troops on eighteenth century European battlefields, Professor Duffy's body of work constitutes essential reading. In order to accomplish this task, it is first necessary to briefly address the current historiography covering the development of light troops during the eighteenth century.

As Professor Duffy himself observed, 'The rise of light infantry formed one of the most significant developments in European warfare in the second half of the eighteenth century.'[2] While light infantry formations developed in North America as well, they drew inspiration, at least in part, from European precedents. Certainly, the literature on light forces contains some comparisons between the formations developed in Europe and North America. For instance, in his work *The Age of Battles*, Russell F. Weigley noted, '…much of the impetus toward employing light infantry in skirmishing tactics rolled across Europe not eastward

---

1   Light troops constitute a generic term, which I apply to include various forms of irregular forces such as Pandours, Croats, Freikorps and Jäger as well.

2   Christopher Duffy, *The Austrian Army in the Seven Years War Vol. 1. Instrument of War* (Chicago: The Emperor's Press, 2000), p.240.

from North America but westward from the Ottoman Empire.'[3] He further observed, 'The Turks like the North American Indians made much use of unconventional tactics, skirmishing, concealment and ambuscades, but with rather more forethought, discipline, and tactical control than the Indians usually managed.'[4] Europe, however, constituted the main theatre for the development of light troops and irregular warfare in the eighteenth century. In addition, it is the region most examined by Christopher Dufy. It stands to reason that this theatre of the war should serve as the focus of the following essay.

Duffy, as well as the present author, Brent Nosworthy, Henry Pichat and Gunter E. Rothenberg, who have examined the development of light infantry in Europe in the eighteenth century observe that the emergence of these troops occurred initially during the War of the Austrian Succession or First Silesian War.[5] At the outset of the conflict, Empress Maria Theresa, strapped for manpower, called upon the inhabitants of the borderlands between her empire and the Ottomans to bolster her armies.[6] These efforts yielded numerous irregular formations such as the Pandours of Francicus von der Trenck.[7] In addition to the Pandours, there were the Grenzer and Croats. These men were accustomed to conducting a low-level conflict with their Ottoman neighbours which centred on raids and ambushes. These troops brought their own tactical approach to the battlefields of Central and Western Europe. Tactically, these irregulars stood as consummate experts in raids and setting ambushes, practices which came under the headings of *kleiner Krieg, petite guerre* or the war of posts. Regardless of the terminology employed, these troops applied their tactics in an adept manner, and the regular field armies in Central Europe initially encountered great difficulty in countering them. Thus, as Professor Duffy remarked, 'In the eighteenth century the great majority of light forces came to their trade through natural habits

---

3   Russel F. Weigley, *The Age of Battles: The Quest for Decisive Warfare from Breitenfeld to Waterloo* (Bloomington: Indiana University Press, 1991), p.269.

4   Weigley, *Age of Battles*, p.269.

5   Other historians who have specifically examined the emergence of light infantry and trace it back to the War of the Austrian Succession include Brent Nosworthy, *The Anatomy of Victory: Battle Tactics, 1689-1763* (New York: Hippocrene Books, 1990), James R. McIntyre *The Development of the British Light Infantry, Continental and North American Influences, 1740-1765* (Point Pleasant, NJ: Winged Hussar Publishing, 2015); Henry Pichat (Trans. George Nafziger), *Maurice de Saxe's 1745 Campaign in Belgium* (West Chester, OH: The Nafziger Collection, 2011); Sandrine Picaud-Monnerat, *La Petite Guerre au XVIIIe Siècle* (Paris: Economica, 2010); Gunther E. Rothenberg, *The Military Border in Croatia, 1740-1881: A Study of an Imperial Institution* (Chicago: University of Chicago Press, 1966).

6   The general histories of this conflict as of the current writing are M.S. Anderson, *The War of the Austrian Succession 1740-1748* (London: Longman, 1995) and Reed Browning, *The War of the Austrian Succession* (New York: St. Martin's Griffin, 1993). See also, Dennis Showalter, *The Wars of Frederick the Great* (London: Longman, 1996), pp.38-90.

7   For an incredibly self-serving autobiography of Pandour Trenck, but one in which details many of his operations, see Francicus von der Trenck, *Memoirs of the Life of the Illustrious Francis Baron Trenck* (London: W. Owen, 1748). Among the more objective accounts of his life are Kurt Sonntag *Trenck, der Pandur und die Brandschatzung Bayerns* (Munchen: Nusser, 1976) and Oscar Teichman, *Pandour Trenck: An Account of the Life of Francicus von der Trenck, 1710-1749* (London: John Murray, 1927). For a more condensed version of the exploits of the Pandour leader, see James R. McIntyre, 'A Scoundrel's Scoundrel: The Life and Exploits of Baron Francicus von der Trenck, Pandour Leader', *The Journal of the Seven Years War Association*, 19:1 (2014), pp.27-42.

of life, or through an enterprising and semi-critical turn of mind.'[8] The men in these units certainly earned the title irregulars, as their activities fell outside the normative missions assigned to the infantry or cavalry.

These troops performed several roles. First and foremost, they acted as scouts, ascertaining enemy numbers and, if possible, intentions. Secondly, and often in combination with the first, they were to raid into the enemy's territory, and thus work to disrupt their plans. When the enemy advanced, they were to interdict their movements, often through the use of a well-laid ambush. Ambushes were intended to slow an enemy attack and weaken it while giving time to the light troops' own forces to prepare to meet the assault. Still, on some occasions, they so disconcerted the plan for an attack that the enemy gave up their design altogether. Historian Gunther Rothenberg summarized their actions as follows, 'They screened the Austrian main body from surprise attacks and, constantly hovering around the flanks and rear of the enemy, forced him to devote a considerable part of his forces to defending his depots and line of communication.'[9]

To help in performing these specialized tasks, irregular troops often sported different arms as well. While generally armed with smoothbore muskets, some records make mention of 'Croat Rifles,' which may indicate some sharpshooter companies.[10] Martin Rink offers additional support to the preceding possibility, 'The process of fighting from cover and aimed fire was not unknown on the Habsburg frontier.'[11]

When these troops entered the battlefields of Central Europe, they exerted a pronounced effect on the conduct of operations. M.S. Anderson described how 'From early in their invasion of Silesia the Prussians found themselves harassed, their communications threatened and their supplies interrupted, by *grenzers* and *pandours*, irregular units originally raised in the Hapsburg military frontier areas in Croatia, which soon became known and feared for their mobility and their propensity to plunder and destroy.'[12] Anderson's observation is reinforced by Duffy's assessment, 'The principal modes of action of the light forces were raids and ambushes, and secrecy and speed, were vital to success in both.'[13] Clearly, as Weigley noted, 'The development of light infantry and the new forms of cavalry could measurably improve reconnaissance and flank security for the army on the offensive, while also increasing opportunities for the defender to harass both the enemy's main body and lines of communications.'[14] The advantage did not remain restricted to the Austrian forces for long, however, as success often breeds emulation. Consequently, it should come as no surprise that numerous other states quickly developed their own light or irregular troops.

---

8   Christopher Duffy, *The Military Experience in the Age of Reason 1715-1789* (New York: Hippocrene Books, 1987), p.267.
9   Rothenberg, *Military Border*, p.19
10   Jim Purky, 'Light Infantry Forces in the Austrian-Prussian Theaters of the SYW', *Seven Years War Association Journal*, 8:4 (1996), p.40.
11   Martin Rink, 'Der kleine Krieg: Entwicklung und Teens asymmetrischer Gewalt bis 1740 bis 1815', *Militärgeschichte Zeitschrift*. 65:2 (2006), p.363
12   Anderson, *War of the Austrian Succession*, p.221. Italics in original.
13   Duffy, *Military Experience*, p.275.
14   Weigley, *Age of Battles*, p.270.

In many of the German states, for instance, leaders looked to their game wardens and recruited the famed Jäger.[15] These recruits had to demonstrate 'undisputable loyalty,' and be 'able to move stealthily in any terrain and hit his target unfailingly even at long distances.'[16] Duffy keenly summarizes the commonalities among these diverse light formations, observing 'The German Jäger, the French chasseurs and their counterpart in other lands were yet another category of light infantry whose skills came from their peacetime occupations, in this case as huntsmen or gamekeepers on the estates of the crown or the great landowners.'[17] One of the major roles these troops performed entailed hanging on the fringes of his main force and act as a skirmisher (*der Plänker*). As one source continued, 'He also scouted, carried messages, and could form the army's vanguard or cover its retreat.'[18] The various belligerents reacted in a number of ways to this military innovation. Brent Nosworthy asserts that the Prussians reacted to this new threat through a greater emphasis on order, as he observes, 'they took a number of systemic precautions to counter this threat.'[19] Likewise, the French began to raise their own troops, such as the Arquebusiers de Grassin, embodied as a direct response to the activities of irregulars of Maria Theresa's empire. In the event, the Pandours, and other units such as the Croats, enjoyed great success not only in upsetting the Prussians' plans, but in harrying the operations of the French in Bohemia as well. The fighting in Bohemia in late 1741 and early 1742 marked famed French leader Maurice de Saxe's first exposure to these troops.[20] Saxe quickly seized upon the merits of these irregular soldiers and worked to inculcate them into the French army.

On his return to France, Saxe began to develop similar forces in the French Army. There is little information currently available concerning how they were recruited and trained, but it is certain that Saxe employed these troops in the campaign of 1745 in Flanders.[21] The Flanders campaign is commonly remembered for the battle of Fontenoy fought on 11 May 1745; however, both before and after Fontenoy a significant amount of partisan clashes occurred in the surrounding region. One of the units raised and employed by the French specifically to counter the irregulars of the Austrians hussars and Pandours during the 1745 Flanders campaign were the famous Arquebusiers de Grassin, a unit raised by a Royal Ordnance on 1 January 1744 by Simon-Claude Grassin de Catigny.[22]

---

15   On the background of the Jäger, see Thomas M. Barker and Paul R. Huey, '"Military Jäger": Their Civilian Background and Weaponry', in *The Hessians: The Journal of the Johannes Schwalm Historical Association*. 15 (2012), pp.1-15.

16   Arno Storkel, 'The Anspach Jäger', *The Hessians: Journal of the Johannes Schwalm Historical Association*. 14 (2011), pp.4

17   Duffy, *Age of Reason*, p.272.

18   Barker and Huey, '"Military Jäger"', p.1.

19   Nosworthy, *Anatomy*, pp.211.

20   This campaign is described in Browning, *War of the Austrian Succession*, p.91-93. On Maurice de Saxe, see Jon Manchip White, *Marshal of France: The Life and Times of Maurice, Comte de Saxe, 1696-1750* (Chicago: Rand McNally, 1962). See also, James Falkner, *The Battle of Fontenoy 1745: Saxe against Cumberland in the War of the Austrian Succession* (Barnsley: Pen and Sword Books, 2019), pp.47-55.

21   On the background for Saxe's campaign in the Netherlands, see Browning, *War of the Austrian Succession*, pp.199-213

22   Sandrine Picaud-Monnerat, *La Petite Guerre*, p.361. See also Brent Nosworthy, 'Arquebussier de Grassin', *Seven Years War Association Journal* 13:1 (Winter 2003): pp 22-23.

A few examples of their activities prove their utility at the sort of irregular warfare already discussed in Eastern Europe. These troops, akin to their eastern forerunners, specialized in scouting, foraging and ambushes. These examples demonstrate the transmission of irregular tactics into Western Europe as well. In the first instance, the Grassins placed themselves in an ambush around a bend in the Scheldt River to interdict a crossing by allied forces. They were quite successful in slowing the allied river crossing.[23] The second action was probably the most significant partisan engagement that took place during the campaign. It occurred in connection with the battle of Melle, fought on 9 July 1745, 'tactically, a most interesting affair', in the words of J.A. Houlding.[24] The action itself consisted in a minor encounter battle. In the aftermath of this engagement, at dusk, the commander of the contingent from the Pragmatic Army, Philipp Freiherr von Moltke, encountered a substantial number of French Grassins, and believed he could take a number of them prisoner. As the Pragmatic forces attacked, the Grassins gave way, falling back off the road they had occupied at the outset. They then barricaded themselves in a chateau surrounded by a wide ditch, a solid defensive position. Since Moltke possessed no artillery with his force, which was essentially an advanced guard for the main Pragmatic Army, he could not force the Grassins from their position. As a result, Moltke broke off his assault after about an hour. Strangely, Moltke failed to inform British Brigadier General Thomas Bligh of the troops occupying the chateau, and the allied army continued its advance on the road to Melle. As the forces under Bligh's command fought the French along a brook, the Grassins made their way out of the chateau and attacked the British baggage train. They managed to take the baggage, tents, equipment and bat horses of the British force, as well as a number of prisoners, forcing Bligh to break off and retreat with heavy losses.[25] As one of the chief authors on this engagement notes, 'The attack by the Grassins on the rear of Bligh's force would not have been so damaging had adequate precautions been taken.'[26] Thus, much of the blame for the Grassins' success falls on Moltke who did not inform Bligh of the threat, probably because he did not believe light troops would act in that fashion. By the same token, the success of the attack on the rear of the British column demonstrates just how effective irregulars could be at undermining the operations of regular forces. As a result of their attack, the British force had to fall back to its original position, minus a significant amount of its equipment. Incidents such as the above showcase, as well, how small war was fast becoming a constant between the main forces of the belligerents.

M.S. Anderson noted fascination with the new formations raised during the War of the Austrian Succession: 'Much more eye-catching and interesting to contemporaries, however, was the considerable use now being made by several armies of light troops of a kind hitherto

---

23   Pichat, *Campaign in Belgium*, pp.57. See also, Russell, 'Redcoats in the Wilderness: British Officers and Irregular Warfare in Europe and America, 1740-1760', *William and Mary Quarterly* 3:35 (1978), p.631.
24   J.A. Houlding, *Fit for Service The Training of the British Army, 1715-1795* (Oxford: Clarendon Press, 1981), p.359.
25   This engagement is covered very well in J.E.O. Screen, 'A "New" Account of the Action at Melle, 9 July 1745', *Journal of the Society for Army Historical Research*, 73: 296 (Winter 1995), pp.275-77, and 'The Action at Melle, 9 July 1745', *Journal of the Society for Army Historical Research*, 77:310 (Summer 1999), pp.88-99. See also, Pichat, *Campaign in Belgium*, pp.32-34, and Picaud-Monnerat, *La Petite Guerre*, p.365.
26   Screen, 'Action at Melle', p.97.

little seen in western Europe.'[27] Still, as Weigley notes, 'light troops remained of secondary importance.'[28] While Weigley's remark is directed at the inability of the light formations to change the indecisive nature of battle, his primary concern, it implies another issue as well. His statement belies the fact that these troops brought several significant liabilities to their new theatre of operations.

While these troops were extremely capable when it came to the small war which gnawed at the periphery of the main forces, as Professor Duffy notes, 'Almost every regiment [in the Prussian Army] owned a horror story of some episode when it had been caught at a disadvantage by the Croats.'[29] By the same token, they could often strike terror into the hearts of civilians, and, on these occasions, the irregulars were very poor at differentiating friendly from enemy non-combatants. Likewise, they were not always especially concerned with whether the people they were abusing were subjects of an enemy's state or their own. The random nature of their conduct towards civilians bred indiscipline in the ranks of these units. Their indiscipline, in turn, undermined their military effectiveness. In essence, military leaders had to be able to count on these irregular formations to complete their missions, and not simply assault and plunder civilians whenever the opportunity arose. If the formations were undependable in this regard, then they were not useful to the leadership. As a result, there developed a trend across the middle of the eighteenth century to attempt to make these troops more disciplined in some regards. In essence, the goal of the reforms made in various armies should be understood as an attempt to focus the violence of these troops to where it would serve the tactical and operational purposes of the state.[30]

Regardless of how one might judge their actions towards civilians, the inescapable fact was that the Pandours and other irregular formations were incredibly effective militarily. As Johannes Kunisch observes, the retreats Frederick II undertook from Bohemia in both 1744 and 1745 were not the result of lost battles so much as the difficulties the Prussians encountered in combating the actions of the Austrian irregulars.[31] Clearly, the activities of these irregular formations caused significant concern among the Prussian leadership. As one historian of these light troops observed, that 'While Frederick discounted their effect in public, privately he held the Austrian light infantry in high regard'.[32]

Following the War of the Austrian Succession, there occurred a period of intense debate as military commentators sought to distil the lessons learned from the recent conflict. Light troops constituted a particular area of interest and attention within their discussions. Among the first to enter into the fray was Pandour Trenck who published his self-serving autobiography in 1748. Within its pages are several accounts of well-orchestrated irregular

---

27   Anderson, *War of the Austrian Succession*, p.271.
28   Anderson, *War of the Austrian Succession*, p.271.
29   Christopher Duffy, *The Army of Frederick the Great* 2nd edition (Chicago: The Emperor's Press, 1996), pp.131. Croats, as well as Grenzer, were irregular troops recruited by the Hapsburg monarchy, along with the pandours, from the Balkan Peninsula.
30   Peter H. Wilson, 'Social Militarization in Eighteenth-Century Germany' in *German History*. 18:1 (January 2000), pp.21-23.
31   Johannes Kunisch, *Der Kleinen Krieg: Studien zum Heerwesen des Absolutismus* (Weisbaden: Steiner Verlag, 1973), p.13.
32   Purky, 'Light Infantry Forces', p.38.

operations. One example he related was indicative of both the assets and liabilities of the first generation of irregulars,

> I received orders to go out upon a party against the enemy, who was then encamped by *Strehlen*, which I willingly complied with. I marched two nights successively, hiding myself by day in the woods, till I arrived and took post at *Zitenberg*, where I was well situated for cutting off the enemy's convoys. Here I took several wagons with provisions and drove back above 300 people with wheel-barrows, after having taken away their provisions, and drubbed them roundly into the bargain. Among other prizes, one of my outposts seized a wagon loaded with linen, together with four merchants in a coach, who being inhabitants of *Schweidnitz*, and consequently the queen's subjects, I stopped them for carrying on an illicit trade with the enemy…[33]

Interesting in his account is the manner in which Trenck organized his movements, travelling at night in order to conceal them enemy detection.[34] Likewise, he set his force up in a position from which to conduct their operations.

In the words of Professor Duffy, these troops had now become an 'established feature of warfare.' He further observed that 'Their character and their modes of action were now explored by authorities of the calibre of Turpin de Crissé (1754) and Silva (1778), as well as in a library of specialized literature (Grandamison, 1756; Jeney, 1759; Griesheim, 1777; Wissel, 1784, et al).'[35] Surveying the publication dates, the aforementioned works bridge the period from the War of the Austrian Succession into the Seven Years War. Joining in the discussion on the use of light troops shortly after Trenck were the Frenchmen de la Croix and Grandmaison.[36]

Little biographical information is available on de la Croix save for the fact that he was a French officer who commanded light troops during the War of the Austrian Succession. His *Traite de la Petite Guerre pour la Compagnies Franches*, first published in Paris in 1752, stood among the first works on irregular warfare widely read by military professionals of the day.[37] De la Croix's book seems to have enjoyed a critical success as a German edition

---

33 Trenck, *Memoirs*, pp.56-7. Here as with other quotations from primary source material, I have remained true to the spelling, capitalization and punctuation of the original.
34 It is worth noting that this same tactic was often utilized by Native Americans in North America. On this point, see Patrick Malone, *The Skulking Way of War Technology and Tactics among the New England Indians* (New York: Madison Books, 1991).
35 Duffy, *Military Experience*, p.269. The specific works Duffy alludes to in the preceding include: Marquis Silva, *Pensées sur la tactique, et la stratégique* (Turin, 1778); C. Griesheim, *Pflichten des Leichten Reuters* (Warsaw, 1778); M. Grandmaison *La Petite Guerre, ou Traité du service des troupes légères en Campagna* (Paris, 1756); Captain Jeny, *The Partisan: Or the Art of Making War in Detachments* (English edition, 1760); George Wissel, *Der Jäger im Felde oder kurze Abhandlung wie der Dienst bei leichten Truppen im Felde zu verrichten* (Göttingen: Johann Ghristian Dietrich, 1784).
36 Kunnish, *Der Kleinen Krieg*, p.5-6.
37 Both John Grenier, *First Way of War: American War Making on the Frontier* (Cambridge: Cambridge University Press, 2005), p.98 and Peter Paret, 'Colonial Experience and European Military Reform at the End of the Eighteenth Century', *Bulletin of the Institute of Historical Research*, 37 (1964), p.57 agree that this was the first widely read work on irregular warfare.

appeared soon thereafter.[38] De la Croix's *Traite* addressed a number of significant points concerning the use of light troops. His main themes included such topics as the discipline that should be observed when marching, and more interestingly, the manner of making night attacks.[39]

After de la Croix, the next discussion of the use of light troops derived from the pen of Thomas Auguste Le Roy de Grandmaison (1715-1801). Grandmaison, the scion of a family descended from the old nobility of France, aimed his previous experience with light troops in the War of the Austrian Succession. His *La Petite Guerre ou Traite des Troupes legeres en Campagne* first appeared in 1756, just at the outset of the Seven Years War. In describing the raising and employment of light troops, Grandmaison stressed the importance of the commander chosen to lead such formations.[40] He went on to explain,

> If on the contrary, merit is preferred, he only considers people of reputation, of experience, and of (good) behaviour. One easily feels the difference that a leader must place between the former and the latter; his advancement, his glory, his reputation, and that of his regiment, are dependent on it.[41]

While European commentators busied themselves with digesting the lessons of these new irregulars, the English remained generally outside of this wave of publications. The main work then in use to train their forces, Humphrey Bland's *Treatise of Military Discipline*, while designed to train a new generation of officers based on practical military experience, was composed prior to the dramatic expansion in light forces which occurred during the War of the Austrian Succession.[42] Only with the publication of Thomas Bell's *A Short Essay on Military First Principles* in 1770 would there be a work by an Englishman dealing specifically with light infantry.[43] Clearly, significant attention was being given to the lessons learned concerning light troops from the War of the Austrian Succession. As in all times, professional soldiers considered how their experiences could be put to use in subsequent conflicts. They would not have long to wait.

Aside from Prussia, the great powers of Europe were generally displeased with the outcome of the War of the Austrian Succession. Certainly, Maria Theresa of Austria sought to regain the lost province of the Silesia, and through the diplomacy of Count

---

38   Paret, 'Colonial Experiences', p.57.

39   M. de la Croix, *Traite de la Petite Guerrepour la Compagnies* (Paris: Franches, 1752), pp.25-26 and 31-33 respectively.

40   Thomas Auguste Le Roy de Grandmaison, *La Petite Guerre or Traite des Troupes legeres en Campagne* (Paris: Knoch, 1756), pp.28.

41   Grandmaison, *Traite*, p.29. Translation by the author..

42   On this see, James R. Mc Intyre 'Vanished into Obscurity: Humphrey Bland', *Seven Years War Association Journal* Volume 14:3 (Fall 2005), pp.80-82. See also 'Enlightened Rogues: Light Infantry and Partisan Theorists of the Eighteenth Century, 1740-1800', *The Journal of the Seven Years War Association*, 18:2 (Fall 2013), pp.4-28. The edition then current of Bland's Treatise would have been Humphrey Bland, *A Treatise of Military Discipline; In which is Lain Down and Explained the Duty of the Officer and Soldier thro' the Several Branches of the Service* (London: D. Midwinter, J. and P. Knapton, 1743).

43   Thomas A. Bell, *A Short Essay on Military First Principles* (London: Printed for T. Becket and P.A. De Hondt, 1770).

Wenzel Kaunitz worked to construct a coalition designed to answer that end.[44] All that remained was a spark to set the great powers of the European continent in conflict with one another once again. The trigger, in this instance, emanated from the backwoods of Pennsylvania and travelled across the Atlantic to the halls of power in the various European states.[45] There ensued the Diplomatic Revolution, which upended alliances that stood for over a century and replaced them with new coalitions, many of which would not survive the coming conflagration.

France, the inveterate foe of Austria on the European Continent, transformed into Austria's ally, as did Sweden and Russia. Prussia, once a supporter of France, now turned on her and entered the British camp. The smaller German states of Central Europe negotiated alliances with these great powers based on a number of factors, including geographic position, religion, familial affiliation, and the potential for territorial gain, or at least defence.

By the coming of the Seven Years War, the importance of light troops in Europe stood as a given. As one of the first historians of that conflict, Johann von Archenholz, noted, 'The want of light troops was the cause of the Swedes being often obliged to give up the best formed projects, and the Prussians harassed them on all sides with a few men and cut off all their supplies.'[46] The preceding is certainly an exaggeration; the Swedes did in fact raise their own light forces.[47] Still, it does drive home the point of the perceived importance of light troops among contemporaries.

Thus, as the great armed hosts of the various belligerents organized and started to march forth, many of the states likewise sought to raise fresh contingents of irregular troops. Although they had demonstrated their utility in the last conflict, no permanent place for these formations existed in the military establishments of the various powers. The closest any power came to possessing a permanent establishment of light troops were the Austrians who maintained their units of Croats, Grenzer and Pandours as a local first line of defence along their border with the Ottoman Empire.

The Austrians led the way in light troops at this time. By the same token, they had embarked on a series of reforms in the interwar years aimed at bringing these troops more in line with the regular establishment. Concerning these reforms, Professor Duffy notes, 'The changes as they affected the Croatian light infantry were an unsatisfactory compromise, for they deprived the Croats of something of their warrior virtues, without endowing them with the solidity of "German" infantry.'[48] Many of the other European states once again turned to their royal gamekeepers and raised contingents of Jäger. As noted above, the Swedes followed this practice. The Jäger were respectable, in Duffy's estimation, however, 'it

---

44   On this point, see Franz A.J. Szabo, 'Prince Kaunitz and the Balance of Power', *International Historical Review* (1979), pp.399-408.

45   On the incident at Jumonville's Glen, which set in motion the Seven Years War, see Fred Anderson, *Crucible of War: The Seven Years War and the Fate of Empire in North America, 1754-1766* (New York: Alfred A. Knopf, 2000), pp.52-58.

46   Johann Wilhelm von Archenholz, *Prussia and the Seven Years War 1756-1763* (Bohn: Hamburg, 1787), pp.66-67.

47   Jeff Leach, 'Swedish Jäger Units of the Seven Years War', *Seven Years War Association Journal* 10:1 (Winter1997), pp.33-42.

48   Duffy, *Force of Arms*, p.12.

is much more difficult to generalize about the hundreds of free corps regiments, battalions or companies which sprang up in wartime and hung around the fringes of the armies.[49]

The Freikorps or Free Corps that Professor Duffy refers to stood as an expedient raised by the different powers, mainly the Prussians, as a means to quickly bulk up their light forces. Duffy further discerned that, 'For hard-pressed governments one of attractions the light troops was that they could be raised so quickly and cheaply.'[50] These formations call for some detailed analysis as they formed a bridge between the older means of raising troops hearkening back to the medieval era, and the newly emerging bureaucratic state. Initially, the term applied to any unit that was not attached to a standing regiment. At their inception, these troops were utilized to garrison fortresses, thus freeing up more line units for active service in the field.[51] As Peter Wilson has observed, all these corps, no matter their respective state, shared one common characteristic, 'they were raised on the initiative of a private individual rather than the government.'[52] The prospective commander was awarded a cash payment by the government to cover any costs incurred in recruiting the unit. Most often, the contract would appoint the prospective recruiter as the unit's commander. It usually allowed him a fair degree of personal latitude in the appointment of his subordinates as well. Once raised, the unit would be paid and fed at the expense of the state it served. The above practice allowed the ruler to quickly raise large formations of irregular troops without having to expand the bureaucracy of the state in order to administer them. The chief drawback to this method lay in the fact that the ruler possessed a very limited amount of control over the formation as it was in essence the property of the commanding officer. This lack of control hindered oversight of the unit as well. It made it difficult for the state authorities to ensure that the unit was actually worth the money invested in it or that the money was not simply being embezzled by the commander. At the same time, the Freikorps were not entitled to the same level of support received by troops in more permanent formations during peacetime. They could be raised at the beginning of hostilities and dismissed as soon as the state deemed their service unnecessary. They consisted of all types of troops including dragoons, hussars, infantry, Jäger, lancers, and at times possessed their own artillery as well. [53]

The sorts of actions the Freikorps engaged in during wartime distinguished them from regular formations as well. By the same token, they were quite akin to the duties of the light troops. For instance, they were often tasked with raiding enemy supply lines. In addition, they were at times sent against enemy outposts with the objective of securing prisoners in order to gain information on enemy troop dispositions. In time of battle, the Freikorps were often given the job of occupying wooded areas in order to secure the army's line of retreat. They were often assigned the post least likely to engage the enemy main forces as well. This deployment was intentional as it was feared that when confronted with large numbers of regular troops prepared for battle, the Freikorps would simply melt away. In

49   Duffy, *Force of Arms*, pp.272-273.
50   Duffy, *Age of Reason*, p.274.
51   Peter Wilson, 'Glassenapp's Freikorps', *Seven Years War Association Journal* 10:4 (Summer 1999), p.10.
52   Wilson, 'Glasnapp's Freikorps', p.10
53   Stephen Summerfield, *Prussian Freikorps and Jäger of the Seven Years War* (Huntingdon, England: Ken Trotman Publishing, 2018), p.5.

addition, they were routinely sent scouting ahead of a main force, especially if the terrain was considered too difficult for the regulars to operate in successfully. Finally, they were tasked with controlling occupied territories during winter.[54] As Stephen Summerfield aptly summarizes, 'the Freikorps were given the tasks that regular troops were unwilling to do'.[55] Summerfield's point is quite valid considering that these formations were ad hoc in nature so their loss would not be felt as keenly by the state as units that were painstaking raised and trained in peacetime.

In many ways the system of raising Freikorps hearkened back to the approach used to raise entire armies in the early to mid-seventeenth century. The heyday for these formations, however, overlapped with the Seven Years War, roughly the middle of the eighteenth century. During this period, they could be found in the armies of most European states. As Wilson aptly observes, 'The *Freikorps* were one of the last bastions of this old-style military entrepreneur-ship.'[56] At the same time, 'this was not the sort of unit for the sons of the high aristocracy to make their careers in.'[57] Rather, the Freikorps offered their founders, who often derived from the lesser nobility or were even of common ancestry, the opportunity of attaining officer status. As Wilson observes these men were often 'low-ranking officers who lacked the necessary wealth to buy a higher commission, or whose promotion was blocked by a string of superannuated superiors serving out their time.'[58] For men in this position, raising a Freikorps opened up several avenues of opportunity. Once they secured the commission to recruit the unit, they could make a profit simply by purchasing substandard arms and equipment. It should come as no surprise then, that service with the Freikorps tended to attract the more avaricious type of would-be officers. While many were honest men out to rise in a system stacked against them, the Freikorps gained an at times deserved reputation for seediness.[59] In sum, they were contingency formations which could be raised swiftly in time of need to fulfil a specific role and dismissed just as easily when circumstances changed.

The Austrian Croats, Grenzer, Pandours and Hussars allowed them to compensate for the existence of the Prussian Free Battalions. Still, in the press to mobilize at the outset of the new conflict, the Austrians too raised their own Freikorps, as did the Hanoverians.[60] In the Austrian case, 'the existence of light or irregular forces enabled the Austrians to attract Prussian deserters who would otherwise have wandered off or gone back to the enemy.'[61] Not only did the Austrians once again raise units of Grenzer and Pandours as well as Hussars, they added to their mix of light troops by raising their own contingents of Jäger.[62]

---

54   Wilson, 'Glasnapp's Freikorps', p.11.
55   Summerfield, *Prussian Freikorps*, p.5.
56   Wilson, 'Glasnapp's Freikorps', p.11.
57   Wilson, 'Glasnapp's Freikorps', p.11.
58   Wilson, 'Glasnapp's Freikorps', p.11.
59   Duffy, *Age of Reason*, p.273.
60   On the Austrian Freikorps, see Purky, 'Light Infantry Forces', p.41. On the Hanoverians and Prussians see Bruce Bassett-Powell, *Freikorps of the Seven Years War Hannover and Prussia* (Weatherford, TX: Uniformology, 2008). See also, Joachim Neimeyer, *The Hanoverian Army during the Seven Years War 'Gmundener Prachtwerk'* (Copenhagen: Bent Carlsens Forlag,1977).
61   Duffy, *Instrument of Wae*, p.240.
62   Duffy, *Instrument of War*, p.241.

By the Seven Years War, the British, as well, realized that light troops would be essential in the coming contest on the continent.[63] They therefore began to raise special units in Hanover. As one authority on the Hanoverian contingent notes, 'These troops were raised for the duration of the war only, and their uniforms and equipment differed considerably from the usual patterns, giving them a somewhat motley appearance.'[64] Not only were these troops uniformed with whatever materials could be procured, they were often armed and equipped with weapons taken from the enemy. Clearly such contingencies made maintaining them in the field as a combat-capable force a challenge of epic proportions, it contributed as well to the varying descriptions of these formation in the primary sources.[65] It just as likely contributed to their reputation for plunder as they could easily be confused with marauders.

The vogue for light troops not only spread in central and western Europe but captured the attention of eastern European states as well. As Professor Duffy observed, the Russian commander, Petr Aleksandrovich Rumyanstev considered augmenting the Russian army with light forces for some time. He frequently discussed this possibility with a Captain Lambert, the two men meeting at Riga in 1757. The captain observed that when it came to his ideas on light troops, Rumyanstev 'was a complete imitator of Turpin de Crisse.'[66] The impetus that moved Rumyanstev from talk to action came in the Russian operation against Colbert which demonstrated the need for troops who could act against the Prussian Jäger and free battalions. He therefore began to raise a light infantry force of 1,040 infantry. As in the light troops of other European powers, Rumyanstev hoped to draw the soldiers from men in possession of previous hunting experience, and who had already formed close binds by serving together in the same regiment.[67]

As the new units were quickly raised, a fresh group of partisan leaders would gain fame through their exploits in the unfolding Seven Years War. These included such men as Johann Christian Fischer, Andreas Hadik, Friedrich Wilhelm von Kleist, and Nikolaus von Lückner. All would achieve either fame or infamy, depending on one's side, for their daring exploits. Among the Hanoverian formations, Lückner's Hussars were probably the most famous. They served in almost every action in the war which involved light cavalry. Through their service, they gained a reputation in these various endeavours for 'a courage verging on recklessness.'[68]

Lückner himself entered the Hanoverian service in 1757 with the rank of captain. By the following year he had achieved the rank of lieutenant-colonel, and in 1759 he earned his colonelcy. In 1760, he was promoted to major-general, and by 1761, at the improbable age of 39, he was made a lieutenant-general. Neimeyer aptly describes this as 'A truly meteoric rise'.[69] Certainly a factor in Lückner's rapid ascent through the officer corps may have been

---

63 On the development of the British light infantry on the continent, see David Gates, *The British Light Infantry Arm c.1790-1815* (London: B.T. Batsford Ltd. 1987).

64 Neimeyer, *Hanoverian Army*, p.69.

65 Neimeyer, *Hanoverian Army*, p.69.

66 Lambert, quoted in Christopher Duffy, *Russia's Military Way to the West: Origins and Nature of Russian Military Power 1700-1800* (London: Routledge and Keegan Paul, 1981), p.120.

67 Duffy, *Russia's Military Way to the West*, pp.120-121.

68 Neimeyer, *Hanoverian Army*, p.71.

69 Neimeyer, *Hanoverian Army*, p.71.

the fact that in 1757 he managed to capture one of the great French proponents of skir-mishing tactics, Grandmaison.[70] The experience of the Lückner Hussars in the Seven Years War certainly lends credence to historian Martin Rink's assertion that while the Hussars were not the only light troops of the eighteenth century, 'they are probably the best embodi-ment of the type.'[71]

While the various states raised and dispatched new light contingents, as Professor Duffy keenly observes, 'There was still a great deal of uncertainty as to how the light forces could best be employed at the middling level of war, in formal combat.'[72] Conversely, there were many who felt that they should operate completely independently of the main battle line.

Even while the first salvos of what would become the Seven Years War thundered across Europe, several authors sought to make their ideas on the use of light troops available to other military professionals. These men included M. La Cointe and, of course, M. Jeney. Both believed that the best role for the light troops was on detached service, away from the main force. Jeney, for his part, began with the idea that 'There is no military Employment that requires more extraordinary Talents than that of a Partisan.'[73] He further observed that the partisan 'should be blessed with an Imagination fruitful in Projects, Strategems [sic] and Resources.'[74] Professor Duffy echoed this sentiment, noting that, 'The best kind of partisan leader was a man who was fertile in projects and ruses. He combined a grasp of terrain and languages with a touch of wildness'.[75]

As an early author on partisan tactics, it was important for Jeney to define terms, which he did throughout the work. For instance, he defined ambushes as 'An Ambuscade is a body of Men concealed in a Wood, or otherwise with an Intention to surprise the Enemy.' He elabo-rated, 'There are no Strategems [sic] of War which afford a Partisan better Opportunities of displaying his Genius and Resolution.'[76] Concerning ambushes Christopher Duffy noted: 'The security of the ambush demanded some attention. The chosen site was best approached by a roundabout route, and the hoofmarks and other spoor were to wipe out with branches.'[77]

A factor that distinguishes Jeney's work is that he provided advice to his readers on a topic, then noted how it would aid their career if they followed his prescriptions. While security could present a major concern while conducting raids, in general it was something that the writers on light troops and detachments gave significant attention to. For instance, Cointe observed, 'We have often seen officers attacked at the instant when they had nothing to do, but to take, at their leisure, the proper measures to remain with the security in the post they had taken possession of.'[78]

---

70   Neimeyer, *Hanoverian Army*, p.71.
71   Rink, 'Der kleine Krieg', p.363.
72   Duffy, *Age of Reason*, p.277.
73   Jeney, *The Partisan*, p.6.
74   Jeney, *The Partisan*, p.6
75   Duffy, *Age of Reason*, p.273.
76   Jeney, *The Partisan*, p.106
77   Duffy, *Age of Reason*, p.276.
78   M. la Cointe, *The Science of Military Posts, for the use of Regimental Officers, who Frequently Command Detached Parties, in which is shewn the manner of Attacking and Defending Posts* (Royal Academy at Nismes, 1761), pp.92-93.

La Cointe certainly saw service with detached forces as a means to gain a reputation as well. As he emphasized, 'Therefore it is only when a private officer, having the chief command of a party can make a gallant defense, or can execute an enterprise to be talked of, that he may thereby be the instrument of his own glory, may merit the commendations of the army, and the favour of the court.'[79] La Cointe reinforced this theme, stating, 'What satisfaction must a young soldier feel, when by various devices he so opposes his enemy, that he secures himself from surprises, resists his attacks, disconcerts his projects and makes him abandon his enterprise!'[80] Following his initial injunctions in praise of the merits of detached service for young officers who want to make their mark, Cointe spent the remainder of the work offering practical advice for officers in a variety of tactical situations. For instance, when defending a house, Cointe advises the officer to post his men on both floors. He further enjoins the officer 'Also make several holes, through the floor, of four inches diameter, to fire from above on the enemy below.'[81] These small holes would allow the men to fire through the floorboards easily should the enemy take the lower level.

After delineating the various methods an officer could use to establish himself safely in a house, Cointe observes:

> But if an officer has not time for all those works that I have spoken of; which happens when a General has a mind to forage, and throws some foot into the houses, of farms, to form a line; an officer ought then to lay directly two trees across before the door, and cut holes through the floors, stop up the windows, and prepare for a vigorous defense, which will give time to the foragers to retire, or to detachments to arrive to succour them.[82]

Thus, the author not only presented his readers with an ideal state but provided them with possibilities for contingencies as well. At times, the practical nature of Cointe's advice transcends the specifics of time and place. For example, he implores officers, 'As to war, when you form a plan of good defence, it is better to take a thousand useless precautions, than to neglect one good one; because the least neglect may disconcert the best measures.'[83] The preceding placed La Cointe in the camp of the cautious commander, to an extent. At the same time, considering the context in which partisans operated, giving consideration to numerous possibilities stood as sound advice.

Both of the above works warrant consideration as they formed an intellectual bridge between the actions of light troops in the War of the Austrian Succession and what would be practice in the unfolding Seven Years War. Both the western and eastern European theatres of the conflict present numerous examples of partisan activity. The examples that follow are culled predominantly from the eastern theatre, as this constituted the focus of the bulk of Professor Duffy's research.

---

79   La Cointe, *Science of Posts*, p.6.
80   La Cointe, *Science of Posts*, pp.6-7.
81   La Cointe, *Science of Posts*, p.57.
82   La Cointe, *Science of Posts*, p.61
83   La Cointe, *Science of Posts*, p.71.

Probably the most ostentatious raid by light forces to occur in the European theatre was conducted by the Austrian commander Andreas Hadik. Professor Duffy describes the Austrian commander as 'Overweight and heavily married', who 'did not appear to the a natural commander of light forces, but he was a hard rider and an effective leader, and his attention to detail ... made him his own chief of staff.'[84] Still, it would he Hadik who managed to take advantage of the Prussian's condition in the summer of 1757 and pull off an operation remarkable for its audacity and its strategic effects.

In September of 1757, while the Austrians sought to counter any possible offensive moves by Frederick of Prussia, they noticed that due to Frederick's advance into Saxony and Bevern's slow retreat on Breslau a gap had opened up exposing the approaches to Berlin. The opportunity thus presented came to the attention of the Austrian commander, Prince Charles of Loraine, who ordered Hadik to attempt to capture the Prussian capital. Hadik led a force composed of 3,400 men, mostly Croats and Hussars.

The raid came as such a complete surprise to the Prussian defenders that the raiders actually managed to capture the city despite being outnumbered by the Prussian garrison, Hadik's force consisting of some 3,400 men against a garrison of 4,000.[85] While the difference in the two forces was small, consider contemporary opinion held that at least a three to one ration in favour of the attackers stood as a necessary prerequisite for attacking a fortified post.

Hadik occupied the city on 16 October 1757 after his four Grenzer companies succeeded in taking the Silesian Gate. Once in possession of Berlin, the Austrian commander exacted a ransom from the city which included 500,000 thalers, 10,000 of which was given directly to his troops to dissuade them from plundering the residents. In a move further designed to spare the inhabitants of the city, as well as conceal his movements, Hadik left Berlin at ten o'clock that night, 'Fourteen confiscated coaches were groaning with whatever the Berliners had been able to raise at such short notice and the rest was made up in paper monetary instruments.'[86] Supposedly, the commander further exacted a tribute of numerous pairs of gloves stamped with the city's coat of arms to provide to the empress Maria Theresa.[87] Initially, Professor Duffy assessed the raid in the following terms, 'The episode is interesting on account of its irrelevance, for it shows that at this juncture the survival of Prussia depended little on the capital, but very much on the king and his army.'[88] Upon further reflection, however, he noted 'Hadik's excellently-managed expedition had thrown Frederick's strategy into disorder and created opportunities for Soubise and Hildburghausen and the allied forces in central Germany.'[89] To a certain extent, however, this is the point of irregular

84   Duffy, *Force of Arms*, p.67. For a brief biography of Hadik, see James R. Mc Intyre, 'Heavyweight of the Lights: Andreas Count Hadik von Futak', in *Journal of the Seven Years War Association*, 22:3 (Spring 2019), pp.5-19

85   On Hadik's raid, see Duffy, *Army of Frederick the Great*, p.264; See also Duffy, *Force of Arms*, p 67-71, and Szabo, *Seven Years War in Europe*, p.101. For an in-depth examination of the raid itself, see James R. Mc Intyre, 'The Raid on Berlin, 1757', in *Journal of the Seven Years War Association* 22: 3 (Spring 2019), pp.20-42.

86   Duffy, *By Force of Arms*, p.70.

87   Duffy, *Army of Frederick the Great*, p.264.

88   Duffy, *Army of Frederick the Great*, p.264.

89   Duffy, *By Force of Arms*, p.70.

warfare. Its purpose is to be disruptive of the intended order of things and throw the best laid plans into consternation.

The following year, 1758, offers several illustrative examples of the work of light troops. The first occasion involved troops once again under the command of Hadik. The source on this occasion is the anonymous author of the journal which forms the core of *Zweybrücken in Command: The Reichsarmee in the Campaign of 1758*. He describes how, on 19 August 1758, 'The Commandant-General, the Prinz von Pfalz-Zweybrücken, went out early in the morning to inspect the position of General Hadik, commanding the Advanced Guard, on the heights of Gersdorf.'[90] The account continues, 'He then went on to reconnoitre the enemy camps at Sedlitz and Kohlberg, and the fortress of Sonnerstein. He did not return until evening.' All the preceding actions were indeed preparations for the night's work.

> That same night, Colonel Baron von Reid, at the head of his battalion of Gradiscaners and a company of Liccaners, entered the Prussian camp above Kohlberg. They put to the sword nearly 100 men in their tents and dispersed the remainder. Colonel Reid then returned to camp having no more than eight wounded; but captain of the grenadiers had the misfortune to be killed and the lieutenant was injured. The Croats captured seven horses and much booty, but, since the enemy occupied the camps at Sedlitz and Maxen in considerable strength, they were not able to carry off more than one prisoner.[91]

The above raid, conducted at night, presents a prime example of the type of work light irregular forces excelled at. In some respects, it is reminiscent of the battle of Paoli in the American War of Independence.[92] In both instances, there was a well planned and executed night attack, which threw the opposing side into confusion. In addition, attacks such as the one detailed above often exercised intermediate-term effects as well, in that the units on the receiving side being held on greater alert, which could sap the resiliency of the men for further operations.

Probably the most significant partisan work of the Seven Years War in Europe occurred between 28 and 30 June 1758 when two Austrian forces combined to assault and destroy a massive Prussian column bringing supplies and reinforcements to Frederick II's forces besieging the fortress of Olmütz. The convoy itself stretched over some 32 kilkometres. To provide cover to the long line of wagons, a force consisting of six battalions of fusiliers, and two of grenadiers along with three battalions of recruits and convalescents with 1,000 horsemen provide an escort. The raids were conducted first by Ernst Gideon Loudon working alone on 28 June, then by the combined forces of Loudon and Joseph Siskovics on the 30th. The second raid demolished the Prussian supply convoy, capturing 58 officers and 2,328 men out of the covering force, and destroying 3,000 out of 4,000 supply wagons. In the words of one of the first histories of the conflict, as a result of this raid, 'This was a fatal

90   Neil Cogswell (trans and ed.), *Zweybrücken in Command: The Reichsarmee in the Campaign of 1758.* (Warwick: Helion and Company, 2019), p.58.

91   Cogswell (trans. and ed.), *Zweybrücken in Command*. P.58.

92   On the connection to the battle of Paoli, 20 September 1777, sometime referred to as the Paoli Massacre, see Thomas McGuire, *The Battle of Paoli* (Mechanicsburg, PA: Stackpole Books, 2000).

stroke; for had it arrived safe, the place would not have held out above a fortnight longer.'[93] The lack of supplies, in turn, forced Frederick to lift the siege of Olmütz. A tactical success thus exerted a strategic effect, a testament to the potential of *kleine Krieg*.[94]

Successful operators in the art of *kleine Krieg* took advantage of environmental conditions as well. As numerous manuals of the period observe, 'The best time to attack an enemy camp or garrisoned village was about one hour before daybreak, when most of the troops were still asleep, and you could still enjoy the cover of darkness if you found you had stirred up a hornets nest.'[95] An additional example of just such a raid can be found in the history of the Schaumburg-Lippe Karbinier Corps in 1759. The following exploit of this unit, well known for its distinctive armour, is included to demonstrate that much the same sort of actions as occurred in the eastern theatre were part of the activities of partisans in the western theatre as well. Here, the Jäger of the Karbinier Corps responded to a raid on their post:

> On the night of April 28, an enemy detachment about the post of Herneburg tried to invade. In spite of Herneburg's hurrying patrol, he also managed to sneak undetected to one of the corps' advanced posts and blast it, killing three Jäger with the bayonet. But as the Jäger gave fire, noise arose in other places; the corps had been on the march through the night. At the first alarm, it was instantly in flight. The cavalry moved out immediately and towards the enemy, while the Jäger held the castle. The enemy saw his plan undone and withdrew under the shadow of darkness.[96]

On the above occasion, the attacking force broke off under just the sort of alarm professor Duffy describes. The result not only were the attackers driven off once the alarm was raised, but a contingent of the Karabiners set off in pursuit under the leadership of a Captain Lieutenant Friedrich Baum.[97] Actions such as those presented above continued throughout the Seven Years War.

Service in the various formations of light and irregular troops was highly active. In addition, 'The light forces took prisoners less frequently than did the regular troops, and they could expect little mercy in their turn.'[98] As a result, it came with a high casualty rate. Neimeyer projects that over the last two years of the war, the light troops sustained a

---

93   Anonymous, *A Complete History of the Present War, from its Commencement in 1756, to the End of the Campaign, 1760* (London: W. Owen; L. Davis and C. Reymers; and J. Scott, 1761), p.264.

94   On the raids at Domstadtle and Gunersdorf, see Duffy, *By Force of Arms*, p.105-113. See also Peter Wilson, 'The Ambush of the Olmütz Convoy at Domstadtl, June 28-30, 1758' *Seven Years War Association Journal* 8:4 (Winter, 1996): pp.10-25.

95   Duffy, *Age of Reason*, p.275.

96   G.W. von Düring, *Geschichte des Schaumburg-Lippe-Bückeburgeschen Karabinier- und Jäger- Korps im Siebenjährigen Kriegs* (Berlin: Graf Sigfried Mittler, 1828), p.66. Translation by the author.

97   During, *Geschichte des Schaumburg-Lippe*. p.66 This officer would later fall, as a colonel in the Brunswick service, at the battle of Bennington on 16 August 1777. See Col. Michael R. Gadue, 'Lieutenant Colonel Friedrich S. Baum, Officer Commanding, the Bennington Expedition A Figure Little Known to History', *The Hessians: Journal of the Johannes Schwalm Historical Association*. Vol. 11 (2008), p.37.

98   Duffy, *Age of Reason*, p.277.

casualty rate of about 50 percent.[99] Beyond the highly active nature of their service, some additional factors may contribute to this high casualty figure. First off, the light troops were often composed of the cast-offs from the regular formations. This was especially true in the Prussian service.

As the war wound down in 1763, men who had served on the various sides once again sought to make sense of their own experiences. Furthermore, they worked to codify those experiences and draw the cogent lessons from them in anticipation of the next conflict.

For the Austrians, while they clearly led the way in the development of irregular forces, they did not make much effort following the War of the Austrian Succession to write down their experience with the practice of small war.[100] Of those who served in the Seven Years War, and set down their experience in writing, among the more notable is Wilhelm von Zanthier. While Zanthier is most known for being the populariser of Marcenado, he did set down the experiences he gained while serving with the Sincère infantry regiment.[101] A number of others attempted to commit their experiences to paper as well. One of the most significant among these was Johann Ewald, then a junior officer in the Regiment von Gilsa. Ewald's first book, *Gedanken eines hessichen Officier uber das, was man bey Fuhrung eines Detachements im Felde zu thun hat* (Thoughts of a Hessian officer about what he has to do when Leading a Detachment in the Field) was published in 1774. As indicated by the title, the work concerned the command of detached forces, in other words, small units operating under the command of a junior officer. His work was therefore dedicated to *petite guerre*, or *kleine Krieg*.[102]

In his *Gedanken*, Ewald first employed the writing style which he would utilize through the rest of his writing career and would draw the approbation of no less a military thinker than Carl von Clausewitz.[103] Ewald would present a tactical situation or problem, provide a solution, and then support his recommendation based upon his own experience in the field.

To these works could certainly be added Johann Gottlieb Tielke's *The Field Engineer Or, Instruction upon every Branch of Field Fortification: Demonstrated by Examples which occurred in the Seven Years War between the Prussians, Austrians and the Russians*, which detailed some of the author's reflections on light troops during the conflict.[104] All of this writing, in turn, would influence yet another group of practitioners of irregular warfare in

---

99   Neimeyer, *Hanoverian Army*, p.69.

100   Kunisch, *Der Kleinen Krieg*, pp.5-6.

101   On Zantheir's service with the Sincère Regiment, see Kunnish, *Der Kleinen Krieg*, p.5. For a brief biography of Zanthier, see James R. Mc Intyre, 'The Popularizer: Friedrich Wilhelm von Zanthier and the Works of Santa Cruz de Marcenado' *Journal of the Seven Years War Association*. 22:2 (Winter 2018-19), pp.16-19.

102   Johann Ewald (trans. and ed. James R. McIntyre), *Thoughts of a Hessian officer about what he has to do when Leading a Detachment in the Field* (Point Pleasant, NJ: Winged Hussar Press, 2020). On Johann Ewald, see James R. Mc Intyre, *Johann Ewald Jäger Commander* (New York: Knox Press, 2020).

103   On Ewald's influence on Clausewitz, see Carl von Clausewitz (trans. and ed. Christopher Daase and James W. Davis), *Clausewitz on Small War* (Oxford: Oxford University Press, 2015), p.167; Peter Paret, *Clausewitz and the State: The Man, his Theories, and his Times* (Princeton: Princeton University Press, 1985), pp.191-92.

104   Johann Gottlieb Tielke, *The Field Engineer Or, Instruction upon every Branch of Field Fortification: Demonstrated by Examples which occurred in the Seven Years War between the Prussians, Austrians and the Russians* (London: J. Walter, 1789).

the next conflict, the American War for Independence. This later conflict would, in its turn, produce its own commentators on the subject, including John Graves Simcoe and Banastre Tarleton. Most importantly, it would see the maturation of the ideas of Johann Ewald.[105]

While the eighteenth century witnessed a re-emergence of light troops, they were not universally accepted.[106] Martin Rink notes how these policies often encountered resistance from military conservatives.[107] Part of this difference most likely traces back to discipline. For, as another commentator has emphasized, 'What was considered cowardice and indiscipline in one helped the other to achieve unpredictable agility and absolute freedom of movement.'[108] Simply put, what constituted liabilities in the regular infantry often stood as tactical assets for the light troops and irregulars. The problem then became how to integrate these forces into something resembling a cohesive whole. This process would work out over the course of the wars of the French Revolution and Napoleon. These developments fall outside the scope of the current writing.

At this juncture, several things are quite clear concerning the development of light infantry in the eighteenth century. First, that the development of light forces constituted a continuum across the middle of the century that began at the outset of the War of the Austrian Succession and continued through the Seven Years War. During the latter conflict, the use of these troops reached previously unseen levels, and their actions could sometimes exert strategic results. The raids on the Prussian convoy to Olmütz stands as cases in point. Second, that the works of Christopher Duffy over his long and productive career are essential in understanding that continuum. Whether the focus is on the general development of light forces across the eighteenth century, or the particulars of the emergence in the armies of Austria, Prussia and Russia, his works serves as a necessary starting point for fresh research on the topic of light forces, as well as a litmus test for theories. This is especially so concerning the critical period of the Seven Years War. His bibliographies are invaluable springboards for their primary source materials and he has set a high bar of academic integrity which current and future scholars can only hope to meet.

---

105 John Graves Simcoe, *Simcoe's Military Journal* (New York: Bartlett and Welford, 1844); Banastre Tarleton, *A History of the Campaigns of 1780 and 1781 in the Southern Provinces of North America* (Dublin: Colles, Exshaw, White, H.Whitestone, Burton, Byrne, Moore, Jones, and Dornin, 1787), and especially Johann Ewald, *Abhandlung von dem Deinst der Leichten Truppen* (Schleswig: J.G. Schloss, 1790 and 1796).

106 Some would push this development back to the seventeenth century, See George Satterfield, *Princes, Posts, and Partisans the Army of Louis XIV and Partisan Warfare in the Netherlands (1673-1678)* (Leiden: Brill, 2003).

107 Rink, 'Der kleine Krieg', p.365. See also the same author's 'The Partisan's Metamorphosis: From Freelance Military Entrepreneur to German Freedom Fighter, 1740-1815', *War in History*. 17:1, pp.6-36.

108 Kunisch, *Der Kleinen Krieg*, pp.22.

Further Reading

Primary Sources

Johann Ewald (trans. and ed. James R. McIntyre), *Thoughts of a Hessian Officer on What has to be done During a Tour with a Detachment in the Field* (Point Pleasant, NJ: Winged Hussar, 2020).

Grandmaison, Thomas Auguste Le Roy de, *La Petit Guerre ou Traite de Service les Toupes Legeres en Campagne* (Paris: Knoch, 1756).

Jeney, M. de, *The Partisan: Or the Art of Making War in Detachments* (London: R. Griffiths, 1760).

Tielke Johann Gottlieb, *The Field Engineer Or, Instruction upon every Branch of Field Fortification: Demonstrated by Examples which occurred in the Seven Years War between the Prussians, Austrians and the Russians* (London: J. Walter, 1789).

Trenck, Francicus von der, *Memoirs of the Life of the Illustrious Francis Baron Trenck* (London: W. Owen, 1748).

Secondary Sources

Duffy, Christopher, *The Military Experience in the Age of Reason 1715-1789* (New York: Hippocrene Books, 1987).

Duffy, Christopher, *The Army of Frederick the Great* 2nd ed. (Chicago, IL: Emperor's Press, 1996).

Duffy, Christopher, *The Austrian Army in the Seven Years War Vol.I Instrument of War* (Chicago: The Emperor's Press, 2000).

Duffy, Christopher, *The Austrian Army in the Seven Years War Vol.II By Force of Arms* (Chicago: The Emperor's Press, 2008).

Fuller, J.F.C., *British Light Infantry in the Eighteenth Century* (London: Hutchinson & Co., 1925).

Grenier, John, *The First Way of War: American War Making on the Frontier* (Cambridge: Cambridge University Press, 2005).

McIntyre, James R., *British Light Infantry Tactics* (Point Pleasant, NJ: Winged Hussar Publishing, 2015).

Picaud-Monnerat, Sandrine, *La Petite Guerre au XVIIIe Siecle* (Paris: Economica, 2010).

Rink, Martin 'The Partisan's Metamorphosis: From Freelance Military Entrepreneur to German Freedom Fighter, 1740-1815', *War in History*. Vol.17, No.1 (January 2010) pp.6-36.

9

The Extraordinary Life and Times of Military Engineer Charles Bisset

Petr Wohlmuth

When I opened pages of Christopher Duffy's *Fire and Stone* for the first time almost 15 years ago, it was at the very beginning of my university studies. The book was so fascinating that it sealed the choice of my research interest. The gripping story of the siege warfare and especially its subterranean dimension, as an almost forgotten, but crucial aspect of early modern wars, especially in the Occident, made me reconsider many previous beliefs I held. I embarked on a voyage that eventually led me to academic research in historical anthropology and military history at Charles University, Prague, Faculty of Humanities. Books by Christopher Duffy have accompanied me from the very start right to this moment, and I feel honoured and privileged to contribute to this Festschrift.

My chapter will return to the very problem, which caught my attention at the beginning: the subterranean component of early modern siege warfare. More specifically it will try to understand the complex meanings associated with the short but highly interesting career of a British physician, military surgeon and military engineer Charles Bisset (1717–1791), whom I discovered almost 10 years ago, during archival research for my MA thesis. Bisset sailed to the War of Austrian Succession in 1744 as an Ensign of the famous Black Watch Regiment, *Am Freiceadan Dubh*. He was fascinated with the phenomena of the underground war, but unlike me, he went through an excruciating direct experience with this kind of warfare. The brutal epiphany which happened during the 1747 siege of Dutch fortress Bergen op Zoom, completely changed his life. He became a military engineer and an author of a respected 1751 volume on fortification and siege warfare. Nevertheless, he was reduced to half-pay, side-lined, and discharged a few years later. Why? First, let us go back to the historical moment which set the scene for Charles Bisset and his short military life.

A sequence of bad news shook European military culture as well as the knowledgeable general public during the latter phase of the War of Spanish Succession.[1] It stemmed from a

---

1 The author subscribes to the concept that Western Europe shared a common military culture from the period of War of Spanish Succession to the French Revolutionary Wars (see above, p.50). See also Ilya Berkovich's concept of Europe united by 'single and relatively stable military culture', Ilya

particular detail related to three momentous siege operations; after a very long investment, a crucial role during the siege was played by underground mine warfare. All fortresses involved, Savoyard Turin (1706), French Lille (1708) and finally Tournai (1709), were examples of modern or significantly updated designs, equipped with a permanent countermine system comprising a labyrinth of underground corridors built under the outermost defensive layer of the fortress, the glacis. Within these corridors, a heavy charge of gunpowder – a mine – could be placed and detonated under the enemy assault trenches, which slowly ran towards the fortress under a heavy cannonade and almost incessant musketry. Eventually, these mines could be detonated even under the besieger's breaching batteries – which were at last successfully placed after a long and often cruelly arduous effort to fire from a close range to the inner defensive layer in order to produce the breach in the fortress walls, through which the infantry could lead a final charge.

The art of military mining had been known for almost two centuries and it had already proved a decisive factor in siege operations, for instance, during Ottoman sieges of Candia, which fell in 1669, and Vienna in 1683, which resisted only thanks to the arrival of allied relief force routing the besiegers. Nevertheless, the details of the underground mine warfare at Turin, Lille and Tournai were gruesome. Moreover, they arrived at a time when many military engineers intensely sought to develop new methods to bolster the defensive potential of bastioned fortresses. Especially in Western Europe, these fortresses regularly fell victim to the method of the so-called regular siege. This was developed by the highest authority in the field at that time, the French *Maréchal* Vauban, during the last quarter of the seventeenth century. Widely known and admired especially after Vauban's famous quick reduction of Ath in 1697,[2] this method combined above all a skilful placement of artillery batteries, firing in ricochet, taking advantage of basic geometric features of bastioned fortresses and also laborious and bloody, yet systematic, running of assault trenches towards the fortress. It provided a near certain guarantee that any fortified place, designed and built according to the bastioned system, could be reduced in due course.[3]

Nevertheless, the 1706 siege of Turin was an utter failure. The besieging army lost too many days, from 2 June to 7 September, in front of the fortress citadel and was finally challenged by a relief force, led by Prince Eugene. The result was a complete rout of the French. Much precious time was lost mainly because the Savoyard defenders made good use of the permanent countermine system of the citadel. Many defensive mines were sprung, the attackers had to descend underground and fight their battles against the enemy well versed in military pyrotechnics. More than 90 days of resisting the regular siege represented a great

Berkovich, *Motivation in War. The Experience of Common Soldiers in Old-Regime Europe* (Cambridge: Cambridge University Press, 2017), p.7. See also Robert Frost's concept of 'Occidental' culture of war, Robert Frost, *The Northern Wars 1558–1721* (Harlow: Longman, 2000), pp.16-19. This view of a specific Western military culture is supported also by Brian J. Davies (ed.), *Warfare in Eastern Europe 1500–1800* (Leiden and Boston: Brill, 2012), pp.1–18.

2   The best contemporary English resource is an ego-document by Goulon, see Louis Goulon, *Memoirs of monsieur Goulon being a Treatise on the Attack and Defence of a Place. To Which is added a Journal of the Siege of Ath in the Year 1697* (London: C. Bathurst and A. Milan, 1745).

3   For an analysis of the reduction of Ath, see Jamel Ostwald, *Vauban under Siege. Engineering Efficiency and Martial Vigor in the War of the Spanish Succession* (Leiden and Boston: Brill, 2007), pp.21–45.

achievement.[4] For the first time in many years, the Vaubanian method of regular siege failed thanks to the application of the permanent countermine system.

The 1708 saw the siege of Lille, when allied armies under the command of Marlborough and Prince Eugene besieged the city adorned with the famous citadel designed by Vauban himself. The siege was ultimately successful but again, the human cost was enormous with losses exceeding 16,000 men after the garrison widely employed the art of military mining.[5] The year1709 saw the culmination of that year's campaign in siege of Tournai, also a first rank fortress, this time designed by senior French engineer Jean de Mesgrigny. Surviving ego-documents and reports from the siege of Tournai provide graphic accounts of underground warfare which was labelled as an 'infernal' struggle, almost beyond human faculties, greatly feared by the deployed troops. Lieutenant-Colonel John Blackadder, who served with the Cameronian Regiment, wrote the following in his diary:

> The enemy having wrought all the ground into mines, which rendered it unsafe to approach from the hazard of explosion. Every step they took was under the apprehension of being blown into the air. Hostilities were carried on chiefly underground, and in total darkness. In counter-mining, it frequently happened that adverse parties met and fought with their shovels, spades and pick-axes. In these subterraneous attacks, the besiegers had to contend with new and appalling dangers. They were sometimes crushed by the failing in of the earth, or destroyed by the springing of the mine. Great numbers perished in this manner... sometimes they were inundated with water which the garrison let in upon them, or suffocated with the smoke of straw or hemp and gun-powder.[6]

There were truly a myriad of horrific ways of being killed in action.[7] Blackadder estimated that no fewer than 4,000 soldiers fell during the attack on the Tournai citadel, and it was extremely difficult not only to succeed in purely military terms, but also to culturally render this kind of experience. Tournai finally fell as well but it was indeed a Pyrrhic victory, again thanks to the vigorous use of a permanent countermine system. Another English ego-document, related to the same siege, the journal of Sergeant John Wilson, mentions that it was extremely difficult to discipline the soldiers, engaged in the underground struggle: 'The Siege being now so farr advanced and the Ingineers perceiving that the troops were very disconsolate and shock't, spar'd noe pains to perswade and also to infuse into the troops full confidence and beliefe that wee were out of any damage from the Enemy from below

---

4   For an analysis of siege of Turin see G. Cerino Badone, *1706. Le Aquile & I Gigli. Una storia mai scritta* (Torino: Omega Edizioni, 2007), pp.129–151.

5   James Falkner, *Marlborough's Sieges* (Stroud: Spellmount, 2007), p.161.

6   Andrew Crichton (ed.), *The life and diary of Lieut. Col. J. Blackadder, of the Cameronian regiment, and Deputy Governor of Stirling Castle; who served with distinguished honour in the wars under King William and the Duke of Marlborough, and afterwards in the rebellion of 1715 in Scotland* (Edinburgh: H. S. Baynes, 1824), p.346.

7   For more detailed description see Christopher Duffy, *Fire & Stone. The Science of Fortress Warfare 1660–1860* (Edison: Castle Books, 2006), p.141.

ground.'[8] The major problem was the cultural variable of horror, which struck the soldiers who were supposed to be deployed in the sector of the mine attack. 'Even the boldest men in the Army then on this service have turned their backs and given way. Nay, even those, who had seen death in all its shapes above ground was struck w'th horror to stand (as he supposed) on the topp of the mine in danger of being blown up every minute', added Wilson in order to explain the feelings of his men.[9]

The spectre of hellish underground struggle, which haunted the scene for some years after Turin, Lille and Tournai, slowly receded into the background, and for some time, it only survived in the form of cultural collective memory of British soldiers, engineers and educated readers. However, after almost four decades, the phantasm was back in full swing. In 1747, during the final phase of the War of Austrian Succession, British soldiers unexpectedly once again experienced the horrors associated with sieges of Lille and Tournai. This new war not only represented one of the watersheds in European military history in the sense that it effected many changes in politics and tore up old alliances, but it also caused a process which came to be known as the *crisis of permanent fortification*. Between 1745 and 1748, Low Countries became one of the crucial theatres of war of this conflict. French forces under Maurice de Saxe and Ulrich von Löwendahl managed not only to win three major field engagements at Rocoux, Fontenoy and Lauffeld but, above all, they scored an impressive and uninterrupted string of victories during major siege operations. Many old Barrier fortresses were reduced in Austrian Netherlands and altogether 28 fortified places fell victim to the victorious French army.[10] Not a single garrison was able to successfully resist. When the dust finally settled and the Treaty of Aix-la-Chapelle was signed in April 1748, military engineering experts on both sides started to evaluate the experience of the Low Countries campaign and several unpleasant facts began to emerge. Field reports were sent in, siege journals were published and, again, they were full of horrors of the underground war.

The reason was primarily one siege, clearly standing out of all other operations: that of the Dutch fortress of Bergen op Zoom in 1747. Among the participants, there were also British Army units, officer observers and military engineers who left some specific historical sources, immediately displaying impressive representations of the underground mine warfare. One of the two published British Bergen siege journals is even titled with a quotation from Milton's *Paradise Lost*, using the same kind of 'hellish' metaphors to describe the underground war as can be found in the 1709 Tournai diaries: 'Under ground they fought in dismel Shade, Infernal noise! War seem'd a Civil Game to this Uproar; horrid Confusion heap'd Upon Confusion rose.' The verses continue with even stronger expressions of the

8   David G. Chandler and Christopher L. Scott, 'The Journal of John Wilson, an "Old Flanderkin Serjeant" of the 15th Regiment and Later of the 2nd Troop of Life Guards, who served in 1694–1727', in David G. Chandler, Christopher L. Scott, Marianne M. Gilchrist and Robin Jenkins (eds), *Military Miscellany II. Manuscripts from Marlborough's Wars, the American War of Independence and the Boer War* (Stroud: Sutton Publishing Limited, 2005), p.75.
9   Chandler and Scott, 'The Journal of John Wilson', p.75.
10   See Anon., *Plans et Journaux des Sieges de la Derniere Guerre de Flandres, Rassemblés Par Deux Capitaines Etrangeres Au Service de France* (Strasbourg: Pierre Gosse Jun., 1750).

immediate results of the mine warfare: 'And now all Heaven Had gone to wrack, with ruin overspread.'[11]

Unluckily for the French, Bergen-op-Zoom represented a *magnum opus* of the celebrated Dutch military engineer Menno, Baron van Coehoorn, who infused this project with many insidiously effective features of his most advanced method of fortification. Moreover, Bergen was the only place which Coehoorn was able to fortify completely anew during his career and where his talent was not constrained by any older structures which had to be preserved.[12] 'This Place is said to be the Master-piece of the great Military Architect, Coehorn, it is fortified well', noted the author of the Owen's siege journal right from the start.[13] Once the French saps had reached the edge of glacis during the night of 5 August 1747 between bastions Pucelle and Coehoorn, the besiegers entered a killing zone of extensive and well prepared permanent countermine system.[14] There was no other way to continue their effort but to descend underground. An anonymous British author of Owen's siege journal noted that 'Our whole Discourse this Day is turned upon the Enemy's Mining, and our Engineers having viewed all within the Walls, and some part of the Lines, think that they shall be able to make their Mining the most expensive Action in the Loss of their Men, that they have as yet undertaken.'[15] This prophecy was indeed fulfilled, as the underground struggle within the front of the attack turned out to be extremely costly in terms of time, materiel as well as manpower. One episode of the first night will perhaps suffice to illustrate the intensity of the combat. The besiegers detonated their first assault mine during the first night close to the salient angle of the glacis near the Coehoorn bastion and a bloody struggle ensued immediately:

> About Eleven this Night the French sprung a Mine… which making some Way for them, they forced themselves into the Covered Way, where they proposed to make a Lodgement… but we… fell upon them with such Fierceness and Determination, that in a little Time they were repulsed with a most dreadful and unparallel'd Slaughter… During the time of the Assault, the Garrison sprung a Mine, which did fearful Execution, blowing up in a moment, two Companies of Grenadiers of the Regiment of Normandy…[16]

---

11 In *Paradise Lost* see Book VI, pp667-670. Anon., *An Authentic Journal of the Remarkable and Bloody Siege of Bergen-op-Zoom by the French under M. de Lowendahl in the Year 1747 etc.* (Dublin: Joshua Kinneir, 1747), title page.

12 Gosewijn Theodor Baron van Coehoorn and J. W. Van Sypesteyn, *Het leven van Menno baron van Coehoorn* (Leeuwarden: G. T. N. Suringar, 1860), pp.114–116.

13 Anon., *An Authentick and Accurate Journal of the Siege of Bergen-op-Zoom, with a Plan of the Town… By an English Officer of Distinction, who was a Volontier both in the Lines and Town etc.* (London: William Owen, 1747), p.10. Henceforth, 'Owen's journal'.

14 Anon., *An Authentic Journal of the Remarkable and Bloody Siege of Bergen-op-Zoom by the French Under M. De Lowendahl… By an English Volunteer, Late of the Garison at Bergen-op-Zoom etc.* (London: Ralph Griffiths, 1747), pp.23-24. Henceforth, 'Griffiths' journal'.

15 Anon., *An Authentick and Accurate Journal*, p.30–31.

16 Anon., *An Authentick and Accurate Journal*, p.44–45. Most references like this can be verified by comparing with not only Griffiths' but also Becket's journal, here Anon., *Military Operations of the English and French Armies, Commanded by His Royal Highness The Duke of Cumberland, and Marshal Saxe, During the Campaign of 1747. To which are added, I. Military Principles and Maxims drawn from*

This part of the siege, the struggle for the glacis and the covered way, which lasted 40 days, became a brutal contest fought mostly using mines and countermines. In total, 77 of them were sprung,[17] which was unparalleled in early modern European siege warfare; the glacis between bastions Pucelle and Coehoorn became a maze of saps and mine craters, covered with charred and destroyed war materiel, and adding yet another level to the horrors of war, also by a multitude of unburied bodies since the opposing sides did not agree upon the terms regarding the usual humanitarian concerns, and for many weeks rejected any ceasefire.[18] British military engineer William Bontein, who sprung a defensive mine under lunette Zeeland on 11 August, killing 200 French soldiers in a single blow, and who was subsequently heavily injured and evacuated, described his experience in these words: 'The siege produced an unintermitting scene of horror and destruction: nothing was to be seen but fire and smoke, nothing heard but the perpetual roar of bombs and cannon – the town was laid in ashes, the trenches filled with carnage.'[19] The author of Owen's journal later summarized his experience of the underground warfare in front of Bergen using these telling words, which fell nothing short of the former expressions of traumatic memory of Lille 1708 and Tournai 1709:

> You express a Curiosity to hear, nay, I think too, to see how Matters appear among the Assilants and the Defendants: Truly it is a Sight you would be very soon sick of… there you may behold the Remains of a human Carcass so disfigured, that all the Resemblance of the Divine Image is lost, scorched, blackened and mangled so frightfully… Scores half buried in the Ruins of a Mine, and what appears above Ground horribly spread over with Blood and Brains and torn Intrails; un short, this is now a Place where nothing but the most shocking Sights are the Objects of Amusement.[20]

---

the Remarks, II. *The Siege of Bergen-op-zoom. By an Officer* (London: Thomas Becket, 1760), p.140. Le Blond's anonymous author also provides very similar description, see Anon., *Journal of the Siege of Bergen-op-Zoom*, p.234. See also Anon., *Plans et Journaux des Sieges*, p.90, where this particular combat situation is described similarly.

17   This reference and many others from both British journals (Owen's and Griffith's) are also supported by a preserved siege journal, written from French perspective by Swedish-Livonian military engineer Lieutenant-Colonel Jacob von Eggers, who was an observer, present in French camp. See both editions Anon., *Journal du Siege de Bergopzoom en MDCCXLVII. Redige par un Lieutenant-Colonel Ingenieur volontaire de l'Armée des Assiegeans* (Amsterdam and Leipzig: Arkstee & Merkus, 1750) and Anon., *Journal du Siege de Bergopzoom en MDCCXLVII. Redigé par un Lieutenant- Colonel Ingenieur Volontaire de L'armée des Assiegeans… Nouvelle Edition* (Amsterdam and Leipzig: Arkstée & Merkus, 1770).

18   This was caused by a complicated cultural misunderstanding, which affected the initial negotiating ritual. This problem represents a subject of author's monograph, which includes transcript of Owen's journal, see Petr Wohlmuth, *Krev, čest a hrůza. Historická antropologie pevnostní války na příkladu britských deníků z obléhání pevnosti Bergen op Zoom z roku 1747* (Prague: Scriptorium, 2017). [Blood, honour and horror. Representations of siege warfare in siege journals of British defenders of Bergen op Zoom in 1747]

19   Whitworth Porter, *History of the Corps of Royal Engineers* (London: Longmans, Green & Co., 1889), Vol I. p.164.

20   Anon., *An Authentick and Accurate Journal*, p.2.

Despite all vigorous defensive measures, the French eventually managed to plant their breaching batteries. After 10 days of the final artillery duel, when the French breaching batteries were repeatedly badly damaged and dismounted by the defender's fire, a desperate attempt at general storm was made, and against all expectations of the defenders, it did succeed. A three-day long brutal pillage ensued.

The siege and defence of Bergen-op-Zoom gradually acquired an almost taboo status in both British/Dutch and French military cultures. Remembering Bergen was undesirable. On the one hand, it was labelled as a shameful loss with a suspected treachery on part of the Dutch garrison and on the other, it was a victory too bloody and costly, moreover spoiled by the final ruthless sack of the town, to be remembered as a marvellous and honourable feat of arms by the French.[21] Even the official history of the French Royal engineering corps treats it only superficially.[22] The siege and defence of Bergen-op-Zoom, though an operation of almost unparalleled magnitude and arguably the toughest episode of early modern European siege warfare, slowly started to sink into oblivion. Immediately afterwards, it was an event which wildly stirred the imagination of European public opinion. The siege was extensively covered in the British press,[23] ballards about the siege and fall of Bergen were sung, various anonymous prints defending the military honour of the garrison were released, and even a theatrical play was written and performed.[24] Despite all the interest and epic dimensions of the siege and many feats of self-sacrifice and gallantry equal or surpassing those displayed at Lille 1708 or Tournai 1709, its memory became obscured, mostly in favour of the memory of major field engagements such as Fontenoy.

Nevertheless, there was a man, a British physician, officer and military engineer, who participated intensively in the defence of Bergen-op-Zoom and refused to engage in the cultural amnesia.[25] The man survived the final storm and sack of the town, did not come to terms, culturally speaking, with the healing process of forgetting the slaughter of Bergen

---

21   Only 39 years later had Louis XVI. commissioned two (surprisingly small) paintings, representing the siege and capture of Bergen-op-Zoom, to be displayed in *Gallerie des Batailles* in Louvre. Both works, *Le siége de Bergen Op Zoom* (National Museum of Versaille and Trianon INV19360) and *Prise d'assault de Bergen Op Zoom* (INV 19362) were painted by Louis Nicolas van Blarenberghe. Especially the second one represents a carefully doctored version of the final assault and sack, avoiding any drastic detail and representations of the destruction.

22   Antoine-Marie Augoyat, *Aprecu Historique sur les fortificationes les ingénieurs et sur le corps du génie en France. Tome deuxieme* (Paris: Ch. Tanera and J. Dumaine, 1862), p.414–428.

23   See for instance Sylvanus Urban (ed.), *Gentleman's Magazine and Historical Chronicle, Volume XVII for the Year MDCCXLVII* (London: Edward Cave, 1747), p.328–329, 344–345, 346 (July issue of The Gentleman's Magazine for July 1747) and p.378–379, 401–402 (August issue) and p.409–413 (September issue). There is an extensive official coverage of the final phase of the siege in official Gazette. See *The London Gazette, Published by Authority*. From Saturday September 19 to Tuesday September 22, 1747. No. 8677. Reports are present already in the issue No. 8659 (July 18th 1747).

24   Anon., *Ballad on the taking of Bergen-op-zoom* (London, 1747), Anon., *Die Ehre der Holländer bey Berg-op-Zoom, Oder Historische Erzelung von der Schicksalen dieser Stadt in den alten etc.* ('s-Hertogenbosch: Gerhard Cornelius van den Dreesch, 1747) or Anon., *Der verlohrne Cranz Der gewesenen Jungfer Berg op Zoom. Ein Lust-Spiel etc.* (Kyck in de Pot, 1747).

25   Latter manifestation of this cultural amnesia can be found, for instance, in the advanced 2007 doctoral dissertation, examining the organization and education of British military engineers in the 18th century. Only Tournai, Gent or Ostende are listed when dealing with 1744-1748 Low Countries campaign. Bergen-op-Zoom is completely missing. Andrew Philipson, 'The Business of Engineers.

and finally, even after being discharged from the army, devoted significant efforts to bring up the painful subject time and again, almost until his final days. His name was Charles Bisset.

Little is known about military engineer Charles Bisset now although he published a major volume on the theory of fortification and, for a certain time, his military career looked very promising. He was born in 1717 and, as his short autobiography suggests, he first served in 1741 as surgeon's mate in the Royal Navy and, later, as a surgeon in a military hospital in Jamaica. In 1745, he had to return home because of bad health and in May of the same year, he purchased an Ensigncy in the 43rd Regiment of Foot (later the 42nd, or Black Watch) and 'began to study Fortification',[26] which became his lifetime devotion. When deployed in 1746 around Sandberg in Flanders with his Regiment, he made a sketch of Dutch fort and its environs, which was passed by his regimental commander, Lord John Murray, to William, Duke of Cumberland. The regiment was then ordered to move to Bergen-op-Zoom and Bisset made another sketch, this time of the fortress, which was also forwarded to the allied supreme commander. Cumberland was so pleased with Bisset's work that he ordered him to move to the town and 'send him, by Express, every second or third day, a particular account of the daily progress of the Attack, with the conduct of the Besieged.'[27] This was a dangerous duty indeed but Bisset performed it more than satisfactorily, and after the fall of the town, Cumberland obtained for Bisset a Warrant as Engineer Extraordinary and shortly after, he was promoted to Lieutenant.[28] From all Bisset's reports only one survived, dated 20 August 1747, showing him as a skilled and competent observer.[29]

Bisset became a sort of protégé of Cumberland and spent next four years studying the art of fortification and finally in 1751, he published a book titled *The Theory of Construction of Fortification*, dedicated to William, Duke of Cumberland, which reflected a great deal upon the siege of Bergen-op-Zoom.[30] The book was submitted to the Board of Ordnance in high hopes of recognition and Bisset was right to describe his treatise in his 1755 letter to Robert Dodsley, publisher of his medical works, as 'being the only original Performance of this kind in our language', available at the time.[31] Despite all his exertions, Bisset did not receive

---

The Organization and Education of Military Engineers during the Eighteenth Century' (PhD Thesis, University of Portsmouth, 2007), p.20.

26   Charles Bisset, 'Essays on Fortification; Illustrated with new Designs. To which is added An Essay on The Attack and Defence of Temporary Defensive Works' (Unpublished manuscript, British Library ADD MS 19695, 1778), Preface. Page numbering is unclear, so the text is referenced as Essay/Chapter/Paragraph.

27   Bisset, 'Essays on Fortification', Preface.

28   The National Archives (TNA), WO 55/494/194, John Duke of Montague to Charles Bisset, Engineer Extraordinary. Bisset was named as a replacement for engineer Harry Gordon, advanced.

29   The Royal Archives (RA), CP/MAIN/25/441–444. 'At the moment the enemy succeeded in destroying the salient angle of lunette Utrecht by springing a mine, but did not manage to lodge in the breach thanks to a vigorous counter-attack.' There are fragments and partial transcripts of other Bisset's reports in The National Archives, SPF/ME – SP 87/23–240 and 23–268.

30   Charles Bisset, *The Theory and Construction of Fortification, illustrated with several new Designs. By Lieutenant Charles Bisset, Late an Engineer Extraordinary in the Brigade of Engineers which served in the Netherlands in the last War* (London: A. Millar, D. Wilson and R. Dodsley, 1751).

31   James E. Tierney (ed.), *The Correspondence of Robert Dodsley 1733-1764* (Cambridge: Cambridge University Press, 1988), p.203.

any official answer and eventually was discharged and put on half pay. His career, which seemed truly promising, took an abrupt downward turn and after some more time spent waiting for the satisfying answer, Bisset gave up and returned to his practice as a physician, in which he was successful and in 1762, he obtained a degree of doctor of medicine at St Andrews. In his 1755 letter to Dodsley, Bisset described the attitude of Board of Ordnance as reserved at best after he repeatedly attempted to gain the Board's attention:

> I was in hopes of being re-established as Engineer; but found the Gentlemen of the Board of Ordnance rather less favourable than the former: they took [no] notice of me till after making application; and then promised to [e]mploy me as practitioner Engineer, a Rank that is only possessed by the youngest Novices, and much Inferior to mine in the last war, which I rejected with great Contempt.[32]

Notwithstanding the adversity, Bisset never gave up his interest in fortification and in 1778, he finished a lengthy manuscript called *Essays on Fortification; Illustrated with new Designs. To which is added An Essay on The Attack and Defence of Temporary Defensive Works*, dedicated to George, Prince of Wales, representing a further advancement of his original 1751 study. His second work was never published and Bisset passed away in 1791. The obituary published in the *Gentleman's Magazine* again mentioned, besides his numerous medical endeavours and publications, his 'brave and skilful performance of duty' during the 1747 campaign in Flanders.[33]

Bisset's treatises, his 1751 book and 1778 manuscript, were no works of an 'insane' amateur, proposing yet another unworkable system of fortification, to be justly discarded by authorities. His book features an impressive list of 213 subscribers, which reads like a who-is-who of the British military establishment of the time, including, for instance, Lieutenant Generals Cope, Howard, Huske and Wolfe, Bisset's former commander Lord John Murray, and many other generals and colonels, plus numerous military engineers such as Captain Cunningham, Lieutenant Colonel Elliot or Colonel Robert Napier or even Adam Ferguson, at the time chaplain to the 43rd Regiment of Foot. Bisset was understood as a man of authority and knowledge who had something to say regarding the matter. He is even mentioned in Porter's *History of the Corps of Royal Engineers* as a young officer who volunteered for a dangerous job and had shown 'such energy and capacity', that rightly earned him a promotion.[34] So why was his contribution almost completely ignored by the Board of Ordnance after his services were amply recognized and Bisset was promoted and even obtained an engineer warrant? This is a question which this chapter will try to answer.

The military career and life story of Charles Bisset had been apparently marked by two key issues of military engineering affairs of the time. The first was the matter of military mechanics: the perceived crisis of permanent fortification and subsequent attempts to overcome it. The second was a matter of cultural nature: the complex of meanings associated with the uneasy cultural status of underground mine warfare, based upon a permanent

---

32   Tierney (ed.), *The Correspondence of Robert Dodsley 1733-1764*, p.203.
33   Sylvanus Urban (ed.), *The Gentleman's Magazine: and Historical Chronicle. For the Year MDCCXCI. Volume LXI. Part the Second* (London: John Nichols, 1791), pp.965–966.
34   Porter, *History of the Corps of Royal Engineers*, Vol I, p.164.

countermine system, as a powerful means to assist in overcoming this crisis. The crisis itself was produced by a conjunction of several factors, especially a series of improvements in artillery: first and foremost, by improved methods of casting gun barrels, invented by Johann Maritz, and also the introduction of tables for calculating propellant charges and correct elevations for both cannon and mortar.[35] The older practice, as explained for instance in the third (1745) edition of old Saint Remy's *Mémoires d'artillerie*, had begun to be significantly updated.[36] Military ballistics was also subject to a gradual change and improvement and for instance, British mathematician and military engineer Benjamin Robins was in his 1742 *New Principles of Gunnery* the first to tackle the problem, nowadays known as Magnus effect, causing an inherent inaccuracy of smoothbore weapons.[37]

The result was a sort of 'new' or rather 'accelerated' type of attack. During the Flanders campaign in 1744–1748, small fortifications were often not subjected to any formal siege but vigorously bombarded from numerous cannon and especially mortar batteries, which usually resulted in most of the artillery being dismounted quickly and the defenders suffering heavy losses. Such was the case, for instance, of Fort Sandvliet, guarding the southern approaches to Bergen op Zoom, which was reduced in less than a day on 10 July 1747. Other lesser fortifications also did not stand the test of the improved siege trains. Jacob von Eggers, present in the French camp, praised Count von Löwendahl precisely for using this new kind of attack.[38] The new practice seemed to represent a fresh upgrade to old efforts to accelerate the siege, exerted during the War of Spanish Succession, where the old engineer paradigm of 'engineering efficiency' started to be replaced with a concept of 'martial vigour', as explained by Ostwald in his seminal volume.[39]

It is generally agreed that no comparable development which would bolster the defence occurred on the part of the art of fortification during the 1720s-1740s. The shocking experience of Bergen op Zoom in 1747 greatly influenced the decision to found the *École royale du génie* at Mézières in 1748. This was supposed to stabilize the situation and improve the art of defence. Nevertheless, the badly needed modernizing impetus never came from this direction. The School of Mézières provided elite education to its students, who had to go through six years of rigorous curriculum, but it also failed to conceptually transcend in any way the classic post-Vaubanian concepts, as elaborated by Louis de Cormontaigne who avoided even the two most advanced Vauban's designs, his Second and Third method. The

35   Christopher Duffy, *The Fortress in the Age of Vauban and Frederick the Great 1660-1789. Siege Warfare Volume II* (London, Boston, Melbourne and Henley: Routledge & Kegan Paul, 1985), p.154. One of the most important publications was Bernard Forest de Bélidor, *Le Bombardier Francois, ou nouvelle methode de jetter les bombes avec precision* (Paris: L'Imprimerie Royale, 1731).

36   Pierre Surirey de Saint-Remy, *Mémoires d'artillerie* (Paris: Rollin Fils, 1745). In the British environment see for instance John Muller, *A treatise of artillery etc.* (London: John Millan, 1768).

37   Benjamin Robins, *New Principles of Gunnery: containing, The Determination of the Force of Gunpowder and The Investigation of the Difference the Resisting Power of the Air to Swift and Slow Motions* (London: J. Nourse, 1742).

38   Bisset noted that intensity of mortar fire during sieges of Flanders campaign was unparalleled and it seemed to him that lesser places could be reduced using only intensive mortar bombardment. Bisset, *Essays on permanent and temporary Fortification*, 2/104 and Bisset, *The Theory and Construction of Fortification, illustrated with several new Designs*, p.61

39   Jamel Ostwald, *Vauban under Siege: Engineering Efficiency and Martial Vigor in the War of Spanish Succession* (Boston – Leiden: Brill: 2006).

'new' concepts were just a re-incarnation of the old orthodoxy. Apart from that, a number of 'more or less insane alternatives to the regular bastion trace' were proposed, such as the systems of now forgotten Cugnot, Pirscher or Robillard.[40] But what about Charles Bisset? Is his contribution in any way comparable to Mézières? We will try to answer this question through an examination of three chief alternations and updates to the classic bastioned trace, proposed by Bisset.

Bisset's book represents an outcome of four years of an intensive private study and a long journey around the continent, about which the author did not give any additional information, but which was probably sponsored by the Duke of Cumberland. Bisset also mentioned his mentors in the engineering corps, Colonel Napier and Lieutenant Colonel Scott.[41] Bisset's concepts were original but his claim that in his 1751 book he 'neither borrowed from, nor imitated, any preceding Author', which he made in his 1755 letter to Dodsley, is without a doubt exaggerated.[42] Bisset was the first and above all a prolific commentator on Coehoorn and his systems of fortification. He stood in awe in front of Bergen-op-Zoom, the chef d'oeuvre of his master, which he could thoroughly study after the 1748 Treaty of Aix-la-Chapelle. He concluded that Bergen's design not only represented the cream of the crop of the Western military engineering, but also a method to be followed and further developed in order to overcome the crisis of the permanent fortification. The first 37 pages, the whole three chapters of his book are devoted to a meticulous analysis of the Bergen project and 1747 siege:

> General Coehoorn's Method of the several Fronts of the Fortification of Bergenopzoome... approaches the nearest, perhaps, of any hitherto invented, to that ultimate Degree of Perfection which is the principal Aim of every Method, or particular Arrangement of defensive Works; and which consists in Strength and Simplicity, in the highest Point these are capable of being obtained together, at any determinate expense...[43]

Bisset primarily recognized the powerful arrangement for flanking defence of Coehoorn's short fronts, which was attained mainly thanks to strong bastions with concave flanks and additional high flanks, hidden behind orillons. Their artillery was able to successfully confront, dismount and ruin even the French breaching batteries and lodgements on the covered way during the final phase of the siege. Bisset's challenge is based primarily on the practical field experience and it differs profoundly from the well-known debate between Montalembert and Ramecourt, where the original challenge was at first purely theoretical.[44]

---

40 Duffy, *The Fortress in the Age of Vauban and Frederick the Great 1660-1789*, p.157.

41 Bisset, *The Theory and Construction of Fortification etc.*, Preface.

42 Tierney (ed), *The Correspondence of Robert Dodsley 1733-1764*, p.203.

43 Bisset, *The Theory and Construction of Fortification etc.*, p.1-2.

44 The first of ten volumes of the Montalembert's challenge was published in 1776, see Marc René de Montalembert, *L'Art défensif, supérieur à l'offensif etc.* (Paris: Didot, 1776). The semi-official reply by the senior of the Royal engineering corps was published in 1786, see Charles-René Fourcroy de Ramecourt, *Mémoires sur la fortification perpendiculaire* (Paris: Nyon, 1786). The whole debate is analysed in Janis Langins, *Conserving the Enlightenment: French Military Engineering from Vauban to the Revolution* (Cambridge (Massachusetts) – London: The MIT Press, 2004).

Bisset in both his 1751 book and 1778 manuscript mainly aims at returning the art of military engineering to its roots, to a sophisticated method opposed to new accelerated ways of attack relying on the overwhelming firepower and massed infantry assaults. Bisset came to the conclusion that contemporary post-Vaubanian concepts of fortification had become outdated and must be further developed in order to match the latest developments in the art of attack. Bisset's texts contain a profound critique of Vauban and his systems, and his attitude to the Grand Master substantially differs from that displayed by the doyen of the British engineering corps, John Muller, who in 1750s still considered Vauban's systems as valid and requiring only minor updates.

Bisset built his case against Vauban by employing an argument of the inseparable connection between reason and experience in military engineering. His ideal engineer possesses both 'practical' experience and theoretical knowledge, and thus can recognize that 'Imperfections naturally flow from Inexperience in the Practice of the Art' and more fundamentally 'Imperfection is inseparable from human nature.'[45] At first his Rules, Principles and Remarks relative to Permanent Fortification, as explained in the first Chapter of his manuscript, closely resemble those of old Vauban, express the same pragmatic spirit, and reject any 'particular regard for Beauty or Taste… in military Architecture.'[46] The Preface to his book also displays his aversion to abstract claims to perfection in style. The art of attack and defence 'seems incapable of being demonstrated geometrically, or mechanically, or by any Method that will amount to a mathematical Certainty; because the Attack and Defence consists in Variety of Circumstances that can neither be exactly determined, not admit of being wholly reduced under certain and general Rules…'[47]

1) Deconstruction of the New Italian School of Fortification

The assault on Great Master begins with a discussion over one of the chief upgrades to the *trace italienne* introduced by the New Italian School in the second half of the sixteenth century, which became a standard feature of bastioned systems – a ravelin, naturally included in Vauban's concepts which, according to Bisset, were in essence mostly updated variants of older designs from Count Pagan's treatises, again drawing heavily from the classic New Italian designs.[48] Bisset recapitulates that the original intention of designing a ravelin was to place an additional obstacle into the main ditch, which could pose a danger to the besieger's breach batteries and would prolong the siege. Bisset argues that there is a hidden and irreparable flaw in the concept of having such outwork:

> For, in order to have the Flank and shoulder of the Bastion well covered by the Ravelin, either the face of the Bastion, which is the weakest part of an Enceinte, must be extended to too great a length, which, besides, by enlarging the Bastion,

---

45   Bisset, *The Theory and Construction of Fortification etc.*, Preface.
46   Bisset, 'Essays on Fortification', 1/1/2.
47   Bisset, *The Theory and Construction of Fortification*, p.38.
48   Bisset, 'Essays on Fortification', 1/1/27.

will greatly add to the Expence, or too great a breadth must be given to the Gorge of the Ravelin…[49]

Such a setup is indeed possible but too expensive according to Bisset, and he argues that it would be more practical to replace this standard New Italian – French feature with something clearly 'heretic', with 'three Great Lunettes in the Covered-Way, as they are constructed and disposed in the first and fourth of the following Methods of regular Fortification. These indeed are a substitute both for a Ravelin and Tenaillons; affording in a great measure the advantages of these expensive Outworks, without their disadvantages…'[50] The source of his inspiration is very clear indeed, for it is almost a direct quotation of Coehoorn's projects for Bergen op Zoom (and also Nijmegen). Bisset had already written in his book that 'The great reveted Lunettes… in the inward Places of Arms of the covered Way, are, indisputably, the most masterly, and most advantageous Works in this Fortress [Bergen]; they are most powerfully commanded by the Body of the Place…'[51] The only way to reduce them was through sapping, which in the face of the permanent countermine system meant an intensive mine warfare because lunettes were 'so contrived as to put them under a Necessity of opening them by Mines' and moreover, in Nijmegen Coehoorn 'very ingeniously disposed them… in Chains, which consist of three or four Lunettes each Chain, as to render it impracticable to cut them off by Sap…'[52]

In his manuscript Bisset summed up the basic design features of such Coehoorn-like lunettes, emphasising especially the necessity to compute exactly its levelling as the horizontal placement of the lunettes was of great importance. In the second chapter, paragraph 39 of his manuscript he wrote:

> A great Lunette in the Covered Way should either have no Ditch at all, or but a very narrow one, and be of a due height so as that the Cannon that are planted upon its Rampart may Just bear over the Crest of the Glacis so as to raze it; by this means its Cannon may be fired with far greater certainty against the Enemy's Batteries in the Field, and against the head of the Sap, and will be far less liable to be dismounted or disabled by the Enemy's Cannon, than if the Lunette were higher, and at a greater distance from the Crest of the Glacis, or than Cannon planted in the face of a Bastion, or Ravelin.[53]

Following the paragraph brings us to a conclusion that replacing a New Italian style ravelin with three Coehoorn-like lunettes is not only economical, but it also adds a considerable strength to the outer defensive layer. Bisset basically argued that:

> a) the crowning of the covered way would be greatly complicated, and a much longer and complex trench must be run around the three lunettes.[54]

---

49   Bisset, 'Essays on Fortification', 1/1/8.
50   Bisset, 'Essays on Fortification', 1/1/8.
51   Bisset, *The Theory and Construction of Fortification*, p.8.
52   Bisset, *The Theory and Construction of Fortification*, p.101.
53   Bisset, 'Essays on Fortification', 1/2/39.
54   In these aspects, Bisset's concepts are similar to later designs by Bousmard, see Henri Jean Baptiste Bousmard, *Essai général de fortification et d'attaque et défense des places* (Paris: Anselin, 1814), in

b) the enemy breaching batteries would be situated close to the lunettes of the neighbouring fortification fronts, which means that these lunettes must also be reduced. It means to enlarge the attack sector at least twice because the adjacent lunettes control the glacis with their fire and can be easily equipped with numerous batteries of small Coehoorn mortars, greatly disturbing the enemy trying to run saps towards the central 'chain' of three lunettes (as was the case during the defence of Bergen).[55]

c) before the crowning of the covered way can be achieved, the besieger must reduce nine lunettes.

Bisset could imagine only one way to achieve this extraordinary feat: to destroy them using the underground mine attack. The besieger must therefore descend underground to face all the old horrors and spectres of Turin, Lille and Tournai – and that is where the besieged would be waiting for him in their permanent countermine system, carefully listening and ready to spring their countermines. In case the besiegers would fail to recognize the tactical value of such lunettes, the siege would almost fatally stumble upon them exactly as in the case of Bergen op Zoom in 1747, which means more time and materiel consumed and much higher losses suffered.[56]

2) The principle of 'non-salient' design

Bisset then postulates another principle representing a critical analysis of older designs, the principle of 'non-salient' or 'compressed' design: 'The more saliant any Piece or Portion of a Front of Fortification is, the more it will be exposed to the Attack of the Enemy, and the more easily approached.'[57] Later, during discussing his Fifth method of fortification, he mentions the principle again: 'As any defensive Work, or member of a Front becomes weaker and more easily approached in proportion as it is more saliant and more acute, particularly with regard to the Bastion...'[58] This stands in opposition to the older practice using complex hornworks and other detached works to add depth to the defence, which was often the case of Vauban's design but also of the School of Mézières introducing new detached works in the form of a ring of single lunettes, detached in front of the glacis. Bisset reiterates here his old concept that such works are of little value because it is very difficult to cover them by fire from the inner enceinte.[59]

This leads to the conclusion, expressed in Bisset's manuscript, that a curtain wall is stronger and more useful for defence than bastions with their long faces, easily commanded

---

particular Pl.59.

55   Bisset, *The Theory and Construction of Fortification*, p.9.
56   Bisset, *The Theory and Construction of Fortification*, p.12.
57   Bisset, 'Essays on Fortification', 1/1/10.
58   Bisset, 'Essays on Fortification', 1/5/80.
59   Bisset, *The Theory and Construction of Fortification*, p.44.

by ricochet fire.[60] It is a truly revolutionary statement. Bisset supported his conviction again by explaining the situation of Bergen bastions Coehoorn and Pucelle, in the front of the siege attack:

> It appeared in the last Siege of Bergenopzoome that while the direct Batteries of the Enemy in the Field, and the Ricochet Batteries on the flanks of the Attack, kept playing against the faces of the Demibastions of the Front attacked, these were rendered quite inserviceable;[61] their Guns were soon dismounted or disabled, and as the fire of the Besiegers was superior, it would have been imprudent to have persisted in opposing the Batteries in the Field from the faces of the Bastions attacked...[62]

Bisset then quotes French engineer Alain Manesson Malett, who already in his 1684 treatise *Les Travaux de Mars ou l'Art de la Guerre* opposed the bastions with long faces, considered them to be the weakest parts of the fortification and argued for new systems of fortification which would not rely on them.[63] This is a key lesson of the siege warfare for Bisset. His solution to the problem is revolutionary: to use the curtain as the main artillery position to be used for the counter-battery fire, the curtain by 'containing more Cannon, Howitzers, Mortars and Musqueteers, and commanding more effectually the Outworks', would be, by its 'retired' position, 'secure from the Attack of the Enemy.'[64] In the following points 21–23, Bisset further elaborates this concept, which closely resembles later principles espoused by Montalembert, subsequently adopted by polygonal systems of fortification. Bisset states that the exclusive role of the bastion is to provide the heaviest possible flanking fire to the area of the main ditch and covered way, and nothing more. The counter-battery fire would be much more effectively provided from the curtain positions. In consequence, Bisset implicitly started the process of morphing bastions into another type of structure, resembling the later caponier.

3) Disrupting the Vauban Method

This process was not straightforward as Bisset at first also proposed a host of minor improvements which would primarily bolster the bastion's capacity to provide flanking fire. As early

---

60   Bisset, 'Essays on Fortification', 1/1/11.
61   Bisset's report dated 20 August states: 'We have very few Cannon on the Bastions... but what have their carriages broke or have some other blemish about them that renders them at present unserviceable. The Mortars and Coehorns are at present of the greatest use to us...' RA, CP/MAIN/25/441–444, p.2.
62   Bisset, 'Essays on Fortification', 1/1/12.
63   Allain Manesson-Mallet, *Les Travaux de Mars ou l'Art de la Guerre*, Vol. II (Paris: Denys Thierry, 1684). Bisset apparently quotes from Vol. 2, p.16, section 'De la longuer des Faces des Bastions de l'Auteur.'
64   Bisset, 'Essays on Fortification', 1/1/19.

as 1751, he suggested taking inspiration from an old project by Franceso di Marchi[65] and providing bastions with 'S' shaped ('the concave and convex') flanks,[66] which according to him was safer and more economical than covering the batteries in orillons frequently used by both Vauban and Coehoorn.[67] In particular Bisset's Seventh method, explained in the manuscript, is used to demonstrate the advantages of new, less salient and flatter bastions: 'By consequence our angular Bastion will be approached with far more difficulty and danger, and be more spacious, and derive a much greater degree of defensive power from the two collateral Bastions, and, on the whole, be considerably stronger, than the common acute angled angular Bastion...'[68]

Bisset adds that his 'less salient' bastioned front would force the besieger to build a much greater amount of siege works, make much longer lines of circumvallation and contravallation, and it would be more difficult and laborious to site ricochet batteries because of the necessary obtuse firing angles. Thus, the siege as a whole would require substantially higher amount of time, materiel and manpower.

It seems that the overall rationale behind Bisset's proposals and experimental designs is to find a way to disrupt as much as possible the old Vauban's method of regular siege. He proposes to reshape substantially the outer layer of defences by omitting the ravelin and instead use three lunettes arranged *a la tenaille* which would be skilfully placed according to Coehoorn's project as to present a smaller, inconspicuous and almost indistinct target.[69] We have already discussed his proposal to profoundly reshape bastions in order to make ricochet fire more difficult and defensive flanking fire more effective. Bisset also claims that he discovered an insidiously effective defensive feature of Coehoorn's method, as displayed in Bergen. The levelling of the glacis was computed so effectively so that:

> [After] the approaches shall have reached the top of the Glacis: at this Period the Enemy's field batteries, the Ricochet Batteries on the flanks of the attack excepted, must cease firing, and the Body of the Place may then be completely repaired, and a sufficiency of Cannon should then be mounted therein for destroying the Enemy's Works on the Crest of the Glacis, and obstructed the erecting of Counter-Batteries there...[70]

Bisset also mimicked the practice displayed during the defence of Bergen not to listen to Vauban or Cormontaigne and to equip the outer defensive layer with artillery and actively use it against the enemy saps as intensively as possible for the longest possible period of the siege. He proposed to plant no fewer than 14 cannon in each lunette chain and, judging from his experience of the defence of Bergen, he supposed this measure to be highly efficient.

---

65   Francesco de Marchi, *Della architettura militare libri quattro. Opera nuovamente data in luce* (Brescia: Comino Presegni, 1599).

66   Bisset, *The Theory and Construction of Fortification*, p.76.

67   Again, more than 40 years later Bousmard proposed very similar design of bastion flanks, see Bousmard, *Essai général de fortification et d'attaque et défense des places*, in particular Pl. 60.

68   Bisset, 'Essays on Fortification', 6/84.

69   Bisset, *The Theory and Construction of Fortification*, pp.17–18.

70   Bisset, 'Essays on Fortification', 2/1/57.

However, what was perhaps most disruptive was that Bisset computed the methods of defence of his new fortification systems as to inevitably include the heavy use of the permanent countermine system. His perhaps most important innovation proposal, to omit the ravelin and to plant three Coehoorn-style lunettes in the covered way, necessarily presupposed the existence of Bergen-style countermines.

Bisset's status of an outsider and 'amateur' who did not complete any standard engineer curriculum but acquired his knowledge in the field and got his rank as a reward for his gallantry and capacity was to his advantage, but it was also his curse. It allowed him to take direct inspiration from a minority tradition in the art of fortification, to transcend and leave behind contemporary orthodoxy and to see old post-Vaubanian concepts with fresh eyes. It inevitably led to a conflict with the establishment of the time. Within the British engineering corps around the middle of the eighteenth century, it was certainly undesirable to mount such an attack to the established principles, as expressed for instance already in 1746 in John Muller's *A treatise containing the practical part of fortification*.[71]

What is even more important, Bisset's stubborn insistence on a permanent countermine system as an extremely useful defensive feature and one of the keys to overcome the existing crisis of defence clashed with the prevailing cultural perception of its deployment. Immediately after Bergen, many representations of gruelling underground duels in front of bastions Pucelle and Coehoorn were available, either in form of siege journals, newspaper articles or anonymous prints. But engineering hierarchy was slow in learning from the Bergen example. Six years after Bisset's book, a new edition of the authoritative engineering textbook *The Attac* [sic] *and Defence of Fortified Places* by Professor John Muller, director of Royal Military Academy at Woolwich, was published.[72] Although Muller devoted the whole Part III of the book to the military mining and insisted that 'The Art of Mining has become one of the most essential parts of the Attack and Defence of Places: so much Artillery is used that nothing above the ground can withstand its effect', his text is purely descriptive, borrows heavily from Le Blond and Valliere and omits discussing any historical field experience, including Bergen-op-Zoom.[73]

The cultural trauma associated with the underground warfare was nonetheless greatly deepened only five years after Muller published his textbook. During one of the most dramatic episodes of the Seven Years War, Prussians besieged Schweidnitz in Silesia, held by an Austrian garrison. Prussian miners were under the command of Simon Lefebvre, 'who had assisted at the siege of Bergen-op-Zoom' and was conversant with the newest deadly invention in the field of military mining: the so-called overcharged mine, essentially an extremely powerful mine calculated to create a massive crater which would be used as a new forward position. This new method was 'unsophisticated' in terms of older mining because in fact, it represented a way to achieve a gradual pyrotechnic destruction of the zone of attack. Lefebvre took inspiration from the latest works of French engineer Bernard Forest de Bélidor who was the first to experiment with overcharged mines (*globe de compression*,

---

71   John Muller, *A treatise containing the elementary part of fortification, regular and irregular etc.* (London: J. Nourse, 1746).
72   John Muller, *The Attac and Defence of Fortified Places. In three Parts etc.* (London: J. Millan, 1757).
73   Muller, *The Attac and Defence of Fortified Places*, pp.206–207.

or *Druckkugel*).[74] During the attack, Lefebvre focused on Jauerniger Fort, detonating four overcharged mines with great effect, and this new method represented further tactical and also cultural escalation of the underground warfare.[75] The crater of the first overcharged mine was 30 metres wide and six metres deep and the explosion and subsequent destruction was of large scale.[76]

Several published siege journals and various ego-documents provide many drastic details and representations of the extreme danger and horrors associated with this kind of warfare.[77] The new method of mine attack caused the assault sector to be small and narrow in comparison with Turin, Lille, Tournai or Bergen, which guaranteed an unparalleled intensity of firepower and military pyrotechnics.[78] After Schweidnitz, the discussion concerning underground warfare almost ceased for a long time. What is apparent is the cultural problem with the 'total' character of such combat technique, causing not only technical, but also cultural difficulties in finding enough willing, competent and disciplined specialists. Bergen and Schweidnitz became examples of a tactical situation extremely challenging for both attack and defence and contemporary authorities slowly shifted towards warnings against any more such operations to be undertaken. Mouzé wrote in 1804 that 'available information from this siege [Schweidnitz] and all others, where countermines were used, prove without a doubt, that the attacker must prevent at any price to be drawn into such unhappy underground war, which will only result in heavy loss of manpower, time and materiel.'[79] Gillot added the following year that 'it is generally known that countermines are effective especially because of causing fear among besiegers' and without competent veterans, well versed in this art, the mine attack is almost hopeless and he quoted Bergen-op-Zoom as an example of an effective defence using countermines.[80] Finally, in 1817 the Austrian authority in military engineering, Maxmilian de Traux, concluded that after Bergen and Schweidnitz, there was a general tendency not to engage in a siege where countermine system would be used.[81]

---

74   Later published as Bernard Forest de Bélidor, *Oeuvres Diverses de M. Belidor, Concernant L'Artillerie Et Le Genie* (Amsterdam – Leipzig: Arkstée & Merkus, 1764), see chapter 'Nouvelle Theorie Sur la Science des Mines propres à guerre, fondée sur un grand nombre d´Expériences', pp.320–391.

75   Simon Le Febvre, *Oeuvres complètes de M. Le Febvre* (Maastricht: Dufour and Roux, 1778), Pl. II, III and IV. See pp.281–328 for detailed siege journal, 'Journal du siege de la ville de Schweidnitz En l´An 1762'.

76   Le Febvre, *Oeuvres complètes de M. Le Febvre*, pp.304–305. For more analysis see J.J. Wilson, 'Notes on the Mining Operations at Schweidnitz, Silistria and Brailow, accompanied by an Account of Recent Experiments in Germany', in: P.J. Bainbrigge (ed.), *Papers on Subjects connected with the Duties of the Corps of Royal Engineers* (Woolwich: W.P. Jackson, 1858), pp.65–66.

77   See also Johann Gottlieb Tielke, *Die Drey Belagerungen und Loudonsche Ersteigung der Festung Schweidnitz, in den Feldzügen von 1757 bis 1762* (Freiberg: Trattner, 1781), pp.264, 265, 272–273.

78   Peter de Guasco, *Relation de la défense de Schweidnitz, commandé par le général feldmaréchal lieutenant comte De Guasco etc.* (Paris: Corréard, 1846), pp.31-32.

79   Mouzé, *Traité de fortification souterraine: suivi de quatre mémoires sur les mines* (Paris: Levrault, Schoell and Cie and Magimel, 1804), p.215.

80   C. L. Gillot, *Traite de Fortification Souterraine ou Des Mines offensives et défensives* (Paris: Magimel, 1805), p.vi.

81   Maxmilian de Traux, *Die beständige Befestigungskunst* (Wiener Neustadt: Fritsch, 1817), pp.473–474. Also see Georg von Hauser, *Die Minen und der unterirdische Krieg* (Wien: k. k. Hof- und Staats-Aerarial-Druckerey, 1817). For Bergen, see pp.73–86 and Schweidnitz pp.86–95.

This brings us to a conclusion regarding Charles Bisset and his concepts and proposals. Even if he had been humble enough to swallow a bitter pill of being reactivated only in the inferior rank of Practitioner Engineer, his position in the corps would have been a precarious one. He was an educated and strongly opinionated person who proved himself in combat and did not hesitate to question many prevailing concepts in the art of attack and defence, surely to the displeasure of more experienced engineers. Moreover, the solutions he suggested would openly conflict the prescribed curriculum at Woolwich Royal Military Academy. Here, the authoritative textbooks by John Muller were predominantly used. Bisset's thinking was analytical but also heretical. An application of his innovations was inconceivable in the country which, at the time, neither felt any particular need for updating its fortifications nor a need to build any new fortified places and whose defence was best guaranteed by its maritime power. Apart from that, Bisset laid strong emphasis on combat methods which were technically extremely demanding and culturally problematic, to say the least. Bisset was not humble enough to work his way up once again from the bottom of the engineering hierarchy. He wanted to fight again, but on his own terms. His military career thus fell easy victim to these unfavourable circumstances. Nevertheless, his contribution represents an intriguing chapter in the history of military engineering and Bisset should be remembered as an original and inventive British author whose concepts predated many later foreign developments.

Further Reading

Anon., *An Authentick and Accurate Journal of the Siege of Bergen-op-Zoom, with a Plan of the Town… By an English Officer of Distinction, who was a Voluntier both in the Lines and Town etc.* (London: William Owen, 1747). For a complete English transcription see Petr Wohlmuth, *Krev, čest a hrůza. Historická antropologie pevnostní války na příkladu britských deníků z obléhání pevnosti Bergen op Zoom z roku 1747* (Prague: Scriptorium, 2017). [Blood, honour and horror. Representations of siege warfare in siege journals of British defenders of Bergen op Zoom in 1747]

Bisset, Charles, *The Theory and Construction of Fortification, illustrated with several new Designs. By Lieutenant Charles Bisset, Late an Engineer Extraordinary in the Brigade of Engineers which served in the Netherlands in the last War* (London: A. Millar, D. Wilson and R. Dodsley, 1751).

Duffy, Christopher, *Fire & Stone. The Science of Fortress Warfare 1660–1860* (Edison: Castle Books, 2006)

Duffy, Christopher, *The Fortress in the Age of Vauban and Frederick the Great 1660-1789. Siege Warfare Volume II* (London, Boston, Melbourne and Henley: Routledge & Kegan Paul, 1985),

Falkner, James, *Marlborough's Sieges* (Stroud: Spellmount, 2007),

Ostwald, Jamel, *Vauban under Siege. Engineering Efficiency and Martial Vigor in the War of the Spanish Succession* (Leiden and Boston: Brill, 2007)

Section Three

Voices from the Past

10

Pastor Täge's Account of the Siege of Cüstrin and the Battle of Zorndorf, 1758

Adam L. Storring[1]

Christopher Duffy has done so much to make the history of the armies of eastern and central Europe during the long eighteenth century accessible to English-speaking audiences. It is therefore fitting that this volume should present a translation of a source describing the Seven Years War from the perspective of a Prussian subject who served in the Russian army. Christian Täge (born 25 July 1724) was a candidate to become a deacon when the Russian army arrived in his home town of Marienwerder in East Prussia in February 1758. The Russian commander in chief, General of Cavalry Villim Villimovitch Fermor – himself a Baltic German and a Lutheran – obliged Täge to join his army, since his many German Lutheran officers lacked a chaplain who could hold Lutheran services.[2] Täge has left a lively account of the 1758 campaign, describing the operations of the Russian army from the perspective of a non-Russian and a civilian but one whose position placed him close to the Russian commander in chief. This article presents a translation of the six chapters of Täge's account describing the climax of the 1758 campaign, including the Russian bombardment of the Prussian fortress of Cüstrin on the Oder river from 15 August, the Battle of Zorndorf on 25 August, and its consequences.

The translation opens with Täge's arrival at Cüstrin. Having occupied East Prussia in January to March 1758, the Russian army had advanced slowly across Poland through the spring and summer to reach the core territories of the Prussian state, attacking Cüstrin on

1   I am grateful to Tim Blanning for his supervision of my master's thesis on the Zorndorf campaign, to Ilya Berkovich for urging me to produce an English translation of Täge's memoir, and to Alexander Burns and Jasper Heinzen for their helpful comments on drafts of this chapter. I would also like to record my grateful thanks to the Arts and Humanities Research Council and the Lichtenberg-Kolleg / Göttingen Institute for Advanced Study, who funded the research that made this chapter possible.
2   August Samuel Gerber (ed.), *Christian Täge's, ehemaligen Russischen Feldpredigers, Lebensgeschichte* (Königsberg: Göbbels und Unzer, 1804), pp.7, 123, 127-137. On Fermor, see Christopher Duffy, *Russia's Military Way to the West: Origins and Nature of Russian Military Power 1700-1800* (London: Routledge & Kegan Paul, 1981), p.81.

15 August.[3] As Täge describes, the explosive shells of the Russian howitzers quickly set the town within the fortress walls on fire, and within hours it had been reduced to ashes. The Russians, however, had been unable to bring their siege artillery across Poland, and the field guns they had with them were unable seriously to damage the fortress walls. Moreover, the marshland surrounding the fortress, crossed only by a narrow causeway, meant that they could not dig trenches and saps towards it. Fermor perhaps hoped to frighten the fortress into surrender through bombardment, a tactic Frederick himself had tried at Prague the previous year and would try again at Dresden in 1760. As Täge notes, however, the fortress commandant, Colonel Schach von Wittenau (Täge variously spells his name 'Schack' and 'Schaak'), rejected Fermor's demand to surrender. Täge notes that the Russians continued their fire even after the town had been reduced to ashes (actually in order to use up their explosive shells, since they did not expect to undertake any other siege during the campaign). In the following days, however, the fire of the Prussian defenders became greater than that of the attackers, and on 20 August they succeeded in setting on fire the suburb outside the walls of Cüstrin, where the Russians had positioned themselves.[4]

Reflecting his closeness to Fermor, Täge refuses to accept that the Russians were not properly prepared for the siege of Cüstrin. He argues that the bombardment at least gave the lie to critics who claimed that Fermor did not prosecute the war against Prussia with the proper determination, an accusation that reflected the political disputes within the Russian high command throughout the Seven Years War.[5] However, rather than engaging with contemporary military histories of the war such as those of Henry Lloyd and Friedrich von Tempelhoff, Täge instead references the *Fatherland-Historical Pocket Book* of Friedrich Eberhard Rambach (1767–1826) and the memoires of the French diplomat Louis-Alexandre

3   Dieter Ernst Bangert, *Die russisch-österreichische militärische Zusammenarbeit im Siebenjährigen Kriege in den Jahren 1758-1759* (Boppard am Rhein: Harald Boldt, 1971), pp.46-52, 82-99; J.G. Tielke (trans. C. Crawford and R. Crawford), *An Account of Some of the Most Remarkable Events of the War Between the Prussians, Austrians and Russians from 1756 to 1763: And a Treatise on Several Branches of the Military Art with Plans and Maps*, 2nd edition (London: J. Walter, 1787-1788), Vol.II, pp.12-22, 47-52, 55, 57, 66-67, 70-71, 83-84, 89, 95, 97-98, 101, 104-109, 112-120, 122-123, 127-128.

4   Christopher Duffy, *The Fortress in the Age of Vauban and Frederick the Great, 1660 – 1789* (London, Boston, Melbourne and Henley: Routledge and Kegan Paul, 1985), pp.118, 120, 125; Duffy, *Russia*, pp.67-68, 86; Großer Generalstab Kriegsgeschichtliche Abteilung II, *Die Kriege Friedrichs des Großen. Teil III: Der Siebenjährige Krieg 1756-1763. Band VIII: Zorndorf und Hochkirch* (Berlin: Ernst Siegfried Mittler und Sohn, 1910), pp.78-87; Dmitri Thedorovich Masslowski (trans. Albert Christian Karl von Drygalski), *Der Siebenjährige Krieg nach russischer Darstellung. Teil II: Der Feldzug des Grafen Fermor in den östlichen Gebieten von Preussen (1757-1759)* (Berlin: R. Eisenschmidt, 1891), pp.143-148; Friedrich August von Retzow, *Charakteristik der wichtigsten Ereignisse des Siebenjährigen Krieges in Rücksicht auf Ursachen und Wirkungen von einem Zeitgenossen* (Berlin: Himburgische Buchhandlung, 1802), Vol.I, pp.310-312; Georg Friedrich von Tempelhoff, *Geschichte des Siebenjährigen Krieges in Deutschland zwischen dem Könige von Preußen und der Kaiserin Königin mit ihrer Alliirten als eine Fortsetzung der Geschichte des General Lloyd* (Berlin, 1783-7), Vol.II, pp.217-220; Tielke, *War between the Prussians, Austrians, and Russians*, pp.128-142; Jürgen Ziechmann (ed.), *Journal vom Siebenjährigen Kriege von Friedrich Wilhelm Ernst Freiherr von Gaudi. Band V: 1758* (Buchholz: LTR-Verlag, 2003), pp.222-228.

5   H.M. Scott, *The Emergence of the Eastern Powers, 1756-1775* (Cambridge: Cambridge University Press, 2001), pp.46-47.

Frotier de La Messelière (1710-1777). This is a reminder that he was a civilian recounting his personal experiences, not a professional military commentator.[6]

Täge's memoires frequently bewail the destruction of war: a reminder that, despite attempts to 'tame' Bellona, eighteenth-century warfare remained terribly brutal and destructive for those caught up in it.[7] The burning of Cüstrin was one of a number of notorious bombardments of towns during the Seven Years War, and Täge fully expresses his own horror at the consequences not only of the Russian bombardment but also of Prussia counter-fire for the civilians living in Cüstrin and its environs.[8]

The Prussians now counter-attacked, as King Frederick II took a force northward from Silesia. On 21 August he joined the detached army of his subordinate Lieutenant General Count Christoph zu Dohna, which was confronting the Russians from the opposite side of the Oder river. An additional corps brought by Frederick from Silesia arrived on 22 August. Judging it impossible to attack the Russian position at Cüstrin frontally, Frederick marched his combined army northwards on the night of 22–23 August, crossing the Oder at Alt-Güstebiese and thus cutting the Russian army in two, dividing Fermor's main force at Cüstrin from a detached Russian corps under Major General Petr Aleksandrovich Rumyantsev at Schwedt to the north. As Täge notes, there is some controversy over how quickly Fermor learnt of the Prussian crossing. Some accounts state that the Russians had already noticed the Prussian preparations to cross the river on 21 and 22 August, and that the Cossack pickets of Colonel Nikolai Chomutov (Täge calls him Lieutenant General Kumatof, and later Colonel von Chumatof) reported Frederick's crossing on the morning of 23 August. Chomutov failed to dispute the crossing, however, and other sources maintain that Fermor only definitely learnt that the Prussians were across the river late on 23 August. Unsurprisingly, given his closeness to Fermor, Täge places the blame on Chomutov.[9]

6   Gerber, *Christian Täge's Lebensgeschichte*, pp.144, 158; Louis-Alexandre Frotier de La Messelière, *Voyage à Pétersbourg, ou Nouveaux mémoires sur le Russie* (Paris: Ve Panckoucke and Gérard, 1803), pp.235-236; Friedrich Eberhard Rambach, *Vaterländisch-historisches Taschenbuch auf alle Tage im Jahr: ein Lesebuch zur Unterhaltung für die Freunde der Vaterländischen Geschichte und zur Belehrung für die vaterländische Jugend* (Königsberg: F. Nicolovius, 1808).

7   Erica Charters, Eve Rosenhaft and Hannah Smith, 'Introduction', in Erica Charters, Eve Rosenhaft and Hannah Smith (eds), *Civilians and War in Europe 1618-1815* (Liverpool: Liverpool University Press, 2012), pp.1-17; John Childs, *Armies and Warfare in Europe, 1648 – 1789* (Manchester: Manchester University Press, 1982), pp.2-27; Gerber, *Christian Täge's Lebensgeschichte*, pp.105, 108-109, 115-117, 161.

8   Johann Wilhelm von Archenholz (trans. Frederick Adam Catty), *The History of the Seven Years War in Germany* (Frankfurt am Main: C. Jugel, 1843), pp.160-161; Duffy, *Fortress in the Age of Vauban*, pp.120, 125; Marian Füssel, 'Theatrum Belli. Der Krieg als Inszenierung und Wissensschauplatz im 17. und 18. Jahrhundert', *Metaphorik* 14 (2008), p.217, <https://www.metaphorik.de/sites/www.metaphorik.de/files/journal-pdf/14_2008_fuessel.pdf>, accessed 6 August 2021.

9   Andrew Bisset (ed.), *Memoirs and Papers of Sir Andrew Mitchell, K.B., Envoy Extraordinary and Minister Plenipotentiary from the Court of Great Britain to the Court of Prussia, from 1756 to 1771* (London: Chapman & Hall, 1850), Vol.I, pp.422-426; Vol.II, pp.37-41; Duffy, *Russia*, p.86; F.A. von Etzel, *Die Operationen gegen die Russen und Schweden im Jahre 1758 und die zweitägige Schlacht bei Zorndorf am 25. und 26. August* (Berlin: Abelsdorff, 1858), pp.154, 170; Großer Generalstab, *Zorndorf und Hochkirch*, pp.90-103; Stefan Hartmann, 'Eine unbekannte Quelle zur Schlacht bei Zorndorf', *Zeitschrift für Ostforschung* 34 (1985), pp.176, 184-185; Max Immich, *Die Schlacht bei Zorndorf am 25. August 1758* (Berlin: Speyer & Peters, 1893) pp.61-63; Masslowski, *Der Siebenjährige Krieg nach*

Täge, like many commentators both at the time and since, is critical of the position that Fermor now took up to fight what became the Battle of Zorndorf. Indeed, Täge's criticism is particularly striking given his stated admiration for Fermor. Breaking camp in front of Cüstrin in the early morning of 24 August, Fermor was joined later in the day by the Observation Corps, a private army created by the Russian Master General of Ordnance, Count Petr Ivanovich Shuvalov, which had marched more slowly across Poland behind the main army (Täge calls it the Nuwo Corpus). The Austrian liaison officer General St André and the Saxon Prince Charles urged Fermor to deploy on high ground near the village of Groß-Cammin, covering his line of retreat, but Fermor instead chose to deploy his army further west, south of the swampy Mietzel river, while leaving his heavy baggage at Groß-Cammin, detached from the main army. While the Mietzel offered a formidable obstacle against frontal attack, King Frederick was able in the early morning of 25 August to march around the Russian army's eastern flank and, as Täge notes, could easily have captured the exposed Russian baggage train. Täge's surprise that the Prussian king did not take advantage of this opportunity has been shared by many later commentators.[10]

Benefitting from the hugely greater mobility of his soldiers, Frederick instead marched them clockwise around the Russian army to attack from the south, the Prussian army taking up its famous oblique line formation with its strength concentrated against the Russian western flank.[11] Täge's description of the 'magnificent' appearance of the Prussian soldiers during this march, which inspired awe in Russian observers, is a reminder that eighteenth-century armies were intended not only to be militarily effective but also visually impressive, as representations of the power of their states.[12] Täge calls the arrival of the Prussians 'solemn' ('*feierlich*'), the same word that he uses to describe Holy Communion, and a word that could also be applied to ceremonies at a ruler's court. He also describes the '*Feierlichkeit*' of the Prussian advance, a word that could mean 'solemnity' or 'ceremony'.

---

    russischer Darstellung, pp.149-154; Tempelhoff, *Geschichte des Siebenjährigen Krieges*, pp.220-222; Tielke, W*ar between the Prussians, Austrians, and Russians*, pp.146-148, 152-156; Ziechmann, *Journal vom Siebenjährigen Kriege*, pp.217-219, 228-229.

10   Bangert, *Militärische Zusammenarbeit*, pp.101-102; Duffy, *Russia*, pp.73, 86; Etzel, *Operationen gegen die Russen und Schweden*, pp.154-156, 170; Großer Generalstab, *Zorndorf und Hochkirch*, pp.101-104, 123-125, 162-163; Hartmann, 'Unbekannte Quelle', pp.176-177, 186-189; Immich, *Schlacht bei Zorndorf*, pp.65-69; Johannes Kunisch, *Friedrich der Grosse. Der König und seine Zeit* (Munich: C.H. Beck, 2004), pp.387-390; Masslowski, *Der Siebenjährige Krieg nach russischer Darstellung*, pp.155-156, 160-166; Johann D.E. Preuss (ed.), *Œuvres de Frédéric le Grand* (Berlin: R. Decker, 1846-56) Vol.IV, pp.230-231; Adam L. Storring, 'Subjective Practices of War: The Prussian Army and the Zorndorf Campaign, 1758' *History of Science* (OnlineFirst 2020), <https://doi.org/10.1177/0073275320958950>, accessed 9 August 2021; Tempelhoff, *Geschichte des siebenjährigen Krieges*, pp.222-224; Tielke, W*ar between the Prussians, Austrians, and Russians*, pp.156-172; Ziechmann, *Journal vom Siebenjährigen Kriege*, pp.230-231.

11   Christopher Duffy, *Frederick the Great: A Military Life* (London: Routledge & Kegan Paul, 1985), pp.164-165; Hartmann, 'Unbekannte Quelle', p.178; Dennis E Showalter, *The Wars of Frederick the Great* (London and New York: Longman, 1996), pp.213-214.

12   Jürgen Luh, *Kriegskunst in Europa 1650-1800* (Cologne, Weimar, Viena: Böhlau Verlag, 2004), pp.11, 149, 173-174, 177-208, 219-223. On this phenomenon specifically at Zorndorf, see Marian Füssel, 'Das Undarstellbare darstellen. Das Bild der Schlacht im 18. Jahrhundert am Beispiel von Zorndorf (1758)', in Birgit Emich and Gabriela Signori (eds), *Kriegs / Bilder in Mittelalter und Früher Neuzeit* (Berlin: Duncker & Humblot, 2009), pp.339, 349.

Like other contemporary sources, Täge states that the Russian army was in a square formation, and Frederick in his own account argued that this reflected Russian practice fighting against the Turks. Although the Russians actually seem to have fought the battle in a linear formation, their troops were certainly packed into a narrow and entirely defensive position, with marshes to the north and ravines to the east and west.[13]

Täge gives a moving description of his feelings before the battle and of the rituals of both soldiers and officers for coping with their fear. He describes how Russian officers spoke openly about the likelihood of death, and notes the importance of religious ceremonies for both sides. Katrin and Sascha Möbius have emphasized that the song *Now Lord I am in Thy Keeping* (*Ich bin ja Herr in deiner Macht*), which the Prussians sang as they advanced to battle at Zorndorf, 'is centred around the expectation of death', and recent research has shown that, unlike their modern counterparts, eighteenth-century soldiers openly described the danger they faced and often saw their preservation as dependant on the will of God.[14]

Although Täge prudently withdrew inside the Russian formation before the battle actually began, his account vividly captures one of the most important features of this battle: the ferocious Prussian artillery bombardment. The experience of highly effective Austrian artillery fire in the early battles of the Seven Years War had led Frederick II to support his own attacks with concentrated firepower, and two batteries, with a combined 60 heavy cannon ('an un-heard-of number for that era', as Dennis Showalter commented) supported the initial Prussian attack on the Russian right flank, bombarding it for two hours from 9:00 to 11:00 a.m. Täge emphasizes the number killed and wounded even among those standing well back from the front line, and his account is particularly valuable in underlining the shattering psychological effect of being exposed to such a bombardment.[15]

---

13   Archenholz, *History of the Seven Years War*, p.164; F.S. Flint (trans.), *Frederick the Great: The Memoirs of his Reader Henri de Catt (1758-1760)* (London: Constable and Co., 1916), Vol.I, pp.291-292; Duffy, *Frederick the Great*, p.165; Etzel, *Operationen gegen die Russen und Schweden*, p.155; Großer Generalstab, *Zorndorf und Hochkirch*, pp.124-5; Immich, *Schlacht bei Zorndorf*, pp.65, 79-90; Masslowski, *Der siebenjährige Krieg nach russischer Darstellung*, pp.162-164, 192-194; *Œuvres*, Vol. IV, pp.230-231; Tempelhoff, *Geschichte des Siebenjährigen Krieges*, p.223; Tielke, *War between the Prussians, Austrians, and Russians*, pp.165-167; Ziechmann, *Journal vom Siebenjährigen Kriege*, p.231.

14   Ilya Berkovich, *Motivation in War: The Experience of Common Soldiers in Old-Regime Europe* (Cambridge: Cambridge University Press, 2017), pp.226-227; Katrin Möbius and Sascha Möbius, *Prussian Army Soldiers and the Seven Years' War: The Psychology of Honour* (London and New York: Bloomsburg, 2020), pp.17, 35, 78-79, 90-92, 97-99, 102-103, 135-137, 155-157, 168, 170, 172 (quotation, p.156); Sascha Möbius, *Mehr Angst vor dem Offizier als vor dem Feind? Eine mentalitätsgeschichtliche Studie zur preußischen Taktik im Siebenjährigen Krieg* (Saarbrücken: VDM Verlag Dr. Müller, 2007), pp.60-63, 101, 106-110, 137-138; Denis Sdvižkov, 'Landschaft nach der Schlacht. Briefe russischer Offiziere aus dem Siebenjährigen Krieg', *Forschungen zur Brandenburgischen und Preußischen Geschichte* NF 22 (2012), pp.39-40, 46-48, 52-54; Denis Sdvižkov, *Pis'ma s Prusskoi voiny. Liudi Rossisko-imperatorskoi armii v 1758 godu [Letters from the "Prussian War". The People of the Russian Imperial Army in 1758].* (Moscow: Novoe literaturnoe obozrenie, 2019), p.676.

15   Duffy, *Russia*, pp.88-89; Duffy, *Frederick the Great*, pp.165-166; Etzel, *Operationen gegen die Russen und Schweden*, pp.156-157, 164; Hartmann, 'Unbekannte Quelle', p.178; Luh, *Kriegskunst in Europa*, pp.167-174; Showalter, *Wars of Frederick the Great*, pp.34-35, 141, 154-155, 160-164, 214 (quotation, p.214); Sdvižkov, 'Landschaft nach der Schlacht', p.48; Tempelhoff, *Geschichte des Siebenjährigen Krieges*, pp.225-226; Tielke, *War between the Prussians, Austrians, and Russians*, pp.177-181;

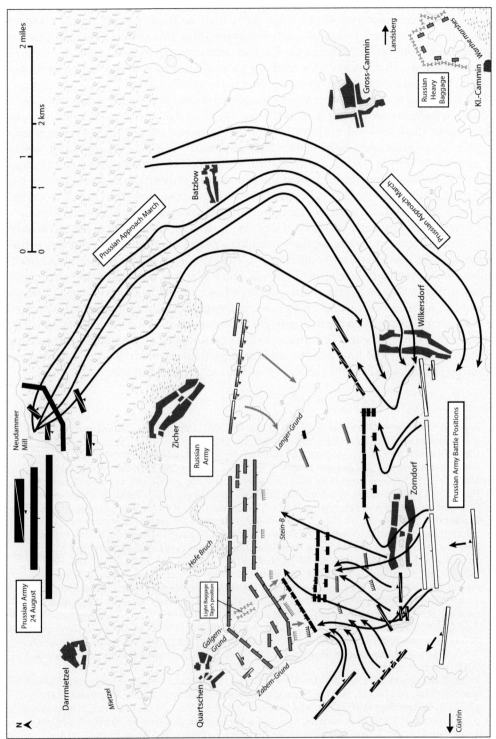

The Battle of Zorndorf, 25 August 1758.

Täge was positioned in a hollow with the Russian light baggage, and Marian Füssel has noted that the clouds of dust thrown up in the baking hot August weather greatly restricted visibility on the battlefield, so that Täge's account focuses on the sounds and emotions of the battle rather than the manoeuvres of the armies.[16] Täge does not describe the initial attack of the Prussian infantry or the responding Russian counter-attack. The Prussian cavalry, however, was now able in turn to fall upon the counter-attacking Russians so successfully that virtually the entire Russian right flank was routed or cut down. Täge records the Prussian Malachowsky Hussars breaking through near to him, and he now tried to flee. The Russian position was divided in two by the deep Galgen Grund ravine, and Täge seems to have tried to escape via the eastern flank of the Russian army, which remained intact and scarcely damaged by the first phase of the fighting.[17]

As Täge's account makes clear, he was far from being the only one to flee. St André and Prince Charles of Saxony both fled the field at this point, while Fermor himself, suffering from a light wound, was caught up in the mass of fugitives. Russian soldiers plundered their own baggage, and both contemporaries and modern historians have argued that, in the course of the battle, it was only the impossibility of retreat across the marshes of the Mietzel that kept the Russian army fighting. Täge describes how the wounded 'Brigadier von S.' – almost certainly Brigadier Joachim Christian von Sievers, who commanded the Murmansk and Riazan Infantry Regiments, which formed part of the second line of the Russian right flank, and who was ultimately captured by the Prussians – exerted his authority to enable Täge and himself to escape from the Russian battle formation.[18] Denis Sdvižkov noted that 'the [Russian] high command temporarily abandoned the battlefield', so that decisions devolved upon 'regimental officers and individual isolated generals'. The experience greatly weakened hierarchies between ranks, and a soldiers' song after the battle mockingly described how:

. . . the little generals with the little brigadiers trembled,
And the colonels with the majors fled away.

Ziechmann, *Journal vom Siebenjährigen Kriege*, p.232. On the psychological effect of artillery fire in the long eighteenth century, see B.P. Hughes, *Firepower: Weapons Effectiveness on the Battlefield, 1630-1850* (London: Arms and Armour Press, 1974), pp.85; John Keegan, *The Face of Battle* (London: Pimlico, 1991), pp.159-161, 177-178.

16   Füssel, 'Das Undarstellbare darstellen', pp.321, 339-340.

17   Immich, *Schlacht bei Zorndorf*, pp.64-65, 68, 93-96; Tempelhoff, *Geschichte des Siebenjährigen Krieges*, pp.226-227; Tielke, *War between the Prussians, Austrians, and Russians*, pp.181-186; Ziechmann, *Journal vom Siebenjährigen Kriege*, pp.234-235.

18   Archenholz, *History of the Seven Years War*, p.166; Bangert, *Militärische Zusammenarbeit*, p.104, Bisset, *Memoirs and Papers of Sir Andrew Mitchell*, Vol.II, pp.43-44; *Memoirs of Henri de Catt*, p.294; Christopher Duffy, *The Army of Frederick the Great* 2nd edition (Chicago, IL: The Emperor's Press, 1996), p.280; Füssel, 'Das Undarstellbare darstellen', p.340; Marian Füssel, *Der Preis des Ruhms. Eine Weltgeschichte des Siebenjährigen Krieges, 1756-1763* (Munich: C.H. Beck, 2019), pp.242-244; Großer Generalstab, *Zorndorf und Hochkirch*, pp.139-140, 149, 8a*; Hartmann, 'Unbekannte Quelle', pp.178-9, 206-207; Masslowski, *Der siebenjährige Krieg nach russischer Darstellung*, pp.174-175, 179, 187; Retzow, *Charakteristik der wichtigsten Ereignisse*, pp.318, 321-322; Tempelhoff, *Geschichte des Siebenjährigen Krieges*, pp.227, 230; Tielke, *War between the Prussians, Austrians, and Russians*, pp.185-186, 189-190, 192-193.

Only the non-commissioned officers fired from the cannons,
And the sutlers distributed lead and powder.[19]

The determination of the Russian army at Zorndorf, which kept fighting even though almost half its soldiers were killed or wounded, has been depicted as a classic example of Russian soldiers' capacity for stoic self-sacrifice.[20] Antony Beevor has shown, however, that such stereotypes may conceal a more complex reality, revealing cases of flight and desertion even in the Red Army at the battle of Stalingrad.[21] Täge's account is a reminder that not all members of the Russian army at Zorndorf faced death with equal fortitude.

Täge and his colleagues tried to escape across the woods and swamps of the Mietzel, but found their way barred by what he calls 'freebooters'. They tried to approach a village, but were fired on. This is one of a number of instances in Täge's account where Prussian civilians apparently used (or at least prepared) arms to defend themselves against the Russians.[22] This first village may have been Zicher, north-east of the Russian position – although contemporary accounts describe it as being occupied and set on fire by Cossacks – or it may have been Batzlow further to the east. Ultimately, Täge and his companions sought shelter in a village near to one of the Prussian batteries, where they were captured. Since the Prussians were originally south of the Russian position, this may have been the village of Wilkersdorf. Täge says that he and his colleagues were then taken the next day to a village called 'Damm' – presumably Neudamm, north of the Mietzel. This would make sense, as the fighting on the afternoon of 25 August had seen the Prussian right flank drive back the Russian left in a counter-clockwise direction, so that by the end of the day the two armies were left perpendicular to their original positions, with the Prussians to the east and the Russians to the west.[23] Neudamm, safe in the new Prussian rear and protected behind the Mietzel river, was a logical place to bring prisoners.

Täge notes the bitterness of some Prussians against the Russians, as a local pastor refused to lend him the implements for performing the last rites. Täge's own account records the depredations of Russian Cossacks, including against Täge himself, and it seems clear that both Prussian soldiers and civilians were animated with a desire for revenge. The Prussian Lieutenant Christian Wilhelm von Prittwitz said that Frederick indirectly told his troops

---

19   Sdvižkov, 'Landschaft nach der Schlacht', pp.40, 43-47 (quotations, pp.43, 47); Sdvižkov, *Pis'ma s Prusskoi voiny*, pp.674, 676. See also Duffy, *Russia*, p.91.

20   Carl von Clausewitz, *Hinterlassene Werke des Generals Carl von Clausewitz über Krieg und Kriegführung* (Berlin: Ferdinand Dümmler, 1837), Vol.X, pp.85-86; Paul Hartig (ed.), *Henri de Catt: Vorleser Friedrichs des Großen. Die Tagebücher 1758-1760* (Munich und Berlin: Deutscher Kunstverlag, 1986), p.63; Tielke, *War between the Prussians, Austrians, and Russians*, p.180; Charles Emmanuel de Warnéry, *Campagnes de Fréderic II, Roi de Prusse de 1756 à 1762* (1788), p.275. For a distinctly pejorative perspective on this phenomenon, see Archenholz, *History of the Seven Years War*, pp.165-166;

21   Anthony Beevor, *Stalingrad* (London: Viking, 1998), pp.xiii-xiv, 90-91, 115, 117, 128, 136-137, 143-144, 166-172, 206, 232.

22   Gerber, *Christian Täges Lebensgeschichte*, p.152. On the wider phenomenon, see Charters, Rosenhaft and Smith, 'Introduction', pp.16-17.

23   Retzow, *Charakteristik der wichtigsten Ereignisse*, pp.320-323; Tempelhoff, *Geschichte des Siebenjährigen Krieges*, pp.229-231; Tielke, *War between the Prussians, Austrians, and Russians*, pp.188-193; Ziechmann, *Journal vom Siebenjährigen Kriege*, pp.235-237.

to 'annihilate' the Russians, and that this was interpreted as an order to take no prisoners. The Prussian Lieutenant Carl Wilhelm von Hülsen (who, like Prittwitz, fought in the battle) and the historian and Prussian officer Johann Wilhelm von Archenholz claimed that Frederick specifically ordered his troops to give no quarter, and that the Russians learnt of the order and declared that they would also take no prisoners. Täge states that the Russians only heard of such an order later, but his account makes clear that the Russians were well aware of the merciless animosity that the Prussians felt for them, and the British envoy Sir Andrew Mitchell, who accompanied Frederick's army, argued that this knowledge inspired the desperate Russian resistance.[24] However, while Täge notes that Russian soldiers hid in the woods for days after the battle rather than give themselves up to the Prussians, he also describes the good treatment given to Russian officers and some medical care given to wounded Russian common soldiers.[25]

Zorndorf was one of the bloodiest battles of the age, with 12,800 Prussians and 18,000 Russians killed and wounded (respectively 35 percent and 42 percentof their armies).[26] Contemporaries wrote of their shock at the violence, and the Russian Brigadier Petr Ivanovich Panin called it an 'unexampled event'.[27] Täge describes in moving terms the sufferings of the wounded, and says that he gave the last rights to a captured and mortally wounded Russian 'brigader': probably Major General Johann von Manteuffel-Zöge, who commanded a brigade in the second line of the Russian left flank.[28] Neither side had the strength to engage on the day after the battle, and on the night of 26–27 August Frederick allowed the Russians to slip past him without hindrance. As Täge notes, and as Marian Füssel describes at length in his contribution to this volume, both sides claimed victory. On the night of 31 August – 1 September the Russians withdrew further back to Landsberg, where Täge joined them on his release from captivity. Frederick soon afterwards hurried southwards to confront the Austrians, and Täge describes the impression he made as he passed through Cüstrin. After moving into Pomerania, and unsuccessfully attacking the Baltic port of Kolberg in October, the

---

24 Archenholz, *History of the Seven Years*, pp.162-163, 170; Bisset, *Memoirs and Papers of Sir Andrew Mitchell*, Vol.I, pp.423-424, 431, 438, Vol.II, p.44; *Memoirs of Henri de Catt*, p.280; Duffy, *Frederick the Great*, p.164; Duffy, *The Army of Frederick the Great*, pp.276-277, 281; Füssel, 'Das Undarstellbare darstellen', p.340; Füssel, *Der Preis des Ruhms*, pp.243-244; Gerber, *Christian Täge's Lebensgeschichte*, pp.149-152; Hans Werner von Hugo and Hans Jessen (eds), *Unter der Fahne des Herzogs von Bevern: Jugenderinnerungen des Christian Wilhelm von Prittwitz und Gaffron* (Breslau: Korn Verlag, 1935), p.216; Helene von Hülsen (ed.), *Unter Friedrich dem Großen: Aus den Memoiren des Aeltervaters 1752-1773* (Berlin: Gebrüder Paetel, 1890), pp.86-87; Immich, *Schlacht bei Zorndorf*, pp.70-71; Möbius, *Mehr Angst vor dem Offizier als vor dem Feind?*, pp.115-116; Retzow, *Charakteristik der wichtigsten Ereignisse*, p.310; Sdvižkov, 'Landschaft nach der Schlacht', pp.36, 46; Sdvižkov, *Pis'ma s Prusskoi voiny*, p.674; Ziechmann, *Journal vom Siebenjährigen Kriege*, p.236.

25 Möbius, *Mehr Angst vor dem Offizier als vor dem Feind?*, p.116 makes a similar point.

26 Duffy, *Russia*, p.90; Duffy, *The Army of Frederick the Great*, p.277; Großer Generalstab, *Zorndorf und Hochkirch*, pp.484-485, 9*-10*.

27 Füssel, *Der Preis des Ruhms*, pp.242-244; Sdvižkov, 'Landschaft nach der Schlacht', pp.36-37, 40 (quotation, p.36); Sdvižkov, *Pis'ma s Prusskoi voiny*, p.674.

28 Großer Generalstab, *Zorndorf und Hochkirch*, p.8a*; Hartmann, 'Unbekannte Quelle', p.206.

Russians went into winter quarters in November in Täge's home town of Marienwerder, bringing the campaign of 1758 to a close.[29]

Täge later became the pastor of the East Prussian town of Pobethen, and was still alive – and 80 years old – on the publication of his memoir in 1804. The book consists of three parts, of which the first and last were written by the book's editor, August Samuel Gerber, in consulation with Täge.[30] The translation that follows has been made using the copy of Täge's memoires held in the Herzogin Anna Amalia Bibliothek in Weimar.[31] The translated chapters come from the longest, second part of the book, which was written by Täge personally and describes his adventures in Russian service. The footnotes within the translation are Täge's own. The page numbers of the original German edition are given in square brackets. When the text refers to a mile, this means a German mile, which was approximately 7.5 kilometres. Although Täge's account is written primarily in the past tense, he also uses the historic present at moments of excitement, and the translation follows this. In places, additional words have been added in square brackets in order to make the meaning of the text clearer. Names are given as Täge writes them, although his transliteration of Russian names is certainly not to be relied upon. Täge's quotation of Russian phrases is essentially accurate, reflecting his considerable experience of Russian life, although again his transliteration varies slightly from modern forms. On two occasions, Täge also shows off his Latin, breaking off his account of the bombardment of Cüstrin with the phrase '*manum de tabula*' ('[take your] hand away from the board / [writing] tablet': an exhortation not to over-do something).[32] He later quotes Virgil's *Aeneid* as he bewails '*oh bella! oh horrida bella!*' ('oh wars, oh horrid wars!').

Further Reading

Christopher Duffy has written excellent accounts of the Zorndorf campaign, accessible to the general reader, from both the Prussian and Russian perspectives, in:

Duffy, Christopher, *Russia's Military Way to the West: Origins and Nature of Russian Military Power 1700-1800* (London: Routledge & Kegan Paul, 1981)
Duffy, Christopher, *Frederick the Great: A Military Life* (London: Routledge & Kegan Paul, 1985)
Duffy, Christopher, *The Army of Frederick the Great* (2nd edition, Chicago, IL: The Emperor's Press, 1996)

---

29   Bisset, *Memoirs and Papers of Sir Andrew Mitchell*, Vol.I, pp.440-441; Duffy, *Russia*, p.91; Ernst von Frisch, *Zur Geschichte der russischen Feldzüge im siebenjährigen Kriege nach den Aufzeichnungen und Beobachtungen der dem russischen Hauptquartier zugeteilten österreichischen Offiziere, vornemhlich in den Kriegsjahren 1757-1758* (Heidelberg: Winter, 1919), pp.85-88; Großer Generalstab, *Zorndorf und Hochkirch*, pp.154-161; Tempelhoff, *Geschichte des Siebenjährigen Krieges*, pp.231-232, 236-238; Tielke, W*ar between the Prussians, Austrians, and Russians*, pp.195-200, 209-214.
30   Gerber, *Christian Täge's Lebensgeschichte*, pp.vi, 3, 324-336.
31   The original work has been digitized and is available online at <https://haab-digital.klassik-stiftung. de/viewer/image/1714397483/1/LOG_0000/> last accessed, 27 August 2021.
32   I am grateful to Ilya Berkovich for his help with Täge's use of Russian, and to David Woodhead for his thoughts on the phrase '*manum de tabula*'. Any errors are mine alone.

For the most recent scholarship on the Zorndorf campaign, see:

Füssel, Marian, 'Das Undarstellbare darstellen. Das Bild der Schlacht im 18. Jahrhundert am Beispiel von Zorndorf (1758)', in Birgit Emich and Gabriela Signori (eds), *Kriegs / Bilder in Mittelalter und Früher Neuzeit* (Berlin: Duncker & Humblot, 2009), pp.317-349

Sdvižkov, Denis, 'Landschaft nach der Schlacht. Briefe russischer Offiziere aus dem Siebenjährigen Krieg', *Forschungen zur Brandenburgischen und Preussischen Geschichte* NF 22 (2012), pp.33-56

Sdvižkov, Denis, *Pis'ma s Prusskoi voiny. Liudi Rossisko-imperatorskoi armii v 1758 godu [Letters from the "Prussian War". The People of the Russian Imperial Army in 1758].* (Moscow: Novoe literaturnoe obozrenie, 2019)

Storring, Adam L., 'Subjective Practices of War: The Prussian Army and the Zorndorf Campaign, 1758' *History of Science* (OnlineFirst 2020)

The Biography of Christian Täge, former Russian Army Chaplain
Prepared according to his own statements and published by the author
of the novels of Doro Caro
With the accurate portrait of this remarkable man

Königsberg, 1804

On the commission of Göbbels und Unzer

Second Section

Täge as Russian Army Chaplain

[p.166]

Sixth Chapter

Täge arrives at Cüstrin to see it turn into a pile of rubble. Again [a] somewhat polemic [passage]. The extraordinary survival of two cellar-dwellers. A preacher in need and Fermor's humanity. The siege is lifted. The King of Prussia crosses the Oder. The Russian army withdraws toward Zorndorf.

It was in the middle of August, around nine o'clock in the morning, when I approached the town of Cüstrin [p.167]. A forest still lay between it and me, but the rising smoke and the ceaseless roaring of the cannons and mortars already announced to me an appalling woe, of which I should soon be an eyewitness. I arrived in the camp. Before lay Cüstrin, behind [me] a wood. Cüstrin was on fire! Not at one or the other end, but simply the whole of it: no single place in the extensive town without fire and smoke. Count Fermor had begun the bombardment around five o'clock in the morning and the very first bombs filled with incendiary materials struck a magazine of straw and were the main cause of the great fire that destroyed the whole of Cüstrin. The fire from the Russian side raged incessantly against the town. Already by midday, it had been reduced to a smoking pile of rubble, but nevertheless the bombs continued to pelt the unfortunate town, probably in order [p.168] to prevent any possible rescue or extinguishing.[33] Hundreds of inhabitants had sought safety on the road from the rain

---

33   In my view, this destruction of Cüstrin – undoubtedly shocking to any feeling heart – very much vindicates Count Fermor. If de la Messeliere accuses him of having made agreements with the King of Prussia, this single circumstances refutes him, and if Rambach in his pocket books on the history of the fatherland p.356 portrays the system of Count Fermor as consisting of pillaging and burning, he does not consider, that, given the mood of the Russian court against the Prussian at that time, a commander in chief had to proceed more according to

of fire from above, or through delay had lost their lives through the collapse of the buildings. The largest part escaped naked and bare, leaving behind their possessions, to the other side of the Oder [p.169], to the suburb, or to villages, where the fire of the Russians could not follow them.

But *manum de tabula* ['away from the [writing] tablet']. The destruction of Cüstrin is often depicted but never more truthfully [than here], as I experienced it myself. It is known that untold numbers of people who had fled to the cellars were killed by the collapse of these or smothered by smoke and vapour. The following anecdote, however, which I learnt later on, is perhaps less well known.

When the Russians lifted the siege on 21 August, the inhabitants who had fled dared to return to the town in order to dig out whatever sad remains of their property might still be there. While doing this they hear through air holes from a deeply buried cellar a muffled voice begging for rescue. At once a hundred hands are ready to clear away the rubble. After an hour they are successful in opening the cellar and pull forth a [p.170] man and his maiden: pale, starving, and shrivelled from the heat. Determination and fortitude had saved their lives. The cellar was deep and drew water. With this they had continually cooled the hot walls until the complete dissipation of all strength reduced them to pitiful cries for rescue. Through judicious care, however, their health was soon restored again.

While we camped next to Cüstrin, I was quartered in a well-furnished house in a village whose name has slipped my memory. This building belonged to a rich man in Cüstrin and served as his summer seat. From here, since I was without employment and wanted to get myself away as far as possible from the sight of the destruction, I took many walks in the surrounding area. On one of these, I become aware of a village nearby with a church. At once the idea occurred to me [p.171] to visit the preacher and perhaps, by this thought, I came to his rescue.

As I enter the house the pastor comes toward me dressed in his full robes. When I had introduced myself to him, he said gravely and with dignity, 'I am completely alone in my house. Loyal to my high obligation, I have not left my post, and I await with complete resignation whatever the enemy will inflict on me.' I comforted him in every way, described to him the humanity of the commander in chief, and promised him that I would ensure the maintenance of his peace and his possessions.

He sent me away more reassured, but the following morning had scarcely dawned than he stood already before my bed in my quarters. He showed me a bunch of keys. 'This is the only thing,' he said with a thousand tears, 'this is the only thing that I have saved. Since you parted from me, the village was fired on by the Prussians and my house and my [p.172] belongings in it were completed burnt down. I flee now for nothing more than the last thing that I still have: for my life.' Hearts that are

---

instructions than according to the feelings of a humanely-thinking heart. I knew him as a humanitarian, and I never felt more compassion for him than when he had to deny his most noble feelings because of a higher interest.

accustomed to sympathise with others will be able to imagine my feelings at this peti-tion! *O bella! O horrida bella!* ['Oh wars! Oh horrid wars!']

I at once reported, with him, to the Count [Fermor], but we were only admitted at ten o'clock. The misfortune of this indeed very worthy man moved him deeply. He gave him princely gifts, and gave him a pass that should bring him to whatever place he chose. The further fate of this good man is completely unknown to me.

Famously, on this day Count Fermor lifted the siege of Cüstrin, after he had vainly demanded that the commandant of the fortress, von Schack, should surrender.[34] Soon thereafter [p.173] the Count received certain news that the king is approaching the Oder and wanted to find a crossing. Lieutenant General von Kumatof was at once ordered to oppose him with an observation corps. Wherever the responsibility may lie, Kumatof does not notice the king, [p.174] and the latter – successfully completes the crossing of the Oder.

Therefore the order is: on the morning of 24 August the whole army will set off. This was done. As night was breaking we reached the area of Zorndorf – to witness the most terrible spectacle I have seen thus far in my life.

Seventh Chapter
Battle of Zorndorf. The Russians are reinforced by the Nuwo Corpus.
Battle order at midnight and holding of Holy Communion. *Prussac idiot.*
Benediction of the Russian army. Solemn arrival of the Prussians. The
cannonade begins.

We were at the place that Fermor had chosen for the battlefield. Some claim that neither the place nor the dispositions were advantageous for the Russian army [p.175]. This is a decision for the tacticians. The unbiased observer will, however, always be struck by the observation that both sides had a certain right to claim victory, as indeed happened.

I do not by any means involve myself in a formal description of this murderous battle, as I am no expert in the art, still less will I draw the missing material from other books, but merely recount thoroughly what I experienced and felt.

Despite all valour, anyone in the army with a sensitive heart had to face this coming battle with a certain shudder. One knew the bitterness that once reigned between

---

34   If Rambach claims that Fermor was not in the least [p.173] equipped for a formal siege then I ask, as does everyone who does not only know war from books but as an eyewitness, whether such a terrible destruction of a large town, which happened in the space of a quarter of a day, could be achieved by anything other than a full siege train? Fermor's retreat was in fact due not to the disappointed hope of taking the fortress, but rather to the approach of the king, who wanted to relieve the fortress and to attack Fermor. It is the pedantic spirit of the historian, if the sources are there and one or the other approach must be chosen, to give the chosen one the most negative meaning.

both armies, one could anticipate that the terrible destruction of Cüstrin would have brought the King and his troops to the greatest extremity, as we later truly learnt, the king allegedly ordered before the battle [p.176] that no quarter should be given to any Russian. So there was nothing to do but to await the terrible scenes.

Having arrived at the place of our destiny, the soldiers were given a short time for rest and then just before midnight battle order was formed. Just then, 10,000 Russian troops joined us, who were called the Nuwo Corpus[35] and commanded by Lieutenant General von Czernizef. Thus, our army was 50,000 men strong. Famously, all the troops formed themselves into a vast square. The light baggage, alongside the junior staff, among whom I was also, were brought into the middle of this square, where there was a kind of depression or hollow, around which several single trees stood. The heavy baggage, in contrast, was posted a quarter mile away, formed a lager of waggons, and had 8,000 men as cover.

[p.177] Here, however, I must honestly admit that the position of this heavy baggage did not seem to be advantageous. The king with his great army had to be by no means far away, and could in fact easily have swept them away. Indeed it was apparently his first decision, although he desisted, for reasons that I cannot say.

It was midnight: one of the brightest that I have experienced. However, the sight of the pure heavens and the clear, scarcely flickering stars could not quiet my heart, which was filled with fear and expectation of the things that must come. Could I be blamed for that: I who was not raised to look the horrors of a bloody war so brazenly in the eye? I, a preacher of the religion of peace? 'How will it look after twenty four hours? If you should indeed bear your life and a healthy body out of it, which is not yet decided; how many hundreds of them, who [p.178] you know, how many of them who you love, will not already be dead, or tortured by a thousand agonies and entreating God for a speedy death?'

In the midst of these feelings, which rent my heart apart more even than if a ball had had mercy on me and dashed my life to pieces, an officer came to me and said with feeling, 'Chaplain, Sir, I and many officers want right now to receive communion from your hands. Tomorrow perhaps we will be no more. We want to be reconciled with God, deliver any valuables to you, and entrust to you our last wills.'

Shaken to the core, I at once make arrangements for this solemn act. Since the baggage had not been unpacked and thus no tent pitched, I had to hold it under the open heavens. A drum served me as sacramental table. Above us arched the blue heavens, which with the light of the breaking day [p.179] began to redden. I have never held a sacrament in a more poignant, inspiring and, as I hope to God, uplifting way, but equally I have never again been in a similar situation. After the service, we parted from each other more speechlessly than eloquently, after I had received their

---

35   New, or Auxiliary and Reserve Corps.

testaments and valuables. Indeed many, many of these officers I never saw again. They went to their graves accompanied by my benediction.

The great exertion of my soul had relaxed my nerves. I sank into a deep sleep, from which I was woken, in bright sunshine, by the dreadful cry of the soldiers around me: *Prussac idiot.*[36] Encouraged, I compel myself, with others, to horse, in order to see the advancing Prussians. From a hill I caught sight of them. Their weapons flashed in the glare of the risen sun, a sight that would in any [p.180] other situation have been magnificent, but was now terrible enough. In a few instants, however, another spectacle distracted me from these matters.

Solemnly, the Archpriest [of the Russian army], surrounded by junior priests and a mass of servants, all furnished with holy banners, rode along the inner side of the square and blessed the soldiers. After they had received this benediction, each [soldier] grasped the leather bottle that hung on his belt, drank, and finished with a loud 'Hurrah!': proof of their readiness to receive the advancing enemy.

Never will I forget this approach. Majestically beautiful, and in still, quiet order, the Prussians advanced. Suddenly – and here I wish that the reader could truly feel this terrifyingly beautiful view – suddenly the Prussians deployed, and henceforth presented a long line in oblique order. The Russians themselves were astounded by this unwonted sight, which, as [p.181] is generally maintained, was a great triumph of the great king's tactic of that time. We already heard the terrible noise of the Prussian drums, although we could not yet discern the music. But in solemn march they come ever closer. Now we hear their oboists, they play 'Now Lord I am in Thy Keeping!' On this music [I say] no word of my feelings. Anyone who is capable of feeling will find it hardly surprising that in my later life this melody has always brought forth the most fervent stirrings of sadness in me.

In all of this din, and all the solemnity with which the Prussians advanced, the Russians army stood unmoving, and so still as if no man were there. But now the thunder of the Prussian canon burst forth, and I withdrew back into the square and into the hollow.

[p.182]

Eighth Chapter
Battle of Zorndorf. Decision. Things become very precarious in the hollow. Täge tries to save himself, but in vain. The Brigadier von S** [von Sievers] helps him out. Perils of the flight. Täge is captured by the Prussians

For those who have never had such an experience, it now seemed that Heaven and Earth were about to end. The ghastly roar of the big and small guns raged ferociously.

---

36   That is 'the Prussians are coming'.

A thick vapour engulfed the whole area of the square from the side of the attack. In the following hours, even the position in the hollow became no longer secure. One continually heard the whiz of the balls in the air and for a short time these smashed against the trees where we stood, and many Russians who had climbed up to see the great [p.183] spectacle better fell down at my feet dead or ripped to pieces. A young man, born in Königsberg – I no longer know either his name or his station in life – speaks with me, removes himself by four paces and – a ball at once lays him dead before my eyes. In the same instant a Cossack falls from his horse close by me. I stood holding the bridle of my horse, now more numb than feeling, more apathetic than in a condition to take a particular decision. However, a sight yet more terrible woke me from my apathy. I become aware that the square has been broken by the Prussians. Hussars from the Regiment of Malachowski have broken through and [attacked] the Russians in the rear.

Should I now wait longer and bring myself certain death or certain captivity, with all of its sad consequences? I throw myself on my horse, abandon everything, and ride to [p.184] the opposite side of the battle order, which the Prussians could not yet have reached. The Officer who commanded at the exit of square, however, a Russian, whose language I could now understand quite well, calls out to me: 'Who are you?' – The Lutheran chaplain. – 'Where the Devil are you going?' – Out of here, to save my life! – 'Back! No one may pass here.' – Consequently I was obliged to take up my old place again.

Scarcely have I arrived than Brigadier von S** [von Sievers] comes up to me: 'Chaplain, Sir,' he said, 'I have received two dangerous wounds, can now no longer serve, and I request that you accompany me to wherever I can be bandaged.' I explained to him the difficulty of leaving the square, but he answered me: 'just let me do it.' I threw myself again on horseback, he was with [p.185] difficulty put on his, and we came to the earlier spot.

The commanding officer still did not want to open [the way]. 'First you go where I was!', said the Brigadier, but this argument also availed nothing. Now, however, von S** spoke with a louder voice:

> 'In the name of Our Most Serene Empress, who wants to know that her wounded officers are preserved, I the Brigadier order you to open the way out for us.'

That worked. Saluting in the name of their empress, he orders the soldiers to open. We ride out.

It was one o'clock in the afternoon. The horrors of war had, however, multiplied themselves without end. A mass of men surrounded us. The screams of the wounded and dying rang in our ears. The Prussian balls reached the Russians even in this position. Even as we were let out, a ball smashed against the cauldron of a Cossack, with [p.186] a crash that almost deprived me of sight and hearing.

Nevertheless, while we did not find it emptier of people outside the battle line, we certainly found it safer. Our way led us in a few minutes to a wood close by, where we came upon both wounded and unwounded officers and their attendants. Still we could not tarry here too long near to the roaming Prussians. But where to go in safety, since we had to choose a route in this completely unknown region without maps and simply at random? A lieutenant, perhaps the bravest of all, calls out: 'I am riding on the right hand. I want at least to reconnoitre. Chaplain, Sir, accompany me.' – My courage had recovered as danger grew further away; I follow him.

Scarcely a short distance away from our companions, we came to a swamp over-grown with bushes, which, unknown to us, enabled enemy freebooters to [p.187] lay ambushes. These fired three shots at us, but without hitting. Calmly we ride further and came to a village. Probably it was Zorndorf. Here too, gunshots were fired from the garden hedgerows at us. Now it was time to retreat. Unhurt, we reached the place where we had left our comrades. We found none of them, but only their un-plundered horses stuck in the morass. A birch grove, which we reached after a while, showed us our missing brothers. We re-united in order to seek our further salvation. We soon found a large road, only it seems to all of us that the road leads again to Zorndorf. Now one must choose carefully. Off to the side lies another village: here we will perhaps find quiet and the wounded can have themselves bandaged. The decision was quickly taken. We leave the route to Zorndorf and go to this unknown [p.188] village. Nothing hostile, no outposts, no fixed sentinels can be seen. We ride more calmly down along the pretty fences that tastefully surrounded the orchards of this village. But right in the middle of our greatest assuredness, a mass of Prussian soldiers leap from the narrow path between two gardens, seize the bridles of our horses and cry:

'You are our prisoners!'

Patiently we had to yield to the superior power and let ourselves be led into the village.

[p.189]

Ninth Chapter
The Proviantkommissarius D** wants Täge's horse. He is deservedly sent on his way. Hard-heartedness of a Christian preacher and great good-heartedness of a Prussian grenadier. Conditions of the poor prisoners. Their further transport to Cüstrin

In this village stood a Prussian field battery with its covering troops. It was they who had captured us. The village administrator distributed us around the village, a courier went to inform the headquarters of our capture, and already at midnight an escort arrived to bring us into the interior of the Prussian states. These were dragoons and hussars. With break of day we were ordered to set off. Country wagons were in readiness for the wounded officers, and I was allowed to ride my own horse. But this I had [p.190] first to achieve by sheer obstinacy. A Proviantkommissarius D**, who was well known to me from Königsberg, where his father had a public position, does not want to have the horse brought out of the stable for me. 'According to the generally known laws of war, it supposedly belongs to him.'

'Mr D**, I answered him calmly, if you were a man of the sword and not of the pen, I would let this pass. The soldier may take what the laws of war allow him; the civilian who arrogates such a thing to himself clearly commits robbery. Nevertheless, take my horse in any case. It costs a hundred rubles for me, but your father will pay me three times as much, and only a single letter from the Russian General in Chief to the governor there will be necessary [to arrange that].' Ashamed, he slunk away, and amidst the loud laughter of the Prussian officers I was able to mount my own horse.

[p.191] Our way led us across a part of the battlefield, where the unfortunate victims of this terrible encounter lay on top of each other in a terrible aspect, some fully dead, others still half living with faint and thus all the more heart-rending cries. We were brought to the little town of Damm, where we met many Russians who had been captured before us. One of these, a brigadier, was very dangerously wounded, saw his end at hand, and on the news of my arrival demanded to receive the last rites from my hands. I had nothing with me: I had had to abandon my things for the sacrament, many valuables and letters entrusted to me, and two thousand rubles of my own property. However, I turn to the local pastor and ask him to lend me the holy vessel.

Was it due to the bitterness of this unseasonable zealot that a born Prussian should preach the peaceful religion of Jesus to the enemies of the state? Or was it base [p.192] avarice, that [he] hoped himself to gain some advantage from this ceremony? Enough; with the harshest expressions he rejected my request and . . . – but I may no longer repeat for him, who already for a long time moulders in his grave, the mortifications that he let me hear.

Deeply moved, I leave this hard-hearted man, firmly determined to give the dying the sacrament in the way the circumstances would allow it. But, given the weak nature of humans, one can forgive bitterness against such an un-Christianly-minded Christian preacher. However, Providence did not wish that such feelings should be dominant in me. It prepared a scene for me immediately afterwards that should reconcile me with humanity all the more, as a true Christian heart beat in the bosom of a most unlearned but truly virtuous enemy.

[p.193] I returned from the pastor across the churchyard. Russian soldiers who had not yet been able to be accommodated were imprisoned here. They seemed to be suffering from deprivation, and stared with dulled senses into the distance, leaning on the churchyard wall. Close in front of me goes a very big Prussian grenadier, also partly a victim of the battle, lamed by a ball, with a crutch under his arm, at the same time heartily eating a large bread that he had in his hand. A Russian soldier looks greedily at him, and savours with his tongue as if he were himself eating. 'Brother enemy!', he calls out to him in broken German, 'I am really very hungry.' Earnestly the Prussian grenadier remains standing, reaches into his pocket, takes out his knife, divides the bread, and gives half to the Russian, saying without a change in expression: 'You may be as brave a fellow as I.' This stroke of pure humanity [p.194] comforted me fully about the hard heart of the preacher.

Shortly before our departure from Damm, where we remained several days, I was obliged to make a very harsh sacrifice to the circumstances, namely to surrender my beautiful and expensive horse to the landlord for twenty-five thalers, which was not even the price of the saddle and accoutrements. It had not received the slightest fodder since our arrival, and moreover the landlord firmly refused to provide this, on the pretext that he could not get hold of any. When, out of pity for the beautiful animal, I relinquished it to him, Ach!, then he knew how to get hold of fodder for it. So is it for poor prisoners.

From here we were transported to Cüstrin, and on the way we had the sad spectacle that powerless Russians stumbled to us out of a wood. Clearly they had fled, but now [p.195], completely prostrated from hunger, preferred to give themselves up to the Prussians. In Cüstrin we were assigned the casemates as our quarters.

Tenth Chapter
Täge's establishment in captivity. Sad ruins of Cüstrin. Falling-out with an unknown young officer. Täge takes care of provisions. He is arrested, released, and meets Lieutenant General Czernizef. Something on the consequences of the last battle. The King of Prussia rides through Cüstrin. Dignified and humane treatment of Czernizef. Täge is ordered to the commandant and then to the Prussian camp and – exchanged.

Since I was quartered with several very course officers, whose morals and behaviour disgusted me, I made an agreement [p.196] with some others who were more genteel and we quartered ourselves in the former guardroom, which had no windows and doors because they had all been respectively melted and burned in the fire, but which nevertheless afforded us a secluded and tranquil residence. Here we established ourselves as the circumstances permitted.

On the following morning I walk along the walls and see with profound sorrow the destruction of this beautiful town. Everything [was] veiled in thick smoke and fog, so that we could procure still-burning coals for our fires. While I walk thus, lost in contemplation, past a casemate, a young Russian officer – I knew him not – walks out of it and washes himself. 'Who are you?', he calls out to me. Humbly I introduce myself to him. He replied, 'you must have prayed badly, since we lost the battle.' Angered by his remark, I replied audaciously 'Sir! It may perhaps [p.197] be put down to thy poor swordplay or, if thou art the one responsible, to thy miserable dispositions.' He laughed and I wanted to go further, but officers who know me call me back into the casemate. 'Chaplain, Sir,' they say, 'no one will stop you from going out of the gate into the suburb. Please take a couple of boys with you and buy provisions. We are suffering from a shortage of everything and you know, if one has money, one can live well in captivity.' I could not refuse this request, I am given abundant money, am, after making a sign, allowed out of the gate without difficulty, buy what is necessary for sustenance but also for delicacy and – am arrested at the door as I return.

Apparently Colonel von Schaak, commandant of the fortress, has been at the gate during my absence and has inquired as to what happened. On the mention of my departure [p.198], he has ordered me to be arrested and brought to him.

Therefore I was taken between two soldiers and, led by a corporal, brought to him. He examined me long and sharply, but finally dismissed me very politely with the request to visit him, which was however prevented by various circumstances.

Delightedly, a handsome feast was made from the materials I had brought. Many persons who I did not know took part but, what a horror for me, the young man who I had spoken to in the morning at his washing was addressed as 'Excellency'. I nudge my neighbour and ask, 'who is he?' 'He is Lieutenant General von Czernizef.' Horrified, I step nearer and ask for forgiveness, in case I should have spoken some-what too freely. Smiling he answered me, 'It was a pleasure to me that you showed yourself to me in a light in which I certainly [p.199] would want to see a righteous and determined young man.'

Only three days did we remain in the casemates, then the generals, along with me, were quartered in the suburb with citizens, where we indisputably found things much more comfortable. Here I learnt the consequences of a ferocious battle from the most harrowing perspective. A Russian soldier who had had one foot half shot away and the other completely smashed had dragged himself to Cüstrin, crawling all the way. Humanity wins over bitterness. People take the unfortunate Russian in, care for him, and give him into the care of the doctor. I was present at the operation. A cut with a round knife cut a part of his leg from him. He remained steadfast. Now, however, the saw goes through his bones and this was beyond human endurance, his feelings over-flowed into horrible shrieking and I turned my back – every [p.200] sensitive heart will know with what feeling.

Scarcely had I arrived in my quarters from this operation than a spectacle presented itself that for me, as a born Prussian, could not be other than deeply pleasant. Our great King Frederick rode through the suburb, naturally with the most distinguished retinue. All the Russian prisoners who were there dashed to the windows to see the hero of the century. Among them was Lieutenant General von Czernizef, who prob-ably wanted to make himself noticeable to the king in view of a possible exchange. Right under the window of Czernizef, however, the king turned his face to the other side – it seemed to me to be deliberate – and did not notice the great Russian. It was, however, certainly on the prior orders of this nobly-thinking king that a senior court chamberlain, following a certain distance behind, called to the lieutenant general: 'Does Your Excellency recognize [p.201] this horse? It is your own. I undertake that it shall be well looked after until it is returned to you.' All of us who heard these words were of one opinion as to their meaning. Thus the great king knew how to strike the right tone, through which he on one side ceded nothing from his royal dignity but on the other side made plain very clearly his will toward a high born prisoner.

Three weeks passed during my imprisonment in Cüstrin: not unhappily, but nevertheless uncomfortably due to the total lack of reasonable employment. After the passage of this time I am suddenly ordered to the commandant of the fortress, Colonel von Schaak. I come to him, and a coach stands at his door. Still I do not realise that this is for me. The commandant says a few friendly things to me, and then announced that in the [p.202] coach below I should travel at once to the Prussian camp – which was close in front of the town. My consternation at all of this was understandably great. I ask humbly but also fearfully what they plan to do with me. 'That I myself do not know', said the colonel, smiling, 'but I suspect that no evil will befall you. His Excellency Count von Dohna will explain the rest to you.'

I had to obey. An officer sat next to me, a non-commissioned officer [sat] on the box. As the light failed we arrived at the headquarters, but were at once allowed before the lieutenant general. Here I was, if possible, received even more kindly. After a few words he announced to me that I was, at sovereign command, to be exchanged. Someone will at once conduct me to the Russian camp. I asked for a delay until morning. 'That is against all orders.' [I asked] simply for rest [p.203] for one single hour. This was permitted to me.

At midnight a staff trumpeter from the Regiment Malachowsky awakened me, led a saddled horse before me, and obliged me to follow him. So I went once again toward the Russian army.

Eleventh Chapter
Arrival in the Prussian camp. Täge is dispatched with a trumpeter toward Landsberg. Ruse of the trumpeter at a mill. His anxieties of the heart. *Chto idiot?* Täge and his companion are plundered by the Cossacks. A German saves both. Joyful reception in Landsberg. The rear guard sets off to unite with the advance guard. Overnight quarters in a destroyed village. *Paschar.* Täge, even poorer, if possible, marches on with the army.

We came to the Prussian camp, where I was permitted a little rest in the sutlers' tents. [p.204] The proprietor looked after me with the true spirit of a fellow-countryman. However the rest was short, we soon had to set off again. The route went toward Landsberg, where the Russian rear guard still stood. The trumpeter who accompanied me, and who was no better informed of the route in this pitch-black night, spots the light of a night lamp to the side and down from the road. We ride there. It is a mill. The trumpeter makes a fearful racket on the door. The miller is thereby woken up, comes, and opens up. We make ourselves known to him and the trumpeter asks for a coal to light his pipe. The miller brings it but scarcely is the business finished than the trumpeter grabs the miller by the scruff of the neck and orders him to be our guide to Landsberg.

Such measures are certainly harsh, but in war sad necessity demands and permits them. Vainly the miller prevaricated as much as he could. Vainly [p.205] he suggested that the route to Landsberg was troubled by Cossacks. A pistol held against him taught him to position himself between our two horses and to be our guide.

As we came further, however, the trumpeter who accompanied me seemed to become sick at heart. The way went through bushes and woodland. 'Can you speak Russian?' he asked me, in a voice whose tone was comparable to the sunken quicksilver in a barometer, if the contrasting properties of the hearing and the face permit a comparison. I answered him that my proficiency in the Russian language was most insubstantial, that I had been for too short a time with the Russian army, and that I would under no circumstances be able to make myself understood with an actual Russian. 'Then it looks very bad for us', he answered, and immediately afterwards the shout resounded in our ears 'Chto idiot?'[37]

[p.206] At once we were surrounded by a mass of Cossacks. The miller disappeared: I never saw him more. My guide blew on his trumpet to prove that he was an emissary, but the Cossacks did not understand this, or did not want to understand it. In any case, they took us prisoner, led us into a bush off to the side, and plundered us of everything we had. My companion even lost his trumpet. To our great misfortune, we could not in any way make ourselves comprehensible to them. The worst was that they brandished their riding whips over us and thereby obliged us, in order not to have to endure pain while they plundered us, to observe the deepest silence.

We stood there robbed of everything when a new troop of Cossacks came to us, probably with the intention of snatching away a part of the booty of the first. The trumpeter and I meanwhile raised plaintive cries and protestation in German. Fortunately there is someone among [p.207] the newly-arrived troop who understands German. He at once speaks to the Russians and, as I later learnt, gives them to understand that they should hold back, as this must be an important person. He now spoke to me in German, and scarcely had he learnt that I was the chaplain of the general staff than he at once made it known in Russian to the others. Not even in a well-appointed theatre does a scene change as quickly as then. The common Russian soldier fell to the ground with abject apology, and the officer asked me touchingly not to inform the commander in chief of this incident. All the things taken from us were returned and a quite considerable detachment of Cossacks brought us to the place we specified, that is Landsberg. A quarter mile from the town we passed the camp of the Cossacks: a romantic view for one seeing it for the first time. On a wide plain in disorderly rows were scattered individual [p.208] straw huts, lighted by the starlight of heavens from

---

37   Who's there? Who goes there?

which the clouds were gradually clearing, the whole thing apparently concealing the otherwise well know character of this people.

We reached Landsberg. Still the day did not dawn. The trumpeter's eyes were bound, and we were lead to the commandant of the town, Colonel von Chumatof.[38] This gentleman at once left his bed to deal with us. The trumpeter was graciously dismissed, received 25 rubles as a gift and an escort of Cossacks to bring him safely into the Prussian camp. At my request, I was given my quarters in the post house, where I had already previously lodged.

It can easily be understood that, with the happiness of being able to rest in a clean and soft feather bed after so much fatigue, I sank at once into the deepest sleep. However, I did not enjoy it for long. A loud racket [p.209] wakes me up. Half terrified, I listen for what it might be. It is music, whose sound unites with the glow of the coming day. I hear my name called, the music quietens just for long enough to bring me a vivat, then blares even louder with trumpets and trombones in this vivat. I jump up, inform myself what is happening, and learn that the corps of officers here, full of joy at my return from imprisonment, wanted to greet me in this way. One can well understand that we now embraced joyfully and ate a choice breakfast with the loudest attestations of friendship.

Yet in the middle of these most blissful sentiments of happy reunion comes suddenly the order from Colonel von Chumatof: the rear guard will set off to unite with the vanguard. Everything was in the best order, and already at 11 o'clock in the morning we were on the march.

[p.210] With dusk that evening we reached our overnight quarters, where at least the staff (and also I) spent the night in a village. This village[39] gave a sad picture of war, which devastates everything. No living souls there, all houses empty, plundered, with windows and doors smashed out. The fine schloss on the Edelhof was similarly ravaged, and the way to the pastor's house could be seen from the books strewn here and there. My lodgings, directly above those of Colonel von Chumatof, showed me even more clearly the horror of the devastation. Everything in this farmhouse parlour that a person had not been able to carry away was smashed, broken, destroyed, the beds cut into pieces and the feathers strewn across the room. I chose a room that contained fewer ruins, laid myself on a pile of straw, and had the Cossacks who had been assigned to me lie down around my bivouac. For a few hours I slept quietly.

[p.211] 'Paschar, Paschar!'[40] sounded suddenly in my ears. Shocked, I rose. The dark night showed me all the more clearly the bright light of the flames of a burning building nearby. Vapour and smoke penetrate into my quarters and surrounded

---

38   He has already been mentioned.
39   The name has escaped me.
40   "Fire! Fire!"

me with fog. I hear the storm roar, which will tremendously increase the danger of the fire. Leaping from my chamber, I open the door of the large parlour, but flames already beat against me. A side door saves me and my Cossacks. I could only grab a couple of pieces of clothing, and a bearskin blanket that Colonel von Chumatof had given me. All the rest was burnt. The fire had started in a neighbouring house because of a badly-kept fireplace. It could not be extinguished, but instead destroyed seven quarters in a row. The most terrible thing was that from most of the roofs came sharp gunshots [p.212], which were not without sad consequences for those who still wanted to save something. Probably the inhabitants, who had previously fled, had hidden these [muskets] in the attics for defence in case of need, and the heat of the fire had caused them to shoot.

So, in this night too, the rest that I had so fervently hoped for after many exertions was again thwarted. At break of day we had only enough time to collect the little that we had saved and then to get ourselves ready for the further march that might at any moment be ordered.

11

Fighting in Frederick II's Favourite Musketeer Regiment: A Unique Series of Prussian Soldiers' Letters from the Seven Years War

Katrin and Sascha Möbius

Hochkirch in Saxony, 14 October 1758, 05:00 a.m.: an uncle and nephew from the Zander family, almost the same age, from the Brandenburg village of Nitzahn, privates in the famous Infantry Regiment Nr.13, commanded by Lieutenant General August Friedrich von Itzenplitz, are among the Prussian soldiers who hastily jump out of their tents, grasp their muskets and try to defend themselves against a large-scale Austrian surprise attack. At the end of the day, the two were dead, together with all other men from their village serving in the regiment. Altogether, their unit had lost six officers and 437 men dead and 12 officers and 365 men wounded. Most probably, both Zanders were killed during the vain attempt to recapture the village of Hochkirch.[1] Another, very famous member of the regiment, Ulrich Bräker, could also have met his fate on this day, had he not deserted during the Battle of Lobositz at the beginning of the Seven Years War. Bräker's story has often been quoted,[2] but this chapter focuses on the two young Zanders, who would have been totally forgotten if a descendant of their family had not found and published their letters from the front 250 years after their death at Hochkirch.[3]

---

1   Christian F. Zander, *Fundstücke – Dokumente und Briefe einer preußischen Bauernfamilie (1747-1953)* (Hamburg: Verlag Dr. Kovac, 2015), pp.111-113.
2   The unwilling Swiss mercenary has been portrayed as the archetype of the thousands of foreign mercenaries, who had been 'pressed into the Prussian military service by ruses or violence, perfectly drilled with the stick and (socially) disciplined by the threat of cruel punishments.' Jürgen Kloosterhuis, former director of the Prussian archives has already shown that a careful reading of Ulrich Bräker's reminiscences presents a much more differentiated picture. See Jürgen Kloosterhuis, 'Donner, Blitz und Bräker: Der Soldatendienst des "armen Mannes im Tockenburg" aus der Sicht des preußischen Militärsystems', in Alfred Messerli and Adolf Muschg (eds), *Schreibsucht: autobiographische Schriften des Pietisten Ulrich Bräker (1735–1798)* (Göttingen: Vandenhoeck & Ruprecht, 2004), pp.136-138.
3   Zander, *Fundstücke*, p.15.

To honour Christopher Duffy, who produced the first in-depth English study of the Prussian army of Frederick II,[4] we want to present the first analysis of these unique and newly-found letters which represent the most important collection of ego-documents of Prussian soldiers from the Seven Years War.[5] We pay special attention to the *Kanton*, on which Duffy wrote: 'Finally the local associations of the cantonal-based regiment helped to promote comradeship on campaign.'[6]

The Zanders' and Bräker's regiment was not only one of the most effective in the Prussian army but has often been presented as a unit with a most strict internal regime and a relationship between soldiers and their NCOs and officers characterized by iron discipline, total submission of the privates and brutal punishments. Jürgen Kloosterhuis has already shown that this verdict needs qualification.

A first debate amongst historians focused on the relationship between the regiments' effectiveness and different schools of leadership. Hans Bleckwenn developed a theory that the regiments built on strict discipline (the 'Dessau school') were able to fight successfully as long as they were victorious, but tended to loose heart after a defeat or severe losses, while those built on a humanitarian culture of leadership and moral encouragement of the soldiers (the 'Schwerin school') were able to recover even after the loss of two-thirds of their complement in one battle. Bleckwenn's thesis was questioned and qualified by Christopher Duffy, who pointed out that Schwerin had also been a strict disciplinarian and 'meted out death penalties much more readily than Frederick, and the armies under his command won general admiration for the restraint they exercised in enemy territory (…). Altogether the Schwerin code of discipline appears to have been more effective, more consistent, and less sentimental than the better-known Dessau variety.'[7] Jürgen Kloosterhuis presented a study of the regiments from Berlin and Brandenburg and found out that Bleckwenn's analysis of the combat efficiency of the different units was at least questionable.[8]

The Zander letters give new and unique insights into the internal regime of the regiment and the relationships between its different sub-groups. The following analysis will deal with the regiment's type of hierarchy, and the interaction between the different groups of soldiers.

The Itzenplitz Regiment

The regiments were at the core of any European army of the early modern era. The regiment was the most important permanent organizational military structure. Like the other Prussian infantry regiments, Infantry Regiment Nr.13, owned by its *Chef*,[9] Lieutenant

---

4   Christopher Duffy, *The Army of Frederick the Great* (New York: Hippocrene, 1974).
5   Parts of the letters have been analysed and translated in Katrin and Sascha Möbius, *Prussian Army Soldiers and the Seven Years War. The Psychology of Honour* (London: Bloomsbury, 2019).
6   Christopher Duffy, *Frederick the Great. A Military Life* (Oxford/New York: Routledge, 2016), p.12.
7   Duffy, *Frederick the Great*, p.14
8   Power Point Presentation from 2011, we are indebted to Jürgen Kloosterhuis for providing it.
9   The term *Chef* is the original German one. The regiment's *Chef* was also called the *Inhaber* (owner, proprietor) in German. The term is somewhat misleading as the owner was responsible for all dealings of the regiment but in the end the regiment was the King's.

General August Friedrich von Itzenplitz, numbered 1,832 men in 1756.[10] The monarch provided the funds and the *Chef* had to invest the money into the regiment, often also using his own money to augment the regiment's chest. Itzenplitz had a brilliant reputation for recruiting good-looking and able soldiers. Already in 1739, the Soldier King had complimented the young Itzenplitz, that he had made so many companies 'handsome'.[11]

Itzenplitz was an experienced soldier who had risen through the ranks and was directly responsible to the king for the raising and maintaining of the unit. He was aided by his staff, consisting of the colonel, or commander, who was responsible for the day-to-day business of the regiment, a lieutenant-colonel, a major and several captains. These officers were also owners of the 12 companies of the regiment. The Itzenplitz regiment had ten companies of musketeers and two of grenadiers. The noble officers of the regiment were volunteers. In times of peace, it was nearly impossible for commoners to become officers. In times of war, the regimental *Chefs* often made exceptions and able NCOs became officers, sometimes faking their certificates of nobility.[12] Like the Zanders, about 36 percent of the privates of the regiment were *Kantonisten*.[13] These were subjects of the Prussian king, who lived in the recruitment district of the regiment (*Kanton*). All male peasants and artisans, who were not exempt for economic or religious reasons[14] and tall enough to serve (taller than 175 cm), were registered in the lists and trained. After their basic training, they were annually called to arms for the summer manoeuvres for two or three months. About 15 percent were subjects of the Prussian king who were exempt from the *Kantonsystem* but served as mercenaries or were sons of soldiers. 48 percent were real foreigners, either from the Holy Roman Empire of the German Nation (37.5 percent) or other European countries (11.5 percent) like Ulrich Bräker, who was from Switzerland.[15] In wartime, the two grenadier companies were detached from the regiment and put together with the grenadier companies of Infantry Regiment Nr.26 (Meyerinck) forming an independent grenadier battalion. The grenadiers were used as light infantry in the war of posts, ambushes and foraging parties against the enemies' light troops. In battle, they were also used as shock troops. Grenadiers were distinguished by their high 'mitre' caps but were not taller than the musketeers. Actually, Frederick II had erased the prescriptions for choosing grenadiers from the ranks of the musketeer and fusilier regiments in the 1743 *Reglement*, so the officers were free to send any men into the grenadier companies. In spite of the special honour connected with being a grenadier, it seems that some officers sent unwanted men off to the grenadier companies, because it was a

---

10   Johann Heilmann, *Die Kriegskunst der Preußen unter König Friedrich dem Großen* (Leipzig and Meißen: F.W. Goedsche'sche Buchhandlung, 1852), Vol.1 p.97.

11   Karl Friedrich Pauli, *Leben großer Helden des gegenwärtigen Krieges* (Halle: Christoph Peter Francke, 1760), Vol.V, pp.225-226.

12   Letter XXII, in Zander, *Fundstücke*, p.76.

13   Kloosterhuis, 'Donner, Blitz und Bräker', p.159.

14   The only sons of peasants, who kept the farm running, village administrators (*Dorfschultzen*), burghers of certain cities, and pacifist religious communities like the Quakers were exempt.

15   Kloosterhuis, 'Donner, Blitz und Bräker', p.159; Martin Winter, *Untertanengeist durch Militärpflicht? Das preußische Kantonsystem in brandenburgischen Städten im 18. Jahrhundert* (Bielefeld: Verlag für Regionalgeschichte, 2005), pp.167–170; Matthias Ludwig von Lossow, *Denkwürdigkeiten zur Charakteristik der preußischen Armee unter dem Grossen König Friedrich II. Aus dem Nachlasse eines alten preußischen Offiziers* (Glogau: Carl Heymann, 1826), pp.2–7.

good possibility to get rid of them. Being a grenadier was much more dangerous than being a musketeer.[16] The 10 musketeer companies were divided into two battalions of five companies each, which formed the smallest tactical unit of the Prussian army.

The Itzenplitz regiment was an elite unit. It had already earned a prodigious reputation during the War of the Austrian Succession. Afterwards, in the Seven Years War, it was instrumental in the victories at Lobositz and Prague and won eternal fame for its role as vanguard during the Battle of Leuthen, when the Prussians defeated a much stronger Austrian army using the famous oblique order of battle.[17] It suffered horrific losses at Hochkirch but kept its elite status until the end of the war and long after. The regiment got many outward signs of honour. For example, Alex Burns was able to point out in his PhD thesis, that it was honoured by Prince Henry of Prussia after the Seven Years War.[18] This Prussian general and younger brother of Frederick II had led the regiment in person during the Battle of Prague. Every year, he invited all members of the regiment who had been present at this battle to a representative dinner. The regiment's *Chef* was often honoured by the king, including a substantial present after the Battle of Lobositz. The Itzenplitz regiment gained one of the most sought for favours. Although only Nr.13 according to its *ancienneté*,[19] it was allowed to march directly behind the guards and the oldest regiment, Nr.1, when parading in front of the king. This was due to the king's praise for its fighting capacities. It also had the right to beat the grenadiers' march on its drums.[20] Its soldiers and officers often got substantial material rewards for their successes in combat.

The Zanders and their Letters

There is a collection of 18 letters from Christian Friedrich (13 letters) and Joachim Dietrich Zander (five letters), uncle and nephew from a village administrators' family from Brandenburg, both serving in the famous Regiment von Itzenplitz.[21] Another five letters of the two had been excerpted by a relative of the family, Professor Friedrich Schultze, when he visited the Zanders' farmhouse in 1919 but have been lost since then. Schultze was also able to give some information provided by his relatives about other letters, which had already been lost by 1919. These lost letters had probably contained the description of the regiment's participation in the battles of Lobositz, Roßbach and Leuthen.[22] Yet, Schultze's information

---

16   Möbius and Möbius, *Soldiers*, p.22.
17   Curt Jany, *Geschichte der Preußischen Armee vom 15. Jahrhundert bis 1914* 2nd edition (Osnabrück: Biblio, 1967), Vol.2, pp.454-455.
18   Alexander Burns, "'The Entire Army Says Hello": Common Soldiers' Experiences, Localism, and Army Reform in Britain and Prussia', 1739-1789 (PhD thesis, West Virginia University, 2021), p.202.
19   That is, the age or seniority of the regiment. Leopold von Anhalt-Dessau had researched the ages of the different regiments and produced a ranking ('*Dessauer Spezifikation*'). Given the crucial importance of the age when it came to defining a person's or groups honour, the oldest regiments were also the most honourable ones.
20   Möbius and Möbius, *Soldiers*, pp.158-159; Möbius, *Ein feste Burg*, pp.261-290.
21   'Itzenplitz Infantry', *Kronoskaf Seven Years War*, <http://www.kronoskaf.com/syw/index. php?title=Itzenplitz_Infantry>, accessed 13 October 2018; Zander *Fundstücke*, p.88.
22   Zander, *Fundstücke*, pp.15-16.

on these letters is very meagre. The letters are written on sheets of paper measuring 340 by 208 millimetres, which had been folded once, thus producing four pages.[23] Unfortunately, none of the letters from Nitzahn to the two musketeers have survived.

We know a lot about the family background of the two musketeers: Both musketeers belonged to a well-off peasant family of *Dorfschulzen* (village administrators). Johann Matthias Zander was *Dorfschulze* of Nitzahn, a Brandenburg village near Plaue an der Havel and the head of the Zander family until his death in 1752. As the head of his family, he was exempt from military service but his position did not prevent his relatives from being drafted into the army. His younger brother, Christian Friedrich Zander (21 August 1725 – 14 October 1758), and his eldest son, Johann Dietrich (15 December 1729 – 14 October 1758),[24] both served in the Regiment von Itzenplitz Nr.13. Together with his brother, Christian Friedrich had unsuccessfully tried to obtain his dismissal from the army. This process is covered by most of their letters written before the Seven Years War.

Christian Friedrich was a 'brewer'[25] and burgher of Plaue and had unsuccessfully tried to get his dismissal from the army in 1749; this failed, but he seems to have gained a substantial leav as there are only two letters between 1749 and the outbreak of the war and both stem from the manoeuvre period of 1753. His exact legal status concerning the *Kantonspflicht* (draft) is not clear. He had already been drafted before moving, in whatever way, to Plaue and had most probably no house and farm (*Haus und Hof*) in Plaue.[26] Johann Matthias Zander died in 1752 and his second son, Johann Wilhelm Zander, inherited the position as *Dorfschulze*, by which he automatically became exempt from military service. He is the main recipient of the letters written during the Seven Years War. It is not clear, why Johan Dietrich as eldest son did not inherit the farm and position as *Dorfschulze* but had to go and join the colours. A normal reason would have been his illegitimate birth. However, information provided by his descendant and Jürgen Kloosterhuis, the former director of the Prussian archives, rules this out and points to a family quarrel.[27] Johann Wilhelm was Christian Friedrich's nephew and Christian Friedrich addresses him as 'Vetter' (nephew) in his letters.[28] That they were from a well-off and educated peasant family of village administrators does not seem to have been exceptional for Prussian *Kantonisten*. Two other writing privates were also sons of the local *Dorfschulzen* (village administrators) and Christian Friedrich Zander mentions the death of the son of the *Dorfschulze* of Möthlitz, a village bordering on the Zanders' village of Nitzahn.[29]

The king valued their regiment Itzenplitz as an elite unit.[30] For the soldiers, this meant that they had *Immediatverkehr* with the king, and were thus allowed to address the king directly in all matters concerning their job. The two Zanders did not take part in the Battle

---

23   Zander, *Fundstücke*, p.16.
24   Zander, *Fundstücke*, pp.83-84, 86.
25   This did not necessarily mean that he worked as a brewer, as every house-owner had the right to brew beer. Zander, *Fundstücke*, p.86.
26   We are indebted to Jürgen Kloosterhuis for this information.
27   We thank Christian F. Zander and Jürgen Kloosterhuis for this information.
28   For modern readers this can be misleading as the modern German word *Vetter* is translated as cousin, while in early modern German it means uncle of nephew. *Zedler's Universal Lexicon*, Vol.48, p.373.
29   Möbius and Möbius, *Soldiers*, pp.62, 194; Letter XIII, in Zander, *Fundstücke*, p.49.
30   Kloosterhuis, 'Donner, Blitz und Bräker', p.135.

of Prague as they were ill at that time. Seven months later, however, both were present at the regiment's famous charge as part of the vanguard of the army at the Battle of Leuthen. They also took part in some minor actions and were killed during the Battle of Hochkirch along with all the other *Kantonists* from their village. One can easily imagine how disastrous this loss was for the social structure of the rural community.

The Zanders play a central role in the community of *Kantonisten* from their village as they were the hub for exchanging information by letters between the village and the army due to their reading and writing skills and their affiliation to the family of the *Dorfschulzen*.[31] Christian Friedrich and Johann Dietrich were central to a network that secured the presence of the village at the front and the presence of the front at the village. At the same time their position as intermediaries between the noble authorities and the peasantry in civil life is reflected by their way of dealing with their officers. Christian Friedrich does not hesitate to approach the owner of his regiment and even the king to get his dismissal and Johann Dietrich approaches his captain on behalf of an acquaintance from the village whom they try to prevent from becoming a grenadier.[32] They fail in both cases, but their challenge to the officers' decisions is perceived as a perfectly normal procedure by them and their commanding officers alike. The strong position of the Zanders stems from their rank in civil society, where the officers need the support of the local administrators when it comes to recruiting the *Kantonisten*.[33]

Their friends and relatives were not all in the same musketeer company; one friend and one relative served in one of the grenadier companies. We know this, because they mention them in their letters; they seem to be their peer group and they were more important than the men they were fighting side by side with.

Their letters show how they care for their relatives, who were also to receive the information contained in their letters. We can imagine that receiving a letter from the front was a major event for the family. The linguistic performance of the texts has to be kept in mind, especially, when the content was also to be received by other family members and friends from the village.[34] We can imagine that the letters were meant to be read aloud in front of an audience made up of relatives and neighbours. Johann Dietrich addresses his letters to his mother and siblings. When they are read aloud to this audience their contents will surely be transmitted to the entire village community and thus the reality of the community is changed by the act of communication. In example, the news of the prominent role of the regiment during the Battle of Lobositz immediately strengthened the self-consciousness of the peasant community in its dealings with the military authorities, when it came to getting back some requisitioned horses.[35] Although Christian Friedrich addresses his letters only to his nephew, numerous other people are mentioned and it can be taken for granted, that at

31   This corresponded to the role of the *Dorfschulzen* as 'brokers of information' (*Informationsmakler*) in civil life; see Löffler, *Dörfliche Amtsträger*, p.185.
32   Möbius and Möbius, *Soldiers*, p.202.
33   Which was also a source of corruption. Winter, *Untertanengeist*, p.311.
34   Marvin Carlson, *Performance. A Critical Introduction*, 3rd edition (Abingdon: Routledge, 2017); Noam Chomsky, *Language and Mind*, 3rd edition (Cambridge: Cambridge University Press, 2006); Uwe Wirth (ed.), *Performanz: Zwischen Sprachphilosophie und Kulturwissenschaften*, 5th edition (Berlin: Suhrkamp, 2002).
35   Letter IX, Zander, *Fundstücke*, pp.40-41.

least parts of these letters were also read to other people in the village with the same effect as Johann Dietrich's letters. Thus, a direct transmission of information is ensured. This fact also has to be remembered when we deal with the unique concept of honour discussed below.

Most striking is their fear that younger relatives will also be drafted. They are honourable men in their village and also honourable soldiers at the front. Their direct influence on the draft is small but that it exists at all increases their standing. Yet, when they write about their role in combat, they seem to be very reluctant to provide details, although they were part of one of the elite regiments of the Prussian army and their relatives were often asking for details from the front. The Zanders' letters do not contain as many religious allusions as other soldiers' letters but the religious aspects of their texts multiply when they write about the hardships of their service or the danger of combat.[36]

Ulrich Bräker was a Swiss, whose father had sent him to Schaffhausen together with two acquaintances, obviously to get him hired as a mercenary by one of the many regiments looking for recruits in this town. Bräker was lucky, as he got hired by a Lieutenant 'Makroni' (Second Lieutenant Arnold Friedrich von Marck) from the Itzenplitz Regiment. Due to his lack of height, 'Makroni' hired him as a servant and not as a musketeer. Yet, upon his arrival in Berlin, Bräker had to find out that the commander of his company thought differently about this and he was made a musketeer in the Itzenplitz Regiment. Bräker decided to learn the soldier's trade in order to be taken to the front and thus get a chance to desert. This chance came, when his regiment took part in the successful attack on the Loboschberg during the Battle of Lobositz (1 October 1756) and Bräker was able to get home to Switzerland.[37] Later on, Bräker became an important figure in pietist and enlightened circles, where he was praised as a common man turned writer. His memoires were published in 1789, where he also describes his time in the Prussian army.

The Owner of the Regiment, August Friedrich von Itzenplitz

The regiment's *Chef* was responsible for the regiment and could run it along his own lines as long as he stuck to the regulations and was successful. It is thus worthwhile to have a look at the personality of the *Chef* during the first years of the Seven Years War. The regiment has been described as a 'tightly run regiment' and the generally excellent *Kronoskaf Seven Years War* website claims that the unit was called the 'Donner und Blitzen' (Thunder and Lightning) paraphrasing the name of its allegedly super-severe *Chef*, August Friedrich von Itzenplitz.[38] Itzenplitz' characterization is solely based on Ulrich Bräker's memoires.[39] A second similar characterization of the regiment's *Chef* by the Swiss historian Franz Ludwig

---

36   Zander, *Fundstücke*, p.99. For examples of more overtly religious letters, see those from the Alt-Anhalt and Hülsen regiments: Möbius and Möbius, *Soldiers*, p.67.

37   Kloosterhuis, 'Donner, Blitz und Bräker', pp.136-179.

38   'Itzenplitz Infantry', *Kronoskaf Seven Years War*, <http://www.kronoskaf.com/syw/index. php?title=Itzenplitz_Infantry>, accessed 13 October 2018

39   Ulrich Bräker, *Lebensgeschichte Und Natürliche Abentheuer Eines Armen Mannes Von Tockenburg* (Zurich: Hans Heinrich Füssli, 1789), p.141.

Haller, can be dismissed as taken from Bräker and not based on another source.[40] Thus, Bräker's verdict, or what has been seen as Bräker's verdict, should be questioned. Karl Friedrich Pauli, author of a compendium of short biographies of Prussian officers of the Seven Years War, *Leben grosser Helden des gegenwärtigen Krieges* (Lives of Great Heroes of the Ongoing War), offered a totally different characterization of Itzenplitz, when he called him 'the gentle father of two promising children',[41] and underlined that Itzenplitz always tried to help lesser persons and to defend 'the just cause of a low-born man against someone who had more power and reputation'.[42] Pauli's appraisal of Itzenplitz' style as a commander is most interesting:

> When his trade demanded strictness and severity, he did not act out of a natural inclination to be cruel, but because he followed the king's orders with the utmost precision and also demanded from others to do this. But any soldier, who did what he was supposed to do, did not find a commanding general in him but a gentle father: and his entire regiment will testify for this.[43]

Pauli describes an ideal commander of the age of enlightenment,[44] and his mixture of gentle paternalism and strict discipline and military drill is totally in line with the Prussian regulations, that call for a harmony in the regiment based on professionalism, care (from above) and subordination (from below).[45] It might be objected that Pauli, being a professor of philosophy and history at the University of Halle (Saale), right in the heartlands of the Brandenburg monarchy, drew too positive a picture of the deceased general and tried to present an ideal rather than a realistic presentation. Yet, Pauli was no palliator. Proof for this is his biography of Georg Friedrich von Manstein, colonel of the Alt-Anhalt Regiment. Pauli depicts Manstein as an incorruptible, courageous, and loyal man, but also underlines his strictness: 'He kept discipline like the strictest Romans, like Manlius Torquatus … this made many people think bad of him and fear him … But he was only tough and did not

---

40   Franz Ludwig Haller, *Militärischer Charakter und merkwürdige Kriegsthaten Friederich des Einzigen Königs von Preußen : nebst einem Anhang über einige seiner berühmtesten Feldherren und verschiedene Preußische Regimenter* (Berin: Oemigke, 1796), p.318. Firstly, Haller was from Switzerland and does not seem to have had access to sources from eyewitnesses. Secondly, he also uses the word '*Schärfe*' (severeness) as Bräker does and calls the general himself (and not the regiment, like Bräker) '*Donnerblitz*' (thunderbolt). Also Haller also uses a similar formulation as Bräker when he describes the fighting on the Loboschberg during the Battle of Lobositz ('from wall to wall', Haller, p.318, Bräker, p.154.) All this indicates that Haller used Bräker and spiced up his source.

41   Carl Friedrich Pauli, *Leben grosser Helden des gegenwärtigen Krieges* (Halle: Christoph Peter Franke, 1760), Vol.V, 253.

42   Pauli, *Leben*, Vol.V, p.255.

43   Pauli, *Leben*, Vol.V, p.255.

44   See for example Carlos III's attempt to introduce enlightened mentalities to the Spanish army. Katrin and Sascha Möbius, 'Honour, Faith and Professionalism. The Transfer of Military Values and Knowledge from Prussia to Spain in the 18th Century', in Peter Burschel and Sünne Juterczenka (eds) *The Sea. Maritime Worlds of Life in the Early Modern Era* (Cologne and Weimar: Böhlau, 2021), pp.41-53.

45   *Reglement vor die Königl. Preußische Infanterie*, Berlin 1743, pp.423-424.

listen to any complaints when he had been provoked by the wicked to hate them.[46] The allusion to Torquatus is crystal-clear, as this ancient Roman commander had sentenced his son to death for disobeying his father's orders. Officers serving under Manstein describe him as a most rude and insulting, yet courageous man.[47] We may thus conclude that Pauli in general drew quite realistic pictures which were only slightly sugar-coated as he was writing about soldiers who had fallen in combat. So, we can believe that Pauli's informers from Itzenplitz's regiment did not see him as a yelling and ranting thunder-god. Actually, it seems as if Bräker misunderstood or made up the meaning of the soldiers' nickname of their regiment. This seems particularly so inasmuch as Bräker never saw Itzenplitz. Most probably, the soldiers did not mean their regiment's *Chef* when calling it '*Donner und Blitz*' but the fighting capacity of the regiment.[48] Above all, Pauli's verdict should make us rethink the regimental culture of the Itzenplitz Regiment. With all due caution, we can summarize that one of Itzenplitz's noticeable personal features was his inclination to do justice to inferiors and not tolerate any abuse of power.

The Interaction Between Different Groups of Soldiers

At the core of the culture of a given group of people are the interactions between its sub-groups and the individuals forming the group, especially the expectations of other comrades' behaviour. Knowing the regulations and customs of the regiment and having a perception of other members' knowledge of these regulations and customs can be seen as an essential prerequisite of any regimental culture. Concerning the subject of gender and marriage, Hurl-Eamon has shown in her ground-breaking study that the knowledge of regimental or even company deviations from the official rules of the army were essential for the shaping of their specific cultures.[49]

The Soldiers of the Itzenplitz Regiment and the King

The men are obviously well informed, which is shown by another scene, they relate in a letter from August 1758. The paragraph deserves to be translated completely:

> A victory was celebrated in the camp of Sprottau on August 3rd, 1758, because the king had beaten the Russians at Zorndorf. The king is pretty cheerful, happy, and fresh … there is hardly any charge in which he does not participate. After he had returned from the Russians, he rode behind our regiment one time. There some of

---

46   Pauli, *Leben*, Vol.I, p.272.
47   Eduard von Bülow (ed.), *Aus dem Nachlasse von Georg Heinrich von Berenhorst*, Vol.1 (Dessau: Verlag von Aue, 1845), XVI; Lemcke, *Kriegs- und Friedensbilder*, p.28.
48   It had fought most efficiently during the first two Silesian Wars. See: Gieraths, *Kampfhandlungen*, p.50; Jany, *Geschichte*, Vol.II, p.135.
49   Jennine Hurl-Eamon, *Marriage and the British Army in the Long Eighteenth Century: 'The Girl I Left Behind Me'* (Oxford: Oxford University Press, 2014), p.39.

our lads stood. He saluted them and said: Good morning, lads, are you still pretty healthy? Yes, the lads answered, but you should have taken us along to the Russians. He answered: You do not have to be around everywhere. Be patient. You shall soon make money with the Austrians. There you shall get good Kremnitz Ducats[50] as a booty. They are better than rubles.[51]

The soldiers of the regiment Itzenplitz are well informed. Their remark that the king should have taken them along to the Russians must be analysed against the background that Frederick had tried to present Zorndorf as a great and easy victory to the army and to the general public. He had published a number of Prussian casualties, which was more than ten times (!) lower than the actual number, 1,200 instead of 13,000.[52] In fact, Zorndorf had been a tactical draw at a very high cost, especially, as Frederick II had expected to make quick work of the 'clumsy' and 'barbarian' Russians. In the end, the Prussian army had been saved from total catastrophe only by the cavalry under the command of Lieutenant General Seydlitz, and the battle had been a bloody and confused massacre.[53] In spite of all the king's efforts, the men of the Itzenplitz regiment got this information and reminded the king of the elite status of their regiment telling him that the battle would have ended better if they had taken part in it. The king seems to overhear this and appeals to their desire for booty. This is of course no insult, as the king takes it for granted that the regiment will be victorious and make booty. Furthermore, the king's answer shows again, how important material incentives were. Next to this, the Zanders mention the king's place at the head of the troops. This is not only honourable for a regiment often deployed in the vanguard of the army and thus advancing together with the king. It also underlines the soldiers' idea that honour is gained by suffering and being in danger, especially when they are near the king.

The king addresses the men, and thereby the regiment, as a collective and both sides strengthen the collective of the army by asserting their belief in future victories. Transmitting this incident home and reading it to the villagers also meant to strengthen the collective of the rural community, which was linked to the men in the field honoured by the king.

Christian Friedrich also relates a story from hearsay to his audience in Nitzahn:

General Braun [Browne], who commands the Austrian army has spoken to our captive officers: Sirs, do you think that we have done battle?[54] No, these were only my pickets, that have come too close and they have had a little skirmish amongst themselves! Our king answered to that: If that had been his pickets, it would have been my flank-patrols, two files from every platoon and an NCO![55]

---

50   'Kremnitz Dukaten' were gold coins produced in the Habsburg mint in Kremnitz (today Kremnica in Slovakia) and valued for their purity.
51   Zander, *Fundstücke*, pp.109-110.
52   Friedrich der Große, *Geschichte des Siebenjährigen Krieges*, p.139.
53   Möbius and Möbius, *Soldiers*, pp.71-72.
54   He obviously means the battle of Lobositz, which was won by the Prussians after the Austrians had put up a hard fight and had nearly defeated the astonished Prussians.
55   Letter VIII, in Zander, *Fundstücke*, p.39.

Here, the king's honour is at stake and is defended by the story. It has to be stressed that Browne does not claim that his pickets had given the whole Prussian army a hard time but that Lobositz had in fact only been a skirmish amongst the Austrian outposts themselves. This is an insult to the king as Commander in Chief of the Prussian army at Lobositz and it is thus answered by the king himself, who claims that an even smaller Prussian force would have defeated the Austrians. When it comes to the actual conduct of operations, the Zanders show a very sober assessment of the king's decisions. In a letter from August 1757, Christian Friedrich tells his readers that the king wants to attack an entrenched Austrian position, but the 'General-Field-marshals advise him not to do this and he calls off the attack.'[56] Johann Dietrich adds another aspect as he stresses the importance of the king's favour for getting back some horses, which had been requisitioned by the army from the relatives in Nitzahn. He sees a good chance to get them back, as their regiment is still valued by the king for its conduct in the Battle of Lobositz.[57]

Bräker is also honoured when the king is near him and his image of the king is actually much more positive and emotional than the Zanders'. Although he had never been in the front line together with the king, Bräker is also proud of having served him[58] and likes to remember when the king had been near to him on the drill square in Berlin.[59] He even takes sides with Frederick in his evaluation of the reasons of the Seven Years War and sees him as the victim of his adversaries' machinations. In comparison, the Zanders' attitude to the king as a source of rewards, favours and guarantor of the regiment's elite status seems much more professionally realistic than Bräker' nostalgic adoration.

We want to stress explicitly that at this time the king was not only the head of state but also the head of their church and sacred person and the God-given ruler of their lives and destinies. Being near to him, to see him and to hear his voice, was in itself a rare grace and increased the honour of the men tremendously. It was even more honourable to talk to the king. If one imagines the presentation of the letters in front of the village public, the honour is transmitted directly from the front to the village and not only the sons, who have to serve, are honoured by it but also the members of their rural community. Furthermore, this fact leads to economic advantages when it comes to negotiations with the authorities. Often enough the honour of their fallen boys was the only solace left to the devastated villagers.

How to Avoid the War: Hierarchies and Interactions between Privates, NCOs and Officers

The Zanders' attitude towards their superiors is characterized by pragmatism and materialism. The attempt to obtain Christian Friedrich's dismissal is a telling example for the hierarchies in the regiment during the time of the predecessors of von Itzenplitz, who became the regiment's *Chef* in November 1750.[60] The family had tried to get the dismissal

---

56   Letter XVII, in Zander, *Fundstücke*, p.62.
57   Letter IX, in Zander, *Fundstücke*, pp.40-41.
58   Kloosterhuis, 'Donner, Blitz und Bräker', pp.182-183.
59   Kloosterhuis, 'Donner, Blitz und Bräker', pp.170.
60   Gieraths, *Kampfhandlungen*, p.47.

some time before December 1745 from the *Chef* of his company, Major Martin Sigismund von Aschersleben.[61] As Christian Friedrich was not positively exempt from the draft,[62] His elder brother, the *Dorfschulze* Johan Matthias Zander, had given 60 Reichsthaler to von Aschersleben to obtain the dismissal. Like many financial dealings of the time, when personal relationships were still as important as state structures, these 60 Reichsthaler were somewhere between a fee and a bribe. They helped to make the officer willing to dismiss Zander and could partially be used as a bounty for purchasing a new soldier.

Unfortunately, Aschersleben was killed during the Battle of Kesselsdorf (15 December 1745). The 60 Reichsthaler were lost with the death of Aschersleben. The Zanders had now approached the new *Chef* of the company, Gerson von Zastrow, who had declined the request. Of course, as he had not been the recipient of the money and did not know of its whereabouts.

The *Dorfschulze*, Johann Matthias Zander, had also bribed Lieutenant Friedrich Bogislav von Miltitz with two *Louisdor* (about 10 Reichsthaler) in order to put pressure on Zastrow to dismiss his brother.[63] In addition to this, Johan Matthias had also written to the king, asking for the reimbursement of the money paid to the late von Aschersleben.[64] The king had transferred the file back to the regiment's owner, Philipp Bogislav von Schwerin.[65] This was a normal bureaucratic procedure, as Johan Matthias as a civilian should not have approached the king in this case. Only his soldier brother had the right to approach the king directly in military matters. Furthermore, it was upon the regiment's owner to settle this case. Schwerin in his turn seems to have handed the case over to Zastrow informing him of Johan Matthias' request in June 1749. Zastrow got the file from the general, checked the matter amongst others with the regiment's auditor (military judge and juridical expert of the regiment),[66] and made Christian Friedrich come to him. Zastrow showed him that he knew how much money had been given to Miltitz, asked for the sum given to Aschersleben and threatened Zander that 'even if he had bribed all NCOs with hundreds of Reichsthalers, [Zastrow] would treat him like a foreigner [mercenary, who served in the garrison as fulltime soldiers] and keep him at the garrison for earning the money [to reimburse Zastrow]' in case Zastrow should be forced to pay the money back to him. Zander did not seem intimidated and answered that he had not asked for a reimbursement but for his dismissal. Zastrow then told Zander that his brother should ask his lord and justice, the civilian authorities, for the

---

61   We thank Jürgen Kloosterhuis for the information on the names of the mentioned officers.
62   The Zanders claimed that he was a burgher of the small city of Plaue and thus exempt. But this was either not the case in a legally binding sense or the authorities did not accept the claim. Letter III, Zander, *Fundstücke*, p.23.
63   Letter II, Zander, *Fundstücke*, p.22. The lieutenant is Friedrich Bogislav von Miltitz. He died as captain after the skirmish near Salesel. He was an important contact of the Zanders amongst the officers and highly esteemed by the king. Frederick II, 'Relation de la campagne 1756', in Johann Gustav Droysen (ed.) *Politische Correspondenz Friedrichs des Großen* (Berlin: Duncker und Humblodt, 1886), Vol.14, p.93. We are indebted to Prof. Jürgen Kloosterhuis for the information about the Bogislav von Miltitz.
64   Our source is Christian Friedrich's letter to his brother Johan, No.II, Zander, *Fundstücke*, pp.22-23. In this letter it is not clear if Johan Matthias had only asked the king for the reimbursement of the money given to von Aschersleben or also the dismissal of Christian Friedrich.
65   Letter III, Zander, *Fundstücke*, pp.23-24.
66   *Zedler's Universal Lexicon*, Vol.2, pp.2013-2015.

reimbursement and sent him to the regiment's auditor to tell the auditor the name of his brother's lord.

Zander went to the auditor and got detailed legal advice. The legal expert of the regiment took down the name of the lord and judge and wanted to send the files there. At the same time, he seemed to have advised Zander that his brother should write another memorial to the general (the regiment's owner, von Schwerin) asking for his dismissal. Then the auditor asked Zander for the dismissal certificate by von Aschersleben. Zander replied that he thought that the auditor had this document and that his brother had given it to the auditor. However, the auditor had never received it. After having related these proceedings to his brother, Christian Friedrich advised his brother to approach a certain H. Becker, who had promised to write to the king concerning this issue.

In 1747, Johann Dietrich Zander had also tried to get dismissed. He had approached a certain Mr Arendt on this matter but Arendt had not known a way to realize his wish. Instead, he had promised to speak to the Major (most probably von Zastrow) or take him to an (unidentifiable) 'count Nachen'. Johann Dietrich tried to encourage his old father to take action on his behalf by pointing to another acquaintance of the Zanders, 'old Buschow', who had asked for the dismissal of his son, which had been more or less granted by the captain of Buschow's son's company.[67]

Obviously, they failed to get their dismissals in both cases.

The conflict highlights several important features of the regiment's and even the army's power structure. The Zanders are at the bottom of the military hierarchy and actually not in a good position to get their dismissal, because both are either legally obliged to serve in the army or else their legal claims are not recognized by the authorities. Nevertheless, they use all legal means to obtain the longed-for dismissal. They even try to approach the king, although they should have written to the regiment's owner or their civil authorities first. It is interesting to see that Zastrow tries to intimidate Zander but still sends him to the auditor who then gives him proper and impartial legal advice on the case. It also has to be added that Zastrow was rightfully infuriated as the Zanders had more or less bypassed him and approached and bribed several people around Zastrow. Given these circumstances, Zastrow's rebuke is relatively mild, and it is most interesting that he tries to stick to the legal procedures. Furthermore, it should be mentioned that Johann Diederich's letter on his own attempted dismissal shows clearly that the knowledgeable 'Mr Arendt' also advises him to first go to the Major (von Zastrow!), the legally responsible person. At the heart of the conflict is that the Zanders see the payment to the late Major von Aschersleben as binding the regiment, while Zastrow, the general and the King see it as something happening inside a legitimate network of patronage, but with the patron Aschersleben gone, the 'bribe' and the promise of Christian Friedrich's dismissal were also gone from the authorities' point of view. Although the Zanders were at the bottom of the military hierarchy of the regiment, their social role as *Dorfschulzen* in the *Kanton* was high and Aschersleben depended on them when he needed to draw new recruits for his company. Thus, Aschersleben was a superb patron for the Zanders' dealings. If it had worked out, it would have bene a win-win situation. Christian Friedrich would have gotten his dismissal and von Aschersleben would have

---

67   Letter I, Zander, *Fundstücke*, p.21.

been rewarded with a most obliging *Dorfschulze* when it came to improving his company by first class recruits from Nitzahn. Obviously, the patronage was also located in a grey area of legality. That is shown by the missing 'receipt', the dismissal paper, that Aschersleben should have given them immediately after paying him. The auditor makes clear that one needed the dismissal paper to receive a legal dismissal. The Zanders had received neither, as the money had been given to Aschersleben to smoothen a time-consuming process of dismissal. The patron had fallen before initiating this process. When the regiment was transferred from von Schwerin to von Itzenplitz in 1750, both Zander boys were thus active members of the Itzenplitz Regiment.

Although neither Zander got his dismissal, because they were legally subject to the draft (*kantonpflichtig*), the proceedings show that the Zanders did not expect their superiors to be arbitrary or brutal, but they saw a good chance to get what they saw as their right or even get the dismissal by using their connections. They did not perceive the regiment as a legal vacuum. On the contrary, they expected their superiors to stick to the rules or at least to have ample room to manoeuvre to pursue their goals. The sources also demonstrate that the Zanders had a vast network of supporters reaching up to their lieutenant and even their captain. The Zanders also try to gain their captain's favour by giving a serious amount of peas to him during the summer manoeuvres of 1753.[68] The amount of money that is given to all persons involved in this affair is remarkable. Sixty *Reichsthaler* for Aschersleben and two *Louisdor*, worth ten *Reichsthalers*, for Miltitz are a small fortune. It has to be remembered that two Reichsthaler were the monthly wage of a musketeer. Thus, 70 Reichsthaler would have sufficed to sustain a common soldier for nearly three years.

The Zanders' relationship to their officers on campaign is also characterized by this typical mid-eighteenth-century system of clientelism and 'bribes'. When their superiors are mentioned in the Zander letters from the front, it is mostly in the context of their fear for relatives being recruited into the regiment.[69] Their report of the man-hunts in Dresden, which the Zanders have witnessed themselves in March 1757, shows that they know the kin's need for fresh recruits, which can make it more difficult to avoid the draft of relatives. But they also notice that the Prussian subjects caught in the press-ganging were released, while only the foreigners, Saxons and Poles, were forcibly kept in the Prussian army.[70] Again, the *Kantonisten* know that the extra-legal activities of strong-arm recruitment can make things more difficult, but they perceive their legal protection as intact, especially when they or their relatives are able to back it up by 'treating' their NCOs and officers.

In 1752, the old Dorfschulze Johann Matthias Zander died and his younger son Wilhelm had succeeded him. The Zanders also consider bribing the recruiting NCO in order to prevent the young *Dorfschulze* from being drafted into the regiment.[71] The passage on the NCO is especially interesting, as Christian Friedrich assumes that the man envies[72] him and Johann Dietrich but has no doubt that a bribe will solve this problem. The background

68   Letter V, Zander, *Fundstücke*, p.27.
69   Letter XII, Zander, *Fundstücke*, p.45; Letter XXI, Zander, *Fundstücke*, pp.71-72.
70   Letter XV, Zander, *Fundstücke*, pp.50-51.
71   Letter XIX, Zander, *Fundstücke*, p.65.
72   Zander uses the French loanword '*schalu*' = *jaloux*; Letter XIX Zander, *Fundstücke*, p.65.

is that the *Dorfschulze* is exempt from military service[73] and that an illegal attempt of the NCO to draft him could be thwarted by 'treating' (bribing) the NCO. The Zanders are also sure that even if the NCO brought the young *Dorfschulze* to the front, they would find a way of getting him back to Nitzahn. Obviously, the *Dorfschultze* feared being drafted in spite of his exemption from the *Kantonsystem* to such a degree that he even considered running away. Later, the Zanders are informed by the *Dorfschulze*, that he had actually given two *Reichstaler* to the NCO but they tell him, that this does not mean anything to the man, as he has been given 20 or even 30 *Reichstaler* by other soldiers who wanted to avoid the draft of their relatives. The NCO had obviously taken advantage of the king's need for recruits and raised the price for bribing him.[74] This goes on, as Christian Friedrich later writes to his cousin, the *Dorfschultze*, that he shall offer coffee and wine to the recruiting officer and treat him like the captain himself.[75]

Again, this is an important hint that the letters directly changed the reality in the village. Here, the communication between the front and the rural community is essential for developing strategies for the avoidance of the life-threatening military service in times of war and horrendous losses on the battlefields and in the hospitals. They even seem to go as far as hiding from their captain the fact that the farm hand of another villager, acquaintance or relative, could be legally drafted.[76] The Zanders themselves were steadily longing for peace as they knew that disease and losses in battle meant that being a soldier equalled a death-sentence in the long run.[77] This was reason enough for wanting to leave the colours but, unlike the mercenaries, the Zanders had a solid social basis at home. That they did not consider deserting like the Swiss mercenary Bräker did, was rooted in the fact that they and their relatives would have lost their integrity amongst the members of their social network as well as their complete economic basis.

The mercenary Bräker, in comparison, was settled in Switzerland. His social network and family ties did not play any role that was in the leas comparable to that of the Zanders. His desertion never meant that his father and siblings would become outcasts in their village and lose their property, or that they would be condemned to become day-laborers and the dishonoured scum of the earth. Nevertheless, even Bräker got problems when he had to prove his honesty in later dealings with his enlightened literary society and when he wanted to get a mortgage. In both cases his broken oath as a Prussian soldier posed severe difficulties for him.

The Zanders also seem to have had other contacts amongst the officer corps, which they used for getting information as they write to their relatives on 13 August 1758 that 'no officers knows what the king wants to do.'[78] They are also well informed about the whereabouts of the officers of their regiment and of the regiments of their relatives, especially when the officers are promoted.[79]

---

73   Letter of Prof. Jürgen Kloosterhuis to Christian Friedrich Zander, 14 June 2015.
74   Letter XXI, Zander, *Fundstücke*, pp.71-72.
75   Letter XXVI, Zander, *Fundstücke*, p.81.
76   Letter XXII, Zander, *Fundstücke*, p.77.
77   Letter XIX, Zander, *Fundstücke*, p.65.
78   Zander, *Fundstücke. Ergänzungen*, p14.
79   Letter XIX Zander, *Fundstücke*, p.66. The mentioned officers have been correctly identified by the letters' editor Christian Friedrich Zander. For example, their former colonel Johann Siegismund von Lattorff has taken over Regiment Nr.1; General von Meyerinck (Dietrich Reichard von Meyerinck)

Interactions and Comradeship Between Privates

For the Zanders, the 'young lads' (recruits) from their village or region, not belonging to their family could also be a source of material gains. As they paid their officers for favours, the Zanders themselves did not hesitate to take 'presents' from young *Kantonisten* who expected their protection and support.[80]

The Zanders' network amongst the privates consisted of *Kantonisten* from villages within a 30–40 kilometre radius from Nitzahn.[81] They write a lot about soldiers from this region, especially about their health and whereabouts, or they convey greetings. That fact particularly underlines the performative situation of the letters. We must assume that the public reading of the letters made the contents spread at least within a radius of 40 kilometre. The recipients of these letters are thus not only located in their village but in the entire district. As we know, that 80 percent of the male population in this region was literate and the Zanders also mention other soldiers' letters, we can easily imagine the hailstorm of information from the front going down on the home region. Every bit of news could be compared to information coming from another writer or hub. That meant that every kind of misbehaviour, be it moral or military, would be transmitted home immediately and received by the entire social network. This cemented the community of the *Kantonisten* in the field and on campaign and it forced them to adhere to a codex of behaviour which was at the roots of their personal and collective honour.[82] The framework of this codex were the 10 Commandments. The main problem for a soldier was that his trade implied breaking the sixth commandment, 'thou shalt not kill'. Although killing as a soldier was sanctioned and even rewarded by the church and the authorities, the men felt uneasy with it, especially when their own hands were stained with human blood due to actions involving close combat.[83]

We can thus assume that there was a tacit consent amongst the men not to write about their personal acts of killing enemy soldiers and taking their lives in single combat with butt and bayonet.[84] However, acts against other commandments like adultery or sexual offences were very well reported and this had serious repercussions.[85]

Given this general problem of the communicative network, another problem for the soldiers' letters which we can also find in the Zander letters, is the compete absence of the

---

has been granted leave and Carl Heinrich von Wedel has become Chef of the Meyerinck Regiment (Nr.26). It has to be noted that the regiments Itzenplitz and Meyerinck/Wedel were often brigaded together; for example, they formed the vanguard during the Battle of Leuthen and were commanded by Wedel. Duffy, *Frederick the Great*, p.150.

80   Letter XXII, Zander, *Fundstücke*, p.75.

81   Letter from Christian Friedrich Zander (the author of *Fundstücke*) containing correspondence with the former director of the Geheime Staatsarchiv Preußischer Kulturbesitz, Jürgen Kloosterhuis.

82   *Zedler's Universal Lexicon*, Vol.8, pp.419–421.

83   Möbius and Möbius, *Soldiers*, p.77; Jutta Nowosadtko, *Scharfrichter und Abdecker. Der Alltag zweier unehrlicher Beruf ein der frühen Neuzeit* (Paderborn: Ferdinand Schöningh, 1994), pp.21–24. On the Brandenburg hangmen and the ambivalent character of their dishonour, see Marita Genesis, *Scharfrichter in der Stadt Brandenburg. Betrachtung eines Berufsbildes* (MA diss., Fachbereich Landesgeschichte des Historischen Instituts der Universität Potsdam, Potsdam 2006), pp.67–74.

84   Möbius and Möbius, *Soldiers*, pp.86–89.

85   Möbius and Möbius, *Soldiers*, p.192. A corporal from CR Nr.7 is accused by his fellow troopers of having had an extra martial relationship with a preacher's daughter.

mercenaries serving in their regiment. Not even the mercenaries from their tent-comrade-ship are mentioned.[86] There are two possible solutions to this problem. Either, the Zanders remained in their rural community while on campaign. Or, the absence of non-Nitzahn-region-soldiers in the letters is caused by the recipients of the letters, as the Zanders do not want to write home about people that their family members do not know and who are thus of no interest for them. A solution can be found in the other letters and memoires we possess.[87] Bräker only mentions the comrades from his quarters and the other Swiss in the regiment. The ones he trusts are the Swiss,[88] and he only mentions the *Kantonisten* as being especially ferocious during the Battle of Lobositz. Many of the NCOs seem to have led a hermetic existence as they do not mention any comrades when writing to their families. The other *Kantonisten* follow the Zander-pattern and only mention comrades from their districts. Dominicus' diary and letter to this brother show that he does not even seem to know the names of the men fighting next to him. He is shocked by their gruesome deaths but does not mention a single name. Thus, we have a strong indicator that the men did not develop strong links to comrades who were not from their villages. And it is also a strong indicator for the *Kantonisten* prevailing civilian identity, which was at least stronger than any regimental identity.

The Zanders are very aware of the promotion of their acquaintances from their region. Being long serving veterans with a very good position in their peasant community, they are also connected to many NCOs,[89] some of whom were even promoted to higher ranks. Christian Friedrich mentions in May 1758 that a former classmate, an NCO, has been promoted to lieutenant. Another NCO, who has become an ensign, had faked his patent of nobility and three others are still thinking about becoming officers.[90] This not only sheds new light on the recruitment of officers during the Seven Years War, but it also shows that the Zanders' network of comrades from their region was extensive and they kept in contact even if the status of these men had changed.

Actually, Bräker's description of his comrades in his quarters[91] validates Lossow's thesis that the core of the Prussian army and also of a positive identification with the army and the regiment were the long-serving *Ausländer*, mercenaries, who had deliberately chosen the trade of a soldier and for whom the regiment was the centre of their social life.[92] Concerning military training, they also formed the backbone of the battalions, as they were drilled all year long unlike the *Kantonisten*, who got their basic training and then two to three months during the summer, when they had to join the colours during the manoeuvres. Bräker's

---

86   The men in the tent were not necessarily men from their home village or district, but the next tallest or smallest men in the line of battle. Still, one might assume that during a campaign some kind of bond would develop between the men of the tent-comradeship. Gabriel Christian Benjamin Busch, *Handbuch der Erfindungen* (Eisenach: Wittekindsche Hofbuchhandlung, 1816), Vol.8 p.16. Möbius, *Soldiers*, p.20.

87   Möbius and Möbius, *Soldiers*, pp.57-62.

88   Bräker, *Lebensgeschichte*, p.148.

89   This is also underlined by their company owner's angry outburst, that he would not let Zander go, even if he had bribed the NCOs and corporals of the company. Letter II, p.22.

90   Christian Friedrich Zander, Letter XXII, Zander, *Fundstücke*, p.76.

91   For example Bräker, *Lebensgeschichte*, pp.118-121.

92   Möbius and Möbius, *Soldiers*, p.138.

memoires also contain another important hint. His housemate, Zittemann, is a long serving mercenary, who helps Bräker a lot. Zittemann calls the soldiers of the regiment 'brethren',[93] a designation, which is also used by many other soldiers.[94] Unfortunately, we do not have any letters written by men like Zittemann, but the existing evidence shows a strong bond of solidarity amongst the soldiers, especially the mercenaries. The old hands help the new men to get used to military service and to cope with the confusing movements on the drill square. This makes sense from a tactical point of view, as a frightened or badly trained soldier could cause the entire unit to be cut down.[95] Yet, this argument does not seem to tell the whole story. In every army at every time the members of a given unit depended upon each other. This was also true for armies, which even had a culture of older recruits bullying or even torturing the younger ones.[96] Thus, it was a question of culture and although we do not know its origins, we know that at least the soldiers of the Itzenplitz Regiment adhered to the regulations' call for harmony in the ranks.

Conclusion

Bräker and the Zanders match completely in one central point: they do not want to be where they are. Bräker correctly fears for his life and the Zanders have a solid civilian material basis as peasants so that military service is only a burden and also life-threatening. Therefore, Bräker deserts and the Zanders try to get their dismissal and to prevent the draft of their relatives by legal means. Yet, the regiment was not kept together by brutal physical force. To be sure, the threat of force played a role. The Zanders knew that a desertion would destroy their material basis of existence and Bräker feared the gauntlet or the gallows in case of a failed desertion. As long as the soldiers did not desert and tried to act in accordance with the *Reglement*, military law and the officers' commands, they were treated well and had a *Chef*, who defended common men against abuses of their superiors. The relationship between them and their officers was characterized by predictability and a juridical framework, which clearly favoured the officers but gave the privates ample room to manoeuvre as long as they had enough money to bribe their officers and the possibility to directly address the king and their superiors.[97]

The *Kantonisten* and the mercenaries lived in different worlds. In peacetime, this was natural as the *Kantonisten* were in their villages and the mercenaries in their garrisons. However, it is one of our important findings from the Zander letters, that it was also true in wartime. With the exception of combat, when both depended on each other, the *Kantonisten* had totally different networks of survival, as they depended on their families and rural communities at home. The mercenaries depended on the army and their fellow mercenaries.

---

93   Bräker, *Lebensgeschichte*, p.119.
94   Bräker, *Lebensgeschichte*, pp.151, 153, 155, 156.
95   Showalter, *Frederick*, pp.513-519.
96   The Russian/Soviet *Dedovshchina* ('reign of grandfathers') has gained notoriety for the brutal psychological and physical abuse of young conscripts by older recruits.
97   Möbius and Möbius, *Soldiers*, p.62.

Yet, both groups saw their fellow-soldiers as brothers and sought for harmonious coexistence among the privates.

Both *Kantonisten* and mercenaries were well-trained and their training was so good that they were able to master all tactical situations ranging from a pitched battle in line formation to night fighting against light infantry. This professional training is in contrast to the men's reluctance to kill even their enemies. In combat, the aim of the Zanders is to defend their honour in the collective framework of their regiment. They do this because a loss of honour amounts to a loss of their and their families' social basis. Even Bräker got lifelong problems as his desertion and the related breaking of his oath made him untrustworthy for many acquaintances and even put him in the vicinity of dishonourable people. The Prussian system was not based on brutal force but on a mechanism, which brought the soldiers into a position of a potential loss of honour upon joining the colours – either by desertion or by military failure. The threat of losing one's social position was much more effective than any officer's cane. An additional factor tying the men to the regiment was the comradely behaviour of the privates amongst each other. Especially, in the case of the *Kantonisten*, this was rooted in their provision of verifiable information from or about themselves to the people of their district.

What made the Prussian soldier fight so efficiently, was the forced continuous connection to his social structure as a Prussian peasant, the permanent drill and leadership by competent officers and the will to survive and come home with their honour intact.

Further Reading

Duffy, Christopher, *Frederick the Great. A Military Life* (Oxford/New York: Routledge, 2016).

Engelen, Beate, *Soldatenfrauen in Preußen. Eine Strukturanalyse der Garnisonsgesellschaft im späten 17. und 18. Jahrhundert* (Münster: Lit Verlag, 2005).

Hagen, William W., *Ordinary Prussians: Brandenburg Junkers and Villagers, 1500-1840* (Cambridge: Cambridge University Press, 2003).

Kloosterhuis, Jürgen, 'Donner, Blitz und Bräker – der Soldatendienst des "armen Mannes im Tockenburg" aus der Sicht des preußischen Militärsystems', in Alfred Messerli and Adolf Muschg (eds), *Schreibsucht – autobiografische Schriften des Pietisten Ulrich Bräker. (1725–1798)* (Göttingen: Vandenhoeck & Ruprecht, 2004) pp.129–187.

Muth, Jörg, *Flucht aus dem militärischen Alltag. Ursachen und individuelle Ausprägung der Desertion in der Armee Friedrichs des Großen. Mit besonderer Berücksichtigung der Infanterieregimenter der Potsdamer Garnison* (Freiburg i. Breisgau: Rombach, 2003).

Rischke-Neß, Janine, *Subjektivierungen und Kriminalitätsdiskurse im 18. Jahrhundert. Preußische Soldaten zwischen Norm und Praxis* (Göttingen: V&R Unipress, 2021).

Showalter, Dennis E. *Frederick the Great. A Military History* (Barnsley: Frontline Books, 2012).

Wilson, Peter H., 'Social Militarization in Eighteenth-Century Germany', *German History*, 18, no 1 (2000), pp.1-39.

Winter, Martin, *Untertanengeist durch Militärpflicht? Das preußische Kantonsystem in brandenburgischen Städten im 18. Jahrhundert* (Bielefeld: Verlag für Regionalgeschichte, 2005).

Section Four

New Perspectives

12

Clearing the Fog of War: Archaeological Research on the Battle of Kunersdorf, 2009-2019

Grzegorz Podruczny

I have had the pleasure of meeting Christopher Duffy only once. It was in October 2016, when I was showing him and a group of military history enthusiasts around the Kunersdorf battlefield, near modern Słubice, Poland. My archaeological research on the battle had not been completed at the time and I was unable to match those incomplete results with the conclusions made by military historians using traditional sources. I am extremely happy that I can now present the first attempt to verify those findings based on archaeological sources here, in the volume devoted to Christopher Duffy, the outstanding scholar specializing in the military of the eighteenth century.

Most historical battles were fairly chaotic, which makes them difficult to describe. The same is true of the battle of Kunersdorf, one of the greatest battles of the Seven Years War. The encounter has been described by many historians, each of whom reconstructed it in a substantially different way. It is beyond the scope of this paper to refer to all the available source literature; hence, I will only present four different versions of the events.

First, however, I will provide some basic information about the battle. The battle of Kunersdorf took place on 12 August 1759. It was one of the largest and most bloody battles of the Seven Years War. It involved the Prussian army as the attackers against the Russian-Austrian coalition. The Prussian army included approximately 50,000 soldiers. The Russians had more or less 60,000 soldiers on the battlefield, and Austrians about 20,000. The Prussians were led by Frederick II, Russians by General Pyotr Semyonovich Saltykov, and Austrians by General Loudon. The Russian/Austrian army settled in a broad fortified camp extending from the forest east of the village of Kunersdorf to the Oder river bank near Frankfurt (Oder). It was located on a plateau. To the north of it, there were low, wetland meadows of the Elsbusch valley, and to the east, the camp bordered the Mühlberg hill. Approximately one kilometre west of the hill, the camp was cut through by the Kuhgrund ravine. Several hundred meters to the south of it, there was a fortified hillock called Spitzberg. Another series of hills had their beginning about three kilometres from Mühlberg. In the eighteenth century, the hills were collectively called the Judenberg, with relation to the Jewish cemetery located on one of them. Initially, the Prussians had the advantage in the battle, but the day ended with the defeat of that army: one of the heaviest defeats during the whole war. More details can be found in historians' accounts. Below I present the versions by three authors from the eighteenth century and a more extensive description made by military historians from the Prussian general headquarters on the basis of the sources they collected.

According to the first author, Georg Friedrich von Tempelhoff, a participant of the battle and later a Prussian general, the battle began at approximately 11:30 a.m. with fire from three Prussian artillery batteries against the Russian posts on the Mühlberg. Half an hour later, the attack of Prussian vanguard began. Eight battalions of grenadiers walked through the abatis and easily captured Russian fortifications and destroyed the Russian troops in that flank. The Russian soldiers were shattered. The Prussians reorganized their troops and formed a short battle line. The vanguard was followed by Finck's corps, which gathered on the southern slopes of the Mühlberg, and by the rest of the main army infantry. The troops had to reorganize, and the Russians used that time to form the lines again and throw new troops into the fray. They resisted the next Prussian assault with more success, yet the Russian formations soon disintegrated anyway. The Russian line, supported with Austrian troops, was re-formed behind the Kuhgrund, running from Kunersdorf towards the Elsbusch meadows. This time, the formation resisted the onslaught of Prussians, who had to retreat. The same happened in all the (many) subsequent attacks at that terrain post. Infantry assaults via the village of Kunersdorf at the post which commanded the terrain, the strongly fortified hill Spitzberg, did not succeed, either. The hill was also attempted from the south by the cavalry led by Lieutenant General Seydlitz, but the attack failed as a result of strong small arms and artillery fire and of the threat posed by the Russian/Austrian cavalry. The two successive attacks of the cavalry from the north (led by Generals Württemberg and Puttkammer) also failed. Finally, exhausted by the fighting, the Prussian troops began to retreat. The threat from the enemy cavalry aroused alarm among the soldiers and led to the disintegration of the Prussian army, which left the battlefield in panic and chaos.[1]

Another participant of the battle, Friedrich Wilhelm Ernst Freiherr von Gaudi, described it in a completely different way. In his account, the initial phase was similar. From 11:30 a.m. to approximately midday, the Prussians were firing at the Russian posts on the Mühlberg from three sides. Then, the vanguard attacked, going through the abatis, entering the fortifications and capturing them. Directly behind them there were the troops of the main army advancing in two groups, and from the side, also Finck's infantry. The Russians made a line formation but were destroyed. The vanguard reached the Kuhgrund. Its line was extended by the troops of Finck's corps, so the Prussian line reached from the village of Kunersdorf to the Elsbusch meadows. Russians and Austrians formed another defence line behind the Kuhgrund in several echelons, each of three or four battalions. Their resistance stopped the vanguard but the support of reserves allowed the Prussian army to overcome the Russian defence. By 5:00 p.m., approximately two-thirds of the Russian camp was conquered, and a similar proportion of forces were defeated on that side. The vanguard troops reached as far as approximately 800 steps from Judenberg. The situation of the defending Russian/Austrian troops was dramatic, because they did not have any ways of retreat (Frankfurt and the

1   G.F. v. Tempelhoff , *Geschichte des Siebenjährigen Krieges in Deutschland zwischen dem Könige von Preussen und der Kaiserin Königin mit ihren Alliirten als eine Fortsetzung der Geschichte des General Lloyd vom G.F. v. Tempelhoff, part 3, Feldzug von 1759* (Berlin: Unger, 1787), pp.215-222.

bridges were controlled by the Prussian forces from Lebus). All the other troops of the alliance were positioned on the Judenberg with plentiful artillery. Lieutenant General Finck did not want to risk further attacks because the soldiers were very tired, yet the king decided to continue the storm so as to destroy the enemy. However, the resistance strengthened, losses on the Prussian side were growing as a result of the fire of infantry and artillery, and no more ground was captured despite throwing more and more fresh troops into the fray. The Russians and Austrians did the same, and the difference was that they had more resources. The impasse was to be broken by the Prussian cavalry. The first attack came from the south but it failed because of strong fortifications, *trous de loup* and cannon fire. In addition, the Prussian cavalry was chased away by the Austrian/Russian cavalry, and while fleeing, the Prussian cavalrymen dispersed their own infantry. Then, generals Württemberg and Putkammer tried more cavalry assaults, yet these also failed. About 6:00 p.m., the decisive move was made by General Loudon, who led the Russian and Austrian cavalry against the sides and rear of the Prussian infantry. The latter began to retreat, followed by the infantry and cavalry of the allied forces. After an unsuccessful Prussian attempt to form an infantry line behind the Kuhgrund, Loudon attacked again with his cavalry. This attack was the decisive one: Frederick II's troops fled in disarray.[2]

Another participant of the battle, the Prussian King Frederick II, described the encounter in still another way.[3] According to him, the battle began with artillery fire from Finck's corps at the Russian posts on the Mühlberg, which drew Russians' attention away from the manoeuvres of king's troops. Then, the Prussians set artillery batteries on the hills around the Mühlberg and started concentric fire. This enabled the Prussian vanguard to attack and easily capture the Russian fortifications. The rest of the army followed through. After the assault, the Russian troops were dispersed and lost many cannons and soldiers. The Prussians captured the area extending from the Mühlberg to Kunersdorf and the local cemetery. At the time, Friedrich Eugen, Prince of Württemberg, attacked the Russian infantry on the Judenberg but was resisted. This, however, made the Russians abandon the great battery on the Judenberg and the Prussians advanced towards it. Their troops were only 800 steps from the post. Yet, they did not manage to capture it, because just before them, Austrian soldiers led by Loudon reached the place and started cannon fire from a close distance. The Prussian line was dispersed, and the artillery resisted the subsequent attacks. As soon as Loudon noticed the Prussians' weakening energy, he threw the cavalry toward them from the right and from the left. The Prussians became disorganized and began to flee, the battle ended, and the Prussian king barely avoided captivity.

These three eighteenth-century descriptions of the battle are only part of the output of historians studying that issue. In the eighteenth and nineteenth centuries, further reconstructions of the events appeared, some of which were scientific and some were not. Most of them were authored by military historians from the Prussian general headquarters. The battle was described in a series devoted to the history of the Seven Years War from the

2   Jürgen Zeichmann, *Journal vom Siebenjährigen Kriege, von Friedrich Wilhelm Ernst Freiherr von Gaudi. Forschungen und Studien zur Friederizianischen Zeit, Sonderband F, Band. 6, 1759, Bearbeitet von Patrick Neuhaus* (Buchholz: LTR Verlag, 2009), pp.201-206

3   Gustav Berthold Volz (ed.), *Die Werke Friedrichs des Großen: in deutscher Übersetzung; V. 4, Geschichte des Siebenjährigen Krieges* (Verlag von Reimar Hobbing, Berlin 1913), pp.14-17.

third decade of the nineteenth century and in a lengthy article prepared for the hundredth anniversary of the battle.[4] Each time, much effort was made to collect sufficient data to reconstruct the events properly. For example, in 1858, as part of works on the article for the hundredth anniversary of the battle, the authors not only visited the battlefield but also made a detailed plan of it with measurements, which was to serve as the basis for a map reconstructing the events.[5] The culminating treatment of the battle, the one included in the volume on the wars of Frederick the Great by the German General Staff, did very extensive archival research before the beginning of that monumental work.[6] The version of the course of the battle provided in that work will be the last I present here.

In this version, the battle began at approximately 11.30 a.m., when the Prussian batteries opened fire: first, three batteries, and then, the fourth one. The fire was directed at the Russian posts on the Mühlberg. It lasted almost an hour, resulting in considerable losses in the Observation Corps. Then, the attack of the Prussian vanguard began. Its soldiers quickly walked through the abatis, captured the fortifications, formed a line and defeated the Russian troops forming their own lines. Due to the very narrow terrain, the line of the attacking infantry was only four or five battalions wide. Later, it even formed three groups. After the first success, the Prussian regiments rearranged themselves and artillery was brought up. At the same time, Russians reorganized their formations as well. They managed to form a battle line, which was, however, quickly broken. The same happened to the next line formed approximately 200 metres east of the Kuhgrund. The allied reinforcements, including Austrian battalions, did not help in the defence, because after a short fight they also retreated. Everything changed after reaching the Kuhgrund. Although the Prussians continued attacking the western slope of the ravine, they were unsuccessful. Many repeated storms only allowed them to reach it on the northern end and to move the Russian and Austrian troops toward the Tiefe Weg, a shallow valley behind the Kuhgrund. This post was repeatedly attempted, both by the infantry and the cavalry from both sides, but with no effect. Prussian soldiers, attacking from the village of Kunersdorf toward the Spitzberg fortifications, had no success either: they encountered rapid fire of artillery and musketry. All the repeated attacks in this location were ineffective. The Prussian soldiers were tired, and Russians received more and more reinforcement. Finck's corps was the first to retreat, exposing the flank of troops fighting for Kunersdorf from the north. It was replaced by Prussian cavalry, trying to change the situation with a sudden assault. Sheltered by the hills, the Prince of Württemberg advanced eastward and reached the Mühlberg approximately 1.5 kilometres from the Kuhgrund, but his attack broke down, just like the subsequent one. The cavalry attack against the Spitzberg from the south, led by Seydlitz, did not succeed either, being likewise met by artillery fire and a counter-attack of Russian/Austrian cavalry.

---

4   Grosser Generalstab, 'Schlacht bei Kunersdorf am 12 August 1759. Nach archivalischen Quellen bearbeitet, nebst 5 Beilagen, Beiheft zum Militair-Wochenblatt für das 1ste Quartal 1860, redigirt von der historischen Abtheilung des Generalstabes', in *Geschichte des siebenjährigen Krieges: in einer Reihe von Vorlesungen, mit Benutzung authentischer Quellen bearbeitet von den Offizieren des großen Generalstabs*, dritter Theil, der Feldzug von 1759, Berlin 1828; Schlacht bei Kunersdorf am 12 August 1759 (Berlin: Armee Verlag, 1859).

5   Staatsbibliothek zu Berlin, Stiftung Preußischer Kulturgüter, Db1.1292 o/2, Db1.1292 o/3.

6   Geheimes Staatsarchiv Stiftung Preußischer Kulturgüter IV HA Rep 15 A, Großer Generalstab, Kriegsarchiv der Kriegsgeschichtlichen Abteilung.

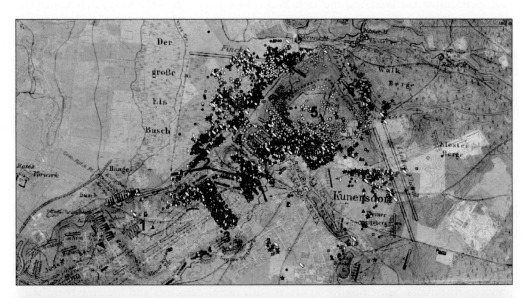

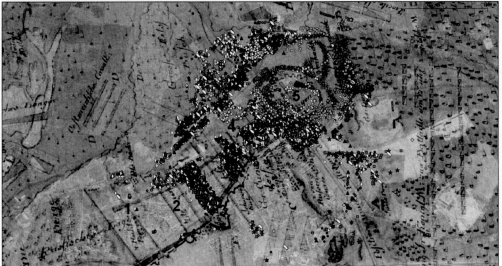

Georeference of archaeological finds and archival maps. At the top one can see a reconstruction of the course of the battle, in its final phase, from Grosser Generalstab, *Die Kriege Friedrichs des Grossen, Der Siebenjährige Krieg*, V. 10 plan 26 C , at the bottom an eighteenth century map from the resources of SBB SPK ref. Db1. 1292q/2. In both cases a contemporary aerial photograph and the present layout of the buildings can be seen in the background.
1. Location of a mass grave found in 2019. 2. Maximum progress of Prussian infantry shown on the map. 3. Grosse Spitzberg. 4. Kuhgrund. 5. Mühlberge. 6. Cluster of canister shots – trace of shelling by Prussian infantry storming Mühlberge in the first phase of the battle.

In the meantime, the fight near the Tiefe Weg transformed into static firefight, in which the Russian and Austrian coalition began to be victorious, as they had a constant inflow of fresh forces. About 5:30 p.m., Prussian troops began to retreat behind the Kuhgrund, and a new defence line was formed there but was soon broken. Finally, the Prussian army was attacked by the cavalry that had gathered behind the Spitzberg and advanced toward the Prussian lines. About 6.00 p.m., the battle was lost for Prussians.[7]

As we can see, all the accounts present the course of the battle in the same way until the moment of the fight for the Kuhgrund, but differ significantly in the description of later events. The situation was perfectly well described by Christopher Duffy in his description of the battle included in *Frederick the Great. A Military Life*:

> The cannon smoke of Kunersdorf not only obscured the battlefield, but has ever since made it almost impossible for historians to determine how much more of the enemy position fell into Prussian hands, and when and where the formations of the Prussian cavalry came into action.[8]

Fortunately for military historians working in the twenty-first century, today's technology grants different avenues for exploring the past, than simply relying on the written word of previous historians. Searching for artifacts with metal detectors and locating them with GPS receivers and Geographic Information System (GIS) devices, we are able to clear some of that smoke from the Kunersdorf battlefield.

I began my study of the battlefield of Kunersdorf in 2006. At that time, I became interested in the battle and made my first visit to the battlefield. Even during that first visit, some atypical earth structures found in the woods of Kunersdorf, a kind of artificial terrace, attracted my attention. Since the field fortifications of the Russian fortified camp were located there, I supposed the terrace was the remainder of those structures. In the subsequent years and visits to the battlefield, more anomalies like this were found, and in 2008, they were surveyed. In addition, I carried out archival research at the Staatsbibliothek in Berlin, resulting in the discovery of the archival cartography of the battle, mostly including handmade plans from the eighteenth century, which have never previously been published.[9] Thanks to the analysis of the field and archival findings, I managed to hypothesize that the structures found in the woods were the remainder of the line of abatis before the proper fortifications of the camp. The analysis of eighteenth and nineteenth treatises on fortification architecture showed that abatis were definitely used in combination with earthen works.[10] What is more, the plans suggested the existence of abatis in other fragments of the Russian fortified camp, near today's bridges on the Oder river, between the town of Słubice

7   Grosser Generalstab, *Die Kriege Friedrichs des Grossen, Der Siebenjährige Krieg* (Ernst Siegfried Mittler und Sohn, Berlin, 1912), Vol.10, pp.245-278

8   Christopher Duffy, *Frederick the Great: A Military Life* (London: Routledge, 1985) p.186.

9   SBB SKP Db1. 1-39.

10 Filip Nereusz Meciszewski, *Fortyfikacya polowa* (Warszawa: Glücksberg 1825) pl.XI; Johann Gottlieb Tielcke, *Unterricht für die Officiers, die sich zu Feld Ingenieurs bilden....* (Dresden, Leipzig: Johann Nicolaus Gelrach Verlag, 1769) pl.XIX

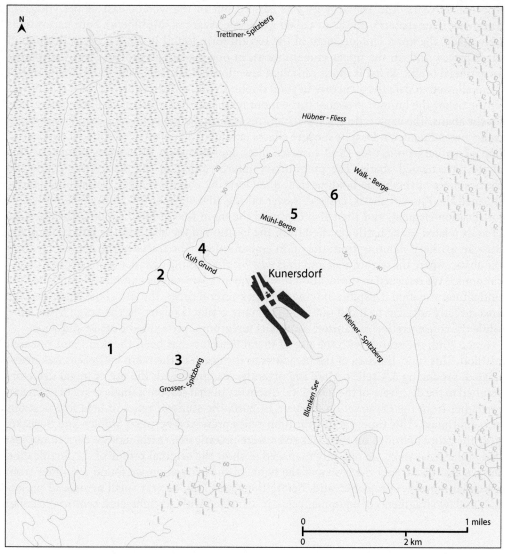

The Kunersdorf battlefield after map in Duffy's *Army of Frederick the Great*. Numbers 1-6 correspond to key to images showing georeference of archaeological finds.

and the village of Świecko. Field visits to those places confirmed the existence of interesting earthen structures.

After initial preparation, the proper archaeological investigation of the battlefield began in July 2009. Naturally, the aim for that season was to verify the earthen structures found in previous years. The archaeology was carried out in the woods, east of the village of Kunowice (Kunersdorf), on the so-called Młyńskie Wzgórza (Mühlberg). Four excavations were made, the lower embankment of the terrain form found in 2006 was cut through in three places, and, in the upper embankment, in one place. The profiles clearly displayed an artificial origin. What is more, although few movable artifacts were found there, one of them allowed to date the structure beyond doubt: in one of the profiles, a musket flint was sitting below the humus, probably thrown out by the soldier who was building the terrace for the abatis. The exploration of the structures was supplemented with a search of the area using a metal detector. Despite meagre effects (a total of 57 objects), we found a concentration of artillery projectiles (lead canister shot) approximately 250 metres before the line of the investigated abatis. The preliminary interpretation of the discoveries confirmed the accounts of the battle holding that, after forming columns, eight Prussian battalions stormed the Russian abatis, crossed it over taking advantage of the faulty location of this fortification element, and then also captured the main line of fortifications. The shortage of finds related to the battle resulted from the location of the abatis in the blind spot of the Russian artillery shooting from the main embankment. The traces of the fire are far from the abatis, where the terrain rose and thus was within striking distance of the fire of Russian cannons.[11] We returned to the location in subsequent years and our new finds confirmed the initial interpretation. Despite studying the place several times, the site of the abatis and the area directly adjacent to it did not produce many artifacts related to the Seven Years War, while the concentration of canister shot in its foreground proved to be dense and wide.

Since 2010, the search with the use of metal detectors has been the dominant research method. This time, the area of the meadows to the north of the main battlefield was investigated, producing 374 relics. More importantly, searching with the use of metal detectors resulted in the discovery of the most vital discovery of that season: a single grave of a Russian grenadier from the Observation Corps.[12] In 2010, the study of relics of field fortifications also continued. This time, the fortification relics preserved between Słubice and Świecko, near the railroad bridge on the Oder river, were investigated. Although we carried out just one probe excavation, we not only managed to show the original profile of the fortification but we also discovered the traces of the fight. In the excavation we found a splinter from a Russian howitzer projectile, and, before the abatis line, several small arms lead projectiles and two fragments of equipment clearly identified with an eighteenth century Prussian

---

11   Grzegorz Podruczny, Jakub Wrzosek, 'Lost elements. Earthworks of the fortified camp of the Russian Army from the time of the battle of Kunersdorf in the light of the recent research', *Archeologia Postmedievale* 14, (2010), pp.65-80.

12   Grzegorz Podruczny, Jakub Wrzosek, 'Lone Grenadier: An Episode from the Battle of Kunersdorf, 12 August 1759', *Journal of Conflict Archaelogy*, Vol. 9 No.1 (January 2014), pp.33-47; Grzegorz Podruczny, Jakub Wrzosek, 'Znalezisko szczątków grenadiera rosyjskiego poległego pod Kunowicami/ Kunersdorf (1759) w świetle zwyczajów chowania poległych w czasie wojny siedmioletniej', *Kwartalnik Historii Kultury Materialnej* 64 (2), pp.225-237.

Volunteers Andrzej Kazana and Norbert Piatkowski during the research of the mass grave of the soldiers from the battle of Kunersdorf. March 2019. (Author's Photo)

uniform: a buckle from the main belt and a much wider buckle, probably from the belt of a cavalry pouch. We were able to return to this place in 2018. More finds allowed us to identify more precisely the unit whose representative was killed there: we found a characteristic belt ending, several fragments of a cavalry carbine, two fragments of sword crossguard, and several Prussian uniform buttons. All these elements clearly look like the equipment of a Prussian cuirassier.

In 2011 and 2012, the only task performed was searching with metal detectors. The area of the meadows, as well as the fields to the north of the buildings of the present village of Kunowice, were searched through. The effect was finding 646 and 1,303 movable artifacts, respectively. In 2012, during the search with metal detectors, human remains (a fragment of a skull and long bones) were also found, lying on the surface of a recently ploughed field. The context of the discovery – several dozen Russian uniform buttons and traces on the bones – allowed to identify the artifacts as the remains of one of the casualties of the battle. In 2013, the search with metal detectors concentrated on the area of the discovery from the previous year. We found more bones and Russian uniform buttons, which displayed clear concentration in the planigraphy. Suspecting the existence of a mass grave, we decided to look for it using probe excavations. Despite four excavations with the total surface of 1.6

acres, we did not find any trace of a mass grave, but we found traces of a settlement from the early Bronze Age.[13]

In the following years, the rhythm of the research did not change: the yearly search with metal detectors, more and more completely covering the battlefield, was supplemented with repeatedly seeking the mass grave. Since 2016, the search was again carried out in the woods. In the years 2015-2017, we searched the undeveloped area south of the former village of Kunersdorf, and in 2017, also the area of the south end of the settlement Zielone Wzgórza in the contemporary town of Słubice. Generally, by May 2019, the search with the metal detector had produced almost 12,000 movable artifacts. Apart from mass finds (bullets, canister shot, buttons), we have found several unique objects, both single items – a bulla, a medieval seal[14] – and whole deposits: in 2016, a deposit of 132 firearm projectiles, a trace of collecting ammunition by the Russian soldiers after the battle, and in 2017, a deposit of decorative objects connected with military equipment (a total of 29 items).[15]

Table 1: Moveable Artifacts Recovered on the Kunersdorf Battlefield

Year	2009	2010	2011	2012	2013	2014	2015	2016	2017	2018	2019
Number of Finds	57	374	646	1,303	1,236	1,109	1,934	1,865	1,530	1,430	460

With regard to the search for a mass grave, non-invasive (geomagnetic, GPR and electroresistance) research was carried out twice (in 2015 and 2017), and the identified anomalies were also probed twice (in 2016 and 2018). Sadly, each time, the probes revealed natural structures in the sites of anomalies. The search was finally discontinued in September 2018. The failure in the planned search for soldiers' graves was compensated by an incidental discovery made during the excavation for the foundations of a house in the Zielone Wzgórza district of Słubice in March 2019. Human remains and some uniform buttons were found then. The archaeological exploration of the site showed that at the place of the planned investment there was a grave with 15 soldiers killed in the battle. Apart from bones found in the grave, many movable artifacts were discovered. The vast majority of them were buttons (292), most of which can be directly attributed to Prussian uniforms. More than 10 Austrian and a similar number of Russian buttons were found as well. The buttons also included many fragments of uniform fabric with small artifacts such as pins or hook-and-eye fastenings. Other relics were much less frequent, which means that the soldiers were buried in their uniforms (or parts of uniforms) after being robbed of valuable objects. However, the robbers overlooked three very interesting items: a seal and two coins. So far, we have only been able to identify one of them: a golden Dutch ducat from 1742 (weight: 3.55 grammes, diameter:

---

13   Jakub Affelski, Michał Bugaj, Marcin Dziewanowski, Jakub Wrzosek, 'Nieznane stanowisko kultury łużyckiej w Kunowicach, pow. słubicki, woj. lubuskie', *Archeologia Środkowego Nadodrza* 2015, V. XII, pp.217-232

14   Zbigniew Misiuk, 'Bulla papieska z Kunowic, pow. słubicki. Przyczynek do interpretacji znalezisk niektórych zabytków z późnego średniowiecza i początku XVI wieku', *Archeologia Środkowego Nadodrza* 2013, V. X. pp.155-165.

15   Grzegorz Podruczny, 'Depozyt pobitewny z Kunowic', *Biografia Archeologii* <http://archeo.edu.pl/biografia2017/2017/09/21/depozyt-pobitewny-z-kunowic>, accessed: 5 April 2019.

22 millimetres). The other, a silver, coin with the diameter of 32 millimetres, cannot be identified at the moment. It was found under the arm of one soldier in a double fragment of material. Probably it was sewn under the lining of the uniform and therefore not stolen. In addition, in the grave, mostly near the skeletons, 17 lead projectiles were found.

The 2018 season proved to be unique, because we managed to implement on a small scale one of the research ideas; that is, the study of lead content in the soil to try to find out whether the lead from the projectiles of the eighteenth century still affects the natural environment. This was carried out in June 2018 by Dr Aleksandra Ibragimow. Samples of soil were collected from the sites where the lead projectiles had been found and are currently being analysed. The only sample analysed so far is the sample of soil from the deposit of small arms projectiles, in which the lead content was 16,000 times higher than the acceptable value.[16]

As compared to the many of the battles of that period, the battlefield at Kunersdorf is relatively small. The core area where the main fighting took place, is only approximately four square kilometres. By the standards of battles from the *Kabinettksriege* era, this is not large. For archaeological research, however, it is a huge area. Therefore, its investigation was time-consuming and required considerable human workforce. In total, in the 10 seasons of field research, it involved 1,248 man-days.

In each season, myself and Jakub Wrzosek (initially the National Centre for the Documentation and Research on Monuments *[KOBiDZ]*, later the National Heritage Board of Poland *[NID]*) took part in the works. Jakub Wrzosek was the principal investigator of the whole project in the years 2009-2011 and the principal investigator of the probe research in 2013, 2016 and 2018. I was the principal investigator in the search with metal detectors and from the beginning coordinated the research works, the organization of the whole project and auxiliary activities. I also personally took part in the research.

Apart from these two scholars, more people were engaged in each research season. In the first season, in 2009, one archaeologist from the National Centre for the Documentation and Research on Monuments also participated in the research, beside two voluntary explorers and 30 students of Spatial Management from Adam Mickiewicz University in Słubice. In 2010, two archaeologists and four voluntary explorers were engaged. The next year, three voluntary explorers and three student volunteers took part in the research. In the fourth season, four voluntary explorers and 30 students of Spatial Management from Collegium Polonicum were involved. In 2013, two archaeologists, three voluntary explorers and 12 students were engaged. In 2014, for the first time, broader collaboration was established with an organized group of explorers *(LGE Nadodrze)*, so a total of 45 researchers took part in the works. In the following years, however, collaboration with organizations was not continued, and only individual explorers were engaged. The number of volunteers willing to help was constantly growing. In 2015, apart from four archaeologists, four voluntary explorers and 10 students took part in the works. In the eighth season of research at Kunersdorf, one archaeologist and 20 voluntary explorers were actively participating. A similar number of

---

16   Unpublished data from Dr Ibragimow. More information can be found in Aleksandra Ibragimow, Grzegorz Podruczny, Marcin Siepak, 'The Environmental Consequences of Historical Battles on the Lead Contamination of Soils and Sediments. International Conference on Heavy Metals in the Environment', abstracts of conference held 22-25 July 2018, University of Georgia, p.112.

explorers assisted in 2017: beside two extra archaeologists and one geologist, 18 voluntary explorers took part in the works. Larger-scale works were carried out in the tenth research season, when 10 people (including eight volunteers) worked at the probe excavation, and 16 students of Spatial Management from Adam Mickiewicz University, one archaeologist and as many as 49 explorers (including 34 people from associations *(Eksploracja Kołobrzeg Parsęta, Sulęcińskie Stowarzyszenie Przyjaciół Historii "DENAR", and Grupa Historyczno-Eksploracyjna Pomerania)* and many independent explorers were involved in the search using metal detectors. The participation of one scientist representing natural sciences (environmental protection) was something new in that year. The number of man-days in each season and the number of participants from different groups are illustrated by the two tables below.

Table 2: Time Spent on the Kunersdorf Battlefield, 2009-2019

Year	2009	2010	2011	2012	2013	2014	2015	2016	2017	2018	2019
Number of man-days	175	30	30	200	145	88	140	100	120	1,430	460

Table 3: Participants in the Research at the Kunersdorf Battlefield, 2009-2019

Year	2009	2010	2011	2012	2013	2014	2015	2016	2017	2018
Archaeologists	2	3	1	1	3	1	5	2	3	2
Explorers	3	44	3	4	3	45	7	20	18	49
Students	25	0	3	30	12	0	10	0	0	16
Volunteers	1	1	1	1	1	1	1	1	2	9

From the beginning of the search with metal detectors, the artifacts were recorded using a GPS receiver. In the first three seasons, it was Garmin Foretrex 301. This is a very simple device (which is an advantage in the investigation of battlefields) but it has one serious disadvantage, in that the waypoints cannot be copied in a file format. This resulted in the need to copy GPS coordinates from the device by hand, which sometimes generated errors. The later purchase of a Garmin Gpsmap 64 made it possible to copy the waypoints in the form of gpx files. Since 2012, the planigraphs of the finds have been made in the QuantumGis/QGIS program.

The use of modern tools of battlefield archaeology not only allowed the reduction of the fog of war referred to by Christopher Duffy, but it also allowed to add new elements to the story. Chronologically, the first thing determined as part of the research was the role of field fortifications in the battle. During the preparation for archaeological research, some terrain forms were found, which as a result of the probe excavation in 2009 were identified as the relics of Russian abatis. In the area of the abatis, just like in the foreground, few movable artifacts were found. Large concentrations of artifacts (mostly lead canister shot) were only discovered 200 meters before the abatis line. In accordance with cartographic sources, the abatis was approximately 100-250 meters before the main bulwark of the Russian fortification camp. In other words, the concentration of canister shot is located approximately 300-450 meters from the line of fortifications, which means that it was the limit of effective canister fire. The absence of canister shot and generally any finds within the abatis zone can be easily explained: the area was in the blind spot of the Russian cannon fire. Most likely, the Prussian columns intending to storm the edge of the fortification camp were under canister fire for a very short time, at the edge of its range, in a narrow, 100 metre strip; thereafter, they advanced relatively safely in the blind spot of artillery fire. The abatis did not help much: it definitely slowed down the Prussian infantry, but it did not contribute to its losses because it was not covered with artillery fire. This discovery casts some new light on the causes of Prussian success in the initial phase of the battle.

Each season of the research produced new discoveries. A great many of finds were discovered on the meadows (Elsbusch) to the north of Kunersdorf. On the surface, it should not be surprising, because that was the way of the attack of Finck's corps, aiming to help the weakening storm of the main army stopped near the Kuhgrund. However, the amount and density of the finds, as well as their origin, excludes their relation to this event only. Small arms projectiles have been found, and the density of their occurrence is similar to the other sectors of the battlefield. Apart from that, many uniform buttons were found, both Prussian and Russian, as well as decorative elements from Prussian and Russian soldiers' uniforms. A single grave of a soldier was also discovered there. The soldier's grave and the four emblems from a grenadier's hat can be clearly related to soldiers from the Russian Observation Corps, fighting to resist the Prussian onslaught on the Mühlberg. The finds from the meadows are probably the remains of the main battle, which apparently was not only taking place on the plateau, within the Russian fortified camp; the lines of the fighting armies reached as far as the meadows.

Other information comes from the investigation of the arable land between the Mühlberg and the eastern end of the present village of Kunowice. Especially important is the field located south of the fortification line of the Russian camp. The account of the battle clearly says that the fights took place only within the camp. For this reason, not many artifacts were expected outside of it. As a result of the research, numerous finds related to the battles were also discovered outside the fortified camp. Interestingly, objects related to artillery, especially Russian lead canister shot, were found in particularly dense groups. The comparison of the planigraphy of these artifacts and the maps of the battle clearly shows the concentration of the discovered canister shots approximately 100-200 meters from the line of fortifications of the Russian fortified camp. It also proves that the fortifications were stormed, and that, after the capture of the Mühlberg, the fight continued. Not only vanguard grenadiers and the left flank of the Prussian army, but also the troops from the central formations were fighting on.

Another finding is not associated with the discovery of many artifacts but, to the contrary, with their relative shortage. The accounts describing the battle point to the fight for the Kuhgrund as its key element. This is especially true of the account by Tempehof and the reconstruction in the tenth volume of the *Kriege Friedrichs des Grossen*. According to them, the fight for this terrain obstacle was the end of the Prussian army's success, as both sides attacked it many times. However, relatively few objects were found in the Kuhgrund and on the fields nearby. Perhaps fighting did take place there, but this is not evidenced by the archaeological discoveries. What is interesting, however, is that the farther westward from the Kuhgrund, the more relics connected with the battle have been found. The planigraphy of the finds compared with the coordinates of the map reconstructing the course of the battle and the maximum range of Prussian infantry published in the tenth volume of *Kriege Friedrichs des Grossen* clearly shows that the spot of the highest concentration of finds, probably being the site of the most intense combat, is not only far away from the line of the Kuhgrund but also far away from the line regarded as the maximum range of attack on the map provided in the appendix to the above-mentioned *Kriege Friedrichs des Grossen*. It is impossible to determine now how far to the west the Prussian attack reached, but we can conservatively assume that it was more than a kilometre farther than the line. That is the place of the grave of Prussian soldiers discovered in 2018. Interestingly, this location overlaps with the range of Prussian infantry presented on eighteenth-century plans and well matches the accounts of the course of the battle known from Gaudi's description.

Apart from supplementing or adjusting the knowledge on the events described by historians, the investigation of the battlefield allowed to discover an event in the battle that was completely absent from historical reports: an attack by Prussian cuirassiers at the western end of the Russian fortified camp. The traces of that event were found during the exploration of the Russian abatis between the contemporary town of Słubice and the village of Świecko. It probably involved only few troops and was therefore ignored by the historians who described the battle. This is also confirmed by the scarcity of finds, limited to several buttons and about a dozen fragments of military equipment. Most probably, Russians saw a group of Prussian soldiers in front of the abatis and fired at them (which is evidenced by a splinter from a howitzer shell found in the profile of the abatis in 2010), killing one soldier. Although no grave was found, the death of one soldier is evidenced by the buckle from the main belt found near the abatis. Whereas just losing a button, a pouch, or a gun may have been accidental, the loss of the belt which held the soldier's breeches apparently means that their owner lost his life.

The artifacts help to identify the troops fighting there. The buckle from the main belt has the shape and dimensions typical of the buckles of Prussian soldiers, both from infantry and from cavalry. Only hussars did not use such buckles, so they can be safely excluded. The wide buckle found in 2010, as well as the belt fitting of the same width discovered in 2018, can be unambiguously identified as fragments of a cuirassier's carbine belt. The discovered fittings of firearms – a lock sideplate, a broken trigger guard and buckles regulating the length of the belt suit the cuirassier's carbine. The greatest interpretation doubts refer to the two discovered fragments of cold weapon: the fragments of a crossguard. The leaflike guard could suggest an officer's épée, but épées did not have sweeping hilts, and yet four broken sweepings were found. On the other hand, the guards of the known copies of cuirassiers' rapiers have fully covered guards, not sweepings. At the moment, it is hard to identify this artifact beyond doubt.

The research of battle graves provides information of a completely different kind. It has already been mentioned that the discovery of the grave of a Russian grenadier from the Observation Corps allowed us to expand the range of the fighting armies to the north, and the mass grave found in 2019 moved the range of the Prussian attack further to the west. Equally important new information is provided by the movable artifacts found by the remains of the soldiers.

Information obtained as a result of the discovery and exploration of graves (the individual one and the mass one) shows that in both cases, the soldiers had been robbed before the burial. However, unlike what might be expected from the analysis of historical accounts of other battles, the soldiers were not buried naked but had their uniforms on. What is more, this was intentional action, not the result of haste, because there was enough time to carefully rob the dead soldiers of all elements of equipment, money, and personal items. Other conclusions result from the analysis of the objects found in the mass grave in the years 2012-2018. The occurrence of two concentrations of uniform buttons, totalling over 300 objects, including buttons with fragments of uniform fabric and with torn shanks may prove an organized action of undressing the killed soldiers before burying them.

The individual grave of a Russian soldier found in 2010 provides important information concerning the uniforms of the Russian army. The most important artifact was the fragments of the hat worn by the soldier: two leather pieces, the from the front and the neck of the cap. On the front fragment, there were still the pieces of brass decorations, and on the neck part, there was a cast emblem. What was lacking was the main, 'head', part of the cap. It is hard to imagine that the robber only removed the middle part of the hat and left the rest. Probably the lack of that part results from the fact that it was made of canvas, and so did not survive to the present day. This relic is different from the appearance of grenadiers caps known from the contemporary iconography and from museum collections, which are fully made of leather. Perhaps this was a kind of hybrid: only the front and the part covering the neck were made of leather, and the middle part was made of canvas. Another important piece of information relates to the buttons. By this same soldier we found almond-like buttons made up of two convex brass pieces soldered together. The button shank, fixed in two holes, was made of a thin brass wire. Buttons of this shape, construction and size were later found in great quantity on the battlefield. Thanks to that discovery, they could be easily identified as belonging to Russian soldiers. Another important information was the way of attaching the buttons. This does not only refer to the finds from the individual grave of the Russian grenadier, but also from the mass grave found in 2019. Many buttons still have the thin strap drawn through the shank. Interestingly, some of the buttons found in the grave discovered in 2019 had a more primitive way of attachment: a thin wooden piece stuck in the shank. Another interesting piece of information obtained as a result of the exploration of the grave found in 2019 was the way of fixing the gaiters. Although the soldiers were buried in uniforms and gaiters, only one buckle was found that could be identified as a gaiter buckle. However, several brass pins were found located near the soldiers' knees, being the trace of an alternative method of fixing the gaiters.

The last new and noteworthy discovery that changes our view of the battle of Kunersdorf was the objects proving the use of hand grenades. They were found in two locations. The first discovery was made by illegal relic hunters approximately in 1999 in the area of the meadows near Kunersdorf. About 70 hand grenades were then discovered, located relatively close to each other. Unfortunately, we do not know much more about those objects. The other discovery was made in 2017. In August 2017, a deposit of elements of soldiers' equipment was found, including a Russian grenadier slow match case. One month later, during the exploration of the close proximity of that discovery, 132 splinters of hand grenades were found, mostly located within a small area of approximately 50 metres by 50. While the discovery from 1999 only proves that such grenades were possessed by the army during the battle, the one from 2017 proves beyond doubt that they were used in the fight in the field. They were definitely not used in the attack or defence of the fortification, as is evidenced by the comparison of the planigraphy of the artifacts with the coordinates of the archival map, showing that the fortifications were located approximately 150 meters to the south from the place of finding the splinters of hand grenades. This means that the discovery from 2017 is probably the trace of the last use of that weapon in the field battle by soldiers fighting in the line. Hand grenades were not used again in the field until the First World War.

As we can see from the example of the study of the battle of Kunersdorf, battlefield archaeology is a great instrument for a historian studying old conflicts. Unfortunately, in the course of or research, we have seen many times that it is not a perfect instrument. First of all, it requires much more work than typical historical research. Additionally, unlike historians, battlefield archaeologists are limited by the contemporary space and its current use. The researchers are also dependent on the owners of the area and their willingness to cooperate. Sometimes the exploration is impossible or difficult, even if the area is accessible and the owner is agreeable. An excellent example was the Elsbusch meadows, which for most of the time were overgrown with very tall grass, making the search with a metal detector impossible. The search in the woods was very difficult, too. Finally, we must not forget that apart from the official research, the battlefield has been searched many times by relic hunters. We know that such actions still taking place as recently as the 1990s. All these factors affect the planigraphy of the finds. It cannot be treated as the ultimate proof but only as a kind of filter through which we can filter the sources used so far by historians and thus assess their reliability. As we can see, the use of both the traditional methods of historical research and the battlefield archaeology will allow to present new, more reliable reconstructions of military events, and thus, reducing the fog of war covering the events of 12 August 1759.

Further Reading

Grosser Generalstab, *Geschichte des siebenjährigen Krieges: in einer Reihe von Vorlesungen, mit Benutzung authentischer Quellen bearbeitet von den Offizieren des großen Generalstabs, dritter Theil, der Feldzug von 1759* (Berlin: Armee Verlag, 1828).

Grosser Generalstab, *Die Kriege Friedrichs des Grossen, Der Siebenjährige Krieg*, V. 10 (Ernst Siegfried Mittler und Sohn, Berlin, 1912).

Podruczny, Grzegorz, Wrzosek, Jakub, 'Artillery Projectiles from the Battles of Zorndorf/Sarbinowo (1758) and Kunersdorf/Kunowice (1759)', *Fasciculi Archaeologiae Historicae*, XXV, 2012, pp. 77-86

Podruczny, Grzegorz, Wrzosek, Jakub, 'Lost elements. Earthworks of the fortified camp of the Russian Army from the time of the battle of Kunersdorf in the light of the recent research', *Archeologia Postmedievale* 14, 2010, pp. 6580.

Podruczny, Grzegorz, Wrzosek, Jakub, 'Lone Grenadier: An Episode fron the Battle of Kunersdorf, 12 August 1759', *Journal of Conflict Archaelogy*, Vol. 9 No.1, January 2014, pp.33-47.

Tempelhoff, G.F. von, *Geschichte des Siebenjährigen Krieges in Deutschland zwischen dem Könige von Preussen und der Kaiserin Königin mit ihren Alliirten als eine Fortsetzung der Geschichte des General Lloyd vom G.F. v. Tempelhoff, part 3, Feldzug von 1759* (Berlin: Unger, 1787).

Volz, Gustav Berthold (ed), *Die Werke Friedrichs des Großen: in deutscher Übersetzung*; V. 4, *Geschichte des Siebenjährigen Krieges* (Verlag von Reimar Hobbing, Berlin 1913).

Zeichmann, Jürgen, *Journal vom Siebenjährigen Kriege, von Friedrich Wilhelm Ernst Freiherr von Gaudi. Forschungen und Studien zur Friederizianischen Zeit, Sonderband F, Band. 6, 1759, Bearbeitet von Patrick Neuhaus* (Buchholz: LTR Verlag, 2009).

13

The Primacy of State Violence in the Austro-Bohemian Lands: Subjects, Soldiers and Shifting Social Boundaries, 1792-1815

Kurt Baird[1]

The threatening skies and the thunderstorms of the coming war drew nearer on the western horizon that bordered France. All the parade grounds of Vienna were covered deep into late Autumn with Landwehr and troops of the line rehearsing, and even though it was above our station, we reserve men were needed as instructors for the Landwehr, attending every Sunday and on holidays. Already it was a matter of public communication and deliberation that the new outbreak of war, a very serious one that brought about extraordinary constrictions and preparations, was a foregone conclusion.[2]

So began the memoir of Johann Schnierer, the son of a poor barber, recounting his military service during the Napoleonic Wars. Born in 1790 in the suburb of Wieden, just outside central Vienna, Schnierer worked as his father's assistant up until he was 18. He lived on the street of Waaggasse growing up only a few blocks behind the infantry barracks of Infantry Regiment Deutschmeister Nr.4, which bordered the Grain Market (*Getreidemarkt*) on the outskirts of the imperial city. The Deutschmeister was one of the preeminent regiments in the Habsburg army, its connection with the Grand Master of the Teutonic Order and its affiliation with the seat of the dynasty served to link the Habsburg Monarchy to the Holy Roman Empire and the post tridentate Catholic faith of southern Germany. It represented not only the dynasty's reach in Central Europe, but also the loyalty of the Viennese locals, who were conscripted to fill Deutschhmeister's ranks.

---

1   The author would like to thank the participants of *The Violent State in Historical Perspective Network*, particularly Dr Shaul Mitelpunkt, Dr Simon Toner, and Dr Sean Fear for their encouragement and advice.
2   Johann Schnierer (ed. Hans Rieder), *Aus der Franzosenzeit (1809-1816): Aufzeichnungen eines österreichischen Soldaten* (Linz: J. Stampil, 1910), p.7.

The early militarisation of Habsburg society during the eighteenth and early nineteenth-centuries, that is the restructuring of rural life, its rhythms, and processes to better serve the military's need for soldiers and materials, in which Schnierer played a small part, was first articulated in its fullest extent by Christopher Duffy. Since then, historians have built on the mighty foundations he set, his expertise, and incredible grasp of primary source material to explore the Habsburg army's centrality to the dynasty's 'imperial project'.[3] A period from the beginning of Maria Theresia's reign in 1740 lasting until the end of the First World War, where the dynasty introduced various cultural, social, and intellectual frameworks that sought to create loyal Habsburg subjects out of the many early modern particularisms and prejudices found within the territories of the House of Austria.[4] It is his work that has provided historians interested in the effects of frontline experience and military service on the culture of the Habsburg Monarchy, now a vibrant field, with the tools to articulate the integrative nature of the army. An imperial institution which allowed individuals and groups to inhabit layers of identities, creating intersections which strengthened the multi-national Habsburg state.[5]

The zenith of the Habsburg army's integrative function, a time that contained little of the ethnic and national friction found in the Monarchy's later years, was during the Coalition Wars. The Grain Market which stood during that time is now gone, replaced by the *Ringstrasse* and the 'golden cabbage' of the Secessionist Building, but during the life of Schnierer the barracks that sat alongside the market housed thousands of soldiers who, when not on duty along the walls of the inner city or practising their drill on the glacis embankments, would entertain themselves in the guest houses of the suburbs and buy goods from the markets. Soldiers and soldiering were on constant display in the city of Vienna and its surrounding areas, indicative of the army's central presence in most local societies throughout the Monarchy. Furthermore, it was in these villages and suburbs that surrounded Vienna that many of the recruits and reserves of the regiment were drawn from, going about their daily lives, like Schnierer, with the knowledge that military service

---

3   The quote is taken from Pieter Judson, *The Habsburg Empire: A New History* (Cambridge, MA: Harvard University Press, 2016), p.4; The best analysis of the army in Habsburg society written in English since Duffy's is Michael Hochedlinger, *Austria's Wars of Emergence, 1683-1797* (London: Routledge, 2003). For the army of the Monarchy's late period see Laurence Cole, *Military Culture and Popular Patriotism in Late Imperial Austria* (Oxford: Oxford University Press, 2014).

4   See recent works on this topic from Paula Sutter Fichtner, *The Habsburgs: Dynasty, Culture and Politics* (London: Reaktion Books, 2014); William D. Godsey, *The Sinews of Habsburg Power: Lower Austria in a Fiscal-Military State 1650–1820* (Oxford: Oxford University Press, 2018); Charles Ingrao, *The Habsburg Monarchy, 1618-1815*, 3rd ed (Cambridge: Cambridge University Press, 2019); Marco Bellabarba. *Das Habsburgerreich 1765-1918* (Berlin: De Gruyter Oldenbourg, 2020). For an earlier examination see Ernst Wagermann, *The Austrian Achievement 1700–1800* (London: Thames & Hudson 1973).

5   The work of Laurence Cole in *Military Culture and Popular Patriotism*, best exemplifies this. As does the analysis of local allegiances and its links to dynastic loyalty in Laurence Cole (ed.), *Different Paths to the Nation: Regional and National Identities in Central Europe and Italy, 1830-1870* (Basingstoke: Palgrave Macmillan, 2007); Ibid, 'Differentiation or Indifference? Changing Perspectives on National Identification in the Austrian Half of the Habsburg Monarchy', in Maarten van Ginderachter and Marnix Beyen (eds), *Nationhood from Below: Europe in the Long Nineteenth-century* (Basingstoke: Palgrave Macmillan, 2012), pp.96-119.

was a probability, and with some understanding of the duties, expectations, and performance of the soldier long before they were conscripted into the local regiment. It was during the Monarchy's war with Revolutionary and Imperial France that the soldier became an everyday presence, existing in society alongside civilians, living with families and friends as symbols of imperial power. For those who would serve the Emperor Francis, the boundary between the peacetime role of subject, rural labourer or artisan, and the wartime identity of the dutiful soldier was a porous one. In some places it did not exist at all.

The 23-year struggle with France saw the culmination of a 40-year process started by Maria Theresa that sought to eliminate the boundaries which separated the Monarchy's standing army from society. As the memoirs and journals of those subaltern officers and common soldiers who fought against France from 1792 to 1815 attest, the Habsburg army was a constant presence in wider society and the extended nature of the war brought the civil and military spheres of the Austro-Bohemian lands closer together. These men write of a time where the Habsburg army and its system of conscription, created from the 1780s onwards, meant that there was little boundary between subjects or soldiers. Ilya Berkovich and Micheal Wenzel make this argument using an army-wide analysis of regimental roll calls to show the Monarchy as an 'empire-in-arms' long before France became a 'nation-in-arms'.[6] What this current work elucidates is the lived experience of the social transformation identified by these two scholars, where the socialisation of the military using native-born men was crystallised and reached its zenith during the struggle with France. Throughout the war conscripts who had been recruited from the surrounding villages of the towns in which regiments were garrisoned, and officers who had been appointed by the regiment from influential local families, served as an ever-present symbol of the monopoly the monarch had on violence and the right to conscribe men. The recollections of these soldiers show the rising number of native-born men in uniform placed more soldiers in civil society, drawing those not in uniform closer to the experiences of combatants and cementing military service for this generation of Habsburg subjects as an accepted part of life long before universal conscription was introduced in 1868.

As briefly sketched earlier in this chapter, the authoritative voice on the beginnings of the Habsburg Monarchy's use of the state to support its military project is Christopher Duffy. His work on the army during the reign of Maria Theresa has revealed, in exacting detail, the primacy of the Habsburg military in the society of the Austrian Hereditary Lands and the Kingdom of Bohemia from the middle of the eighteenth-century onwards. *Instrument of War* and *By Force of Arms*, two works published since 2000, are both considered evolutions of Duffy's first published study on the armed forces of Imperial Austria: *The Army of Maria Theresa*.[7] The first volume, *Instrument of War*, is the definitive text on how the

---

6   Ilya Berkovich and Micheal Wenzel make this argument using an army wide analysis of regimental roll calls, 'The Austrian Army', in Alan Forrest (gen. ed.), *The Cambridge History of the Napoleonic Wars* (Cambridge: Cambridge University Press, 2022), Vol.2, Part 2, Chapter 28 [Forthcoming]. I would like to thank Dr Berkovich and Michael Wenzel for graciously allowing me to consult their manuscript before publication.

7   Christopher Duffy, *Instrument of War: The Austrian Army in the Seven Years War, Vol 1* (Michigan: The Emperor's Press, 2001); *By Force of Arms: The Austrian Army in the Seven Years War, Vol 2* (Michigan: The Emperor's Press, 2005); *The Army of Maria Theresa: The Armed Forces of Imperial Austria, 1740-1780* (Hippocrene Books: New York, 1977).

Habsburg Monarchy simultaneously worked with and coercively shaped the traditions, particularisms and the demographics of its population to create an army that would protect its sphere of influence in Central Europe. Whilst capturing in vivid detail the campaigns of the Habsburg Monarchy, and expertly evaluating the tactical acumen of the army's leaders during its struggles with Frederick the Great of Prussia, the most methodologically enlightening and intellectually stimulating approach of Duffy's work on the Austrian army has been his use of memoirs and military sources to document the lives of those who were at the sharp end of the Monarchy's struggles against Prussia.

Before historians began studying the impact of the military and state violence on the social and cultural landscape of the Atlantic world, Duffy's *Military Experience in the Age of Reason* opened the many ways in which we can investigate how military processes and practices influenced the cultural attributes and representations of war in the eighteenth and early nineteenth century. In the 'alien landscape' of the Age of Reason, Duffy used the lived experiences of the common soldier and the officer to chart the impact systems of recruitment, training and military norms had on the lives of those in the uniform of the state, whilst also relating peacetime routines, civil-military interactions, and the way the mad, frightening, and terrible encounters of battle were understood by combatants.[8]

Importantly, Duffy stressed the primacy of historical context in understanding the way societies existed in war, and how individuals experienced it. His approach, which related the military institutions of the eighteenth-century at their moment, as opposed to part of a wider revolution in military affairs, allowed a more purposeful and revealing examination of the way attitudes to gender, identity, class, and enlightened concepts of human experience all played a role in influencing the way the military and military service was understood by contemporaries. Moreover, Duffy revealed that even as Old Regime armies constrained men's choices, soldiers at the same time held a diverse range of personal reasons for submitting to the authority of the military, which contributed to the fighting cohesion of a unit.[9]

Current academic approaches to war in the Age of Reason and Revolutions are twofold, and are influenced by the methodologies primarily used by historians who study conflict in the twentieth century. On one hand there are those who address how certain society's systems of meaning allow people to experience, narrate and understand war.[10] On the other hand, there are those who investigate how the social and cultural beliefs of people influence the motivations, behaviours and institutional values of the military.[11] Criticisms of both approaches have highlighted the lack of attention and contextual weight some historians of war, culture and society give to military tactics, organisation, systems of recruitment and strategy. These arguments stress the importance military practices had on the decisions, values, and approaches to war, which together influenced the way men and women

---

8   Christopher Duffy, *Military Experience in the Age of Reason* (London: Routledge and Kegal Paul, 1987).

9   For a work that fundamentally revises our understanding of the motivations of the common soldier see Ilya Berkovich, *Motivation in War: The Experience of the Common Soldiers in Old-Regime Europe* (Cambridge: Cambridge University Press, 2017).

10   Catriona Kennedy, *Narratives of the Revolutionary and Napoleonic Wars: Military and Civilian Experience in Britain and Ireland* (Basingstoke: Palgrave Macmillan, 2013).

11   Cole, *Military Culture and Popular Patriotism.*

experienced it. For example, a better understanding of Prussian linear tactics and rate of musket fire, and how it was perceived by Austrian contemporaries during the Austrian War of Succession, would better illuminate why the Habsburg army subsequently placed an importance on centrally recruited and trained men when narrating the impact of the military on local communities in the lead up to the Seven Years War.

In Duffy's *Instrument of War*, we are presented with a chapter that not only uses the two above contemporary approaches to the cultural and social history of war, but also firmly grounds them within the context of eighteenth-century military strategy, tactics, and organisation to describe the military experience of the private soldier in the army of Maria Theresia. *Adam Bauer – The Austrian Private Soldier*, chapter eight in *Instrument of War*, is mastery of marshalling historical sources in such a way as to provide a snapshot into the lives lived at the bottom of a social hierarchy.[12] It charts the military systems that governed the experiences of young men in the Monarchy between 1750 and 1765, documenting the way central bureaucrats, military authorities and periphery contractors, like regional noble landowners, mobilised local populations for war. Beginning with who was to be selected by local authorities for service in the army, and investigating the intellectual reasonings that attempted to make military service desirable for native-born men, Duffy reveals the conditions the soldier faced, the physical requirements service demanded, and the culture of an army embroiled in a life-or-death struggle with Prussia. Pay, military leave, the plight of prisoners of war and the motivations of honour, which was instilled within the men by the deeds and words of their officers, are all covered in a chapter that does more than reveal the military life of the common soldier. It is a study of how historical actors and social groups immediately exposed to the stresses and strains of war understood it, which masterfully reveals the struggles found in attempting to integrate the ideals of modernity with the corporate traditions of old Europe.[13]

Duffy's work on the Habsburg army during the time of Maria Theresia, and at Austerlitz, his 'thick description' of military experience, and consummate understanding of the military organisation of Old Regime armies, is an approach which historians focusing on the lived experience of the 'Age of Revolution' should explore if they wish to properly historicise the links between war, culture, and society. It is the intention of this present work in the space allowed, using the memoirs and documents of soldiers, to relate a period when fighting for the Habsburgs was constant. I will attempt to extend, in homage, the historical narrative of Duffy's work and borrow his approach to show how the porous boundary between the life of a subject and the life of a soldier benefitted the imperial project of Monarchy in its war against France.

The Evolution of Military Service in the Habsburg Crownlands, 1765-1792

The culmination of the military reforms and transformation of some of the corporate particularisms of early modern Austria, Bohemia and Moravia, which began in the 1740s

---

12   Duffy, *Instrument of War*, pp.198-227.
13   Duffy, *Instrument of War*, pp.18-34.

in response to Prussia's conquest of Silesia, was the creation of a massive standing army that could protect the dynasty's sphere of influence in Europe. It was this army, created in the late eighteenth century, which challenged and eventually ended French power between 1792 and 1814. As Michael Hochedlinger has shown, the Austro-Bohemian lands were more militarised than Prussia even before the beginning of the French Revolutionary Wars, and this process only accelerated as the struggle with France intensified. It was this process of militarisation which provided the manpower to sustain the successive campaigns needed to defeat France. [14]

Debates over how militarised Habsburg society should be began as early as 1761, when manpower shortages were understood by generals to have stymied their efforts against Prussia. This discussion continued after the war, lasting until 1769 as members of the central government argued vigorously over the purpose of the military, its impact on society and the realm of the civilian. The Foreign Minister Wenzel Anton von Kaunitz advocated for an increased use of volunteers from outside the crownlands to prevent a slowing of domestic growth and reform, whilst the Field Marshals Leopold Joseph von Daun and Franz Moritz von Lacy and then the young Emperor Joseph II argued, in a series of memoranda put to Maria Theresia, for a system of recruitment like their enemy Prussia. Joseph wanted a practice reliant largely on the native-born men of the crownlands as he believed that 'the duties of a citizen and a soldier have never appeared and still do not appear to me incompatible'. [15] These debates were a determining factor in the type of system introduced by the central government for the raising of troops, as well as influencing the way men were treated in the army after Maria Theresia sided with her son in 1769. What followed in the 1770s was the first dismantling of the social, economic, and cultural boundaries that separated the Habsburg military from the rest of society.

The Monarchy attempted to address the military failures of the Seven Years War by introducing cantonal recruitment (*Konskriptions- und Werbbezirkssystem*) in March 1770, modelled on the Prussian system, with its full implementation in the Austro-Bohemian Lands occurring between 1779 and 1781. [16] This system of building an army to defend against Prussian aggression was forever championed by Joseph II and reinforced by his transformation of agrarian economies and noble landlord rights between 1780 and 1788. [17] The intended consequences of these reforms, amongst other things, was to make available able bodied men for military service. [18] This enlightened reform, or absolute rule, or even enlightened

---

14   Hochedlinger, *Austria's Wars of Emergence*, pp.291-297.

15   Franz A. J Szabo, *Kaunitz and Enlightened Absolutism, 1753-1780* (Cambridge: Cambridge University Press, 1994), p.288.

16   Szabo, *Kaunitz and Enlightened Absolutism*, pp.278-295. Michael Hochedlinger, 'Das Stehende Heer,' in Michael Hochedlinger, Petr Maťa and Thomas Winkelbauer (eds), *Verwaltungsgeschichte der Habsburgermonarchie in der Frühen Neuzeit, Band 2, Hof und Dynastie, Kaiser und Reich, Zentralverwaltungen, Kriegswesen und landesfürstliches Finanzwesen* (Vienna: Böhlau, 2019), pp.655-760.

17   Edith M. Link, *The Emancipation of the Austrian Peasant, 1740-1798* (New York, Columbia University Press, 1949), pp.89-142; Jerome Blum, *Noble Landowners and Agriculture in Austria, 1815-1848: A Study in the Origins of the Peasant Emancipation of 1848* (Baltimore: The John Hopkins Press, 1948), pp.45-88.

18   Hermann Rebel, 'Peasantries under the Austrian Empire', in Tim Scott (ed.), *The Peasantries of Europe: From the Fourteenth to the Eighteen Centuries* (Harlow: Longman, 1998), pp.191-227, in

despotism, has been covered extensively by Derek Beales, Peter Dickson, Timothy Blanning, Hamish Scott, William Godsey, Franz Szabo and others, but it is enough to say here that after much debate, reform, centralisation, negotiation and compromise a fiscal and military system was put in place by 1781 that allowed the Monarchy to field an army by 1789 that was the largest, on paper at least, in Europe with a pool of potential reserves totalling a million and a half men.[19]

As part of this new military system infantry regiments were each given a region where recruiting parties would select unmarried men between the ages of 18 and 40 for soldiering. As Duffy's research has revealed, men conscripted into the ranks of the local regiment would, it was hoped, view it as their 'second home and family'.[20] The regimental authorities were guided by comprehensive surveys (*Seelenkonskription*) of the male population, which had been done almost annually since 1770.[21] How local authorities and these representatives of the regiments agreed on who would be conscripted is unknown, but, as was the case with all the armies of the time, conscription into the infantry regiments of the Monarchy fell most heavily on the poorest of the rural population and the lowliest of village artisan. The cantonal recruiting departments of each regiment benefited from the excluding nature of peasant societies and the inefficiencies of manor economies, which meant almost half of all males in the Austro-Bohemian lands were deemed by military and civilian authorities as excess to local requirements.[22] This is hardly an amount that can be placed under the rubric of undesired fringe dweller. Most of the conscripts were men without a fixed profession, that is they were not employed in one of the trades that was protected by guild rights or deemed essential. Again, this does not mean they were just unemployed vagabonds or delinquents. Most often the common soldier had been an agricultural labourer, or house servant working within peasant economies that could only sustain a casualised workforce and where excess labour was a systematic factor.

Those deemed too important for rural economies and exempted from military service were property owners and tax-paying peasant tenants. As were their heirs and the master apprentices to most skilled artisan workers. However, as the war with France continued and more men were required, younger apprentices were conscripted, as were some sole apprentices in towns and cities. Further exemptions were given to those in skilled manufacturing and mining. Urban professionals such as lawyers, bookkeepers and civil servants were also

---

particular 223-224; Michael Hochedlinger, 'The Habsburg Monarchy: From "Military-Fiscal State" to "Militarization"', in Christopher Storrs (ed.), *The Fiscal-Military State in Eighteenth-Century Europe: Essays in Honour of P.G.M. Dickson* (Farnham: Ashgate Publishing, 2009), pp.55-95.

19   Derek Beales, *Joseph II: In the Shadow of Maria Theresa, 1741-1780* (Cambridge: Cambridge University Press, 1987; Ibid, *Joseph II: Against the World, 1780-1790* (Cambridge: Cambridge University Press, 2013); P.G.M. Dickson, *Finance and Government under Maria Theresia 1740-1780* (Oxford: Clarendon Press, 1987) Vols.1&2; Timothy C.W. Blanning, *Joseph II* (London: Routledge, 1994); Hamish Scott (ed.), *Enlightened Absolutims: Reform and Reformers in Later Eighteenth-Century Europe* (Basingstoke: Palgrave Macmillan, 1990); Godsey, *The Sinews of Habsburg Power*; Szabo, *Kaunitz and Enlightened Absolutism*. See note 3 for other scholars.

20   Duffy, *Military Experience*, p.93. Quoted from Duffy's transcription of General Creutz's report for the *Nostitz-Rieneck Hofcommission*, which was held 1791-1796.

21   Anton Tantner, *Ordnung der Häuser, Beschreibung der Seelen – Hausnummerierung und Seelenkonskription in der Habsburgermonarchie* (Vienna: Studienverlag, 2007).

22   Dickson, *Finance and Government*, p.45.

exempt.[23] Of course the nobility was not forced to join the army, but the lesser nobles were socially expected to voluntarily commit to service in the army as regimental officers. Many of the lesser noble families provided generations of men who served together in the local regiments. Often a son served as an ensign (*Fähnrich*) in his father's company before he rose in the ranks. Despite the vast exemptions put in place to safeguard against a society so militarised that it amounted to what Kaunitz labelled as a 'Prussian slavish military system' and thus the inevitable retardation of noble landowners' profits, the conscription system of the Habsburg Monarchy was efficient in filling the ranks of its standing army before, during and after each major campaign against France and its allies.[24]

The Experience of Conscription and War, 1792-1815

By the beginning of the First Coalition many male subjects of the noble landowners were soldiers in waiting. Soldiering was firmly part of rural society and the military institution of the Monarchy impinged upon most people's daily lives and consciousness. Whilst this militarisation of the rural populace did not lead to a level of militarism that asserted the primacy of the army in all aspects of social, cultural and political life, or the manifestation amongst all native born men the desire to serve in the army, it did create a culture where soldiering was not for outsiders, vagabonds and want-away-sons, but an extension of the patrimonial society that existed throughout the rural landscape of the Austrian Hereditary lands and the Kingdom of Bohemia.[25] A culture of service that only grew as the war with France progressed.

The extent to which military service became an embedded part of life in the Austro-Bohemian lands is exemplified by the reflections of the Moravian conscript Johann Schnerer on his time as a soldier, which he wrote down in an unpublished manuscript for his family in 1857.[26] Born in Kanitz (now Dolni Kounice) in Moravia in 1778 to a volunteer soldier from Bavaria and a local woman, Schnerer was marked by manor officials and regimental authorities for service in the Infantry Regiment Loudon Nr.29 when he was a nine-year-old boy. Before being conscripted Schnerer attended a school run by the regiment where he learnt to read and write in rudimentary German as well as geography, astronomy, and

---

23   Hochedlinger, 'Das Stehende Heer', p.732.
24   Szabo, *Kaunitz and Enlightened Absolutism*, p.271-295. For quote see p.291.
25   Ilya Berkovich, 'Military Recruitment in the Habsburg Monarchy, 1740-92', in William Godsey and Petr Mat'a (eds), *The Habsburg Monarchy as a Fiscal-Military State, c. 1648-1815: Contours and Perspectives* (Oxford: Oxford University Press), Chapter 7 [Forthcoming]. I must thank again Dr Berkovich for kindly allowing me to consult this manuscript before publication. See also Michael Hochedlinger, 'The Habsburg Monarchy: From "Military-Fiscal State" to "Militarization"', in Christopher Storrs (ed.), *The Fiscal-Military State in Eighteenth-Century Europe: Essays in Honour of P.G.M. Dickson* (Farnham: Ashgate Publishing, 2009); Arthur Mark Boerke, 'Conscription in the Habsburg Empire to 1815', in Donald Stocker, Frederick C. Schneid and Harold D. Blanton (eds), *Conscription in Napoleonic Europe: A Revolution in Military Affairs?* (New York: Routledge, 2008), pp.66-83.; Cole, *Military Culture and Popular Patriotism*, pp.33-37.
26   Österreichisches Staatsarchiv (Austrian State Archives, hereafter ÖStA), Kriegsarchiv (KA), Militärische Nachlässe (NL), 1396 (B) Schnerer, fol., *Manuskript Bruckstucke aus meinen leben, 13 Bogen, verfasst nach März 1857*. Not to be confused with Johann Schnierer from Vienna.

religion. Schnerer's military education was not unique. Across the Monarchy regimental schools took in the sons of respected NCOs with the goal of creating the next generation of exemplary soldiers. These boys would be entrusted with maintaining the cohesion, health and motivation of the regiment at a company level once they were conscripted into the ranks and obtained a position of leadership.[27] Writing in 1857, Schnerer tell us that 'all the boys specified for Conscription were taken whilst the regiment was on campaign' in late 1795.[28] He was part of a new wave of men who would replace the losses Loudon had sustained along the Rhine during the previous campaign season. Included in the group of conscripted boys from the recruiting district of Brunn (*Brunner Kreis*) were two of Schnerer's childhood friends, Leopold Wolf and Joseph Kampel.[29] Together under the watchful eye of Second Lieutenant (*Unterleutnant*) Baron Presing, the conscripts were marched 18 miles to the regimental depot in Brunn. There Schnerer and another of his childhood friends were placed in the Reserve Division of the regiment after they were paid the usual bounty of three Florins given to conscripted men at the beginning of their service. From 1796 to 1798, whilst the regiment's third battalion was stationed in Lemberg, securing the Monarchy's new territories after the third partition of Poland, the young soldier spent two years escorting newly raised conscripts from the regiments supplementary district (*Aushilfbezirk*) in Galicia to Brunn, foreign volunteers from Rositz in Thuringia to Vienna and Moravians to depots in Budweis. His education, familiarity with the regiment and position as the son of a corporal, made him the perfect candidate to accompany the recruiting parties of the Reserve Division, showing to new conscripts the ideal model of emperor Francis' soldiers.[30]

The duration of the recruiting trips Schnerer lists, and the length of how far they ranged, reveals the extent to which infantry regiments in the Monarchy went about finding able bodied men. The Regiment Loudon was an institution highly visible to the people living in the district of Brunn. Soldiers were not absent from the community they had once inhabited as subjects of the noble landowner. The muster rolls and the monthly transfer lists of the Regiment Loudon from 1792 to 1802 elucidate the almost monthly regularity the Reserve Division sourced men from the local manors surrounding the garrison town of Brunn, trained them, and then sent them to the battalions fighting in Italy. In March 1797, the Reserve Division had 827 common soldiers listed as part of the unit, with 556 of those men identified as locals.[31] Of the full list of common soldiers, 644 had yet to be classed as effective as they were still in training. In the preceding 15 months beginning in January 1796, a total of 1,233 men had been conscripted from Moravia and Galizia and 907 sent on to the two field battalions in a monthly stream. All men would have been escorted by capable and trusted soldiers like Schnerer, both to the regimental depots for training and then on to the frontlines to replace the sick, the dead and those who had

---

27   Hochedlinger, *Austria's Wars of Emergence*, p.314.

28   ÖStA, KA, NL, 1396 (B) Schnerer, fol., *Manuskript*, p.1.

29   ÖStA, KA Personalunterlagen (Pers), MLST I Infanterie IR 29 2522. By 1802 Wolf, or Wolff as he was listed it in the *Musterlisten*, had advanced to the rank of *Fourier* in the staff company (Staab) of IR 29. His understanding of the regiment from such a young age and his ability to read and write made him the perfect candidate to assist the majors in its day-to-day administration.

30   ÖStA, KA, NL, 1396 (B) Schnerer, fol., *Manuskript*, 1; KA Pers MLST I Infanterie IR 29 2517 Revisionslisten, 1795-1797.

31   ÖStA, KA, Pers, IR 29 2517 Revisionslisten, 1795-1797, fol., *Reserve Division Revisions Liste, Marz 1797*.

deserted. In the military district of Brunn we can conclude that it was a hive of military activity, with recruiting parties constantly scouring the land for young men. Moreover, what these numbers indicate, is that Loudon operated as part of a military system that expected regimental attrition, planned for it, and knew how to maintain the fighting effectiveness of the two field battalions. Therefore, even when the regiment was on the frontlines, its men still played a significant part in the economic and social functions of rural life. As Schnerer's account of his first two years of service in the Reserve Division show, the Regiment Loudon viewed the men of the Brunn district as future soldiers, just as the *Seelenkonskription* had described them.

The process of 'counting of souls' which had identified the usefulness of Schnerer long before he realised he could have any, was the prime reason Loudon could efficiently source replacements for its losses. As part of the introduction of the *Seelenkonskription* in 1770 the military numbered houses, counted every male and draught animal and lodged in exacting detail those who could be used for the army.[32] As Anton Tantner and Hochedlinger had shown using the reports of the first *Seelenkonskription*, the army 'discovered' and mapped the interior of the Habsburg lands for the dynasty. In the process these military authorities revealed the appalling living conditions and demands the subjects of the local manors were forced to abide, thanks mostly to the powers the landowning nobility had over those who lived on their estates.[33] With the help of central legislation, which removed some of the powers of noble landowners, the army became one of the primary institutions of Habsburg life, infiltrating the lives of boys long before they donned the uniform of their monarch, and putting them aside for a time when local officials and military authorities agreed they were needed for 'state necessities'.[34] This was a term the *Seelenkonskription* gave to the numbers of unmarried cottars and smallholders, day-labourers, orphans, and other miscellaneous workers who were available for conscription.

The pervasiveness of conscription and the regularity men were drawn into the regionally based regiments impacted the economic prosperity of the local authorities, leading to obvious resentment, but for some conscripts the army provided them with the ability to escape the restricting confines of pre-industrial agricultural life.[35] The memoirs of Franz Bersling, another Habsburg subject from the Kingdom of Bohemia, is an invaluable source which describes the early impact of the war on Habsburg society. Importantly, Bersling's reflections provides a glimpse into the different ways in which conscription was viewed by young men, as well as the importance of the soldier's visibility in wider society as means to internalise military service as an acceptable part of life. Bersling was born in Gitschin (Jičín) in 1775 to a tailor, and, like the Moravian Schnerer, was a replacement for losses

---

32   Anton Tantner, *Ordnung der Häuser*.

33   Michael Hochedlinger and Anton Tantner, 'Auf dem Weg Zur Allgemeinen Wehrpflicht? Die Einfuhrung des "Konskriptions -und Werbbezirkssystems" in der Habsburgermonarchie', in Anton Tantner and Michael Hochedlinger (eds), *...der größte Teil der Untertanen lebt elend und mühselig: Der Berichte des Hofkriegsrates zur sozialen und wirtschaftlichen Lage der Habsburgermonarchie 1770-1771* (Vienna: Studein Verlag, 2005), pp.1-76.

34   Dickson, *Finance and Government*, Vol.1, p.45.

35   David M. Hopkins, *Soldier and Peasant in French Popular Culture, 1766-1870* (Suffolk: Boydell Press, 2002).

sustained in the army's previous campaigns.[36] Bersling was taken from his father's house in 1791 as part of the influx of enlisted men used to rebuild the artillery regiments that had been involved in the Austro-Turkish war fought from 1788 to 1791. For Bersling conscription into the Habsburg army was a welcome relief from having to learn his father's trade, which he labelled as 'dogsbody' work (*Handlanger dienst*). Soldiering, on the other hand, was a life that Bersling had been drawn to as a young 13-year-old boy where, risking the blows of his father and stepmother, he 'used every eye to watch the hustle and bustle of the soldiers'.[37]

Indeed, whilst working at the table of his father's shop, with needle and thread in hand, peering out of his window towards the Central Bohemian Highlands, all the young Bersling could think of was the troops who gathered in the town square before they marched off to war. Unlike the other boys of his age who were fearful of battle, Bersling notes in his memoirs that he longed to leave the torment of his father's workshop and hoped his early growth spurt would enable him to experience the foreign dangers of war sooner rather than later.[38] It is important to note here that Bersling understood that his view of the army as a potential escape was unique and that the majority of those his age viewed conscription with trepidation and dread. This, however, does not diminish the pervasive nature of the army, but reveals the significant extent to which soldiering and military service dominated the lives of young men.

It was not until the end of the campaign season in 1791 that Bersling, in his eighteenth year, was conscripted into the First Imperial Artillery Regiment stationed in Prague. In Bersling's account he writes, 'In July 1791, when the last campaign against the Turks had ended, recruitment in my home circle and all of Bohemia was renewed in an effort to rebuild the regiments, which had never before suffered so much than in the war just ended.'[39] The height of Bersling at 5 fuss, 6 zoll (1.73 metres) must have persuaded the recruiting corporal to target the young man, and also led the local military officials to reject the 'objections' of his father to his son's enforced military service.[40] Bersling's father had a right to object to his son's conscription as he should have been exempted from military service as a qualified tailor, living in an urban centre and, from what we can tell, the only son of a professional. Yet it seems that the restrictions which should have exempted Bersling from service were ignored by the military, most probably after negotiations at the provincial level between the central government under Leopold II and the representatives of the noble landowners, bishoprics, and wealthy burghers of Bohemia. Bersling himself seems to have understood this when he explains almost 60 years later that after the Austro-Turkish war, 'the emperor needed soldiers, the more the better, as the next year's war against France clearly enough proved.'[41]

---

36   Franz Bersling, *Der Böhmische Veteran. Franz Bersling's Leben, Reisen und Kriegsfahrten in allen fünf Weltteilen* (Schweidnitz: F.D.A Franke, 1840), p.8.
37   Bersling, *Der Böhmische Veteran*, p.10.
38   Bersling, *Der Böhmische Veteran*, p.9.
39   Bersling, *Der Böhmische Veteran*, p.10.
40   Bersling, *Der Böhmische Veteran*, p.10.
41   Bersling, *Der Böhmische Veteran*, p.10.

For the 18 year old Johann Schnierer, whose account opened this paper and who was needed to train the *Landwehr* late into Autumn 1808, the beginning of his military service did not mean he left his kin and civilian life behind even after he gave his oath to the emperor.[42] Whilst his occupation as an apprentice barber would have seen him most probably excused from military service if the Monarchy had designs on a permanent peace with France, the intensity of the conflict and its extended nature forced the government in 1807 to partially reform its system of conscription to include those in the army who had previously been deemed important to local economies.[43] According to Schnierer's account, his wartime service began in 1808 when he was placed on the reserve roll of the Infantry Regiment Deutschmeister Nr.4. Unlike Bersling, Schnierer was initially a reluctant soldier, unhappy to be amongst the company of peddlers (*Scherenschleifern*) and woodcutters (*Holzscheiben*) from the countryside who were usually the men marked out for service. His tent-mates, a group of 8-10 soldiers who acted as a small social group overseen by a senior common soldier, were rural labourers with behaviours the suburban barber viewed with disdain.[44]

However, on swearing his commitment to the monarch and donning the uniform of the regiment just after the Deutschmeister field battalions departed for the Bavaria in early April 1809, Schnierer seems to have accepted the lot of the common soldier and the duty he was to carry out. Initially, the young conscript was stationed in one of the Deutschmeister's billets (*Caserne*) in Wiener Neustadt, a military town home to the Theresian Military Academy (*Theresianische Militärakademie*). The billets in Wiener Neustadt were one of a few located in the urban centres of Lower Austria, the others were situated in Laxemberg, Hainburg an der Donau and next to the Grain Market in Vienna.[45] It was there in the barracks next to the Grain Market that Schnierer and the depot companies were sent to once the war with France was underway. The billets just outside the walls of the city were along the main southern route out of Vienna, *Mariahilferstraße*, which was only a 10-minute walk from the Schnierer's home, and on hearing the news he was to move there the young man rejoiced, knowing he would be able to see his family and friends.

Whilst stationed in Vienna during the early weeks of April 1809, the young Schnierer worked as a clerk for a sergeant in one of the depot companies training the stream of conscripts called up to replace Deutschmeister's initial losses. When not on guard duty, or working as a company clerk, Schnierer tells us he and the Viennese in the regiment, supported by the money of their parents, sang, and laughed in the guest houses of the suburbs, no doubt enjoying their position as soldiers in a city eagerly anticipating victory over France. That these men's wages were supplemented by the money of their parents, indicates military service in the regular army was now impinging upon the lives of the emperor's wealthier subjects. And as the war in Bavaria turned for the worst with Deutschmeister suffering almost 1,700 casualties, Schnierer tells us that although he could have sat out the conflict, helping with the monthly training of replacements, he did not want to be seen by

---

42   Schnierer, *Aus der Franzosenzeit*, p.6.

43   Rothenberg, *Napoleon's Great Adversary*, p.153. For details on how this change was apologetically communicated see the newspaper, *Vaterländische Blätter für den Österreichischen Kaiserstaat*, Nr. 4, 20 May 1808, pp.25-26.

44   For the remaining paragraph detailing Schnierer's account see *Aus der Franzosenzeit*, pp.7-11.

45   ÖStA, KA, Pers, MLST I Infanterie IR 4 349 Musterlisten (1. Teil), 1806, fol., *Muster Tabella*.

his returning comrades as a coward, and as 'a man who sat it out by the fire'. Schnierer was farewelled by the tears and well wishes of his family and left with the rest of the reservists for the regiment in the last weeks of April. Almost immediately after reaching the Bavarian town of Altöttin, Schnierer was assigned to Captain Mehlführer's company, taking part in the counterattack against the French at Neumarkt on 24 April 1809.[46]

Schnierer's account of the early life he led as a conscript elucidates the proximity of soldiers and civilians, and the peacetime similarities between native-born men in uniform and those not. This same proximity and lived experiences are reiterated in the memoir of the gunner Bersling. Though Bersling got his wish to be made a soldier in 1791 he was not removed from Gitschin to live the life of a military man in Prague, and nor could he forget the trade of his father.[47] The military system of the Monarchy, which took men identified as surplus to local manor economies, also provided these same men as workers to provincial and state economies when they were needed.[48] Soldiers would work as agricultural labourers, road builders, artisans and assist in the construction of state projects, such as the building of forts. On Sundays, these furloughed men were ordered to wear their uniform to internalise service as a normal part of the community they lived and worked in.[49]

This oscillation between the life of a soldier and civilian employment was played out in the first two years of Bersling's time as part of the garrison in Prague, which he described as active but financially limited. In the city the new conscript practiced his trade in part-time employment (*Nebenerwerb*), working as a tailor.[50] This not only provided Bersling with extra pay, but as the Habsburg military administrators had envisioned, part-time employment also reduced the need of the state to provide the soldier with a living allowance. Thus, the army was only required to pay soldiers a basic wage, which failed to meet inflation and had been stagnant since the beginning of the eighteenth-century. The account of Bersling's time in Prague is the experience of almost all the conscripts sourced from the Austro-Bohemian lands, where furlough during peacetime placed soldiers within communities they had previous connections to through either trade, proximity, language or kin. It was not until Bersling's artillery regiment was deployed to the Austrian Netherlands in 1793, when it left its barracks and civilian lodgings, that the young man felt 'the actual life of a soldier started, and peaceful pursuits ended for a long time'.[51]

What we can garner from these first-hand accounts, detailing the early experiences of a conscript's military service, is that the divide between the soldier and the potential soldier was blurred thanks to the inescapable nature of the Habsburg military system and the prevalence of the army in the towns and villages throughout the Monarchy. In Kanitz, Moravia, it was the efficiency of the Habsburg military administration and the pervasiveness of cantonal recruitment that made soldiering a visible occurrence, infiltrating the

---

46   ÖStA, KA Pers, MLST I Infanterie IR 4 398 Standestabellen, 1809.01-1809.06, fol., *April: Mehlführer 2nd company*. Johann Schnerer was one of 18 men assigned to Mehlführer from the Reserve Division to replace the 94 casualties the Second Company had sustained in the first two weeks of the campaign.

47   Bersling, *Der Böhmische Veteran*, p.10.

48   Hochedlinger, 'The Habsburg Monarchy', pp.87-88.

49   Hochedlinger, 'The Habsburg Monarchy', pp.87-88.

50   Bersling, *Der Böhmische Veteran*, p.11.

51   Bersling, *Der Böhmische Veteran*, p.11.

villages and towns of the Brunn district, a region and locality created specifically for the Regiment Loudon. In 1788 the town of Gitschin served as an assembly hub for the regiments based in the northern parts of Bohemia before they marched off to fight along the Monarchy's southern border.[52] There in the central marketplace of the town Bersling would have seen soldiers gathered in their companies, their packs strewn on the cobblestone floor and muskets propped up against one another as the uniformed men awaited the order to march. Inhabitants of the town would have carried on as normal around them, or stared out of their balconies down at the milling soldiers who no doubt used their time to club coins together so their corporal could buy last minute comforts for his section. A scene which, as Joseph intended, fostered within Bersling a desire to don the uniform of his monarch.

The increased prevalence of conscription and its alteration of society did not abate as the war with Revolutionary France turned into a struggle to end French imperial power in Europe. Thanks to the duration of the conflict and the ever-growing size of the Monarchy's army, Schnierer's recruitment into the reserve cadre of Regiment Deutschmeister was part of the enlargement of the line regiments across the army in 1808. The process of training reservists who lived as civilians during times of peace to replace those who would fall in the initial stages of a campaign, not only enlarged the military system of the Monarchy, but also increased its visibility and made Sundays a day dedicated to the act of soldiering. The 1808 reforms of Archduke Charles and his advisor Matthias von Fassbender introducing the reserve battalions, enabled men to come to terms with soldiering long before they joined the regiments proper, quickening their transition into frontline soldiers. Unlike today where the mobilisation of fighting men for war is a private and unseen event, where troops move from peacetime barracks to campaign staging points without meeting civilians, the commotion, movement, and spectacle that was the assembly of Habsburg regiments comprised of predominantly local born men would have had a carnival feel to it. Indeed, as Bersling tells us the town of Gitschin was 'no less a scene of military exercise than Prague or Vienna'.[53]

By looking at the early stages of Habsburg conscript's military experiences, the boundary between civilian life and soldiering is shown to be porous and constantly in flux. These men lived in an environment where the physical spaces often associated with civic life, like the town square of Gitschin, the manor of Kanitz, the Grain Market, guest houses and the promenades of Vienna, were also sites for the soldier. This proximity of space did not end when these men were ensconced within the military culture of their regiment, becoming long-term soldiers off on campaign. The soldier also served an important function at home, visually promoting the centrality of the dynasty to its subjects in public spaces, acting as a symbol of authority to be seen by all.

The Common Soldier as a Symbol of Dynastic Power and Local Loyalty

During the Revolutionary and Napoleonic Wars, the soldiers of the Habsburg Monarchy served a double function. Their primary role was to fight on the battlefields of Europe, but,

---

52   Bersling, *Der Böhmische Veteran*, p.9.
53   Bersling, *Der Böhmische Veteran*, p.9.

as the memoirs of Habsburg soldiers reveal, uniformed men were also a significant tool used to project the power and legitimacy of the monarch as part of imperial civic ceremonies.[54] Significantly, the proliferation of soldiers in displays of popular patriotism coincided with a wartime society where greater numbers of men were in service. The need to assert the importance of soldiering in a society exposed to the stresses and strains of war witnessed a more visible inclusion of uniformed men in dynastic culture and regional celebrations. This furthered the prevalence of the army in civic spaces and the connections civilians had with the sphere of the military.

At the very beginning of the war with France soldiers in the Monarchy played an important part in asserting the legitimacy of the dynasty, during time when Monarchianism was openly challenged. One of the first military functions the young Bersling performed was as an artilleryman in the honour guard for the crowning of the 24-year-old Francis as king of Bohemia in 1792. During the ceremony, Bersling's artillery battery was set up in the Royal Garden (*königlichen Garten*) behind St Vitus in Prague. There an immense mass of people was spread far and wide and cheered loudly as the roar of the cannon greeted the new King as he '…rushed from the cathedral'.[55] It was not the first coronation the people of Prague and the garrison had participated in that decade. Only a year before, the 21-year-old cadet, Laurenz Zagitzeck, stationed in Prague with the grenadier companies of Infantry Regiment D'Alton Nr.15, took part in the coronation of Leopold II and witnessed 'many related curiosities'.[56] The grenadiers of D'Alton, large men in their bearskin hats, with waxed moustaches and pristine white uniforms, some conscripted from north Bohemia, would have been a resplendent sight amongst the throng of poorly paid urban artisans, house servants and travelling peasants who tried to glimpse the new king through the ranks of the soldiers.

In both coronations the soldiers provided a spectacle of authority that showcased the monopoly the king had on violence. The assertion of said monopoly through the presence of soldiers was also an important counter-revolutionary symbol during a time when France advocated citizens had the right to carry out violent acts on behalf of the state. Whilst soldiers of the Monarchy represented the king's power, the inclusion of Bohemians from the garrison symbolised the local regions subjugation to him. The presence of this supranational, imperial force at the King of Bohemia's coronation, with recognised regional elements, served to link local regional loyalties to the dynasty.

The daybook of the officer Marcus Hibler, who in 1796 joined Infantry Regiment Stain Nr.50, documents the importance of the military as a symbol of dynastic authority in a composite monarchy where local traditions and legal structures had to be respected.[57] Throughout the war Hibler relates how each of the local regiments garrisoned in the Catholic lands of the Austrian provinces participated in religious-civic ceremonies, providing a

---

54   Bernhard R. Kroener, '"Des Königs Rock". Das Offizierkorps in Frankreich, Österreich und Preußen im 18. Jahrhundert—Werkzeug sozialer Militarisierung oder Symbol gesellschaftlicher Integration?' in P. Baumgart, B. R. Kroener, and H. Stübig (eds), *Die Preußische Armee. Zwischen Ancien Regime und Reichsgründung* (Paderborn: Schoeningh Ferdinand GmbH, 2008), pp.72-95.

55   Bersling, *Der Böhmische Veteran*, p.15.

56   ÖStA, KA, NL, 682 (B) Zagitzeck, fol. 1, *Das Bemerkenswerte meines Lebens, meiner Familie zum Andenken gewidmet, 1840*, p.3.

57   ÖStA, KA, NL, 1143:2 (B), Hibler, fol. 1, *Journal: nebst einigen gemachten Anmerkungen mit anfang des Jahres 1796 bis Ende des Jahres 1837*.

dual link that worked to bind the periphery to the centre and vice versa. Hibler, an ensign (*Fähnrich*) in 1797, recounts the celebration of the emperor Francis' name day in the town of Linz on 4 October. As part of the celebration the companies of the third battalion paraded around the central square accompanied by the city's town guard (*Stadtgardisten*), whose role in the parade was to ceremonially represent the power of the region.[58] Making up the common soldiers of the third battalion was a significant portion of men born in the villages surrounding Linz in the district of Mühlviertel.[59] This district was one of the four quarters of Upper Austria, one which the cantonal system of Joseph II had assigned to the Regiment Stain. Hibler himself mentions the regiment had been stationed in Linz since 1781, and as he marched around the town square behind the files of his platoon, the unit was as much a part of the town's fabric as the traditional town guard.[60]

The celebration of the Monarchy using the name day of the emperor, one that included the local regiment, connected two of the most important pillars the Emperor Francis relied upon to secure his political status in the lands of Austria and Bohemia. As Richard Evans has shown, the standing army and the baroque Catholic faith of the late eighteenth century was one of the fundamental tools with which the early modern Habsburg monarch was able to cement his authority over the myriad of contradictory and convoluted systems of power that made up each kingdom and duchy.[61] What Hibler's account attests to is this power projection and the use of the army was also an important part of wartime culture, where the legitimacy of Monarchianism and primacy of faith was challenged by the political and cultural forces emanating out of France.

In Vienna the *Wiener Zeitung* sighted the day as an important event where 'in every one of the provincial towns there were solemn processions and joyous festivals' calling on God to preserve the emperor.[62] For Linz the name day was significant for three reasons: it asserted the primacy of the monarch to the local population, the influence of the Catholic faith in a province which had been subjected to the full force of the counter-reformation in the preceding century, and it gave a chance for the city to showcase its loyalty during a period of unprecedented European turmoil.[63] The inclusion of the Regiment Stain marked

---

58 ÖStA, KA, NL, 1143:2 (B) Hibler, fol. 1, *Journal*, p.25.

59 ÖStA, KA, Pers, MLST II Infanterie IR 50 10.507 1797, fol., *Monat Tabella October 1797, Der K. K. Feldzeugmeister Graf Stainischen Infanterie Regiments Reserve Division*. The *Stadestabellen* lists the total number of common soldiers in the three companies garrisoned at Linz and who would have taken part in the parade as 371. Of the soldiers, 133 were listed as local conscripts. Most soldiers were Galiziens (171), conscripted in the preceding months to replace the losses in Italy. Galiziens provided a source of men whose enforced military service did not impact the rural economy of Upper Austria. A total of 644 common soldiers were part of the battalion; however, 273 were not fully trained. These men represented the newest conscripts yet to be assigned to a company in the regiment.

60 ÖStA, KA, NL, 1143:2 (B) Hibler, fol. 1, *Journal*, p.24.

61 Robert J. W. Evans, *Austria, Hungary, and the Habsburgs: Central Europe c.1683-1867* (Oxford: Oxford University Press, 2006), p.18; Ibid., *The Making of the Habsburg Monarchy, 1550-1700* (Oxford: Oxford University Press 1979), p.169; Harm Klueting, 'The Catholic Enlightenment in Austria or the Catholic Lands', in Ulrich L. Lehner and Michael O'Neil (eds), *A Companion to the Catholic Enlightenment in Europe* (Leiden: Brill, 2010), pp.127-165.

62 'Inländische Begebenheiten', *Wiener Zeitung*, No.11, October 1797, p.3021.

63 Peter Thaler, 'Peasants and Swedes: The Making of a Habsburg Nightmare in Early Modern Austria', *Social History*, Vol 42, No.2 (2017), pp.205-232.

the monarch's presence in Linz, but it also showcased the town and Upper Austria's commitment to him. Indeed, as many of the soldiers present in the parade were men of the area, the regiment proved that the inhabitants not only gave their blessings on the emperor's name day, as the *Wiener Zeitung* reported, but were also 'faithful subjects' (*getreuen untertanen*).[64]

The links the Regiment Stain had to the region were affirmed in a public baptism of the third battalion's *Ordinärfahne* three weeks after the celebration of the emperor's name day. The banner's godparents, Countess Althann (Althaim), a noblewoman of Linz, and the regiment's second in command, lieutenant-colonel (*Obrist-Lieutenant*) Caraccioli, witnessed the flag, bearing the double headed eagle of the Monarchy on a yellow background, as it was:

> [B]rought to a tent pitched in the square of the town for the sacred ritual, where nails were hammered (attaching the banner to the pole) in accordance with the order and regulations. Each staff officer nailed in three, the remaining officers one each, as did a sergeant major (*Feldwebel*) and three common soldiers. After this, the flags of the major (*Oberstwachtmeister*) von Schönthall were accompanied by the banner with a short form of address. It was then handed to the Auditor before the officer corps escorted the priest to the tent where the blessing was given.[65]

The presence of the countess, a woman whose paternal family holding in Upper and Lower Austria was significant, and whose husband's family was just as influential in the region, represented the regiment's affiliation to the local authorities, and its central position in the society and culture of Linz and its surrounds. The countess as a godparent to the *Ordinärfahne,* representing the battalion, was to advocate for the military body in the community it inhabited. Moreover, Countess Althann provided links not only to the authorities of the area, but also represented to subjects of those authorities that the institution of the regiment was legitimate and by extension so was military service. The solemn ceremony, which combined public displays of military culture, baroque Catholicism and local symbols of authority was, like the feast day for the Emperor Francis, a public act used to legitimise the Monarchy, link local particularisms to it and assert the importance of the army in the region to its inhabitants.

The prevalence of soldiers in displays of dynastic power was a consequence of the policies and court of Francis' uncle Joseph II, who spent his whole reign, and a significant part of his mother's, working to create a society that understood its role in supporting a massive standing army. Instead of the ornate baroque Spanish court of Maria Theresia, Joseph introduce an austere court where he took to wearing the uniform of an Austrian general and styled himself as a military man first and foremost.[66] This, however, was not a sharp break

---

64   'Inländische Begebenheiten', *Wiener Zeitung,* No.11, October 1797, p.3021.
65   ÖStA, KA, NL, 1143:2 (B) Hibler, fol. 1, *Journal,* p.25. The Countess Althaim (Althann) is most likely Maria Franziska Eleonore von Thürheim whose family seat was Schloss Hagenberg, a manor in the Mühlviertel distrcit that passed to the Althann family after she married Count Michael Max Althann. Their four children were all born in Linz between 1798 and 1808, indicating her presence in the city at this time. The Thürheim family were one of the oldest lines in Upper Austria, with 15 estates in the province.
66   Timothy C. W. Blanning, *Joseph II,* pp.125-131.

from the policies of his mother, who played an important role in professionalising the officer corps, opening it up to the middle-class and positioning military honour as a right that was earnt through service and not inherited through birth.[67] The empress also permitted the wearing of military uniforms at court, attaching significant socio-political capital to the wearer. As Hibler, Bersling and Zagitzeck reveal, the descendants of these two rulers continued the tradition of placing soldiers in civic spaces to assert the symbiotic relationship between society, dynasty, and the Monarchy's military. The inclusion of soldiers in public imperial celebrations on the periphery that were used to mark the importance of the dynasty was a way in which conscription in local areas could be internalised as legitimate. During times of war, in a state governed by layers of interrelated authorities, there was nothing more that branded military service as a valid part of life then representing it as both a part of the local area's culture, and the region's recognition of the dynasty's supreme authority.

The Soldier, the Subject, and the Sympathiser

An argument on the prevalence of the military in Habsburg society during this period, and the porous nature between the two cannot conclude without documenting the interactions the fighting men of the Monarchy had with civilians. Using the reflections of these men it is possible to gauge the relationship between soldiers of the Habsburg Monarchy and its subjects by focusing on the way in which they wrote about these encounters. Subaltern officers with company responsibilities socialised with the wealthy and ennobled as befitting their status either as nobles themselves or men of the monarch, whilst common soldiers relied upon the goodwill of the local population to ease the burden of military service. The accounts of the soldiers themselves reveal the proximity they had with locals, the prevalence of combatants in Austria and Bohemia, and the violence these men were unafraid to mete out to civilians of a foreign land.

During times of war the Habsburg soldier was never totally removed from the society they defended. Unlike the French, who campaigned almost exclusively in foreign lands, soldiers of the Habsburg Monarchy found themselves operating in the crownlands of the dynasty, or in the *Reich* where the locals they encountered were subjects of their emperor. These interactions do not carry the mutual dislike described by Jean-Paul Bertaud's analysis of the army of the French Revolution.[68] Instead, they are narrated with a sense of solidarity, shared between those struggling through the turbulence of the war. One example is provided by the young Schnierer, who after his participation in the battle of Neumarkt was forced to wearily retreat into Austria. A moral sapping journey seeing Schnierer and his regiment trudging along tracks 'covered with troops, soaked and full of deep faeces…until the dark night covered the earth'.[69]

---

67   Michael Hochedlinger, 'Mars Ennobled the Ascent of the Military and the Creation of a Military Nobility in Mid-Eighteenth-Century Austria', *German History*, Vol.17, No.2 (1999), pp.141-176.

68   Jean-Paul Bertaud (trans. R.R. Palmer), *The Army of the French Revolution* (Princeton: Princeton University Press, 1988), pp.291-300.

69   Schnierer, *Aus der Franzosenzeit*, p.11.

Arriving into a camp located along a woodland edge near Haag am Hausruck in Upper Austria after a day where 'the sky had still not exhausted, pouring like a cool shower [*Tropfbad*] over us', wearing shoes bought by his parents in place of his water damaged military issued ones, Schnierer left his regiment with a companion in the hope of finding a cobbler in the village or 'a pretext for a few hours under a covered shelter'.[70] Instead of finding a cobbler Schnierer describes approaching the house of a peasant family where he 'succeeded in finding real shelter with the good people, where the full kettles smoked in the kitchen'. Accompanied by his companion the young soldier 'crouched in the same little corner [as the kettles] and deliciously dined on tripe soup [*Flecksuppe*]'. There in the room of 'gold-tilled humanity' Schnierer remarks both soldiers were 'very happy and well-mannered' before being led to a hayloft to sleep. The next day, awoken by the call to march by the drums of the regiment, Schnierer hurriedly left the hayloft with his companion grateful for the generosity of his hosts, still wearing the shoes purchased by his parents.[71] This is a scene of Biedermeier sensibilities, but it does communicate the proximity civilians had to soldiers on campaign, and attests to a knowledge they had of the effects of war on the men who would later return to these communities at its conclusion.

The sick, wounded, imprisoned, and dying were also cared for by the local inhabitants of Austria as the armies of the Monarchy campaigned within the region. In the last months of the 1809 campaign the ensign Karl August Varnhagen, a 24-year-old Prussian volunteer with Infantry Regiment Vogelsang Nr.47 wounded at the battle of Wagram, describes the interactions Habsburg troops had with the inhabitants of Zistersdorf in Lower Austria.[72] His reflections published some 35 years after the war notes the importance of the care the Austrian peasants gave in reviving the soldier's spirits, treating their wounds, and honouring the dead. The treatment of the soldiers and officers in Zistersdorf, which had been turned into a military hospital, was overseen by the local magistrate, who spread the wounded throughout the village in the houses and cellars of the inhabitants. The young ensign was treated by the village doctor, entertained by the magistrate's family and was loaned books which he read in the garden of the house he stayed in. The spiritual needs of the wounded were met by Zistersdorf's parish priest in the cramped confines of the cellars where they died. It was then the task of the local peasant to bury their bodies in unmarked graves. When French light cavalry approached the village it was the magistrate who helped some officers escape, and he later acted as a mediator between the soldiers of France and their Habsburg prisoners.[73] After being captured and giving his *parole d'honneur*, Varnhagen stayed in Vienna where he describes a city full of young women 'a little proud of the accompaniment of their Austrian officer[s]' and who made great shows of their attachment to those in the uniform of the Emperor Francis right in front of their French chaperones.[74] Male Viennese locals also took great pride in associating with captured officers,

---

70   Schnierer, *Aus der Franzosenzeit*, p.11.
71   Schnierer, *Aus der Franzosenzeit*, p.13.
72   Karl August Varnhagen von Ense, *Denkwürdigkeiten des eignen Lebens* (Leipzig: F. A. Brockhaus, 1843), Vol.2, pp.149-165.
73   Varnhagen von Ense, *Denkwürdigkeiten*, Vol.2, pp.151-152.
74   Varnhagen von Ense, *Denkwürdigkeiten*, Vol.2, pp.151-152.

inviting them into their social circles where they overtly made it known of their loyalty in subversive rituals and clandestine gatherings.[75]

During times of peace garrisoned soldiers grew close to the townspeople they shared spaces with. Hibler recounts in his daybook of the kind generosity he was shown by the family he stayed with whilst stationed in Linz. On being assigned to the Staff (*Staab*) company in Bavaria and having to leave the town he writes the 'rich brewer, his wife and daughter treated me during my five-month stay like their own son.'[76] In 1801 Hibler reflects on being stationed in Salzburg where the 12 companies of Infantry Regiment Jordis Nr.59 and six of Stain were garrisoned two soldiers to a house owned by the locals 'who seemed so happy to see us.'[77] The amount of money the regiment brought to the local economy may have offset the difficulties of having soldiers living with Salzburg's citizens, as might have the two regiment's affiliation with the area.

The bond regiments had with local areas was evident on Regiment Deutschmeister's return to their quarters in Vienna at the end of the Fifth Coalition. In October 1809, the fusilier Schnierer describes a scene of triumphant re-entry as the regiment and its local conscripts returned home to the cheers of the city's inhabitants.[78] Alas the young man was sick and 'motionless in the cart and with no other feelings than those of my suffering' as the regiment marched from Polna in Moravia where it had remained after the ceasefire in mid-July. Unable to greet the residents of the city and the families who embraced those able to march with 'the proud attitude of a war-torn warrior', Schnierer was one of the hundreds of soldiers in the regiment who had fallen sick to fatigue, illness, wounds, and malnourishment in the months of August and September.[79]

Regimental affiliation, social standing and the uniform of the emperor did not always guarantee smooth relations between subjects, civilians, and soldiers. Hibler angrily notes after being sent to Linz to recover from wounds in June 1800, 'it infuriated me infinitely that in a city where the regiment had been garrisoning for about 20 years, I was denied accommodation for two or three days.'[80] Later during Regiment Stain's actions in Switzerland the young officer was placed under house arrest for assaulting a mayor who failed to recognise the man's credit.[81] Sometimes, troops of the emperor were turned on his own subjects as the memoir of the cavalry officer Karl Johann von Grueber attests to. His participation in the suppression of bread riots in Vienna in 1804, where he and his section charged down the *Mariahilferstraße* using the flats of the sabres to bloody the heads of the looters, paints a vivid picture of men in the military eager to use violence on civilians.[82] However, Grueber's account is littered with friendly and cordial relationships with the emperor's subjects he

75   Varnhagen von Ense, *Denkwürdigkeiten*, Vol.2, pp.151-152.
76   ÖStA, KA, NL, 1143:2 (B) Hibler, fol. 1, *Journal*, p.8.
77   ÖStA, KA, NL, 1143:2 (B) Hibler, fol. 1, *Journal*, p.40.
78   Schnierer, *Aus der Franzosenzeit*, pp.25-26.
79   Schnierer, *Aus der Franzosenzeit*, p.26.
80   ÖStA, KA, NL, 1143:2 (B) Hibler, fol., 1, *Journal*, p.28.
81   ÖStA, KA, NL, 1143:2 (B) Hibler, fol., 1, *Journal*, p.19
82   Karl Johann Grueber, *Lebenserinnerungen Eines Reiteroffiziers Vor Hundert Jahren* (Vienna: S.W. Seidel & Sohn, 1906), p.37: For information on the riots of 1804 see Karl A. Roider, Jr. 'Austria's Road to Austerlitz,' in Kinley Brauer and William E. Wright (eds), *Austria in the Age of the French Revolution* (Minneapolis: Centre for Austrian Studies, 1990), pp.11-24, in particular p.13.

encountered, suggesting that he and his men were only too willing to harm those that threatened the equilibrium of their emperor's state, and not because they policed their corporate identity as soldiers by inflicting harm on civilians.[83]

If Grueber was prepared to harm those within the Monarchy who challenged the power of the emperor, civilians from outside the borders of the Monarchy, or who had once been subjects of the Emperor Francis, were open to violent retaliatory killings throughout the war. This was especially so with those who had been seen to have helped the French, or resisted the authority of the Emperor Francis. One corporal in Regiment Deutschmeister attests to the violence inflicted on civilians by men of the army after the capture of the Austrian Netherlands city of Liege in April 1793. There soldiers were allowed to loot the city for seven hours, many taking this time to kill the inhabitants who had fired on the men as they stormed the city's gates. This, of course led to violent animosity between French speaking locals and the German soldiers who were ordered leave their weapons loaded and to venture out at night with lights.[84] A year later at Namur, inhabitants of the city who attempted to help the French were 'slaughtered' by Habsburg soldiers perplexed at the decisions and ineptitude of their new enemy.[85]

In Switzerland, the Second Lieutenant Johann Edler Innerhofer, of the Infantry Regiment Kaiser Franz II Nr.1, was forced to prevent his own men from murdering the mayor of Bad Ragaz's family after his regiment stormed the town in the early stages of the Second Coalition. It was only after men from Innerhofer's company began bayoneting the inhabitants who had apparently fired on them that the mayor sank to his knees 'to save and beg for his families protection from death.'[86] Innerhofer's honour permitted him to ward off the advances of his men, but as the young man attests in his day book it did help that his actions gained 'the sincerest thanks of the three most gracious daughter.'[87] During the Monarchy's military campaign in Italy in 1809 Hibler, now serving as a light infantry captain, recounts in his diary his kidnapping by deserting Grenzers during the Battle of Piave in April. There a section of the Croatian skirmishers, led by an experienced corporal, threatened him with death for attempting to curtail their violent and drunken pillaging of the villages north of the present-day Lake Santa Croce in what was once the Monarchy's province of South Tyrol.[88] Looting and murder was also commonplace in the later years of the war, especially during the invasion of Saxony in 1813, where poorly equipped and fed troops took whatever they could from the peasant farms along the border with Bohemia.[89] The occupation of France in 1815 was also violent, with soldiers from the elite *Jäger* battalions wiping out whole villages, to the shame of some, in response to attacks on messengers by unknown vigilantes.[90]

83   Grueber, *Lebenserinnerungen*, pp.26 and 57.
84   Johann Friedrich Löffler, *Der alte Sergeant. Leben des Schlesiers Johann Friedrich Löffler. Ein Beitrag zur Geschichte der Zeitgenossen* (Graz: Barth und Comp, 1836), pp.89-90.
85   ÖStA, KA, NL, 682 (B), Zagitzeck von Kehlfeld, fol., *Das Bemerkenswerte meines Leben*, p.17.
86   ÖStA, KA, NL, 905 (B) Innerhofer von Innhof, fol., *Kriegstagebuch*.
87   ÖStA, KA, NL, 905 (B) Innerhofer.
88   ÖStA, KA, NL, 1143:2 (B) Hibler, fol. 4, *Journal*, p.20.
89   ÖStA, KA, NL, 682 (B), Zagitzeck, fol., *Das Bemerkenswerte meines Leben*, Part 2, p.30.
90   Schnierer, *Aus der Franzosenzeit*, pp.79-80.

It is clear then when focusing on the writings of the Habsburg soldier that these men valued the interactions they had with the subjects who lived in the areas they were garrisoned in and were conscripted from. All knew they relied on local civilians to ease the burdens of military service when they were on campaign. Conversely, subjects of the Emperor Francis sometimes viewed soldiers of the Monarchy as symbols of popular patriotism, whilst rural peasants and local authorities devoted their scarce resources to care for the wounded, the dead, and the dying. This mutual respect did not transcend the borders of the Habsburg Monarchy however, where non-combatants were subjected to reprisals killings and violent looting that officers were sometimes unable to prevent. Such incidents indicate Habsburg soldiers understood the need for healthy civilian-military relations in the areas directly under the control of the Emperor Francis, just as much as they indicate soldiers cared very little for civilians in enemy country.

Conclusion

The experiences of soldiers in the service of the dynasty show us that war with France did not lead to the separation of the military from the rest of society. The Habsburg army relied upon a symbiotic relationship with the rural structures, traditions, and economic particu-larisms of the Austro-Bohemian lands. This relationship and the process of transforming society to meet the needs of the army only increased as the war with France progressed. The canton system altered the geography of the Monarchy, extended the influence of the army in civilian spaces, and provided it with a readily available source of recruits who lived as the subjects of their noble landowning lords with the understanding that fighting in the army of the Monarchy was a real possibility. Yet when these men were conscripted they did not disappear into the sphere of the military, even if they were aware that they were leaving their communities and previous lives behind.

The military experiences of the Habsburg common soldier and subaltern officers also reveal the extent to which men in uniform, representing the monarch and his monopoly on violence, were constantly visible in the civil spaces of Austria, Bohemia and Moravia, always interacting with those not in uniform both as defenders of the state and men of the area. Indeed, the soldier, specifically the native-born conscript, was a constant sight in society. He was billeted on the population, generally from the community he lived in as a civilian, campaigned within the borders of the Monarchy and relied upon the good will of the locals to ease the terrible burden of war. Generally, soldiers positively narrated their interactions with civilians from within the borders of the Monarchy and from their own perspective such relations did not lead to confrontation – even if individual disagreements led to personal grudges.

In the provinces of the Austro-Bohemian lands the regiment served as an institution that allowed the intersection of identities where local particularism, traditions and authorities of an area were aligned with the dynasty's projection of power and legitimacy. In turn, these institutions dominated the social, cultural, and economic life of the regions they were based in, internalising military service for those young men destined for the army and exposing it to those who were not. As the reflections of Habsburg soldiers attest, the extraordinary constrictions of war and the preparations for it created an environment where the physical and abstract boundaries between civilians, subjects and soldiers were porous, always shifting and never delineated.

Further Reading

Berkovich, Ilya, *Motivation in War: The Experience of Common Soldiers in Old-Regime Europe* (Cambridge: Cambridge University Press, 2017).

Boerke, Arthur M., 'Conscription in the Habsburg Empire to 1815,' in Donald Stoker, Frederick C. Schneid and Harold D. Blanton (eds), *Conscription in the Napoleonic Era: A Revolution in Military Affairs?* (Abingdon: Routledge, 2008), pp.66-83.

Brauer, Kinley and William E. Wright (eds), *Austria in the Age of the French Revolution* (Minneapolis: Centre for Austrian Studies, 1990).

Cole, Laurence, *Military Culture and Popular Patriotism in Late Imperial Austria* (Oxford: Oxford University Press, 2014)

Dickson, Peter G.M., *Finance and Government under Maria Theresia 1740-1780* (Oxford: Oxford University Press, 1987).

Duffy, Christopher, *Instrument of War: The Austrian Army in the Seven Years War* (Michigan: The Emperor's Press, 2001).

Duffy, Christopher, *Military Experience in the Age of Reason* (London: Routledge and Kegal Paul, 1987).

Eysturlid, Lee, *Formative Influences, Theories and Campaigns of the Archduke Carl of Austria* (Westport, CT: Praeger, 1999).

Godsey, William D., *The Sinews of Habsburg Power: Lower Austria in a Fiscal-Military State 1650–1820* (Oxford: Oxford University Press, 2018).

Hochedlinger, Michael, *Austria's Wars of Emergence, 1683-1797* (London: Routledge, 2003).

Kuijpers, Erika, Cornelis Van Der Haven (eds), *Battlefield Emotions 1500-1800: Practices, Experience, Imagination* (Basingstoke: Palgrave Macmillan, 2016).

Planert, Ute, *Der Mythos vom Befreiungskrieg. Frankreichs Kriege und der deutsche Süden: Alltag – Wahrnehmung – Deutung 1792-1841* (Paderborn: Brill, 2007).

Rothenberg, Gunther E. *Napoleon's Great Adversary: Archduke Charles and the Austrian Army 1792-1814* (Staplehurst: Spellmount, 1995).

Wilson, Peter H., '"Mercenary" Contracts as Fiscal-Military Instruments', in Svante Norrhem and Erik Thomson (eds), *Subsidies, Diplomacy, and State Formation in Europe, 1494-1789* (Lund: Lund University Press, 2020), pp.68-92.

14

A Crisis of Battle? On Decisiveness in the Wars of Frederick the Great

Alexander Querrengässer

> 'More glory cannot be won, but more decisive, final consequences we still hope to hear, and languish for farther letters from the Prussian army.'
>
> William Pitt the Elder about the Prussian victory at Zorndorf[1]

At his castle in Rheinsberg, Prince Heinrich of Prussia, younger brother of Frederick the Great, established a small room with portraits of military leaders of the early modern period, admired by him and sometimes underrated by his brother.[2] One of them was *Generalfeldmarschall* Leopold von Anhalt-Dessau, a distinguished soldier under Frederick's father, but never really trusted and often sidelined by the great King himself. However, on 15 December 1745 Leopold led a Prussian army to a crushing victory over Saxon forces at the battle of Kesselsdorf, on the heights surrounding the Saxon capital and major fortress of Dresden. The victory was followed by the fall of the city, the retreat of the remaining Saxo-Austrian forces over the border into Bohemia; thereafter, the Treaty of Dresden, signed by Saxony and Austria, ending the Second Silesian War (1744-1745). Despite this remarkable achievement, Kesselsdorf is mainly forgotten and has never been listed in a book of the great battles of world history.[3] While later Saxon historians understandably had few interests in this period of decline – nevertheless, until recently the only major monograph on Kesselsdorf was published in 1912 by Saxon archivist Arthur Brabant – in Prussia it was quickly forgotten, because the history of the Silesian Wars

---

1   Quote in Jeremy Black, *Pitt the Elder. The Great Commoner. Revised Edition* (Stroud: Sutton Publishing, 1999), p.159.
2   Jürgen Luh, *Heinrichs Heroen. Die Feldherrengalerie des Prinzen Heinrich im Schloss Rheinsberg* (Karwe: Edition Rieger, 2007), pp.16-22, 36-38.
3   So also in the probably most famous compilation, which especially asks for the decisive character of battles: Russel Weigley, *The Age of Battle. The Quest for Decisive Warfare from Breitenfeld to Waterloo* (Bloomington: Indiana University, Press 1991).

at first was written by its most prominent figure, Frederick II himself.[4] To Frederick, Kesselsdorf had one tremendous flaw: he did not participate in it. Instead, the decisive encounter of the war was won by one of his father's favourites, a man he never really got warm with and with whom he had a serious falling-out with during the campaign. While personally praising Leopold the day after the battle, when Frederick arrived with his army, he later sneered at him by having a map produced, which showed an old grumpy lion with a long beard – the lion being the heraldic animal of the princes of Anhalt-Dessau. Nineteenth-century historians in their reconstruction of Frederick's life and wars at first examined his personal writings and so it takes no wonder, that Kesselsdorf was never really acknowledged as what it really was: the most decisive battle fought by the Prussian army in the era of Frederick the Great.

But what really is a decisive battle? Historians carry out heated debates on the decisiveness of early modern warfare, with the majority underlining a somewhat indecisive character of seventeenth and eighteenth century battles.[5] John Lynn in his study *Battle* put it to the point by saying: 'In fact, the ancient regime provides few examples of battles that ended major wars; the presence of numerous fortified towns and the dependence on cumbersome logistics made it difficult to turn a victory into a decisive military or political success.'[6] Apart from his explanation, his definition of 'decisiveness' is interesting, as it seems that a battle, according to Lynn, has to be war-ending to be decisive. He further says: 'Frederick the Great may have exploited battle in the Seven Years' War, but he had little choice if he was to hold off the mighty alliance arrayed against him, and his battles did not lead to decision; they just bought him time.'[7]

German historian Marian Füssel in several essays also underlined the indecisive character of battles and even spoke of a 'crisis of battle'.[8] A major problem with this often-resolute discussion is that the character of decisiveness is never really defined. In fact, the critic of indecisiveness implies, that those battles did not change anything and that the military and political situation afterwards was the same as before, but such

---

4   Artur Brabant, *Kesselsdorf und Maxen. Zwei Winterschlachten bei Dresden* (Dresden: Köhler, 1912). There are a couple of essays and articles, also published in Saxon historical magazines, see Karl Theodor Winkler, 'Ein Beitrag zur Geschichte der Schlacht bei Kesselsdorf', *Archiv für Sächsische Geschichte* 9 (1871), pp.225-250; Marc Arndt, 'Vor 250 Jahren – Schlacht bei Kesselsdorf am 15.12.1745', *Sächsische Heimatblätter* 6 (1995), pp.361-365; Dietmar Bode, *Die Schlacht bei Kesselsdorf (15. Dezember 1745)* (=Militärhistorische Schriften des Arbeitskreises Sächsische Militärgeschichte e.V. Heft 3) (Dresden: self-published, 1995) is a small broschure. For the latest work see:Alexander Querengässer, *Kesselsdorf 1745. Eine Entscheidungsschlacht im 18. Jahrhundert* (=Beiträge zur Geschichte des Militärs in Sachsen 4) (Berlin: Zeughausverlag, 2020).

5   Still very influencing in this regard is Weigley, *The Age of Battles.*

6   John A. Lynn, *Battle. A History of Combat and Culture. From Ancient Greece to Modern America. Revised Edition* (New York: Westview Press, 2003), p.129.

7   Lynn, *Battle*, p.199.

8   In the respective article, Füssel also deals with other forms of 'crisis' in battle, for example the critical point of the decision. However, he concludes: 'Praxis demonstrates, that the real outcome of a battle under the structural circumstances of the period war making seldom took a decisive character.' Marian Füssel, 'Die Krise der Schlacht. Das Problem der militärischen Entscheidung im 17. und 18. Jahrhundert', in Rudolf Schlögl, Philip R. Hoffmann-Rehnitz, Eva Wiebel (ed.), *Die Krise in der Frühen Neuzeit* (=Historische Semantik 26) (Göttingen: Vandenhoeck & Rupprecht, 2016), pp.311-332.

an attempt is misleading and deeply flawed. This is most prominently pointed out by Jeremy Black, who also strongly refused the concept of indecisiveness: 'The stereotypical view of eighteenth-century "indecisiveness" is due to a failure to put eighteenth-century operations in context, and equally a failure to define "decisive".'[9] It is interesting to note, that the German term for decision – *Entscheidung* – is often used by Frederick himself in his writing on seeking battle. In his General Principals of War from 1748 he brought it to the point: 'Battles decide the fate of states. Whoever conducts war, has to cause such decisions, be it, to free himself from a miserable situation or to bring the enemy into such a situation or to fight out a struggle, which otherwise would take no end.'[10] So seeking an *Entscheidung* means seeking decisive effects through battle. This sounds rather like Napoleonic war-making, but Frederick also demands prudence. 'A reasonable man must not take any step without good reason. Still less could an army commander offer a battle without pursuing an important purpose. If he is forced into battle, he himself has made a mistake and must have the rules of an engagement being dictated to him by the enemy.'[11]

This understanding is different from Napoleonic war-making, which was based on a much broader base of resources and the ability to mobilise them – especially manpower – so that seeking battle took on much greater prominence.[12] However, short campaigns with quick decisions in battle were also central to Prussian war-making, due to the state's small economic base. Essentially, that Frederick was seeking a war-ending battle as well, but that he was never able to achieve this goal, does not mean that his battles had no decisive outcome. This approach to war was atypical for this time, leading Christopher Duffy to point out 'in the Age of Reason warfare and the military machines were managed in two ways. One was the style of Frederick the Great, and the other was followed by everyone else.'[13] Duffy means the unity of command of both army and state by Frederick as *roi-conné-table*, a role matched only by Charles XII at the beginning of the century. But in this unity was perhaps also created Frederick's aim of achieving political outcomes through military success, while other army commanders were much more prudent and did not want to risk their armies, which were difficult to replace.

Most historians – like Lynn and Füssel – seem to see decisiveness as congruent with 'war-ending'. This approach led Frank Tallett to the opinion, that except for Naseby and Mühlberg, no battle in Europe between 1492 and 1715 could be considered decisive.[14] This definition also underlies Russell Weigley's famous compilation of important battles in the Early Modern Age. This view in turn was criticized by Dennis Showalter as 'a search for the

---

9   Quoted in Jeremy Black, *European Warfare 1660 – 1815* (New Haven, London: Yale University Press, 1994), p.85.
10 Quotation after Gustav Berthold (ed.), *Die Werke Friedrichs des Großen. In deutscher Übersetzung* (Berlin: Hobbing, 1913), here Vol. VII: Antimachiavell und Testamente, p.75.
11 Quotation after Berthold (ed.), *Die Werke Friedrichs des Großen*, Vol.VII, p.75.
12 See for example Jeremy Black, *Western Warfare 1775-1882* (Bloomington, Indianapolis: Indiana University Press, 2001), pp.37-42.
13 Quoted in Christopher Duffy, *The Military Experience in the Age of Reason* (London: Routledge & Keegan Paul), p.151.
14 Frank Tallett, *War and Society in Early Modern Europe, 1495-1715* (London, New York: Routledge, 1992), p.53.

fata morgana of a decisive battle that would in a single day determine a war's outcome by destroying an enemy's army.'[15]

Such a view also appealed to German militarists in the Wilhelmian era, when all future plans for war aimed for a quick decision in one great encounter shortly after the declaration of war. The history of warfare contains very few such examples. Of course, the battles of some nineteenth-century conflicts, such as Königgrätz/Sadowa in the War of 1866, or the Austrian-Italian War of 1859, ended by Solferino, more or less fit into this definition. Yet the vast majority, for example in the American Civil War and especially of the two World Wars, do not. Even the Napoleonic battles, declared by Lynn as paradigm of this definition, do not always meet expectations. They might have ended their respective wars, especially Austerlitz and Wagram, but the peaces dictated by Napoleon could not create a stable political system, so that each peace within months was followed by the next war, which led it appear proper to see all these conflicts not as separate, but as the one unified event known to us as 'The Napoleonic Wars'. This contrasts markedly from the Wars of German Unification, where Bismarck was able either to formulate peace terms which were not regarded as humiliating (1866) or to further isolate defeated opponents (after 1871). This point also reminds us of the fact, that decisiveness cannot just be defined in terms of the military success, but that the political alterations caused by the battle have been even more – to overuse the term once more – 'decisive' to define this respective character of the battles themselves. To put it another way: battles decide nothing (apart from many thousand individual fates), but they can alter the political-military circumstances. Their decisive character emerges from what happened after the last round is fired and depends on a range of factors, first how far the victor is willing –and able – to transform success into results, but also the decisions of the defeated and how far he is willing to accept or resist the consequences of defeat.[16]

With this in mind it becomes clear, that there is a much wider definition of decisiveness apart from war-ending victories. A battle can be decisive – at least for one participant – by successfully denying an enemy's objectives, or, more plainly spoken, to ruin his plans. A battle can be decisive by turning the momentum in a war, without ending it or making it inevitable, that those defeated in battle will necessarily lose the war. Gettysburg is a prominent example, as it broke the backbone of the Confederate Army of Northern Virginia and rendered it incapable of mounting strategic invasions in the North again – Jubal Early's campaign being more a large-scale diversion. In the Second World War El Alamein can be mentioned for the campaign in North Africa, Stalingrad for the Eastern Front, or Midway for the Pacific Theatre of Operations. None of these battles decided the conflict and none of them made Axis defeat inevitable, but all are considered by historians as decisive, as they turned the favour in their respective campaign areas to the Allies.

All these aspects will be considered now for the Wars of Frederick the Great, except the case of what we might call 'Turning Points' because no examples of this type of battle exist in the three Silesian Wars or the Bavarian War of Succession. However, it is clear, that the many battles should not be considered as a useless bloodletting – this view often reflects

---

15   Quoted in Dennis Showalter, *Frederick the Great. A Military History* (Barnsley: Frontline Books, 2012), p.23.

16   Christopher Duffy has pointed out, that '[t]he connection between war and politics was clearly understood in the Age of Reason', see Duffy, *The Military Experience*, p.154.

the humanitarian personal attitudes of modern commentators, but these humanitarian concerns are not valuable for historical analysis. Counterfactual analysis can play a valuable role in discussing decisiveness. This method is still used with reluctance by historians, due to the fact that many people reduce it to the foolish assumption that if a decisive battle would have ended the other way round, the war would have, too.[17] By carefully considering counterfactual possibilities, however, we are also better able to understand the potential of battles to alter the course of events. This potential is also dependent from the political and military situation on the eve of battle.

Avoiding Defeat

The Seven Years War, for Prussia, was a defensive war fought against a coalition of the continental powers, encircling the Central European kingdom from the West (France), South (Austria), East (Russia) and North (Sweden). The first aim for many of Frederick's campaigns and battles fought in this war was not to knock any of these powers out of the conflict. He tried to do so at the beginning by capturing Saxony and invading Bohemia, but lost the initiative to do so during the siege of Prague or, at the latest, after the battle of Kolin, when he was forced to abandon Bohemia.[18]

Following this defeat, Frederick faced the first serious crisis in the war, as all three major powers now started their own offensives, the Russians invading East Prussia, the Austrians Silesia and the French, after they knocked out the Army of Observation, composed of Hanoverian and other German troops under the Duke of Cumberland, at Hastenbeck,[19] marching with one army at the direction of the fortress city of Magdeburg, where huge parts of the Prussian government had fled to, due to the vulnerability of Berlin, and a second one together with Imperial forces through Thuringia into the direction of the important crossroads at Leipzig. The allies could have smashed Frederick, but he now started to profit from the weaknesses in their alliance system. The Russians still had trouble conquering Eastern Prussia. The cost of their victory at Großjägersdorf and logistical problems forced a pause in their invasion. The Austrians waited with their offensive for the French to draw out Prussian forces of Silesia, while the French in turn slowed their progress, as they had no interest in winning the war for the Austrians.[20]

This gave Frederick vital time to block all their offensives separately. He first turned against the French-Imperial army under Prince Soubise and Saxe-Hildburghausen and was able to defeat them at the battle of Roßbach, a day's march from Leipzig. This battle is often

---

17   About this approach see Jeremy Black, *What If? Counterfactualism and the Problem of History* (London: Social Affairs Unit, 2008); *Other Pasts, Different Presents, Alternative Futures* (Bloomington: Indiana University Press, 2015).

18   About this battle see Peter Broucek, *Der Geburtstag der Monarchie. Die Schlacht bei Kolin 1757* (Vienna: Österreichischer Bundesverlag, 1982).

19   English scholarship on this battle is lacking. See Moritz Oppermann, *Die Schlacht bei Hastenbeck* (Hameln: C. W. Niemeyer, 1957); Walther Mediger, 'Hastenbeck und Zeven. Der Eintritt Hannovers in den Siebenjährigen Krieg', *Niedersächsisches Jahrbuch für Landesgeschichte* 56 (1984), pp.137–166.

20   As a history of this 'double campaign', see Christopher Duffy, *Prussia's Glory. Rossbach and Leuthen 1757* (Chicago: Emperor's Press, 2003).

reduced to a historical cornerstone, demonstrating the superiority of the Prussian army as the most effective military machine of its days, over the French, the once mighty force of the era of Louis XIV. But Roßbach was more significant. It definitely was decisive: not just because it thwarted the French attempts to march on Magdeburg and Leipzig. It came close to being – from the Prussian perspective – the knockout blow for France.[21] All this is due less to the invincibility of Frederick's small army, but to the fact that he was able to break the will of his opponents. Soubise's and Saxe-Hildburghausen's army might have been scattered and unable to continue the campaign in 1757, but there was still an even larger French force under the Duc de Richelieu marching on Magdeburg, opposed by no other forces than the fortress garrison. The Austrians, strengthened by their victory at Kolin, invaded Silesia, where they won a victory over the Prussian army at Breslau, following which the Silesian capital fell into their hands. So, despite Frederick's victory, his strategic situation was still critical. That Roßbach became more important was first due to the fact that Richelieu, without need, abandoned the march on Magdeburg. The French felt cheated by the Austrians, who delayed their invasion of Silesia until Frederick had turned against Soubise. Second, Frederick used his victory at the political table and immediately convinced the British envoy in Prussia, Mitchell, that George II should not ratify the Convention of Closter-Zeven, according to which the British would withdraw from the continent. Mitchell, in a personal meeting with the king at Merseburg on 11 November, tried to convince Frederick to follow up his victory and push the French back over the Rhine but Frederick wisely declined. According to Mitchells report:

> The King answered plainly it was impossible, that he must immediately go into Silesia to endeavour to save Schweidnitz, and, when I pressed again to this point, he answered with great warmth: "Sure, it is but just that I should take some care of my own country; what assistance have I had of any sort? You know, you have seen what I have suffered by the Hanoverian convention, and from your nation I have nothing but good words." I replied I hoped they would soon be realized, and that this act of generosity on his part of helping to drive the French out of Hanover, would forever secure to him His Majesty's friendship and the gratitude of the English nation. "Well," says he, "but, in the meantime, the Austrians will get a settlement in Silesia; will the Hanoverian troops help me to recover it?"[22]

Mitchell's report is a reminder of the possibilities that offered themselves to the victor of battle and that it was important to make the right choice in order to achieve decisive outcomes. Frederick was not going to win Britain's war, as the French were not going to win that of the Austrians. Roßbach was the battle that avoided the further intermingling of the two conflicts: the global Franco-British and the continental Austro-Prussian. Frederick sent small number of troops, which, together with British, Hanoverian and Brunswick forces,

---

21   See Alexander Querengässer (ed.), *Die Schlacht bei Roßbach* (=Beiträge zur Geschichte des Militärs in Sachsen 2) (Berlin: Zeughaus Verlag, 2017); published in English as *The Battle of Rossbach: New Perspectives on the Battle and Campaign* (Warwick: Helion, 2022).

22   Quotation after Preußische Akademie der Wissenschaften (ed), *Die politische Correspondenz Friedrichs des Großen* (Berlin: Hobbing, 1888), Vol.16, Nr. 9498, S. 15.

formed a new army under the Prince of Brunswick, who in the following years was able to successfully fend off any further attempts of the French to conquer Hanover and win a pledge for a possible peace treaty with Britain, which, in the meantime, was crushing the French colonial Empire. Brunswick in 1759 won another major victory at Minden, which, due to the prominent participation of British troops, is one of the more famous continental battles in the Anglophone world.[23] It blocked the last major attempt of French forces to overrun George II's electorate and perhaps march on to Magdeburg. Minden is a victory comparable to Roßbach, in so far as it avoided an Anglo-Prussian defeat and denied the French victory. However, the importance of Roßbach becomes even clearer if one understands that, without this Prussian victory and the following British decision to re-enter the war on the continent, there would never have been a battle of Minden.

After Roßbach Frederick then turned eastwards against the Austrians and defeated them at Leuthen, probably his most famous battle. Leuthen was not a knockout blow either, but that was due to the different interests of Fredericks opponents. For the French, Prussia was not the prime target, this honour had been reserved for Britain, but, for Austria, Silesia was the Hesperidian apple they wanted to win. Nonetheless, Frederick forced them to abandon this province, and so won an important operational victory, as he has saved both Saxony and Silesia as winter quarters. These provinces, due to their economic strength, were vital for the Prussian ability to sustain this war. Roßbach and Leuthen were also important in reversing the results of former defeats – in so far that they were turning points within their respective campaigns – namely Hastenbeck and Breslau. Both of these battles could have been decisive, as they turned the military, and in case of Hastenbeck even the political, situation strongly in favour of the French and Austrians. But they were not able to turn these successes into results and, with his two crushing victories, Frederick avoided defeat and turned the tables again. A window of opportunity, opened by the former battles, was closed by the latter.

The same is true of Zorndorf, which in a tactical sense was a narrow victory and sometimes is even considered as a stalemate. However, after the fall of Eastern Prussia all that Frederick wanted to achieve was to block the further advance of the Russians over the River Oder or prevent the capture of a strategic foothold on this river, like Küstrin. Zorndorf was decisive in preventing a further Russian advance.[24]

Lobositz, the first big encounter of the Seven Years War, is also seen as a tactical draw, even if the Austrians retreated from the battlefield, but definitely had decisive consequences. It blocked Frederick's advance into Bohemia, which he was keen to take in 1756 in the hope to knock Austria out of the conflict. But it also blocked any further attempt of Field Marshal Ulysses Browne[25] to relieve the Saxon army, besieged on the heights between the fortresses

---

23   A very valuable and detailed account of this army is Walther Mediger, *Herzog Ferdinand von Braunschweig und die alliierte Armee im Siebenjährigen Krieg (1757-1762). Für die Publikation aufgearbeitet und vollendet von Thomas Klingbiel* (Hannover: Hassarowitz, 2011).

24   A valuable overview of the Russian campaigns in this war is given by Christopher Duffy, *Russia's Military way to the West. Origins and Nature of Russian Military Power 1700 – 1800* (London: Routledge & Keegan Paul, 1981), pp.55-124.

25   Christopher Duffy, *The Wild Goose and the Eagle. A Life of Marshal von Browne 1705-1757* (London: Chatto & Windus, 1965).

of Königstein and Pirna.[26] The Saxons surrendered a few days later. While the capitulation of Struppen is often seen as a low point of Saxon political ambitions, the siege of Elector Frederick August's forces still had grave consequences. The Saxons held out longer than expected by Frederick II and so won vital time for the Austrians to prepare their forces in northern Bohemia. Thus, the siege and the often-neglected Battle of Lobositz seriously influenced the course of the war.

Saving Territory

Eighteenth-century warfare in Western and Central Europe in many cases revolved around gaining and protecting territory and Frederick's wars were no exception. For Prussia, provinces like Silesia and the electorate of Saxony were central to its capacity in war making, due to their economic strength. Prussian victories like Mollwitz, Leuthen or Burkersdorf had decisive effects, as they saved Silesia as vital economic base. The same is true of Lobositz, Torgau and Freiberg with regard to Saxony. During the Seven Years War, Prussia gained about 48 million Thaler in contributions from Saxony, about 38.4 percent of the total costs for war.[27] So every battle that helped Prussia to keep control of the electorate must be considered decisive due to its economic consequences.

On the other hand, conquests could be important for further campaigns. Thus, with Saxony and Silesia in hand, Prussia was able to mount invasions into Bohemia and threaten Prague, while on the other hand, the Austrians were able to attack Berlin after they took Silesia late in 1757. The validity of this point is further proven by the War of the Bavarian Succession 1778-1779, a short struggle, which is often regarded as a sign for a decline in Prussian military capability and a lack of vigour on part of the king due to his age.[28] While

---

26 Marcus von Salisch, *Treue Deserteure. Das kursächsische Militär und der Siebenjährige Krieg* (=Militärgeschichtliche Studien 41) (Munich: Oldenbourg, 2009).

27 See Bernhard R. Kroener, 'Die materiellen Grundlagen österreichischer und preußischer Kriegsanstrengungen 1756 – 1763', in Bernhard R. Kroener (ed.), *Europa im Zeitalter Friedrichs des Großen. Wirtschaft, Gesellschaft, Kriege* (=Beiträge zur Militärgeschichte 26), (Munich: Oldenbourg Verlag, 1989), pp.47-78, here p.76; Carl Görler: Carl: 'Studien zur Bedeutung des Siebenjährigen Krieges für Sachsen', *Neues Archiv für Sächsische Geschichte* 29 (1908), pp.118-149; Jürgen Luh, 'Sachsens Bedeutung für Preußens Kriegführung', in *Sachsen und Dresden im Siebenjährigen Krieg* (=Dresdner Hefte. Beiträge zur Kulturgeschichte 68) (Dresden: self-published by the Dresdner Geschichtsverein, 2001), pp.28-34; Katrin Keller, 'Der Siebenjährige Krieg und die Wirtschaft Kursachsens', in: *Sachsen und Dresden im Siebenjährigen Krieg* (=Dresdner Hefte 68) (Dresden: self-published by the Dresdner Geschichtsverein, 2001), pp.74-80; Alexander Querengässer, '"Ich bin Meister vom Lande, und es muß geschehen, was ich befehle" – Die Bedeutung Sachsens für die preußischen Kriegsbemühungen im Siebenjährigen Krieg', in Querengässer (ed.) *Die Schlacht bei Roßbach*, pp.149-170

28 Modern military studies about this conflict are lacking. The author is actually writing one for Helion, which should be published in 2023. Jürgen Ziechmann, *Der Bayerische Erbfolge-Krieg 1778/1779 oder Der Kampf der messerscharfen Federn* (Südmoslesfehn: Edition Ziechmann, 2007); Marvin Thomas Jr.; *Karl Theodor and the Bavarian Succession, 1777–1778: a Thesis in History* (Philadelphia: Pennsylvania State University, 1980). About the Prussian army see Christopher Duffy, *The Army of Frederick the Great* (London, Vancouver: David & Charles, 1974), pp.204-205. There is still no better single-volume monograph available.

there might be some truth about this, there are other important factors which also influenced its outcome. One was the improved effectiveness of the Austrian army, which denied the Prussians a decisive battle, a tendency which had already been demonstrated in the later stages of the Seven Years War. By pinning the Prussians down close at the border of Bohemia, the Austrians denied them the possibility to draw resources from outside their kingdom. This was a crucial factor in Prussian's ability to wage war in the Seven Years War, when Prussian troops held most of Saxony which paid for almost 40 percent of the total costs for war. But this time, Saxony was a Prussian ally. The War of the Bavarian Succession as a continental conflict was also not intermingled with the American War of Independence, in the way that the French and Indian War and the Third Silesian War had been two parts of the Seven Years War, when Britain paid financial subsidies to Prussia and so further supported its war making capability. Without any financial support Prussia's ability to wage war were limited from the beginning and a successful outcome depended on victories in the field. So, the failure to force battle on the Austrians and drive them deeper into their own country and gain contributions was decisive in ensuring the short duration of the war.

Another important battle insofar as control over territory is concerned was the Russian victory at Großjägersdorf in East Prussia in 1757, as it saved this Prussian province for Russia until Tsar Peter III came to power in 1762. Because of the tremendous distance between the Russian core provinces and the Prussian heartland around Berlin, the Russians faced grave difficulties in mounting campaigns spanning only one season. The possession of East Prussia shortened communication lines, as the province was big enough to serve as a springboard for further campaigns and even than the Russians faced huge logistical difficulties. To stress counterfactuals once more it seems appropriate to ask, what would have happened, if the Russians lost Großjägersdorf? In this case, they would not have been able to save East Prussia and so they would have been unable to mount a campaign on the Oder in 1758 and probably even 1759 – depending on how long they would need to reoccupy East Prussia during the next campaign. This in turn would have seriously altered the campaigns of 1758 and 1759, as it would have given Frederick a free hand to operate against the Austrians and concentrate more men and resources. In all likelihood, he would have been able to invade Bohemia once more and win a battle against the Austrians instead of suffering serious defeats like Hochkirch, Kunersdorf or Maxen. Without a prospect of help from its major allies, Austria might have been willing to seek peace. This scenario of course is – like all counterfactuals – not inevitable but it offers a realistic alternative and is definitely helpful to underline the importance of the lesser-known battle of Großjägersdorf.

Lost Victories

Victors in the battles of the Silesian Wars often failed to use their success to achieve decisive results. Kunersdorf is the most prominent example.[29] The Prussian army was virtually annihilated, Frederick's will to continue the war was – at least for a moment – broken and

---

29   Scott Stephenson, 'Old Fritz Stumbles: Frederick the Great at Kunersdorf, 1759', in *Studies in Battle Command. Combat Studies Institute, US Army Command and General Staff College* (Fort Leavenworth, KS.: Diane Publishing, 2012), pp.13–20. With nothing new to add to the discussion see Klause

apparently the king considered suicide. The road to Berlin was wide open to the Austrian-Russian forces. Kunersdorf could and should have been the decisive knockout blow of the war. But it was not. Instead of following up their victory, the Russian and the Austrian army split up, the former retreating to East Prussia, the latter into Silesia. What Frederick later called 'the Miracle of the house of Brandenburg' is attributed by modern historians to a serious lack of supplies on part of the Russians.[30] The Russian commander Piotr Saltykov relied on the Austrians to bring up supplies along the Oder and was disappointed. This does not explain, however, why he did not try to find them to the west of the river or at Berlin, at this time a major city of Europe, which was a mere two-day march from the battlefield. The fact that the allies did not follow up their victory closed the window of opportunity created by Frederick's desperateness in the hours after the battle. He quickly regained his confidence, and this was all he needed, to rebuild his forces. The very fact, that the allies very often were been able to follow up their victories, notably at Kunersdorf or at Hochkirch in the year before, might run counter to the argument, that defensive successes of the Prussians, like at Roßbach, Leuthen or Zorndorf, denied them victory. But this argument can not undermine the importance of those battles for stabilising the critical strategic position of Prussia.

Frederick himself also won a victory he could not follow up on, at Prague in 1757. Marian Füssel quotes the memoires of the Russian officer Andrej Bolotow about this battle, to underline his argumentation about an indecisive character of contemporary battles. The Russian wrote:

> However bloody the already mentioned and most terrible battle of Prague might have been and while within a few hours thirty thousand men of both sides have been killed or crippled, nothing changed of the actual situation, the ferocity of the war did not reduce, no hope for peace sprouted. This battle is especially remarkable, because, while everybody thought and expected it would have mighty results, this was not the case and it had none[31]

Bolotow's remark is not wrong. It is certainly correct for this battle, but not for Frederician battles in general. Like the Austrians after Hochkirch or Kunersdorf, Frederick was definitely willing to follow up his success, but the Austrians were not willing to abandon Prague without a siege nor the were Prussians able to conduct one.

Jürgen Bremm, *Kunersdorf 1759. Vom militärischen Desaster zum moralischen Triumph* (Paderborn: Ferdinand Schoeningh 2021).

30   John L. H. Keep, 'Die russische Armee im Siebenjährigen Krieg', in Bernhard R. Kroener (ed.), *Europa im Zeitalter Friedrichs des Großen. Wirtschaft, Gesellschaft, Krieg* (=Beiträge zur Militärgeschichte 26) (Munich: Oldenbourg Verlag, 1989), pp.133-169, here p.160

31   Quoted in Andrej Bolotow, *Leben und Abenteuer des Andrej Bolotow von ihm selbst für seine Nachkommen aufgeschrieben*(Munich, Weimar: Verlag Gustv Kiepenheuer, 1990), Vol.1 p.1990; see also Füssel, 'Die Krise der Schlacht', p.330.

Limitations of Battles

Frederick too was unable to use his victories on occasion. Prague was probably his most bloody victory. The Prussians defeated the Austrian army and drove it behind the gates of the golden city. But Frederick's army always lacked the capabilities in siege warfare displayed by the French under Vauban or Maurice de Saxe and the English under Marlborough, and as a result the Prussians were unable to take Prague. A comparison with Kesselsdorf is obvious. In the battle of 1745, the Saxon army was defeated, and the Saxon-Austrian high command decided to abandon the capital of Dresden, despite the fact that a large undefeated Austrian army under the Prince of Lorraine was at hand. Supply problems might have played a crucial role, as the Austrians suffered from ice covering the natural supply route, linking Dresden with the Austrian depots in Northern Bohemia. However, in the end, the Prussians were able to transform success into results, following up their victory at Kesselsdorf with the fall of Dresden and the treaty signed at the same place.[32] Prague did not lead to the same results, as the Austrians successfully defended their city and the Austrians were able to turn the tables at Kolin, itself a decisive encounter, as it forced Frederick to abandon Bohemia and gave the allies the initiative, with the Austrians invading Silesia and the French marching on Magdeburg and Leipzig. However, counterfactual comparisons have their limitations as it appeared doubtful, that a fall of Prague would have led Austria to abandoning the war. The Austrians lost the city twice in the First and Second Silesian War and did not seek for peace when a European coalition was fighting against them, so it appears doubtful that they would have done so in 1757, when only one kingdom was fighting with them. However, in comparing Kesselsdorf with Prague, battles fought within comparable military parameters, it becomes clear that the decisiveness of these encounters depended on the measures taken by victors and defeated alike after the battle.

Frederick always faced serious problems when operating in Bohemia. The country was too thinly populated to feed his army and the population was generally hostile to his troops. Even after his victories at Chotusitz (1742) in the First Silesian War and Soor (1745) in the Second, Frederick was not able to control Bohemia. Although acknowledged Prussian victories, none of these battles led to an Austrian rout. They could retire to a safe position while light troops harassed the Prussian lines of communication, always forcing Frederick to abandon the country. This is a reminder of the fact, that the broader general political and military frame can have more influence on the outcome of a campaign or war, than a single battle. In the end political and not military events, most notably the death of Tsarina Elisabeth, saved Frederick from defeat in the Seven Years War.[33] Frederick was never able to appreciate this, writing in his *Die Generalprinzipien des Krieges und ihre Anwendung auf die Taktik und Disziplin der preußischen Truppen* in 1748: 'Because the capture of a provision

---

32   For a modern study, see Querengässer, *Kesselsdorf 1745*.

33   It is interesting to note, that Marian Füssel placed his counterfactual approach to the Seven Years War not on the case, that the allies followed up their victory at Kunersdorf, but that Elisabeth did not die in 1762, see: Marian Füssel, 'Das Debakel des Hauses Brandenburg 1762: Ein anderer Ausgang des Siebenjährigen Krieges', in Christoph Nonn, Tobias Winnerling (eds), *Eine andere deutsche Geschichte. Was wäre wenn…* (Paderborn: Verlag Ferdinand Schoeningh, 2017), pp.87-102 and pp.274-277.

train or the loss of a magazine will not end the war immediately and only battles bring a decision, so one must use both means to achieve ones goals.'[34]

Another pair of battles, also fought in the Seven Years War, but within the Anglo-French conflict, makes the importance of circumstances plainly clear: the battles of the Plains of Abraham and Sainte-Foy. The first was fought on 13 September 1759, when a British army was besieging Quebec. Parts of the French garrison under the Marquis de Montcalm decided to attack the English under James Wolfe on the Plains of Abraham, but they were severely routed. The French still had a substantial garrison within Quebec but surrendered shortly afterwards. The second battle was fought in the next spring on 28 April 1760, when Montcalm's successor the Chevalier de Lévis marched a 7,000 strong army to Quebec. The English garrison repeated Montcalm's mistake and, instead of waiting for the French to start a siege of the strong fortifications, attacked them at the Plains of Abraham in what became known as the battle of Sainte-Foy. They suffered a serious defeat, with losses higher than in the first battle, and retreated into the walls of Quebec. But this time the French were not able to recapture the city. That was due to British naval power, which brought support to the British defenders, while denying it to the French in 1759. British control of the St Lawrence River decided the outcome of both sieges and victory in the field had virtually no influence on it.[35]

Conclusions

It should be clear, that the decisive character of battles should not be judged by the fact of how many of them were fought in a war that was finally ended through mutual attrition, like the Seven Years War. This underlines the willingness especially of Austria and Prussia to fight to the end and the difficulty to translate military victories into political success. But that of course does not mean that the many battles fought in this war did not gravely alter the operational or strategic situation; this is something totally different from an indecisive battle in which the situation afterwards is the same as before, which could happen but was seldom the case.

This analysis is obscured by the fact, that Frederick himself held to the concept of battle as the war-ending event, a notion that through time became deeply rooted in German military culture, especially following quick victories in the Wars of German Unification with Düppel (1864), Sadowa (1866) and Sedan (1870).[36] This military tradition led to the fatal approach of

---

34   Quotation after Berthold (ed.), *Die Werke Friedrichs des Großen*, Vol.VI, p.13.

35   A good account of these actions is Stephen Manning, *Quebec. The Story of Three Sieges. A Military History* (London: Continuum, 2009).

36   There is extensive scholarship regarding this topic. Sven Lange, 'Von Leuthen zum Schlieffenplan – Friderizianische Militärtradition im Kaiserreich', in Thorsten Loch, Peter Andreas Popp (eds), *Wie Friedrich „der Große" wurde. Eine kleine Geschichte des Siebenjährigen Krieges 1756 bis 1763* (Freiburg i.Br., Wien. Berlin: Rombach, 2012), pp.267-272; Gustav-Adolf Caspar, 'Die Nachwirkungen Friedrichs des Großen im preußischen und deutschen Heer', in Militärgeschichtliches Forschungsamt (ed.), *Friedrich der Große und das Militärwesen seiner Zeit* (=Vorträge zur Militärgeschchte 8) (Herford, Bonn: E.S. Mittler & Sohn, 1987), pp.176-192; Manfred Messerschmidt, 'Nachwirkungen Friedrichs II. in Preußen-Deutschland', in Bernhard R. Kroener (ed.), *Europa im Zeitalter Friedrichs*

subordinating operational realities to tactical needs; that is to say, planning campaigns with the ultimate target of forcing the enemy to a battle of annihilation which would automatically lead to the end of the war. This concept failed in two world wars when Germany was fighting alliances in which operational goals had to serve general strategic aims.

It is indisputable that most battles impacted the chronological progression of events, and, therefore, exerted a decisive influence on history. In order to sufficiently grasp this, historians must understand why commanders sought to fight, but also why they attempted to avoid battle. Both of these decisions, to fight or deny battle, were firmly grounded in the knowledge that the potential engagement would alter the course of the campaign.

Further Reading

Jeremy Black, *European Warfare 1660 – 1815* (New Haven, London: Yale University Press, 1994).

Marian Füssel, 'Die Krise der Schlacht. Das Problem der militärischen Entscheidung im 17. und 18. Jahrhundert', in Rudolf Schlögl, Philip R. Hoffmann-Rehnitz, Eva Wiebel(eds), *Die Krise in der Frühen Neuzeit* (=Historische Semantik 26) (Göttingen: Vandenhoeck & Rupprecht, 2016), pp. 311-332.

Alexander Querengässer, *Kesselsdorf 1745. Eine Entscheidungsschlacht im 18. Jahrhundert (=Beiträge zur Geschichte des Militärs in Sachsen 4)* (Berlin: Zeughausverlag 2020).

Alexander Querengässer, *Eine Militärische Evolution. Militär und Kriegsführung in Europa 1300-1815* (Berlin: Zeughausverlag 2021).

Russel Weigley, *The Age of Battle. The Quest for Decisive Warfare from Breitenfeld to Waterloo* (Bloomington: Indiana University, Press 1991).

---

des Großen. Wirtschaft, Gesellschaft, Krieg (=Beiträge zur Militärgeschichte 26) (Munich: Oldenbourg Verlag, 1989), pp.269-288.

15

Embattled Representations: Indecisiveness and the Making of Victories During the Seven Years War

Marian Füssel

When I started working on the cultural history of battle around 2004, 'cultural history' was still an embattled category itself.[1] In the intervening time, the heated discussion has almost ceased, the old trenches have been filled and the once edgy 'cultural' has turned into the new mainstream, at least in German historiography. A lot has been published on the cultural history of warfare, but to radically historicize battle as we have done with political rituals or witch trials is still a challenge.[2] Among the many approaches located under the large roof of cultural history, three seem to have been particularly productive with regard to battles: the 'face of battle' approach following the seminal work of John Keegan – a contemporary and colleague of Christopher Duffy at the RMA Sandhurst; the cultural representations of battle; and the memory cultures of battles.[3] While the face of battle approach is generally hard to realize given the scarcity of early modern eye-witness accounts, memories and representations have no shortage on source material. Alongside these well-trodden paths of research, the diverse cultural turns such as gender, emotions, space, time, materiality, images or sound have also left their traces on the subject.[4]

---

1   As an example of the language of war in the debate on cultural history see Ute Daniel, 'Clio unter Kulturschock. Zu den aktuellen Debatten der Geschichtswissenschaft', *Geschichte in Wissenschaft und Unterricht* 48 (1997), pp.195–218 and 259–278.

2   Jeremy Black, *War and the Cultural Turn* (Cambridge: Polity Press, 2012); John Keegan, *A History of Warfare* (London: Hutchinson, 1993).

3   John Keegan, *The Face of Battle* (London: Pimlico, 1976); Olivier Chaline, 'La Bataille comme objet d'histoire' *Francia* 32:2 (2005), pp.1–14; Hervé Drévillon, *Batailles. Scenes de guerre de la Table Ronde aux Tranchées* (Paris: Éditions du Seuil, 2007); Yuval Noah Harari, *The ultimate experience: battlefield revelations and the making of modern war culture, 1450–2000* (Basingstoke: Palgrave Macmillan, 2008); Marian Füssel and Michael Sikora (eds), *Kulturgeschichte der Schlacht* (Paderborn: Schöningh, 2014).

4   Doris Bachmann-Medick, *Cultural turns: new orientations in the study of culture; translated by Adam Blauhut* (Berlin/Boston: de Gruyter, 2016); Gary Wilder, 'From Optic to Topic: The Foreclosure Effect of Historiographic Turns', *The American Historical Review* 117:3 (2012), pp.723–745.

In the work of Christopher Duffy we find many of these questions addressed without engaging too loudly in the academic culture clashes.[5] Duffy tries to get as close as possible to the event, giving context – be it the physical environment or the political – its due course and opening up multiple perspectives, not privileging one side. One of Duffy's main fields of inquiry, the Seven Years War, provides the ideal background for a cultural history of eighteenth century battles.[6]

In the following chapter I want to highlight a particular feature of early modern battle, in order to put the cultural approach to the test: the question of decisiveness or, more precisely, the cultural negotiation of winning or losing a battle. The assumption that battles have decided the fate of monarchs and nations within a day, or sometimes only several hours, is a strong conviction that motivates much of the historical interest in the subject. Anthologies of decisive battles of the world prove at least enduring popular interest in the decisive character.[7] Recent scholarship has instead argued that the seventeenth and eighteenth century lacked decisiveness. Russel F. Weigley, for example, describes the 'Age of Battles' from Breitenfeld (1631) to Waterloo (1815) as an era of undecidedness: 'The swift decisions almost never came. If war's one virtue was its capacity to produce decisions at a tolerable cost, it had lost its virtue before the age of battles commenced.'[8] For Weigley, the era between Gustav Adolph and Napoleon showed a hiatus between the hope of politics to bring about decisions on the battlefield and the actual indecision of the battles, which alone lead to enormous losses of people and resources. He therefore sees the warfare of the time not as a continuation of politics, but as its 'declaration of bankruptcy'. More recently, James Q. Whitmann's study *The Verdict of Battle*, however, has once again brought movement into the discussion.[9] Whitmann argues from a legal-historical perspective that the so-called 'pitched battle' as a quasi-juridical decision-making procedure is basically the most humane form of warfare to date. The transition of the battle from a 'rule of law' to a 'rule of force' in the late nineteenth century is read by him as the story of a loss. Whitmann, too, is aware that only a few battles just of the eighteenth century showed directly decisive character. But even the undecided battles were a 'blessing', compared to the alternative of marauding war across the country.

My point here is not to engage in that debate but to question how contemporaries negotiated the outcome of a battle in terms of victory or defeat, not its subsequent consequences

---

5   Christopher Duffy, *The Military Experience in the Age of Reason* (London: Routledge, 1987); Ibid., *Friedrich der Große. Die Biographie* (Düsseldorf: Albatros, 2001); Ibid., *Prussia's Glory: Rossbach and Leuthen* (Chicago: Emperor's Press, 2003); Ibid., *By Force of Arms. The Austrian Army in the Seven Years War* (Chicago: Emperors Press, 2008).

6   For a cultural history of the war, see Marian Füssel, *Der Preis des Ruhms. Eine Weltgeschichte des Siebenjährigen Krieges 1756-1763* (München: Beck, 2019).

7   This popular genre was founded with Edward Shepherd Creasy, *Fifteen Decisive Battles of the World: from Marathon to Waterloo* (New York: Harper & Brothers, 1851); see also Yuval Noah Harari, 'The Concept of 'Decisive Battles' in World History', *Journal of World History* 18:3 (2007), pp.251–266.

8   Russel F. Weigley, *The Age of Battles. The Quest for Decisive Warfare from Breitenfeld to Waterloo* (Bloomington: Indiana University Press, 1993), pp.XII–XIII, here p.XVIII.

9   James Q. Whitman, *The Verdict of Battle: the Law of Victory and the Making of Modern War* (Cambridge, Mass.: Harvard University Press, 2012).

for a campaign or a whole war.[10] On the German theatre of the Seven Years War we find several events that raised contemporary debate, such as the battles of Lobositz, Hastenbeck, Zorndorf and Torgau. The different arguments developed by the belligerents can work as a kind of tracer to the question of what a 'true' battle was and it delivers the cultural construction of battle. To speak of a cultural construction does not mean questioning the reality of battles but rather accepting that they produced multiple realities at least in their representations.

In an interview with Zurich's *Weltwoche* in 2004, Peter Sloterdijk stated:

> All commanders in the age of American wars [the War on Terror] base their actions on the recognition that there are always two wars in one or two battlefields that overlap each other, with the battlefield of images playing an increasingly important role. [...] the pictorial theater, the theatrum belli of the imaginary, can no longer be neatly separated from the actual events of war. The picture war has become the actual, the perpetual war.[11]

He thus argues in line with the French media philosopher Paul Virilio, who at the end of the 1980s already came to the radical conclusion that 'the history of battle is primarily the history of radically changing fields of perception'. In other words, war consists not so much in scoring territorial, economic or other material victories as in appropriating the 'immateriality' of perceptual fields'.[12] These quotations refer to the two central concepts we are concerned with here: on the one hand the spatial dimension of the battlefield and on the other its media representation.

Performing Decision

The battle was theoretically conceived a precisely choreographed but extremely contingent event with a high risk for both sides. They had to agree to a certain extent to fight each other, otherwise people spoke of an 'encounter' (*Treffen*) not a battle and attributed a different value to victory and defeat. For some contemporaries, as well as today's researchers, this agreement brought battle close to being a legal decision-making process or a duel. Repeatedly there is explicit talk of a '*rencontre*' (encounter). In contrast to duels, however, a battle could involve up to 120,000 men on a field covering several square kilometres. This mass event

---

10   See also Marian Füssel, 'Die Krise der Schlacht. Das Problem der militärischen Entscheidung im 17. und 18. Jahrhundert' In Rudolf Schlögl et.al. (eds), *Die Krise in der Frühen Neuzeit* (Historische Semantik 26) (Göttingen: Vandenhoeck & Ruprecht, 2016), pp.311–332; Alexander Querengässer, 'Ungehöriges Risiko oder Handlungsvorteil? Der Roi Connétable in der Frühen Neuzeit', in Martin Clauss andChristoph Nübel (eds), *Militärisches Entscheiden. Voraussetzungen, Prozesse und Repräsentationen einer sozialen Praxis von der Antike bis zum 20. Jahrhundert* (Frankfurt a. M.: Campus, 2020), pp.313–340.

11   Peter Sloterdijk, 'Es gibt keine Individuen', in Ibid, *Ausgewählte Übertreibungen: Gespräche und Interviews 1993-2012* (Berlin: Suhrkamp, 2013), pp.187–195, here p.191.

12   Paul Virilio, *War and Cinema: The Logistics of Perception* (London/New York: Verso, 1989), p.7.

was a huge challenge both logistically and epistemologically.[13] To get into the planned battle order as quickly as possible required a high degree of discipline and coordination; to keep an overview and to know what was going on was no less challenging.

The seventeenth- and eighteenth-century pitched battle was a complex cultural performance. Some of its elements can be compared to court ceremonies but the event as whole went far beyond that.[14] The *ordre de bataille* formed a symbolic order of rank and status that caused the same problems with ranking as civil ceremonies like processions or diets did. For example, in multi-confessional armies like the Holy Roman Empire's Imperial Army (Reichsarmee) the Protestant field chaplains quarrelled with their Catholic colleagues about whether they would preach on the left or the right side of the order of battle.[15] The battle itself followed the patterns of ritual: the beginning was marked symbolically by chants, a speech of the general or the drinking of alcohol, than the main course of the action was a time of violent competition with an open outcome, like a duel, and at the end the event was closed again by religious chants, the burying of the dead and so forth. A cultural approach to the history of battle should therefore overcome supposed distinctions between the true and proper core of military action and the 'merely cultural', its representations etc. This 'jargon of authenticity' (Adorno) is a legacy of nineteenth- and early-twentieth-century military doctrine that had no sense of the proper historicization of early modern battles, which appeared as a men's ballet in the theatre of the tamed Bellona.[16] But issues of rank and honour mattered and they mattered also for the outcome of battles.[17] At the battle of Minden (1759) we find quarrels over rank within both parties: the united British and German forces under the command of Ferdinand of Brunswick faced a striking example of military obstinacy, when Lord Sackville refused a cavalry charge ordered by Ferdinand. Among the French forces a rivalry between Marshal Contades and Lieutenant General Broglie over the beginning of the attack caused comparable problems.[18] Although disagreements regarding rank and obedience did well continue

---

13   On logistics, see Marcus Warnke, *Logistik und friderizianische Kriegsführung: eine Studie zur Verteilung, Mobilisierung und Wirkungsmächtigkeit militärisch relevanter Ressourcen im Siebenjährigen Krieg am Beispiel des Jahres 1757* (Berlin: Duncker & Humblot, 2018); on epistemology and knowledge see Ewa Anklam, *Wissen nach Augenmaß. Militärische Beobachtung und Berichterstattung im Siebenjährigen Krieg* (Herrschaft und soziale Systeme in der Frühen Neuzeit 10) (Berlin u.a.: Lit, 2007).

14   Jürgen Luh, *Kriegskunst in Europa 1650-1800* (Köln/Weimar/Wien: Böhlau, 2004); Jan Philipp Bothe, '"Martialische Lustbarkeiten". Die Inszenierung des Zeithainer Lagers (1730) zwischen Hof und Militär', *Archiv für Kulturgeschichte* 101:2 (2019), pp.29–60.

15   Max Plassmann, 'Bikonfessionelle Streitkräfte', in Michael Kaiser and Stefan Kroll (eds), *Militär und Religiosität in der Frühen Neuzeit* (Münster: Lit, 2004), pp.33–48.

16   Stig Förster, Markus Pöhlmann, and Dierk Walter, Vorwort, in Ibid. (eds), *Schlachten der Weltgeschichte. Von Salamis bis Sinai* (München: Beck, 2001), p.8; Winfried Mönch, '"Rokokostrategen': Ihr negativer Nachruhm in der Militärgeschichtsschreibung des 20. Jahrhunderts. Das Beispiel von Reinhard Höhn und das Problem des "moralischen" Faktors', *Aufklärung* 11:2 (1999) [Special Issue *Die Kriegskunst im Lichte der Vernunft: Militär und Aufklärung im 18. Jahrhundert* Teil I], pp.75–97.

17   Armstrong Starkey, *War in the Age of the Enlightenment, 1700 – 1789* (Westport, Conn.: Praeger, 2003), pp.69–103.

18   See Carl Renouard, *Geschichte des Krieges in Hannover, Hessen und Westfalen von 1757 bis 1763* (Kassel: Fischer, 1863-64), Vol.2, pp.252–258; see also Luh, 'Kriegskunst', p.209f. The best overview on

in the nineteenth and twentieth centuries, precedence played a special role in the culture of the *ancien régime*.[19]

In the eighteenth century, the battlefield was understood as a precisely defined place, as a manageable stage. In Zedler's universal encyclopaedia, the concept of the battlefield appears under the article '*Wahlstatt*':

> Wahlstatt, French Champ de Bataille, is the name of the field and the place where two enemy armies fight a battle against each other, and the one who, whether he lost the same or far more people (*Volck*) than the other, when the other must withdraw himself, keeps the field Maitre du Champ de Bataille, is called master of the field, or of the Wahlstatt.[20]

Thus, the Zedler already names the most important symbolic criterion for the decision of a battle since the Middle Ages: the occupation of the battlefield.[21] The highest criterion for the outcome of a battle in Europe has been the possession of the physical battlefield. The main goal of every army commander was to displace the enemy troops from the *Walstatt* and to hold the field.[22] In the age of linear tactics, this went hand in hand with disorder or even dissolution of the enemy lines. When the sources say that the formation was disordered, this is usually a firm sign of a looming defeat. But it was not that simple.

Ambiguities

The Battle of Hastenbeck, an example of a typical indecisive battle during the Seven Years War, was fought on 26 July 1757 between an Allied army led by the Duke of Cumberland and the French army led by Marshal d'Estrées. Due to misjudgements of the situation both army leaders gave the order to retreat, so that there were basically neither victors nor losers, which led the Prussian great general staff to the statement that the Battle of Hastenbeck would 'always take an peculiar position in the history of war'.[23] For, while there were some examples of both parties claiming the field of battle and later attributing victory to themselves, it is extremely unusual that both opponents 'for fear of being bypassed and involved in a catastrophe, retreat almost at the same time, and then the one who notices the departure of his opponent at the earliest advances again, occupies the already abandoned battlefield and becomes the victor only through this.

---

the Battle of Minden is Martin Steffen (ed.), *Die Schlacht bei Minden. Weltpolitik und Lokalgeschichte* (Minden: Bruns, 2008).

19   See Marian Füssel and Thomas Weller (eds), *Ordnung und Distinktion. Praktiken sozialer Repräsentation in der ständischen Gesellschaft* (Münster: Rhema, 2005).

20   'Wahlstatt', in Johann Heinrich Zedler, *Grosses vollständiges Universal-Lexicon aller Wissenschafften und Künste* (Leipzig/Halle: Zedler, 1747), Vol.52, Col.846–847, here Col.846.

21   Malte Prietzel, 'Blicke auf das Schlachtfeld. Wahrnehmung und Schilderung der Walstatt in mittelalterlichen Quellen', *Das Mittelalter* 13 (2008), pp.28–45.

22   Keegan, *Face of Battle*, pp.162–163.

23   Großer Generalstab (eds), *Der Siebenjährige Krieg 1756-1763. vol 5. Hastenbeck und Rossbach* (Berlin: Mittler, 1903), p.108.

The entire war history offers no example of this'.[24] Even if the Battle of Hastenbeck is therefore considered to have a certain exceptional character, two general phenomena can be observed in it. On the one hand, the aim for protecting one's own troops, in view of the threat of complete destruction or inadequate opportunities for retreat – the Duke of Cumberland had only one bridge through the swampy lowlands of the rivers Hamel and Remte at his disposal. At 1:00 p.m. he decided to withdraw and not to risk complete destruction and to leave Hannover defenceless to the French, although he still had the entire right flank and the cavalry at his disposal.[25]

On the other hand, the significance of the performative occupation of the battlefield for the claim to victory is once again evident. Even in one of the last battles of the Seven Years War, near Torgau in 1760, it was apparently difficult to find a clear winner. The historian and Prussian officer Johann Wilhelm von Archenholz therefore reports:

> Since nobody knew how the Wager of Battle would turn out, both parties had agreed to recognize the power that would have claimed the field at the dawn of the [following] day. At sunrise, however, the illuminated 'corpse field' apparently offered a clear scenario. Friedrich became aware that there were no more Austrians to fight here. He saw himself in possession of the entire battlefield; the victory was completely decided, and Saxony claimed.[26]

These examples make it clear that the question of decision was strongly dependent on coping with scenarios of undecidedness. It was not the classical worries of military theorists that a battle could actually end in a devastating and unequivocal defeat that were under discussion here, but rather the symbolic struggles to produce an officially recognized result in the distribution of victory and defeat. Battles continued in the public sphere.

Media Battles and Early Modern 'Fake News'

In recent times battles have frequently been analysed as media events.[27] A media event is not just the mirroring of the original action, it rather constitutes a reality of its own, it is a second order event.[28] This meant that in the case of events did not have unambiguous results, battles were sometimes fought a second time in the public sphere.

---

24   Großer Generalstab (eds), *Siebenjährige Krieg 1756-1763*, Vol.5, p.108.
25   Moritz Oppermann, *Die Schlacht bei Hastenbeck. Zum 250. Jahrestag* (Hameln, C.W. Niemeyer, 2007), p.25.
26   Johann Wilhelm von Archenholz, *Geschichte des siebenjährigen Krieges in Deutschland von 1756 bis 1763* (1793), in Johannes Kunisch (ed.), *Aufklärung und Kriegserfahrung. Klassische Zeitzeugen zum siebenjährigen Krieg* (Bibliothek der Geschichte und Politik 9) (Frankfurt a. M.: Dt. Klassiker-Verl., 1996), pp.9–513, here pp.358–359.
27   Sebastian Küster, *Vier Monarchien – vier Öffentlichkeiten: Kommunikation um die Schlacht bei Dettingen* (Münster: Lit, 2004); Thomas Weißbrich, *Höchstädt 1704. Eine Schlacht als Medienereignis; Kriegsberichterstattung und Gelegenheitsdichtung im Spanischen Erbfolgekrieg* (Paderborn: Schöningh, 2015); Jürgen Wilke, 'Krieg als Medienereignis – Konstanten und Wandel eines endlosen Themas', in Kurt Imhof and Peter Schulz (eds), *Medien und Krieg – Krieg in den Medien* (Zürich: Seismo, 1995), pp.21–35.
28   See Niklas Luhmann, *The Reality of the Mass Media* (Cambridge: Polity Press, 2000).

Shortly after the emergence of the first newspapers in the seventeenth century, the spread of false news of victory and defeat was the subject of heated debate. A particularly influential media reflection in this context proved to be the *Dissertation sur les libelles diffamatoires* by the French enlightened thinker Pierre Bayle (1647-1706), printed in the appendix of his famous *Dictionnaire*.[29] Bayle described the question of news policy as a feather-war in the spirit of raison d'état:

> Since cunning is allowed in war anyway, one must excuse the tricks of the news-paper writers. The diligence they use to meet the enemy's news is a kind of war, and it is for this reason that their writings are considered as weapons of the pen by some political writers.[30]

A partial translation in German was later included in the article '*Zeitung*' in the Zedler *Lexicon* and became the subject of an anonymous pamphlet during the Seven Years War on the question 'Whether it is advisable according to the rules of statecraft to deny the loss of a battle, or to spread false victories and advantages.'[31] Its author was the well-known political-economist Johann Heinrich Gottlob Justi (1720-1771) – author of a whole series of mostly anonymous military pamphlets – who later even included the text in an edition of his Collected Political and Financial Writings.[32] Justi assumed that his current readers shared Bayle's judgment in principle and 'the newspapers sixty years ago were already similar to what they are now, namely a mixture of truth and lies, without the majority of

---

29 Pierre Bayle, *Dictionnaire historique et critique*. Nouvelle Édition (Paris: Desoer, 1820), Vol.15, pp.148–189.

30 '*Outre que le ruses étant permises dans la guerre, il faut excuser les artifices des nouvellistes; car le soin qu'ils prennent de contrecarrer les relations de l'ennemi sont une espèce de guerre, et de là vient que leurs écrits ont été comptés parmi les armes de plume*,' Bayle, *Dictionnaire*, p.179.

31 '*Zeitung*', in Johann Heinrich Zedler, *Grosses vollständiges Universal-Lexicon aller Wissenschafften und Künste* (Leipzig/Halle: Zedler, 1749), Vol.61, Col.899–911, here Col.901f.; Anon., *Zwey Abhandlungen von der Kriegs-Zucht, und Ob es nach den Regeln der Staats-Kunst rathsam ist, den Verlust einer Schlacht zu läugnen, oder falsche Siege und Vortheile auszubreiten* (Berlin: Unknown Publisher, 1760) the same already printed in Goettingen 1757 and contained in *Teutsche Kriegs Canzley* 1757, Vol.3, Nr. 67, pp.392f.

32 Johann Heinrich Gottlob von Justi, *Gesammelte politische und Finanz-Schriften. Über wichtige Gegenstände der Staatskunst, der Kriegswissenschaften und des Kameral- und Finanzwesens* (Kopenhagen and Leipzig: Rothe, 1761; reprinted Aalen: Scientia, 1970), Vol.1, pp.1–340, here pp.33–46. Following his own accounts already printed before as Johann Heinrich Gottlob von Justi, *Deutsche Memoires, oder Sammlung verschiedener Anmerkungen, die Staatsklugheit, das Kriegswesen, die Justiz, Morale, Oeconomie, Commercium, Cammer- und Polizey- auch andere merkwürdige Sachen betreffend, welche im menschlichen Leben vorkommen, von einigen Civil- und Militairbedienten, auch von andern gelehrten und erfahrnen Personen aufgezeichnet und hinterlassen worden* (Leipzig: Unknown Publisher, 1741-1744). However, some texts contain current references to the Seven Years War, so they have been revised. On Justi's engagement as a 'political writer', see Ferdinand Frensdorff, 'Über das Leben und die Schriften des Nationalökonomen J. H. G. von Justi', *Nachrichten der Königl. Gesellschaft der Wissenschaften zu Göttingen: Phil.-histor. Klasse* 4 (1903), pp.356–503, here pp.391–412 and pp.417–438; Viktor Heydemann, 'Deutsche und Französische Broschüren aus der Zeit des Siebenjährigen Krieges', *Zeitschrift für Bücherfreunde* N. F. 20 (1928), pp.94–98, here pp.95–97.

newspaper writers themselves being to blame for much of it.'[33] In his subsequent reflections, however, von Justi did not entirely agree with Bayle's view and pleaded for a (media) policy that was appropriate to the situation but fundamentally sincere. Among the most striking cases of contested truths from the Seven Years War were the battles of Lobositz (1756) and Zorndorf (1758). The belligerents argued about the exact location of the battlefield, because the successful claim of victory depended on it. Thus, battles often developed a second reality as media events in which the assertions of prevalence met again.

Lobositz: 'une affaire indécise'[34]

After Frederick II had invaded Saxony in August 1756 the Prussian army managed to surround the Saxon Army at Pirna and the Prussian king went on to Bohemia in search of a quick decision in battle.[35] But the question of decision proved to be a difficult one.

On 1 October 1756 the first battle of the war on the European mainland was fought at Lobositz.[36] Frederick II, with 28,000 men, engaged the 35,000-strong Austrian army under the command of Field Marshal Maximilian Ulysses Browne (1705-1757).[37] Already a few days after the battle, on 6 October, the *Wiener Diarium*, the official Austrian newspaper, reported a stand-off. Both armies went back to their camps after battle 'thus the victory between both parties remained doubtful'.[38] The Prussians, in contrast, had on 3 October already publicly announced via postillions the news of 'a complete victory' in Berlin and Dresden.[39]

The Prussian side could claim to have driven the Austrians from the hard-fought vineyards (where the Swiss-born soldier Ulrich Bräker famously deserted) and the town of Lobositz itself and forced them to retreat to Budin.[40] In a contemporary printed chronicle in 'Jewish style', Christoph Gottlieb Richter wrote 1758:

33   Justi, 'Schriften', p.41.

34   Quoting Count Vitzthum in [Karl Friedrich Vitzthum von Eckstädt], *Die Geheimnisse des Sächsischen Cabinets. Ende 1745 bis Ende 1756* (Stuttgart: Cotta, 1866), Vol.2, p.182.

35   The best account of the events in Saxony is Marcus von Salisch, *Treue Deserteure. Das Kursächsische Militär und der Siebenjährige Krieg* (München: Oldenbourg, 2008).

36   See Duffy, *Friedrich*, pp.150–159; Ibid., *By Force of Arms*, pp.22–31; from the older literature see Großer Generalstab (ed.), *Kriege Friedrich des Großen: Der Siebenjährige Krieg, Vol.1: Pirna und Lobositz* (Berlin: Mittler, 1901), pp.262–285; Franz Quandt, *Die Schlacht bei Lobositz, 1. Okt. 1756*, Diss. Berlin (Charlottenburg Pfeiffer, 1909); Max Immich, 'Zur Schlacht bei Lobositz', *Forschungen zur Brandenburgisch Preußischen Geschichte* 6 (1893), p.355–376; Herman Granier, *Die Schlacht bei Lobositz am 1. Oktober 1756*, Diss. Berlin (Breslau: Trewendt, 1889); Alfons Dopsch, *Das Treffen bei Lobositz, sein Ausgang und seine Folgen* (Graz: Styria, 1892).

37   See Bernhard Jahn, 'Die Medialität des Krieges. Zum Problem der Darstellbarkeit von Schlachten am Beispiel der Schlacht von Lobositz (1.10.) 1756) im Siebenjährigen Krieg', in Wolfgang Adam and Holger Dainat (eds), *'Krieg ist mein Lied'. Der Siebenjährige Krieg in den zeitgenössischen Medien* (Göttingen: Wallstein, 2007), pp.88–110. On Browne see Christopher Duffy, *Feldmarschall Browne. Irischer Emigrant – Kaiserlicher Heerführer – Gegenspieler Friedrichs II. von Preussen* (Wien: Herold, 1966), pp.280–301.

38   *Wienerisches Diarium* Nr. 80, Mittwoch den 6. Oktober 1756. See also Manfred Schort, *Politik und Propaganda. Der Siebenjährige Krieg in den zeitgenössischen Flugschriften* (Frankfurt a. M.: Peter Lang, 2006), p.264–267 and pp.412–416.

39   See Hans Jessen, 'Die Nachrichtenpolitik Friedrichs des Großen im 7jährigen Krieg', *Zeitungswissenschaft* 15 (1940), Heft 11:12, pp.632–664, here p.635.

40   See Jürgen Kloosterhuis, 'Donner, Blitz und Bräker. Der Soldatendienst des 'armen Mannes im Tockenburg, aus der Sicht des preußischen Militärsystems', in Alfred Messerli and Adolf Muschg

As soon as the enemy fled, Browne gave the signal for retreat and fought no more, but kept quiet during the night and returned to his camp at Budin early in the morning. The Prussians instead rested on the battlefield from which they had forced the enemy back. And it is the custom of all nations that victory is ascribed to the one who has gained the battlefield. [...] And it is true that this battle did not decide the fate of both armies, and that is was due to the Austrians' neglect that they lost, although the facts show something different.[41]

On the Austrian side it was soon recognised that it had been a mistake to keep Browne's official relation rather modest, so that the Prussian king was now claiming the victory. As an ex-post-facto argument against that pretension, a dispatch by Count Kaunitz emphasized that the Austrians had retrieved Prussian wounded and had buried their dead.[42] Because only the party who controlled the battlefield was able to do this, in the eyes of the Vienna officials this was a clear argument that the Prussians were wrong. On 13 October the *Wiener Diarium* announced in an official relation: 'Our army rested the whole day and whole night until early the next day on the battleground and had to bury the dead of the enemy.'[43]

The claim to have held one's ground was mediated in three different ways. First through the performative practices of taking possession of the concrete physical battleground, secondly by the definition of that particular space, and thirdly by the legitimate representation of that space in the public sphere and its media. So much depended upon the assumption of which battlefield or which part of it one was talking. At one end of the fighting zone near Sullowitz the Austrians were in control and it was feasible to care for their wounded soldiers. On the right wing and in the centre of the battlefield that would hardly have been possible. Claims of victory thus depended on a commonly-accepted definition of place. Among the performative practices through which pretensions for victory were made were the singing of the *Te deum*, the fire of gun salutes and celebratory prayer and devotion. Prussian musketeer Johann Jacob Dominicus notes in his diary: 'On the 17th we held a thanksgiving and on the 18th we fired three times with all canons. The Thanksgiving at Lobositz was celebrated on

(eds), *Schreibsucht. Autobiographische Schriften des Pietisten Ulrich Bräker* (Göttingen: Vandenhoeck & Ruprecht, 2004), pp.129–187.

41   [Christoph Gottlieb Richter], *Die Historie des Kriegs zwischen den Preussen und ihren Bundsgenossen und den Österreichern und ihren Bundsgenossen von dem Einfalle in Sachsen an bis zu dem Friedensschlusse zu Hubertusburg von R. Simeon Ben Jochai* (Nürnberg: [Raspe], 1758-1763), Vol.1, 1758, p.42f.

42   Alfred Ritter von Arneth, *Geschichte Maria* (Wien: Wilhelm Braumüller, 1875), Vol.5, p.472 with note 26: '*Il est sûr que ce Prince a fait une grande perte à la journée de Lowositz, et s'il s'est attribué la victoire, il ne doit ce avantage qu'à la modestie de notre général, qui n'a point relevé dans sa relation des circonstances décisives pour le gain de la bataille. Il ne nous a point dit qu'il avoit fait retirer du champ de bataille les blessés prussiens, qu'il avoit fait enterrer leurs morts, et maintes autres particularités qui, ajoutées à celles qu'il nous mandoit, nous auroient mis en droit de célébrer par des rejouissances publiques la bataille gagnée. Mais faute de ces notions, nous la jugeames douteuse, et par conséquent point qualifiée à des démonstrations. Nous ne voulons en rien ressembler au Roy de Prusse ; nous soutiendrons ce principe en tout et partout ; il n'y a aura jamais rien d'équivoque dans notre conduite.*'

43   Extra-Blatt zum Wienerischen Diarium Nr. 82 den 13. Oktober 1756.

the 3rd of October with the singing of the 152nd and 151st psalm, but without any sermon, because the preacher was among the wounded.[44]

The ambiguities of the whole affair become evident from the later perspective of Austrian veteran and renegade Jacob de Cogniazzo (1732-1811) in his *Confessions*:

> The Prussian's fired victory salutes on the battlefield: we contented ourselves with firing a parting shot in retreat (*Retraitschuß*) into the camp of the winners, where we had sounded reveille in the morning. They were rightly celebrating the victory: we thanked the Lord of Hosts under the roaring of our guns, on occasion of the highest saint's day of the emperor, for our reconcilable fate– at least Frederick had not encountered the old Austrians, although we again encountered the old Prussians, the winners in five field battles under their commander rich with laurels.[45]

The explanation given by Cogniazo in the footnote is very telling:

> These celebrations by Browne's army had something of an ambiguous appearance. The celebration declared a victory, but that it could hardly be, although in Prague there was held a solemn mass for that memorable day and in Vienna they held devotions for nine days for the officers and soldiers killed in that battle. Prince Piccolomini had no order for any such celebration and in his camp at Königgrätz not a musket was fired in honour of the battle of Lobositz. All this illuminates the falseness of the pretension that the Austrian side had claimed the victory.[46]

For Prussian eyewitnesses like Frederick's page (*Leibpage*), Prussian possession of the field was out of question. His page Georg Karl Ganz Edler zu Putlitz wrote: 'They were concerned with their retreat und left the battlefield to us.'[47] Beyond the battlefield the pretension of victory or stand-off was enforced in the media through official 'relations'. Communication thus shifted away from the field of combat into the virtual space of the European public sphere. In Berlin's newspapers the news of the victory was repeated again and again through stories about the celebrations of victory, which were held in early November in

---

44   'Den 17. hielten wir das Dankfest, und den 18. wurde auß allen Canonen 3 mahl gefeuert. Das Dankfest bei Lobositz wurde den 3. October gehalten mit Absingung des 152. und 151. Gesangs; wurde aber keine Predigt gehalten, weilen der Prediger bey den Bleßirten war.' Dietrich Kerler, *Aus dem siebenjährigen Krieg. Tagebuch des preußischen Musketiers Dominicus* (München: Beck, 1891; Reprinted Osnabrück: Biblio.-Verl., 1972), p.6f. The Nr. 151 is 'Herr Gott dich loben wir' and Nr. 152 'Nun danket alle Gott'.

45   Jacob de Cogniazzo, *Geständnisse eines österreichischen Veterans in politisch-militärischer Hinsicht auf die interessantesten Verhältnisse zwischen Oestreich und Preußen, während der Regierung des Großen Königs der Preußen Friedrichs des Zweyten mit historischen Anmerkungen gewidmet den königlich preußischen Veteranen von dem Verfasser des freymüthigen Beytrags zur Geschichte des östreichischen Militär-Dienstes* (Breslau: Gottlieb Löwe, 1788–1791; reprinted 4 vols. Bad Honnef: LTR-Verlag, 1982), Vol.2, pp.216–255, here p.238f.

46   Cogniazzo, *Geständnisse eines österreichischen Veterans* Vol.2, p.238n. See also von Archenholz, *Geschichte*, p.31.

47   Curt Jany, 'Aus den Erinnerungen eines Leibpagen des Großen Königs (Puttlitz)', *Hohenzollernjahrbuch* 16 (1912), pp.73–85, here p.76.

Potsdam, Dresden, Wriezen and Stargard.[48] The genuine event of the battle was replaced by a second-order media event. On the Austrian side an anonymous pamphlet entitled *Letter by Sr. of *** to Sr. N.N. from the Camp at Budin* was published and drew a lot of attention, notably in Regensburg, the seat of the imperial diet, because it claimed a stand-off and downplayed Prussia's triumph.[49] The Austrian envoy Freiherr von Buchenberg (1701-1769) as well as the envoy of Bohemia ordered reprints at local printer Neubauer and sold them publicly. Prussian envoy Erich Christoph Edler Herr und Freiherr von Plotho (1707-1788) was not amused. He complained to the urban magistrate and ordered the city's treasurer to confiscate the prints. Buchenberg was enraged and took the prints under his protection, selling a thousand more. Plotho, in contrast, did not succeed in having the Prussian version of truth printed in the local newspaper, so he decided to reprint it himself, and distributed the prints among the envoys of the diet. The Austrians retaliated with another broadsheet that attacked the Prussian proclamation of victory and explicitly referred to its communication in acoustic terms:

> Since the King of Prussia undertook to deceive the public his ministers, his presses and newspapers are only occupied with spreading the strangest fictions and the most palpable lies. But these voices bawling so loudly do not suffice: he also needs post-horns to disturb common sense. Does a prince who gained so much glory and reputation in the last war need a trumped-up victory (*une victoire postiche*) to maintain this reputation?[50]

The Austrian Jesuit J.P.C. Michael Denis (1729-1800), in his *Poetic Pictures of most of the events of war in Europe, since the Year 1756*, was one of the few Austrian literary voices in the war of propaganda. His work can be seen as a pendant to the far more popular *Prussian War Songs* by Johann Wilhelm Ludwig Gleim (1719-1803). Denis's point was, how could the Prussians dare to claim victory when their casualties were so great:

> The Austrian retreated, but what made him retreat? Was it Fredericks Cavalry, which was dispersed so quickly? The King won. But where are the symbols of victory [...] You Braggarts! [...] Its clearly evident that most of you were left on the field [dead][51]

Gleim himself wrote in a letter to Kleist on 24 October 1756:

---

48   Jessen, 'Nachrichtenpolitik' (1940), p.635.
49   Printed in [Karl Friedrich Vitzthum von Eckstädt], *Geheimnisse*, Vol.2, pp.177–182, see also for a detailed account Schort, 'Propaganda', p.264f. On the Diet and situation in Regensburg, see Michael Rohrschneider, *Österreich und der Immerwährende Reichstag: Studien zur Klientelpolitik und Parteibildung (1745-1763)* (Göttingen: Vandenhoeck & Ruprecht, 2014).
50   Eckstädt, *Geheimnisse*, p.177.
51   Michael Denis, *Poetische Bilder der meisten kriegerischen Vorgänge in Europa seit dem Jahr 1756* (Wien: Kurtzböck, 1760-1761), Vol.I, p.13, quote after Johannes Birgfeld, 'Kriegspoesie für Zeitungsleser oder Der Siebenjährige Krieg aus österreichischer Sicht. Michael Denis' *Poetische Bildern der meisten kriegerischen Ereignisse in Europa seit dem Jahr 1756* im Kontext des zeitgenössischen literarischen Diskurses', in Adam and Dainat (eds), '*Krieg ist mein Lied*', p.223.

The Austrians claim victory in the battle of Lobositz and write impertinently that they gained the field of battle and rested there during the night after the fighting. I think their generals made the empress believe it. They also pretend our Army was 50-60 thousand men strong. They are badly wrong; it was 130 thousand men strong. With one hundred and thirty thousand men Frederick fought the Austrians. Because he alone was a hundred thousand men![52]

Not only in the city of the imperial diet did the newspaper coverage cause disturbance. Beyond the political public sphere contemporary observers privately took notice of events and commented on them. One of the most famous sources for contemporary media reception in Germany, next to Goethe's *Truth and Poetry*, was the correspondence of authoress Meta Klopstock (1728-1758), wife of German writer Friedrich Gottlob Klopstock (1724-1803), which has become kind of an 'icon of reception'.[53] Mrs Klopstock laments in a letter of 16 October 1756 to her sister in Hamburg about the curiosity for news of battle. Everyone is gathering while the messenger is approaching and the whole household is hungry for news:

> What might have happened? What in Bohemia, what in Saxony? Klopstock always argues about what Browne should do or what he wishes that he does not. The Saxons who form the biggest party over here chasten themselves about what their nation *might* do, but probably *will* not do.[54]

Instead of debating, she wants to read her sister's letters quietly and undisturbed.

> But now it is shouted: Prussia! Browne! Lobositz! and so on, what do I know what is shouted in confusion and what disturbs me, maybe while hearing you telling me something about your kids! […] Last post day I was angry about Klopstock because as I wanted to read him out the message about your [Hamburg] flood he said: Oh! Oh! Let me read about the battle first. […] By this you see on which side Klopstock is. But to be honest, I could not like it myself when the King of Prussia would lose a battle.[55]

The battle can be 'read', and the Klopstock family become virtual participants of the battle who share the excitement of single manoeuvres in a way we more likely know today from sporting media events. The Hamburg flood mentioned in the letter is a good indicator of competing issues in the media. The debate about on whose side victory fell lasted until the next media event overrode it. During the Seven Years War the next battle usually occurred

---

52   Gleim to Ewald v. Kleist, 24 October 1756, in *Ewald von Kleist's Werke, Dritter Theil Briefe an Kleist* (Berlin: Hempel, 1882, Reprinted Bern: Lang, 1968), Nr. 58, pp.154–156, here pp.155–156.

53   See Martin Welke, 'Die Legende vom "unpolitischen Deutschen". Zeitunglesen im 18. Jahrhundert als Spiegel des politischen Interesses', *Jahrbuch der Wittheit zu Bremen* 25 (1981), pp.161–188, here p.176f.

54   Meta Klopstock geborene Moller, *Briefwechsel mit Klopstock ihren Verwandten und Freunden, Herausgegeben und mit Erläuterungen versehen von Hermann Tiemann* (Hamburg: Maximilian-Gesellschaft, 1956), Vol.2 1754-1758, pp.529–531, here p.529f.

55   Klopstock, *Briefwechsel mit Klopstock*, Vol.2 1754-1758, p.529f.

within a few months. But the labelling controversies continued up to the nineteenth century. In 1892 Lobositz-born Austrian Historian Alfons Dopsch (1868-1953) published a book on the battle, which he named the *Treffen* (encounter) at Lobositz in contrast to his Prussian colleagues speaking of a battle. In contrast to the pitched battle, the 'encounter' happens accidentally. A defeat thus cannot be labelled as a strategic mistake, and a victory counts less.

Zorndorf: Contested Places

One of the most debated battles of the Seven Years War was fought at Zorndorf on 25 August 1758.[56] Carl von Clausewitz considered the Battle of Zorndorf 'without contradiction [as] the strangest in the seven-year war, perhaps in all recent war history, because of its strange course'.[57] Zorndorf's importance is also emphasized in current research.[58] Dennis Showalter, for example, writes: 'Zorndorf was arguably far more significant for the Seven Years War than either Leuthen or Rossbach. Unlike its predecessors, the battle created a new paradigm.'[59] Showalter sees this new 'paradigm' above all in the significance of the Russian army, which was demonstrated there. Despite immense losses – the Russians lost between 18,000 and 21,500, the Prussians more than 12,000 men – contemporaries did not agree on who had won the battle and who had lost. As a result, a massive journalistic conflict arose over the outcome of the battle. Andrei Bolotov (1738-1833), a contemporary Russian officer, wrote in his memoirs:

> Never has so much been written about a battle as by the Zorndorfer or, as some also called them, the Küstriner. Because both sides wanted to attribute victory to themselves, both together initially lied a lot, either in things they signed or by attributing several things to each other, which gave both sides cause for multiple and different replies, explanations, and evidence. And that's why the newspapers of that time were so interesting.[60]

In the aftermath of the battle, confusion about the past event dominated its perception. Henri de Catt, his conversation partner through the campaigns, was asked by Frederick

56   Duffy, *Friedrich*, pp.237–247. Most of the older literature on the battle has now been collected and reprinted in Ulf-Joachim Friese (ed.), *Die Schlacht bei Zorndorf am 25./26. August 1758 und die Tage davor und danach in preußischer, russischer und österreichischer Darstellung*, 2 vols. (Buchholz: LTR-Verlag, 2010). More recent works include Stefan Hartmann, ‚Eine unbekannte Quelle zur Schlacht bei Zorndorf', *Zeitschrift für Ostmitteleuropa-Forschung* 34 (1985), pp.176–210; Simon Millar, *Zorndorf 1758. Frederick faces Holy Mother Russia* (Oxford: Osprey, 2003); Marian Füssel, ‚Das Undarstellbare darstellen. Das Bild der Schlacht im 18. Jahrhundert am Beispiel Zorndorf (1758)', in Gabriela Signori and Birgit Emich (eds), *Kriegs/Bilder in Mittelalter und Früher Neuzeit* (ZHF Beiheft 42) (Berlin: Duncker & Humblot, 2009), pp.317–349.
57   Carl von Clausewitz, ‚Die Feldzüge Friedrichs des Großen von 1741–1762', in Ibid., *Hinterlassene Werke über Krieg und Kriegführung*, Vol.10 (Berlin: Dümmler, 1837), pp.29–254, here p.83.
58   See Adam Storring, 'Zorndorf 1758: Prussian War-Making at the Mid-Point of the Seven Years War', in *Mars & Clio* 36 (2013), <http://www.bcmh.org.uk/wp-content/uploads/2019/05/StorringZorndorf.pdf>
59   Dennis E. Showalter, *The Wars of Frederick the Great* (London/New York: Longman, 1996), p.219.
60   Andrej Bolotow, *Leben und Abenteuer des Andrej Bolotow von ihm selbst für seine Nachkommen aufgeschrieben* (München: Beck, 1990), Vol.1, pp.310–315, here p.310f.

after the battle: 'Have You conceived everything this devilish day?' And he responded: 'Sir, I conceived well the march and all the dispositions taken before the battle, and I even observed well the beginning of the battle; but everything else I missed. I understood nothing of the moves that have been made.' Frederick obviously almost felt the same when he responded: 'You are not alone, my friend, you are not alone, take comfort!'[61]

A stroke of luck for written records is the fact that one month after the Battle of Zorndorf, during a sally from Neu-Stettin, a Russian courier was arrested, from whom a bag full of official correspondence and about a hundred private letters were captured.[62] In the royal chancellery, they were translated shortly afterwards by the Swiss mathematician and member of the Prussian Academy of Sciences Leonhard Euler (1707-1783) into a selection to be used for the journalistic epilogue of the battle. There is hardly a battle of the Seven Years War that has been fought in such detail for a second time in public as Zorndorf.[63] In political journalism, an extensive conflict of interpretation arose over the outcome of the battle, which was also commented on by newspaper readers and diarists. The dispute centred on four main topics: a) the assertion of the *Walstatt* b) the amount of losses c) the booty d) the cruelty of the Russians. Of these, only the first will be examined in detail below.

As it turned out later, it was of utmost importance that the Prussians claimed the possession of the field of battle on the first day. Frederick's aide-de-camp Friedrich Wilhelm Ernst von Gaudi (1725-1788) writes: 'The army remained under arms on the battleground and in the midst of the enemy dead until the 26th full day.'[64] Now Gaudi comes to the delicate question of the controversial victory:

> It was this circumstance that subsequently gave the Russians the opportunity to dare to attribute to themselves the victory to which they were otherwise not entitled to make the slightest claims. In order, however, to give himself the prestige of having won the *Bataille*, General Fermor had the previous night written to Lieutenant General Count Dohna requesting a truce to bury the dead and collect the wounded, but he was told that since the king had remained master of the battlefield, he would not fail to take care of this.[65]

This question has also been passed down by various other observers. British Envoy Andrew Mitchell writes in a letter of 29 August:

---

61   Friedrich der Große (ed. Willy Schüssler), *Gespräche mit Henri de Catt* (München: DTV, 1981), pp.230–241, here p.237.

62   Denis Sdvižkov, 'Landschaft nach der Schlacht. Briefe russischer Offiziere aus dem Siebenjährigen Krieg„ *Forschungen zur Brandenburgischen und Preußischen Geschichte* NF 22:1 (2012), pp.33–56, here pp.33–34; see also Ibid (ed.), *Letters from the 'Prussian' War. The People of the Russian Imperial Army in 1758*, Денис Сдвижков, Письма с Прусской войны Люди Российско-императорской армии в 1758 году (Moscow, Novoe literaturnoe obozrenie, 2019).

63   Already see Füssel, 'Das Undarstellbare darstellen', pp.330–335.

64   Jürgen Ziechmann (ed.), *Friedrich Wilhelm Ernst Freiherr von Gaudi: Journal vom Siebenjährigen Kriege* (Forschungen und Studien zur Friedericianischen Zeit, Sonderband E) (Buchholz: LTR-Verlag, 2003), Vol.5: 1758 Bearbeitet von Manfred Löffelholz, pp.230–251, here 237.

65   Ziechmann (ed.), *Friedrich Wilhelm Ernst Freiherr von Gaudi*, p.238.

The day after the battle he [Fermor] sent a trumpet to ask a suspension of arms for three days to bury the dead, which was refused, as it belongs to him who has the field of battle to bury the dead, and to take care of the wounded; but the burning of villages, &c., has ceased since that time.[66]

The concern for the dead and wounded, which the respective army – as in this case – was mostly overburdened with, was used to produce criteria for victory or defeat, as was already the case with Lobositz. Friedrich was therefore probably well aware of the consequences that Fermor's request could have.[67]

On the day after the battle, 26 August, when cannon fire still continued, Mitchell wrote a letter to the Earl of Holdernesse giving a brief overview of the course of the fighting:

The action began at nine in the morning, near the village of Zorndorf, and lasted till seven at night. The fire of the artillery was terrible on both sides, and continued almost without interruption till the end of the action. What added to the horror of this spectacle was that the Cossacks and Kalmucks had set fire to the villages all round, and great number of Russian powder wagons blew up in the woods which surrounded the field of battle. The beginning of the action was very favourable to the Prussians, and if the infantry placed on the left (I mean that of General Dohna's army) had done what was expected from them, the victory would have been most complete; but, unhappily, they neither charged with the spirit of Prussian soldiers, nor showed that firmness which they have done on other occasions. I have it from the mouth of a Russian officer, prisoner, that if they had, the whole Russian army would have been destroyed. In one word, those battalions gave way, got into confusion, and many of them left the field of battle, which now began to be very doubtful, till Lieutenant-General Seidlitz, with his own regiment, that of the gardes du corps and the gens d'armes, broke through the Russian cavalry into their infantry, and restored our affairs; the rest of the Prussian cavalry likewise behaved well, so that one may fairly say this battle was won by the cavalry.[68]

The decisive question now turned out to be the possession of the battlefield during the second day. Even during the second day an observer like Andrew Mitchell was not at all clear whether the Prussians had won the battle: 'To this I most readily agreed as I thought the affair far from being decided'.[69]

---

66 Andrew Bisset (ed.), *Memoirs and Papers of Sir Andrew Mitchell. K.B., Envoy Extraordinary and Minister Plenipotentiary from the Court of Great Britain to the Court of Prussia, From 1756 to 1771* (London: Chapman & Hall, 1850), Vol.1, p.438. On Mitchell, see Patrick Francis Doran, *Andrew Mitchell and Anglo-Prussian diplomatic relations during the Seven Years War* (New York: Garland, 1986).

67 On burial of the dead during the Seven Years War, see Marian Füssel, 'Ungesehenes Leiden? Tod und Verwundung auf den Schlachtfeldern des 18. Jahrhunderts', *Historische Anthropologie* 23:1 (2015), pp.30–53.

68 Bisset, 'Memoirs', p.429f.

69 Bisset, 'Memoirs', p.432.

The debate left its traces in diaries all throughout Germany. Silesian noblewomen Juliane von Rehdiger (1713-1784) noted for example: 'Both sides are appropriating the victory, which I do not want to decide, but so much is certain, that many people were left [dead] on the field and almost all humanity has been set aside.'[70] The Krefeld-based Mennonite and bookseller Abraham ter Meer (1729-1804) was also a keen newspaper reader, and his diary repeatedly contains notes on battles.[71] On 1 September, ter Meer noted: 'As news one hears that the king completely defeated the Russians near Zorndorf on August 25.'[72] But this unambiguous verdict should not be the end of the story. Duchess Luise Dorothée of Saxe-Gotha wrote to her correspondent Voltaire on 16 September:

> The unique thing about this victory is that the newspaper writers in Vienna and Berlin reported it so differently. The first say that the Russians had been defeated on August 25, but that the battle would have started again the next morning all the better, the Russians have recaptured territory, and that only eight thousand men and some cavalry detachments of the entire Prussian army had been saved. The Berliners cover the battlefield with twenty thousand Russians [casualties], one hundred and three cannons conquered by the Prussians, twenty-seven standards, the entire field treasury, all ammunition, two thousand prisoners; according to them, a complete victory.[73]

For Voltaire, the matter was quite clear when he replied

> The new victory of the King of Prussia at Küstrin can only be denied in writing, it seems to me. That the Russians were beaten is surely very clear, because they do not show themselves. If they were victors, they would be in Berlin and the King of Prussia would not be in Dresden.[74]

An important symbolic means for celebrating victory in battle was performing the Te deum laudamus all over the country.[75] Here we can add another notion of meaning to an observation by Christopher Duffy, who claimed that Frederick tried to obscure the horrible bloodshed of Zorndorf by ordering the Te deum to be sung.[76] After all, the Te deum was part of

---

70   Paul-Ulrich Flashar (ed.), *Familienbuch Michaelis- von Tschirschky, Bd. 2: Memoiren der Eleonore Juliane von Rehdiger verw. Freifrau von Lüttwitz geb. von Falkenhayn 1713-1784; Das Tagebuch der Urahne; ein Lebensbild aus dem 18. Jahrhundert* (Bielefeld-Senne: Gottfried Michaelis, 1996), p.129.

71   Next to the French newspaper of Cologne, the *Gazette de Cologne*, ter Meer read the *Lippstädter* and *Harlemer Zeitung*. See Gottfried Buschbell (ed.), *Das Tagebuch des Abraham ter Meer (1758-1769)* (Krefeld: Zelt-Verlag, 1936), p.41f., 45, 49, 53; see Miriam Müller, 'On dit. Die Nachrichtenrezeption des Krefelders Abraham ter Meer im Siebenjährigen Krieg', *Annalen des Historischen Vereins für den Niederrhein insbesondere das alte Erzbistum Köln* 215 (2012), pp.73–96.

72   Buschbell (ed.), *Das Tagebuch des Abraham ter Meer*, p.27.

73   Gotha, 16 September 1758, Bärbel Raschke (ed.), *Der Briefwechsel zwischen Luise Dorothée von Sachsen-Gotha und Voltaire* (1751-1767) (Leipzig: Leipziger Universitäts-Verlag, 1998), p.141.

74   Raschke (ed.), *Briefwechsel* Aux Délices, 26 September 1758, p.142.

75   See Michèle Fogel, *Les cérémonies de l'information dans la France du XVIe au milieu du XVIIIe siècle* (Paris: Fayard, 1989).

76   Duffy, *Friedrich*, p.423.

the fixed traditional repertoire of the symbolic assertion of victory. However, the fact that both armies thought they had won or at least intended to claim victory was symbolized by the singing of the Te Deum and a salute on 29 August. So Austrian Major General St André, who served with the Russians, wrote: 'on the 29th both from our side and the enemies the Te Teum laudamus was celebrated and we fired guns and also muskets'.[77] Prussian musketeer Dominicus notes in his diary:

> On the 28th came 20 trumpeting postilions who sounded their trumpets and brought the message that the king on the 25th of August between Küstrin and Landshut had beaten the Russians very well, where the Russians lost 55,000 men dead and wounded; they had 288 canons, of which we captured 247; their army was 130,000 men strong and ours 80,000 men. We lost eight hundred men dead, and six hundred men wounded. The 29th Victoria was fired 3 times out of all the canons, and salutes were fired 3 times from our small guns. Then the 'Te deum laudamus' was sung, and the sermon on the 89th Psalm V. 22-24 was preached, and then 'Now thank we all our God' was sung."[78]

A few days later, victory celebrations were held on both sides in many cities: In Berlin on 3 September, in Konigsberg on 6 September, in St Petersburg on 10 September and also in Vienna.[79]

In Berlin's newspapers, the media war over Zorndorf is clearly articulated:

> It will be difficult to find an example in the stories that someone has invented so many untruths to obscure such a great event. But they will not succeed in doing so with the rational world. The position of the armies on both sides after the day of the 25th, the retreat of the Russians after Landsberg, the number of prisoners, and numerous signs of victory, […] and finally the own confession of the commanding general, are so many proofs which leave no doubt in the minds of the unbiased. Meanwhile, one can leave the counterpart the comfort that, if he cannot obtain the victories in the field, he seeks to fight through his newspaper writers and thereby make a blue haze for the common people.[80]

In a pro-Russian Konigsberg newspaper, it says however:

> How little cause the Prussians have to attribute victory to themselves, and to have this trumpeted by many Postillions, is to be seen from enough the above, since

---

77   Relation by St André, in Ernst von Frisch, *Zur Geschichte der russischen Feldzüge im Siebenjährigen Kriege nach den Aufzeichnungen und Beobachtungen der dem russischen Hauptquartier zugeteilten österreichischen Offiziere vornehmlich in den Kriegsjahren 1757/58* (Heidelberg: Winter, 1919), p.113.

78   Kerler, 'Tagebuch', p.41.

79   *Danziger Beyträge*, (Berlin) p.402; (Russia) p.395, (Vienna), p.607.

80   Gottlob Naumann and Karl Friedrich Wernich (eds), *Beyträge zur neuern Staats- und Kriegesgeschichte* (Danzig: Schuster, 1756-1764) [= Danziger Beyträge] Vol.6, 1759, St. 55-58, pp.433–437, here p.436f.

undisputedly the Russian Imperial Army claims the field, and consequently had more reason to hold a thanksgiving because of the enemy's weakened position than they [the enemy] did.[81]

The *Berliner Zeitung* was indignant: 'that the Russian side does not only want to contradict the relation made known by the Battle of Zorndorf itself, but also to drive even the impertinence so far as to pretend that the Russian army has claimed the field of battle'.[82] The Russians had obviously exaggerated the figures in their favour and had also misrepresented the actions of the individual units. However, the Prussian relations finally argue with all their might against the Russians' assertion of the Walstatt, whereby it turns out that it was by no means clear where exactly the battlefield was. At the beginning of the battle, the Russian army had been located between Quartschen and Zorndorf and had been driven by the Prussian into the swamps to a forest extending from Zorndorf towards Küstrin. So, the battlefield was the place 'where the Russian army stood at the beginning of the action, between Quartschen and Zorndorf. It was completely driven from the same, and in the evening, was half a mile away from it. His Royal Majesty, however, pitched his camp in the middle of the Walstatt and spent the night there'.[83] The symbolic assertion of the Walstatt and thus the victory clearly depended on who succeeded in defining the Walstatt as a place at all. The performative act of occupation alone was obviously not enough. Additionally, the Prussian side denied that the second day of fighting was a real battle. Instead, it was conceived as a mere artillery duel without close combat. Defining what was no battle helps us to understand what a 'proper' battle was for the contemporaries.

Even the dead carried on with the debate. In a broadsheet entitled *Dialogue between a Prussian Black Hussar and a Moscovitian Cossack about the bloody battle at Zorndorf,* the Prussian Hussar laments in the underworld: there are so many different and contradicting rumours circulating about the battle, that:

> [O]ne wants to get mad when one tries to judge upon it. For my part I died under the bayonets of your already retreating infantry last August the 25th, and I died with the proud opinion that we were the winners. And now I see that since then there have been reports which partly diminish, partly entirely neglect our advantages. Damn News-Vendors! So you are entitled to fool the public as in the upper world as well as in the underworld![84]

---

81 Danziger Beyträge 1758, St. 45-48, pp.392–395 here p.394. On the situation in Königsberg see [Johann George Bock] (ed. F.W. Schubert), 'Die Occupation Königsbergs durch die Russen währen des siebenjährigen Krieges', *Neue preußische Provinzial-Blätter, dritte Folge* (Königsberg: Tag & Koch, 1858), [part 1] Vol.1 (1758), pp.153–178, [part 2] Vol.1 (1858), pp.201–217, [part 3] Vol.2 (1859), pp.59–78, [part 4] Vol.2 (1859), pp.140–153, quote here [part 2], pp.213–215.

82 *Berliner Nachrichten*, Nr. 109, Dienstag 12. September 1758, p.470; *Teutsche Kriegs Canzley* 1758, Vol.2, Nr. 134, pp.1050–1056, here pp.1051–1052.

83 *Teutsche Kriegs Canzley* 1758, Vol.2, Nr. 134, p.1053.

84 [Anonymous], *Gespräch zwischen einem preuß. Schwarzen Husaren und einem Moscowitischen Cosacken über die blutige Schlacht so den 2. Augusti 1758 bey Zorndorf ohnweit Cüstrin vorgefallen* (Unknown Publisher, 1758), p.5.

The Prussian field chaplain Täge, serving with the Russian Army, later looked back at the events in his Autobiography trying to mark a slightly irenic middle ground position: 'It will always come to the unbiased observer the remark, that both parties, as indeed happened, had a certain right to claim the victory for their side.'[85]

Conclusion

During the Seven Years War the rapid dissemination of news became an important means of politics, and Frederick II recognized this in a way none of his adversaries did.[86] In Hamburg in 1757 a significant rumour circulated that, according to the official news from Berlin, Frederick wanted to call himself 'King of the Presses' rather than King of Prussia, 'because on the one hand he put the printing press into constant motion, on the other hand he said 'I have against me several kings and many gazetteers'.[87] However, the king was also aware that the media alone could not decide the war. To the Marquis d'Argens, with whom he regularly corresponded about pamphlets and poems he had written, Frederick wrote in a letter of 19 February 1760: 'Unfortunately, this war will not be decided by the pen, but by the sword. If it were only a matter of writing, we would soon have hunted down the Austrians, the Russians, the Imperial Army and the Swedes'.[88]

The relationship between space and media was followed on three levels around the battlefield. The concept of the 'theatre of war' expresses various dimensions of how space is mediated through the media: The theatre of war as a geographical space of fighting, its theatrical representation as a form of knowledge show, for instance in maps of the same name, and

---

85   [Christian Täge], *Christian Täge's ehemaligen russischen Feldpredigers Lebensgeschichte, herausgegeben vom Verfasser der Novellen von Doro Caro* [i.e. August Samuel Gerber] (Königsberg: Degen, 1804), p.175. On Täge see the contribution by Adam Storring in this volume.

86   See Patrick Merziger, 'Der öffentliche König? Herrschaft in den Medien während der drei schlesischen Kriege', in Bernd Sösemann and Gregor Vogt-Spira (eds), *Friedrich der Große in Europa. Geschichte einer wechselvollen Beziehung* (Stuttgart: Steiner, 2012), Vol.1, pp.209–223; Hedwig Pompe, 'Im Kalkül der Kommunikation: Die Politik der Nachricht', in Adam and Dainat, '*Krieg ist mein Lied*', pp.111–136. Frederick had only slowly learned the 'news war' himself in the first two Silesian Wars, but soon perfected it, see Hans Jessen, 'Die Anfänge der friderizianischen Nachrichtenpolitik', *Zeitungswissenschaft* 15:7 (1940), pp.303–321; Karl Kurth, 'Grundzüge der friderizianischen Nachrichtenpolitik im 1. und 2. Schlesischen Kriege', in *Zeitungswissenschaft* 15 (1940), pp.606–631.

87   Alfred Dreyer, 'Hamburgische Stimmungsbilder aus den ersten Jahren des Siebenjährigen Krieges', *Hamburgische Geschichts- und Heimatblätter* 4 (1929) [45. Jg. Der Mitteilungen des Vereins für Hamburgische Geschichte], pp.58–67, here p.62. Dreyer evaluated the 'political mood reports' ('*Stimmungsberichte*') from Johann Matthias Dreyer to Legationsrat Alaradus von Canthier, head of foreign affairs for the bishop of Eutin; see Alfred Dreyer, *Johann Matthias Dreyer 1717-1769. Ein Hamburger satirischer Dichter und Holstein-Gottorper-Diplomat. Ein Beitrag zur Geistesgeschichte Hamburgs um die Mitte des 18. Jahrhunderts* (Hamburg: Christians, 1934) (= Veröffentlichungen des Vereins für Hamburgische Geschichte, 8).

88   Letter from Freiberg, 19 February 1760, in Friedrich der Grosse (ed. Hans Schumann), *Mein lieber Marquis. Sein Briefwechsel mit Jean-Baptiste d'Argens während des Siebenjährigen Krieges* (Zürich: Manesse, 1986), p.194.

finally the battlefield as the stage of a play with a deadly outcome.[89] The control of the battle-field as a space was also identified as the decisive criterion for victory or defeat in a battle, the assertion of which depended above all on media representation. Thus, control of the represented space in the media became at least as important as actual control of the space. It was only here that it was finally decided who could claim victory. After all, it is the memory of a battle that manifests itself in places of memory, and this is dependent on symbolically represented space as well as physical space. The spaces of war, here concretely the battle-fields, thus prove to be manufactured spaces in various ways. Battlefields only become a significant space through the action of fighting, to which the media representation is added as an additional virtual battlefield. The fiction of achieving a complete overview, as well as of a spatially limited battle, can be described as characteristic of this period. At all times, major field battles proved to be hard to control, but the seventeenth and eighteenth centuries reacted in a special way to the problem of confusion and un-representability with the use of theatre metaphors. The stage could be overlooked by the viewer. Theatres of knowledge conveyed complex processes and relations in a synoptic overview. The geometrical repre-sentation of the battle simultaneously conveyed the image of a containment of war within a precisely limited space. The civilian population appears only as spectators, not as victims. A new look at media representations of pre-modern battlefields thus shows that, even in the eighteenth century, war was always a war for the control of the fields of perception, and that many aspects of the new wars are therefore perhaps not so new or already follow a long history.

Further Reading

Clauss, Martin, and Nübel, Christoph (eds), *Militärisches Entscheiden. Voraussetzungen, Prozesse und Repräsentationen einer sozialen Praxis von der Antike bis zum 20. Jahrhundert* (Frankfurt a. M.: Campus, 2020).
Duffy, Christopher, *Prussia's Glory: Rossbach and Leuthen* (Chicago: Emperor's Press, 2003).
Marian Füssel, *Der Preis des Ruhms. Eine Weltgeschichte des Siebenjährigen Krieges 1756-1763* (München: Beck, 2019) [English translation in preparation with Columbia University Press].
Füssel, Marian, and Sikora, Michael (eds), *Kulturgeschichte der Schlacht* (Paderborn: Schöningh, 2014).
Lynn, John A., *Battle. A History of Combat and Culture* (Boulder: Westview, 2003).
Querengässer, Alexander, *Kesselsdorf 1745. Eine Entscheidungsschlacht in der Frühen Neuzeit* (Berlin: Zeughaus Verlag, 2020) [English translation in preparation with Helion and Company].
Weigley, Russel F., *The Age of Battles. The Quest for Decisive Warfare from Breitenfeld to Waterloo* (Bloomington: Indiana University Press, 1993).
Weißbrich, Thomas, *Höchstädt 1704. Eine Schlacht als Medienereignis; Kriegsberichterstattung und Gelegenheitsdichtung im Spanischen Erbfolgekrieg* (Paderborn: Schöningh, 2015).

---

89   See Marian Füssel, 'Theatrum Belli. Der Krieg als Inszenierung und Wissensschauplatz im 17. und 18. Jahrhundert', *Metaphorik* 14 (2008), pp.205–230.

16

'...when it comes to fightin'...they'll shove me in the stalls': Africans, Indians, and Imperialism's Great War

Dennis Showalter[1]

At first glance this essay may seem the proverbial white crow in a Festschrift honouring Christopher Duffy. His recognized milieu is early modern Europe. What place can an article focusing on the First World War have a claim to inclusion? But a bit of reflection—and familiarity with recent scholarship—demonstrates that the defining military event of this period, namely the Seven Years War, is increasingly interpreted and presented as the true First World War. Moreover, Christopher has contributed to the literature on the First World War with his excellent, *Through German Eyes: The British and the Somme*. Since this volume honours his wider career, I am grateful to the editor for allowing its inclusion. Both the First World War and the Seven Years War reached literally into every corner of the globe, from West Africa to the Philippines, from Tannenberg to Tanga. Willingly or not, indigenous cultures contributed men to fight both of these wars—frequently alongside Europeans.[2]

In the colonial era, local soldiers bore the brunt of British, Dutch, and French military effort in South Asia. North American ways of war developed in a tension between the methods of Europeans and those employed by the continent's First Peoples. South American wars of liberation, too, were shaped by officers who had observed the Prussian military experience. Experience and necessity, then, combined with intention to give Europe's military culture a global perspective and a multi-ethnic seasoning. Neither should be exaggerated. Seasoning is not the same as flavour; indigenous troops remained marginalized exotics –cultural successors to the Croats of the eighteenth-century Habsburg army and the Scots Highlanders under British colours in that era. Nevertheless, both were present over the next century and a half. Often maligned by European populations, these soldiers

---

1   Dr. Showalter's family has kindly given permission to include this essay in the volume posthumously.
2   See particularly the anthology Mark Danley and Patrick J. Speelman (eds), *The Seven Years' War* (Leiden: Brill, 2012).

could equally share in the complaints of Kipling's white soldier in *Tommy*. But in another World War these indigenous soldiers experienced the fundamental process of moving from history's stalls to its centre stage.

In the final months of 1914, a dance of the furies began. Choreographed by hatred and suspicion, self-justification and self-righteousness, it would transform Europe fundamentally. An aspect of that transformation often overlooked began in August as the first battalions of *tirailleurs algeriens* disembarked in the ports of southern France. It expanded in September when an Indian Corps joined a hard-pressed British Expeditionary Force. Tsarist Russia had a significant number of non-Russians in uniform. By 1914 the Habsburg army invited description as a transnational force. But in these cases, the 'outsiders' were officially direct subjects of their respective states.[3] In French and British contexts, for the first time in literal centuries, non-Europeans fought in strength, not as auxiliaries, not as exotics, but as integral, indeed crucial, elements of their parent armies in a heartland campaign. The Indian Corps froze and bled to the point of exhaustion in a Flanders winter, fighting an embryonic trench war alien to their experience, suffering 35,000 casualties in fourteen months. The North Africans paid a no less heavy toll in the battles of the frontiers. A single battalion lost 500 of its 900 men in a single day at Charleroi. War Minister Adolphe Messimy was only marginally hyperbolic in praising the *tirailleurs'* decisive role at the Marne: on the Orcq and in the marshes of St Gond.[4] In perhaps the Great War's most comprehensive exercise in cultural displacement, battalions from sub-Saharan Africa played a critical role during First Ypres in defending the ruins of Dixmude in a desolation of freezing muck. In both France and Britain, the front experience was an entering wedge. While racialized considerations remained a factor among the European soldiers, they were increasingly balanced by a sense of common participation in a common experience and a common cause. The balancing process was enhanced by a generalized sense of colonial soldiers as shock troops – a trope, ironically, nurtured by an enduring sense of colonials as 'others', better attuned to the demands of the trenches than 'civilized' and sensitive Europeans.[5]

The notion of colonial soldiers as patriots at one remove, faithful participants in the imperial process, was of course a construction – but not a complete fiction. Colonial soldiers were, arguably fundamentally volunteers – 'true volunteers' like Britain's Indian army, or French subjects eligible to be drafted, by methods that as the war continued increasingly amounted to dragooning and impressments. Given, however, the loopholes and vagaries of French colonial administration it was also possible to avoid service by flight or hiding; a situation inviting comparison with the US Selective Service system during the Cold War.[6]

---

3   Joshua Sanborn, *Drafting the Russian Nation: Military Conscription, Total War, and Mass Politics, 1905-1925* (De Kalb: Northern Illinois University Press, 1993); and Istvan Deak, *Beyond Nationalism: A Social and Political History of the Habsburg Officer Corps, 1848-1918* (New York: Oxford University Press, 1990).

4   Adolphe Messimy, *Mes souvenirs* (Paris: Plon, 1937), p.178.

5   Elizabeth Stice, 'Men on the Margins; Representations of Colonial Troops in British and French Trench Newspapers of the Great War', *The Journal of Military History*, 83 (2019), pp.435-454. Claude Markovits, *De l' Indus a la Somme: des Indiens en France pendant la Grande Guerre* (Paris: Éditions de la Maison des sciences de l'homme, 2018), offers a useful and neglected perspective.

6   Self-mutilation and suicide were also responses to conscription. Sikh Myron J. Echenburg, 'Paying the Blood Tax: Military Conscription in French West Africa, 1914-1929', *Canadian Journal of African*

This conceptual matrix generates two sets of questions. First, how did the west's major colonial powers evolve from regarding locally raised troops as marginal auxiliaries and emergency expedients, to accepting them as bulwarks not merely of empires, but of the respective homelands? Second, what inducements and compulsions could Imperial powers offer to keep their ranks full? And on the other hand, why would a Sikh or a Kabyle seek out a recruiter or accept answer a draft call?

The answers involve two factors. First was availability. In India decades of war and revolution had generated a pattern of displacement. Specifically, soldiers of fortune – and misfortune –drifted south, like sand in a boot. Seeking familiar employment, they found places with European trading companies seeking guards and escorts. As Britain's Honourable East India Company expanded its commercial and political horizons it militarized these ad hoc detachments – often under Indian officers.[7] As the Company moved north it encountered a fully developed culture of an armed and assertive peasantry for whom soldiering was a familiar post-harvest, dry-season occupation, and who found the British no more than another in a catalogue of alien paymasters.[8] In Algeria, then essentially a geographic expression, France raised its first ad hoc indigenous unit almost as soon as they landed, then began working with the Berber Zwawas, who had long supplied fighting men to the Ottoman Empire's local forces. The first Zouave battalions were formed from volunteers in 1830. Initially intended to reduce costs and mortality rates – death ratios of ten to one were not uncommon in metropolitan units deployed to North Africa in the early years of empire – the North Africans rapidly won a reputation as an elite.

That reputation informed the second factor in the evolution of local forces: effectiveness. The Zouaves indeed were so highly regarded that Frenchmen were integrated into their ranks, and eventually they were complete Gallicized – an early case of cultural military appropriation! But though retitled *tirailleurs algeriens*, the North Africans retained and enhanced their status. Still volunteers, with a mixed French/indigenous officer corps, they were deployed in the first line against Algeria's unending rebellions and insurgencies and counterinsurgency operations. At mid-century they served in Europe itself – the Crimea in 1854 and Italy in 1859 – with distinction, albeit on battalion scales.[9]

Studies/Revue Canadienne des Etudes Africaines, 9, pp.171-192; Christian Koller, 'Between Acceptance and Refusal-Soldiers' Attitudes toward War (Africa)', *1914-1918 Online*, < https://encyclopedia.1914-1918-online.net/article/between_acceptance_and_refusal_-_soldiers_attitudes_towards_war_africa>.

7   C. Wickremeseka, *"The Best Black Troops in the World:" British Perceptions and the Making of the Sepoy, 1746-1805* (Delhi: Manohar, 2002).

8   Dirk A. Kolff, *Naukar, Rajput, and Sepoy: The Ethnohistory of the Military Labour Market of Hindustan, 1450-1850* (Cambridge: Cambridge University Press, 1990); S. Alavi, *The Sepoy and the Company: Tradition and Transition in Northern India,1770-1830* (Delhi: Oxford University Press, 1994).

9   'La creation de l' Armee d'Afrique' and 'La conquete d'Algerie', in *Champs de Bataille Thematique*,28, *La onquete de l'Empire Colonial Francais*, 28 (2012), pp.18-47, combine for a useful introduction. Jennifer F Sessions, *By Sword and Plow: France and the Conquest of Algeria* (Ithaca: Cornell University Press, 2011), is an up-to-date overview.

The British Indian Army: Organization and Motivations

The sepoy regiments of the East India Company demonstrated similar adaptability – most significantly to India's version of the eighteenth-century battlefield. Armed and trained identically with their British counterparts, Indian battalions played equivalent parts on stricken fields from the mid-eighteenth century Carnatic Wars through the Mahratta Wars to Sobraon against the Sikhs. Increasingly they outnumbered European battalions, both the Crown's and the Company's. These were otherwise unavailable, considered too expensive, or – especially in the case of Company Europeans – were increasingly recruited from the dregs of the recruitment pools. Even the cavalry regiments bore the dismissive nickname 'dumpies', because of their large number of physically undersized and underdeveloped troopers.[10]

Class, caste, and race were flexible, when not protean, concepts in the early British imperial period. Successful commanders made no significant ethnically based distinctions. In the ranks, veterans spoke of putting '… religion into our knapsacks whenever the colours were unfurled.' Making full allowance for nostalgia and for telling superiors what they wished to hear, the trope reflected the reality of caste being significantly open to negotiation and manipulation.[11] The erosion of that structure, the evaluation of potential soldiers by race instead of caste, began well before the Revolution of 1857.[12] Its roots were complex; its construction was convoluted. The concept of 'martial races' fuelled by Social Darwinism was as widespread among Indian as British theorists. It was cultural as well as biological, ethnological as well as ethnographical. From perspectives of respect, admiration, and affection, the Indian Army's British officers utilized group identification as a shortcut to comprehending individual characteristics. The best example of the result is the dominant tone of the numerous memoirs produced by British officers who in general considered their men, whether Nepalese Gurknas, Jat Sikhs, or Punjabi Muslims, as faithful, valiant, and dense, dependent on Westerners to do their higher-order thinking.[13]

Both for internal security and external power projection a substantial number of Indians under arms was essential. The reconfigured military system was in good part based on incorporating a higher percentage of British troops, and British control of most of the artillery. In specifically India contexts it involved developing alternate recruiting grounds, especially in

10 See Richard Holmes, *Sahib: The British Soldier in India* (London: Harper Collins, 2005); Peter Stanley, *White Mutiny: British Military Culture in India* (New York: New York University Press, 1998). and 'Imperial Vice: Sex, Drink and the Health of British Troops in North Indian Cantonments, 1800-1858', in David Killingray and David Omissi (eds), *Guardians of Empire* (Manchester: Manchester University Press, 1999), pp.25-52

11 Often cited in this context, and not much less often criticized, is Sita Ram Pande's narrative memoir, *From Sepoy to Subedar*. The best evaluation of its authenticity and context is Alison Safidi, '"From Sepoy to Subedar" Khvab-o-Khayal and Douglas Craven Philpott', *Journal of Urdu Studies*, 25 (2020), pp.42-65. The quotation is from Simon Millar, *Assaye 1803: Wellington's First and Bloodiest Victory* (Oxford: Osprey, 2006), p.23.

12 Douglas Peers, '"The Habitual Nobility of Being": British Officers and the Social Construction of the Bengal Army in the Early 19ith Century', *Modern Asian Studies*, 25 (1991), pp.545-569.

13 See Heather Streets, *Martial Races: The Military, Race, and Masculinity in British Imperial Culture, 1857-1914* (Manchester: Manchester University Press, 2004); and David Omissi, '"Martial Races": Ethnicity and Security in Colonial India, 1858-1939', *War and Society*, 9 (1991), pp.1-27.

the Punjab, where loyalty in 1857 resulted in a spectrum of economic, political, and cultural rewards that significantly reshaped that region – not to mention an opportunity to rebalance accounts with longstanding foes of Hindustan.[14]

The Indian Army nevertheless remained a local and regional force, despite some minor short-term deployments in East Africa. That pattern reflected racial and ethnic considerations, highlighted by the definition of the Second South African War as a 'Sahib's war', with Indian regiments not needed, not wanted, and not welcome.[15] Increasingly as well it reflected an understanding that high-end regional wars were becoming increasingly demanding. The traditional frontier opponents were more and more technologically, tactically, and not least politically sophisticated to a point where standard orders of battle not only brigaded British and Indian battalion evenly – two apiece – but selected the Indian units from a limited pool considered best capable by culture and training of meeting the Frontier's operational demands. As for the increasingly perceived threat posed by Russia in Asia, the British strategic hope was that logistics, rear-area uprisings, and forces of relatively lower quality than the European army corps would combine to balance odds that as a rule were considered uneven.[16]

Raising the Indian Army's overall effectiveness to the point of large-scale commitment against cutting-edge Western-pattern forces was considered a chimera.[17] This was not entirely for the often-cited fear of revolution that for decades kept Indian rifles a generation behind those of their British counterparts. India's arms industry was marginal even in the context of India's limited general industrial development.[18] British investments emphasized railways and textiles. Nor could the home country readily fill the weapons gap from its own relatively limited capacities. Recruiting patterns were also adjusted to favour those groups that had remained loyal during the Revolution. Here however ethnography played as wide a role as politics. The Indian Army's British officers were frequently sophisticated, if limited, cultural anthropologists. From a perspective of respect, admiration, and even affection,

14 David Omissi, *The Sepoy and the Raj: The Indian Army, 1860-1940* (Basingstoke: Palgrave Macmillan, 1994); Bruce Collins, 'The Military Marketplace in India, 1850-1869', in N Arielli, B. Collins (eds) *Transnational Soldiers. Foreign Military Enlistment in the Modern Era* (New York: Palgrave Macmillan, 2013), pp.69-86. See also Kaushik Roy, 'Logistics and the Construction of Loyalty: The Welfare Mechanism in the Indian Army, 1859-1913', ed. P S Gupta and A. Deshpande (eds) *The British Raj and its Indian Armed Forces. 1857-1939* (Delhi: Oxford University Press, 2002), pp 98-124

15 Balasubramanyan Chandramohan, '"Hamlet with the Prince of Denmark Left Out"? The South African War, Empire and India', in D. Lowry (ed.) *The South African War Reappraised* (Manchester: Manchester University Press, 2000), pp.150-168, is a nuanced analysis of this complex question.

16 See Kaushik Roy, *Frontiers, Insurgencies and Counter-insurgencies in South Asia* (Oxford: Routledge, 2015), pp.10-67; and the general analysis by T.R. Moreman, *The Army in India and the Development of Frontier Warfare, 1847-1947* (Basingstoke: Palgrave Macmillan, 1998)

17 Three works published recently and almost simultaneously combine for an excellent overview of the Indian Army in the Great War. Alan Jeffreys, *The Indian Army in the First World War: New Perspectives* (Warwick: Helion, 2018), is a comprehensive scholarly anthology; George Morton-Jack, *Army of Empire: The Untold story of the Indian Army in World War One* (London: Basic Books, 2018), is as perceptive as it is comprehensive; Kaushik Roy, *The Indian Army in the First World War, 1914-1918* (New Delhi: Oxford University Press, 2018), is a masterful study from the doyen of modern Indian military history.

18 Kaushik Roy, 'Equipping Leviathan: Ordnance Factories of British India, 1859-1913', *War in History*, 10, pp.398-423, takes a more sanguine view of production potential.

they utilized group identification as a shortcut to comprehending individual characteristics – behaviour that indeed was generally discouraged. 'Going native', getting 'too close' to those perceived as ultimately inscrutable Orientals, was a widely accepted norm in the eighteenth century. It became an increasingly culpable aberration in the nineteenth.[19]

Perhaps the best example of the result is the dominant tone of memoirs produced by British officers of Gurkhas, who in general considered their men as faithful, valiant, and dense – if you will, precursors at best of *Star Wars*' Wookies.[20] The end result by 1914 was an Indian Army that was in Imperial contexts a thing apart structurally and a specialized work tool operationally. The comprehensive Kitchener reforms of the early twentieth century focused the Indian Army even more on the frontier, towards Afghanistan, and towards a Russian threat that even after the Entente of 1907 loomed far larger in Delhi than London.[21] From the Indian perspective, the reconfigured army's internal ground rules were clearly understood and well accepted, from the support of religious festivals and activities to the convention that wounded men were not returned to the front, provided a source of status and profit for the Indian officers, the subadars and jemadars, who functioned as an O-ring and a communications link between the sahib-log on one hand and the sepoys and sowars on the other. In a wider context the military structure provided leverage in terms of culture, class, caste, and family: direct, personal access to the governing establishment, an inside track on such economic developments as irrigated farmland with veterans' preference.[22] One might speak of a new form of mediating elite, eventually a potential fifth order added to the traditional Hindu four. The Indian Army was in short what in China would be called a 'rice bowl': a stable, satisfying livelihood and way of life. It was a long distance from an imperially configured instrument of war.[23]

The French African Forces

The *tirailleurs algeriens*' experience in the nineteenth century's second half was significantly different. Their strength remained token: three regiments, then four. Their focus remained North Africa: counterinsurgency and 'pacification', though token forces were sent

---

19   Kaushik Roy, 'The Construction of Regiments in the Indian Army, 1859-1913', *War in History*, 8, pp.127-148; and Douglas M. Peers, 'The Martial Races and the Indian Army in the Victorian Era', in D. Marston and C.S Sundaram (eds), *A Military History of India and South Asia from the East India Company to the Nuclear Era* (Bloomington: Indiana University Press, 2008), pp.34-52.

20   Lionel Caplan, *Warrior Gentlemen: Gurkhas in the Western Imagination* (Providence: Berghan Books, 1995).

21   Tim Moreman, 'Lord Kitchener, the General Staff, and the Army in India, 1902-1914', in D. French, B. Holden Reid (eds), *The British General Staff: Reform and Innovation, c. 1902-1939* (London: Routledge, 2002), pp.57-74.

22   Tan Tai Yong, *The Garrison State: The Military Government and Society in Colonial Punjab, 1849-1947* (New Delhi: Sage, 2005).

23   An insider's perspective is provided in De Witt C. Ellinwood (ed.), *Between Two Worlds: A Rajput Officer in the Indian Army 1905-21: Based on the Diary of Amar Singh of Jaipur* (London: Hamilton, 2005.) An aristocrat's account, it can by no means dismissed as special pleading. Cf. for context Tony McClenhagan, *For the Honour of My House: The Contribution of the Indian Princely States in the First World War* (Warwick: Helion, 2019)

to Senegal, Indochina, and Mexico in the 1860s. In the Franco-German War, however, the 'turcos' moved to the centre ring as part of a larger redeployment from Algeria to eastern France. They gave the Germans expensive lessons in minor tactics while providing fodder for endless denunciations of employing 'black savages' in a war between civilized peoples. [24]

In Algeria's economically undeveloped, continually disordered, social system, 'conscription by destitution' was as much rule as exception. The principal motivation for enlistment was economic: employment at regular pay for acceptable risk. Initially service could be for as long as 25 years, with regular reenlistment bonuses, and the rank and file were correspondingly isolated from their original communities, dismissed (with solid justification) as religiously lax winebibbers. On the other hand, the support of caids and clan notables for military service was regularly sought through financial and political means, and as regularly received – not least because the demand for recruits was sufficiently limited that, if anything, indigenous pressure was to expand the numbers in the ranks for the sake of expanding influence. Increases in numbers were in turn checked by opposition from an expanding *colon* population which had no Indian counterpart. These immigrants, themselves economically and socially marginal, had ethnic and economic reasons to keep guns as far away from as many *indigenes* as possible.[25] As the legal incorporation of Algeria into France increasingly became a political reality under the Third Republic, colon influence grew. The massive – and still little known – *indigene* uprising of 1871, structured by drought, famine, and plague, was sparked by a mutiny of soldiers resisting shipment to France in the war's late stage – in the light of Britain's recent experience, a pragmatic reason to limit the number of *indigenes* under arms, and also limiting their geographic deployment. Most of the *tirailleurs'* activity was in Algeria, and most of that in small detachments. Several battalions were deployed as well to Indochina, where the climate proved no less debilitating than it did for Europeans and where the Algerians acquired a significant reputation for looting and atrocities, both reflections of long-standing patterns generally accepted in Algeria as combat bonuses.[26] In effect the Algerians were more and more being considered not as a force specifically adapted to specific North African conditions, but as part of *France militaire outre-mer.* Further steps in their integration involved expanding the number of battalions – to 37 by 1914 – despite continued colonial opposition. This reflected France's growing involvement in Morocco, increasing tensions in Europe, and a growing concern that in an age of mass war, France's metropolitan population was increasingly lagging behind that of Germany. That last point connected with significant domestic opposition to increasing conscription requirements that under the Third Republic featured more and more loopholes and exemptions. The Law of 1905 requiring two years under arms and allowing only medical exemptions, amounted to a political compromise. Making up the difference from the empire became an increasingly attractive bridge in military, political, and not least intellectual circles.[27]

---

24   Christian Koller, *'Von Wilden aller Rassen niedergemetzelt:' Die Diskussion um die Verwendung von Kolonialtruppen zwischen Rassismus und Militaerpolitik (1914-1930)* (Stuttgart:Franz Steiner, 2003).

25   David Prochaska, *Making Algeria French: Colonialism in Bône, 1870-1920* (New York: Cambridge University Press, 1990), is a useful case study.

26   See for context Michael P.M. Finch, *A Progressive Occupation? The Galleni-Lyautey Method and Colonial Pacification in Tonkin and Madagascar, 1885-1900* (Oxford: oxford University Press, 2013).

27   See in general Gerd Krumeich (Trans. S. Conn), *Armaments and Politics in France on the Eve of the First World War: The Introduction of Three Year Conscription* (Famington: Berg, 1984)

Arguably the major justification for the Third Republic's empire was the concept of the 'civilizing mission'. It was not merely pith-helmeted colonialists who internalized the position that France was unique among Europe's great powers in extending the benefits of Western culture and Western governance to less enlightened regions and peoples. However, that process had grown increasingly expensive in terms of lives, money, and diplomacy. With the turn of the century an argument developed and expanded that France could and should no longer maintain a one-sided paternal position.[28] The benefits of civilization had a price; a blood price, or more euphemistically and acceptably, a blood tax. After all, was not Western civilization itself sustained by its taxes? Did not the colonies, in particular north and west Africa, possess 'reservoirs of men', uncounted, untapped, and surplus to economic requirements?[29] And if military service was regarded even on the Left in France as a means of transmitting French Republican values to the youth, why would it not have the same results in the overseas communities? Perhaps service, specifically compulsory service, might prove a means of developing native subjects into French citizens – eventually, of course!

The matrix of a system for civilization through militarization was already in place. Tunisia, ruled by France since 1881, had possessed the framework of a conscription system, not universal but rather on the selective service model mentioned earlier. This was retained, and periodically considered as a model for Algeria as well.[30] In a wider context, moreover, Algeria was increasingly integrated into the metropolitan war plan: organized and numbered as an army corps, expected to provide two standard divisions for general service in time of war. That in turn required significant, systematic *indigene* participation.

An aside worth mentioning, in both French and British contexts, is that during the second half of the nineteenth century colonial soldiers acquire a patina of exotic glamour. The widespread adoption of Zouave pattern uniforms in the US before and during the Civil War is the most familiar example. But as war correspondents, war photography, and colour illustrations became more comprehensive and familiar, 'native' troops took a literal stage centre compared to their workaday European counterparts. If they looked good, a logical deduction was that they could fight well.[31]

In the French context a wild card appeared on the board in 1910. A hitherto obscure Colonel Charles Mangin published *La Force noire*. France had been systematically recruiting in its coastal sub-Saharan African possessions since the 1850s. The *tirailleurs senegalais* had, by companies and battalions, played a central role in the successful French expansion in central Africa, and were sufficiently effective in Morocco to lend gravitas to Mangin's case that eventually they could play a vital role replacing the sons that French women were unwilling to bear and French men were unable to father. He argued black Africans were better suited to contemporary industrial warfare than over civilized Europeans. Mangin contended that the men possessed physical endurance, indifference to pain, less developed

---

28   See Dino Constanti and Juliette Ferrand, *Mission civilisatrice: le rôle d'histoire colonial de l'identité politique francaise* (Paris: La Découverte, 2008).

29   The phrase is from Shelby Cullom Davis, *Reservoirs of Men: A History of the Black Troops of French West Africa* (Geneva: Impr. réunies, 1934).

30   Anthony Clayton, *France, Soldiers, and Africa* (London: Brassey's, 1988), p.246.

31   See Thomas S. Abler, *Hinterland Warriors and Military Dress: European Empires and Exotic Uniforms* (Oxford: Bloomsbury, 1999).

nervous systems that limited their susceptibility to stress – these were the characteristics of the warriors France needed if she hoped to recover the lost provinces of Alsace and Lorraine.[32]

Mangin's proposal never received official approval. Jean Jaurès spoke for many on the Left when he argued that Black soldiers might be used to suppress protest and dissent – an argument given weight by the widespread and widely publicized use of metropolitan troops in domestic disturbances. Nevertheless in 1912 a decree enabled conscription of African men for up to four years. Keeping the decree's administration in local hands enabled significant abuses familiar in earlier centuries in Europe. 'Undesirables' of various sorts, those without influence, found themselves in uniform, with corresponding negative effect on whatever public enthusiasm existed. Some were outright slaves, or as close to it as made no difference.[33] By 1914 only 15,000 'Senegalese' (the generic name for Black African *tirailleurs*) were in French service, while the original manpower crisis seemed on the way to being appropriately addressed by the 1913 increase of the metropolitan term of service to three years.

The 1905 reduction of the conscription term in metropolitan France to two years, however, had brought the issue of conscription to the forefront of Algerian politics. The 1912 decrees imposing conscription on Algerian Muslims reflected Minister of War Adolphe Messimy's grandiloquent proclamation that 'we do not govern the indigenous people; we commend them.'[34] What debate existed focused on the need for responding to the German threat. There was no serious discussion of the issue of colonial resistance, much less considering Muslim reaction in any systematic fashion. That proved a mistake. A significant number of draft-eligible men fled to other parts of the Islamic world. Newspapers and activists demanded compensation for an arbitrarily imposed blood tax. In particular a Young Algeria movement, generally assimilationist in orientation, insisted on a spectrum of reforms built around granting such rights of citizenship as suffrage – without granting citizenship itself. That, the reformers understood, would mean giving up Muslims' existing right to be governed in many civil matters by Koranic law – a status far more widely popular than projected and ephemeral benefits of citizenship to be acquired by accepting conscription. The government, nevertheless, fearing unrest, compromised sufficiently to satisfy the Young Algerians, removing some administrative restrictions immediately and declaring the rest negotiable.[35]

Most were met – in a law passed on 15 July 15, 1914! The catch-22 was obvious: such major changes must await victory – to which Algerians would contribute as a down payment in what was generally expected to be a short-term process. In the event over 250,000 North Africans and above 150,000 sub-Saharan Africans served France in uniform, in addition to hundreds of thousands of civilian laborers. Their performance in battle earned them first-line status – shock troops, not, as some anti-colonialist accounts have it, mere bullet-stoppers – was confirmed when for the projected campaign of 1919 an exsanguinated France

32   Charles Mangin, *La Force noire* (Paris: Hachette, 1910); and *La Mission des troupes noires* (Paris: Comité de l'Afrique française 1911).
33   Joe Lunn, *Memoirs of the Maelstrom: A Senegalese Oral History of the First World War* (Portsmouth, NH: Heinemann Educational, 1999), pp.45ff.
34   Adolphe Messimy, *Le Statut des Indigènes Algériens* (Paris: Charles-Lavauzelle, 1913).
35   Savannah Pine, 'Conscription, Citizenship, and French Algeria', *KU ScholarWorks*, 2016, pp.44-54.

proposed to replace a metropolitan regiment with a North African one in an increasing number of divisions. In material terms North Africa and the colonies subscribed over a billion francs in war loans and donations and provided around five and a half million tons of raw materials—and that from people and places described as 'underdeveloped', owing whatever progress they experienced to the *mission civilaisatrice!*

European Fears and Colonial Service in Europe

Recruitment in north and sub-Saharan Africa was de facto by a mixture of volunteering and compulsion – though increasing numbers of 'volunteers' were generated by coercion that grew less and less subtle as the casualty lists mounted. Direct resistance was overall limited and ephemeral. Grievances involved military specifics: promotion, home leave, benefits. The army –still to the surprise of some contemporary scholars – could provide better conditions than Algeria's civil administration, even if they reflected an egalitarian sharing of misery. Muslim social and religious perquisites were generally honoured, despite an enduring suspicion that Islam somehow rendered its adherents less reliable. In fact, the limited deployment of French Muslims against the Ottoman Empire minimized direct foci of religious/cultural conflict. Initial encounters, whether in rural or urban contexts, tended to generate anxiety and mistrust. These generally gave way to curiosity. Curiosity evolved – or devolved – into a tolerance of acceptance and indifference that was a noticeable contrast to the behaviour of whites in the colonies.[36]

The principal European racial fear: contact with 'white women', proved essentially a constructed flash point. The off-duty African soldiers were closely supervised, officially to protect them from degenerate European vices. Their knowledge of French was limited; for the sub-Saharan *tirailleur* it was based on an official pidgin known as *petit-negre*. And again, taken collectively the Africans most seem to have preferred least a semblance of cooperation in matters sexual. That in turn might be gained by money, friendliness, or, especially in a countryside denuded of healthy men, cheerfully pitching in to chores reminding them of home. The Senegalese, indeed, acquired in popular culture something of the status of exotic pets. One postcard shows a black rabbit in *tirailleur* uniform and a white rabbit in woman's clothing sitting cosily on a park bench as the *tirailleur* declares in broad *petit-negre* that after the war they will go to Africa and make little black and white rabbits for France.[37] More familiar and less threatening was the long-standing advertisement for the chocolate drink

---

36   The best overviews are Richard S. Fogarty, *Race and War in France: Colonial Subjects in the French Army, 1914-1918* (Baltimore: Johns Hopkins University Press, 2008); and Jacques Fremeaux, *Les Colonies dans la Grande Guerre Combats et epreuves des peoples d' outre-mer* (Paris: 14-18 Éditions, 2006). For Algeria see Gilbert Meynier, *L'Algérie revelee: La Guerre de 1914-1918 et le premier quart du XX siècle* (Geneva: Librairie Droz, 1981); Marc Michel, *L'Appel d' Afrique: Contributions et reactions a l'effet de guerre en A.O.F 1919-1918* (Paris: Publications de la Sorbonne, 1982) remains standard for the Senegalese. See generally William F. Dean, 'Morale among French Colonial Troops on the Western Front during World War One: 1914-1918', *Scientia Militaria. South African Journal of Military Studies*, 38 (2010), pp.44-61.

37   Dick van Galen Last with Ralf Futselaar, *Black Shame. African Soldiers in Europe, 1914-1922* (London: Bloomsbury, 2015), pp.87-93, introduces this complex and still-fraught issue. The postcard in

banania, featuring ape caricature of a grinning *tirailleur* and the pidgin slogan 'Y'a bon'.[38] In the views of Europeans: exotic, alien, fundamentally 'other', black or brown, Muslim or animist, Africans were nevertheless fighting for France in its direst hours – and often literally side by side with whites.

If France's colonial soldiers were in its metaphoric front room, Britain's primarily remained in the back garden. In 1914 Britain declared war in the name of its empire, seeping consent from neither dominions nor possessions. Nevertheless, significant initial enthusiasm for the war existed in India. Motives were usually specific, based on hopes of group or individual benefit from being first on side. Objectively, in hindsight from a British perspective in made best operational and logistical sense to base any Indian contingent in Egypt. But George V, who took seriously his status as King Emperor, wished his Indian subjects to participate at stage-centre in what was expected to be a short and splendid war, and his opinion could not be dismissed. The Viceroy, Lord Hardinge, was more concerned for internal security than imperial defence. But he had successfully improved relations with a still embryonic nationalist opposition and saw the war as a means of giving 'advance' Indian opinion a political stake in the Raj. Kitchener, now Secretary of State for War, wished to see his handiwork tested. The exigencies of war, moreover, were impelling the withdrawal of all but a few British battalions from India and removing the best of the Indian regiments would diminish the prospects of a military-focused revolt on the lines of 1857.[39]

Britain withdrew the Indian Corps from the Western Front in 1915, leaving only a token presence of cavalry. The decision reflected a still-debated combination of operational and cultural reasons. The winter of 1914-1915 was bitter, and conditions alike at the front and in the rear primitive. Artillery, machine guns, and barbed wire created a tactical environment no less alien than the ecological one. The sepoy's relationship to the army was strongly contractual: an 'if-then' pattern. If most sepoys came from rural areas, significant numbers even of Gurkhas came from backgrounds of freeholding cultivators were understanding one's legal and cultural rights in dealing with markets, moneylenders, and officials was a requisite of survival. Plainly put, this was not an expeditionary force of yokels – and certainly not expendable yokels.

'Working conditions' were further exacerbated by heavy casualties. The few British officers in a battalion were its almost literal lifeline to a new and random world. They took their responsibilities seriously. Their losses were proportionally heavy, and they could not be replaced even in terms of warm and willing British bodies, to say nothing of any linguistic and cultural qualities. Nor was the replacement system generally prepared for anything like the continuing casualty lists of the Western Front. Increasingly entire companies were transferred from regiments still at home, to be replaced by recruits and inserted unceremoniously into the attenuated battalions in the trenches. By the armistice only a single pre-war Indian battalion would have the same four companies it had in 1914. The effects of this

question is included in the illustrations for Michel; see also Stepan Likosky, *With a Weapon and a Grin: Postcard Images of France's Black Colonial Troops in WWI* (Alglen PA.: Schiffer, 2017)

38   Richard S Fogarty, 'The French Empire', in E. Gerwarth and E. Manila (eds), *Empires at War, 1914-1923* (Oxford: Oxford University Press, 2014), p.124.

39   David Omissi, 'The Indian Army in Europe, 1914-1918', in Eric Storm and Ali Tuma (eds), *Colonial Soldiers in Europe, 1914-1918* (New York: Routledge, 2016), pp.120-123.

process on unit cohesion in a combat zone were swingeing. Even more significant was the accompanying policy of returning recovered lightly wounded men to the ranks instead of sending them home which was standard policy on the Indian frontier.

The initial result was a 'concealed strike' – or perhaps better said, a challenge to breach of contract. Increased sick calls and small injuries were complemented by a growing number of self-inflicted wounds too obvious to be explained away. Severe responses, including flogging and the death penalty (more likely to be imposed and suspended than actually inflicted) diminished these overt indirect protests. Withdrawn for rest and refitting at the turn of the year, the Indian Corps did well in the next fighting season, especially at Neuve Chapelle. But the continued high losses and the exposure to gas war at Second Ypres increased the number of shellshock cases and generated a persistent rumour that Indians were being sacrificed to spare British lives. In fact, casualties were more or less proportional. But in estaminets, latrines, and even letters home, the image of 'grain that is flung back into the ocean' persisted.

By summer it was plain that the British New Armies would provide an increasing and predictable source of men. It was no less clear that these new divisions would make heavy material demands on an economy still in the process of mobilizing for war. Were the Indians still needed, especially in the context of facing another winter? Desertion had been limited and reflected 'workplace' grievances as opposed to fundamental reaction of the British war and the British raj. Nor had unsanctioned sexual contact with British ladies or French women proved significant; more significant, at least, than the increasing concern at policy levels for the effect in India of continued large-scale participation on the Western Front.[40]

Initially, concern for the loyalty of Muslim troops once Turkey entered the war had led to their exclusion from Gallipoli.[41] As 1915 waned, however, looming defeat at Gallipoli and developing stagnation in Mesopotamia encouraged an increased Indian presence in the Middle East. Britain was fighting to maintain and enhance the Empire as well as to win the war. Palestine, Syria, the Mesopotamian provinces were vital elements in a stable overland link to India. The region's oil was central to Britain's continued status as the world's leading naval power. Yet Britain's operational reach had consistently exceeded its military grasp, a fact illustrated and exacerbated by the contradictory, not to say duplicitous, nature of the Sykes-Picot Agreement, the Balfour Declaration, and the McMahon-Hussein correspondence.[42]

From both necessity and choice, Indian troops, specifically the fire-tried Indian Corps, provided a chance to rebalance the books. Reassigned at the end of 1915, its two divisions were the core of a revitalized Mesopotamian campaign, and of the Palestine triumph of 1918

---

40   Omissi, 'The Indian Army in Europe, 1914-1918', pp.123-127, is a good introduction to the subject; the quotation is on p.125. George Morton-Jack, *The Indian Army on the Western Front.: India's Expeditionary force to France and Belgium in the First World War* (Cambridge: Cambridge University Press, 2014), is the most recent and best balanced of the substantial number of recent studies of the Indian troops in France.

41   Peter Stanley, *Die in Battle, Do Not Despair: The Indians on Gallipoli, 1915* (Warwick: Helion, 2015).

42   Scott Anderson, *Lawrence in Arabia: War, Deceit, Imperial Folly and the Making of the Modern Middle East* (New York: Doubleday, 2013), is an award-winning page-turner. See also and more soberly David French, 'The Dardanelles, Mecca, and Kut: Prestige as a Factor in British Eastern Strategy, 1914-1916', *War and Society* 5 (1987), pp.45-61.

– both of which were accomplished essentially by Indian units and formations, many newly created. The two cavalry divisions that remained in France as a token presence were also sent to Palestine in early 1918 and helped turn a British victory into a military triumph that, for good an ill, underwrote a century-long restructuring of the Middle East. The theatre of operations might have been a secondary one militarily. But its consequences established put the Indian Army squarely in the front lines of the British Empire.[43]

As the war progressed and its demands on India increased, the British government raised the level of its promises to extend Indian self-government generally, and specifically to 'Indianize' the Indian army by opening the King's Commission to Indians. On the other side of the line was a nationalist movement whose pre-war attitude to the army had been largely indifferent when not hostile. Now politically involved Indians began pressuring the government on issues of military reform as part of the path to self-rule, and eventual partnership in an expanded British system.[44]

Wartime recruiting abuses and inflation sustained disaffection in traditional recruiting grounds. Demobilized soldiers participated in the post-war demonstrations in the Punjab and elsewhere. The interwar use of Indian troops against nationalist demonstrations tested their loyalty and identity to new limits.[45] The issue of commissioning Indian officers proved a thorny one – not least because of the question of the effects of the change on the Indian officers, whose lack of Western educations essentially excluded them from the process.[46] Yet on the whole the Indian army built on its Great War experience to lay the foundations for greater success in a larger conflict.

Conclusion

This was only the beginning. For Britain, the key to maintaining an overextended Asian position by projected large-scale external deployments became the Indian Army.[47] France compensated for a declining birth rate by importing the largest non-indigenous force seen in Europe since the Roman Empire.[48] The global nature of the later war and the Axis victories of 1940 meant colonies could not be relegated to the margins. Their contributions could not be treated as 'nice to have'. Their fighting men could not be regarded as dispensable

43   See Matthew Hughes, *Allenby and British Strategy in the Middle East, 1917-1919* (New York: Routledge, 1999); and Kaushik Roy, 'The Indian Army in Mesopotamia, from 1916 to 1919: Tactics, Technology, and Logistics reconsidered', in I. Beckett (ed.), *1917: Beyond the Western Front* (Leiden: Brill, 2009), pp.131-158.

44   Sir Algernon Rumbold, *Watershed in India, 1914-1922* (London: Athlone, 1979), remains a useful overview.

45   Nick Lloyd 'The Indian Army and Civil Disorder, 1919-22' and Rob Johnson, 'The Indian Army and Internal Security, 1919-1946', in Kaushik Roy (ed), *The Indian Army in the Two World Wars* (Leiden: Brill, 2012), pp.335-358 and 359-390.

46   Pradeep P. Barua, *Gentlemen of the Raj: The Indian Army Officer Corps, 1817-1949* (Westport: Praeger, 2003), provides an overview and background.

47   Pradeep P. Barua, 'Strategies and Doctrines of Imperial Defence: Britain and India, 1919-1945', *Journal of Imperial and Commonwealth History*, 25 (1997), pp.240-266.

48   Tarak Barkawi, *Soldiers of Empire: British and Indian Armies in World War One* (Cambridge: Cambridge University Press, 2017).

auxiliaries. By 1945 'colonial' had become a retrograde description. Liberating France from the Nazis was essentially the achievement of the French Empire, especially North Africa, which furnished most of the men and suffered most of the casualties.[49]

To wage war in South Asia Britain was constrained to raise history's largest colonial army –increasingly by expanding recruiting parameters and internal procedures to a point where by 1945 it was approaching a national institution culturally – and politically as well. Perhaps the key signifier was the increasing use of a new word to describe and identify its rank and file. For decades Indian soldiers had been cast in subordinate, even childlike, roles. Now they were '*jawans*': young *men*. Indian and North African recruitment pools grew significantly larger in the First World War. Tones were nevertheless set by the same classes and cultures heavily recruited in the First World War, and they retained and transmitted comprehensive collective memories of the experience of colonial soldiering that were not overwhelmingly positive. What were the origins and outgrowths of colonial service: Societal conditions: ethnicity and communalism? Ideological developments: nationalism and anti-colonialism? Economic factors: comprehensive change in attitudes towards getting, spending, and having? Military organizations themselves: their evolving appeals and compulsions in an age of globalized war? Answers vary widely, but their roots are common: they lie in the eighteenth century – and correspondingly shed long-range light on the work of Christopher Duffy.

Further Reading

Barua, Pradeep P., *Gentlemen of the Raj: The Indian Army Officer Corps, 1817-1949* (Westport: Praeger, 2003).

Fogarty, Richard S., *Race and War in France: Colonial Subjects in the French Army, 1914-1918* (Baltimore: Johns Hopkins University Press, 2008).

Morton-Jack, George, *The Indian Army on the Western Front.: India's Expeditionary force to France and Belgium in the First World War* (Cambridge: Cambridge University Press, 2014)

Storm, Eric, and Tuma, Ali (eds) *Colonial Soldiers in Europe, 1914-1918* (New York: Routledge: 2016).

Streets, Heather, *Martial Races: The Military, Race, and Masculinity in British Imperial Culture, 1857-1914* (Manchester: Manchester University Press, 2004).

---

49   For the context see Eugenia C. Kiesling, *Arming against Hitler: France and the Limits of Military Planning* (Lawrence: University Press of Kansas, 1996).

Index

From Reason to Revolution – Warfare 1721-1815

http://www.helion.co.uk/series/from-reason-to-revolution-1721-1815.php

The 'From Reason to Revolution' series covers the period of military history 1721–1815, an era in which fortress-based strategy and linear battles gave way to the nation-in-arms and the beginnings of total war.

This era saw the evolution and growth of light troops of all arms, and of increasingly flexible command systems to cope with the growing armies fielded by nations able to mobilise far greater proportions of their manpower than ever before. Many of these developments were fired by the great political upheavals of the era, with revolutions in America and France bringing about social change which in turn fed back into the military sphere as whole nations readied themselves for war. Only in the closing years of the period, as the reactionary powers began to regain the upper hand, did a military synthesis of the best of the old and the new become possible.

The series will examine the military and naval history of the period in a greater degree of detail than has hitherto been attempted, and has a very wide brief, with the intention of covering all aspects from the battles, campaigns, logistics, and tactics, to the personalities, armies, uniforms, and equipment.

Submissions

The publishers would be pleased to receive submissions for this series. Please contact series editor Andrew Bamford via email (andrewbamford@helion.co.uk), or in writing to Helion & Company Limited, Unit 8 Amherst Business Centre, Budbrooke Road, Warwick, CV34 5WE

Titles

No 1 *Lobositz to Leuthen: Horace St Paul and the Campaigns of the Austrian Army in the Seven Years War 1756-57* (Neil Cogswell)

No 2 *Glories to Useless Heroism: The Seven Years War in North America from the French journals of Comte Maurés de Malartic, 1755-1760* (William Raffle (ed.))

No 3 *Reminiscences 1808-1815 Under Wellington: The Peninsular and Waterloo Memoirs of William Hay* (Andrew Bamford (ed.))

No 4 *Far Distant Ships: The Royal Navy and the Blockade of Brest 1793-1815* (Quintin Barry)

No 5 *Godoy's Army: Spanish Regiments and Uniforms from the Estado Militar of 1800* (Charles Esdaile and Alan Perry)

No 6 *On Gladsmuir Shall the Battle Be! The Battle of Prestonpans 1745* (Arran Johnston)

No 7 *The French Army of the Orient 1798-1801: Napoleon's Beloved 'Egyptians'* (Yves Martin)

No 8 *The Autobiography, or Narrative of a Soldier: The Peninsular War Memoirs of William Brown of the 45th Foot* (Steve Brown (ed.))

No 9 *Recollections from the Ranks: Three Russian Soldiers' Autobiographies from the Napoleonic Wars* (Darrin Boland)

No 10 *By Fire and Bayonet: Grey's West Indies Campaign of 1794* (Steve Brown)

No 11 *Olmütz to Torgau: Horace St Paul and the Campaigns of the Austrian Army in the Seven Years War 1758-60* (Neil Cogswell)

No 12 *Murat's Army: The Army of the Kingdom of Naples 1806-1815* (Digby Smith)

No 13 *The Veteran or 40 Years' Service in the British Army: The Scurrilous Recollections of Paymaster John Harley 47th Foot – 1798-1838* (Gareth Glover (ed.))

No 14 *Narrative of the Eventful Life of Thomas Jackson: Militiaman and Coldstream Sergeant, 1803-15* (Eamonn O'Keeffe (ed.))

No.15 *For Orange and the States: The Army of the Dutch Republic 1713-1772 Part I: Infantry* (Marc Geerdinck-Schaftenaar)